SERIAL PUBLICATION IN ENGLAND
BEFORE 1750

'*This Method of Weekly Publication allures
Multitudes to peruse Books, into which they
would otherwise never have looked.*'

THE GRUB-STREET JOURNAL,
NO. 148, (OCTOBER 26, 1732)

Numb. 3.   *Dec. 3, 1745*

PROPOSALS

For Printing Weekly by SUBSCRIPTION,

With His MAJESTY's ROYAL PRIVILEGE and LICENCE,

(GENTLEMEN sending in their Names only)

A New General COLLECTION of

VOYAGES and TRAVELS,

MORE

Copious, Methodical and Accurate, than any hitherto published:

Consisting of above

Five Hundred of the most esteemed RELATIONS,

(Many of them now first Translated from Foreign Languages.)

Being designed,

Both to supply the Imperfections of Dr. HARRIS's Collection,
And continue it down to this TIME.

The Whole interspersed with the most remarkable

EXPEDITIONS, SEA FIGHTS, SHIPWRECKS, CAPTIVITIES, ESCAPES,

AND OTHER

Entertaining ADVENTURES, as well by LAND as SEA;

AND

Improved not only with select CUTS, taken from the several AUTHORS;
and CHARTS and MAPS entirely new, accommodated to the WORK;

BUT ALSO

With so much of MODERN HISTORY and GEOGRAPHY, as may serve to illustrate
the present State of all NATIONS.

CONDITIONS.

I. THIS Work, which will contain about 400 Sheets, will be printed in Four Volumes, Quarto, on the same Letter and Paper as the Account of the Design hereto annexed; and for the better Accommodation of the Purchasers, Three Sheets (which will contain as much as Six of the common Octavo or Folio Sheets) will be deliver'd every Week, Stitch'd in blue Paper, at the Price of Six pence.

II. Every Chart or Map, which will be entirely new drawn, to be reckon'd as Two Sheets, tho' the Expence of Drawing and Engraving will be equal to Three; and every Half Sheet of Cuts as One Sheet.
III. The following Numbers will be publish'd regularly every Saturday Morning, till the Whole is finish'd.
IV. The Purchasers of the first Number shall be welcome either to return or exchange it for any other Book, if not approved of.

PROPOSALS are deliver'd, and SUBSCRIPTIONS taken in by THOMAS ASTLEY, at the Rose in St. Paul's Church-Yard, London: as also by the Booksellers at the two Universities of Oxford and Cambridge; and by the Booksellers and Printers in all the Cities and noted Towns in Great-Britain and Ireland.

1. Proposals of Astley's *Voyages*

SERIAL PUBLICATION
IN ENGLAND
BEFORE 1750

BY

R. M. WILES

Professor of English, McMaster University
Hamilton, Ontario, Canada

CAMBRIDGE
AT THE UNIVERSITY PRESS
1957

CAMBRIDGE UNIVERSITY PRESS
Cambridge, New York, Melbourne, Madrid, Cape Town, Singapore,
São Paulo, Delhi, Dubai, Tokyo, Mexico City

Cambridge University Press
The Edinburgh Building, Cambridge CB2 8RU, UK

Published in the United States of America by Cambridge University Press, New York

www.cambridge.org
Information on this title: www.cambridge.org/9780521170680

First published 1957
First paperback edition 2010

A catalogue record for this publication is available from the British Library

ISBN 978-0-521-17068-0 Paperback

CONTENTS

Illustrations . . . . page VII

Preface IX

Note on Dates XIII

Chapter   I. 'Nimbly through the Nation'   I

II. Series, Serials, and Supplements   15

III. The Earliest Number Books (1678-1731) .   75

IV. Fascicules in Full Spate (1732-1733) . . .   105

V. The Law and the Profits   133

VI. Production, Promotion, Distribution . . .   195

VII. For Every Taste and Pocket   232

Appendix A. Text of the first Copyright Act (8 Anne. c. 19)   261

B. Short-title Catalogue of Books Published in
Fascicules before 1750   267

C. Names and Addresses of Booksellers, Printers,
and Others Who Had Some Share in the Production and Distribution of Number Books
before 1750   357

Bibliography   367

Index   371

ILLUSTRATIONS

1. Proposals of Astley's *Voyages*, printed on the blue paper cover of the third number, published December 3, 1743 . . . . *Frontispiece*

2. Two columns of serialized fiction in a daily newspaper, 1743 . . . . *Facing page* 50

3. Title-page of the earliest successful book published in fascicules, 1677 (i.e. 1678) 80

4. Title-page of the first monthly number of Rapin's *Acta Regia*, translated by Stephen Whatley, published in octavo numbers, 1725-1727 . . . 97

5. Title-page of a four-page leaflet advertising the beginning of Jacques Lenfant's *History of the Council of Constance*, translated by Stephen Whatley for publication in fascicules, 1728 103

6. Title-page of Teresia Constantia Phillips's *Apology*, signed by the author as a guarantee of authenticity 145

7. Printed text of the Royal licence issued to Dennis de Coetlogon for his *Universal History of Arts and Sciences*, published in weekly fascicules, 1741-1747 163

8. Official licence of Astley's *Voyages*, published in weekly fascicules, 1743-1747 168

9. Memorandum of assignment of a one-sixth share in Elizabeth Blackwell's *Curious Herbal*, published in 125 weekly numbers, 1737-1739. . . . 176

PREFACE

This book began as a brief introductory essay prefixed to a list of about 150 titles of works published in 'numbers' during the first half of the eighteenth century. As the list of titles grew, the introductory essay expanded into half a dozen chapters. What was at first intended only as a mildly interesting note for librarians has turned into a treatise on an important phase of England's literary history. Evidence of the growth of the reading public had earlier been seen in the phenomenal increase in the number of newspapers and other periodical publications. What is here discussed is a curious and extensive development of the book trade brought about by an entirely new mode of publishing and vending books. This was the device of issuing books in instalments. Publishers discovered that hundreds—even thousands—of people not previously interested in books would buy them if they could get them in inexpensive parts, piecemeal. It became quite the thing to buy books in monthly or weekly fascicules—that is, in small batches of printed sheets, folded, collated, and stitched in blue paper covers—at prices everyone could manage. Many of the books issued in fascicules (then called 'numbers') were reprints; but the publishers of several important new books deliberately chose to put them before the world in successive portions rather than in complete volumes. More than three hundred new and reprinted works were so issued before 1750, on almost every conceivable subject: history, theology, biography, fiction, travel, drama, music, mathematics, geography, architecture, astronomy, botany, anatomy, medicine, calligraphy—even carpentry. The extent of the trade is indicated by the sheer bulk of the short-title catalogue in Appendix B, and it is quite probable that within a year after this book is published a dozen or more works missing from the list will be reported.

This new branch of the book publishing business has not previously been studied with any thoroughness. Evidence brought forward here shows that during the first few decades after it was introduced, publishing in numbers became both highly competitive and highly remunerative for the booksellers, if not for the authors and compilers; it was big business. But for most readers this study will have its chief value as an account of a hitherto unrecognized stimulus to increased literacy among the lower and middle classes of the English people two centuries ago.

The material examined has been principally the books themselves, now to be found in considerable numbers as bound volumes on the shelves of public and private libraries. Modern readers, and even some librarians, are unaware that these particular volumes were made up of sheets originally issued in weekly or monthly fascicules. Were it not for newspaper advertisements, indeed, relatively few eighteenth-century books would now be recognized as having been published in fascicules; certainly this present book could not have been written had the information which the newspapers provide not been available. Primary evidence as to the mode and frequency of publication, the selling price of each number, the dates on which runs began, sales, and profits, is to be found in these contemporary newspaper advertisements, in editorial comments, letters, trade-sales catalogues, printers' ledgers, and in other records, both printed and in manuscript.

I have not managed to see a copy of every book published in numbers before 1750, and I confess that I have not read very far into those I have examined. My bookworm zeal ordinarily took me through scores of massive volumes from cover to cover with no more than a swift and purely physical nibbling; it did not often happen that a work which I knew to have been published in fascicules proved so engaging that I suspended my search in order to feast on mental sustenance. Perhaps I was warned by the fable of the man who laboured long to separate wheat from chaff and at the end of the task was given the chaff as reward. Among the number books there is no lack of dusty chaff. It will perhaps distress some readers to find that my object has been to display the variety of number books rather than to appraise their intrinsic worth one by one or to describe them with bibliographical exactitude.

For courteous assistance in finding these books, records, advertisements, and other materials I am happy to record my thanks to the librarians of the British Museum, the Bodleian, the Cambridge University Library, the National Library of Scotland, the Library of

Lambeth Palace, the Sion College Library, the Public Record Office, the Worshipful Company of Stationers and Paper Makers, the Folger Shakespeare Library, the Library of Congress, the Harvard College Library, the Harvard Law School, the Yale University Library, the New York Public Library, the American Archaeological Society, the Parliamentary Library at Ottawa, the Ontario Legislative Library, the University of Toronto Library, the Toronto Reference Library, Osgoode Hall, the Nova Scotia Barristers' Society, the Hamilton Law Association, and the McMaster University Library. To these librarians and their courteous assistants I am grateful, for they have enabled me to spend many pleasant hours in a harmless and often diverting piece of research. I feel, and here record, a special kind of gratitude toward McMaster University, whose liberal grants enabled me to visit great libraries in Britain and America.

For particular kindnesses I should also like to express cordial thanks to Messrs Longmans, Green and Company, to Mr. Cyprian Blagden, to Mr. Graham Pollard, to Dr. Laurence Hanson, to Mr. Sidney Hodgson, to Mr. R. A. Austen-Leigh, to Dr. Giles E. Dawson, and to Professor James Sutherland. I have good cause also to thank the staff of the Cambridge University Press for unfailing courtesy and efficiency at every stage in the publishing of this book. To no one am I more indebted or more grateful than to my wife, upon whom (in Dogberry's phrase) I have bestowed all my tediousness, chapter by chapter. It will give her much relief to see this book in print.

R. M.W.

Hamilton, Ontario, Canada
December 1955

NOTE ON DATES

For two quite different but often confused reasons, literary historians dealing with the eighteenth century have to be especially careful in citing dates. One of these is the matter of Old Style and New Style. Until the Gregorian reform of the calendar was adopted in England in 1752, English dates were normally given in Old Style, which during the first half of the century differed by eleven days from the New Style already in use in Scotland and on the Continent. England's January 25, for example, came on the day which France and Scotland dated February 5. When the change was effected by Act of Parliament in 1752, the eleven days were dropped, Wednesday, September 2 being followed by Thursday, September 14. This particular anomaly does not have to be considered in the present work, for no document, book, fascicule, or newspaper referred to here as having been written or published in England before September 14, 1752 either was or is dated in New Style, and all dates given herein from September 14, 1752 onwards were and are in New Style. The universal use of Old Style in England prior to the official change to New Style is mentioned in this note only in order to emphasize the fact that this practice did not affect the dating of a publication except from the point of view of a person living outside of England.

The other and more noteworthy reason why special care is needed in giving eighteenth-century dates is that, until New Style replaced Old Style in England, the date that officially and, for many people, unofficially marked the beginning of a new year was March 25, not January 1. Some Englishmen preferred to consider —as all Englishmen do now—that one year ended and a new one began when the clocks ticked their way past midnight on December 31; for them, December 31, 1735 was followed by January 1, 1736. But the majority of people called that day January 1, 1735, on the well established principle that the change of year would not come until Lady Day, nearly three months later. More often than not, newspapers, letters, and documents both in manuscript and in print bearing dates between January 1 and March 24 were assigned —as entries in the Stationers' Register and in the Journals of the House of Lords and the House of Commons invariably were—to the year we now consider to have ended the preceding December 31. For example, the *Tatler* number 93 was dated November 12, 1709; *Tatler* number 147, issued four months later, bore the date March 18, 1709, but clearly was published in the year we now call 1710. The eighteenth-century Englishman recognized the possibility of uncertainty or mistake, for double dates were sometimes used, in the forms

$$\text{January 9, } 173\frac{6}{7}, \text{ February 12, } 17\frac{25}{26}, \text{ and March 21, } 1741/2.$$

In the present work all newspapers and fascicules published between January 1 and March 24 inclusive have been regarded as falling within the same year as those published during the nine months which followed March, and where necessary the year dates have been silently adjusted accordingly. This has also been done with the dates of entries in the Stationers' Register. Dates in imprints of volumes have not been altered, however, even when it is known that the imprint date is one year early because of publication between January 1 and March 24.

In addition to the slightly confusing before-or-after-Lady-Day principle of dating, the works published piecemeal present a special problem of chronology, for the date that was printed on the title page of a book published in numbers depended on whether that title page was issued with the first fascicule of a volume or with the last. It is easy to see that if the general title page was issued with the last fascicule, as was usually done, the date in the imprint might be a year, or even two years, later than the date on which No. 1 was issued, the gap depending on the time of year at which the series began and on the length of the run. On the other hand it sometimes happened that the title page was issued as part of the first fascicule, in which case the date in the imprint might be as much as a year or two in advance of that on which the work was completed. So far as consistency is both desirable and possible, each number book mentioned in the text or chronological Catalogue of the present work is assigned to the January-December year in which the first fascicule reached the subscribers, no matter what date appears in the imprint of the completed volume. Particular examples are discussed in the introductory paragraphs of Appendix B.

Dates of the month are given in the form which most eighteenth-century writers preferred: August 15, 1736, not 15 August 1736.

'NIMBLY THROUGH THE NATION'

For two hundred years the potential market in the English-speaking world has been large enough to absorb vast quantities of periodical literature and large editions of many books. The twentieth-century book-buying public is enormous, and it is likely to continue to be so unless rising costs of book production make retail prices too high or the charms of television permanently allure readers' eyes away from the printed page. These threats to the trade, however, are slight in comparison with the problems confronting the publisher at the beginning of the eighteenth century, when relatively few people could either read books or afford to buy them. There were then, as there have always been since the invention of printing, persons of means and discrimination who would willingly pay as much for a choice book as for a suit of clothes. There was then, as now, a limited group of learned and professional men to whom good books were as necessary as food and air—the men who bought most of the works listed in Robert Clavell's quarterly *Catalogue of Books Printed and Published at London* (1670-1709), in the *History of the Works of the Learned; or, An Impartial Account of Books Lately Printed in All Parts of Europe* (monthly, 1699-1712), and in the catalogues published by Lintot (1714-1715) and Wilford (1723-1730). These lists included many publications at moderate cost—playbooks, sermons, pamphlets, little volumes of fiction and poetry—which even the less 'polite' sections of the population would buy. Yet the bulk of the population at the end of the seventeenth century either had no money to spare for books or had no desire to buy them, for the good and sufficient reason that they could not read. Exact figures showing the extent of literacy are not available for that period, but it is probably reasonable to conjecture that in the early years of the eighteenth century the ratio of readers to non-readers in the whole population of the British Isles was lower than it has been in any decade since, and the figures for London by itself were probably not much better. In the present century books are bought by hundreds of thousands of readers, and there are literally millions of persons who do not hesitate to buy a well printed paper-covered book of three or four hundred pages for half a crown or half a dollar. In the year 1700 the equivalent of a twentieth-century half-crown or half-dollar would not have bought anything larger than a very thin pamphlet, for no publisher could hope to sell enough copies of a sizable quarto or octavo volume to justify his bringing out a large edition at a low retail price. The reading public was simply not big enough to absorb editions of more than a few hundred copies. The economic law correlating price, supply, and demand was inescapable; the problem was how to influence the demand so as to bring about an expansion of the trade—to induce more people to buy more books.

There is no doubt whatever that the book trade did expand. As the century advanced, more and more people were discovered to be interested in buying books. There are several reasons for this accelerated development of the market: new and improved schools substantially added to the number of persons who could read; prosperity brought notably increased purchasing power to the middle classes; and a strong impetus to reading was given by the *Tatler* and the *Spectator*, by the newspapers, which rapidly became numerous in town and country, and by the spirited writings of Defoe, Swift, and Henry Fielding. In addition to all these influences there was one remarkable innovation which must certainly have accelerated the book trade more than any other single force affecting the reading habits of our ancestors between 1700 and 1750. This was a new method of persuading people to buy books —big, expensive books— and the publishers themselves must take the credit for the discovery. The plan, admirably simple and amazingly successful, can be expressed in these terms: if the customer cannot or will not buy a book because he has not enough money, then sell it to him in portions, so many pages each month or each week, at a cash price so low that he cannot possibly resist. The plan worked. As was observed in the *Grub-Street Journal* number 148 on October 26, 1732, 'This Method of Weekly Publication allures Multitudes to peruse Books, into which they would otherwise never have looked.'

It now seems surprising that no one had thought of the principle earlier, for it offered advantages to everyone concerned. A book, no matter how big it is, has to be written page by page, and it is read page by page. Why not sell it page by page, or in batches of pages —exactly, indeed, as it is set up in type? For books are made up of sheets of paper which have been printed on both sides and then folded once, or twice, or thrice, or four times, according to the size of the page desired, the type having been set appropriately. Fold the sheet once and you have four folio pages; fold it twice and you have eight quarto pages, all accessible when the folded edges are cut open or trimmed off; fold it thrice and you have sixteen octavo pages; and so on. The sheets used for the printing of any one work will naturally have to be of uniform size, though in the eighteenth century other sizes were available[1] in addition to the standard, which was approximately sixteen by twenty inches. It takes 150 sheets to make a folio volume of 600 pages. Half that number will do for a quarto volume of 600 pages, since each sheet makes eight pages of moderate size instead of four large ones. What the eighteenth-century publisher discovered was that people who would not pay thirty shillings for a thick folio volume were quite willing to purchase the same book, three sheets at a time, by paying sixpence a week as they received the successive numbered parts (each a fascicule or 'number'). It was a principle which the author and the publishers of *The Pickwick Papers* and *Nicholas Nickleby* found useful in the 1830's; indeed it was the common practice of Dickens, Thackeray, Surtees, Trollope, and several other Victorian novelists to publish a new work in 'parts' before issuing it as a complete book, though the nineteenth-century 'parts' or 'numbers' —unlike those of the preceding century—were complete units, beginning and ending with unbroken sentences. The fact is that the piecemeal publishing of books was well established a hundred years before Dickens put pen to paper.

Little attention has hitherto been paid to the earlier phases of serial publication. Since the age of Fielding and Johnson stands significantly in the records largely because of Fielding and Johnson themselves, together with a few of their most distinguished contemporaries, literary

[1] See Graham Pollard, 'Notes on the Size of the Sheet', *Library*, 4th ser., XXII (Sept.-Dec. 1941), 105–37.

historians and bibliographers have quite properly focussed attention upon these important writers, the great 'producers' of literature. In reviewing the cultural trends of England in the eighteenth century, however, one should not ignore the 'consumers', especially when their number increased so remarkably in that period. Increase in the number of readers can be looked upon both as a symptom and as a cause of cultural advance. There is something to be said, then, for observing how the practice developed of retailing literature in small parcels, both as instalments in newspapers and magazines and as numbered consecutive parts issued independently at regular intervals at low prices.

It is easy to assume that when the proprietors of eighteenth-century newspapers reprinted consecutive portions of books in their columns they did so because they were hard pressed for material and took to instalment printing as the least expensive method of filling space. It will be shown presently that such an assumption is not always justifiable. As for number books, it is equally easy—and much more erroneous—to suppose that only the most disreputable of printers would stoop so low as to wheedle pennies from soft-headed illiterates by specious promises of culture at bargain prices when (it is assumed) all they could offer was twopenny or sixpenny fragments of hack-written history, fourth-rate fiction, and dull theology, badly printed on poor paper. To a few of the number books issued before 1750 these harsh terms apply. Investigation shows, however, that although this issuing of books in numbered parts was sometimes only a paltry money-grubbing enterprise undertaken by a handful of book pirates on the outer fringes of the publishing business, it was a much more respectable and impressive thing than that, even in the course of the first few decades after the idea caught on.

Books had been published in parts as early as the last quarter of the seventeenth century, but it was not until a few works advertised in the *Tatler* (1709-1711) had proved successful that the possibilities of developing the piecemeal publishing of books into a thriving business began to be recognized. Prior to 1725 only a score of works were issued in consecutive parts; but during the second quarter of the eighteenth century the new experiment in book publishing expanded with phenomenal success. The first real boom came in 1732, and (as the chronological register in Appendix B shows) the next eighteen years saw the number-book trade well established. Aggressive rivalry soon sprang up among booksellers, who hoped for large gains from the publishing of books in fascicules. It was reported in the *Grub-Street Journal* number 247 (September 19, 1734) that the Knaptons were expected to clear between eight and ten thousand pounds by their publication—first in monthly and then in weekly numbers—of Rapin's *History of England* in the English translation by Nicholas Tindal, in spite of the fact that a rival translation by John Kelly was at the same time being published in numbers by J. Mechell. Profits on other number books must have been considerable, too, for many works issued in fascicules were owned jointly by one or other of the 'congers' or by large groups of individual firms in temporary partnerships, the shares sometimes being in very small fractions indeed, such as one tenth of one third, one fifty-seventh, or three sixty-fourths. There is evidence showing that in the 1730's and 1740's the editions in numbers were in some cases as large as two or three thousand copies, and that in numerous instances particular numbers had to be reprinted because the demand for the work far exceeded the proprietors' expectations.

By the third quarter of the eighteenth century a majority of the books published piecemeal were mere pot-boilers; but they *did* sell. Lest it be supposed that the number-book business dwindled after 1750, attention should be drawn to the very extensive sale enjoyed by Smollett's *History of England* when published in weekly numbers by James Rivington and James Fletcher. There is in the British Museum a manuscript record[1] of the financial affairs of these two business partners at the time when Rivington's share was being taken over by William Johnston. This interesting document shows that Smollett was paid three guineas per sheet for writing the 332 sheets (making four volumes) of the *History*, plus five hundred pounds for revisions and additions; it shows that the sum of three hundred pounds was spent on advertising, two hundred pounds for printing 'very large Quantities of Proposals', and other sums for engraving maps, 'heads', etc.; it shows

[1] British Museum, Add. MS. 38730.

that 13,000 copies were printed of each of the first fourteen weekly numbers, and that for the next eighty-three numbers 2,739,000 sheets of paper were required; it shows that 2281 reams of blue paper were used 'for the Wrappers of the said History'; it shows that Richard Baldwin of Paternoster Row was paid £7589. 5s. 'for printing and publishing four hundred and twenty one thous^d six hundred and twenty five Numbers of Dr. Tobias Smollett's History of England', which numbers Baldwin had delivered to Rivington and Fletcher between February 25, 1758, and January 1, 1760. As literature and as history this work of Smollett's is undistinguished; but the figures in this financial statement make it hard to maintain that reading in England two centuries ago was restricted to a small inner-circle group of statesmen, aristocrats, and professional men who bought only *whole* books.

As will presently be shown, many of the substantial works which English readers were prevailed on to buy in weekly or monthly parts not only put money into the pockets of publishers but did much to stimulate both book buying and book reading. In 1839 C. H. Timperley, testifying to the enormous sums of money made by Alexander Hogg, John Cooke, and James Harrison by the publication of number books in the second half of the eighteenth century, declared that these Paternoster-Row numbers were 'calculated to catch the attention of mechanics'; but he did not hesitate to add that although it might be customary to kick the ladder down when it was of no further use, publications of this sort 'must be confessed to have greatly contributed to lay the foundation of that literary taste and thirst for knowledge which now pervades all classes'.[1] A little later Charles Knight asserted that the number-book trade was 'a necessary offshoot of that periodical literature which sprang up into importance at the beginning of the eighteenth century'. Periodical literature, he added, 'in all its ramifications, has had a more powerful influence than that of all other literature upon the intelligence of the great body of the people'.[2] If it be

---

[1] C. H. Timperley, *A Dictionary of Printers and Printing* (London: Johnson, 1839), p.838n.
[2] Charles Knight, *The Old Printer and the Modern Press* (London: John Murray, 1854), p. 217.

objected that only the least intelligent readers would ever bother to buy a number book, and that men of letters like Fielding and Johnson would scorn such lowly sheets, let it be remembered that the inherent goodness or badness of a book does not depend on the number of its sheets released at a time; Johnson's own *Dictionary* was none the worse for being reprinted in weekly numbers shortly after the two folio volumes of the original edition had appeared in 1755. People who could not or would not spend money for a whole book were willing to buy it in inexpensive parts, paying the same total price in the end but being less conscious of the outlay. Such arrangements are common enough to-day, though seldom for the purchase of books.

Sometimes, of course, a book foisted on a too-gullible public was worthless. Fielding clearly implied in the introductory chapter to Book XIII of *Tom Jones* that booksellers of his time often turned the dead loss of an unsaleable remainder into clear gain, or made capital of an antiquated tome, by issuing it in instalments, for thus 'the heavy, unread, folio lump which long had dozed on the dusty shelf, piecemealed into numbers, runs nimbly through the nation'. Fielding was here denouncing an unscrupulous practice and at the same time testifying to its success, for by 1748, when these words were written, scores and scores of books —not all of them heavy folio lumps by any means —had run nimbly through the nation precisely because they had been piecemealed into numbers. Six years earlier Fielding, in the chatty introductory chapter in Book II of *Joseph Andrews*, had poked fun at the parcelling out of books. There the satirical novelist facetiously declared that even Homer not only divided his great work into twenty-four parts but 'according to the opinion of some very sagacious criticks, hawked them all separately, delivering only one book at a time (probably by subscription)'. It was Homer, indeed, that 'was the first inventor of the art which hath so long lain dormant, of publishing by numbers'! Even dictionaries were divided and exhibited piecemeal to the public, said Fielding derisively. But he was hardly fair when he added that one bookseller, to encourage learning and ease the public, had 'contrived to give them a dictionary in this divided manner for only fifteen shillings more than it would have cost them entire'.

In the half century before Fielding wrote the words quoted from
Tom Jones at least three hundred separate works in English were sold
in numbered parts to subscribers and casual purchasers in London, in
the provinces, and (a few of them) in the American colonies. Many
other works were printed as serials in the columns of London and
provincial newspapers or attached as supplements thereto. All these
publications have significance in the history of our ancestors' reading,
but particularly the number books, since the combined parts made up
real folio, quarto, octavo, or duodecimo volumes. Booksellers of the
present century often list them among other valuable second-hand sur-
vivals of earlier times without knowing that they once reached the
original buyers in the form of slender packets of sheets, delivered at
intervals of a month, a week, or a fortnight. Many a fat volume now
given space on the shelves of a national or a university library is made
up of sheets originally issued in groups of two or more, stitched together in blue paper covers, the first sheet in each fascicule having its
special signature — 'Numb. VII', or 'No. LXXVI' — to mark its place
in the series. Except for this consecutive numbering of parts, these
sheets differed in no respects from those used in making up any other
book. Librarians may even be unaware that some of the most impressive looking volumes on their shelves are number books, for a fair proportion of the books published in weekly or monthly parts had no
special signatures, the serial numbers being printed on the blue paper
covers of the separate fascicules, which were removed when the work
was bound.

Since it was common in the eighteenth century for books to be sold
in sheets instead of in volumes ready bound, the only difference between buying, say, the $512\frac{1}{2}$ sheets of Chambers's *Cyclopædia* (fourth
edition, 1741) at one transaction and buying the same work three
sheets at a time was that the latter arrangement enabled the customer
to acquire the two folio volumes by paying sixpence a week instead of
four guineas in a lump sum. What came back from the binder was the
same in either case, though the buyer of the numbers could begin
reading the early sheets of his book many months sooner than the man
who preferred to wait until the whole had been printed, since more

often than not the regular subscribers got the book in parts some time before the complete volume was on sale in the shops. That was naturally true of works written or translated especially for the number-book trade, for not all number books were reprints.

Whether reprints or originals, however, the books issued in numbers represent a surprisingly wide range of interests among the polite as well as among the less affluent sections of the population. Number books were commonplace when George Crabbe wrote *The Library* (1781), for many people were then finding their palates 'Cloy'd with a folio-Number once a week'.

> Bibles, with cuts and comments, thus go down:
> E'en light Voltaire is number'd through the town:
> Thus physic flies abroad, and thus the law,
> From men of study, and from men of straw . . . .

If fewer palates were cloyed half a century earlier it was not for lack of numbers. Between 1725 and 1750 all the important publishers of London were delivering every month or week great quantities of number-book parts to the houses of subscribers, or sending them 'smoking forth, a hundred hawkers' load',[1] to be sold in the streets.

The variety of subjects is remarkable. You could buy the Bible in numbers, with or without annotations; you could buy *Paradise Lost*, or *Don Quixote*, or Foxe's *Book of Martyrs;* you could buy collected sermons, songs, maps, plays, Latin classics, and reports of scientific research; you could buy the biography of Christ, of Cromwell, of Sir Walter Ralegh, of Queen Anne, of Quarll the hermit, of Peter the Great, of the kings of England, of the most notorious female robbers and 'pyratesses'; you could buy histories of England, of Ireland, of Scotland, of America, of China, of Rome, of the Ottoman Empire, of the British navy, of the Jews, of the Christian Church, of the Inquisition; you could buy dictionaries, encyclopedias, books of travel, records of famous trials, collections of rare documents; you could buy treatises on architecture, astronomy, conveyancing, painting, penmanship, physics, mathematics, topography, officinal herbs—everything, in fact, from anatomy to logarithms.

[1] Pope, *Epistle to Dr. Arbuthnot*, l. 217.

The mere enumeration of these subjects is enough to show that, whether frail or substantial, the number books were designed to appeal to a wide range of interests. At prices that sometimes were as low as a single farthing, sometimes went as high as half a crown, but usually were based on a rate of three halfpence or twopence per sheet, the weekly and monthly numbers would doubtless attract readers of moderate income. Again and again the advertisements make the claim that 'the Design of publishing Books in this manner Weekly is to lighten the Expence of them'. But the lists of subscribers make it perfectly clear that some, at least, of the more significant works published in numbers were taken by the most distinguished aristocrats in the kingdom as well as by ordinary citizens, university men, lawyers, schoolmasters, clergymen, surgeons, and tradesmen. Warren Hastings owned and used Claude Du Bosc's number-book edition[1] of *The Ceremonies and Religious Customs of the Various Nations of the Known World*—published in weekly numbers from 1733 to 1739—not the rival edition published by Nicholas Prevost in whole volumes. According to Thomas Tyers,[2] Samuel Johnson, in his desire to develop an elegant style of writing, 'set for his emulation the preface of Chambers to his Cyclopedia', and it was the edition published in numbers in 1741 that Johnson had in his own library.[3] It can hardly be supposed that only lightermen, porters, and chimney sweeps bought the consecutive numbers of Rapin's *Acta Regia*, Elizabeth Blackwell's *Curious Herbal*, and the *Harleian Miscellany*. No one can be sure how many persons were really interested in reading works printed serially in newspapers, for the man who bought a newspaper got the instalment or the literary supplement willy-nilly, and if he glanced at anything besides news and advertisements it may often have been because he had

[1] Each of the seven volumes in the British Museum has the autograph of Warren Hastings on the title page.

[2] Thomas Tyers, *A Biographical Sketch of Samuel Johnson* (1785), reprinted as the Augustan Reprint Society's Publication No. 34 (Los Angeles: William Andrews Clark Memorial Library, 1952), which see, p. 8.

[3] Item No. 487 in *A Catalogue of the Valuable Library of Books, of the Late Learned Samuel Johnson, Esq; LL.D. Deceased; Which Will Be Sold by Auction, (By Order of the Executors) By Mr. Christie, At His Great Room in Pall Mall, On Wednesday, February 16, 1785, and three following Days.*

no other use for his time and his eyes; at best the continued pieces in newspapers have only a temporary interest. But the man who deliberately surrendered a small coin for the twelfth number of Francis Moore's *Travels into the inland parts of Africa*, or the thirtieth number of *An Appendix to the Greek Thesaurus*, or the hundred and fifty-first number of Dr. James's *Medicinal Dictionary*, had only one object—to complete his set, to get the whole book in order to read it—or at least to own it.

If some of these number books, when bound in calf or sheepskin, served only as ornaments in the best room of an upper-class or middle-class house, they were certainly not the only books used primarily for that purpose two centuries ago, nor can it be said that only 'mechanics' bought books for purely decorative uses. It appears from contemporary satire that even men of considerable wealth left their books unopened. Daniel Defoe's posthumously published *Compleat English Gentleman* describes the library of a country squire as comprising a Bible, a volume of family records, three massbooks, four or five prayer books, some old newspapers, a few ballads, an old bass viol, two fiddles, and a music book. 'What should I do with books?' the squire asks a friend. 'I never read any.' Then the friend remonstrates: 'O but, Sir, no gentleman is without a library. 'Tis more in fashion than ever it was.'[1] Unfortunately both country squires and gentlemen were sometimes content to own books without bothering to read them.

It must have been such a state of affairs that gave point to a satirical though of course fictitious letter in the Edinburgh *Echo* number 79 (July 8, 1730). A servant girl describes the various households in which she has worked, among them that of a wealthy baronet. Upon first coming into the family she thought her master a very learned man and her mistress much given to reading, for he had a large library of fine books and the lady 'a Closet of choice Books curiously bound, gilt and letter'd'. But the girl soon discovered that her master never went into the library except to show it to company, and the lady's books were rarely taken out of the case except to be dusted. She could not

[1] Daniel Defoe, *The Compleat English Gentleman*, ed. Karl Bulbring (London: David Nutt, 1890), p. 135.

imagine why people who did not read should put themselves to the
expense of buying such a number of books and fitting up a library, till
she was informed that 'a Study is as necessary in a Nobleman or
Gentleman's House, altho' he does not read, as a Chappel, tho' he
never hears Prayers'.

Non-reading book-owners are more mercilessly ridiculed in the *Lay-
Monk* number 8 (December 2, 1713) and in the *Universal Spectator*
number 254 (August 18, 1733). The former describes an 'Upholsterer
in Learning', Sir Gregory Bookworm, a country gentleman of wealth
who orders books by the yard to fill his shelves. The letter in the
Universal Spectator, obviously based on this paper in the *Lay-Monk*, is a
request for a shipment of books to stock up the library of Sir Tinsel
Wormius. 'In pursuance of this Scheme', writes Sir Tinsel's chaplain,
'I'm to order you to send down with Expedition, five yards of Folios,
Theologists, Philosophers, Schoolmen or Romances; but particularly
five Foot of Common Law, and seven of the best Civil.' Neither Sir
Gregory nor Sir Tinsel would have found number books acceptable
for ornamental purposes, at least not until the complete sets had been
bound. Indeed, the spaces in their libraries could be filled better with
imitation books, wooden dummies, like those found by Mr. Spectator
when he browsed through Leonora's library (*Spectator* number 37,
April 12, 1711).[1]

A further stroke of satire against illiterate gentility is administered
in Patrick Delany's Dublin *Tribune* number 11 (November 25, 1729),
a delightful essay on the relative merits of reading and drinking. 'Many

---

[1] In the following century counterfeit books were used to give the impression of
erudition in households. A correspondent writing from Berlin in December 1849
records in *Notes and Queries* (1st. ser. 1, 166) that upon purchasing at St. Petersburg
the library formerly owned by an old Russian nobleman of high rank he was
astounded to find many dummy volumes, 'all very neatly bound in calf, gilt, and
with red morocco backs', and bearing such titles as *Oeuvres de Voltaire, Oeuvres de
Swift*, and even *Oeuvres de Miss Burney*. He learned subsequently that during the reign
of Catherine every courtier who hoped to win her approval was expected to have a
room fitted up with mahogany shelves filled with books, though he was not required to read them. To meet this demand for a sumptuous library a tradesman
named Klostermann used to provide 'books' at prices ranging from fifty to a
hundred roubles per running yard, according to the binding.

of our Gentry seem to think Learning not only a needless, but an impertinent Qualification', says the author; and he adds, 'The State of
Conversation among us is such as to require a well furnish'd Wine-
Cellar, much more than a Library, for its Support.' Then he observes
that many landed proprietors have no use for books at all, though
their wives may have a few novels and the servants a handful of chap-
books:

> I my self know several rural Esquires of good Estates, who sit down
> every Day to a Dinner of ten Dishes of Meat, and to a Supper of five,
> and consume two or three Tuns of *French* Wine yearly, and yet never
> once look on a Book, or have any such furniture in their Houses. I must
> indeed except a *Bible*, a *Prayer-Book*, and a *Week's Preparation*, which are
> the Property of the Lady of the House, who is generally the better
> Scholar, as well as the better Christian of the two. Her Woman also
> may happen to have a *Robinson Crusoe*, *Gulliver's Travels*, and Aristotle's
> Master-piece, both for her own Edification, and the Instruction of the
> young Ladies, as soon as they are grown up; not to mention *Tommy
> Pots*, *Jack* the *Giantkiller*, the *Cobbler* of *Canterbury*, and several other
> notable Pieces of Literature carried about in the Baskets of itinerant
> Pedlars, for the Improvement of his Majesty's Liege People.

It is unlikely that the baskets of itinerant pedlars contained many number books even after the trade spread to the provinces in the second
quarter of the eighteenth century, for the sons of Autolycus could
hardly expect their rural customers to buy odd parts of an incomplete
book. Broadside ballads and chapbook synopses would go better with
those who favoured *Tommy Pots*.

Among the number books mentioned in the following chapters there
are, it is true, a dozen or more which presumably would appeal only
to the chambermaid mentality. But from the best of the titles that
were sold in 'numbers' in the second quarter of Johnson's century a
very respectable shelf of books could be selected, books of which
Johnson himself would undoubtedly approve, and not solely because
he had a hand in the preparation of several of them. Many twentieth-
century readers would find something of impermanence in a book accumulated a few sheets at a time, but on the other hand the eighteenth-
century buyer did not suffer the ignominy of having his books picked

out for him by the official selectors in a 'book club'; he bought an inexpensive sample or two first, and, if he liked the work, kept on buying the parts at a price he could afford. The plan has much merit. Some customers may occasionally have felt that keeping on paying for the parts of a 'heavy' book was only flinging good money after bad, but they were at liberty to stop when they chose.

There is evidence that a few of the number books failed for want of support; but most of them brought financial satisfaction to the proprietors and must therefore have met with approval among the subscribers. The satiric journalists implied that country gentlemen bought books only to be in the fashion; there must have been many people who bought books because they valued them as books rather than as furniture. One such man was Henry Purefoy, whose personal library at Shalstone Manor in Buckinghamshire contained several hundreds of volumes, and who frequently sent to London for books that interested him. Purefoy regularly commissioned 'a Schoolmaster at Brackley' by the name of Cooper to bind various books for him, among them the successive half-yearly volumes of Thomas Salmon's *Modern History,* published from 1724 to 1738 in monthly numbers at a shilling each.[1] That was the only way in which the work could be purchased.

There is nothing wrong with buying or selling books on the pay-as-you-go basis. The sale of number books would have to be condemned as bad for the customers only if fraudulent misrepresentation or deceptively 'low' prices were used to lure people to purchase books inherently pernicious or feeble. Some of the number books were bad in every sense of the word; most of them, whether reprints or originals, did something to make John Bull read for pleasure and instruction. If the publishers of number books substantially assisted in the promotion of general literacy in England two hundred years ago by creating a market for books, they deserve praise, not blame or neglect.

---

[1] See letters 406 (February 18, 1736), 408 (March 2, 1738), and 410 (June 14, 1738) in *Purefoy Letters* 1735-1753, ed. G. Eland (London: Sidgwick & Jackson, 1931), II, 274-7.

CHAPTER II

SERIES, SERIALS, AND SUPPLEMENTS

Many an eighteenth-century bookseller —that is to say, publisher — like his twentieth-century successor, must on occasion have looked at his overloaded shelves with sinking heart, wondering why his unsold stock had not run nimbly through the nation. What he desired more than anything else was to have his editions sold out completely in a few months so that he could go ahead with the publishing of another and still another book. It must have occurred to him that the only sound basis for expecting his hope to triumph over his less satisfactory experiences was either to publish what the people wanted or to induce them to want what he published. He knew that he could count on a fairly solid body of buyers if his books were small and inexpensive, for like his predecessors in the book trade he often made money with controversial pamphlets, single sermons, and playbooks, all of them small and cheap. It was one thing, however, to bring out an occasional quarto pamphlet containing the text of a popular play, a sensational sermon, or a lively discussion of a current political issue; it was quite another thing to keep the presses busy with a staple of profitable printed matter when topical writings were scarce. From the bookseller's point of view what had to be done was to find some way of inducing more customers to hand more cash over the counter.

I. SERIES

One way of multiplying the number of cash sales was to bring the same customers back repeatedly by publishing a cumulative series of little books, each one low in price but collectively amounting to something. One sort of publication —the quarto, octavo, or duodecimo play-book —offered special possibilities for sequential sales, for it was supposed that people who bought a single play by Nathaniel Lee, for example, would be interested in buying others by the same author if subsequently published in similar format. That publishers succeeded in persuading people to accept the principle of the continuing series is apparent from the existence of composite volumes made up of separate quarto editions of individual plays by Otway (with general title page dated 1692), Shadwell (dated 1693), and Dryden (dated 1695). In 1712 R. Wellington reprinted one by one a numerous series of Lee's plays, each with its own pagination and separate title page, the set making two octavo volumes, for which Wellington provided a general title, *The Works of . . . Nathaniel Lee*, dated 1713. Within the same decade W. Mears published an assortment of plays by various authors, each text having an independently dated title page and separate pagination. The whole *Collection of Plays by Eminent Hands* made four duodecimo volumes when the several pieces were brought together under this general title in 1719. Into such compounded volumes it would be easy to incorporate remainders of earlier printings, though it is not likely that the imprint dates of the separate plays were falsified, as were those in a more famous Shakespearean fraud a century earlier.

What is notable in the development of playbook publishing in the 1730's is that plays by various Restoration and other dramatists began to appear at *regular* intervals, once a month or once a week. John Watts, who had earlier printed single plays, in 1732 brought out in eight monthly pocket volumes, duodecimo, at two shillings and sixpence each, a *Select Collection of Moliere's Comedies in French and English*. William Feales, and presently Jacob Tonson and Robert Walker, also saw that it was the connected series rather than the single play that gave most hopeful promise of wide sales. These men realized, moreover, that they could attract large numbers of new readers only by setting the price really low. During the years 1734 to 1736 there appears to have been a heated rivalry among these three booksellers, with a price war and a glutted market in playbooks.

For a while there issued from the presses of one or another of these publishers a 'new' play almost every day of the week. And the boom spread into the provinces, where the London booksellers were now finding an expanding market through their agents. Several letters and other documents preserved in the British Museum reveal the ups and downs of this newly developed business, and although the few exact figures which survive do not tell us how many copies of the threepenny, fourpenny, and sixpenny texts were actually printed, it is obvious that William Feales and his partners looked for substantial returns on their investment. Feales certainly put money—or at least promissory notes—into the venture. On February 14, 1733/34, G. Van der Gucht signed a statement that he had that day 'Received of Mr Feales a Note for nineteen pounds nineteen Shillings which when paid (with five pounds five Shillings before received) is in full for Designing & Engraving twelve plates for Lees plays'.[1] On June 17 of that same year Henry Woodfall gave Feales a receipt for notes amounting to £ 34. 10s. 6d. 'on account for Printing a Volume of Lee's Plays'.[2] Indicative of the extent to which Feales went in the attempt to flood the market is a list[3] dated August 1, 1734, of 158 titles, in alphabetical order, of plays in twelves to be sold by him 'to Booksellers only for the present Month, at two Pounds ten Shillings per Hundred, Ready Money'. He warned the tradesmen that there were 'but small Numbers of some of the Plays'. Opposite the titles in the British Museum copy of this list have been added in ink the quantities of each play in someone's inventory—perhaps that of Feales himself—at some time during the sale. The figures range all the way from 305 (Cato), 247 (Fair Penitent), 165 (Hamlet), and 163 (Orphan), through 137 (Conscious Lovers), 96 (Jane Shore), 88 (Recruiting Officer), 77 (Merry Wives of Windsor), and 43 (Man of Mode), down to 19 (Sophonisba), 13 (Country Wife), and 1 (Constantine the Great).

It is startling to find the name of Feales linked with that of his rival, Tonson, in a letter[4] from an Oxford book dealer on the last day of 1734:

Mr Feales

We have Sometimes had Dealings for Plays, if you will furnish me wth those wch you & Mr Tonson are now printing in a Cheap manner, I shall be glad to hear from yu; let me know ye Names of wt are already publish'd, & Ile order ye Number, & Send ye Money imediatly upon y Receipt of ym.

[1] British Museum, Add. MS. 28,275, item 313.
[2] Ibid., item 316.
[3] Ibid., item 317.
[4] Ibid., item 344.

Let me know w^t price & allowance.

I am S^r y^r Humble Servt

A^Y PEISLEY

Oxon Decr 3 1st. 1734

Feales cannot have been very businesslike in his relations with the provincial dealers, for on April 18, 1735, Thomas Burn wrote from Oxford that he had not received any of Lee's plays 'since ye 15th of Last Inst' (whatever that means). He requested Feales to send '25 of Each Publish'd Since Constantine ye Great', and particularly demanded that the copies should be dry, 'for Several of ye others is Mildew'd'. Burn, who wrote also on behalf of a Mrs. Fletcher, indicated that there might be a sale for other plays in the same series: '. . . if you have any other at ye Price of Lees Send weekly wth ye 6^d ones'. But he still did not know what allowance he and Mrs. Fletcher were to receive on the plays: 'I desire that you'll Send a Small Note that I may know what you Charge ye 6^d ones at I only going upon Supposition as Relating to y^r Prices.' It is understandable, then, that some time later[1] Thomas Burn felt justified in returning large numbers of unsold playbooks, the reason being 'occasion'd by every Bookseller dealing in them here, And a Decline of ye Sale Among Gentlemen they being almost a weary of this Scheme'. In his letter to Feales Burn sent ten pounds and eleven shillings in payment for 575 books at nine shillings per quarter-hundred, but he added that Feales need not send any more, 'Y^e Profit of ye Sale not paying Charges'.

On June 19, 1735,[2] Joseph Pote, a dealer in Eton, returned 101 copies of Lee's plays to Feales, and on June 2, 1736,[3] wrote a letter which shows that in Eton the trade had by then completely shrunk into nothing: 'I desired when last in town that you would send no Plays my Sale being quite ended, have since rec^d two Parcells or three of which have not sold one.'

But Feales and his associates still had playbooks to sell, for only the preceding week he had advertised in the *London Daily Post, and General*

---

[1] The letter in B.M. Add. MS. 28,275, item 349, has no decipherable date.

[2] British Museum, Add. MS. 28,275, item 355.

[3] *Ibid.*, item 368.

Advertiser number 4[88] that on that day (Tuesday, May 25, 1736) there had been published at sixpence, 'Pursuant to the Printed Proposals', a correct and beautiful edition of Lee's tragedy *Constantine the Great*. The subscribers were 'desired to give in their Names and Places of Abode to W. Feales, A. Bettesworth, F. Clay, R. Wellington, C. Corbet, and J. Brindley'.

Meanwhile the aggressive and often aggrieved Jacob Tonson had tried to undersell Feales, but had discovered that his threepenny single plays of Shakespeare and later dramatisis were not bringing in enough clear profit. When he announced that he intended to reprint these plays more attractively at sixpence, he stirred into active rivalry a man against whom Tonson subsequently had to obtain an injunction, and who will have to be given the credit of publishing more number books than any other single bookseller before 1750. This was Robert Walker, whose name will occur frequently hereafter.[1] On January 24, 1734/35, Robert Walker sent forth from his printing establishment at Shakespeare's Head in Turnagain-lane, Snow-Hill, London, proposals for printing 'by Subscription' a select collection of tragedies, comedies, operas, and farces, written by 'the most celebrated poets'. The authors named, not in chronological order, seem to have been assembled in an effort to make the list as impressive as possible, though some of them certainly did not deserve to be labelled 'celebrated':

[1] Walker had begun to publish plays of Shakespeare in single duodecimo volumes in the autumn of 1734. The Folger Shakespeare Library in Washington has two different editions of *The Merry Wives of Windsor* bearing Walker's imprint and dated 1734. Dr. Giles E. Dawson of the Folger Library has drawn my attention to an 'Advertisement' dated 6 September 1734 in Jacob Tonson's edition of the same play, also dated 1734, in which Tonson asserted that Walker had issued proposals for printing some plays of Shakespeare and other authors in single sheets weekly at one penny each sheet, and that Walker had already published two wretchedly printed sheets of *The Merry Wives of Windsor*. It was Walker who five years later published in weekly numbers thirty-six plays by Shakespeare, Otway, Congreve, and other dramatists under the general title *The Beauties of the English Stage; or, Select Plays from the Best Dramatick Authors*. This was not a series of separately published single plays but a real number book in nine volumes, each volume comprising four plays but made up of nine or ten consecutively numbered and separately published fascicules. Each of the thirty-six plays has its own title page, with imprints dated 1739, 1740, or 1741.

Shakespeare, Jonson, Wycherley, Banks, Beaumont and Fletcher, Lord Orrery, Dryden, Etherege, Congreve, Addison, Rowe, Farquhar, Sir Robert Howard, Steele, Otway, Southern, Vanbrugh, Shadwell, Philips, Cibber, Trapp, Fenton, Day, Young, and 'the rest of the English poets'. Obviously Walker was hoping to drive both Feales and Tonson out of the serial-book business, though it was mainly in opposition to Tonson that the stipulated 'Conditions' and the attached 'Advertisement' were drawn up.

Walker's 'conditions' are worth examining, for they follow the pattern which by 1735 had become the standard form for announcing books published in fascicules. They show that Walker was determined to get a share of the weekly-books business by offering to readers of moderate means, at a price one third lower than Tonson's, complete texts of English plays, well printed on fine imported paper.

CONDITIONS

I. These Plays will be printed in Twelves, on a new Elziver [thus] Letter and superfine Dutch Demy Paper, in the most beautiful Manner, with a curious Frontispiece to each; which will far exceed any former Editions printed either in England or Holland.

II. One Play compleat, stitch'd in blue Paper, shall be delivered every Monday at the Subscribers Houses, or any Place they shall appoint, at the Price of Four-Pence and no more, which is but one third Part of the Price they were formerly sold for: and being one third cheaper than what is designed by *J. Tonson* and the Body of Booksellers, who vainly oppose this Undertaking.

III. The original Dedications, Prefaces, Prologues, and Epilogues shall be printed with each Play, so as to render them perfectly compleat.

IV. General Titles beautifully printed in Red and Black shall be given to the Subscribers to bind up with each Author's Works.

V. The first Play will be published and delivered on Monday next, being the 27th of this Instant January, and on every Monday following till the whole is compleated.

In an 'Advertisement' attached to these printed proposals Walker carried on publicly his quarrel with Tonson, saying that what he had foretold some time before had now been verified, namely that 'as soon as he had glutted the Town with his bad and incorrect Editions at Three-pence he would then print the same Plays . . . at an advanced

Price'. He ventured to prophesy that when 'Tonson and Comp.' had stocked the town with their new editions of plays at sixpence each, they would then 'form a second Specious Excuse' and double the price again.

Walker himself had already begun to issue the plays of Shakespeare, and he announced that thereafter he would publish two plays every week, 'Lee's on a Monday, 'till his Works are compleated, and every Thursday one of Shakespeare's, 'till his Works are compleated'. By the first week of February he had published both *The Rival Queens: Or, the Death of Alexander the Great* and *Sophonisba;* and his advertisement in the *Daily Advertiser* number 1255 (February 5, 1735) showed how easily new customers could obtain these and later plays:

The Subscribers are desir'd to give in their Names and Places of Residence to Robert Walker, Printer, at Shakespear's Head in Turn-again-lane, Snow-hill, or at his Shop in Exchange-alley, Cornhill; at which Places Proposals may be had, and the Plays sold; also Proposals are given gratis, and Subscriptions taken in by the Hawkers, who also sell these Plays.

By such means Walker obviously hoped to attract not just casual buyers but regular subscribing customers who would keep the business steady. Walker assured the public that if after they had bought any of his fourpenny plays they did not find them as correct and printed on as good a letter and paper as Tonson's sixpenny plays he would return their money.

Feales, Tonson, and Walker, with their threepenny, fourpenny, and sixpenny playbooks, were not the first publishers who tried to establish the series rather than the single work as the basis of publication and purchase. That had been done and continued to be done even when there was neither continuity in the substance nor regularity in the interval between the successive units. For several years early in the eighteenth century Paul Lorrain issued at irregular intervals under the title *The Ordinary of Newgate* single sheets giving accounts of criminals recently executed,[1] and as the century advanced it became a regular

[1] Donald A. Stauffer, *The Art of Biography in Eighteenth-century England* (Princeton: Princeton University Press, 1941), pp. 156, 162, 179.

practice for publishers to issue numbered threepenny or fourpenny pamphlets six or eight times a year under this title or under the title *The History of Executions*.

It is apparent that even such individually complete and separately published pamphlets as *The Ordinary of Newgate* and *The History of Executions* were regarded as in the aggregate making up a whole 'book', which at the year's end would find a place on the customers' shelves as a full sized single volume with title page and index. Evidence of this expectation is to be found in advertisements in the *Grub-Street Journal* in 1730. Number 10 (March 12, 1730) announced as published that day the first number of *A Compleat History of Executions*, printed by R. Newton at St. John's Gate, and sold by A. Dod[d] at Temple Bar, E. Nutt at the Royal Exchange, and at the pamphlet shops. The price 'in common Paper' was fourpence, and the advertisement indicated that the several accounts[1] would 'at the Year's end . . . make a handsome Volume; for which Purpose a compleat Index will be given with the concluding Number'. Advertisements of later numbers of the series in 1730 (for example, in the *Grub-Street Journal* number 20, dated May 21, 1730) indicate that the work had met with encouragement, that it would be continued 'every Sessions', that the numbers would be published regularly 'soon after the Execution', and that the series would 'make a compleat Volume at the Year's End'.

Several other publishers sought to make money from the same sort of morbid series. In 1733 John Applebee of Bolt-Court, near the Leg Tavern, Fleet Street, had his name in the imprint of 'Numb. V for the said Year' of *The Ordinary of Newgate, His Account of the Behaviour, Confessions, and Dying Words, of the Malefactors, who were Executed at Tyburn, On Saturday the 6th of this Instant October*, 1733. *Being the Fifth Execution in the Mayoralty of the Rt. Hon. The Lord Mayor for the Time being*. These threepenny publications, often the suspiciously lurid reports prepared by the prison chaplains, were numerous throughout the century.

[1] In the initial number these were 'The Life, Writings, and Crimes of Williamson Goodburn, of the University of Cambridge, lately executed at Tyburn: With an ingenious Letter to his Friends, and part of a Poem of his Writing . . . , Remarks on the whole Life and various Actions of John Everett, the noted Highwayman, and an Account of Henry Nowland and Thomas Westwood, Footpads.'

These Newgate chaplains were not the only men of the cloth who published little works in series. It was a clergyman, Dr. Richard Willis, who in 1697-1698 published a succession of essays under the title *The Occasional Paper;* and various clergymen contributed to a similar series published monthly under the same title in 1716-1719. Among those whose essays were published in the latter series was Dr. Samuel Wright, whose sermons were later (in 1741) issued in a numbered series at fourpence each under the title *The Occasional Preacher.* The Rev. James Robe, minister at Kilsyth, published pamphlets as numbered parts of a series in local church history, under such titles as *A Faithful Narrative of the Extraordinary Work at Kilsyth* (1742) and *A Short Narrative of the Extraordinary Work at Cambuslang* (1742). Though inferior in appearance, these tiny booklets were announced as numbered units of a connected series and are therefore in the same category as the more scholarly publications of the versatile Rev. William Stukeley[1] (1687-1765), whose *Palæographia Sacra; or, A Discourse on Monuments of Antiquity that Relate to Sacred History* (1736) and later *Palæographia Britannica; or, A Discourse on Antiquities in Great Britain* (1747) were announced as to be published in numbers, though neither series progressed very far.

The same can be said of some other series which started impressively. The skimpy series of old royal proclamations and acts of Parliament which came out in weekly numbers in 1715 without imprint under the title *Faithful Collections* may be ignored. No greater success seems to have attended *The Sailor's Advocate,* the first two and perhaps sole numbers of which were published at sixpence in 1728. No. 1 of Richard Savage's *An Author to be Lett* was listed in the *Monthly Chronicle* for April 1729, but no later numbers appeared, though a second *Author to be Lett* was advertised repeatedly. Savage's seven occasional odes, published in March of each year from 1732 to 1738 under the title *The Laureate Volunteer,* were numbered consecutively, but they do not comprise an integrated whole. It appears that John Entick planned a

[1] For a modern account of this most interesting man of many sciences see Stuart Piggott, *William Stukeley: An Eighteenth-century Antiquary* (Oxford: Clarendon Press, 1950).

succession of volumes in language study when his sixpenny manual was issued ('Sold by G. Strahan, J. Batley, R. Williamson, and J. Pote') in October 1728 with the persuasive title, *Speculum Latinum: Or, Latin made easy to Scholars, by an English Grammar only, neither tedious nor obscure, composed on natural Principles, and instructing the young Beginner in Latin, by English Rules adapted to the meanest Capacities, for the use and Benefit of Schools and Families.* But it was not until a year later that *Speculum Linguarum No. 2. Or Greek made easy to Scholars* was printed 'for J. Pote near Suffolk-Street, by Charing Cross'.

A similar effort had earlier been made by 'Orator' John Henley, whose series of ten grammatical treatises was published with some irregularity, beginning with No. 1 for the month of August 1719 ('Being a Grammar of the Spanish Tongue') and continuing through Italian, French, Greek, Latin, Hebrew and other languages, under the general title, *The Compleat Linguist, Or An Universal Grammar of all the Considerable Tongues in Being, In a Shorter, Clearer, and more Instructive Method than is extant.* The title page indicates that the series was intended to be published monthly, 'one distinct grammar each month, till the whole is perfected'. The first three grammars sold for a shilling each; later numbers were issued for two or three months at a time and sold for two shillings, though No. 10, not published until 1726, sold for one shilling and sixpence.[1] There were even greater gaps of time between successive numbers of *Oratory Transactions*, the first number of which was listed in the *Monthly Chronicle* for June 1728 as to contain 'the Rev. Mr. Henley's Life, Education, Studies, Degrees, and Orders, Chaplainship and Promotion, Correspondence . . . &c. with the Cause of this Institution. By Mr. Welstead'. The second number did not come out until 1729. J. Roberts, one of the two publishers responsible for *The Compleat Linguist*, was also the publisher who in 1731 brought out in sixpenny numbers Henley's *Course of Academical Lectures*, which stirred up a hornet's nest of adversaries,[2] as did the other specious

[1] Henley would have been happy to know that a twentieth-century London bookseller, Colin Richardson, would in 1951 offer a complete set of the ten numbers for £30.

[2] The most violent abuse of Henley was printed in the *Grub-Street Journal*. See James T. Hillhouse, *The Grub-Street Journal* (Durham, North Carolina: Duke University

enterprises of this irrepressible master of various arts. 'O Henley! thou eldest son of effrontery! renowned for thy Grammars, no less than for thy oratory! how shall thy Fame be transmitted to after-ages as it deserves?' So exclaimed a journalist quoted in the *Gentleman's Magazine* for March 1731. But Henley continued to use his gilt tub[1] to lecture on the belles lettres, on forming a fine taste, on the languages ancient and modern, on art and imagination, publishing his lectures monthly at sixpence apiece.

So long as the price per book was only fourpence or sixpence numerous readers were doubtless willing to buy the plays of 'celebrated' dramatic writers, the biographies of contemporary malefactors, and possibly even the 'fluent nonsense'[2] of Henley. There was still the problem of how to induce these same readers to buy full-length books, for the increased sale of pamphlets alone cannot have affected very significantly the volume of business. If the numbered series of single plays, sermons, and lectures did anything toward bringing a new prosperity to the trade, it was mainly by making readers acquire the habit of purchasing successive units of the series at regular intervals, much as they were becoming used to receiving successive issues of newspapers and periodicals.

II. SERIALS

There is no doubt that the rapid development of newspapers and periodicals in the first half of the eighteenth century did much to multiply the number of habitual readers in England, and that the inclusion of free 'literary' matter in the newspaper columns prepared the public to accept the principle of piecemeal publication of books. Newspapers as such are transitory things; unless they contain more than advertisements and brief reports of current happenings their readers, whether numerous or not, cannot properly be called consumers of literature.

Press, 1928), pp. 120-32. Forty-three quarto volumes of 'Heads of lectures delivered by John Henley' in the years 1728-1756 (the latter being the year of his death) are in the British Museum (Add. MSS. 10346-10349, 10576-10578, 11768-11801, and 12199-12200).

[1] Pope, *The Dunciad*, II, 2.

[2] *Ibid.*, III, 201.

Many of the eighteenth-century periodical publications did contain literary matter substantial both in bulk and in quality. Steele and Addison through their *Tatler* and *Spectator* essays sought to 'bring philosophy out of the closets and libraries . . . to dwell in clubs and assemblies, at tea-tables and coffee-houses'.[1] With less lofty motives scores of newspapers, like those of our own time, reprinted in their columns some of the day's best-sellers and standard works in history, biography, fiction, and literature of travel. In some of these papers the instalments outgrew the columns and became detachable supplements, which were often indistinguishable from the independently published number books. Before the new mode of issuing books in fascicules is examined, therefore, some attention should be paid to the newspapers of the time, and to the great mass of 'literary' material which they offered daily, or weekly, or at some other regular interval.

There is one obvious difference between the printing of consecutive instalments of a complete book in the pages of a literary periodical or a newspaper and the issuing of that book either as a complete work or in the form of numbered parts issued by themselves periodically. Normally the readers of a newspaper or periodical do not plan to have the instalments of a work printed serially therein bound into a book to be placed on the library shelf alongside 'real' books, for those instalments are of irregular length and of inconvenient shape for binding; number books, on the other hand, are ostensibly printed with the intention that the consecutive parts will be preserved and bound. Yet even newspaper instalments were sometimes kept. It is obvious that the two most extensive surviving runs of the *Original London Post; or, Heathcote's Intelligence* have been preserved precisely because on the first two pages Heathcote printed consecutive instalments of lengthy works evidently of sufficient interest to be kept and bound as volumes. One of the works thus printed piecemeal three times a week is a detailed descriptive history of the several counties of England. The numbers from 801 (January 20, 1724) to 914 (November 2, 1724) all have on the first two pages portions of a description of Kent, each instalment filling the whole space, often beginning and ending in the middle of a

[1] *Spectator* number 10 (March 12, 1711).

sentence, and with a catchword at the bottom of page 2 linking each excerpt with the one which begins on the first page of the following issue. This scarce run of the *Original London Post* would not likely have been preserved at all if someone had not valued the description of Kent so much that he had the instalments bound as a book.

Preserved for a similar reason, and substantially bound for the Right Honourable Thomas Grenville,[1] are pages 1 and 2 of the *Original London Post* from numbers 125 (October 7, 1719) to 289 (October 19, 1720), in which the first two parts of *Robinson Crusoe* are printed in thrice-a-week portions. It is quite possible that the third page[2] of the numbers of this run contained other works reprinted thus a page at a time, for the extant numbers for 1723 and 1724 have the third page filled with instalments of *The Fanatical Persecution* (ending in number 809, dated February 7, 1724), and of a small tract entitled *The Fate of Majesty* (ending in number 815, dated March 16, 1724). Heathcote's statement in number 862 (July 3, 1724) testifies to the public's interest in these works:

> The History of the Fanatical Persecution, (lately inserted in this Paper), having given wonderful Satisfaction to our Readers in general, a Continuation of the same, in the Lives of those execrable Villains who dar'd to imbrue their vile Hands in the Sacred Blood of their dread Sovereign, the Royal Martyr K. Charles I. of blessed and pious Memory, (together with Lives of several other notorious Schismaticks), we hope will be equally as acceptable.

Justifying himself by this blurb, Heathcote reprinted a serial account of the Regicides.

Adding further variety to his *Original London Post*, Heathcote inserted in numbers 867 (July 15, 1724) to 889 (September 4, 1724) a piece of fiction to which he gave the title, 'The surprising and fatal Effects of rash and violent Love. Illustrated in the following faithful History of two Noble, but Unfortunate Lovers.' Although this was announced as having been 'Done from the French', it was an unacknow-

---

[1] This volume is in the British Museum.
[2] The third and fourth pages of the *Original London Post* are not preserved in the Grenville volume in the British Museum.

ledged reprinting of Eliza Haywood's novel, *The Fatal Secret; or Constancy in Distress*, first published by J. Roberts in May 1724, and reprinted the same year. Heathcote changed the heroine's name from Anadea to Celia, wrote 'the Chevalier De . . .' and 'Count . . .' for Mrs. Haywood's 'Chevalier De Semar' and 'Count Blessure', but otherwise copied the story word for word. Of equal interest to students of prose fiction is Heathcote's reprinting[1] of two remarkably effective epistolary novels by Mrs. Hearne, *The Lover's Week* (1718) and its sequel, *The Female Deserters* (1719). Heathcote once again made no mention of the author, and not only disguised the works under a vague title, 'Tales of Love and Honour, Being some very Curious and Diverting Tales, Written by an English Lady', but printed the two novels as a single work, lopping off the final paragraph of *The Lover's Week*, inserting the whole of *The Female Deserters*, and then tacking on the last few lines of the earlier story. These modifications, trifling though they are, suggest that the proprietor of the *Original London Post* hoped to conceal the fact of his borrowing current novels by Mrs. Haywood and Mrs. Hearne.

However unscrupulous Heathcote may have been in attempting to evade the copyright law that ought to have protected the literary property of Daniel Defoe, Eliza Haywood, and Mary Hearne, he deserves credit for choosing praiseworthy material. It appears, moreover, that he may have made some business arrangement if not with the authors at least with the publishers of the works he reprinted. In connection with his use of *Robinson Crusoe* he mentioned in numbers 220 and 289 of the *Original London Post* that William Taylor, the publisher of Defoe's novel, had the three volumes for sale at 'the Ship in Pater-noster Row', though if Heathcote was really on good terms with Taylor it is curious to find in numbers 632 (December 26, 1722) and 633 (December 28, 1722) an advertisement offering what one supposes to have been a piratical abridgment of the book: *The Life and Most Surprising Adventures of Robinson Crusoe of York, Mariner*, 'the whole Three Vols. done into one, with Cutts. Price 2*s.* 6*d*. Printed for M. Hotham, at the Black Boy on London Bridge'. Again, after an-

[1] In the *Original London Post* numbers 816 (March 18, 1724) to 861 (July 1, 1724).

nouncing in number 890 (September 7, 1724) that he proposed to reprint piecemeal in the *Original London Post* 'A General History of the Pyrates',[1] Heathcote printed the Preface and an outline of the contents, followed by a statement in number 900 (September 30, 1724) claiming authorization for the reprinting:

> Note: The History begins next; which being taken from the Original Copy, with the Consent and Approbation of the Proprietor, must be more satisfactory and Diverting than what is Piratically and Clandestinely inserted in another Paper.

Here, surely, is the pot calling the kettle black. The other paper was *Parker's London News*, and in it, for a time, the same group of biographies ran serially. Parker's side of the case is made clear by a statement in number 907 (September 9, 1724) of his paper:

> Since our Opposers in the Printing of Half-Penny Posts have begun the History of the Pyrates in their Papers of Monday last, we think the same to be as free to be copy'd by us as by them, and therefore intend to continue it from the Beginning to the End, to oblige our Customers, but with this Regard to Mr. Mist, the Proprietor thereof, that if he can prevail with others to desist, we shall cheerfully do the same.

Apparently Mr. Mist in some way or other prevailed, for the unfinished narrative is interrupted in *Parker's London News* number 930 (November 2, 1724) without explanation. Parker's curious proposal to 'desist' is worth a moment's thought, for it shows that Mist, as proprietor of a work just off the press, was apparently helpless to prevent two newspapers from reprinting it in instalments.

A few months later this same piratical and pirated work proved to be the subject of a heated dispute between Andrew Brice of Exeter and his rival fellow-townsmen, Samuel and Edward Farley. The doughty Andrew declared in *Brice's Weekly Journal* number 23 (Oc-

---

[1] This is the very popular work by Charles Johnson, first printed in 1724, with several other editions in the next few years. It was translated almost immediately into Dutch and French, and not only ran serially in the halfpenny papers of Heathcote and Parker but was also a bone of contention between two rival journalists in Exeter. It was issued as a number book in 1733, 1742, and in 1747.

tober 15, 1725)[1] that he had decided against inserting portions of *The History of the Pyrates*, reflecting, as he said, that

> such was the Practice of the *Grub-Street* Authors alone, and might be pleasing only to Vulgar Readers; for that if it prov'd *taking*, but a very few would be unfurnish'd with the Original, which might be had at every Bookseller's Shop, before I had gone a Quarter Way thro' the same.

But, as Brice explained, since his rivals had subsequently begun to print *The History of the Pyrates* in *Farley's Exeter Journal*, he decided to run an abridgment in his paper too, 'lest the Want of *any Thing* in *mine* should be urged by *any* to its *Prejudice*'. Both papers continued to print brief instalments of Charles Johnson's work, but it is clear that Brice felt no more eagerness to do so than did Parker in London, for he sometimes deliberately omitted the instalments, and in the number for March 18, 1726, printed disparaging remarks submitted by a correspondent who, writing from an inn, frankly 'thought it more entertaining to listen to the talk at a neighbouring Table than to read an Hum-drum History concerning a Crew of Rogues'. But Brice did not conclude the abridgment until August 12, 1726.

The issuing of a new and popular work in instalments, then, would seem to have been a very casual affair, since the proprietor of a London newspaper said he would 'chearfully' stop printing it and an Exeter journalist frankly admitted that he was using the book only because his rival had already started to print it in weekly portions. Whatever arrangements Heathcote and Farley respectively may have made with the proprietor of *The History of the Pyrates*, neither Parker nor Brice seemed to feel that there was any moral or legal or financial impediment to their reprinting considerable portions of one of the season's best-sellers. One wonders whether Brice had made any financial arrangement to reprint in his earlier paper, the *Postmaster*, Defoe's *Captain Singleton* (within the year of its first publication, 1720), and in later issues an 'Account of the Plague at Marseilles', the record of the famous 'Trial of Counsellour Layer', and 'Mr. H. Treby's Narrative of his

[1] In the new series which began with the resumption of the Stamp Tax on April 25, 1725.

Unfortunate Shipwreck'. Copyright restrictions do not seem to have affected serial publication very much.

There was, however, a law which might well have kept serialized matter to a minimum in the columns of newspapers. The Act of 10 Anne, c. 19, which was intended to be effective for thirty-two years from August 1, 1712, required all copies of newspapers of half-sheet size to be printed on paper on which a halfpenny stamp had been impressed, and those of a whole sheet to be printed on paper bearing a penny stamp.[1] As *Spectator* number 445 (July 31, 1712) duly recorded, the imposition of the tax caused some of the less firmly established papers to cease publication; and the same thing happened when the tax was resumed in 1725 after notorious evasions in the preceding years. It is a fact, however, that in many newspapers before and after 1725, full-length works of history, biography, theology, and fiction were reprinted in instalments. It is probable that in some of the cheapest newspapers —those whose proprietors habitually defied the law by using unstamped paper —the instalments were used mainly to fill space not required for news and advertisements. But in many papers the serialized matter regularly occupied the whole front page, or even the first two or three pages, of a four-page journal printed on stamped paper, and it is hard to escape the conclusion that the piece 'to be continued' was regarded as a special feature to make the customers feel that they were getting a bargain and thereby to keep the circulation steady. It has been suggested that there was a stronger financial reason for printing books serially in newspapers.[2] With the utmost clarity the law required that newspapers of one sheet or a half sheet be printed on stamped paper; it said nothing about newspapers filling a sheet and a half. The Stamp Act stipulated that publications larger than a single sheet but less than book size were to be classed as pamphlets, the only tax payable for these being at the rate of two shillings for every sheet in a single copy, regardless of how many copies were

[1] The mechanical process by which the sheets and half sheets were stamped is clearly described in Sydney R. Turner, *The Newspaper Tax Stamps of Great Britain. The First Issue, 1712-1757* (pub. by Sydney R. Turner [1936]).
[2] See Stanley Morison, *The English Newspaper* (Cambridge: University Press, 1932), p. 83.

printed in the edition. It was therefore easy enough for publishers of newspapers to avoid paying the penny-a-sheet stamp tax by swelling the size of each issue to one and one-half sheets or more, and that could be inexpensively done by stuffing the columns with almost any kind of printable matter. For an impression of six hundred copies of a news-paper filling a half sheet the stamps would cost twenty-five shillings; to print six hundred copies of a publication filling a sheet and a half would cost more for paper and type-setting, but the tax would be only three shillings. The saving would be much greater if a whole-sheet newspaper were increased to a sheet and a half.

Unless proprietors were willing to absorb the stamp tax, therefore, the only way to avoid increasing the selling price of a newspaper was to alter the size of the paper. Some proprietors reduced the size and printed the news on half sheets bearing halfpenny stamps; others preferred to expand each issue to a sheet and a half of unstamped paper, paying only three shillings for the whole impression and yet not violating the strict letter of the law.

It was not until 1724 that Parliament recognized and dealt with this clever means of dodging the stamp tax. That there were many who circumvented the law by using tax-free paper is clear from the preamble to the relevant part of An Act for Continuing the Duties upon Malt . . ., and for Explaining a Late Act in Relation to Stamp-Duties on News-Papers . . . (11 George I, c. 8), wherein it is asserted that

the Authors or Printers of several Journals, Mercuries, and other News-Papers, do, with an Intent to defeat the aforesaid Payments, and in Defraud of the Crown, so contrive as to print their said Journals, and News-Papers, on One Sheet and Half-Sheet of Paper each, and by that Means they neither pay the afore-said Duties of One Pen[n]y for each Sheet, nor a Half-pen[n]y for the Half-Sheet, as by Law they ought to do, but enter them as Pamphlets, and pay only Three Shillings for each Impression thereof, whereby his Majesty hath been much injured in his Revenues, and the Printers of other News-Papers, who do regularly pay the said Duties, are great Sufferers thereby.

It was therefore enacted that 'such Journals, Mercuries, and News-Papers, so printed on One Sheet and Half-Sheet of Paper' should not for the future be classed as pamphlets. From and after April 25, 1725, when the statute took effect, publishers of newspapers were required to pay the stamp tax at the penny-a-sheet rate, whatever size of paper they decided to use.

It was, of course, possible within limits to use sheets of larger breadth and length and still pay only a penny per sheet or a halfpenny per half sheet, though 'large paper' would doubtless cost more per ream. A sycophantic note sent by Edmund Curll to the Lords of the Treasury in March 1731[1] did not succeed in persuading them to set a legal limit on the size of the sheets that might be used for printing newspapers. In course of time larger sheets were used,[2] though apparently not primarily for the purpose of printing instalments in the columns. The necessity of using stamped paper rendered space so costly that no intelligent publisher would print instalments of books as mere fillers, and if continued pieces are found in newspapers after April 25, 1725, therefore, it may be taken as self-evident that the proprietors looked upon the instalments as a successful means of retaining customers and of obtaining new ones. The fact is that instalment printing in English newspapers was more extensive after 1725 than before.

It is worth noticing that the two Exeter newspapermen mentioned above — Brice and Farley — deliberately chose to fill space with the text of Johnson's *History of the Pyrates* at the very time when the renewed stamp tax put space at a premium. Required by law to print his weekly journal on stamped paper, Andrew Brice had to suffer the loss of customers unwilling to pay the increased price; but he did not think it wise to discontinue the printing of instalments. On the same day

[1] Edmund Curll (of all persons!) formally proposed to Sir Robert Walpole and the other Lords of the Treasury that Parliament should limit the size of paper on which newspapers could be printed and the number of lines which could be used in newspaper advertisements, thereby increasing the revenue by more than £10,000 per annum. The Commissioners of Stamp Duties reported on June 1, 1731, that they had a well qualified Register of Pamphlets and Advertisements and did not think it necessary to put the Government to the expense of engaging an inspector of newspapers and advertisements. Curll's representation and the Commissioners' report are filed as Treasury Board Papers CCLXXVI, No. 14. See *Calendar of Treasury Books and Papers. 1731-1734*, ed. W.A. Shaw (London: H.M. Stationery Office, 1898), p. 65.

[2] See. Graham Pollard, 'Notes on the Size of the Sheet', *Library*, 4th. ser., XXII (1941), 105-37.

(October 15, 1725) on which Brice began to print instalments of *The History of the Pyrates* he expressly stated that now more than ever he must compensate for the loss of half his customers by providing varied entertainment. Obviously the suggestion that books were reprinted serially only to fill space is untenable with reference to newspapers printed after April 25, 1725. Many proprietors reduced the size of their papers because of having to use stamped paper, yet they continued to print instalments of books.

While it is undoubtedly true that the renewal of the stamp tax put an abrupt end to many papers and caused an immediate shrinkage in the size and circulation of others, there is no way of knowing for certain how the renewed tax affected papers of which only one or two single issues have survived. The *Half-Penny London Journal* printed by W. Parks and J. Lightbody, with its two-page instalments of *The Life of John Sheppard* seen (in number 14, November 17, 1724), may have been forced out of existence by a rival paper of similar title rather than by the demands of the Stamp Office. The *Half-Penny London Journal; or, The British Oracle,*'printed for the Author, by T. Read', had the first two of its six pages filled with instalments of the partly fictitious *Voyages, Dangerous Adventures and Imminent Escapes of Captain Richard Falconer,* 'Written by Himself, now Alive' (published in 1720 by W. Chetwood). Single copies of number 10 and number 17 (January 12 and 28, 1725) seem to be the only ones now extant, but Read's paper may have continued to appear until the tax brought about a reduction in size and an increase in price. At any rate the *Penny London Post* which Read began to publish on April 26, 1725, comprised four pages printed on a large stamped half sheet, and it regularly had its first two pages filled with continued pieces. The extant numbers for 1726—numbers 109 (January 3) to 267 (December 30)—have instalments of the Philips translation of *Don Quixote,*[1] a series of 'historical novels' (followed by *Modern History; or the Present State of All Nations*), *Chinese Tales* (followed by Penelope Aubin's *Life and Adventures of Lady Lucy*) and *Gulliver's Travels*. Read's penny paper was smaller than

[1] See William A. Jackson, 'Two Unrecorded Serial Editions of *Don Quixote*', *Harvard Library Bulletin*, I (1947), 309-10.

the halfpenny one had been, but it gave one half of its space to serialized matter instead of one third, and these continued pieces were invariably given first-page and second-page space.

The change in size resulting from the renewal of the stamp tax on newspapers is most strikingly exhibited in a paper already mentioned, *Parker's London News*, and its successor, *Parker's Penny Post*. The former of these came to an end as a six-page Monday-Wednesday-Friday newspaper with the publication of number 1005 on Saturday, April 24, 1725, instead of on the following Monday, when the tax would come into effect. Parker complained about the tax, but announced his determination to comply with the Act. He said he proposed to 'put out a Stampt News Paper, to be vended for one Penny, resolving and no ways doubting to give as much if not more Satisfaction to his Readers by his Penny Paper, than is to be met withal in those of a higher Price'. He flattered himself, moreover, that all his former readers 'and all the well Wishers to the Rights and Privileges of this Great Metropolis' would give his new paper a kind and favourable reception. When on Wednesday of the following week *Parker's Penny Post* began to appear, it had only four pages, and each number was printed on stamped paper. Even thus much restricted in size the paper still printed instalments of *The Arabian Nights' Entertainments*, resuming the series which —to the number of 355 parts, each with a catchword to the next instalment—had already appeared in *Parker's London News*. Without interruption the work continued to be a front-page feature of Parker's paper until instalment 445 brought 'the End of the Twelfth and last Volume of the Arabian Nights Entertainment' in number 89 (November 24, 1725). In the meantime Parker, desiring to divert his readers to the utmost of his power, had begun in number 48 (August 16, 1725) to reprint in numbered instalments the *Exemplary Novels*[1] of Cervantes, this translation and that of *The Arabian Nights' Entertainments* appearing side by side on the front page until one was completed and the other unceremoniously halted part way through the 'Story of the Liberal Lover', in number 109 (January 10, 1726).

[1] These, translated by John Ozell, had earlier appeared in the successive numbers of the *Monthly Amusement*, beginning in number 1 (April 1709).

Soon after *The Arabian Nights' Entertainments* ran out, Parker began to print instalments of Robert Samber's translation of *Aventures merveilleuses du mandarin Fum Hoam, contes chinois* (1723) by Thomas Simon Gueullette, prolific author of pseudo-oriental narratives.[1] When the series was interrupted for a few issues early in 1726 Parker's subscribers protested, for in number 121 (February 7, 1726) Parker wrote:

Being requested by some of my Readers to continue the *Chinese Tales*, I have therefore (to oblige these Persons) inserted them again and begun at the Place where my former Paper Number 113 left off, and hope they will give a diverting Pleasure and Satisfaction to every Purchaser of my Paper.

It was doubtless a similar hope of giving pleasure and satisfaction that led Parker to print serial instalments of the Countess D'Aulnoy's *Relation of a Voyage to Spain* in numbers 118 to 306 (January 31, 1726 to April 19, 1727), and likewise the four parts of Swift's *Gulliver*, beginning in number 246 (November 28, 1726) precisely one month after the book had first been published. These *Travels*, said Parker, 'having for the Variety of Wit and pleasant Diversion become the general Entertainment of the Town and Country', were inserted 'in small Parcels, to oblige our Customers, who are not otherwise capable of reading them at the Price they are sold'. Other substantial works reprinted serially in *Parker's Penny Post* in later years included *The Four Years' Voyages of Captain George Roberts*[2] in numbers 308 to 414 (April 24 to December 29, 1727) and thereafter in numbers not seen; a frequently reprinted novel called *Cynthia. With the Tragical Account of*

---

[1] According to Esdaile, two other translations of this work were advertised in 1725, one for J. Roberts, 'Made English by Mr. Macky', and the other for H. Curll, 'translated by Mr. Stackhouse'. For an account of the work see Martha P. Conant, *The Oriental Tale in England in the Eighteenth Century* (New York: Columbia University Press, 1908), pp. 32-6.

[2] Published by A. Bettesworth in 1726 and believed to be partly Defoe's work. On the question of authorship see W. P. Trent, *Daniel Defoe: How to Know Him* (Indianapolis: Bobbs-Merrill, [1916]), p. 262, and Paul Dottin, *Daniel De Foe et ses Romans* (Paris: Les Presses Universitaires, 1924), pp. 774-8.

the Unfortunate Loves of Almerin and Desdemona,[1] in numbers 392 to 414 (November 8 to December 29, 1727) and thereafter; and *The Life of Cromwell*,[2] seen in numbers 1186 to 1302 (November 27, 1732 to August 24, 1733) but obviously running before and after these dates.

Special attention has here been given to Parker's newspaper and its serialized matter; but this was only one of many papers that in the first half of the eighteenth century reprinted works of fiction, biography, history, and travel, with little or no additional cost to the subscribers. Among these papers the earliest to contain more than four instalments of a continued work was the *Rhapsody*, a thrice-weekly half-sheet paper 'Sold by John Morphew', with the motto, 'Quod Veteres Scripsere, mea est farrago'; numbers 11 to 17 (January 24 to February 7, 1712) contained an English translation of Sophocles' *Electra*. Toward the end of the same year the *British Mercury*, official 'house organ' of the Sun Fire Office, printed on the first two or three of its eight pages weekly instalments of various works, among them *A Brief Historical and Chronological Account of all the Empires . . . of the World . . . from the Creation, to this present time* in numbers 397 (February 11, 1713) to 470 (July 7, 1714), and an entertaining little picaresque novel, *The Rover*, in consecutive numbers from 471 (July 14, 1714) to 482 (September 29, 1714). After printing briefer works in geography, the proprietors made it clear in number 519 (June 11, 1715) that thereafter 'only such Subjects as may be short and pleasing' would be printed in the *British Mercury*; but the paper itself apparently ceased publication soon after this announcement was made. An entertaining serial might conceivably have kept it alive.

---

[1] Esdaile lists editions of this anonymous work in 1687, 1700, 1703, 1709, 1726 ('The Eighth Edition'), and another, 'The Tenth Edition', without date.
[2] This, presumably, is the work entitled *The Life of Oliver Cromwell . . . Impartially collected from the Best Historians and Several Original Manuscripts*, first published in 1724 and ascribed by Halkett and Laing to Isaac Kimber. See Godfrey Davies (ed.), *Bibliography of British History: Stuart Period, 1603–1714* (Oxford: Clarendon Press, 1928), p. 83. There was a third edition in 1731, and in the *Gentleman's Magazine* for September the Register of Books lists the fourth edition, enlarged, sold by Brotherton at five shillings.

Certainly the proprietors of other papers thought that continued pieces would please their customers. In 1720 the author of the *Penny Weekly Journal; or, Saturday's Entertainment. With Freshest Advices Foreign and Domestic* hoped that his paper would find 'a favourable Reception from every candid Reader', and courted custom by deliberately imitating the proprietors of other papers who had 'so ingeniously pleased their Readers by various Performances taken from the *Tryals of State Criminals,*[1] *Arabian Nights Entertainments,*[2] *Robinson Crusoe of York, Mariner,*[3] and others'. His *pièce de résistance* was Edward Ward's 'Matrimonial Dialogues in Verse'.[4] In spite of the proprietor's assurance that these dialogues merited the praise of the learned and the acceptation of everybody, 'being so Natural and easie to be understood by the meanest Capacities', and in spite of his hint in number 15 (February 4, 1721) that readers were getting a bargain—'the Book from whence the Dialogues are taken being Ten Shillings Price'—the enterprise was on the verge of collapse after three months, as the admission on February 4 indicated:

The Author of this Journal, finding the Charge of carrying it on greater than his Expectations, has thought fit to lay it down; but the kind Acceptance which the Dialogues have met with, by People of all Parties, Ranks, and Abilities, encourage [thus] the Printer and Publisher to continue them.

The title of the paper was changed to the *London Mercury; or, Great Britain's Weekly Journal*, and the price was raised to three halfpence. But even the pompous title and the claim that the dialogues were 'certainly Pieces of excellent Wit and most diverting Amusement' were unable to keep the paper alive. The point to notice, however, is that

[1] This work was then running serially in Read's *Weekly Journal; or, British Gazetteer*, and was later printed serially in the *London Journal* (John Trenchard's weekly newspaper) along with *The Lives of the Sovereigns* and *The Tryal of Counsellour Layer*.
[2] Portions of this translated work were printed in early numbers of the *Churchman's Last Shift; or, Loyalist's Weekly Journal*, which began on May 14, 1720. Reference has already been made to George Parker's reprinting of the entire work in his *London News* in the years 1723 to 1725.
[3] Printed serially in the *Original London Post* in 1719, as was indicated above.
[4] Presumably either *Marriage Dialogues; or, a Poetical Peep into the State of Matrimony* (1708), or *Nuptial Dialogues and Debates* (2 vols., 1710).

the proprietor based his appeal for support on the continued piece rather than on any other department of his paper.

Continued pieces were notably successful in sustaining certain other newspapers in the same period. Heathcote and Parker had by no means cornered the market for such wares. Two other enterprising printers, John Applebee and James Read, conducted without interruption for many years separate weekly journals containing not only 'fresh advices foreign and domestick' but a great variety of essays, letters, and long serials. Read's paper, the *Weekly Journal; or, British Gazetteer*, in the course of its first few years printed by instalment several relatively short works of fiction and also such works as *The Czar of Muscovy's Travels thorugh Holland and France, The Tryals of State Criminals*, and *The Lives of the English Sovereigns*. That these were not mere space fillers is obvious from Read's note in the number for July 13, 1723:

> Several of our Readers having complain'd that our Accounts of the Kings of England, and also of the State Trials, have not been so entertaining as we would desire, by Reason of the Shortness of them, and the Scantiness of the Paper rendring [thus] it impossible to make them longer, while they are both in one, we have resolv'd, for the time to come, to insert them separately, in every other Paper.

In later issues of the *Weekly Journal* there were several long works of biography and history. Beginning in April 1732 Read reprinted substantial portions of Voltaire's *Life of Charles XII of Sweden*, just two months after it was first published. An abridgment—probably that attributed to Rev. Thomas Stackhouse—of Bishop Burnet's *History of His Own Time*, in 179 instalments, filled the front page of Read's *Weekly Journal* from March 30, 1734, to August 27, 1737. This was followed by a biography of Bishop Burnet himself, ending in number 692 (December 10, 1737). Read's note in this number shows that he deliberately chose to print serials as a means of pleasing his customers:

> Having gone through Bishop Burnet's *History of his own Times*, which we hope, and have reason to believe, has been thought an agreeable Entertainment to our Readers; we shall supply the Place of it, by another History not less entertaining, and which we hope will give the same Satisfaction, viz. The Life of that most famous Hero of Antiquity,

Alexander the Great, translated from Quintus Curtius, with the Supplements of the learned Freinshemius, &c.[1]

During the next two years Read continued to fill the front page of his paper with consecutively numbered instalments of the translation of Quintus Curtius.

In the meantime John Applebee had printed a number of continued pieces in his *Original Weekly Journal*, among them a spurious continuation of Swift's *Gulliver* (beginning April 13, 1728), a 'Narrative of the Shipwreck of the Nottingham Galley (1710)' (beginning September 27, 1729), and in ninety-three instalments running from June 2, 1733, to June 14, 1735, *The Sultanas of Guzarat, or the Dreams of Men Awake. Mogul Tales*, a pseudo-oriental work specially translated from the original French of Thomas Simon Gueullette.[2] Applebee continued to make a specialty of foreign fiction, usually printing two or three columns of translated French or Spanish novels on the front page—the work of Cervantes, Margaret of Navarre, Madame de Gomez, and other 'celebrated Writers'. Of more interest than these selected stories is the instalment printing of two full-length works of early romantic fiction, both in fresh translation: *The Pilgrim*, from the Spanish of Lope de Vega,[3] and *Diana*, by Jorge de Montemayor.

With few exceptions—among them these translations in Applebee's *Original Weekly Journal*—the books parcelled out as serials in English newspapers and low-priced miscellanies during the second quarter of the eighteenth century were neither expressly written nor expressly translated for instalment printing, though sometimes, as has already been pointed out, the proprietors had the temerity to reprint a book just off the press. That is what happened when the anonymous *Celenia; or, the History of Hyempsal, King of Numidia*, published at six shillings in

[1] In December 1739 A. Millar published in two volumes, duodecimo, price six shillings, the second edition of a work listed in the *London Magazine* as 'Quintus Curtius's History of the Wars of Alexander. Translated by John Digby, Esq.'
[2] *Les Sultanes de Guzarete ou les Songes des hommes éveillés, contes mogols* was first published in three volumes in 1732. Applebee's translation was published in two duodecimo volumes under the title *Mogul Tales, or Dreams of Men Awake*, six months after the end of its run in his weekly paper.
[3] Of this work, which was first printed in Spanish in 1584, Esdaile lists English translations dated 1621 and 1623.

March 1736 by E. Davis, was given first and second column space in the *London Tatler*, the only two extant numbers of which (dated November 6 and December 4, 1736) both have instalments from the first of the two volumes. Likewise the *Weekly Amusement; or, Universal Magazine*, a twopenny miscellany which J. and T. Dormer published from November 1734 to January 1736, printed a translation of Claude Prosper Jolyot de Crébillon's *L'Ecumoire, histoire japonaise*[1] immediately after *The Skimmer; Or, the History of Tanzai and Neadarne* had been announced in the *Gentleman's Magazine* and the *London Magazine* as having been published in June 1735 in a duodecimo volume at three shillings. The *Weekly Amusement* also reprinted some of the 'Letters of Abelard and Heloise', various other series of notorious love letters, and a continued 'History of England, by way of Question and Answer'.

Similarly typical of the bargain-counter miscellanies of the time was the sixteen-page *Universal Spy; or, London Weekly Magazine*, which sold for a penny in 1739. Its twenty-six numbers contained instalments of 'Robert Drury's History of Madagascar',[2] 'A Genuine Account of Richard Turpin, who was executed at York, April 7, 1739, for Horse-stealing', and three short works by Edward Ward.

By 1739 instalment printing had become a regular thing in the less distinguished areas of the newspaper world, as is obvious if one examines the scattered remnants of London news-sheets surviving from the 1730's and 1740's, for among them they reprinted a sizable shelf of books, several of them respectable enough in their own time and three or four of them still significant. To list all these works, native and

---

[1] First published in Brussels in 1733. The continued popular interest in the English translation is attested by its inclusion in the list of romances and novels prefixed to Colman's *Polly Honeycomb* (1760).

[2] Published by W. Meadows in 1729 under the title *Madagascar: or Robert Drury's Journal during Fifteen Years Captivity on that Island . . . ,* 'Written by Himself, digested into Order, and now publish'd at the Request of his Friends'. Both W. P. Trent and Paul Dottin agree with S. P. Oliver's opinion that Daniel Defoe had a considerable share in the work. See Samuel P. Oliver (ed.), *Madagascar; or, Robert Drury's Journal . . .* (London: Unwin, 1890), p. 19, W. P. Trent, *Daniel Defoe: How to Know Him* (Indianapolis: Bobbs–Merrill, [1916]), p. 264, and Paul Dottin, *Daniel De Foe et ses Romans* (Paris: Les Presses Universitaires, 1924), p. 793. A slender volume in the British Museum consists of the successive instalments of this work as they were printed in the columns of the *Universal Spy*.

foreign, brief and extended, new and old, might constitute a useful exercise in the detailed bibliography of the eighteenth century and might contribute a minor addendum to the history of English newspapers. As an index to the current tastes in reading at the lower levels of society two centuries ago, however, a few further examples are enough, with those already given, to show what varied works were used to give a touch of culture to the front page of many a cheap London newspaper of the time.

This variety is well illustrated in the four-page penny paper brought out by William Rayner three times a week—Monday, Wednesday, Friday—under various titles from late December 1735[1] to 1742. The first of the full-length works printed on the front page of *Rayner's London Morning Advertiser* was headed, 'The History of Osman the 19th, Emperor of the Turks, and the Empress Aphendina'. This was taken directly from the two volumes printed in 1735, 'faithfully translated from the French, by John Williams', with the title, *The Life of Osman the Great, Emperor of the Turks* . . ., the author being 'Madam de Gomez, Author of *La Belle Assemblee*'.[2] Rayner's instalments continued until number 97 (August 4, 1736). Next came Voltaire's *History of Charles XII, King of Sweden*, which ran to number 166 (January 11, 1737). In that number was a note explaining that many readers had asked to have some account of the Portuguese because 'the Misunderstanding which at present subsists between Spain and Portugal has made a great Noise in the World'. The work offered in compliance with this request was announced as 'The History of the Revolutions of Portugal by the famous M. l'Abbé de Vertot'.[3] The next numbers

---

[1] Number 57 of *Rayner's London Morning Advertiser*, the earliest seen, is dated May 3, 1736. Unless there was some irregularity in the sequence of the first fifty-six numbers, number 1 must have appeared on December 23, 1735.
[2] *La Belle Assemblée*, by Madeleine Angélique Poisson de Gomez, was translated into English by Eliza Haywood in 1724-6. There were later editions of this translation, the 'Fifth', 1743, doubtless being the one reprinted serially in the *General London Evening Mercury* for at least seven months in 1743-4.
[3] Vertot's *History of the Revolution in Portugal*, 4th edition, 'with considerable Improvements', was listed in the *London Magazine* for September 1734 as printed in octavo at 3s. 6d. for the Knaptons, Midwinter, Innys, Robinson, Rivington, Longman, and A. Ward.

seen (with the title the *London Morning Advertiser*, and later the *Generous London Morning Advertiser*) have the front pages nearly filled with instalments of Eliza Haywood's novel, *Love in Excess; or, the Fatal Inquiry*, the first two parts of which had been published in 1719, the third in 1720. The whole work was reprinted in the forty-eight numbers from 938 (September 4, 1741) to 985 (January 6, 1742). Later in 1742 the front page contained instalments of a 'Description of Flanders, Holland, Germany, Sweden, and Denmark',[1] which ended in number 1213 (November 22, 1742). Then followed, in numbers 1216 (November 29, 1742) to 1272 (May 4, 1743), 'The Life of Oliver Cromwell', probably reprinted from the enlarged fourth edition (published in September 1741) of the same *Life of Oliver Cromwell* which Parker had reprinted in his *Penny Post* ten years earlier.

There were in the 1740's several other newspapers offering strong bids for custom; Rayner did not have a monopoly of printing serial instalments. Heavy competition was presented by J. Nicholson in his *Universal London Morning Advertiser* —later called *Penny London Morning Advertiser*, and *Penny London Post; or, the Morning Advertiser* —which contained many extracts from books. The most notable complete books reprinted in this paper were 'The Trial of the Hon. James Annesley vs. Rt. Hon. Richard Earl of Anglesey', which filled the first three columns of numbers 109 to 183 (January 9 to June 29, 1744), a 'History . . . of the Town of Tournay' in numbers 198 to 227 (August 3 to October 10, 1744), and 'at the Request of many of our worthy Customers . . . Commodore Anson's Voyage round the World', in numbers 200 (August 8, 1744)[2] to 228 (March 1, 1745).

[1] This was probably *Travels through Flanders, Holland, Germany, Sweden, and Denmark* . . . , 'Written by an English Gentleman, who resided many Years in Holland in a publick Capacity'. The fifth edition, 'much enlarged', of a work bearing this title was published in London in 1725.
[2] On the preceding Saturday a rival paper, the *General London Evening Mercury* number 198 (August 4, 1744), referred to the 'great Desire the Public seem to have for the Voyage of Commodore Anson to the South Seas', and proceeded to reprint this work in that and successive numbers to 314 (May 4, 1745), pointing out that readers would have it in that form 'as soon as if they took it in Numbers'. This account of Anson's voyage, written by John Philips, a midshipman of the *Centurion*, and published in 1744 under the title *An Authentic Journal of the late Expedition under the*

In number 302 (April 5, 1745) began a series of accounts of criminal trials, the series continuing until midsummer three years later, coming to an end in number 789 (June 3, 1748). Then, after a miscellaneous assortment of brief biographies and fictitious narratives, there appeared 'A Faithful Account of the Sufferings and Hardships of Joseph Pitts, who was many Years a Slave in Algiers; including an Account of the Country; the Turks, and their Religion'. This piece, beginning in number 1004 (September 23, 1748), continued well into the year 1749. It was probably reprinted from one of the editions of *A Faithful Account of the Religion and Manners of the Mahometans, in which is a particular Relation of their Pilgrimage to Mecca ... With an Account of the Author's being taken captive; the Turk's Cruelty to him; and of his Escape*, first published in 1704, ten years after Pitts returned to his home in Exeter.

By far the most interesting newspaper to contain instalments of books in the 1740's was a daily paper called *All-Alive and Merry; or, The London Morning Post*,[1] with imprint 'London: Printed for A. Merryman, and sold by the Hawkers'. But the imprint varies. 'London' is sometimes omitted; sometimes the phrase is 'Printed by A. Merryman'; occasionally the last words are 'and sold by the News-Carriers'; a few numbers have no imprint at all. Even those numbers of early 1740 in which the imprint is 'Printed for A. Merryman, in Silver-Street near Golden Lane' afford little clue to the identity of the proprietor, for it may be assumed that 'A. Merryman' is a fictitious name, a verbal mask concealing someone who had reasons for remaining anonymous. It is tempting to conjecture that he was A. Ilive, especially since Golden Lane was within a stone's throw of the Ilive establishment (Abraham, Isaac, and Jacob, sons of T. Ilive, all of them printers and for a time type-founders) in Aldersgate Street. That *All-Alive and Merry* was printed in that general vicinity seems fairly deducible from the following item of news in that paper for Monday, February 18, (1740):

Command of Commodore Anson, was also published in sixpenny weekly numbers by Jacob Robinson beginning in September 1744.
[1] The subtitle was subsequently altered to *The London Daily Post*, and in the earliest numbers was, for a time, *The Daily Farthing Post*.

A few Nights ago, a young Lad, the Son of a poor Hawker, going with a Parcel of Alive and Merry into Grace-church-street, was met by a Sharper in Cheapside, who taking the News-Papers to be Things of great Consequence, prevailed on the Lad to go to a Tavern to fetch his Hat and Cane, and gave him Sixpence for his Trouble, telling him he would take Care of his Parcel till he returned; with which the Villain made off.

Those familiar with London streets will recognize that a hawker's boy taking a load of papers from Aldersgate Street to Gracechurch Street might easily have been intercepted in Cheapside. But the facts are too sparse and the logic is too thin to be conclusive.

Concerning the price and the life-span of *All-Alive and Merry* there is greater certainty. A manuscript note on one of the British Museum copies of the number dated Tuesday, November 10, [1740], states that 'This paper was a long Time sold for a Farthing.' Corroborative evidence of this low price—evidence which incidentally proves that *All-Alive and Merry* was already circulating early in 1739—is to be found in the following paragraph of a letter printed in *Common Sense* number 116 (April 16, 1739):

It seems, one of your Brothers of the Quill, the ingenious Author of a Paper, intitled, *All alive and merry, or the Daily Farthing Post*, hath not paid all that Respect to the Laws of his Country, as becomes so good a Subject; for, whereas he should have contributed the Sum of one Halfpenny to the Support of the Government for every individual Copy of his Farthing Post, he hath taken the whole Farthing to himself, to the great defrauding of his M[ajesty's] Revenue.

Each number of *All-Alive and Merry* consists of a single half-sheet of unstamped paper, the first column defiantly headed 'Necessity has no Law.'

Certainly the proprietor of the cheapest of all newspapers did his mightiest to give full value for the money, since in addition to Foreign News, Country News, Port News, London News, Irish and Scottish News, stock quotations, tide-times, and a daily (though also weakly) anecdote, A. Merryman reprinted in one or more of his six columns instalments of a most impressive set of works, worth listing as evidence that even farthings—if there were enough of them—could be used to purchase a shelf of books in those days. The titles as they stood in the columns of *All-Alive and Merry* are as follows, with the years during which the runs continued:

1739–40 A New History of England by Way of Question and Answer, extracted from Rapin, and other English Authors.

1740   The Distresses and Adventures of John Cockburne, Esq.

1740   The Trial of Charles Drew of Long Melford, Esq.

1740   The Life and Adventures of Robinson Crusoe, of York, Mariner.

1740–42 The British Traveller: Being a new History of England, Scotland, and Wales; describing all Things remarkable and is the best and truest Description of those Countries ever yet made Publick.

1740–42 The Turkish Spy; or, Hill's General History of the Ottoman Empire.

1741–42 Familiar Letters from a beautiful young Damsel to her Parents.

1743   The History and Cruelties of the Inquisitions of Spain and Portugal.

1743   The History of Tarquinius, Lucretia, and Brutus.

1743   Memoirs of an Unfortunate Young Nobleman &c. Being a Series of Transactions within the Memory of most of our Readers.

1743   The History of the Adventures of Joseph Andrews (Brother to Miss Pamela) and his Friend Mr. Abraham Adams.

Several of these works may be ignored as fourth-rate, though two or three others are of primary importance in literary history. Even the worst ones show that A. Merriman looked upon piecemealed prose literature—no matter how often it had already been reprinted—as useful farthing-bait.

The first work on this list was probably reprinted from the fourth edition, 'corrected and very much improved', of John Lockman's *New History of England by Question and Answer*, 'Extracted from the most celebrated English Historians, particularly M. Rapin de Thoyras, by the Authors of the new Roman History'. This edition, in duodecimo, was listed in the *London Magazine* for March 1739 as just issued at two shillings and sixpence and sold by Thomas Astley. It was doubtless an earlier edition of this book that was reprinted in J. and T. Dormer's *Weekly Amusement* in 1735.

The second book on the list above had been published by Rivington in 1735 as *A Journey over Land, from the Gulf of Honduras to the Great South-Sea. Performed by John Cockburn, and Five other Englishmen.* As late as March 1739 the book was being advertised as 'lately published', at five shillings. Unsold copies of this edition were offered to Rivington's customers in 1740 as 'The Second Edition', with a new title page reading *A Faithful Account of the Distresses and Adventures of John Cockburne, Mariner, and Five other Englishmen.* That the book came down still further in the ranks of vendible commodities is clear from the fact that it was reprinted in the columns of *All-Alive and Merry* during 1740, that it was issued in the autumn of the same year as a weekly number book at twopence per number ('the Whole to be issu'd in six numbers' of thirty-two pages each), and that it was advertised thus in *All-Alive and Merry* for April 6, 1743:

This Day is publish'd, a very entertaining Book, entitled, The Unfortunate Englishman: Or, a faithful Narrative of the Distresses and various Adventures of John Cockburn . . . .

Altho' this Book contains near 200 Pages in Octavo, it will be Sold for One Shilling, neatly stitch'd in blue Paper.

The size and price of this edition, together with the phrase 'stitch'd in blue Paper', justify the suspicion that it was only the unsold remainders of the number book offered now as a complete book instead of in parts. It cannot be merely a re-issue, under a new title, of Rivington's unsold sheets of the 1735 (1740) volume, since that contained 349 pages, the first 264 being filled with Cockburn's narrative. It looks as though the proprietor of *All-Alive and Merry* had by some means or other acquired the publishing rights and tried in various ways to make money out of it.

One suspects that this merry and pseudonymous snapper-up of unconsidered trifles found himself in difficulties when he tried to do the same thing with one of the abridged versions of the world's most popular novel. *All-Alive and Merry* for December 6, [1740], contained half a column from the beginning of a much condensed *Robinson*

Crusoe, and during the next few days the instalments appeared regularly. Then, in the number dated December 11, [1740], the proprietor made this astounding announcement:

The Life of Robinson Crusoe not being so well receiv'd by our Customers as we imagin'd it would, we shall instead thereof insert the following History of the Turks, which cannot but be acceptable to the Publick.

Then followed the first instalment of a work labelled 'The Turkish Spy; Or, Hill's General History of the Ottoman Empire'.¹ Perhaps the man who so boldly declared at his masthead that 'Necessity has no Law' had perforce to recognize some book-pirate's claim to a particular abbreviated edition of Defoe's famous narrative.² It takes a thief to catch a thief. It is entirely possible, on the other hand, that the readers of *All-Alive and Merry* really did disapprove of a garbled *Crusoe*; A. Merryman may have been telling the truth when he said it was proving unacceptable. At any rate, the copyright protection of Hill's book had lapsed in 1731, and the public apparently continued to think it pleasing, since, like *The British Traveller* and *Anti-Pamela*,³ it appeared regularly in *All-Alive and Merry* for over a year.

There may have been nothing reprehensible at all in A. Merryman's piecemeal reprinting of these books in order to eke out the thin fare of a minimum-rate newspaper. But the practice seems to have led to a much more curious kind of skulduggery. Either the proprietor of *All-*

---

¹ Not to be confused with Giovanni Paolo Marana's frequently reprinted work, first published in English translation in eight volumes between 1687 and 1694 and widely known under the title *The Turkish Spy*. Aaron Hill's book, first published in 1709, was entitled *A Full and Just Account of the Present State of the Ottoman Empire*.
² The many editions of *Robinson Crusoe* that appeared within the first dozen years after Defoe wrote the book are discussed by H. C. Hutchins in '*Robinson Crusoe*' *and its Printing, 1719–1731* (New York: Columbia University Press, 1925) and in his article, 'Two Hitherto Unrecorded Editions of *Robinson Crusoe*', *Library*, 4th ser., VIII (1927), 58–72; but the brief run of the abridgment in *All-Alive and Merry* is not mentioned, since it belongs to a later period.
³ The work printed serially in *All-Alive and Merry* during 1741 and 1742 under the running title 'Familiar Letters, from a beautiful young Damsel to her Parents' is really *Anti-Pamela; or, Feign'd Innocence Detected; in a Series of Syrena's Adventures*, published anonymously in London in June 1741 by J. Huggonson, and now attributed to Eliza Haywood.

Alive and Merry was the victim of an unscrupulous rival who deliberately and for gain (why otherwise?) pirated the whole publication during at least a few weeks, using even the same title and imprint, or (the only alternative, surely) A. Merryman himself published two different concurrent editions of his daily half-sheet. The evidence is clear enough, for two copies of *All-Alive and Merry* in the Burney Collection (British Museum) bear the same date, Tuesday, November 10, and although the date-line in *All-Alive and Merry* does not indicate the year, a comparison of the news with that in other papers of known date establishes the year beyond question as 1741. The two issues of identical date are actually for the same day of the same year, though the news differs in detail and the instalments of the three serials running at that time—*The British Traveller*, 'Familiar Letters from a beautiful young Damsel to her Parents', and *The Turkish Spy*—are taken from quite different parts of the three books. In one of these two Tuesday papers, for example, the instalment of the 'Familiar Letters' is from *Anti-Pamela* (1741), pages 181–182; in the other the instalment is from pages 187–188 of the same edition; and part of this second portion of the narrative appeared, with changes of capitalization, in *All-Alive and Merry* for Thursday, November 19, [1741]. The two papers dated November 10 differ slightly in imprint, one having 'Printed for A. MERRYMAN, and sold by the Hawkers', the other, 'LONDON: Printed for A. Merryman, and sold by the Hawkers'. Can it be that the proprietor of this paper, or someone else, prior to November 10, 1741, decided to catch more customers by issuing a rival *All-Alive and Merry* containing similar but not identical news, and instalments of the same three books? It is more likely that the proprietor deliberately prepared a separate edition of his paper for circulation in the provinces, as Robert Walker did with his *London and Country Journal*.[1]

It is likely that duplication of this sort was still going on a year or two later, for in the only extant numbers of *All-Alive and Merry* for 1743 (dated April 6 and April 20) there seems fairly strong evidence that

[1] During 1739–43 (the same years as those in which *All-Alive and Merry* was published) Robert Walker published concurrently two different series of his *London and Country Journal*, one on Tuesdays, the other on Thursdays.

two entirely different sets of continued pieces were being reprinted. It is true that the two pieces running in the number dated April 6 —'The History and Cruelties of the Inquisitions of Spain and Portugal' and 'The History of Tarquinius, Lucretia, and Brutus' —might have reached their journey's end prior to April 20, since neither piece appears in the later paper. But the instalment of *Joseph Andrews* on April 20 consists of some 350 words transcribed without omission from the end of Chapter XVII and the beginning of Chapter XVIII[1] in Book I. Now it is inconceivable that the eleven numbers of *All-Alive and Merry* issued from April 7 to April 19 (omitting April 10 and 17, which were Sundays) should have contained the twenty thousand words that stand in Fielding's novel before the portion printed as the instalment on April 20, even if there had been severe cutting not apparent in the one instalment that does survive. Similarly, the instalment of the second continued piece in the number dated April 20 is taken from pages 48 and 49 in the first of the two volumes published in 1743 under the title *Memoirs of an Unfortunate Young Nobleman*, based on the famous case of James Annesley *versus* the Earl of Anglesey. The preceding forty-seven pages could hardly have been reprinted in *All-Alive and Merry* between April 7 and April 19. If A. Merryman did not have a rival he must himself have conducted a two-handed struggle to win the public's farthings.[2]

'Necessity has no Law', A. Merryman impudently declared; 'Necessity is the Mother of Invention', feebly echoed the similarly pseudonymous 'A. Freeman' when he produced his rival half-sheet, the *London Evening Advertiser*, during the fourth week of October 1740. Imitating *All-Alive and Merry* in every aspect of its form and contents, this new-

---

[1] Misnumbered 'xvi' in *All-Alive and Merry*.

[2] The invasion of a good market by the unscrupulous using of another man's trademarks is illustrated by an announcement in J. Nicholson's *Penny London Morning Advertiser* number 203 (August 15, 1744):

> The Proprietors of an unstamp'd Paper called the *British Intelligencer, or Universal Advertiser*, very remarkable for being stuff'd with old News, stupid Paragraphs, and most scandalously printed, finding their Sales decrease, have changed their Title to the same which this Paper bore . . . .

Nicholson's own paper, the announcement continued, was thereafter to be called the *Penny London Post, or the Morning Advertiser*.

NECESSITY is the Mother of Invention.

Memoirs of an Unfortunate Young Nobleman, &c. Being a Series of Transactions, within the Memory of most of our Readers.

NOTHING could exceed the amazement which the account he gave of himself excited in the person who heard it; but willing to try him farther I am afraid you are a lying boy, said the I know the b on de Altamont very well he had never but one fon and he is dead. Indeed madam, I tell the truth, cryed he, and if any body told you I was dead they lyed, I never was fick but ahcee and that was when I fell down and cut my forehead with a great ftoner here is the mark of it, added he, putting back his hair, and fhewing her a la ge fcar above his eye brow. My Father knows it well enough, faid he, for he came when my head was bound up, and was very angry they had taken no more care of me.

The perfon who was thus inquifitive kept a great eating houfe, and the chevalier Richard came frequently there: And whenever the baron came to town, as he fometime did, tho' very privately this was always the place where he appointed to meet thofe w th whom he had any bufinefs She had heard here was an heir in the Family, and that he was dead; and to be tole he was alive, and reduced to this miferable condition the boy was in, feemed a thing incredible: but then again the particulars he had related, the confidence with which he fpoke, and the innocent grief he expreffed at not being able to find his father, would not fuffer her to believe him an impoftor. She ruminated a good while, and reflecting on the affair of the leafes which fhe was perfecly acquainted with and the baron's fecond marriage, fhe grew affured in her mind, that for the fake of raifing money, and getting a wife, he had renounced his child. The thought of fuch a babarity ftruck her with horror fhe fhuddered at the unnatural deed, and making the child come in, fhe undrefs'd her fervants to clean him and fent one out to buy fome neceffaries for cloathing him, while another fpread a table with fuch food as far a long time he had not tafted. He was almoft befide himfelf at the kindnefs he received, he wept with joy as he had lately done with grief, and was ready to fall down and worfhip his benefactrefs.

Had fhe purfued her firft intention, which was to write to the baron, the young Chevlier might perhaps have a lafting caufe to blefs her; but on recollecting that the chevalier Richard came often to her houfe, fhe thought it better to relate the whole affair to him; in the mean time kept the young penfioner in to be continued

The Hiftory of the Adventures of Jofeph Andrews, (Brother to Mifs Pamela) and his Friend Mr. Abraham Adams.

fhe child nor conceive him pleafed with what had happened, was in her opinion rather a gentler beaft than her miftrefs. Mrs. Tow-woufe, at the interceffion of Mr Adams, and finding the enemy vanifhed, began to compofe herfelf, and at length recovered the ufual ferenity of her temper, in which we will leave her, to open to the reader the fteps which led to a Cataftrophe, common enough, and comical enough too, perhaps in modern hiftory, yet often fatal to the repofe and well being of families, and the fubject of many tragedies, both in life and on the ftage.

CHAP. XVI.

The Hiftory of Betty the Chambermaid and and Account of what occafioned the violent Scene in the preceding Chapter.

BETTY, who was the occafion of all this hurro, had fome fome good qualities. She had good nature, generofity and compaffion, but unfortunately her conftitution was compofed of thofe warm ingredients, wh ch though the purity of courts or nunneries might have happily controuled them, were by no means able to endure the ticklifh fituation of a chamber maid at an inn, who is daily able to the folicitations of lovers of all complex ons: to the dangerous addrefs of fine gentlemen of the army, who fome times are obliged to refide with them a whole year together; and above all are expofed to the carcaffes of footmen, ftage coachmen an drawers; all of whom employ the weole arts lery of kiffing, flattering, bribing, and every other Weapon which is to be found in the whole a mory of love, againft them.

Betty, who was about one and twenty, had now lived three years in this dangerous fituation, during which fhe had efcaped pretty well. A man enfigo of foot was the firft perfon who made an impreffion on her heart; he did indeed raife a flume in her, which required the care of a furgeon to cool.

While the beaut for him, feveral others burnt fo her. officers of the Army, young gentlemen travelling the Weftern circuit, indifferive Squires, and fome of graver character were let affre by her corona!

At length having perfectly recovered the effects of her firft unhappy paffion, fhe feemed to have vowed a ftate of perpetual chaftity. She was long dead to all the fufferings of her lovers, till one day as at neighbouring fair, the Rhetorick of John the hoftler, with a new to be continued

FOREIGN AFFAIRS

Florence, April 6. General Breitwitz, upon the extreal folicitations of the Baron de Neuhoff, having wrote to the great duke to acquaint him with the propofitions which the baron had made, his royal highnefs fent the following anfwer to M. Breitwitz: That how fingular and impracticable foever the propofitions of the baron de Neuhoff were, he took his zeal and kind intention in good part that he might even affure him of this, in cafe he was within the reach of being fpoke or fent to; but that as to his projects, and the fuccour which he had demanded, it was neither convenient for the regency nor the generality to concern themfelves therein in any fort. The baron is ftill with his nephew in a country houfe fix miles from hence. Nothing is more certain, than that of the Corficans are difcontented with him, he is not lefs fo with them on the fcore of their ingratitude, who, after having availed themfelves of the arms and ammunition which he fent them on board fhips freighted by merchants of the returns which they expected in commodities of the produce of the ifland.

Genoa, April 6. The republick has received advice, that the king of Great Britain has fent exprefs orders to admiral Mathews, not to give any affiftance either to carry them ammunition, or any other thing whatfoever; but on the contrary, to put under arreft, and to fufpend the captains who fhall difoboy thofe orders. We are alfo informed by letters from Baftia, that the people of the ifland have lately had a general affembly, at which it was agreed to propofe to the re publick certain conditions, upon its great ing whereof they fhould be content to live under its dominion. So that the royalty of the baron de Neuhoff is now abfolutely out of the queftion. They have provifionally chofen for their chiefs, capt. Grandenio de Tavagna, for what rel t s to military affairs, and dr. Julia na, a lawyer, to have the direction of civil matters.

Milan, April 10. Count Traun has demanded an aid of this city of 10 000 florins for the fervice of the Auftrian army. An extraordinary contribution is likewife fetled by that general in this Dutchy under the name of Quiete viveret

Bologna, April 9. The head quarters of the Spanifh army is at Rimini, and the troops are divided in the neighbouring places, where they are fortifying themfelves, and making a line to fhelter them from any furprize from the Auftrian Hufars: Tis faid they will remain in this pofture till the court of Naples determines upon the march of its troops.

Petersburg. April 1. One hundred and twenty nine Gilleys are defign'd to make a defcent into Sweden. Count Lafcy, who is to embark in them, will have under his command the generals Lewafchew and Keith.

Vienna. April 13 The queen has re

comer in the ranks of cheap newspapers was sold, according to the imprint on the sole surviving copy, 'only by such Hawkers as have *True Hearts and sound Bottoms*'. With the remark, 'Considering the Diversity of Evening Farthing Papers that are dispersed about the Town, it may be thought imprudent to attempt another of the like Kind', the proprietor justified his invasion of the crowded market by insisting that the other papers were very badly printed and gave little or no news, whereas he proposed to spare neither cost nor pains to make his paper 'more agreeable and useful to those who shall be pleased to encourage it than any Thing of the Kind yet published'. It was on the ground that he printed more 'extensive and authentick Intelligence' that A. Freeman claimed encouragement for the new venture, for the formal notice 'to the Publick' made no reference to the two books reprinted in instalments on the front page of this farthing daily. If one may judge from the single surviving sample, the news in the *London Evening Advertiser* was not more extensive than that in *All-Alive and Merry*. It would have been the easiest thing in the world to make good the claim and find room for 'Intelligence' if there had been no instalments of 'The Spanish Historian; being a compleat History of that Monarchy. By Way of Familiar Letters, from a Lady on her Travels to her Kinswoman in London', and of 'The Entertaining Traveller, being an Account of a Voyage round the World'. Obviously A. Freeman believed that these two serials would help to sell his paper, even if, unlike A. Merryman, he did chop off the portions to fit the space that needed filling, regardless of where the sentence-endings came.

Equally eager to make money by this process, though careful to begin and end his instalments with completed sentences, was the unidentified proprietor of a badly printed half-sheet newspaper issued in 1742 with the alluring title, *Robinson Crusoe's London Daily Evening Post*. Only four frail copies survive, but it is obvious that the paper had been appearing for many weeks prior to the earliest extant number, which is dated Tuesday, September 21, 1742. In each number, besides foreign and domestic news, stock quotations, advertisements, theatre notices, news of shipping, and tide times, there appeared on the front page instalments of three prose narratives already in print. Of these by far the most important is headed 'A Continuation of the Familiar Letters of Pamela, &c.' This is Richardson's story, the first two volumes of which, as everybody knows, had been published in November 1740. The passage reprinted in the number dated September 21 is from Volume II of *Pamela*—part of the record for the Tuesday after the heroine's marriage, 'the Sixth of my Happiness' as she calls it. No instalment of *Pamela* appears in the three other extant numbers of this paper, dated November 12, 13, and 18; but in all four, and still 'to be continued', were portions of a work headed 'The Life and surprizing Adventures of Signor Rozelli, late of the Hague'. This was a translation of a French work by Abbé Olivier, first published in English by J. Morphew in 1709 with the title *Memoirs of the Life and Adventures of Signor Rozelli, At the Hague*, 'the whole being a Series of the most diverting History, and surprizing Events, ever yet made Publick', according to Morphew's title page.[1] As the earliest instalment is from page 151 of this volume, there must have been many earlier issues of *Robinson Crusoe's London Daily Evening Post*. That the proprietor planned to continue issuing the paper for some time to come is clear from his announcement in the number dated Saturday, November 13, 1742:

For the better Entertainment of our Readers, on Monday next we shall begin to insert (to be continued every Day, 'till the whole is finish'd) a diverting history, intitled, The Devil turn'd Hermit; or The Adventures of Astaroth, banished from Hell. A satirical Romance.

This translation of *Le Diable hermite; ou avantures d'Astaroth bani des enfers* (printed in Amsterdam in 1741 and attributed to Pierre Lambert de Saumery) had been announced in August 1741 as a new book published by Robinson at two shillings and sixpence. The second volume of the translation was listed by the *Gentleman's Magazine* as among the books published in February 1742.

In spite of the impudent declaration that 'Necessity has no Law' it is quite probable that *All-Alive and Merry* came to the end of its lively

---

[1] The '4th Edition, in 2 Pocket Volumes, with Cuts' was listed at five shillings in the *London Magazine* for July 1740, and *Robinson Crusoe's London Daily Evening Post* for November 12, 1742, advertised the book as published that day at two shillings, 'To be had of the Persons who serve News and Subscription-Books'.

and merry—if unlawful—existence on or soon after the first day of May 1743, along with the *London Evening Advertiser, Robinson Crusoe's London Daily Evening Post*, and other unstamped half-sheet papers that were being sold in the streets by hungry hawkers. By section 5 of the Act of 16 George II, c. 26,[1] all persons peddling unstamped newspapers after May 1, 1743, ran the risk of being taken before a Justice of the Peace and committed to the House of Correction for a maximum of three months; and the Act had teeth in it, for any person reporting an offender could claim a reward of twenty shillings upon producing a signed certificate proving that the alleged offender had been convicted. With a reward so easily won there must have been many a half-starved man or woman ready to swear and forswear for the sake of twenty shillings. Small wonder that A. Freeman in 1740 had declared that his *London Evening Advertiser* was to be sold only by 'such Hawkers as have *True Hearts and Sound Bottoms*'. They would need both. It must have taken courage to start out in the evening with a bundle of freshly printed half-sheets, when enemies or perfect strangers could bring about a windfall for themselves by merely seizing, apprehending, and carrying before a Justice of the Peace 'any such Person so offending as afore-mentioned'.

That many were so apprehended is likely, unless the farthing papers simply ceased publication on the dead-line date. That many had been running the risk prior to the passing of the Act is clear from the preamble dealing with the offence in question, for it is there stated that

great Numbers of News Papers, Pamphlets, and other Papers, subject and liable to the Stamp Duties, and which are not duly stampt according to Law, are daily sold, hawked, carried about, uttered, and exposed

---

[1] This particular Act is a curious omnium-gatherum, for its full title is as follows:
     An Act for continuing several Laws relating to the Allowance upon the Exportation of British made Gunpowder; to the Importation of Naval Stores from the British Colonies in America; to the additional Number of one hundred Hackney Chairs; and to the Powers given for regulating Hackney Coaches and Chairs; for punishing the Venders of unstamped News Papers; for allowing the Importation of Hemp or Flax manufactured in Ireland, though not shown to be of the Growth of Ireland; and for the Relief of Bryan Blundell, in respect to the Duty on some White Salt lost in a Storm at Sea.

to Sale by divers obscure Persons, who have no known or settled Habitation, to the great Loss of the fair Trader, and the Prejudice of his Majesty's Revenue.

A law for remedying and preventing such abuses and offences for the future was particularly needed because of 'several Doubts and Difficulties ... relating to the Execution of the Laws formerly made, and now in Being, for preventing such Practices, and punishing the Offenders'.

The Commissioners of the Stamp Office had for some months been disturbed by the large numbers of offenders, and on March 18, 1742, had sent their solicitor to the Lords of the Treasury with a memorial about unstamped newspapers. A year later (on February 24, 1743) they sent a further communication stating that they had committed some persons for hawking and selling unstamped newspapers, and protested that several Justices of Peace had hesitated to convict the alleged offenders on the ground that no statute gave clear direction as to penalty. The Commissioners desired that a clause should be inserted in 'the Vagrant Act now depending' for empowering the Justices to impose a suitable penalty. Section 5 of the Act of 16 George II, c. 26, had swift and remarkable effects, for the Commissioners found their work so vastly increased as a direct result of that clause 'for preventing hawking and vending of unstamped newspapers' that they had to hire quarters in an adjacent street to house an additional rolling press. A Treasury warrant authorizing the Stamp Commissioners to take a lease of chambers in Lincoln's Inn, at £100 per annum, was issued on June 28, 1744.

Apparently a few convictions were enough to make both hawkers and printers conform, though John Nicholson's complaint of August 15, 1744 (quoted above, p. 50, n. 2) indicates that the proprietors of the *British Intelligencer; or Universal Advertiser* continued to defy the Commissioners of the Stamp Office. Among those who defied the law to their sorrow was John Nicholson himself, who twice in 1743 (June 29 and September 28) sent a petition to the Lords of the Treasury concerning his plight in being prosecuted for publishing unstamped farthing newspapers, only to find that the Lords of the Treasury on both occasions referred the matter to the Stamps Commissioners.[1] The 'divers obscure Persons' who hawked Nicholson's papers doubtless suffered also; but to follow these in their distresses would lead into many a Dickensian dark alley which need not be explored for the purpose in hand. Who really wants to see Autolycus and his tribe in the House of Correction?

The only safe way for hawkers and printers to avoid punishment was for them to obey the law. For the fair traders there was a way by which they could keep the stamp tax they paid to a minimum. Ten years before the law caught up with the tax evaders of 1743 it had been discovered that if the part of a newspaper given over to news and advertisements was duly printed on stamped paper, it was possible to issue along with it, on unstamped paper, a literary supplement which could be counted on to sustain or extend the circulation. Evidence that this was done is to be seen in a plain-spoken attack on Eustace Budgell in the *London Magazine* for May 1733. Budgell, author of the *Bee; or, Universal Weekly Pamphlet*, had apparently neglected to have this six-page weekly paper entered as a pamphlet, and was consequently charged by the Commissioners of the Stamp revenue with breaking the law. Budgell had attempted to defend himself and his publisher (J. Roberts) in a letter on May 21, but J. Wilford, proprietor of the *London Magazine*, printed in the issue for that same month a merciless exposure of Budgell's specious arguments. Under the heading

The Downfall of the Bee: Or, A detection of the notorious Falsehoods in Mr. Budgell's Mendicant Letter of the 21st Instant. Being a True State of the Case, now Depending, between the Commissioners of the Stamp-Revenue and the Publishers of Pamphlets,

the *London Magazine* set forth the chief falsehoods alleged to be in Budgell's letter and at the same time missed no opportunity to refer disparagingly to the *Bee*, calling it 'an Universal Pyratical Pamphlet', and 'a Weekly Hodge-Podge consisting of a very dull Repetition of what was published the Week before'. Budgell had attempted to

[1] The communications referred to in this paragraph are reprinted in *Calendar of Treasury Books and Papers, 1742–1745, Preserved in the Public Record Office*, ed. W. A. Shaw (London: H. M. Stationery Office, 1903).

exonerate himself by insisting that his *Bee*, printed on three sheets, did not come within the provisions of the law. In reply the editor of the *London Magazine* rehearsed the relevant details of the Act:

> The Act of Parliament expressly obliges all Persons to stamp every Pamphlet, of half a Sheet of Paper, with a Half-penny Stamp; and every pamphlet of a whole Sheet of Paper with a Penny Stamp. But all Pamphlets, exceeding a Sheet of Paper, are liable only to a Duty of 2*s*. per Sheet. And all Pamphlets exceeding 6 Sheets in Octavo, 10 in Quarto, and 20 in Folio, are exempted even from the Duty of 2*s*. per Sheet, and have not any Tax upon them, being then accounted Books.

Budgell had complained, moreover, that the action of the Commissioners was aimed at himself in particular; but the writer of the *London Magazine* letter explained very clearly that R. Penny, publisher of the *British Observator*, was guilty of the same evasion, and had in fact been reported to the Commissioners earlier than Budgell himself.

What gives special interest to this letter in the *London Magazine* is the fact that very clear reference is made in it to the charge that Penny filled his pages with serial matter in order to swell the publication beyond the penny-a-sheet size, and thereby, as Heathcote, Parker, and a host of others had done before 1725, to evade the stamp tax.

> Complaint having been made to the Commissioners, that, one Penny, a Printer, publish'd a Weekly Pamphlet of two Sheets of Paper in Quarto called the *Observator*, one Sheet of which was News, and the other Sheet a downright Pyracy of Camden's *Britannia*, and that only added to evade the Stamp-Duty, as the Act of Parliament requires all News-Papers, Daily, or Weekly to pay, Penny was summoned before the Board and told by the Commissioners, that they looked upon his Pamphlet as a Weekly News-Paper, and the making of it two Sheets was only done to evade the Act of Parliament, and insisted upon his laying it down, or publishing it with the Half-Penny Stamp, as all other Proprietors of Weekly-Papers do. To this Penny humbly assured the Board that, 'he thought it would be no more deemed a Crime in him to publish a News-Paper of two Sheets, Weekly, than it was in Mr. Budgell to publish a News-Paper of three Sheets, Weekly; and only desired that his *Observator*, and the *Bee*, might be put upon One and the same Footing'; which he was promised should be done.

Examination of the extant numbers of the *British Observator* shows that, beginning with number 9 (May 5, 1733), Penny reduced the size of his paper from two sheets to one, printing news on the first of the two halves of the sheet, duly stamped with a halfpenny stamp, and printing four quarto pages of Camden's *Britannia* on the other half, which is not stamped. This seems to indicate that Penny, caught by the law in a test case, had to conform to the regulations in respect to the news part of his paper, but that he was prevented neither by the stamp tax nor by the copyright law from issuing *Britannia* as a supplement. Presumably instalment-supplements attached to newspapers were regarded by the Commissioners as portions of whole books, and therefore subject to no tax or duty whatsoever. By the same token, number books published independently as portions of whole books were likewise exempt, since they contained no news.

If the distinction between taxable and untaxable matter in the columns of papers containing news seems clear in principle, there was trouble in practice, since it had still to be determined precisely what the term 'news' designated. When Budgell was accused of not using stamped paper for the *Bee; or, Universal Weekly Pamphlet*, the question was whether the *Bee* was to be considered a miscellany or a collection of news. According to the *London Magazine* for May 1733, the keeper of the register at the Stamp Office refused to enter the *Bee* as a pamphlet liable only to the duty of two shillings per sheet, 'because he look'd upon it as a *Weekly Collection* of News, and therefore ought to be printed in a half Sheet, and bear the Half-Penny Stamp, as all other Weekly Collections of News do'. The implications here seem to be not only that the half-sheet of news must be printed on paper bearing a halfpenny stamp (as the statutes required) but that one half-sheet was recognized as the proper size for the news part of a paper, and that all other matter, regardless of its nature or extent, could be printed on unstamped paper. Budgell protested that his *Bee* was, in respect to the printing of news, much like the *London Magazine* and the *Gentleman's Magazine*. But the proprietor of the former insisted that to put the weekly *Bee* in the same class as these monthly magazines was ridiculous, chiefly because the columns of news in the *London* and the *Gentle-*

man's were really only summaries of reports no longer significant as up-to-the-minute intelligence.

The true *Import* and *Meaning* of the Word *NEWS* is the Return of Intelligence, of any Kind, by the Posts *Foreign* or *Domestick*. But all Transactions of a Month's standing, are, long within that Time, recorded in the *Secretary* of *State's Office*, then, by the Law of Nations, become *Memorials*, and all future Recitals of them, fall under the proper, and only, Denomination of HISTORY. All Monthly Collections are bound up annually with proper Indexes; and any *Attempt* to bring such *Collections* within the *Stamp-Revenues*, might as well include *Josephus, Rapin's* History, and Baker's *Chronicle*.

It was entirely a question of when news ceased to be news.

The point of the reference to Josephus, the translation of Rapin's *Histoire d'Angleterre*, and Sir Richard Baker's *Chronicle of the Kings of England* is that these three works of history were then (1733) being issued in weekly numbers, and whether these numbered parts could be regarded as taxable pamphlets or not, it was patently absurd to regard them as taxable bulletins of news. But when the news was only a month out of date the collectors of His Majesty's revenue insisted that it was none the less current intelligence and tried to force the proprietors of magazines to use stamped paper. Doctor Johnson's account of Edward Cave in the *Gentleman's Magazine* for February 1754 makes it clear that it was Cave who, as publisher of the *Gentleman's*, convinced the Commissioners in the Stamp Office that stamped paper should not be required for the last half-sheet of the magazines, on which the digest of the month's news was printed. 'Mr. Cave alone defeated their claim, to which the proprietors would meanly have submitted.'

One of those who meanly submitted was Robert Dodsley, who in 1741 made the embarrassing discovery that news a week old was nevertheless taxable, and had therefore either to omit the news altogether or raise the price of his weekly paper. Dodsley's sixteen-page miscellany, the *Publick Register; Or, the Weekly Magazine*, printed in double columns on four half-sheets, had been selling for threepence since its first issue on January 3, 1741. Then, in number 12 (March 21, 1741), came Dodsley's regretful but forthright announcement:

We hope not many of our Readers will be disappointed, or displeased, that they find no News in this Number of our MAGAZINE;
the Reason of which is, That we were obliged, if we continued the
News, to stamp every Half Sheet of it, as a News-Paper, and consequently should have been under a necessity of raising the Price, which
we apprehend would have been more disagreeable to the Publick than
the Loss of such News, as the greatest Part of our Readers must have
seen before in the Daily and Evening Papers; and which Loss we shall
use all possible Endeavours to supply with something more entertaining, and, we hope, more material. This, 'tis true, will be more expensive to us, but we chearfully submit to it as a grateful Return for
the kind Reception given to our Labours . . . .

Dodsley said he was surprised that he should have been called to account when other pamphlets of the same sort had been published for
some years without challenge. He protested that his intentions had
been innocent, and he acquiesced in the decision that his *Publick
Register* was, 'according to the Sense and Meaning of the Act', a newspaper. He announced that for the future no news would be printed in
the paper, and he hoped it could then 'in no Sense be deem'd Illegal'.
One phrase in Dodsley's declaration deserves particular notice—the
reference to the added cost of printing 'something more entertaining'
than news. Dodsley implied that he would have to pay a considerable
fee for the privilege of printing portions of a book as consecutive instalments, and that he would look upon this—and obviously expected
that his subscribers would look upon this—as an acceptable substitute
for news.

   With number 13 (March 28, 1741) the *Publick Register* included
each week a portion (complete in itself) of *An Historical and Geographical
Description of all the Counties in England*, 'by J. Cowley, Geographer
to his Majesty'. Neither that nor the 'Memoirs of a certain
Society', which, beginning in the number for May 2, gave thinly
disguised accounts of the current debates in the House of Commons, proved attractive enough to offset the demand for current news.
In number 17 (April 25, 1741) there was an accommodating note:

   As we find that our Readers, particularly in the Country, are very
desirous of having the News in this Paper as usual, we are determin'd

to gratify them, and yet not willing to raise the Price of our Paper. In order therefore to afford it at the same Price to the Publick, we have chosen to print two Pages less than we did, to balance the Expence we are at in Stamping that Half-Sheet which contains the News.

Thereafter each number of the *Publick Register* contained a four-page section (that is, a half-sheet) of news, printed on stamped paper. But in less than two months the paper proved financially unmanageable, partly, said Dodsley, because of the 'additional Expense I was obliged to in Stamping it', more because of 'the ungenerous Usage I have met with from one of the Proprietors of a certain Monthly Pamphlet, who has prevail'd with most of the common News-Papers not to advertise it'.

Other proprietors did not give in so easily, and there were many who managed in spite of the stamp tax to give their customers both news and serialized literary matter. Some of them expected the portions of books reprinted as instalments on the front page not only to be read but to be saved, fastened together consecutively, and given a place on the subscribers' bookshelves. That ,as was pointed out above, is precisely what happened to one subscriber's copies of Heathcote's *Original London Post*, containing *Robinson Crusoe* (in 1719-1720) and a lengthy description of Kent (in 1724). Andrew Brice of Exeter knew that regular readers of his *Post-Master; or, the Royal Mercury* would welcome the notice in number 27 (July 5, 1723): 'The Title-page (formerly promised to all my own immediate Customers) of the Abstract of Mr. Layer's Trial, printed lately in this Paper, is ready to be delivered to such as shall send for it.' On the other hand John Applebee announced in his *Original Weekly Journal* on June 21, 1735 that in response to popular demand the *Mogul Tales*, which had been running serially in that paper for two years, would be published with all expedition in two neat pocket volumes. Applebee assumed that although his readers presumably had enjoyed the serial few of them had kept the successive issues of the paper. Even when, as happened in some papers, the current instalment filled the whole of the front page and had its own serial number, signature, and catchword to the next instalment, the other side of the leaf was filled with news, prices, and advertisements soon out of date.

III. SUPPLEMENTS

Instalments in the front-page columns of a newspaper may well have brought reading matter to people who would not otherwise have seen it, but clippings or odd pages do not make a book. If instalments were to be preserved by anyone other than a few old ladies with a mania for keeping things, the instalments would have to fill both sides of one or more leaves which could be separated from the newspaper itself. What was needed was a detachable supplement, an extra sheet or half-sheet printed exactly like the sheets that went into the making of a regular octavo, quarto, or folio volume.

In the 1730's there were several newspapers which offered this special feature, the work thus issued in separate sheets being usually some sort of history or biography. The *Historical Journal*, for example, which R. Barlow (at the corner of Red Cross Alley, Jewin Street) printed and sold for twopence beginning on June 10, 1732, had the first two of its usual four pages filled with news, the remaining half-sheet (measuring approximately $10\frac{1}{4}$ by $15\frac{1}{2}$ inches) being set up as for a regular octavo and constituting, when torn off and folded, eight numbered pages of *The History of England from the Earliest Accounts of Time Down to the Reign of his Present Majesty King George II*. Although described by Barlow as having been 'Collected from the most Impartial Authors that ever treated of that Subject', the work was simply an adaptation of Rapin's *Histoire d'Angleterre*, Kelly's translation of which had begun to appear in weekly numbers on June 3, 1732, as a rival to Tindal's translation, previously published in monthly numbers by the Knaptons.

Early in the next year (1733), as was pointed out above, Robert Penny of Wine Office Court, Fleet Street, attached as a removable supplement to each issue of his *British Observator* a portion of Camden's *Britannia*. Bound with the five numbers of the *British Observator* (ix to xiii, dated May 5, 12, 19, 26, and June 2, 1733) in volume 80 of the Nichols collection of newspapers in the Bodleian Library are five supplements comprising pages 65 to 84 of *Britannia*. The supplement accompanying each of the first eight numbers of the paper was twice that size, that is, a whole sheet, comprising eight quarto pages. Penny reduced the size of the *British Observator* and of the supplement when the Commissioners of the Stamp Revenue reclassified the publication as a newspaper and required Penny to print the news section —not the supplement —on stamped paper.

It was also in 1733 that James Read, who for a long time had been reprinting books by instalment in the columns of his weekly paper, began to issue Burnet's *History of the Reformation of the Church of England* as a detachable supplement. He advertised in the *St. James's Evening Post* number 2857 (September 27, 1733) that the supplement was to be printed on a good letter and paper in such a manner that it could be bound up by itself. The title page and preface were to be given gratis when the volume was completed. For some three years Read issued a folio sheet of this work every week with his paper —then called *Read's Weekly Journal; or, British Gazetteer* — and during the same period customers who preferred to do so could also purchase two sheets every fortnight or four sheets monthly. The price was uniformly a penny per sheet, whether taken one, two, or four at a time. At that rate the total came to eleven shillings and seven pence, for there were 139 weekly single-sheet numbers, as the signatures indicate. In the preface of the completed volume, which is dated 1737, Read explained that he had published the work in 'small Parcels' in order to make it more universally read, since thereby 'it might be come at with a trivial Expence'. He had reduced the work from three large volumes to one by omitting the supporting documents. These 'original and authentick Papers', he said ,were 'valuable to the Curious' but made the price too high for many readers.

It appears that the proprietor of the *Original London Post; or, Heathcote's Intelligence* made the same sort of change in the form of the serialized literary feature in his newspaper, for he announced in the *Daily Advertiser* number 846 (October 16, 1733) that the paper would thereafter have two separate folio sheets, one sheet consisting of 'the most authentick News, both Foreign and Domestick, Ship News, List of Bankrupts, Bill of Mortality, Price of Stocks, Goods and Grain at Bearkey', the second sheet comprising a portion of *The History of the*

Conquest of Mexico, or New Spain, printed on a good letter and in such a manner that the accumulated sheets could be bound by themselves. The title page, preface, and contents were to be given gratis when the volume was completed. This double bargain, 'being more in Quantity than any thing of the kind hitherto published at that Price' —one penny—was advertised as 'to be continued every Monday, Wednesday, and Friday', and was 'to be had only of B. Buckeridge, in Baldom's Gardens, Leather-lane, and of the Persons that carry the News Papers'.

Likewise offering a weekly bargain of news and a literary supplement at very low cost was a provincial paper advertised in the *London Evening Post* number 1370 (August 28, 1736) combining the two distinct methods of reprinting books piecemeal in or with a newspaper —the front-page instalment, and the separately printed supplement:

On Monday next (Aug. 30) will be publish'd, Price Two-pence, printed on a fine Paper and a beautiful new Letter, *The Reading Mercury: Or, The London Spy.* . . . The first Page will contain that diverting Piece of Wit, Humour, and Satire, The London Spy; and the rest of the Paper will consist of the most authentic Advices . . ., with which will be deliver'd with each Paper as publish'd, a Sheet containing the History and Antiquities of Berkshire, which will be printed on a superfine Paper, and in such Manner as to be fit to bind up, which, when compleated, shall be follow'd with the several Histories and Antiquities of the neighbouring Counties . . . .

The enterprising printer who announced this inexpensive packet to be sold by the news men was William Carnan in Reading Market Place. A year or two later the proprietor of a similar undertaking in the metropolis, the *London Spy Revived,* offered much the same combination of literary features, printing on the front page numbered excerpts from Tom Brown's *Amusements Serious and Comical* and at the same time publishing a supplemental sheet containing successive portions of Ward's *London Spy* and other works. A note in number 225 (December 30, 1737) indicates that although Ward's works had been completely reprinted in the supplement and the second sheet would thereafter contain *The Persian Tales,* the title of the paper would continue to be the *London Spy Revived.*

A somewhat less pretentious and perhaps less successful enterprise comes to light in C. Corbett's notice in the *Daily Advertiser* number 2763 (October 15, 1739) announcing the second number of *Pasquin; or, The Emblematist*. Each monthly number, it was proposed, should contain a beautiful folio print, 'curiously engraven', and two sheets of letterpress. The first sheet was to contain an essay or letter dealing with the subject of the monthly print, followed by a digest of the remarkable occurrences of the preceding month 'to fill up the Remainder of the Sheet'. In the second sheet, Corbett announced, he would carry on a work entitled *The Genius of the Antients; or, The Wisdom of Greece and Rome*, this being 'a Collection of the Sayings, Maxims, Repartees, Allusions, &c. of great Persons mention'd by the Greek and Roman Writers'. This has a very amateurish and experimental tone. How long Corbett's sixpenny monthly package of gnomic wisdom continued to be issued is difficult to ascertain.

One of the most ambitious, though not most successful, of the purveyors of culture in supplements was one Cornelius Cotes, who in 1734 showed an extraordinary eagerness to make good literature accessible to all, for those subscribing to *Cotes's Weekly Journal; or, the English Stage-Player* were regularly furnished, as the subtitle announced, with 'two intire Sheets in Folio, one of a Play, and the other of the most authentic Intelligence both Foreign and Domestic'. Cotes was perfectly frank in his introductory remarks in the initial number (May 11, 1734); he pointed out that though English plays equalled if not excelled those of other nations, 'it requires more Expence to be furnished with a compleat Collection of them than is agreeable to the Circumstances of the Bulk of Mankind, especially to bear it all at once'. This present undertaking, he declared, would remove this inconvenience and enable any person, at the rate of twopence a week, not only to be furnished with the news but in process of time to be supplied with all the plays in the English language. Cotes made a good beginning, for during the course of the summer months in 1734 his customers got two complete plays, Shakespeare's *Julius Caesar* and Fielding's comedy, *The Miser*. Precisely when or why the project collapsed is not clear, but perhaps it was because with a lofty objective before him Cotes alienated potential customers by assuming—and in his prospectus telling them—that they were low and illiterate. Surely few readers would grasp eagerly at the opportunity of getting a sheetful of culture even at twopence a week when they found themselves addressed in such blunt terms as these:

This Design has a natural Tendency to spread Politeness over the most vulgar and obscure Parts of the Town and Country; and an illiterate Artificer or Peasant, of good natural Parts, may learn to be as much delighted with the Works of Shakespeare, Dryden, &c. as with dabbling in Politicks, perusing idle Tales and romantick Histories, or any other Diversions. Thus, by this Means, the Manners of Persons in low Life will be insensibly polished and improved, and an Air of Gentility and Complaisance render their Conversation with one another more agreeable than ever, and at the same time recommend them to the Notice and Esteem of their Superiors.

If the illiterate artificers and peasants of good natural parts did not put profits into the pockets of Cornelius Cotes and his printer (J. Taylor at T. Edlin's in the Strand) it was none the less commendable in him to make this offer.

What Cotes lacked, apparently, was some means of persuading the prospective customers that the opportunity of acquiring an air of gentility and complaisance was too good to miss. There were a few other newspaper proprietors who saw this clearly and were perhaps more successful in drumming up business. One of Cotes's contemporaries, T. Read in White-Fryars, Fleet Street, publisher of the *Weekly Oracle; or, Universal Library* (1734–1737), even offered to deliver his supplement (a series of questions and answers) either one sheet per week with the newspaper, or four sheets per month as a separate publication, 'stitch'd up in Blue Paper . . . at the Price of 6d. to such as are unwilling to take both Sheets weekly at 2d.' Unlike Cotes, Read managed to keep his supplement going for seventy numbers, perhaps because his appeal had been to more 'polite' people. A note on the last page of the final number suggests that he had a superior clientele, though it may only disguise the fact that sales had dwindled:

As the Encouragement given to this Paper has been chiefly among Persons in polite Life, and as the Season of the Year is now coming on, which usually calls such to more agreeable Scenes than the Town can afford, we think it proper to suspend, for a Time, the Progress of our Work, and shut up the Mouth of our Oracle, who has been always unwilling to answer the Impertinences of the Vulgar: But we promise our Readers that we will be ready to attend them again in the Winter Season, tho' perhaps, with some little Alteration in the Form of our Paper.

Read had no particular social class in mind when he printed instalments of a work alluringly entitled *A Collection of State Trials: Being the several Trials of Persons (with their Dying Speeches) for High Treason, Murder, Rapes, Heresy, Bigamy, Patricide, Sodomy, Burglary, Bills of Attainder, Impeachments, &c. from Richard II down to this time.* At frequent intervals during 1733 and 1734 Read gave notice in various newspapers that

A Sheet of this Work is publish'd every Monday, Wednesday, and Friday, in the *Penny London Post*; and twelve Sheets will be every Month stitch'd in blue Paper, for those who are willing to keep them clean, and deliver'd at their Houses, or at such Places as they shall appoint, at the Price of One Shilling.

His advertisements usually added that the general title page and a complete index would be delivered gratis when the collection was finished; and he arranged for a fairly wide distribution in London and Westminster, for customers could obtain copies either at Read's own establishment in Fleet Street or at the pamphlet shops at the Royal Exchange, Temple Bar, and Charing Cross. There, too, they might get former numbers or single sheets to complete their sets.

Read knew, of course, that his was just one of several such collections then being issued in parts, most of them based on Thomas Salmon's earlier *Complete Collection of State Tryals* (1719); but he strove to convince people that only his edition was genuine. In the *Daily Advertiser* number 1119 (August 30, 1734) he announced his thirteenth monthly number ('being the Third of Vol. II'), and solemnly declared that

The Publick having been amus'd with several pretended Editions of the *State Trials*, many of which are no other than very imperfect and inaccurate Abridgments of them; to prevent the like Imposition for the Future, this is to give Notice, that the genuine State Trials are printed by T. Read.

As will be seen in a later chapter, Read's claims were challenged by more than one other publisher who catered to public interest in criminal records by publishing them in monthly batches of eight or more folio sheets.

Read's most pathetic rival in the publishing of criminal biographies was a man for whom, in his particular circumstances, such publications were singularly appropriate. It is descending to the lowest depths of sordid literature to notice two desperate publishing ventures by William Rayner, who attempted in 1733 to gather a few pennies even while he was in jail. This enterprising man announced in the *Daily Advertiser* number 818 (September 13, 1733) that on the following day there would be published 'for the Benefit of William Rayner, Prisoner in the King's Bench', the second number of the *Compleat Historian, or the Oxford Penny-Post*. This paper, which was to be continued every Monday, Wednesday, and Friday, at a price of just one penny, was to be 'more in Quantity and better in Quality than any thing of this Kind hitherto publish'd at that Price'. As one might expect from this hackneyed formula, the first sheet of each number was to consist of authentic news, foreign and domestic; in this first sheet there were to be other useful 'particulars', for the procuring of which, Rayner said, no cost was to be spared. It is gloomily ironic that the imprisoned Rayner should offer, as the second sheet of his projected thrice-a-week bargain, four folio pages of criminal records. Rayner must have been desperately anxious to squeeze every penny from his 'select and valuable Collection of Trials for High Treason, Heresy, Bigamy, Burglary, Sodomy, Murthers and Rapes, &c.', for he added a solicitous note to inform those gentlemen who were willing to encourage the undertaking that they might have the three weekly sheets of this work delivered at their own houses by the news carriers every Saturday at the small price of two pence, or nine sheets 'stitch'd' every three weeks, for sixpence; or the sheets would be sent to any part of the country 'by Stage Coachmen, Waggoners, and Watermen'. A week later Rayner announced in the *Daily Advertiser* number 825 (September 21, 1733) that on the following day the first sixpenny number of *The State Trials* would be sold at his printing office in Marygold Court, near Exeter Exchange in the Strand, and by 'the Book-sellers, Pamphlet-sellers, and News-carriers, in Town and Country'.

Rayner had another string to his bow at this time, for his advertise-ment of September 13, 1733, also announced that local and provincial vendors would 'on Saturday next' be selling the *British Mercury, or Weekly Pacquet*, containing three sheets in folio, price two pence. The first sheet, he said, was to contain observations on the most noted daily and weekly papers, together with the foreign and domestic news of the week. The other two sheets in this weekly packet were to contain 'part of the History of Scotland' (the author is not named) until that work should be completed in 'one handsome Volume fit to bind'. These pot-boilers probably did not benefit Rayner or anyone else for very long.

The most venturesome of all newspaper proprietors who sought to win customers by offering impressive supplements was Robert Walker. Not content with the potentialities of the London market for his wares, Walker sought to exploit the provincial market as well. He had agents in several towns, including Bristol and Canterbury, and had his own shops in Oxford, Cambridge, and Birmingham. Walker attempted to triumph in both worlds by publishing a country edition as well as a city edition of his *London and Country Journal*. The London issues, beginning January 2, 1739, had been appearing regularly every Tuesday for nearly five months before Walker decided to print a separate edition on Thursdays for subscribers living in the provinces. For nearly three years — 149 consecutive numbers — both series of the *London and Country Journal* had as regular weekly supplement a fascicule of *The History of the Old and New Testament*, the work coming to an end in the Tuesday series on November 3, 1741, and in the Thursday series twenty-two weeks later.

Robert Walker initiated many similar enterprises, though not in duplicated series. It is not easy to determine how many of these suc-ceeded, since few of the papers and their supplements have survived. Not long ago Professor James Sutherland was able to examine what may have been the only surviving file[1] of Walker's newspaper, *Queen*

[1] As Professor Sutherland explained in the *Periodical Post Boy* number 6 (March 1950),

Anne's Weekly Journal; Or, The Ladies Magazine, numbers 1 to 175 (November 15, 1735, to March 17, 1739). The title, at first glance curiously anachronistic, may indicate that the paper was accompanied by a supplementary sheet or two comprising one of the biographies of Queen Anne, several of which were published during the 1730's. In the columns of *Queen Anne's Weekly Journal* were advertised seven other papers, now all apparently non-existent, each one of which contained literary supplements. With the kind permission of Professor Sutherland I list these papers, together with details of the supplements:

The Parrot: Or Pretty Poll's Morning Post, 1735 (Two sheets; Monday, Wednesday, Friday; three halfpence; two pages of news, and instalments of a History of England and an English translation of plays by Molière).

The Oxford Journal: Or The Tradesman's Intelligencer, 1736 (Two sheets; weekly; twopence; news, plus instalments of 'Lord Grey's Incomparable Love-Letters to his Sister the Lady Harriot Barclay' and 'All the Expeditions, Sea-Fights, Sieges, etc. from the Time of the Great and Valuable Sir Walter Raleigh . . .').

The Oxford Magazine: Or Family Companion, 1736 (Four half-sheets; twopence; instalments of Aphra Behn's *Oroonoko*).

The Weekly Spectator, and English Theatre, 1736 (Two sheets; weekly; portions of *The Recruiting Officer*).

Walker's Half-Penny London Spy, 1736 (On the first page, portions of *The London Spy* and other works by Edward Ward; news on pages 2, 3, and 4; second sheet, 'printed distinct, so as to be bound up in a neat Volume', has portions of 'The Wonderful Life and most surprising Adventures of Robinson Crusoe, of York, Mariner').

The Distillers Universal Magazine, 1736 (Four sheets, the second of which was to contain 'Mr. Seymour's Survey of the Cities of London and Westminster'; third sheet, 'Voyages, Travels, and Battles').

The New Half-Penny Post, 1738 (Two sheets; first sheet, news, second sheet, 'The Reign of the Victorious Queen Elizabeth').

Professor Sutherland's notes indicate that the last two papers in this list were published by J. Staunton (or Stanton, as the name is elsewhere usually written).

Concerning Stanton and his relations with Walker there is a tale to

this interesting bundle of a previously unknown paper was destroyed by enemy action in the North Atlantic during the Second World War.

be told, though this is not the place for telling it. Both men strove mightily to make money by printing cheap newspapers with pretentious supplements; and one of them, Walker, made more attempts to publish books in numbers than any other publisher who was in business before 1750. Stanton was a printer and publisher only because the Act for Laying a Duty upon the Retailers of Spirituous Liquors and for Licensing the Retailers thereof (9 George II, c. 23) had driven him out of his former business as a distiller. This Act became effective on September 29, 1736. Shortly before that date Stanton disposed of his still, hung up his empty and now useless gallon pot for a sign at his new place of business, and announced in the press that he would forthwith become a publisher. His first venture, advertised in Walker's *Queen Anne's Weekly Magazine* (as it was then called) number 45 (September 18, 1736) and in the *London Spy Revived* number 24 (September 20), was to begin on September 25 and was to be called the *Distillers Universal Magazine*. He assured the public that he would proceed to publish the magazine regularly every Saturday, and said that he desired their encouragement only so long as he merited it. How long Stanton merited encouragement cannot now be determined. Certainly while it lasted the *Distillers Magazine* (as it was called in later advertisements) was a remarkable production for its sheer bulk and impressiveness. No copy seems now to be extant, but if the ten numbers known to have been published maintained the standards set in the successive advertisements, no customer could complain that the price—two pence—was too high. Each issue was printed (so Stanton said) on four sheets of 'exceedingly fine Paper'; it was 'stitched neatly up in purple Covers'; its first sheet contained 'the whole Week's News, collected from all the Daily and Evening Papers extant, with Lists of Bankrupts, Prices of Stocks, Goods, and Grain, Weekly Bill, &c.'; its second sheet comprised successive portions of *A Survey of the Cities of London and Westminster* by John Mottley (alias 'Robert Seymour'), which T. Read had only a few months before completed as a number book; its third sheet, according to the detailed list of contents in the advertisement[1] of the seventh number, consisted of a

[1] In the *London Spy Revived* number 43 (November 3, 1736).

continued work called 'Naval Transactions and Sea Fights of the English Nation, from the year 1693, to this Time: Collected from Lediard's and Burchet's Naval Histories, and other authentick Authorities'; and the fourth sheet was filled with extracts from the *Craftsman, Fog's Weekly Journal,* the *London Journal,* 'Songs, Epigrams, Epitaphs, jocose Tales, and merry Jests', together with 'curious Receipts in Physick, Surgery, &c.' Small wonder that the aggressive ex-distiller made the claim in his advertisements that his magazine was 'the most useful, and entertaining Book extant; and if private Families were once to see it, they would not for that small Matter Weekly be without it'.

One suspects that not enough private families saw the *Distillers Magazine* even once, for although Stanton announced on November 3 that the first six numbers had been reprinted, on that same day he offered as special lure to new customers a series of 'Historical Bible Cuts . . . printed on a superfine Genoa Crown Paper, of a large Quarto size'. There were to be nearly two hundred of these cuts, and all were 'engraved from the Paintings of Theodore Rembrandt'! The first one, showing Abraham offering up his son Isaac, was to be given away with number VII (November 6). The cut to be given gratis with number VIII was (it may be supposed) a trifle more alluring, for it showed 'Adam and Eve in Paradise'.

The giving of free premiums —sure sign of an unresponsive market — was a device also employed by Walker, who on January 7, 1737, advertised in the *London Spy Revived* number 71 that on the following day there would be published the first number of his new weekly paper, the *Oxford Magazine, or Universal Library*. It, too, was to have four sheets, with news in the first, extracts from other weekly papers in the second, the 'Trial at large of Dr. Henry Sacheverell' in the third, and a portion of 'The most remarkable Sea Fights and Expeditions of the English nation from . . . 1665, to this present Time' in the fourth. Walker's free gift each week was to be one of a set of eighty-two 'Common Prayer Cuts . . . printed either for a large twelves Common Prayer Book, or a middling Octavo'. He thought these would be of great service to all families who had any Common Prayer books by them. And the price for this heterogeneous little weekly heap was only two pence.

During the next few years Walker was responsible for parcelling out other cheap once-or-twice-or-thrice-a-week combinations of news and (in a very broad sense) literature, among them one that must have survived for at least several weeks, for a small volume in the Yale University Library contains the complete run of two works which, according to the title pages, were printed by R. Walker and W. Jackson and delivered to customers who took the *Oxford Flying Weekly Journal*. Both works are abridgments of books published earlier, and were obviously issued at the rate of one half-sheet (octavo) per week. One of these bears the arresting title,

The History of the Surprizing Rise and Sudden Fall of Masaniello, The Fisherman of Naples, Who in the Space of Four Days raised 150,000 People in Arms, and in Two Days more made himself Governor, or King of Naples. Containing Very exact and impartial Accounts of the whole Tumults and Insurrections that happened there in the Month of July 1647, by Reason of the Tax laid upon Fruit, and other burthensome Taxes.

This abridgment compressed into 104 pages (about 40,000 words) the story of Tomaso Aniello, by Francis Midon, which C. Davis and T. Green had published in an octavo volume of 226 pages in 1729. The other, likewise an abridgment (in twelve numbers), bore the title.

The Trial of Charles the First, King of England, before the High Court of Justice: Begun Jan. 20, in the 24th Year of his Reign, and continued to the 27th. To which is prefixed, The Act of the Commons of England, assembled in Parliament, for erecting a High Court of Justice, for the Trial of his Majesty; as also the Journal of the said Court, as it was read before the House of Commons. With Additions, by J. Nalson, Doctor of the Civil Laws.

Walker may have been the publisher of a longer version of this story in eleven twopenny numbers of three octavo half-sheets each in 1740, the imprint of the volume being in the anonymous form which he often used: 'London: Printed and Sold by the Booksellers in Town and Country'.

It has been conjectured that the two abridged works just referred to appeared in the *Oxford Flying Weekly Journal* during 1746.[1] About the same time Walker and an associate, Thomas James, made similar efforts to promote the sale of a newly established newspaper[2] in the other university town by offering a *History of the Rebellion* and a biography of Queen Anne[3] as free supplements to purchasers of their *Cambridge Journal and Flying Post*. The mental nutriment thus supplied to Cantabrigians might seem more suitable for an academic community than that provided for Oxonians were it not that the astute proprietors interrupted their reprinting of Hooper's *Impartial History of the Rebellion* long enough to give readers of the *Cambridge Journal* the text of a scandalous novel called *The Unfortunate Duchess; or, the Lucky Gamester.*

Thus far it has been shown that between 1710 and 1750 the proprietors of many English newspapers gave to their subscribers, either in instalments printed in the columns of the papers themselves or as detachable supplements, a wide variety of 'literary' works, and that a few of those same works were also issued in 'numbers' printed independently. It is curious to find that occasionally the usual order of newspaper-plus-supplement was reversed, and that the news became the supplement—a sort of free gift attached to the number book—sometimes serving merely as a dust cover in place of the customary blue wrapper. In Walker's *London and Country Journal* number 149 (No-

[1] The Yale University Library catalogue dates this edition of *The History of* . . . *Masaniello* as '*c*. 1746'. For the *Oxford Flying Weekly Journal* see G. A. Cranfield, *A Handlist of English Provincial Newspapers and Periodicals 1700–1760* (Cambridge: Bowes & Bowes, for the Cambridge Bibliographical Society, 1952).

[2] As number 68 of the *Cambridge Journal and Flying Post* is dated January 4, 1746, the paper presumably began to appear in September 1744. John Nichols (*Literary Anecdotes of the Eighteenth Century* [London, 1812], II, 726) leaves both the date and the title of the paper unspecified. The *Cambridge Journal* lasted for over twenty-two years. See Cranfield, *op. cit.*

[3] John Nichols (*loc. cit.*) said that these two works were Clarendon's *History of the Rebellion* and Abel Boyer's *History of the Life and Reign of Queen Anne;* but R. Bowes declared in 1894 that they were works of similar title by Jacob Hooper and Conyers Harrison, respectively. See R. Bowes, 'On the first and other early Cambridge Newspapers', *Proceedings of the Cambridge Antiquarian Society*, VIII (1895, for 1891–4), 348.

vember 3, 1741) two of these number books wrapped in news were advertised as about to appear. The first was by Laurence Clarke, M.A., and was described as 'an excellent Work, intitled, A Compleat and full History of the Life of our Blessed Lord and Saviour Jesus Christ; with the Lives, Travels, and Sufferings of the Twelve Apostles and Four Evangelists'. It was to be comprised in ninety-nine weekly numbers, with thirty cuts. The price was set at twopence per number, 'in Order to make this Work come cheap, and that the poorer Sort of Families may purchase it as well as others'. The offer was made more attractive by the assurance that one sheet in large quarto would be delivered every week, neatly stitched in covers on which would be printed 'the whole Week's News, Foreign and Domestick, as in all the Weekly Journals'. In the same advertisement a companion work was offered, described as 'A Compleat Collection of the Genuine Works of Flavius Josephus', with 'James Wilson, Gent.' named as the editor. It was to fill 104 sheets, and again one sheet, stitched up in a large cover, was to be delivered every week, with the whole week's news printed on the cover. The price was twopence per number, but customers could save money by subscribing to both number books, in which case one of them would be issued with a plain cover at three halfpence.

A few weeks later, on December 21, 1741, William Rayner (now out of jail) added the word 'Generous' to the title of his *London Morning Advertiser* and announced that the paper would be given gratis to persons who were or would become subscribers to 'the Numbers of the Family Bible, or other Books, publish'd by William Rayner'. When the first number of this piecemeal printing of the Bible had been announced in the *London Morning Advertiser* for October 12 of that year, the conditions were that four large folio sheets, accompanied by a cut, would be published each week at the price of sixpence, that the work would be comprised in about 300 sheets—enough to make 'two handsome Volumes'—and that each weekly part would be covered with *Admiral Vernon's Weekly Journal*, containing not only the common news but 'the Life, History, and Memoirs of that magnanimous and renown'd Admiral'. *Quel embarras de richesse*—for sixpence a week!

CHAPTER III

THE EARLIEST NUMBER BOOKS
(1678-1731)

Long before the bargains mentioned at the end of the preceding chapter were offered in 1741, the number books, independently issued in weekly or monthly parts, wrapped in blue paper covers, had become a common commodity in the publishing business. It was essentially an eighteenth-century innovation, but a few experiments in piecemeal publishing can be found in the last quarter of the seventeenth century. In the search for the earliest examples of books issued in portions one hesitates to recognize as a genuine number book such a trifling thing as the thin batch of badly printed single half sheets—each labelled a 'Tome'—which Roger L'Estrange officially allowed A.P. and T.H. to print 'for the General Assembly of Hawkers' once a week beginning December 10, 1677. Together, the seventeen parts made up a weakly Rabelaisian narrative bearing the title *Poor Robin's Memoirs. With his Life, Travels, and Adventures.*[1] It began with a flippant address 'To the Sour, Sens-less, Cynical, and Censorious Reader'. The hero of the story was one S. Mendacio, and the reader was at liberty to take the initial S. as standing for Sir, Seignior, Sebastian, Samuel, Stephen, or anything else he wished. 'You shall find in the following History', said Henry Care, the author, 'many things worthy of your Curiosity, and as useful and diverting to aftertimes as those of *Garagantua* [thus]; and all within the bounds of modesty and good manners.' In order to avoid surfeiting the reader the author said he proposed to dispense the story in fresh portions every week, since 'it must needs be more acceptable in Penny Chops' than if it were offered 'all at a Lump'. Each 'chop' was a complete and independent unit and the seventeen successive 'tomes' are therefore not strictly speaking fascicules of a whole; but the instalments have a cumulative effect that marks the work off from the

---

[1] With 'Tome the third' (December 31, 1677) the title was altered to *Poor Robin's Memoires: or, The Life, Travels and Adventures of S. Mendacio*; and the imprint became 'London: Printed for D.M. 1677.'

amorphous matter of Care's earlier *Poor Robin's Intelligence*.[1] The character and the escapades of Don Mendacio are less interesting than those of Till Eulenspiegel and Lazarillo de Tormes, though the style has a certain satirical pertness that prevents complete dullness. Mendacio is no angel. 'He was always very arch, spiteful, and mischievous. If any boy had in the least offended him, he would presently bite off his Nose, bore out one of his Eyes when he was asleep, or pour scalding Lead down his Neck.' His natural talent in sophistry having made him a little famous, he took such pride in it that 'he became an everlasting Wrangler, more troublesome in Company than a Wasp buzzing at a mans Nose at Dinner, and his Conversation as insufferable as a Country Fiddler'. He was good at fencing, but 'Singing he could never attain any great perfection in.... Yet he could Dance incomparably a Scotch Jigg with one Leg, and the Friar and the Nun with t'other.' This last accomplishment, along with the statement that 'his Masterpiece was Juggling', leads one to suspect that the whole thing is a thinly disguised political satire, the sort of thing that is more memorably done in the first two books of *Gulliver's Travels* and in Henry Fielding's satirical farces. Description of Mendacio's courtships, of the countries he visited, and of his adventures—for example (in 'Tome the fourteenth') 'How Mendacio trepan'd a Lawyer, and cheated an Innekeeper'—apparently exhausted the audacity or the inventiveness of the author, for even before completing the first dozen numbers this predecessor of Ward and Defoe began to invite readers to communicate further 'Authentick Records' of Mendacio. *Poor Robin's Memoirs* petered out.

Even less significant, though likewise written in the third person and published in weekly parts, was *The English Guzman; or Captain Hilton's Memoirs*, printed for R. Oswel early in 1683. Had this account of the villainies of 'Captain' John Hilton and his brother George continued

---

[1] The eighty-four folio half-sheet parts, marked with consecutive letters, A-Qqqq, instead of numbered, and 'Printed by A. Purstow, for the General Assembly of Hawkers', were issued from March 23, 1676, to November 20, 1677. *Poor Robin's Intelligence* was revived for thirty-eight numbers from September 4, 1679, to May 12, 1678.

beyond the first few numbers it might have achieved a place among the early books published in parts.

A somewhat more sustained[1] though not more admirable effort at vivid narration is to be seen in the work printed for James Orme in St. Bartholomew's Hospital and published in six monthly numbers from September 1696 on, under the title *The Night Walker; or Evening Rambles in Search after Lewd Women, with the Conferences Held with Them, &c'*. This was just one of John Dunton's many flash-in-the-pan enterprises in journalism with an ostensibly moral purpose. He assured his readers that the design was 'not to minister Fuel to Wanton Thoughts, or to please the prophane Pallats of the Beaus and Sparks of the Town, but to display Monthly their Abominable Practises in lively Colours, together with their dismal Consequences, in order to frighten or shame them out of them if possible'. The author began the second number by joyfully declaring that the first one had been 'entertained with a General Applause, and approved as subservient to the design of a publick Reformation'; but one suspects that even the dedicating of the December number to 'the Gentlemen of the Society for Reformation' could not disguise from anyone the fact that the whole thing pandered to the lustful instincts of readers attracted by the title of the publication. Such readers cannot have been numerous. The vulgar realism of the communications from repentant sinners brought to confession by the rambling John Dunton had none of the fascination which Defoe later gave to the ampler disclosures of Moll Flanders, and it is not surprising that this salacious but dull work soon came to an end. *The Night Walker* is mentioned here only because the matter in the successive monthly pamphlets, each with separate pagination and signatures, has a degree of continuity that puts the work into the borderland between a tenth-rate periodical and a tenth-rate book published in parts.

More weighty in contents and more appropriately classed as an early number book is a publication which, if judged by its name, would surely seem to belong to the category of controversial newspapers. Its title, after the first number, was *The Weekly Pacquet of Advice from*

[1] Each of the six parts had five quarto sheets.

Rome,[1] but its substance was simply a history of Rome compiled by Henry Care and published in weekly parcels of eight quarto pages each. What makes this unmistakably a number book rather than a weekly paper is that the signatures and pagination are continuous through each of the five volumes, and—as was regularly so in eighteenth-century number books—each volume has a preface and title page printed *after* the final number in that volume. For instance, the third volume had eighty numbers, the first dated June 4, 1680, the last dated December 16, 1681. Readers had the early numbers of Volume III in their hands before midsummer in 1680, but Henry Care's Preface to that volume is dated December 24, 1681. It is worth noticing also that the imprint on the general title page of Volume III reads, 'London, Printed for, and are to be sold by Langley Curtis, at the Sign of Sir Edmundbury Godfrey, near Fleet-Bridge, 1682.[2] Where also may be had the two former Volumes, or any particular Sheets.' These last words make exactly the same offer to supply missing numbers to complete the customer's set as was frequently printed in the advertisements of number books over half a century later.

It is not surprising that, not long after Henry Care found a market for his anti-Catholic propaganda, weekly 'pacquets of advice' from Geneva and other continental centres of ecclesiastical influence appeared. Of these, only one survived long enough to deserve mention here as an early number book. This was *The Weekly Pacquet of Advice from Germany; or, The History of the Reformation of Religion there*, which appeared on successive Wednesdays from September 3, 1679. Its eighteen numbers, of eight quarto pages each, had continuous pagination and signatures, with the words 'The History of the Protestant Reformation' as a running title at the head of each opening. The author and the proprietor have not been indentified. The imprint

---

[1] The title of number 1 (December 3, 1678) was *Pacquet of Advice from Rome: or, The History of Popery*, and there were several changes of title during the course of the third volume. Three numbers of the sixth volume were published in 1689.

[2] This date is surprising only because at that time the new year date would not normally be introduced until March 25; there may have been a slight delay in sending the Preface and title page of Volume III, but it is unlikely that the delay extended to the end of March. The first number of Volume IV bears the date December 23, 1681.

simply indicates that the numbers were sold at the Phoenix in St. Paul's Churchyard.

Henry Care's *History of Popery*, first published in 240 consecutive numbers,[1] would stand as the first genuine number book of any considerable size to be published in England, were it not for the fact that Joseph Moxon, a member of the Royal Society and 'Hydrographer to the King's most Excellent Majesty', decided nearly a year earlier to write a book called *Mechanick Exercises, or, The Doctrine of Handy-Works*, and to publish only a portion at a time. The first number, 'Printed for Joseph Moxon at the Sign of Atlas on Ludgate-Hill', was dated January 1, 1677 (i.e., 1678), just a little over eleven months before the first *Pacquet of Advice from Rome* appeared. It is a real book, though it reached the buyers in the form of numbered monthly parts, each with a separate title page and a serial number. It is not a periodical, and it is not a series of separate pamphlets, for it has continuous pagination and its signatures run consecutively through the fourteen numbers of Volume I, starting again in the second volume. Until an equally substantial work is found to have been issued in numbers before the first day of January 1678, then, Moxon's *Mechanick Exercises* can stand in the records as the earliest English number book.

It was an interesting venture. Moxon's frank, vigorous Preface, like the book itself, shows him to have been a very practical man. This was to be a useful, trustworthy manual on smithing, joinery, carpentry, and related crafts. Moxon realized that it might not find a ready sale, and therefore, 'because the whole will be both a Work of Time and great Charge', he said, 'I mean to try by the Sale of some few Monthly Exercises what Encouragement I may have to run through all, if I live so long, and accordingly to continue or desist'. He took an extra

---

[1] Volume I has 31 numbers (December 3, 1678, to July 4, 1679), Volume II has 47 numbers (July 11, 1679, to May 28, 1680), Volume III has 80 numbers (June 4, 1680, to December 16, 1681), Volume IV has 35 numbers (December 23, 1681, to August 18, 1682), and Volume V has 47 numbers (August 25, 1682, to July 13, 1683). Thirty-eight competing numbers of Volume V were issued by a rival, William Salmon, from August 25, 1682, to May 17, 1683. It is interesting to note that in 1735–6 this work, somewhat condensed, was again published in numbers, excellently printed on fine paper. See below, p. 297.

month to prepare the fourth number, and after number VI (June 1 to July 1, 1678) there were longer delays, for the remaining numbers of the first volume did not appear until 1679 and the following year. 'The next Exercises' said Moxon at the end of number IX, 'will (God willing) be upon the Art of Turning, Soft Wood, Hard Wood, Ivory, Brass, Iron &c. With Several Inventions of Oval work, Rose work, Rake work, Angular work, &c.' Clearly he did not plan to desist; nor did he, though the second volume, comprising twenty-four numbers and with the general title, *Mechanick Exercises; Or, The Doctrine of Handy-works. Applied to the Art of Printing*, had the date 1683 in the imprint. There were subsequent editions of the numbers and the accompanying plates in both volumes.[1]

Moxon lived until 1700. By April of that year the last monthly part of another piecemeal book had been published. This was *The London Spy*, Edward Ward's colourful and spirited description of London life at the end of John Dryden's century. It was published in eighteen parts, the first being that for November 1698. In October of the following year parts I to XII were gathered together as Volume I and a new series was begun with the number for November 1699, which was marked, 'The Second Volume. Part I'. The first five parts were 'Printed for J. Nutt, near Stationers-Hall'; all the others have in the imprint, 'Printed and Sold by J. How, in the Ram-Head-Inn-Yard in Fanchurch-street [thus]'. Ward, who is identified in the title pages only as 'the Author of the Trip to Jamaica', followed the example of John Dunton in expressing pleasure that the first number had been widely acclaimed:

> The first Part of this undertaking I pop'd into the cautious World, as a Skillful Angler does a new Bait among wary Fish, who have oft been prick'd in their Nibbling; and finding the Publick Snapping at it with as much Greediness as a News-monger at a Gazett, or a City Politician at a new Proclamation, makes me purpose to continue it Monthly, as long as we shall find Encouragement.

[1] When The Typothetæ of the City of New York reprinted Moxon's second volume in 1886 the editor, Theo. L. De Vinne, observed that it was not only the first but the most complete of the early manuals on printing, adding that for a clear understanding of the mechanical side of the art of printing in the seventeenth century Moxon's treatise was indispensable.

MECHANICK

EXERCISES,

OR,

The Doctrine of

𝕳𝖆𝖓𝖉𝖞-𝖜𝖔𝖗𝖐𝖘.

Began Jan. 1. 1677. *And intended to be*
Monthly continued.

By *Joseph Moxon* Hydrographer to the
Kings moſt Excellent Majeſty.

❧❧❧❧
❧❧

LONDON,

Printed for *Joſeph Moxon* at the ſign of *Atlas* on
Ludgate-Hill, 1677.

3. Title-page of 1677 (i.e. 1678)

Ward proposed to keep his readers both edified and diverted with his 'compleat Survey of the most remarkable Places, as well as the common Vanities and Follies of Mankind, both by Day and Night'. He referred to the work as a 'Monthly Journal'. It is indeed a first-person narrative of what are ostensibly actual experiences of the author, much as Dunton's *Night Walker* had been two years before; and the text is obviously written in portions of convenient length for publication in sixpenny packets of four sheets each. 'It now being about Three a Clock, we concluded to go into *Pauls*, an Account of which, I shall give in my next.' So ends Part IV, for the month of February 1699; and the next monthly part ends, '. . . an account of which, for want of Room, I shall defer till my next'. Such signing-off phrases need not lead one to insist that *The London Spy* is merely a set of periodical essays. An essential continuity is easily perceived in the well sustained spright-liness of style and the consistent point of view. In spite of the fact that each part is complete in itself, with separate signatures and pagination, *The London Spy* is just as much a 'book' as *The Pickwick Papers*, which was issued in much the same way 140 years later. The most entertaining of Ward's realistic works continued to find favour, for *The London Spy* was several times reprinted both as a complete volume and as sup-plements to —or instalments in —early eighteenth-century newspapers.

If the search for valuable matter among the books published in numbers before 1750 is at its worst something like the project of trying to extract sunshine from cucumbers in the laboratories of Lagado, the yield thus far has been negligible mainly because up to the end of the seventeenth century the crop of 'cucumbers' was itself slender. Two books started their piecemeal run in 1678, and a third began to take shape twenty years later. Clearly the authors and booksellers had not yet perceived the possibilities in this new mode of vending their wares. It was another decade before any more examples of books in parts were added to the list, and even those have no great significance. The eighteenth century had well begun by the time two more works by Edward Ward[1] reached their first readers in monthly instalments:

[1] The history of early number books would not be appreciably altered if one insisted on including such publications as Ward's *Weekly Comedy as it is Dayly Acted at Most of*

Hudibras Redivivus; or, a Burlesque Poem on various Humours of Town and Country, published in twenty-four monthly parts in 1705–1707, and *The Life and Notable Adventures of that Renowned Knight Don Quixote De La Mancha*, 'merrily translated into Hudibrastick verse' and published in monthly instalments beginning in October 1710. In the latter of these, several proprietors had shares, for the general title page of the first volume, dated 1711, indicates that it was 'Printed for T. Norris at the Looking-Glass, and A. Bettesworth at the Red-Lyon on London Bridge; J. Harding at the Upper-end of St. Martin's Lane; and Sold by J. Woodward in Scalding-Alley, over-against Stocks-Market'.[1] According to the imprint of Volume II, dated 1712, Norris, Bettesworth, and Harding were joined by J. Woodward, E. Curll, and R. Gosling as proprietors; but it is possible that these last three were only vendors without any financial investment in the enterprise. At the outset the proprietors encountered difficulties, for a paragraph in the general Preface written when all the numbers of Volume I were assembled mentions 'the Difficulties this troublesome Task has been forc'd to struggle with'. The greatest of these was 'a generous Combination of some certain Persons . . . in order to stifle the . . . Performance upon its first Publication'; but the author then happily adds, 'The Approbation and Encouragement this elaborate undertaking has met with from those of better Judgment, have, I thank my Stars, deliver'd me, at last, from the grinning Insults of partial Envy, as well as threatning Ignorance.' The statement which follows, that 'the Second Volume is now in the Press, and will be publish'd entire in a little time', seems to indicate that it was the intention to issue the latter half of Ward's doggerel *Don Quixote* complete rather than in numbers. Opposition did not keep the proprietors from eventually putting 952 octavo pages of versified Cervantes into their customers' hands.

the Coffee Houses (in ten weekly numbers beginning May 10, 1699) and the *Infallible Astrologer; or Mr. Silvester Partridge's Prophesies* (the joint work of Edward Ward and Tom Brown, issued in eighteen weekly numbers beginning October 16, 1700).
[1] According to H. C. Hutchins, *'Robinson Crusoe' and its Printing, 1719–1731* (New York: Columbia University Press, 1925), p. 184, it was William Taylor who on January 16, 1710 (i.e., 1711) entered in the Stationers' Register 'Part 3d' of this work on behalf of himself, Norris, Bettesworth, Woodward, and B. Lintot.

Loftily indifferent to threats of opposition was the anonymous author of a work published in threepenny numbers early in the century by J. Morphew (near Stationers' Hall) under the title, *Great Britain's Rules of Health*. The undated title page of number V indicates that this little treatise was to be continued only according to the author's convenience. With delightful candour this self-appointed dictator on public health declared that he could not promise that the papers would be published at any certain time, 'as some do seem to demand', but he promised to continue them occasionally, 'according to his own spare and leisure Hours'. He thought this was probably the best way, since the writing, when hurried or 'too strictly tied down to a particular Time', would be likely to suffer; and besides. he added, 'We are not always in the same itching Humour of scribbling.'

Such candour and such inertia are not conducive to success in the early stages of a new development in book publishing. More energy went into the production of several other works which appeared in monthly numbers early in the eighteenth century, though not all achieved success. Beginning early in 1708 and appearing regularly for nine years was a comprehensive work entitled *Atlas Geographus: Or, a Compleat System of Geography, Ancient and Modern*, 'with Two Hundred new Maps and Cuts', the former by the well-known cartographer, Herman Moll. It was printed by John Nutt (in the Savoy) and the shilling numbers were sold by a group of retailers: Benjamin Barker and Charles King (in Westminster Hall), Benjamin Tooke (at the Middle-Temple Gate), William Taylor (at the Ship in Pater-Noster-Row), Henry Clemens (at the Half-Moon in St. Paul's Church-yard), Richard Parker and Ralph Smith (under the Piazza of the Royal-Exchange), and John Morphew (near Stationers' Hall). The work ultimately made five substantial quarto volumes. When the twelfth number, for the month of April 1709, was advertised in the *Tatler* number 16 (May 17, 1709), the dealers named in the imprint requested those that took the numbers month by month not to bind them 'till Europe be compleated, which will be in about 7 Months'. The numbers dealing with Europe totalled nearly 1800 pages, and at the end of that part of the work a page of 'Directions to the Binder' indicated that these numbers were to be divided into two equal volumes, the second beginning with the sixteenth monthly number; and "tis the Binder's Fault if he don't see they are intirely perfect'. Then came Volume III, on Asia, Volume IV, on Africa, and finally Volume V, on America. The Preface supplied with the title page of Volume I recommends *Atlas Geographus* as both profitable and pleasant to persons of all ranks, and suggests that by reading the book they may 'know all that is curious in the World, without the Fatigue or other Inconveniencies of Travelling'. There were apparently some complaints of prolixity in the work, but while the first numbers were appearing many commendatory letters had been received by the authors and by Mr. Moll. The proprietors, who may have been the eight men named in the imprint of the numbers, said they had spent £ 150 on books needed by the compilers, who had also made extensive use of public and private libraries, among them those of Dr. Hans Sloane and Dr. Tancred Robinson. It was explained that Herman Moll had worked for some seven years at the engraving of the maps, that the introduction dealing with 'the Scientific Part' was done 'by the Direction of the learned Dr. Gregory, late Astronomy Professor at Oxon', and that (upon Dr. Gregory's recommendation) the history and geography were written by 'two ingenious Gentlemen' together with 'some others of University and Liberal Education' who, 'if Health permit, will go through with the Whole'. The proprietors declared that modesty would not allow them to recommend their performance, but they permitted themselves to declare that they had not been wanting in pains, and that their materials were 'much better than ever were used for any Work of this Nature done in England'. That they were justified in mentioning the good reception accorded the first volume is apparent from the printed list of 762 subscribers (subsequently augmented by the addition of 74 names), among them 'Mr. Michael Johnson, Bookseller, in Litchfield', 'Hans Sloane, M.D.', 'Alexander Pope, Gent.', and many other well-known persons.

It is noteworthy that this five-volume work, first published in numbers, was yet not large enough to contain the descriptive accounts and maps of Great Britain and Ireland. These were reserved for a separate work under the title *Britannia & Hibernia Antiqua & Nova*, in which it was intended to include a new and accurate map of each county, 'with the Wapentacks, Laths, Hundreds, &c. and all the Roads exactly mark'd'. Advertisements invited gentlemen to contribute 'what Accounts they think proper for this Design, to John Nutt, . . . paying Postage'. As early as 1711 the proprietors of *Atlas Geographus* —which was 'printed by Eliz. Nutt, for John Nicholson at the King's Arms in Little Britain' —announced on the verso of the title page of the first complete volume that they would begin to print *Britannia & Hibernia Antiqua & Nova* in less than six months, though they expected to fill only one volume with the materials which they somewhat quaintly said they received 'more or less from Gentlemen in the County every Post'. The title page of *Atlas Geographus* number 25, for May 1710, has a crowded note expressing thanks to several gentlemen for communications, 'particularly to the Gentleman from Kilkenny; to the Gentleman that has promised to do North Wales; to another for what he has done, and is doing towards another Part of Wales'. Thanks were expressed also to several other contributors who had sent in accounts of towns and manufactures, 'not forgetting Two Letters wrote in the Style of those call'd Quakers, which, relating to Trade, and the Improvement of two different Manufactures in two different Parts of the Country, and writ intelligibly, shall be faithfully inserted'.

It is obvious that the compiler of *Magna Britannia* (as the work was commonly called) found himself simply swamped with materials, and that the work outgrew its place as an integral part of *Atlas Geographus*.[1] That it was the sheer abundance and complexity of the material which made it impossible to keep the accounts of Great Britain and Ireland within the expected single volume is clear from the 150-word subtitle attached to each of the six volumes of *Magna Britannia & Hibernia Antiqua & Nova or, A New Survey of Great Britain:*

wherein to the Topographical Account given by Mr. *Cambden*, and the late Editors of his *Britannia*, is added a more large History, not only of the Cities, Boroughs, Towns, and Parishes mentioned by them, but

---

[1] The caption for the text of *Magna Britannia* Volume I (1720) is 'Atlas Geographus: or, a compleat System of Geography, Ancient and Modern, for Great Britain and Ireland'.

also of many other Places of Note, and Antiquities since discovered. Together with the Chronology of the most remarkable Actions of the *Britains, Romans, Saxons, Danes,* and *Normans.* The Lives and Constitutions of the Bishops of all our Sees, Founders and Benefactors to our Universities and Monasteries, the Sufferings of Martyrs, and many other Ecclesiastical Matters. The Acts and Laws of our Parliaments, with the Place of their Meeting. A Character of such eminent Statesmen and Churchmen as have signalized themselves by their wise Conduct and Writings. And the Pedigrees of all our noble Families and Gentry, both Ancient and Modern; according to the best Relations extant.

All this was collected and composed by 'an impartial Hand', this being the phrase that concealed Rev. Anthony Hall, fellow of Queen's College, Oxford, and Thomas Cox.[1] The maps were by Robert Morden. It took the collaborators nearly seventeen years to prepare and publish the numbers which made up the six quarto volumes —over 4800 pages —into which the work eventually grew. The earliest numbers of *Magna Britannia* were listed in Lintot's *Monthly Catalogue* in 1714 and 1715, though the title pages of the first and second volumes, printed by Elizabeth Nutt, were both dated 1720. The remainder of this vast work continued to appear in monthly numbers, but as in usual with number books in quarto the signatures give no indication of the fact. Volume III bears the date 1724, Volume IV 1727, Volume V 1730, and Volume VI 1731. The sixth volume closed with the note, 'The End of that Part of Great Britain called England'. Ireland must have proved unmanageable, for it was omitted.[2]

Atlas Geographus, with its offshoot, *Magna Britannia,* deserves special attention as apparently the first number book compiled expressly for

[1] The British Museum catalogue identifies this Thomas Cox as the 'Rector of Stock-Harvard, the Elder'; but the imprint of Volume III of *Magna Britannia,* bearing the date 1724, indicates that the work was 'sold by T. Cox at the Corner of Swithin's Alley, Cornhill'. When Volumes IV, V, and VI were published (in 1727, 1730, 1731) T. Cox was 'at the Lamb, under the Royal Exchange'.

[2] Contemporary manuscript notes on a trade-sale catalogue now in the London offices of Longmans, Green and Company show that at the auction sale of Richard Williamson's stock on Tuesday, November 29, 1737, S. Birt thought it worth while to pay seventeen shillings for numbers 62 to 92 of this work, together with a book listed as *General View of the World,* three volumes and some odd numbers.

publication in monthly parts extending to more than two volumes; but there were other works of considerable merit and extent which began to appear in monthly numbers about the same time. One of these was *A View of the Universe; or, a New Collection of Voyages and Travels into all Parts of the World*.[1] It consisted of seven different works brought together for the first time by John Stevens and published in monthly numbers during 1708, 1709, and 1710. The accumulated numbers made two quarto volumes, which were reissued with new title pages in 1711.[2] The proprietors, J. Knapton, A. Bell, D. Midwinter, W. Taylor, and others,[3] obviously saw in the number books a new kind of venture promising substantial profits. In an 'Advertisement' prefixed to the first number of Stevens's *New Collection* (as it was commonly called) they declared that they did not intend to fill it with 'Persuasives to buy it', but they obviously tried hard to make the work acceptable to intelligent readers. The maps and cuts, they indicated, were to be inserted in their proper places, 'for substantial Information, and not dispers'd at Will to embellish the Book and divert the Ignorant'. Most significant of the publishers' statements are those concerning the method of publication and the consequent advantages to the subscribers. The

[1] Not to be confused with the 364-page octavo volume printed for Edmund Curll (at the Peacock, without Temple Bar) and Egbert Sanger (at the Post-House in the Middle-Temple Gate, Fleet-street) with the title *A General History of all Voyages and Travels throughout the Old and New World*, dated 1708. This was a translation of *Histoire universelle des voyages faits par mer et par terre dans l'ancien et dans le nouveau monde* (Paris, 1707), written (according to the title page of the Amsterdam edition dated 1708) by Jean Baptiste Morvan de Bellegarde, and edited by Du Perier.

[2] It remained on the market a few years longer. When T. Warner, proprietor of the *St. James's Evening Post*, advertised in number 1043 (January 25, 1723) of that paper the books for sale at his place of business (the Black Boy in Paternoster Row), he listed among them 'A Collection of Monthly Voyages, in 2 vols. in 4to, price Bound 1£. 4s.'

[3] The title pages of the separate works, of the two volumes, and of the two volumes reissued in 1711 have differences in the imprints. The number for December 1708 has the imprint: 'London Printed, and Sold by J. Knapton, in St. Pauls Church-Yard; J. Round, in Exchange-Alley, in Cornhill, N. Cliffe, at the Golden Candle-stick in Cheapside, E. Sanger, at the Post-House, and A. Collins, at the Black-Boy in Fleetstreet, 1708.' The number for January 1710 has the imprint, 'London Printed for J. Knapton . . . ; A. Bell . . . ; D. Midwinter . . . ; W. Taylor . . . ; and Sold by J. Round . . . ; N. Cliffe . . . ; A. Collins . . . ; and J. Baker . . . .

plan was to publish every month as much as would make 'a Book of Twelve Pence, or Eighteen Pence, according as it can be contriv'd, without breaking off abruptly, to leave the Relation maim'd and imperfect'. They realized, and warned their customers, that scarcely any of the books to be included in the *New Collection* were so small as to come within the compass of a monthly number. 'Of necessity they must be divided into several Parts, according to their Bulk.'

That is what was done with all seven of the treatises in the *New Collection*. The first work, Argensola's *The Discovery and Conquest of the Molucco and Philippine Islands*, filled the four numbers published in December 1708 and the next three months, each number being stitched so that the buyers could bind all four together. It was promised that great care would be taken that one number would end and the next begin so that there would be no confusion in the binding. The simple procedure of publishing so many sheets in each number, regardless of where the divisions came, had not yet suggested itself to the proprietors as feasible.

But the advantages of buying a book in fascicules were none the less emphatically set forth:

Thus every Person will, at so small a Price, as has been mention'd have a Taste of the Author propos'd to be translated, and of the Performance, before he launches out more Money to purchase the whole, and has every Month something New to Divert and Inform; which, tho' at first it may look slight, as being a Stitch'd Pamphlet, will soon grow upon [thus] into a Compleat Work, as if Printed all at once, and be no less becoming any Gentleman's Study, or Library. No Author is design'd to be Abridg'd, but fairly, and carefully Translated at large; but if any should hereafter be thought fit, for any particular Reasons to be so dealt with, it shall not be done without the Advice and Approbation of sufficient Judges,and the Publick shall have Notice of it, that no Man may have just cause to Complain he is any way Impos'd on. Every Author shall have a particular Preface giving some Account of Him, and his Work, with a fair Title, for the Binding of him up conveniently into a Volume, and every Month, as has been said, so contriv'd, that there may be no Casma, or other Eyesore in the Book. A small number will be Printed on a large fine Paper, for such as are more Curious, at one half more than the Price of the Common Sort.

The monthly numbers in the *New Collection* ran to well over 1300 quarto pages. Stevens may have been an undistinguished translator, but it stands to his credit that he introduced to English readers several first-hand accounts of distant places, among them the contemporary John Lawson's *New Voyage to Carolina*.

Another of the many translations made by John Stevens[1] was also published in numbers a few years later. That was his incomplete rendering of a Spanish historical work by Antonio de Herrera y Tordesillas, first published at Madrid in the period 1601–1615. Stevens' publisher, Jeremiah Batley (at the Dove in Paternoster Row), was wrong in asserting that *The General History of the Vast Continent and Islands of America, commonly call'd the West Indies*, had never been translated to English; a portion at least had been translated by Samuel Purchas for inclusion in his *Hakluytus Posthumus, or Purchas his Pilgrims*, first published just a hundred years before Batley parcelled out Stevens' translation in monthly one-shilling numbers in 1725 and 1726. Both Stevens and Batley, however, would have been delighted to know that a bookseller in 1952 would be offering the six octavo volumes for fifty pounds.[2]

One can understand why publishers in 1708 and 1709 hoped to develop a market for compilations in geography and history, which have always been popular with English readers; it is hard to see what prompted John Nutt to print in monthly numbers a work bearing so learned a title as *Bibliotheca Anatomica, Medica, Chirurgica, &c*, which appeared regularly from November 1709 on for many months, until the three quarto volumes—totalling well over 2000 pages—were completed. This book was a modified and augmented translation of a compilation by Daniel Le Clerc and Jean Jacques Manget, first published in Geneva in 1685 under the title *Bibliotheca anatomica sive recens in*

[1] Interesting information about this versatile man is to be found in Robert H. Murray (ed.), *The Journal of John Stevens containing a brief account of the war in Ireland 1689–1691* (Oxford: Clarendon Press, 1912).

[2] For an illuminating account of books of travel published in the period covered by this study see G. R. Crone and R. A. Skelton, 'English Collections of Voyages and Travels, 1625–1846', in Edward Lynam (ed.), *Richard Hakluyt and His Successors* (London: Hakluyt Society, 1946), pp. 66–140.

anatomia inventorum thesaurus locupletissimus. An advertisement in the
Tatler (number 93, November 12, 1709) indicates that it was on the
second edition, published in two folio volumes in 1699, that the English version was based, but points out that the work now in progress
incorporates 'near double the Number of other Curious Tracts, which
were either omitted in the said *Bibliotheca*, or have been publish'd
since, some of them translated, others faithfully abridg'd'. The imprint
of number 1 lists a large number of dealers:

> In the Savoy: Printed by John Nutt; and sold by W. Lewis in Russel-
> Street, Covent-Garden; Dan. Brown without Temple-Bar; J. Pember-
> ton in Fleet-street; R. Knaplock at the Bishop's Head; R. Wilkin at
> the King's Head; and M. Atkins at the Golden-Ball, in St. Paul's
> Churchyard; W. Taylor at the Ship in Pater-noster-Row; T. Horne
> under the Royal-Exchange; A. Bell at the Cross-Keys, in Cornhill;
> and J. Morphew near Stationers-Hall.

Some or all of these booksellers may have had a financial interest in the
undertaking. This first number, for November 1709, began with
'several Tracts relating to the External Parts of the Body, and of Bones
in general'. It was supposed that bones in general would attract readers
just as well as a new view of the universe. At any rate, the work was
carried on to completion.

Following this venture into the realm of experimental science, a few
years later there began to appear in one-shilling numbers a work bearing
the title *The Compleat Herbal: or, the Botanical Institutes of Mr. Tournefort.*
This treatise by Joseph Pitton de Tournefort (1656–1708), the 'Chief
Botanist to the late French King', was 'carefully translated from the
Original Latin' by John Martyn, 'with large Additions from Ray,
Gerarde, Parkinson, and others'. The title pages of the monthly parts
indicated that the work included 'a full and exact Account of the
Physical Virtues and Uses of several Plants', and 'a more compleat
Dictionary of the technical Words of this Art, than ever hitherto pub-
lished'. The entire work, which ultimately comprised two quarto
volumes, included some five hundred copper plates, representing over
four thousand different figures, 'all curiously Engraven', and was offered
to the public as 'A Work highly Instructive, and of general Use'.

The numbers which made up the first volume (completed in 1719) were published by a group of nine booksellers, whose names stand in the imprint of number XVI in this order: R. Bonwicke, Tim. Goodwin, John Walthoe, Matt. Wotton, Sam. Manship, Rich. Wilkin, Benj. Tooke, Ralph Smith, and Tho. Ward. Like the completed first volume, the numbers were 'to be Sold by J. Morphew near Stationers-Hall'.

The publishers explained in their Preface that they had several reasons for publishing the work in monthly parts: first, 'the Expence . . ., which otherwise would have amounted to too Considerable a sum'; second, the ease with which the undertaking could be dropped with minimum loss, 'if it does not answer the Expectations, nor hit the Taste of the Curious'; third, the possibility of correcting errors, since 'in this Manner of publishing, all Mistakes may be with less Trouble rectified'; fourth, the possibility of including original contributions submitted either to the printer or to the publisher by those who 'wish the Propagation of useful Knowledge' and are inclined to 'communicate some new Observations'. It is not clear whether the work proved unwieldy, but the numbers making up the second volume did not appear until ten years after those of the first volume. Numbers 21 to 41 are mentioned in the *Monthly Catalogue* and other papers as published more or less regularly between February 1728 and October 1730. By 1728 the proprietors had become fewer in number, for they now included only Walthoe, Wilkin, J. and J. Bonwicke (instead of R. Bonwicke), Ward, and two new members of the group, S. Birt and T. Osborn. Early in 1730 there was a further change of proprietors, E. Wicksteed replacing Osborn. Ten years later still, at the auction sale of copies and quirestock of George Conyers, deceased, on Thursday, February 14, 1739/40, Lot 8 consisted of 'Compleat Herbal, with 750 Books'; and at the sale of the stock of Francis Gosling on Tuesday, October 5, 1742, Osborn paid two guineas for '12 Bundles of odd Numbers of Tournefort's Herbal'. One wonders whether Osborn really expected to get his money back, or whether he was too much mellowed by the dinner which usually preceded such sales of copies and remainders.[1]

[1] These details about book auctions are taken from the manuscript notations in

If this record of bundles of odd numbers sold so long after the completion of the printing is surprising, even more remarkable is the long continuance, as an actual monthly publication, of a number book mentioned in Chapter I as in demand by at least one country customer. It is doubtful whether either the buyers or the sellers of Thomas Salmon's *Modern History; or, The Present State of All Nations* realized when it began to appear in June 1724, 'to be continu'd monthly in Pamphlets, till the Whole is finish'd', that ten years later the subscribers would still be paying their shilling a month for this highly successful publication; and it did not stop in 1734, though by February of that year J. Roberts was advertising number 122, 'Being the First Number of the 21st Volume'. This was also reckoned as the first number of the eighth volume relating to Great Britain and Ireland. So popular had the work become that Roberts said he would issue a number every fortnight instead of every month, and by midsummer the frequency was increased to once a week. There were eventually thirty-one volumes in this work, besides the French translation which began to appear in monthly numbers at a shilling each in April 1725, 'beautifully printed for the Use of Schools, as also Gentlemen who are desirous of acquiring the French Language'.

There was another Salmon, Nathaniel (1675-1742), whose first work written for publication in numbers began with Part I in April 1728. This was *A New Survey of England*, 'wherein' (the *Monthly Chronicle* announced) 'the Defects of Camden are supply'd, and the Errors of his Followers remark'd; the Opinions of our Antiquaries are compar'd; the Roman Military Ways trac'd; and the Stations settled according to the Itinerary, without altering the Figures'. The work was to be continued monthly, 'or as often as conveniently it may'. It was not until August 1730, however, that the eleventh and last of the shilling parts was published. J. Roberts was the proprietor of the work as it was issued in parts, though the *Monthly Chronicle* for November 1730

copies of eighteenth-century trade-sales catalogues in the London office of Messrs. Longmans, Green & Company, Limited, by whose permission these and other notes are quoted in the present work. For a description of the trade sales and the catalogues see Cyprian Blagden, 'Booksellers' Trade Sales 1718-1768', *Library*, 5th ser., V (1951), 243-257.

lists the completed work, in two volumes octavo, as printed for J. Walthoe. According to W. M. Sale, Samuel Richardson was the printer of this work.[1]

Nathaniel Salmon was less successful with his next venture in the writing of number books. *The Lives of the English Bishops from the Restauration to the Revolution* was to have been comprised in five parts, published at a shilling each. The first part, printed for C. Rivington, was published in July 1731, and the second part two months later; but the work announced as 'fit to be opposed to the Aspersions of some late Writers of Secret History' encountered either opposition or indifference. The second number was printed for J. Roberts, and it was over Roberts's imprint that the title page of the third part bore the announcement that,

The Author, being advised to discontinue publishing this Work in Parts, and to complete the same in the subsequent Publication, has comply'd therewith, and accordingly the following Sheets in succinct Order finish the Design.

The whole work filled only 402 octavo pages. A few years later (1739–40) another of Salmon's works, *The History and Antiquities of Essex*, came to an abrupt conclusion before completion, perhaps because his historical methods were wrong. Philip Morant, in a letter addressed to Richard Gough,[2] declared that, 'The poor man intended to have comprised the whole County in 21 numbers, for a guinea; but how much he miscalculated, his work shows.' Morant complained particularly about Salmon's inaccurate transcription of epitaphs in churches.

It was probably not the derangement of epitaphs that brought grief and an early halt to *Christianity set in a True Light*,[3] the first number of which was published by J. Peele in 1730. This was doubtless only one of many number books which fell flat after the first two or three fascicules had been issued. Likewise beginning bravely with 'No. 1' but not getting very far was a work listed in the *Monthly Chronicle* for January

[1] W. M. Sale, *Samuel Richardson, Master Printer* (Ithaca; Cornell University Press, 1950), p. 201.

[2] Quoted by John Nichols, *Literary Anecdotes of the Eighteenth Century* (London, 1812), II, 706.

[3] Attributed to Alberto Radicati, conte di Passerani.

1730 under the title *Memorials of Affairs of State, during several of the last Years of the Reign of King William III.* The proprietor, P. Meighan, announced on the title page of the first number that the work would contain authentic dispatches of Sir James Vernon, principal Secretary of State, relating to the foreign negotiations of the Earl of Manchester, and other communications on affairs of importance concerning Ireland; but the enterprise apparently failed to attract readers. Four years earlier, J. Batley and S. Chandler found the public unresponsive when they published 'Numb. I' of *A New Version of all the Books of the New Testament, with a Literal Commentary on all the Difficult Passages.* This ambitious work was 'written originally in French by Messieurs De Beausobre and Lenfant. By the Order of the King of Prussia', and was 'done into English, with Additional Notes' by an unnamed translator. Special additional features were to be 'An Introduction to the Reading of the Holy Scriptures, intended for Young Students in Divinity', 'An Abstract or Harmony of the Gospel-History', and 'A Critical Preface to each of the Books of the New Testament, with a General Preface to all of St. Paul's Epistles'. Perhaps these ponderous titles discouraged potential buyers. Even the excellent paper and good type did not procure customers. The young students in divinity were either indifferent or unprovided with shillings. Within the next quarter century the public eagerly bought *tons* of scriptural commentaries issued in monthly or weekly numbers; this particular one failed.

Greater success, due probably to more energetic publicizing, attended the efforts of a translator who was first announced as 'a Clergyman of the Church of England' but did not long remain anonymous. This was the Reverend Nicholas Tindal, M.A., Vicar of Great Waltham in Essex, whose translations of French works brought great wealth, if not to himself, at any rate to the enterprising publishers for whom he undertook the work. In April 1724 J. Roberts in Warwick Lane, together with S. Wilmot at Oxford and C. Crownfield at Cambridge, began to issue Tindal's *Antiquities Sacred and Prophane; or, a Collection of Curious and Critical Dissertations on the Old and New Testament.* It was announced in the newspapers that this work was 'done into English from the French of the Learned D. Augustin Calmet', that it was illustrated with notes and copper plates, that it was printed on fine paper and in a large character, that each number would be 'a compleat Thing of it self', that the work was 'necessary for all those who desire to have a thorough Knowledge of the Holy Scriptures', and that it would be continued monthly in order to 'render the Charge insensible to the Purchasers'.

As was promised, each shilling number was complete in itself, with separate title page; but the pagination is erratic: it is continuous to page 98 in the first two numbers, begins again at page 1 with the third number, and then, after page 184, begins once again at page 1 part way through number VII. It is possible that this irregularity indicates the employment of more than one printer. The success of the venture is shown by the note on the verso of the title page of number X (published May 27, 1725) to the effect that 'the greatest Part of the first six Numbers being sold off, they are going to be reprinted in order to compleat a certain Number of Vol. I. that will be sold by Subscription'. It was stated that this volume would consist of fifteen numbers, comprising twenty-four of the dissertations and filling about ninety sheets. Except for the cost of a temporary binding, those who subscribed to the whole volume would pay exactly the same as those who took the work in numbers, though people buying the complete volume had to pay down half of the fifteen shillings and the rest at the delivery of the book, bound in pasteboard, the following October. Further evidence of the book's success is to be seen in the larger list of dealers mentioned in the tenth number, for at that time (the end of May, 1725) printed proposals were to be seen and subscriptions booked at the establishments of J. Knapton, W. and J. Innys, J. Roberts, J. Pemberton, T. Woodward, and J. Clark of London, as well as S. Wilmot and W. Wells at Oxford, C. Crownfield at Cambridge, W. Ward at Nottingham, T. Bailey at Bury, Smithurst at Plymouth, and Palmer at Gloucester. Presumably most of these agents had no proprietary interest in the Calmet-Tindal work; but all of them must certainly have had copies for sale. The reprinting of the first, fourth, fifth, and sixth numbers indicates that more people bought the work than was at first expected.

In the eleventh number of Tindal's translation of Calmet notice was given that a few days earlier—that is, before the end of June 1725—the first number of another work translated by Tindal from the French original had been published by J. Knapton. This was Paul Rapin de Thoyras's *Histoire d'Angleterre*. No work published in numbers in the second quarter of the eighteenth century is more frequently encountered in newspaper advertisements than this. Tindal's translation eventually filled fifteen octavo volumes, each made up of five or six monthly numbers. Tindal doubtless spent many long hours in producing the translation, but one must not picture him grinding out copy in a cramped garret or a stuffy vicarage; he wrote much of the book while cruising in an English naval ship off the west coast of Europe. It was not from Great Waltham but from on board the *Torbay* in the Bay of Revel in the Gulf of Finland that on July 12, 1726 he addressed the dedication of Volume II to Sir Charles Wager, commander of the British fleet in the Baltic, and he expressed particular gratitude for 'the Leisure I enjoy under you in your Expedition to the North'. When he wrote the dedication to Volume IV over a year later—on September 4, 1727—Tindal was once again aboard the *Torbay*, this time in Gibraltar Bay. By September 10, 1728, when Volume VI was dedicated, Tindal had returned to his own parish in Essex, but he cannot have spent much time there, for in addressing 'the Gentlemen of the English Factory at Lisbon' he referred to the volume as 'the Fruits of . . . leisure Hours whilst at Lisbon' and mentioned with great satisfaction the privilege he had enjoyed of officiating for five months as chaplain to 'the largest and noblest Factory in the World'. Thanks to the Royal Navy, a country vicar was able to translate for English readers a work which he did not hesitate to call 'the Best and most Impartial History of England yet Extant'. Tindal's translation of Rapin's *Histoire d'Angleterre* proved so popular that while it was still in progress J. Roberts began (in February 1729) to publish in shilling numbers the original French text, together with a French translation of Tindal's notes, these being *'marquées d'un astérisque'*. As soon as the English translation was completed in monthly octavo numbers the Knaptons reprinted it and Tindal's continuations in sixpenny weekly

ACTA REGIA:

OR,

An ACCOUNT of the

TREATIES, LETTERS, and INSTRUMENTS

Between the Monarchs of *England* and Foreign Powers, publiſh'd in Mr. *Rymer's* FOÉDERA, which are the Baſis of the *Engliſh* Hiſtory, and contain thoſe Authorities which rectify the Miſtakes that moſt of our Writers have committed for want of ſuch a Collection of Records.

Tranſlated from the *French* of M. RAPIN, as publiſh'd by M. LE CLERC.

With the Heads of the Kings and Queens, curiouſly engrav'd by Mr. *Vandergucht*.

To be Publiſh'd Monthly.

Number I. for *September*.

Beginning with the Reign of King *Henry* I. and ending with that of *Edward* I.

LONDON:

Printed for J. DARBY, A. BETTESWORTH, F. FAYRAM, J. PEMBERTON, C. RIVINGTON, J. HOOKE, F. CLAY. J. BATLEY, and E. SYMON. M.DCC.XXV. *Price* 1 s.

4. Title-page of the first number of Rapin's *Acta Regia*

folio numbers, beginning on August 5, 1732. The financial returns were so gratifying to the Knaptons that they 'made Tindal a large present'.[1] And well they might; their profits from this one work were said to have been between eight thousand and ten thousand pounds.[2]

Meanwhile another work by Rapin was brought out in fascicules by a group of nine publishers—J. Darby, A. Bettesworth, F. Fayram, J. Pemberton, C. Rivington, J. Hooke, F. Clay, J. Batley, and E. Symon—who in September 1725 issued the first number of a valuable source book formally announced as *Acta Regia: or an Account of the Treaties, Letters and Instruments between the Monarch of England and foreign Powers, published in Mr. Rymer's FOEDERA, which are the Basis of the English History, and contain those Authorities which rectify the Mistakes that most of our Writers have committed for want of such a Collection of Records.* It is surely a tribute to the intelligence of people who bought number books that this learned work was carried to successful completion in twenty-five numbers during the next two years, and in 1732–3 was reprinted in sixpenny weekly parts, a new edition in folio. The earlier edition, 'with the Heads of the Kings and Queens, curiously engraven by Mr. Vandergucht', made four octavo volumes, each with new signatures and pagination. Presumably the translator, Stephen Whatley, was as well paid per sheet as Tindal was for translating Rapin's *Histoire d'Angleterre*; Rapin himself had died in 1725, but even had he lived he would have received nothing from the English publishers of his two works, since the laws of England did not protect books in foreign languages.

In the autumn of 1725 two other translations began to appear in numbers. The *Evening Post* number 2512 (August 31, 1725) announced that on that day was published—'to be continued Monthly till the whole is finish'd'—the first number of *The Life and Actions of that ingenious Gentleman Don Quixote de la Mancha*, 'Wrote by M. Cervantes

---

[1] So Thomas Tyers declared in *A Biographical Sketch of Dr Samuel Johnson* (1785), reprinted as the Augustan Reprint Society's Publication No. 34 (Los Angeles: William Andrews Clark Memorial Library, 1952), which see, p. 15.
[2] See the passage quoted from the *Grub-Street Journal*, below, p. 237.

Saavedra. In Spanish and English; The English being an entire new Translation, with large Notes, explaining the difficult Passages'. The proprietors, T. Woodward (at the Half-Moon over against St. Dunstan's Church in Fleet-Street) and J. Peele (at Locke's head in Paternoster Row), set a high price (one shilling and sixpence) for each number, and may not have been able to keep the work going very long. The translator himself seems to have had some doubts about the success of the undertaking, and frankly stated in his Preface, 'If the present Translation meets a favourable Reception, I shall continue the work Monthly: If not, I shall neither trouble the Publick nor my self with publishing any more.'[1] The most pressing problem confronting Woodward and Peele was not a sluggish market, however. They encountered unexpected difficulties when they were about to publish in two folio volumes Dr. Richard Bundy's translation of *Histoire romaine, depuis la fondation de Rome*, a work by François Catrou and Pierre Jeanne Rouillé, currently being published in Paris. The two proprietors of Bundy's translation, together with their printer, J. Bettenham, found to their great annoyance that another group of booksellers —W. and J. Innys, J. Osborn and T. Longman, G. Strahan, W. Mears, J. Pemberton, and T. Edlin—had engaged John Ozell to make a different translation of the same work, and indeed had already begun to publish it in monthly numbers at one shilling and sixpence each. Edlin, who apparently took the lead in the rival enterprise, advertised in the *Evening Post* number 2507 (August 19, 1725) that he had that day published Number I of *The Roman History complete*. This announcement drew from Woodward and Peele the statement that now they too were determined to publish their translation in numbers. Their own Number I, they declared, would be published 'with the utmost Expedition', and they warned the public against Ozell's translation, 'which often mistakes the Author's meaning and is full of unpardonable Blunders'. This remark touched off a most violent exchange of defamatory charges and recriminations in the newspapers and in a series of pamphlets. All of these make dull reading at this distance, but the

[1] Details are given by William A. Jackson in 'Two Unrecorded Serial Editions of *Don Quixote*', *Harvard Library Bulletin*, I (1947), 309–10.

tone of the contention is amusingly illustrated by the title of an octavo pamphlet published four years later with only J. Roberts's name in the imprint:

> No. I of the Herculean Labour: or, the Augean Stable Cleansed of its Heaps of Historical, Philological and Geographical Trumpery. Being serious and facetious Remarks, by Mr. Ozell, on some thousands of Capital and Comical Mistakes, Oversights, Negligences, Ignorances, Omissions, Misconstructions, Misnomers, and other Defects in the Folio Translation of the Roman History by the Rev. Mr. Bundy.

Ozell began his observations by saying, 'If my Remarks on Mr. Bundy's Book shou'd chance to check the Sale of it, he may thank himself.' But it was Ozell's translation that came to a halt, and he took this opportunity to tell the purchasers of his translation that they would long before have had the whole work 'had not the Booksellers fall'n out among themselves about Paper and Print, &c.' after only sixteen numbers had been published. He assured them that if the 'two Booksellers concern'd' would take in partners that would 'push it' he would go on with the translation 'full as fast as Mr. B . . . and a thousand times more correct'. It was not until three years later, however, that the work was resumed. An advertisement in the *Daily Advertiser* number 397 (May 8, 1732) announced the publication that day of numbers 17, 18, and 19, 'To satisfy those Gentlemen who have subscrib'd, or such as shall subscribe, for Mr. Ozell's Translation of the Roman History; as well as to give a Proof of the intended Expedition with which that Work will now be carried on'. Edlin, the 'Undertaker', promised that three numbers would continue to be published punctually every month, and said that the first sixteen numbers 'in three Volumes sewed up' could be obtained at his own place of business, the Prince's Arms over-against Exeter Change in the Strand, or from Mr. Ozell's residence at No. 3 in Smith Street. A postscript offers gratis to those who subscribe for this work 'Mr. Ozell's Critique on Mr. Bundy's Translation, which will fully convince them of the Preference Mr. Ozell's Version justly deserves'. Bundy's translation, on the other hand, continued to flourish, ultimately filling six handsome folio volumes (dated 1728, 1729, 1729, 1730, 1736, and 1737 respectively) and bringing both honour and reward to Dr. Bundy.[1]

Advertisements in the London and provincial newspapers make it clear that during these years other works had been given to British readers —or rather sold to them at a tidy profit —in monthly parts. On May 5, 1726, fourteen booksellers advertised the first number of *The Ecclesiastical History of M. L'Abbé Fleury*, translated[2] from the French original published in Paris in 1722. This first number contained fifteen sheets 'beautifully printed in Quarto', and the advertisement announced that the same number of sheets would be printed monthly until the whole work had been published. The proprietors, J. Crokatt (in Fleet Street) and W. Innys (in St. Paul's Churchyard), engaged T. Wood to print the work, which continued to appear in monthly parts during the next five years, the five volumes running to more than 3600 pages. Though the price for each number was three shillings, the long list of subscribers indicates that the sale was considerable.

A learned work written originally in Latin, Jacques Auguste de Thou's *History of His Own Time*, also enjoyed extensive sale in a translation by Rev. Bernard Wilson, M.A., Vicar of Newark and Prebendary of Lincoln. As the current issues of the *Monthly Chronicle* show, the first of the two-shilling numbers appeared in February 1728, and the remaining eleven numbers of Volume I followed month by month with fair regularity; the twelve numbers of Volume II, though still numbered individually from 13 to 24, were published quarterly in

[1] A manuscript note found in the ninth volume of the diary kept by the first Earl of Egmont reveals that King George II was so pleased with Volume I of Bundy's translation, presented to His Majesty by Bundy himself, that Bundy was made Royal Chaplain, was presented to the living of Barnet, was made a prebendary in Westminster, and was finally presented to the Church of St. Bride's. See *Manuscripts of the Earl of Egmont*, III (London: H. M. Stationery Office, 1923), 349.

[2] According to a note in the card catalogue of the Harvard College Library, this translation was made by Henry Herbert and G. Adams. One of the copies in the Harvard College Library belonged to Samuel Taylor Coleridge and has his autograph annotations in ink and pencil on the margins of the first two volumes. Joseph Spence quotes in his *Anecdotes, Observations, and Characters, of Books and Men* (London: W.H. Carpenter, 1820), p. 57, a remark by the Chevalier Ramsay (secretary to Fénelon, Archbishop of Cambrai) to the effect that, 'The Abbé Fleury's Ecclesiastical History is allowed, on all sides, to be the best that ever was written, though it is put into the *Index Expurgatorius*.'

groups of three between June 1729 and May 1730. The two handsome folio volumes, beautifully printed on fine paper, are dated 1729 and 1730, but they give no indication of having been published in numbers. The imprint of Volume I shows that it was printed by E. Say, and sold by W. Meadows, B. Motte, T. Worrall, J. Stagg, T. Jackson, and B. Farnsworth (of Newark). The imprint of Volume II does not name the printer, but adds to the list of dealers the names of F. Fayram, T. Green, and J. Roberts, omitting Farnsworth.

Four other books which preceded the real boom in the number book business deserve notice here, though all four of them ran into difficulties. Spread over so long a time as eighteen years were the numbers of an ambitious work by Samuel Parker, M.A., son of the Bishop of Oxford. This was *Bibliotheca Biblica. Being a Commentary upon all the Books of the Old and New Testament*, 'Gather'd out of the Genuine Writings of Fathers and Ecclesiastical Historians, and Acts of Councils'. According to John Nichols the first five monthly numbers of this work were printed by William Bowyer as early as 1717. At that time the publishers were W. Taylor and H. Clemens. 'The sale seems to have been considerable', says Nichols, for one thousand numbers were printed, some of them on large paper.[1] Subsequent numbers were printed at the Theatre (Oxford) for Charles Rivington (at the Bible and Crown in St. Paul's Church-Yard) or for W. and J. Innys, but most of the numbers were published many months late, perhaps because Parker himself was too busy to prepare the copy. Although his *Bibliotheca Biblica* came out with much irregularity, each fascicule, no matter when issued, bore two serial numbers —its number in the series for the year, and its number in the series for the particular book of the Bible with which it dealt. Thus the *Monthly Chronicle* for April 1728 recorded somewhat confusingly that numbers X, XI, and XII for the year 1725 had just been issued, these comprising numbers XXII, XXIII on the Book of Numbers and number I on the Book of Deuteronomy. When the seventh, eighth, and ninth numbers for 1727 (that is, numbers XX, XXI, and XXII on the Book of Deuteronomy) were announced in the *Monthly Chronicle* for October 1730 as just published,

[1] John Nichols, *op. cit.*, I, 139–40 and 140 n.

it was stated that, 'The Author of this excellent Work, now with God,[1] having left Materials for a Continuation of it, it is intended that under the Inspection and with the Assistance of some Learned Friends, it shall be publish'd for the Advantage of the Family of the Deceased, in the usual Method.' But the intentions were not carried out, and the work which was to have embraced all books of the Old and New Testaments did not go beyond the Pentateuch. When the last seven numbers were published in 1735, bringing the fifth volume to an end, a note was inserted in Wilford's *Literary Magazine* requesting 'such Gentlemen as are desirous of compleating their Sets . . . to send their Orders for that Purpose to the Author's Widow, at her House in Oxford; or to Mr. Clements, Bookseller in St. Paul's Church-Yard, London'. This note was never seen by one of the American subscribers, for Cotton Mather died in 1728; but several numbers of *Bibliotheca Biblica* bearing dates 1728 and 1729 were among the books in the Mather libraries until recently.[2]

The early death of the author likewise cut off before completion the work of another Samuel, *The General History of Printing*, by Samuel Palmer, printer, who planned to keep on publishing the work in monthly parts until it should make two quarto volumes. His specimen title page[3] of Volume I, number I, for March 1729 has the imprint 'Printed by the Author, and sold at his Printing-House in Bartholomew-close: also by J. Roberts in Warwick-lane, and by most Booksellers in Town and Country'. The first number contained a 'General View of the whole Design as it now stands', though Palmer declared that he might see cause to alter it in both substance and method 'if any new Discoveries offer'. This warning suggests that Palmer was eager to please his customers, even to the extent of in-

---

[1] Samuel Parker died on July 14, 1730.
[2] See Julius Herbert Tuttle, *The Libraries of the Mathers* (Worcester, Massachusetts: Davis Press, 1910), reprinted from *Proceedings of the American Antiquarian Society at the Semi-Annual Meeting, April, 1910*, p. 51.
[3] Bibliographers may be interested to observe a note in the first number of *The General History of Printing* which indicates that 'This Sheet of Title and Contents is not design'd to be bound with the Work, but a new one shall be given gratis at the conclusion of the first Volume.'

On *Saturday* the 6th of *April*, will be publiſh'd,
Nº· I. of

THE

HISTORY

OF THE

COUNCIL of CONSTANCE.

Written in *French,*

By *JAMES LENFANT.*

Done into ENGLISH, from the laſt Edition, printed at
AMSTERDAM 1727·

Adorned with twenty *COPPER PLATES,* curiouſly Engraved by
the beſt HANDS.

L O N D O N:

Printed for THOMAS COX, at the *Lamb,* under the *Piazza* at the
Royal Exchange; THOMAS ASTLEY, at the *Roſe,* STEPHEN AUSTEN
at the *Angel,* both in St. *Paul's* Church-yard; and LAWTON
GILLIVER, over againſt St. *Dunſtan's* Church in *Fleetſtreet.*

N. B. *The whole Work will make about ten Numbers, containing fifteen
Sheets each Number, beautifully printed in* 4to, *Price* 3 s. *to be continued Monthly, and will be compleated by* Chriſtmas *next at fartheſt.*

5. Title-page of a leaflet advertiſing Lenfant's *Hiſtory of the Council of Conſtance*

corporating their contributions to the text itself. There is a certain solicitous eagerness in the assurance printed at the end of the first number that, 'No. II is in great Forwardness.' But later numbers were slow in coming out, and when Palmer died in 1732 the work was brought to an end by George Psalmanazar.[1] The unexpectedness of Palmer's death is reflected in the imprint of the volume when it was published as a whole in 1732: 'London: Printed by the Author, and sold by his Widow at his late Printing-House in Bartholomew-close....' Copies remaining unsold were reissued in 1733 with a different title page, bearing the imprint of new proprietors, A. Bettesworth, C. Hitch, and C. Davies, all of Paternoster Row. When this volume, beautifully printed on excellent paper, was reviewed in the *Literary Magazine* for February 1735, the reviewer seemed to be trying a little too hard to boost the sales, for his account began, ''Tis natural for one to look, with eagerness, into the writings of a man who undertakes to discourse on any famous and useful art, from the practice of which he has great reputation.' It is on this account, the reviewer declared, that 'Mr. Palmer's history of printing may reasonably be expected to meet with many readers, considering the great importance of that noble art, of which he undertook to give an account, and in which he was himself so eminently distinguish'd.'

Another work which did not succeed in coming out at regular intervals began in April 1728 and was announced as to be completed 'by Christmas next at farthest'. This was *The History of the Council of Constance*, a translation (attributed to Stephen Whatley) of a well received book written in French by Jacques Lenfant, 'Done into English, from the last Edition, Printed at Amsterdam, 1727... and Adorned with twenty Copper Plates'. This publication, undertaken jointly by Thomas Cox, Thomas Astley, Stephen Austen, and Lawton Gilliver, was expected by them to bring in three shillings per customer for each of the ten quarto numbers, each number comprising fifteen sheets. The promise to complete the work by Christmas 1728 was not kept, for there were sometimes gaps of two or three months between consecutive numbers. For the publication of the second number the

[1] According to a note on the Library of Congress card.

four original proprietors named in the printed Proposals were joined by J. Clark, R. Hett, J. Gray, and C. Rivington; and before the two complete quarto volumes were advertised at £ 1. 14s. in April 1730 A. Bettesworth had also joined the group, though he and the others may have been sleeping partners from the beginning.

To close the account of these pioneer volumes that preceded the rush of numbers which came in 1732 and 1733, one may add J. Morgan's *Phoenix Britannicus,* a 'miscellaneous Collection of Curious Tracts' which began to appear early in 1731 in quarto parts at two shillings and sixpence. The proprietors were T. Edlin and J. Wilford. It included such a 'curious' piece as *Prosopopoeia; Or, Sir Walter Raleigh's Ghost* (1622), but did not extend beyond six numbers, and even these probably did not sell, for in 1736 the six numbers were advertised as 'Now collected into One Volume'.

Up to the end of the year 1731, then, the number-book trade, sponsored by over sixty bookseller-publishers individually and in groups for the nonce, provided somewhat heavy learning for their customers and an income for themselves as well as for a good many compositors, printers, and vendors. For the numerous translators, the industrious compilers, and the handful of original authors who supplied the copy, the rewards, with one or two exceptions, were doubtless meagre enough. The books themselves, less than forty in number, are larger in bulk than in literary value, but they represent the incipient stages of a new trend. Within the next twenty years the number-book business increased tenfold.

CHAPTER IV

FASCICULES IN FULL SPATE

There is no doubt that the year 1732 marks the beginning of a real boom in the number-book trade. By that year it had become clear to publishers that large profits were to be made by this relatively new mode of bookselling, and within the next two years more books were issued in numbers than had ever before appeared in that form.

One of the first things to be observed in the number-book trade's initial period of real prosperity is that from 1732 onwards the numbers were issued not monthly but, for the most part, weekly. This meant a great deal more handling for the booksellers, but it also required a smaller periodical payment by the customers. As we shall see, many of the publishers offered to deliver numbers fortnightly or once a month if their customers did not wish to be troubled by a weekly transaction; but once the weekly publication was introduced most of the business continued to be on a weekly basis. Every effort, indeed, was made to exploit the gold mine.

One of the liveliest pieces of contemporary evidence on this new development in the printing business is to be found in the *Grub-Street Journal* number 148 (October 26, 1732) and the *Grub-Street Journal Extraordinary* (October 30, 1732). In what purports to be the conversation of printers' devils who were carrying from the Stamp Office the unsold copies of newspapers after the stamps had been cut off, it was remarked by one of the boys that in time they would grow up to be printers themselves, and that then they would be able to lord it over their errand boys just as their masters now lorded it over *them*, and as the booksellers lorded it over the printers. The booksellers, the boys agreed, were 'an upstart Profession, who have almost wholly ingrossed to themselves the selling of Books, which originally belonged solely to our Masters'. But, said one of the youngsters, the prospects had begun to look brighter for the printers; they no longer depended on the booksellers for business, but had started to develop a business of their own, that of reprinting —especially in number books —works no longer protected by copyright. So well had the number-book trade developed, in fact, that the booksellers were themselves following the lead of the printers.

For, says he, many young, learned, publick-spirited Printers have undertaken to reprint, weekly, at a very reasonable rate, several Books, both original and translated; the Copies of which were purchased by Booksellers, and had been vended by them, as their Property, secured by an Act of Parliament, till the late Expiration of it. This Method of Weekly Publication allures Multitudes to peruse Books, into which they would otherwise never have looked; and it has had a miraculous Influence on some Booksellers themselves, inducing them to follow the Example by publishing in the same Manner, even at a cheaper Rate, and to sell a second Edition, corrected and revised, for much less than half the Price of the First.

The race was on, and if authors gained little by this accelerated sale of printed matter the publishers fought hard to capture a market which they saw to be richly remunerative for themselves.

One of the best evidences that money was being made in the number-book trade is the crowding in of rivals. It will be recalled that seven years earlier (in 1725) two rival translations of a French work began to appear in monthly parts under the name *The Roman History*. Even then the number-book trade had so firmly established itself that Woodward and Peele knew they would lose their market for their intended two-volume edition once Edlin, their inconsiderate rival, began to issue his hack translator's version in monthly parts, for it had been discovered that people were really eager to buy books in small inexpensive portions. Woodward and Peele could do nothing but beat Edlin at his own game and publish their book in numbers too. Precisely the same situation developed in 1732 when James and John Knapton, having completed the issuing in monthly parts of Nicholas Tindal's *History of England* (translated from the French of Rapin), found that a competitor, James Mechell, printer (at the King's Arms, next the Three Cups Inn, High Holborn), had already begun to issue in sixpenny weekly numbers a rival translation by 'John Kelly of the Inner-Temple, Esq.' Rather than acknowledge defeat and let Mechell run away with their market, the Knaptons immediately announced an improved second edition of Tindal's translation, to be issued weekly, 'the Whole to make two Volumes in Folio containing 400 Sheets, at 2£. 2s. in Sheets, including the Copper-Plates'.

Kelly's translation, which began on the first Saturday of June 1732, had an eight weeks' head start, but it was Tindal's that generally received praise. Soon after the Knaptons' weekly numbers of *The History of England* began to appear, Thomas Cooke's short-lived paper, the *Comedian; or, Philosophical Enquirer*, published in its sixth number (September 1732) a letter commenting on this and the rival translation:

> As there has been lately set on Foot a most pernicious Project to discourage Literature by invading the Propertys of honest Booksellers, I mean, by reprinting their Copys in weekly Parcels, I think all Men who have any regard to Honour and Learning should use their utmost Endeavours to put a Stop to it; nor can the Knaptons be too much applauded for the Method which they have taken to vincidate their Right against this infamous Practice.

The Knaptons still had on hand some unsold copies of their earlier edition in octavo numbers, bound in fifteen volumes. The method which they took to vindicate their proprietary rights was to insert a lengthy notice in the *Daily Advertiser* number 443 (July 3, 1732) and later numbers that their own edition in weekly folio fascicules would be both cheaper and better than Mechell's.

> Whereas there is lately set on Foot the Project of a new Translation, in Weekly Pamphlets of four Sheets for Six-pence; and whereas it is affirm'd by the Undertaker, that the Whole will be compriz'd in 400 Sheets, it is evident, on the contrary, . . . that the Number of Sheets will amount to 600; wherefore, that Gentlemen may not be drawn in by such specious Pretences, . . . there will be publish'd every Week, beginning in about 14 Days, five Sheets for 6d. in such a Manner as to contain six of the proposed new Translation; . . . and both Volumes will be publish'd in the Space of a Year, which is but a Quarter of the Time that it can be new done, as it ought, by any one Hand.

The Knaptons issued their Proposals the following week, and published the full text of them in the *Daily Advertiser* number 454 (July 15, 1732), announcing also their removal from St. Paul's Churchyard to the Crown in Ludgate Street, near the west end of St. Paul's. The first number of their folio edition appeared on August 5, and subsequent numbers followed promptly week by week.

The author of the article in the *Comedian* commended the Knaptons and wrote disdainfully of Mechell's translator:

> Some, perhaps, may say that M. Rapin's History, written in French, is as free for one Person to translate as another; which I deny, if the first Translation be a good one, and if Honesty has any Place in the Question . . . . The Knaptons having published a very just Translation of Rapin's History, and that meeting with the Success it deserved, an obscure Person is employed about a new one, in Hopes of putting a little Money in the Publisher's and Translator's Pockets . . .; and, the more easyly to answer their Ends, they publish their rabsodical Translation in Scraps, that the Purchaser may not feel the Price; which Method of Publication the Knaptons are forced to follow, in the second Edition of their Translation, in their own Defence.

This rap on the Mechell and Kelly knuckles must have pleased Tindal and the Knaptons almost as much as the praise for themselves that accompanied it, though no praise could be quite so acceptable as the extensive sale of the weekly numbers themselves.

Though James and John Knapton were 'forced' to issue their *History of England* in weekly numbers, so well did those fascicules sell that before long a writer in the *London Journal* number 696 (October 28, 1732) remarked, "Tis a Pleasure to see such vast Numbers of them sold every Week.' And he added, 'There is no Treatise contributes so much to serve the Interests of Liberty and publick Virtue . . . . This Book should be in every Englishman's Hand.' There were other words of approval in the second number of the *Englishman* (January 23, 1733) and in *B. Berington's Evening Post* on July 14, 1733. Later, in January 1736, Nicholas Amhurst of the *Craftsman*, when discussing a casual censure of Rapin (in the *Daily Gazetteer* for September 11, 1735) as 'the Dullest of Dull Writers', observed that 'no Historian was ever so universally read, by all Degrees of People, in this Kingdom'.

Tributes of praise were accorded also to Tindal's own *Continuation of M. De Rapin Thoyras's History of England*, published in sixpenny numbers by the Knaptons in 1736 and following years. Mechell, incidentally, likewise found it profitable to publish a continuation of

Rapin. In 1735 he advertised himself as the sole proprietor of a continuation written by Thomas Lediard, 'Gent.', and assured subscribers that the total price for the one hundred folio sheets would not exceed 12s. 6d. He announced that every Saturday four sheets 'stitch'd in blue Paper' could be obtained for sixpence at his own establishment (by this time located at the King's Arms next the Leg Tavern, Fleet Street), as also at the booksellers' and pamphlet shops in town and country.

Kelly's translation of Rapin was not the first weekly number book to be published in Britain, for a rare pamphlet[1] by the Rev. Thomas Stackhouse shows that prior to May 1732 'certain Things, publish'd Weekly' had proved successful enough to 'set every little Bookseller's Wits to work' in hopes of making money by issuing books in weekly fascicules. Stackhouse had initiated his literary career ten years earlier with the publication of a pathetic little work, *The Miseries and great Hardships of the Inferior Clergy in and about London; and a Modest Plea for their Right and better Usage; in a Letter to a Right Reverend Prelate.*[2] He had also written larger works, among them *A Compleat Body of Divinity* (1729), which was later (1742) reprinted in numbers, presumably because by then this 'learned and pious but necessitous Divine', as John Nichols called him, had made a name for himself as the author of a 'best-seller', *The History of the Bible.*

The writing of this popular and frequently reprinted work Stackhouse had been persuaded to undertake when, as he tells in *The Bookbinder, Book-printer, and Book-seller Confuted*, he had been invited by John Wilford and Thomas Edlin to a conference in the Castle Tavern in Paternoster Row early in May 1732. He was justly suspicious of both men, but as he owed Edlin a book debt of about three pounds he

[1] *The Book-binder, Book-printer, and Book-seller Confuted: or, the Author's Vindication of himself, from the Calumnies in a Paper, industriously dispers'd by one Edlin. Together with Some Observations on the History of the Bible, as it is at present publish'd by the said Edlin.* 'By the Reverend Mr. Stackhouse, Curate of Finchley . . . . London: Printed for T. Payne . . . , MDCCXXXI.' John Nichols gives a summary of this pamphlet in his *Literary Anecdotes of the Eighteenth Century* (London, 1812), II, 393 n. Excerpts quoted here are taken from a copy of the pamphlet in the Library of Congress.

[2] There was a second edition in 1741, according to the *London Magazine* for October of that year.

was 'forc'd to sit down and hear what they had to propose'. What they wanted was 'something . . . which might be publish'd weekly', but they had no idea what would go well in that form. Edlin had some thought of reprinting in weekly numbers Ozell's translation of *The Roman History*, which, back in 1725, had forced Woodward and Peele to issue Dr. Bundy's translation of the same work in monthly numbers. With 'some heavy Imprecations upon Dr. Bundy', Edlin 'very warmly maintain'd that, with a little Brushing up . . . the Thing would still do in a weekly Manner'. But Wilford refused to have any share in that work. At that point Stackhouse suggested 'a good Expedient, which was, to publish a *New History of the Bible*'. He pointed out that his studies in the preparation of the *Compleat Body of Divinity* qualified him to undertake such a work. 'After a little Altercation' the suggestion was accepted, and Stackhouse was instructed to draw up proposals. Before these were circulated Wilford withdrew from the project, but Edlin decided to go ahead, provided that Stackhouse would 'stand by him'. Feeling that his debt to Edlin hung over him like a Damocles' sword, Stackhouse consented, but at the same time, he later declared, *'Demitto auricules* [*sic*], *ut iniquae mentis asellus, cum gravius dorso subit onus.'* This Horatian lowering of the ears was symptomatic of a burden-bearing which Stackhouse soon found impossible to endure; he was no ass.

Edlin printed the proposals, 'got credit for Paper, brush'd up his old batter'd Letter, pick'd up a poor Compositor or two, . . . and began to be very clamorous for Copy'. But Edlin made three mistakes, and discovered that Stackhouse was a man of spirit as well as of industry. In order to do his work with scholarly thoroughness Stackhouse had stipulated that he be provided with substantial works of reference, but these Edlin refused to supply, arguing that 'the chief of his Subscribers lived in Southwark, Wapping, and Ratcliff Highway; that they had no Notion of Criticks and Commentators; . . . and therefore the less Learning in it the better'. There was an even more infuriating kind of niggardliness in Edlin's crowding of the type in the first sheet; Stackhouse found that by this 'Encroachment' he would, 'in the Compass of the Whole Book', be the loser by some forty or fifty

pounds in copy-money. Again, though he had agreed to write three
sheets a week, he was particularly annoyed with Edlin for releasing the
first number of the Introduction on September 27, 1732, since he had
submitted copy only on condition that forty or fifty sheets would be
finished before one line should be published. The result was a dead-
lock. Letters were exchanged. Edlin visited Stackhouse at Finchley,
'vowing and swearing that he would take away his Books and employ
another Writer'. Edlin tried to get Stackhouse to sign a new contract
binding him and his heirs, executors, and administrators 'in a Penalty
of 50 Pounds, to write well, and finish the History of the Bible for
him'. Without signing this preposterous instrument, the curate of
Finchley indicated his discontent, said he would go on with the work,
but asked for his copy-money. In announcing the first weekly number
Edlin had said that as no money was required from subscribers until
the sheets were delivered, so none would be delivered without the
money. This was a reasonable arrangement; but Edlin used a vastly
different principle in dealing with the long-suffering author whom he
thought he had under his thumb. Eventually Stackhouse got twelve
guineas for the twelve sheets of the Introduction, but relations were
broken off, Edlin engaged Dr. John Campbell to carry on the work,
and Stackhouse found another publisher for his own *History of the
Bible*, which began anew in February 1733.

Meanwhile the heated controversy carried on in the press and in
virulent little pamphlets published by one or the other shows how
well-founded was the ominous warning in the original proposals: 'In so
large and extensive a Work, it is difficult to say, what Things may
occur in its Composition.' On November 30, 1732, Stackhouse as-
sailed Edlin in the *Daily Advertiser* number 572 with a mighty 'whereas'
and many harsh words:

Whereas Mr. Tho. Edlin, at the Prince's Arms, over-against the
Exeter Exchange in the Strand, Bookseller, upon his Disagreement
with me, has himself undertaken (for surely none but himself could
ever write at so sad a Rate) under the Sham Title of *A new and compleat
History of the Bible*, to give us every Week a strange confus'd Hodge-
Podge of I know not what, to the great Reproach and Disparagement

of the Sacred Scriptures; but the better to impose upon his Subscribers has been cunning and confident enough (even contrary to my Remonstrance) to subjoin my Name to his Work: In order to prevent the Publick from being abus'd for the future by such a bare-fac'd Imposture, as well as testify my Abhorrence of such vile Trash, I think my self oblig'd to declare, that the Introduction only is of my composing.

Stackhouse went on to declare that he neither had, nor would have, any concern in what Edlin might at any time write, print, or publish, and that he had made considerable progress in his own *History*, which he hoped to finish in due time 'with the Blessing of God'. He asked his friends and well-wishers to leave their names and addresses as subscribers at St. Paul's Coffee House in St. Paul's Churchyard.

Not more than a fortnight later Edlin printed some of Stackhouse's letters, with uncomplimentary remarks upon their author's poverty and morals. On December 18, 1732, the *Daily Advertiser* number 587 published the clergyman's declaration, dated from Finchley two days earlier, that in a very short time he would 'set that matter in a clear Light'. Before the week was out, the columns of the *Daily Advertiser* carried an announcement of Edlin's *New and Complete History of the Holy Bible*, No. VIII, 'containing a Curious and Critical Account of Noah's Ark', and the same columns contained the full text of Stackhouse's new Proposals, offering his rewritten preface gratis to any persons who would bring in a copy of the other one. Subscriptions were being taken for him, the curate said, by Mr. Ballard, at Paul's Coffee House in St. Paul's Churchyard, by T. Payne, bookseller, at the Crown in Paternoster Row, and by himself or his family, at Mr. Gauden's in King Street, Bloomsbury. The following week Stackhouse advertised that his formal vindication would be published in a few days, and on January 3, 1733, *The Book-binder, Book-printer, and Bookseller Confuted* was announced as published. In that lively pamphlet he soundly belaboured Edlin, adding strength to his language by quoting fragments of Horace to stun Edlin into silence.

Edlin may have been stunned, but he was not silenced. On January 9 he announced that there would be published the following week a verbal blast called *Mr. Stackhouse's last Stack; or, the Curate of Finchley turn'd loose upon the Common*. This, he said, would be delivered gratis to all of his subscribers, and to all booksellers of town and country who had a stock of his earlier *Case* against the recalcitrant author. The total effect of all this bickering cannot now be estimated. One result must certainly have been to stir up a lively interest in the two competing versions of *The History of the Bible*, though it is easy to imagine the most frustrating conversations when a customer asked his bookseller for the current number of *The History of the Bible* and got the wrong one. It might be supposed that the spirited Mr. Stackhouse neglected his parochial duties in order to carry on this and other works published in numbers during the next twenty years; but his literary efforts (including pamphlets of vindication) did not interfere with his being presented to the living of Beenham in Berkshire in 1733. There he wrote other books and pamphlets, among them *A New and Practical Exposition of the Apostles' Creed*, issued in twenty-eight sixpenny numbers from October 1746 onwards 'for the Benefit of the Author and his Family'. But he continued to be known best for his *History of the Bible*, and from it he must have derived most of his income over and above his stipend as Vicar of Beenham. There seems to be no record of how much he received for his copyright when a 'second Edition' of his masterpiece, 'carefully revised, corrected, improv'd, and enlarg'd', was issued in sixpenny weekly numbers by Stephen Austen in 1742. After Stackhouse's death in 1752 a monument erected in the Beenham parish church[1] paid tribute to his literary and spiritual achievements. He is there celebrated as a man *qui pro Christiana fide strenuus admodum propugnator non sine gloria militavit*. Surmounting the inscription is an open book bearing the words, 'The History of the Holy Bible'. What seems like an opportune hint in the inscription—*Qui plus scire volunt, scripta sua consulant*—was presumably not prompted by a mercenary desire to boost the sales of Stackhouse's number books; the words doubtless refer to the unhappy Latin verses entitled *Vana Doctrinæ Emolumenta*, in which, as Nichols says, the poor man 'deplores his miserable condition, in all the keen expression of despair and bitter disappointment'.[2]

[1] John Nichols describes the monument in *Literary Anecdotes*, II, 393 n.   [2] *Loc. cit.*

If the quarrel of Thomas Stackhouse and Thomas Edlin produced much name calling and a somewhat confusing pair of rival works bearing the same title, there must have been equal confusion in the public mind, as there was certainly as much vituperation, over rival translations of Pierre Bayle's *Dictionnaire historique et critique*, first published in Rotterdam in 1697 and frequently reprinted.[1] The first English translation, based on the second edition in French (1702), had appeared in 1710, over the imprint of Charles Harper and ten other proprietors. Fifteen years later the copyright was regarded as valuable, for at the sale of the late Mr. Edward Valentine's copies and shares of copies on Thursday, October 21, 1725,[2] W. Mears paid twenty pounds for a fortieth share of Bayle's *Dictionary*, along with a sixteenth share in the first volume of L'Estrange's *Aesop* and a half interest in Sir Charles Sedley's comedy, *Bellamira*. Two years later, at the sale of copies formerly owned by Awnsham Churchill, deceased, on December 10, 1730, J. Walthoe paid thirteen pounds for two ninth shares of Bayle, together with one half of certain works by Bishop Burnet. Soon after that date a separate group of booksellers decided to offer a new translation of the work, since the fifth edition had just been published at Amsterdam. But the surviving sharers in the translation of 1710 objected, insisting that they were themselves about to produce a revised translation. Then in August 1732 ten aggressive booksellers (J. Brotherton, J. Hazard, W. Meadows, T. Cox, W. Hinchliffe, W. Bickerton, T. Astley, S. Austen, L. Gilliver, and R. Willock) announced in the *London Magazine* that they were about to publish proposals for printing by subscription a new translation of Bayle. 'For the greater Ease and Accomodation of all Sorts of Readers', they said, it would be published in weekly numbers at sixpence.

We advertised this Undertaking near Two Years ago; but on some Clamours raised by several Proprietors of a former wretched Translation of this curious Work, and chiefly upon their assuring the Publick

[1] The account of Bayle in Emile Faguet, *Dix-huitième Siècle. Etudes littéraires* (Paris, [1890]), begins, 'Il est convenu que le *Dictionnaire* de Bayle est la Bible du XVIII siècle....'

[2] A marked copy of the original trade-sale catalogue is in the possession of Longmans Green and Company, London.

that they were carrying on the same Design with all possible Expedition, we thought it proper to desist at that Time: But now, after so long an Interval, it appearing that they have made no Progress in the said Work, we have again resumed the said Undertaking.

To cut off 'all possible Pretext for Altercation and Dispute' the proprietors of the proposed new translation offered to accept as sharers the proprietors of the 'former mutilated Translation' if they cared to signify their acceptance in writing within ten days, though some adjustment was expected because the earlier translation was incomplete. By the time the first volume of the new translation was published (in thirty numbers of thirty-two pages each), the ten proprietors named above had been joined by twice as many others (James, John, and Paul Knapton, A. Bettesworth and C. Hitch, J. Tonson, W. Innys and R. Manby, D. Midwinter, J. Osborn and T. Longman, T. Ward and E. Wicksteed, T. Woodward, B. Motte, J. Walthoe, Jr., E. Symon, A. Ward, D. Browne, S. Birt, H. Lintot, and H. Whitridge), among whom were several of the proprietors of the 1710 translation. This new translation was published as the second edition of *The Dictionary Historical and Critical of Mr. Peter Bayle*, and the fortnightly (rather than weekly) numbers, well printed on excellent paper, eventually filled five folio volumes.

It is symptomatic of the new development in the book trade that within a few months another new translation of the same work was being offered to the public in monthly numbers, at the price of three shillings and sixpence for twenty sheets. The title of the rival translation was *A General Dictionary, Historical and Critical*, and the three men who translated and compiled the work, making many additions, were Rev. John Peter Bernard, Rev. Thomas Birch, and Mr. John Lockman.[1] Eventually this rival undertaking filled ten folio volumes.

The proprietors of the version in fortnightly numbers did not intend to let themselves be robbed of their market. When the first number of the Bernard-Birch-Lockman work was about to appear, the pro-

---

[1] For a discussion of the authorship of the translation, with original additions, see J. M. Osborn, 'Thomas Birch and the *General Dictionary*', *Modern Philology*, XXXVI (1938), 25–46.

prietors found that the printers of six newspapers —the *Daily Courant*, the *Daily Post*, the *Daily Journal*, the *Daily Post Boy*, the *London Evening Post*, and the *Whitehall Evening Post*—had all been instructed not to accept advertisements of the *General Dictionary*. On January 22, 1733, the second page of the *Daily Advertiser* carried an indignant letter from the *General Dictionary's* compilers and extensive excerpts from their Proposals. From then on, the two publications continued to appear at regular intervals, with frequent unfriendly exchanges in the newspapers. In March the promoters of the *Dictionary Historical and Critical* published a persuasive puff for their fortnightly shilling's worth of letterpress, praising both the book and the manner of publishing it. Every reader who could afford a shilling once a fortnight, they said, would in three or four years' time be 'Master of a Library, a great Library in a few Volumes; from whence our common Artificers and Farmers, and even their Wives and Children, may gather much Learning as well as much Entertainment . . . .' The emphasis in this sales talk proved unfortunate, for a correspondent in the *Daily Advertiser* number 691 (April 18, 1733) turned the edge of their 'Pedantic Eulogium' by admitting that the proprietors of the *Dictionary Historical and Critical* showed some judgment when they said the perusal of their version would be beneficial to artificers, farmers, and their wives and children as they sat by their firesides.

For such indeed it seems only calculated; and therefore we would advise 'em not to contend any more with Persons whose Ambition is to entertain the polite, the judicious, and learned Part of Mankind.

So neat a rebuttal doubtless came from the pen of Bernard, or Birch, or Lockman, who continued to be well paid by the proprietors of the *General Dictionary*, a company of seventeen substantial men (T. Osborne, J. Batley, T. Worrall, J. Clarke, T. Hatchett, J. Gray, J. Shuckburgh, C. Ward, J. Crokatt, G. Strahan, J. Wilcox, J. Brindley, A. Millar, C. Corbett, J. Bettenham, E. Cave, and H. van der Esch).

By the spring of 1733 the number-book business had moved into a much wider arena of competition than served before. When two large groups —twenty in one and seventeen in the other —are seen to be engaged in a prolonged contention, and *both* groups achieve a measure of success, the affair has become something more than a pair of dogs quarrelling over a dead bone; hunting is done in packs only when the game is supposed to be alive and plentiful.

There were other pairs of rival publications, though none so vast in extent as the adaptations of Bayle. Readers of the *Daily Advertiser* during the last two weeks of November 1732 must have followed with interest the violent exchange of compliments by Benjamin Cole and Samuel Harding over the publication of Palladio's *Four Books of Architecture*, first printed in Venice in 1570. Cole, announcing in the *Daily Advertiser* number 559 (Wednesday, November 15, 1732) that he would on Saturday of that week begin to publish the first of the four books in weekly folio numbers, pointed out that several editions of the work had already been published at ten shillings, but that his edition, 'engrav'd and printed with as much Exactness and Care as the best of the former Editions', would sell for half that price. His terms, he said, were so easy that all journeymen, apprentices, and others might purchase the great Palladio's work, and he added that if the work met with encouragement he would offer the other books in the same manner and at the same rate—three and a half sheets weekly for sixpence. To Samuel Harding this announcement was disturbing, for he believed he had the copyright to the work and that in any case his edition, not yet exhausted, was superior. A few days after Cole's first number of Palladio had appeared, Harding expostulated in print, offering the remaining copies of the first book at five shillings. This he did purely to preserve the 'Right of Copy against the—Design of one B— Cole'. With indignation somewhat muffled but none the less perceptible behind these dashes, Harding invited prospective customers to compare his complete edition of Book I with 'that—Specimen lately publish'd by Cole'. The subsequent quarrel over the quality of the engravings is now only mildly amusing, but while it was being aired publicly in the columns of the *Daily Advertiser* in November 1732 it must have stirred up wide interest in a number book which otherwise might have fallen flat.

Competition is said to be the life of trade. One may question whether the English reading public in 1732–3 really needed both John Court's

'intire new Translation' of the works of Flavius Josephus, printed in
134 numbers in folio by R. Penny at Mr. Janeway's, and the fifth
edition of the translation which had been made thirty years earlier by
the eighty-six year old Sir Roger L'Estrange, now published in fifty
handsomely printed numbers by a large group of individual booksellers and firms: the three Knaptons, D. Midwinter and A. Ward,
A. Bettesworth and C. Hitch, John Osborn and Thomas Longman,
J. Batley, J. Pemberton, C. Rivington, F. Clay, R. Williamson,
R. Hett, T. Hatchett; and the imprint adds, 'Sold by T. Warner'.
Each of these translations published in numbers ran to about a thousand pages; many pressmen and distributing agents must have been
kept busy with *Josephus* in 1732 and 1733. A year later William
Bowyer, the printer of L'Estrange's fifth edition for Knapton and the
others,[1] had his compositors and other workmen run off for William
Whiston his new translation of Josephus, the full text and accompanying dissertations filling 315 sheets. These were sold in numbers of
twelve sheets each by John Whiston, at Mr. Boyle's Head, Fleet
Street. Evidently the elder Whiston had no hesitation in letting the
publication in numbers begin before he had completed the translation,
for although the final numbers did not appear until 1737, the new
translation in numbers was welcomed early in 1735 by a two-page
notice in the *Present State of the Republick of Letters*. In a note on page
[1023] of his sumptuous edition Whiston said, 'N.B., I began this
version (after I had frequently perused *Josephus* in the original, and
prepared the Preliminary Dissertations, and the Notes beforehand) on
December the 9th, A.D. 1734 (the day that I was 67 years of age)
and finished it on Jan. 6, 1736/37 in the beginning of my 70th year;
having been two years and one month about it.'

Josephus was the order of the day, for these three editions in numbers
continued to be valued by the booksellers. At the auction sale of
Richard Williamson's stock in November 29, 1737, Richard Ware
paid eight pounds for a fourth share in L'Estrange's *Josephus*, and

[1] According to the very careful analysis of Bowyer's records by Keith I. D. Maslen
of Exeter College, Oxford, in his unpublished thesis (now in the Bodleian Library),
'Works from the Bowyer Press (1713–1765)'.

other booksellers bought up odd numbers.[1] In the meantime another group of booksellers[2] had sold in twenty-five eight-sheet folio numbers what purported to be (but was not) a fresh translation 'from the Original Greek and Compared with the Translation of Sir Roger L'Estrange'. The explanatory notes and editorial remarks were on the title page of the completed volume attributed to 'H. Jackson, Gent.' Nor did this pretentious edition mark the end of *Josephus* in numbers before 1750. Attention was drawn in Chapter II to Robert Walker's offer in 1741 to print a quarto sheet of *Josephus* once a week for two-pence, with the whole week's news printed on a large cover without additional charge. In one translation or another the numbers of *Josephus* must have been for several years a staple commodity in many a London bookshop.

Not all books published in numbers during the first year of the boom were dazzling successes. Several of them encountered difficulties and delays. The initial number of *The Traditions of the Jews, with the Expositions and Doctrines of the Rabbins, contain'd in the Talmud and other Rabbinical Writings* was published early in 1732, and Volume I was completed in June of that year with the publication of Number III at four shillings—or two shillings and sixpence to those who had bought the first two numbers; but Volume II was not completed until 1734. *Milton Restor'd and Bentley Depos'd* was obviously intended, along with other publications in 1732, to discredit Dr. Richard Bentley's emendations of *Paradise Lost* in the edition of Milton's poem which Jacob Tonson and John Poulson had just published; it does not seem to have been continued beyond the second number, though Edmund Curll, the proprietor, had the audacity to imply on the title page of Number I that the whole work was addressed to Dr. Bentley by Dean Swift.[3] The first quarto number of *A History of Essex* which the

---

[1] According to manuscript notes in the Longmans, Green copy of the catalogue.

[2] Eight dealers are named in the imprint of this *Compleat Collection of the Genuine Works of Flavius Josephus* (1736); it is doubtful whether many of these were actual proprietors.

[3] See A. T. Bartholomew, *Richard Bentley, D.D., a Bibliography of his Works and of All the Literature called forth by his Acts or his Writings* (Cambridge: Bowes and Bowes, 1908), p. 77.

Knaptons engaged Nicholas Tindal to write was formally announced in April 1732 at one shilling and sixpence; but the second number was two months late, and the whole thing proved unmanageable. It was to have been a very comprehensive work, for Tindal proposed to include an account of all the manors of Essex from the Norman Conquest to his own time, together with many other details of local history. The title page indicated that the compiler was using materials collected by T. Jekyl of Bocking, J. Ouseley, 'sometime Rector of Panfield', and W. Holman, 'late of Halsted, who spent ten Years in a diligent Search after every thing remarkable throughout the Country, and as many in examining Court-Rolls, Wills, Evidences, Deeds, &c.' H. Woodfall was engaged as printer, and the numbers were distributed by the Knaptons in London, Mr. Green at Chelmsford, Mrs. Oliver at Norwich, Mr. Baily at St. Edmundsbury, Mr. Holman at Sudbury, Mr. Humphry at Halsted, Mr. Creighton at Ipswich, and others at Saffron-Walden, Braintree, Colchester, and the rest of the towns of Essex. There is a mingling of hope and anxiety in the advertisement printed on the verso of the title page:

As the Publication of this History depends entirely on the Reception it meets with from the Gentry, &c. of the County of Essex, all that intend to encourage the Work, by taking in the Numbers as they come out, are desired to send in their Names to any of the Places mentioned in the Title-Page, and they will be prefix'd to Vol. I. when finish'd.

Unfortunately, though the work was to have filled three volumes containing between 300 and 400 sheets, publication in numbers proved unacceptable, even though seven sheets were offered in each number. Only the first two numbers were ever printed, and nothing came of the attempt to induce subscribers to take the remainder of Volume I for a guinea (less three shillings already paid for the numbers) and to subscribe to Volumes II and III at a guinea each, payable upon delivery. Philip Morant, who was living with Tindal in 1732, recalled in 1769 that 'Want of due Encouragement, especially Mr. Tindal's being better engaged in the new Folio edition of Rapin's History, took him from this work.' He added that the proportions were wrong. 'As he had begun it, it would have been too bulky and tedious, and could not have been comprehended in less than 6 or 7 Quarto Volumes.'[1]

Three other works struggled to survive in 1732 but apparently failed. One of these, published by J. Batley under the title *The History of the Popes from St. Peter down to Benedict XIII*, began in September and continued for at least four monthly numbers at a shilling each. This was a translation of *Histoire des Papes* by François Bruys, a young Frenchman whose identity was kept secret, as Batley informed his customers. The original work filled five quarto volumes, though only the first two had been published when an unfavourable review was printed in the *Present State of the Republick of Letters* in September 1732.[2] Anonymity cannot have been the worst fault of the translation published in numbers. Equally unsuccessful, though more directly practical in its appeal, was a work which J. Roberts initiated with a sixpenny number on December 15, 1732, under the title *Dr. Colbatch's Legacy; or, the Family Physician*. This treatise was to contain an account of all the diseases incident to the human body, 'alphabetically digested', with a 'plain and rational' discussion of their causes and cures, the receipts for each distemper being put in English and the methods in which the sick were to be treated being carefully explained. *Dr. Colbatch's Legacy* was designed for the 'Universal Benefit of private Families, and the Instruction of young Practitioners'. In thirty-nine small pages the first number dealt with abortion, ague, St. Anthony's fire, apoplexy, and appetite lost; but the work never got beyond blood-spitting, blood-vomiting, and bruises, for 'Finis' is printed on page 90. Only *very* young practitioners can have received much instruction, for some of the methods seem to have been derived from the 'organ recitals' of old cronies discussing their ailments over a glass of something. Chapter X, on Belching or Ructation, incorporates the testi-

---

[1] The letter is in John Nichols, *Literary Anecdotes of the Eighteenth Century* (London, 1812), II, 705. Tindal's abortive *History of Essex* should not be confused with Nathaniel Salmon's *History and Antiquities of Essex*, based on the same sources but published (incomplete) in nineteen folio numbers of six sheets each in 1739–1740, with the imprint 'London, Printed by W. Bowyer, and Sold by J. Cooke, Bookbinder, next to the Red Hart, Fetter-lane'.

[2] Proposals to publish an English translation of the whole work were issued in 1757.

monial of a gentleman who had been afflicted with 'wind' for some twenty years and then suddenly got relief when he was advised to take up pipe-smoking. Nevertheless the benefits of the book proved to be something less than universal. When the two or three numbers were reissued at a shilling and sixpence, with a new title, *The Generous Physician, or Medicine Made Easy*, the author was credited with writing the work for the benefit of those whose narrow circumstances did not enable them to pay the 'exorbitant Fees of a Physician'. But even the sixpence charged by Roberts for each number must have seemed exorbitant; the 'Family Physician' came to an untimely end. No better success seems to have attended a work designed to interest a much smaller body of prospective readers, though C. Price (in the Fleet) may have been able to continue somewhat longer the account of *The Construction and Principal Uses of all Mathematical Instruments* 'by several hands', which he began to issue in fortnightly numbers (four sheets each) at sixpence in December 1732.

There were other books in numbers, however, which succeeded very well, though without achieving the popularity of Rapin, *The History of the Bible*, Bayle, and Josephus. There is a notable variety of subject matter in six number books established during the last three months of 1732, and it is worth noticing that by the end of that year the list of individual booksellers and firms handling number books had increased considerably. A few days after Thomas Edlin had advertised the first number of Stackhouse's Introduction to his *History of the Bible* the *Daily Advertiser* number 604 (October 7, 1732)[1] and other papers announced the first number of Geoffrey Keating's *History of Ireland*, a work originally written in Irish and published in an English translation by Darby O'Connor in 1721. This second edition, printed for B. Creake (at the Red Bible in Ave Mary Lane)[2] and W. Waring (at

---

[1] A few issues of the *Daily Advertiser* were incorrectly numbered in September and October 1732.

[2] In 1724 Creake had published in parts *A Pocket Companion for Ladies and Gentlemen containing all the Opera Songs*, and in 1726 a work in monthly parts entitled *Sepulchrorum Inscriptiones*. See H. R. Plomer. G. H. Bushnell, and E. R. McC. Dix, *A Dictionary of the Printers and Booksellers who were at work in England, Scotland and Ireland from 1726–1775* (Oxford: University Press, for the Bibliographical Society, 1932), pp. 55, 66.

the Bible in Jermyn Street, St. James's), made thirty weekly numbers, which sold (or were intended to sell) at sixpence. On July 14, 1738, Creake advertised in the *Weekly Miscellany* number 290 that he was that day publishing *A General History of Ireland* at fifteen shillings, but this was probably only unsold numbers bound up. Creake and Waring were also sharers in the second edition of Edward Oakley's *Magazine of Architecture, Perspective, and Sculpture*, the first edition of which Oakley and Creake had engaged A. Campbell to print two years before. The first of the eighteen fortnightly parts was published on Monday, October 16, 1732. The regular numbers, each containing ten half sheets 'stitch'd in blue Paper', sold for twelve pence; for 'the Curious' a few copies were printed on Royal paper at 1s. 6d.

One of many collections of songs to be published in numbers in the eighteenth century began in November 1732, when W. Bickerton, T. Astley, S. Austen, and R. Willock advertised their sixpenny numbers of *A Compleat Collection of English and Scottish Songs and Ballads*.

A more serious work, though not necessarily less favourably received, was a second edition, once again in numbers but this time weekly instead of monthly, of Stephen Whatley's translation of Rapin's *Acta Regia*, recommended in the Proposals[1] as 'absolutely necessary to accompany Mr. Rapin's History [of England], now printing Weekly in Folio'. The weekly numbers, each containing five sheets for sixpence, began to appear on November 25, 1732. The earlier edition in monthly octavo numbers beginning in September 1725 had been published by a group of nine sharers, five of whom (A. Bettesworth, J. Pemberton, C. Rivington, F. Clay, and J. Batley) were also concerned in this new edition in folio. The fact that by 1732 shares had been acquired also by C. Hitch (joint holder with Bettesworth), the Knaptons, D. Midwinter, J. Osborn, T. Longman, A. Ward, R. Hett, and T. Hatchett, indicates the increased value of *Acta Regia* as a booksellers' enterprise, for this powerful combination of proprietors would not invest funds in a publishing venture if it promised only a handful of pennies apiece. The complete folio has 215 sheets, well printed on very good paper.

[1] Reprinted in the *Present State of the Republick of Letters* for November 1732.

The same praise can appropriately be given to an attractive folio volume containing 204 sheets printed in double columns on large paper, bearing the title, *The Universal Traveller; or, a Complete Account of the Most Remarkable Voyages and Travels of Eminent Men of our own and other Nations, to the Present Time.* The first number of this work, which was 'collected from the best Authorities, Printed or Manuscript' by Patrick Barclay, D.D., was advertised on the day of publication (December 9, 1732) as 'Sold by[1] Abr. Holbeche, at the Bible and Crown in Barbican; Sam. Hester, at the Corner of White-Friars in Fleet-street; the Widow Davis, in Frying-pan-Alley in Wood-street; and A. Weddell, against Catherine-street in the Strand'. This advertisement indicated that customers could have two sheets delivered weekly for threepence if they preferred that arrangement to taking eight sheets monthly for a shilling. By the time the first volume, dealing with America and Asia, was completed, J. Purser and T. Read had apparently taken over the shares of Holbeche, Wedell, and Mrs. Davis, for the imprint on the title page shows that it was printed for Purser, Read, and Hester. *The Universal Traveller*, like most of the collections of travel literature, is not a particularly distinguished work. It deserves mention as an example of a work first published in numbers, as a work immediately pirated in Dublin,[2] and as a work written in a hurry by an author who frankly expressed disapproval of having to write by the calendar. Dr. Barclay dedicated his *Universal Traveller* to the 'Worthy Merchants of London',[3] saying that if they found his first volume acceptable he would cheerfully go forward with his volume on African and European travels. Either the worthy merchants did not find the first volume acceptable or Barclay did not feel cheerful enough to go forward with the other volume. His Preface to Volume I, containing

---

[1] The advertisements of number 3, published February 15, 1733, read, 'Printed for . . . ' instead of 'Sold by . . .'.
[2] The Dublin edition, dated 1735, was completely reset, in single instead of double columns, and was issued in twenty numbers, each comprising ten small folio sheets (forty pages). The imprint is 'Dublin. Printed by R. Reilly, on Cork Hill, For Stearne Brock, at the Stationers Arms in Castle Street, MDCCXXXV'.
[3] In the Dublin edition the dedication is addressed 'To the Worthy Merchants of the Cities of London and Dublin'.

an apology for defects in its compilation, throws a good deal of light on
what must have been the experience of many a needy literary hack:

> I am very sensible that there are many defects in it. All that I can say
> for them is, that it had been better, if I had been allow'd more time:
> And however easy for readers, and the less rich purchasers of books,
> the modern way of publishing (at so many sheets a week or month) may
> be, I cannot but observe, that it is a great hardship upon an author, or
> compiler, to be hurried, to keep the press going.
> I shall not take upon me to explode this way of writing; I know I
> have a great number of fellow-labourers; who,. perhaps, for reasons
> little different from mine, are concern'd in this way of publishing books
> of different kinds. I wish both them and myself good success, and that
> we may be employ'd in the different ways which our genius and edu-
> cation have fitted us for, and be useful to our country, according to
> the different talents which are entrusted with us.

Barclay did not exaggerate when he referred to a 'great number' of
fellow-labourers engaged in writing books to be published in fascicules.

Yet it is obvious from the list of books published in fascicules
in Appendix B of this present work that most of the number books
were compiled or translated rather than newly written as original
literary creations or fresh technical treatises; some were merely reprinted from earlier editions —the heavy unread folio lumps mentioned
by Fielding in *Tom Jones*. Among these last is a book which, in one or
another of its many editions, must have been on practically every
seventeenth-century shelf of books, Sir Richard Baker's ninety-year
old *Chronicle of the Kings of England*.[1] In an edition of 1730 printed for
S. Ballard, B. Motte and others, two continuations brought the work
to the end of the reign of George I. One suspects that when the same
proprietors in December 1732 advertised an edition in forty-eight
weekly numbers, five folio sheets for sixpence, they were merely trying
to get rid of unsold stock which had been on their shelves for over two
years. Except for the title pages the two editions are identical. Most
folio books published in numbers have distinctive number-book signatures; the weekly fascicules of Baker's *Chronicle* lack these special

---

[1] Mr. Spectator found a copy in Leonora's library (*Spectator* number 37), and Fielding says Joseph Andrews read the book.

signatures,[1] and only the newspaper advertisements show that the work was issued five sheets at a time during the latter part of December 1732 and most of 1733. Those advertisements indicated that the publication in numbers was intended to accommodate subscribers who preferred to spread the cost —£ 1. 4s. —over forty-eight weeks instead of taking the whole work at once. It was clearly seen that books in numbers were more likely to sell than whole books. As Budgell's *Bee* number 1 (February 3, 1733) put it, in reference to a proposal to print the Bible in weekly numbers, 'The Undertakers are in Hopes that by this Means many People who are frightened at the sight of a large Volume, may be unwarily drawn in to read the Scriptures.'

By the early months of 1733 weekly books were pouring from the London presses in full spate, along with a few others issued fortnightly or monthly. Some of the works listed in the monthly magazines or advertised in newspapers as published in numbers had begun to appear in that form several years earlier[2] and were still continuing more or less regularly; and most of those which had started in 1732 continued through at least part of 1733. The short-title listings in the *Gentleman's Magazine* for January of that year include both these continuing numbers (Bayle, Baker, Josephus, *The History of the Popes, Acta Regia, Dr. Colbatch's Legacy,* Oakley's *Magazine of Architecture,* Keating's *History of Ireland,* Barclay's *Universal Traveller*) and several new ones. Newspaper advertisements and other announcements extend the list considerably. By midsummer the *Gentleman's Magazine* (June 1733) could not find space to enumerate the titles, merely noting at the end of the Register of current publications, 'Books Publish'd in Numbers as usual'. Similar comprehensive notices were printed in the Monthly Catalogue of the *London Magazine* in July and August of that year; then for a few months the number books were ignored in the *London Magazine's* list of current publications, until in December 1733 the Monthly Catalogue ended with this note:

[1] The advertisements of this edition—for instance, that in the *Daily Advertiser* number [577] (December 6, 1732)—make no mention of the usual blue paper covers, on which the serial numbers of the weekly parts would also be printed for ease in distinguishing one from another.

[2] See the end of the preceding chapter.

N.B. The Books which are printed in Numbers (as have been already frequently mentioned) continue to be publish'd as usual; to which may be added, *Burket's* Exposition of the New Testament, which is begun to be publish'd weekly at five Sheets for *6d.*

This edition ('the Tenth . . . corrected') of William Burkitt's *Expository Notes, with Practical Observations on the New Testament* (first published posthumously in 1724) was just one of some forty or more number books which, during the year 1733, were sold in the pamphlet shops, hawked about by the news carriers, or delivered at the houses of subscribers.

Number books which began their runs in 1733 are listed in Appendix B and need not be enumerated here, but attention may be drawn to a few of them. There were some notable successes, and of course some failures. Probably nothing came of J. Millan's proposal to publish James Thomson's *Seasons* and other poems, 'adorn'd with six curious Copper Plates design'd by Mr. Kent and engrav'd by Tardieue at Paris'. Millan asserted that the paper, print, and plates were 'full as good' as in the edition published by Thomson himself for a guinea. A notice in the *Daily Advertiser* number 605 (January 8, 1733) was somewhat indefinite as to the price of each fascicule—'2s. or 3s.'—but specified Monday, January 22 as the day on which the first number was to appear. The work was to be continued fortnightly, but may never have started at all. Millan was also the proprietor of Batty Langley's *Young Builder's Rudiments*, apparently a handbook 'teaching by Question and Answer the most useful Parts of Geometry, Architecture, Mechanicks, Mensuration several ways, and Perspective, &c.' In his announcement of the first number (in the *Daily Advertiser* number 605, January 8, 1733) Millan said that the whole book would consist of about twenty large quarto sheets and 32 copper plates, and that the numbers would be published fortnightly at a shilling. It may have failed to interest the 'Gentlemen, Architects, Sculptors, Painters, Masons, and all others concerned in the Noble Art of Sound Building' for whom it was designed. Batty Langley was a man of many practical interests and talents, but he may not have been able to keep two number books going at the same time. One week after the first number of his *Young*

Builder's Rudiments was announced there appeared the first number of a very carefully prepared technical work entitled *The Principles of Antient Masonry, or, a General System of Building.* It was to be the joint product of a group of 'the most experienc'd Practitioners and Workmen in Building, and the several Branches of Learning relating thereto'. When the work was finally completed and published in 1736 with the title *Ancient Masonry, both in Theory and Practice,* Langley inserted on page [2] a notice confidently setting forth his capabilities:

> Young Noblemen and Gentlemen
> Taught to Draw the Five Orders of Architecture,
> To Design Geometrical Plans and Elevations for Temples, Hermitages, Caves, Grotto's, Cascades, Theatres, and other Ornamental Buildings of Delight,
> By the Author.
> By whom Buildings in general are Designed, Surveyed, and Performed in the most Masterly Manner, Artificers Works Measured and Valued,
> And Engines made, for raising Water for the Service of Towns, cities, &c.

Langley's treatise on the principles of ancient masonry was carried to successful conclusion, for it ultimately incorporated nearly five hundred large folio copper plates, and the text (434 pages) was well printed on Royal paper of excellent quality. Langley encountered difficulty with his collaborators in the writing of the work, for in his 'Advertisement' to the reader, dated September 10, 1736 (presumably the date of the final number) he said that none of them produced the parts they had promised,

> ... so that (had not I, of myself, been able to carry on and finish the Whole ...) I should have been a very great sufferer in the Expences that I had been at, for Paper and Printing, and the World disappointed of the Performance also.

Langley's animated discussions on the structure of Westminster Bridge show that he had an eye for modern as well as ancient masonry.

One cannot be sure whether John Mottley, in writing his *Survey of the Cities of London and Westminster,* used the *nom de plume* 'Robert Seymour' merely to conceal his identity or with some hope of overcoming buyer-resistance with a slightly more euphonious name. This useful work, published in 111 numbers (making two folio volumes) by J. and T. Read, beginning in the spring of 1733, survives in more copies than many other number books of this period. But survival seems often to have been fortuitous. It is perhaps only by the merest chance that works published as detachable supplements to newspapers and also offered in fortnightly or monthly batches of sheets were collected and preserved, among them an abridgment of the Bishop of Salisbury's *History of the Reformation of the Church of England*, an anonymous *History of Scotland*, and various collections of trials for all sorts of sordid crimes. The numbers of one or two unusually large works were preserved by the original subscribers perhaps because so much money had been put into the accumulated fascicules. One can still see the seven folio volumes of an anonymous translation of Jean Frédéric Bernard's *Cérémonies et coutumes religieuses de tous les peuples du monde*, with plates after Picart, issued by Claude Du Bosc in shilling numbers, beginning in March 1733, by way of rival to John Lockman's translation published in whole volumes by Nicholas Prevost.

It is not known what success attended G. Bird's *Practising Scrivener and Modern Conveyancer* (eight sheets for a shilling fortnightly, beginning January 25, 1733), John Ozell's renewed attempt to outsell his rival by publishing *The Roman History* in weekly numbers, the edition of John Foxe's *Book of Martyrs* listed in the *Gentleman's Magazine* in January 1733, the similar work by 'Harry Lyndar of the Inner-Temple' which began to appear in sixpenny weekly numbers in July 1733, the second edition of Joseph Champion's *Practical Arithmetick* (the first number of which, containing two half sheets octavo, was published at threepence on March 20, 1733), *The Practical Husbandman*, of which S. Switzer entered number I 'for ye Month of Aprill' in the Stationers' Register on June 8, 1733, and the *Compleat History of the Civil Wars in England* by 'J. Rio, A.M., late Rector of Rodney-Stoke, and Prebendary of Wells in Somersetshire'. The last-named work kept going for six numbers, beginning on June 30, 1733, but then there was an interruption. An engraving of King Charles I was given gratis with the first number, no money was required until each number was delivered,

and customers taking six copies got a seventh copy free; but apparently customers did not visit the designated agents—W. Jackson,
S. Smith, J. Millan, J. Critchley, Mr. Lewis, R. Phillimore, and Mr.
Lye. Over a year later four booksellers (J. Wilford, G. Strahan,
B. Motte, and J. Fox), together with printer W. Jackson, advertised
in the *St. James's Evening Post* number 2933 (August 15, 1734) that the
previous week they had published Proposals for Rio's book, saying
that they had on hand the first six numbers printed, as well as the 'very
neat and curious Cut' of King Charles I given gratis with the first
number. They also printed a special notice which indicates the sort of
contingency several of the weaker number books doubtless had to
struggle against:

N.B. Many People having suspended their Encouragement of this
Work, on a Supposition that they should meet with an ample and
satisfactory Account of the Civil War in the History of England,
which they have been lately entertain'd with by Mr. Tindal; the Proprietors hereof thought proper to discontinue any further Progress in
it, till the Publick had an Opportunity of informing themselves, how
little that History answer'd their Expectation on this Head; and not
doubting but the greatest Number of its Readers are now fully convinced of the manifest Partiality of the Accounts therein contain'd, we
now intend to resume the Publication of This Impartial History;
assuring our Subscribers that no further Delays shall interrupt us, but
all Diligence and proper Means be made use of, in pursuing it to its
final Period, consistent with the Conditions, which may be seen at
large in the Proposals.

Public indifference seems to have been due more often to inadequate
publicity or to inferior book-making than to competing publications,
though there was sometimes strong competition. But some proprietors, as we have already observed, experienced difficulty in publishing
the numbers on time. Delays must have annoyed the customers and
disheartened the proprietors. There was much delay over the issuing
of George Bickham's *Universal Penman*, which began to appear in
beautifully engraved half sheets in August 1733, 'Printed for the
Author, and Sent to the Subscribers, if Living within the Bills of
Mortality'. Bickham and his associates continued to be optimistic

about their publication, but were quite unable to publish the regular quota of four leaves, and they knew that their customers were getting apprehensive. The *Daily Advertiser* number 892 (December 8, 1733) carried a notice 'To the Subscribers to the Universal Penman':

> Whereas it may be imagin'd from some unavoidable Incidents which have lately happen'd, That this Work will not be compleated; These are to assure all those who are pleas'd to encourage it, that it will be carried on with all convenient Speed, till the Whole is finish'd, by
>
> George Bickham, Engraver
> Joseph Champion,   ⎫
> Willington Clark,   ⎬ Writing Masters
> William Leekey, &c.   ⎭
>
> N.B. In a few Days will be published, No. IV.

But it was not until early the next month that the fourth number was announced in the *Daily Advertiser* number 915 (January 4, 1734) as 'just publish'd . . . For the Improvement of Youth in Reading and Writing . . . containing four large Half-Sheets for Six pence'. Bickham was able to produce only five or six numbers per annum. Numbers 5 to 10 are dated 1734, numbers 16 to 21 bear various dates in 1736, there is no number 22, and the next dozen numbers, each (as usual) having four leaves engraved on one side only, are dated 1737 or 1738. It was an interesting and valuable work, for the penmanship of Willington Clark, Joseph Champion, Zachary Chambers, Emmanuel Austin, William Leekey, and several other masters may still be examined with delight.[1]

Less difficulty was naturally encountered by proprietors who merely reprinted in weekly or monthly numbers such works as Herman Moll's *New Description of England and Wales* (first published in 1724), Sir Walter Ralegh's *History of the World* (first published in 1614 and many times reprinted in the seventeenth century), and J. Janeway's combination of Alexander Smith's *General History of . . . the Most Famous*

---

[1] See P. H. Muir, 'The Bickhams and their *Universal Penman*', *Library*, 4th ser., XXV (1945), 162–84 and plates. W. Heffer & Sons Ltd. (Cambridge, England) published *Selected Plates from the Universal Penman* in 1943, two hundred years after the completion of the second and more regular run in weekly numbers at sixpence each.

Highwaymen and Charles Johnson's *Genuine Account of the . . . most Notorious Pyrates.* As antidote to this literature of roguery there was an edition of the New Testament, with annotations by John Court and John Lindsay, offered by Robert Penny at the rate of two sheets weekly for threepence or eight sheets monthly for a shilling; and there were rival collections of songs published monthly for a shilling under almost the same title.

With all this variety in subject, in size, in length of run, in price per number, and in degrees of success, one may say that the issuing of books in fascicules was well established as a publishing practice by the end of 1733; from then onwards the 'new' mode of publishing books was never again experimental. Booksellers knew that the public would unhesitatingly buy fascicules if properly produced and distributed. The question was not whether fascicules would sell; it was the old, familiar one of how to keep to a maximum the difference between the gross income and the net cost.

CHAPTER V

THE LAW AND THE PROFITS

The eagerness with which booksellers and printers entered into the number-book trade from 1732 onwards shows that profits were expected, and there is plenty of evidence that profits were realized by scores of London publishers, who published in numbers because the numbers *went*. Often less money had to be invested than in the ordinary modes of publication, and the returns were swifter. The subscriber to a number book paid cash for each part as it was delivered, an arrangement which every publisher must have welcomed, since a quick sale of the sheets as they were run off made it unnecessary to tie up either money or warehouse space. But it was a booksellers' market, not an authors' market. The men who reaped the financial gains from books published in numbers were not ordinarily the authors or compilers or translators, but the publishers and all those others engaged in the mechanical processes of producing and distributing the printed sheets.

One of the most striking things about the number books, apart from their variety, is the number of persons engaged in their production and distribution. 'It is perhaps not considered through how many hands a Book often passes, before it comes into those of the reader, or what part of the profit each hand must retain as a motive for transmitting it to the next.' So wrote Samuel Johnson to Rev. Dr. Nathan Wetherell, Master of University College, Oxford, on March 12, 1776.[1] The mercenary motive had not altered perceptibly during the preceding forty years. Shrewd men of trade were doubtless capable of benevolence, but anything less than a twenty per cent margin of profit on the sale of ordinary books could hardly keep a retailer in business when he ran the risk of loading his shelves with dead stock. It is conceivable that if number-book sales were brisk the retail dealers would be satisfied with a smaller margin, and in any case they may have looked upon number books as bait to bring customers back into their shops at

[1] No. 463 in *The Letters of Samuel Johnson*, ed. R. W. Chapman (Oxford: Clarendon Press, 1952), II, 113 f.

regular intervals.[1] Book dealers and proprietors of pamphlet shops, however, were not the only sharers in the profits of number books. The makers and importers of paper, those who handled it in the warehouses, the typesetters and pressmen in the printing establishments, the boys who delivered the number books to the subscribers' houses, the vendors, male and female, who hawked them about the streets—all these had a share, if infinitesimal, in the gross income from weekly, fortnightly, and monthly numbers. But the bulk of the profits went to the proprietors, who took all the risks. For them, if for no others, the trade was often highly remunerative. The authors, to their sorrow, found themselves less richly rewarded than they thought proper.

Every author who is not a hack-writer paid by the hour or by the piece has hopes that his book will go into a second edition. When it does, he takes the credit and expects profits; when it fails, he is likely to complain of unfair treatment by the publisher. It is an old contention, and many a pamphlet has been written in defence of one or the other party. In 1758 James Ralph published *The Case of Authors by Profession or Trade, Stated*, asserting that 'Wit and Money have been always at War' and protesting that authors should not be frowned upon for hoping to make money whether they wrote for the booksellers, the stage, or the public. Ralph said it was all very well for the gentleman-writers—'amphibious Things; half 'Squire, half Author, who . . . look down on a poor Pen and Ink Laborer'—to 'make a Compliment of the Profit' to their booksellers, but protested that it would be very foolish for a person who wrote for a living to give up 'the Pittance usually given to the Author'. He complained that, 'To write for the Bookseller is . . . always a Grievance, let the Bargain be driven how it will', and resented the fact that the bookseller, '. . . knowing best what Assortments of Wares will best suit the Market . . . gives out his Orders accordingly, and is as absolute in prescribing the

---

[1] At least one shopkeeper—Stephen Lye, framemaker and printseller—made a point of advertising in 1733 that customers requiring treatment for an embarrassing disease could obtain a 'Specifick Remedy' by visiting his shop near the India House in Leadenhall Street, ostensibly to buy weekly subscription books. There are not many lower uses to which number books could be put than as a blind for quack medications.

Time of Publications as in proportioning the Pay'. Ralph called upon authors to unite. 'Combine', he said, 'and you might out-combine the very Booksellers themselves!' There is no difference between the writer in his garret and the slave in the mines, said this vehement defender of Grub-Street:

> Both have their Tasks assigned them alike: Both must drudge and starve; and neither can hope for Deliverance. The Compiler must compile; the Composer must compose on; sick or well; in Spirit or out; whether furnish'd with Matter or not; till, by the joint Pressure of Labour, Penury, and Sorrow, he has worn out his Parts, his Constitution, and all the little Stock of Reputation he had acquir'd among the Trade; Who were All, perhaps, that ever heard of his Name.

Some of the spirit and feeling in this pamphlet may be attributed to Ralph's own experience as the writer of a *History of England*, 'By a Lover of Truth and Liberty',[1] published in 1744–1746 in weekly numbers. At any rate his defence of authors who wrote for money was much more heated than was an anonymous pamphlet published twenty years earlier in defence of the booksellers.

The writer of *A Letter to the Society of Booksellers on the Method of Forming a True Judgment of the Manuscripts of Authors* (1738) kept his tone subdued as he appeared to speak for the authors but in reality disposed one after another of their complaints against booksellers. The first charge, that booksellers were not always sufficiently ready to print the works submitted by authors, he dismissed as 'entirely groundless'. The second charge, that booksellers did not give authors a sufficient encouragement, but pocketed all or most of the profit for themselves, he dealt with at some length. He conceded that even at best there was very great uncertainty in judging in advance whether a manuscript would meet with good or bad success.

If my Information be just, the Undertaker of the last Translation in Folio of the famous and highly reputed Author, Rap. Thoyras, an

---

[1] For an enlightening account of this journalist and henchman of George Bubb Dodington see Robert W. Kenny, 'James Ralph: an Eighteenth-century Philadelphian in Grub-Street', *Pennsylvania Magazine of History and Biography*, LXIV (April 1940), 218–42.

Undertaking of great Consequence and Importance, after he had published a very considerable Part of this Work, was for some Time not a little dubious, as to its success; and strongly inclin'd to drop his Design; and yet it is well known to what a vast Account it turn'd at last.

The defender of the booksellers had much to say on the services they rendered in having books properly advertised, and contended that no author could achieve fame without their assistance. 'Is it not manifest', he demanded rhetorically, 'that no Author ever did any thing to Purpose, without your Concurrence? . . . You have more Influence in the Sale of Books than Authors themselves . . . .' As to the profits, it had to be admitted that sometimes the booksellers enjoyed extraordinary gains and that the authors received very little for their copies, but he could not see that authors had any just cause to complain, provided they were paid according to the contract, which they had been under no compulsion to sign. These observations must have brought small comfort to authors in 1738, for it is probable that many of the publishers were powerful enough to adopt a take-it-or-leave-it manner when authors inquired what terms they could expect.

Several authors of books published in numbers obviously did not find the booksellers' terms acceptable, or else preferred to retain control of the enterprise and enjoy all the net profits. Back in 1678 Joseph Moxon made his own arrangements with a printer (who is not named in the imprint), and managed to keep his *Mechanick Exercises* going, even without the assistance of backing by a bookseller. Advertisements and imprints of the early numbers of Thomas Salmon's *Modern History*, which began to appear in monthly numbers in June 1724 and continued for fourteen years, indicate that the author was himself the proprietor and J. Roberts the chief selling agent, though during the course of the long run various booksellers (Roberts himself, J. Crokatt, T. Wotton, J. Shuckburgh, T. Osborn) apparently bought their way into this successful enterprise. After A. Bettesworth had reprinted the work in three quarto volumes in 1739, a third edition was published in 143 folio numbers (making three volumes) in 1743-46, a royal patent dated December 30, 1743, granting fourteen years' exclusive rights to T. Longman, T. Osborne, J. Shuckburgh, C. Hitch, S. Austen, and J. Rivington. Salmon's work had proved so successful that these booksellers had apparently taken over his interest at terms acceptable to himself. Thomas Stackhouse's bitter experience with an unscrupulous bookseller in 1732 made him prefer to keep full control of his *History of the Bible* when he started again in 1733, and notices in the newspapers continued to indicate that he remained the sole proprietor and main distributor. For example, in announcing the 25th number (in the *Daily Advertiser* number 915, January 4, 1734) he said that it would be published the next day 'At my House in Theobald's-Court, near Red-Lion-Square', and he declared that no pains would be wanting 'to regulate the Publication, as well as finish and compleat the Work in due Time'. Before a second edition was brought out in 1742-1744, however, Stackhouse transferred the copy to Stephen Austen, a bookseller at the Angel and Bible in St. Paul's Church Yard. A royal patent dated January 8, 1742, recognized that Austen held the sole right and title of the copy and granted him exclusive rights of printing this work for fourteen years.

It appears that Stackhouse also tried to be his own publisher, promoter, and distributor when he wrote another work for publication in numbers. Early in 1746 he began to sell his own *New and Accurate Exposition of the Apostles Creed*, and when he announced in the *Whitehall Evening Post* number 34 (May 3, 1746) that the fifth number would be published on the following Thursday (May 8) he made a statement that shows clearly his intention to remain the sole proprietor:

> The Book, which will consist of about two hundred Sheets in Folio, will be . . . published for the Benefit of the Author and his Family, at his House in Eagle Court in the Strand; where Subscriptions are taken in, and whence Numbers will be sent out, stitched in blue Paper, and consisting of four Sheets each (at the Price of Sixpence) to Subscribers at their own Houses, on Publication Days, which will be on Thursday in every other Week.

Perhaps in hopes of getting more substantial amounts of cash in hand, Stackhouse added that the price to subscribers who preferred not to take the work in numbers would be ten shillings in advance and fifteen more on delivery of the whole. One gathers that the response was disappointing. The well-known author of the *History of the Bible* must have found his sales too small to be of much 'benefit' to himself and family, for new proposals were issued on the following October 1 by a group of booksellers who referred to themselves as the proprietors of the book. It was the same book, but its fascicules of four sheets each were to be published every Saturday instead of every second Thursday. Thomas Longman and Thomas Shewell, Charles Hitch, Richard Manby and Henry Shute Cox, John and James Rivington—these men published number 1 on October 18, 1746, and carried the work through to completion in 28 numbers by the following spring. It is to be hoped that the Stackhouse family enjoyed a tangible benefit in return for the surrender of the copy.

Hoping to make more money than they would get by assigning their rights to publishers, a few other authors retained control of their works published in numbers. Their success varied. Thomas Deacon of Manchester, translator of Tillemont's *Ecclesiastical Memoirs* in 1732–1735, named Wilford of London and Clayton of Manchester as retailers of the numbers, but insisted in the imprint that the work was published 'for the Benefit of the Translator'. Had he chosen to let one or more publishers manage the sales, Deacon's list of subscribers might have been longer and he would not have stopped the publication with the seventeenth number. In 1735 the Rev. William Whiston may have found difficulty in persuading booksellers to undertake the publication of his new translation of Josephus because both Court's and L'Estrange's translations had just been issued in weekly numbers. Title pages of the separate numbers are (as is usual) not extant; but the general title page to the single folio volume (which is excellently printed on fine paper) has as imprint, 'London, Printed by W. Bowyer for the Author: and are to be sold by John Whiston, Bookseller, at Mr. Boyle's Head: Fleetstreet. MDCCXXXVII'. William left the distribution entirely to his son John, but at least there was one commercial agent. John Frederick Fritsch, translator of Gérard de Lairesse's *Art of Painting* in 1737-1738, issued the numbers as 'Printed for the Author', but the imprint lists twenty retailers, some of whom may have had a minor investment in the enterprise. When William Maitland, F.R.S., advertised the first number of his *History, Antiquities, and Present State of the Cities of London, Westminster, &c.* in April 1737, he indicated that the first six sheets would be sold by himself 'at the Dial, opposite the Old Jewry in the Poultry', and said that he would personally undertake to send subsequent numbers to the habitations of all those who subscribed. He did, too, for with the co-operation of his printer, Samuel Richardson, he completed the work by the end of March 1739, and his list of subscribers filled seven folio pages, two columns to a page.

It is natural that a work designed by a professional engraver should be issued by that engraver himself. That is why George Bickham, engraver, retained control of his *Universal Penman* when the first and second impressions in numbers appeared in 1733 and 1741, though when the plates were published together in a volume in 1743 H. Overton was the proprietor. Bickham also preferred in 1743–1749 to distribute from his own shop the 190 engraved leaves of his *British Monarchy; or, a New Chorographical Description of all the Dominions Subject to the King of Great Britain.* He was simply combining the functions of 'author' and publisher.

Authors of printed works published in numbers must sometimes have felt that it would be financially advantageous to retain control of their copies and to engage dealers to handle the numbers for them at set rates. When John Marchant announced in the *Champion* on November 11, 1742, the first number of his *Exposition on the Books of the New Testament*, he included in the advertisement the full text of the royal patent dated two weeks earlier and added his own signed statement 'To the Publick' promising in his own name to give the excess over 220 sheets gratis. 'I shall publish one Number every Wednesday', he said. The notice in the *Champion* also gives interesting details about Marchant's arrangements for the distributing of his *Exposition:*

And I have appointed Mr. Benjamin Cole, Engraver, at the Corner of King's Head Court, Holborn, and Mr. John Pelham, of New Shoreham in Sussex to deliver out the Books for me. And all Persons, by giving Notice as aforesaid, may have the Numbers regularly sent to

their Houses, or where they please to appoint. And all Orders received shall be punctually obey'd, and gratefully acknowledged by their Humble Servant,
                                                            J. MARCHANT.

N.B. All Booksellers, and Venders of News and Subscription Books, may be supplied at the above-said Places.

Between November 24, 1742, and February 2, 1745, Marchant himself entered in the Stationers' Register the 110 successive numbers of the volume on the New Testament, usually two at a time, paying the sixpenny fee for each, signing the book, and depositing the nine copies required by law. From February 8, 1745, to October 22, 1747, he did the same for the 145 numbers of the second volume, the *Exposition on the Books of the Old Testament*, even though by May 1745 he had assigned the copyright of both volumes of his *Exposition* to R. Walker, a smart London publisher with branch offices and agents in the provinces.

The combination of personal attention by the author and the commercial efficiency of booksellers was occasionally offered even from behind the cloak of complete anonymity. William Duff personally entered in the Stationers' Register the successive numbers of his *New and Full Critical, Biographical, and Geographical History of Scotland* between August 5, 1749, and October 1, 1750; but he insisted in the Preface that he had not been prompted to write by any selfish motive or expectation of profit, and named no names on the title page. The work is attributed to 'an Impartial Hand', and the imprint indicates that it was printed in London 'for the Author' and 'sold by the Booksellers of London and Westminster'.

Two extraordinarily interesting examples of the authors' personal acceptance of total responsibility for publication are to be seen in works widely separated in time and place and intention, both first published in numbers. The earlier and more important of these is Rev. Francis Blomefield's *Essay Towards a Topographical History of the County of Norfolk*. The full story of Blomefield's unceasing zeal as author and publisher of a county history is recorded in the numerous notebooks and letters still preserved in Norwich. These show that he spent large sums of money in travel and in the purchase of historical manuscripts. He had a comfortable income and did not write for bread; but he suffered heartbreaking difficulties and set-backs,[1] including the loss of valuable manuscripts by fire, and the theft of many of the plates after they had been engraved. Most remarkable is the fact that when Blomefield found it impossible to make satisfactory arrangements with a publisher or printer he decided to set up his own press in Fersfield. He bought a press in London for £ 7, engaged a workman, Nicholas Hussey, at £ 40 a year, and proceeded to publish at a shilling each the successive folio numbers of his *Topographical History*. The Introduction, dated at Fersfield on the first day of the new year (March 25, 1736), sets forth in friendly terms Blomefield's reasons for issuing the work in numbers and for publishing it himself:

> Several Reasons there are that induced me to publish in this Method, among which, these are the Chief, *viz.* the Improvements that may be made as I go on, by Gentlemens seeing in what Manner I proceed, and helping me, as I come to their Parts, to a sight of old Evidences, of Antiquities, or by Subscribing for Plates of their Seats, Monuments, Arms, Ruins, or other Things worth Observation, which Advantage I could not have had, if I had done it at once; besides, I don't fear but I may hereafter meet with several Subscribers, who will willingly expend a Trifle every month, that would not have chose to lay down half the Price before-hand, (as is the common Way), nor to have expended it all at once . . . . And that this Work may be done to my own Liking, and corrected by myself, I have procured a Workman, who hath put up a Press in my own House, for the Publication of it.

In a letter to a Cambridge bookseller in April 1736 Blomefield reported joyously that he had met with much greater encouragement than he had expected, and added, 'Tho' I have printed a good number above my subscribers that I was aware of, wanted some hundreds, so

[1] A succinct account of these is given in Rev. C. L. S. Linnell's Foreword to the catalogue issued in 1952 by the Public Libraries Committee of the City and County of Norwich with the title *Francis Blomefield 1705–1752 Historian and Topographer: Exhibition . . . in the Central Public Library. On Wednesday, January 16th, 1952*. Other details are in a communication by S. Wilton Rix, 'Cursory Notices of the Rev. Francis Blomefield, The Norfolk Topographer; Chiefly Extracted from his Parish Register Book and from His Correspondence, 1733–7', *Norfolk Archaeology*, II (1849), 201–24.

that I have been forced to reprint it.' A month later he reported to a Norwich correspondent, 'I have had such a run, that I have only eight of those of the first number that I printed off the second time.'[1]

There were delays, however, and the final number of the first volume did not appear until December 25, 1739. Blomefield's enterprising spirit must have been disturbed by 'unjust Reports and unjuster Actions' by opponents, but he acknowledged 'great Favours, Helps, and Assistances' from various churchmen, and was grateful to his 'generous Subscribers'. But some subscribers proved less generous than the busy author at first had reason to hope they would. On the last page of the text in the first volume Blomefield said he proposed to insert at the end of the work a list of 'all such as have stood to their Subscriptions, and another of those who, tho' they subscrib'd, had not Honour enough to stand to it'. He proceeded with the second volume, the first number of which was listed in the *Scots Magazine* in May 1741. The second volume was not completed until May 31, 1745 (page 902 bears that date), and the general title page has the imprint 'Printed at Norwich in the Year of our Lord MDCCXLV'; but the copy in the Cambridge University Library has what must be the title page of one of the numbers, for its imprint reads 'Printed at Fersfield, in the Year of our Lord, MDCCXLI'. The Cambridge copy also has a list of 269 subscribers, among them the Archbishop of Canterbury, the Earl of Oxford, Caius College Library in Cambridge, Richard Rawlinson, LL.D., F.R.S., and a large number of clergy. There is no list of renegade subscribers, but thirty-six of the names are marked with a dagger as having suffered an alternative and presumably worse fate. 'Those with this Mark † before them are dead.' Blomefield himself had brought out only twenty-one numbers of Volume III before he died of smallpox on January 16, 1752. His work was later completed by Rev. Charles Parkyn, Rector of Oxburgh. Blomefield was a genuine antiquarian, and although the paper he used was only fair and the type bad it is pleasant to see his volumes, distinguished by gilt edging and sumptuous bindings, in the Grenville collection on the shelves of the British Museum.

[1] Quoted in S. Wilton Dix, *art. cit.*

Like Blomefield, Mrs. Teresia Constantia Phillips paid unremitting personal attention to the publishing of her one book, which, like his, offered parcels of fact for a shilling and likewise eventually won a place in the Grenville collection; but the sensational details in the numbers of *An Apology for the Conduct of Mrs. Teresia Constantia Phillips* earned a kind of notoriety which no *History of Norfolk* could ever achieve. 'Con.' Phillips' shameful secrets concerning her marriage to 'an eminent Dutch Merchant', Henry Muilman, were disclosed with a combination of pathos and zest obviously calculated to stimulate the circulation. Into the unsavoury details of the story it is not necessary to probe, but it is interesting to observe what steps the indefatigable little woman took to make the most of her temporary fame. She claimed the patronage of the great, she went through the motions of protecting herself against piracy, she tried to prove herself a persecuted victim of underhand business practices and a martyr to official oppression —and all the while she must have been gloating over the attention she was receiving. Some of her *obiter dicta* are worth transcribing here, for they show how much of a scheming minx she really was, and how determined she was to tell and to sell her story.

Like her prototype, Moll Flanders, Mrs. Phillips had unquenchable audacity, and could endure any shame but that of being ignored. In the very first number she complained that the proprietors of four newspapers had refused to print her advertisement, and that only the *London Courant* and the *General Daily Gazetteer* had published it. 'The *Daily Advertiser* look'd upon it, and said, "Oh, this is Mr. Muilman's Affair; I wont touch it upon any Terms".' The *London Gazette*, the *London Evening Post*, and the *General Daily Advertiser* had likewise refused her the use of their columns even at abnormally high rates.[1] But she had other means of attracting attention. In dedicating the first

[1] That the indomitable Constantia really enjoyed publicity is seen in her complaint that when her case was being heard in Doctors' Commons she 'intended to advertise it in all the Papers, that all of the Public . . . might . . . have attended it'. She then found that the printers 'took her Money, but never inserted the Advertisement; which laid her under the Necessity, the Day before the Trial came on, to print a Hand Advertisement, and distribute it upon the Exchange, the Coffee-houses, &c.'

number to the Earl of Scarborough she tucked in a few sentences to
procure readers for her salacious trumpery: '. . . for, all the World will
own, that it is attended with so many shocking Circumstances of
Dishonour, that, without such authentic Proofs as are here produced,
it would scarce be credited'. Eighteenth-century readers liked to be
told that stories submitted for their perusal were (a) true, (b) moral.
Like Defoe before her, Mrs. Phillips sought to satisfy her customers
on both scores. In reply to an objector she protested in the third
number of Volume III that her narrative was a moral treatise especially
suitable for innocent young ladies, for they would be warned by her
unhappy example to keep to virtuous ways. She had the effrontery to
declare that several clergymen had purchased the numbers for their
daughters and had assured her they contained matter well worth a
young girl's perusal. That testimony, she admitted, made her feel that
her labours were amply rewarded. One detects the resourceful sales
promoter rather than the persecuted and penitent sinner in her next
remark: 'I have, to the utmost of my Power, endeavoured to set the
Pleasures of the Life I have led in the lowest and most contemptible
Light . . . .'

This egregious flaunting of soiled linen obviously brought satisfaction of one sort or another to Constantia. Impudently dedicating
the second number to her quondam husband, Henry Muilman, she
complained of the 'repeated Calumnies' she had endured, but said she
had not lost track of his actions: 'There is scarce a Day (as the Sale of
this Apology obliges me to see many People) but some of your Exploits come to my Ears.' Then, declaring that she was not in the least
surprised that their dispute had excited so much public curiosity, she
said she really should not blame him for duplicity, since all his protes-
tations merely made her own share in the drama appear to greater
advantage; 'and it must be confess'd,' she added, 'I have, on that
Account, already reaped considerable Benefit.'

Making sweet uses of adversity, the lady then addressed the 'candid
and impartial Reader', saying, 'as . . . scarce any Story was brought to
Light attended with such strange Circumstances as mine, I may also
venture to say, never was Oppression equal to that attempted to be

A N

APOLOGY

FOR THE

CONDUCT

O F

Mʳˢ· *Teresia Constantia Phillips*,

MORE PARTICULARLY

That Part of it which relates to her
MARRIAGE with an eminent
𝕯𝖚𝖙𝖈𝖍 𝕸𝖊𝖗𝖈𝖍𝖆𝖓𝖙:

The Whole authenticated by faithful Copies
of his Letters, and of the Settlement which
he made upon her to induce her to suffer
(without any *real* Opposition on her Part)
a Sentence to be pronounced against their
Marriage;

Together with such other Original Papers, filed
in the Cause, as are necessary to illustrate that
remarkable Story.

Were ye, ye Fair, but cautious whom ye trust,
Did ye but know how seldom Fools are just,
So many of your Sex wou'd not, in vain,
Of broken Vows and faithless Men complain:
Of all the various Wretches Love has made,
How few have been by Men of Sense betray'd ?
　　　　　　　　　　　　Rowe's Fair Penitent.

N. B. Such extraordinary Care has been taken to intimidate
the Booksellers, in order to stifle this Work, that Mrs.
Phillips is obliged to publish it herself, and sold at her
House in *Craig's Court, Charing Cross*; and to prevent
Imposition, each Book will be signed with her own Hand.

6. Title-page of Teresia Constantia Phillips's *Apology*

put upon me'. Then follows the most remarkable detail in the whole business. She had tried in vain on April 27, 1748, to get the publishers of newspapers to print an announcement concerning the difficulty she was experiencing in distributing her *Apology*. She therefore printed it in her second number:

> Mrs. Phillips begs leave to inform the Publick, that as the House she lives in was Yesterday surrounded with 13 Constables, in order to seize upon and carry her to Newgate . . . she hopes, when any Gentleman calls for her Apology, they will not take it amiss if the Door is not open'd to them, but that her Servant is oblig'd to give it through the Window . . .!

Could there be a better way of attracting attention than to have one's house surrounded by a baker's dozen of constables?

Mildly amusing though all this now seems, it is hard to refrain from applauding the resiliency of Constantia Phillips. Threatened with 'unaccountable Stratagems' to prevent publication (or delay it until 'most People would be gone out of Town'), uncertain how best to publish her precious stuff—for her friends feared it would be 'mangled and pirated by some of the mean underling Booksellers' if she ventured to publish it in numbers—she forestalled invasion of her copyright by entering the successive fascicules in the Stationers' Register,[1] and protected her customers from deception by affixing her own signature to each copy of the successive numbers! The note on the title page is so unusual as to deserve quotation:

> N.B. Such extraordinary Care has been taken to intimidate the Booksellers, in order to stifle this Work, that Mrs. Phillips is obliged to publish it herself, and only at her House in Craig's Court, Charing Cross; and to prevent Imposition, each Book will be signed with her own Hand.

The name 'Teresia Constantia Phillips' in faded brown ink on surviving copies of her *Apology* is a vivid personal reminder that at least one

[1] Only the six numbers of Volume I, beginning on April 11, 1748, and the first three of Volume II were entered; the remaining numbers of Volume II and the six numbers of Volume III were not entered.

author of a book published in numbers managed to get along without the assistance of booksellers.[1]

Unlike the Reverend Francis Blomefield and the unrevered Constantia Phillips most authors shrank from the complicated business of publishing and distributing their works, preferring to accept a certain cash-in-hand sum in exchange for dubious net profits and a great deal of unfamiliar promotion. It is to be supposed that in some cases an author (or someone acting on behalf of an author) approached a particular publisher, showed him a completed manuscript (or perhaps a portion of a work not yet completed), discussed terms, signed a formal agreement, surrendered the manuscript (or arranged to do so later), and thereupon cut himself off from all future financial interest in the work. Or the initiative may have been taken by the bookseller, who approached an author known to have written (or known to be engaged in writing) a saleable work. When a bargain was struck, the transaction would be completed by the formal assignment of the copy for a sum acceptable to both parties. Unless there are contemporary documents giving the details it is seldom possible to determine which party took the initiative and on what terms publication was agreed upon. It is often difficult even to determine who published a particular book, and seldom possible to determine who printed it. One naturally looks at imprints for these details, but some imprints are completely anonymous and information concerning publisher and printer must be sought elsewhere.

When a work was published in twenty-three small quarto numbers in 1739 under the title *England's Triumph: or, Spanish Cowardice Expos'd*, 'By Captain Charles Jenkins', the imprint on the general title page told only that the place of publication was London and that the work had been 'Printed in the Year M.DCC.XXXIX'; there is no reference to a proprietor or a printer. Similarly the ninety folio numbers of *A Compleat and Impartial History of England*, 'faithfully collected from Rapin,

[1] It is astonishing to find that Anthony Trollope, who in his *Autobiography* declared that he had never read 'more detestable trash' than the writings of Aphra Behn, thought enough of Mrs. Phillips' *Apology* to mark his ownership of the three volumes by affixing his personal bookplate. Trollope's copy of the *Apology* is now in the Houghton Library at Harvard University.

Echard, Kennet, and other Historians, by James Robinson, Esq.' and published in 1739, gives no hint of publisher or printer, the imprint on the title page merely indicating that the work was printed in London 'for the Booksellers in Town and Country'. During that same year and in the next two or three years a dozen or more books were published in numbers with that same vague imprint, 'Published for the Booksellers in Town and Country', and it is only by consulting proposals, newspaper advertisements, or the affidavits in Chancery cases that one is led to suspect R. Walker as the unacknowledged proprietor of most of them. It is obvious that Walker sought to evade detection as a book pirate by lurking under the cover of anonymity. As will be pointed out presently, he did not succeed in concealing himself.

Even when one or more persons are named in the imprint, there is often uncertainty as to whether the printer is included, and equal uncertainty as to how many of the persons named are only vendors rather than financially interested proprietors. There was, of course, a clear distinction between 'printed by' and 'printed for', though the same person might be both publisher and printer.[1] When the sixth number in the third volume of Thomas Lediard's *History of England* (a continuation of that translated by Kelly from Rapin) was advertised in the *St. James's Evening Post* number 4062 (January 17, 1736), the announcement stated that the work was 'printed by and for the sole Proprietor J. Mechell, at the King's Arms next to the Leg Tavern, Fleet-street', and then added that the numbers could also be procured from the booksellers and pamphlet shops in town and country. Mechell was obviously both printer and publisher. It would be interesting to see his records, to discover how he reckoned his profits. Whatever they were, he did not share them with others.

Sometimes the imprint names the printer, but gives no hint about the proprietor of the copy. For instance, the twenty-three half-sheet octavo numbers of *The Present State of the Turkish Empire*, 'collected

---

[1] Reference was made above, at the beginning of Chapter IV, to enterprising printers who in 1732 determined to publish as well as to print number books in order to have an investor's share in the profits of a business previously monopolized by the booksellers.

from the best Authors By the Rev. Mr. Purbeck', was, according to the general title page, 'Printed by T. Totteridge, opposite to the Elephant and Castle in Fleet-Lane'. More often the proprietor is named, with no hint of the printer, as is seen in the imprints of the prose translations of Horace and Virgil, 'Printed for Joseph Davidson, at the Angel in the Poultry, Cheapside'. It is only by consulting William Strahan's ledgers[1] that one discovers that he was the man whom Davidson engaged to print the successive numbers from 1739 onwards. On the other hand the title pages of the first two volumes of Blainville's *Travels through Holland, Germany, Switzerland, and Other Parts of Europe* name Strahan as printer, but leave the proprietor unnamed. Strahan's ledger, as also the preface to the third volume, shows that the proprietor was D. Soyer; the imprints indicate that the work was available at the bookshops of J. Noon, at White-Hart, near Mercers-Chapel, Cheapside, and R. Dodsley, at Tully's Head, Pall-Mall, and also 'at the Bar of Old Slaughter's Coffee-House, in St. Martin's Lane'.

Occasionally the several title pages of a work published in numbers were entirely explicit in designating both printer and publisher, as is seen in the imprint of the first volume of William Guthrie's *General History of England*: 'London: Printed by Daniel Browne, for T. Waller, at the Crown and Mitre, opposite to Fetter-lane, in Fleet-street. MDCCXLIV', though Browne's name is omitted in the imprints of Volume II (1747) and Volume III (1751). Browne is also named in the imprint of James Ralph's competing *History of England*, the proprietors named in the imprint of Volume I (1744) being F. Cogan and T. Waller. Cogan's name is omitted in the imprint of Volume II (1746). There is no question that, as the imprint shows, the numbers of Daniel Scott's *Appendix ad Thesaurum grecæ linguæ ab Hen. Stephano* were printed by J. Bettenham and sold by J. Noon ('Londini, typis Jac. Bettenham, veneunt apud Joh Noon, Bibliopolam, in Vico dicto, Cheapside. 1745').

Frequently, both in advertisements and in the imprints, there is no unmistakable reference to either printer or proprietor. The title page of *The Pleasant and Surprizing Adventures of Mr. Robert Drury, During his*

[1] A microfilm copy is in the Bodleian Library.

Fifteen Years Captivity on the Island of Madagascar apparently names merely three vendors: 'London, Printed, and Sold by W. Meadows, in Cornhill; T. Astley, in St. Paul's Church-Yard; and B. Milles, in Houndsditch near Bishopsgate. 1743'. But Bryan Milles must have been the proprietor, for it was he who on December 9, 1741, made formal entry of his copy ('The Whole') in the Stationers' Register, depositing the nine books of number 1, paying the sixpenny fee, and later entering numbers 2 and 3 (January 15 and February 1, 1742).

All of this serves to indicate that the question of who 'owned' the number books and reaped the profits (or suffered the losses) cannot always be settled by examining the imprint or observing the names set forth in proposals and advertisements. The whole matter is further complicated by the fact that often the advertisements listed a large number of dealers from whom the fascicules of a particular work could be obtained, many of these agents presumably having nothing to do with the financial risks and profits from investment. But there is plenty of evidence that not infrequently the publishing (as distinct from the mere vending) of a number book was undertaken jointly by a temporary combination of interested proprietors, sometimes as many as fifteen or twenty sharing in a particular enterprise and all expecting a profitable return in proportion to their individual investments. Lists of proprietors in proposals and advertisements, as well as in imprints, show that multiple ownership was common and that business associates in one number-book venture often had financial fingers in several other pies as well.

There is no doubt that there were both recognized 'congers'[1] and *ad hoc* combinations of proprietors in the number-book trade; it is also clear that a few proprietors in a recognized 'conger' had other interests in which fellow members had no share. It is to be remembered, moreover, that partners in a 'conger' sometimes deliberately assigned their shares to newcomers, and that the shares of a member who died were

[1] A definition cited by the *OED* from Bailey's *Dictionary* (Vol. II, 1731) suggests that the term was applied to a group of ten or more booksellers because 'as a large conger eel is said to devour the small fry, so this united body overpowers young and single traders'. The word was used in something like this sense from the beginning of the eighteenth century.

disposed of by legacy or auction or both. The general title page and advertisements of the weekly numbers leave no doubt that Samuel Ballard, Benjamin Motte, Richard Williamson, Samuel Birt, John Stagg, Thomas Osborne, and Charles Davis were joint proprietors of Sir Richard Baker's old *Chronicle of the Kings of England*, with continuations, when it was published at the rate of five folio sheets for sixpence in 1732-1733. Two of these men, Motte and Birt, were also sharers in the 'seventh' edition of Ralegh's *History of the World*, in weekly sixpenny numbers (1733-1734), and in the 'eleventh' edition of the same work (with a new Life of Ralegh by William Oldys), published in numbers in 1735-1736.[1] Also sharing in the 'seventh' edition were James, John, and Paul Knapton, G. Conyers, D. Midwinter, A. Ward, A. Bettesworth, C. Hitch, J. Tonson, B. Sprint, J. Osborn, T. Longman, R. Robinson, J. Walthoe, Jr., J. Wilford, J. Clarke, T. Wotton, H. Lintot, H. Whitridge, and R. Knaplock.[2] With the exception of Knaplock, Osborn, and Wilford, these same proprietors were responsible for the 'eleventh' edition, as the general title pages of the two volumes dated 1736 show. The Knaptons, Ward, and Longman were joined by Richard Ford, Richard Hett, and Thomas Cox in publishing the fourth edition of Matthew Henry's *Exposition on the Old and New Testament* in 118 weekly shilling numbers during 1736-1738. A few years later eight proprietors—T. Woodward, A. Ward, S. Birt, D. Browne, T. Longman, H. Whitridge, J. Hodges, and B. Dod—were by a royal license dated February 23, 1744, granted exclusive rights of printing, publishing, and vending their edition of John Harris's *Navigantium atque itinerantium bibliotheca. Or, A Complete Collection of Voyages and Travels*, though the imprint on the general title page included also the names of seven others—R. Hett, C. Hitch, S. Austen, J. Robinson, T. Harris, J. Hinton, and J. Rivington—as though they were also proprietors. Whether all fifteen of these men belonged to a

---

[1] The general title pages to Volumes I and II, both dated 1736, bear the words 'The Eleventh Edition'; but a title page dated 1733 has the words 'The Seventh Edition', as have also the advertisements of the numbers published during 1733 and 1734. See below, Chapter VI, pp. 201-2.

[2] Conyers and Knaplock are not named in an advertisement of the fifty-first number (*Whitehall Evening-Post* number 2455, January 24, 1734).

recognized 'conger' or not, they were responsible members of a group handling at least one substantial book. Before the end of 1744—on December 26—a royal license named twenty-two persons as proprietors of *Biographia Britannica*, and six additional ones were included in the imprint of the general title page of Volume I when it was completed in 1747.[1]

What is required to prove multiple ownership is an authentic contemporary document recording the proportional shares held jointly by a combination of proprietors, and it is fortunate that such a document is among the scanty records still extant. It is a large sheet of paper[2] listing the eighty-odd copies and shares of copies owned by one of the self-styled 'congers'. The ten members of the group—Richard Ware, Aaron Ward, John and Paul Knapton, Thomas Longman & Co., Richard Hett, Charles Hitch, James Hodges,[3] Stephen Austen, Henry Pemberton, and John Rivington—had organized themselves into a partnership by articles dated January 15, 1738 (that is, by our reckoning, 1739), and on March 20, 1745 (that is, 1746), drew a formal inventory of their joint holdings of copies purchased at auctions and at other sales. The object was to show what share each of the ten partners had in the several copies and parts of copies. These include five books which had been published or were then being published in numbers. The ten partners each owned one tenth of the whole copy of L'Estrange's *Josephus*, both folio and octavo, which a somewhat different group[4] had published in weekly numbers in 1733. They also owned equal shares in the whole copy, both folio and octavo, of Rapin's *Acta Regia* (presumably the translation by Stephen Whatley), the folio edition of which had been issued in weekly numbers in 1732–

[1] See the appropriate entry in Appendix B.

[2] Bodleian Library, MS. Eng. Misc. b. 44, item 46. I am indebted to Mr. Cyprian Blagden for calling my attention to this document.

[3] Hodges became a member of the conger by purchasing Thomas Bowles's tenth share of the conger's books and copies on June 4, 1742. The original assignment, now at the Houghton Library at Harvard University, shows that Hodges paid Bowles £ 366.14s.3d. for his tenth share.

[4] The Knaptons, D. Midwinter, A. Bettesworth and C. Hitch, C. Rivington, J. Pemberton, J. Osborn and T. Longman, F. Clay, J. Batley, A. Ward, R. Hett, and T. Hatchett.

1733 by almost exactly the same proprietors as were then publishing *Josephus*, the octavo edition having been published in monthly numbers in 1725–1727 by Bettesworth, Pemberton, Rivington, Clay, Batley, and four others. The ten partners in the 'conger' owned equal shares in one half of the copy of Tillotson's *Works*, in folio and octavo, a sumptuous edition of which, in octavo numbers, they had published in 1742–1744, the owners of the other half apparently being J. and R. Tonson, whose names stand in the imprint.

A more complicated division of copies is seen in this 'conger's' shares in a work listed in their inventory as 'Moll's Geography now reprinting under the Title of System of Geography', for Pemberton had no share at all, Austen owned one fifth, and the others had one tenth each; but the 'conger' had title to only 33 shares in 72, the remainder being apparently in the possession of Clarke, Osborne,[1] Whitridge, Comyns, Millar,[2] and Corbett, whose names are in the imprint of the two volumes dated 1747 after the work had appeared in 144 weekly numbers. One of the most popular of the Biblical commentaries was that 'endeavoured' (as the title page said) by William Burkitt (1650–1703), published posthumously in 1724 under the title *Expository Notes, with Practical Observations on the New Testament* and subsequently reprinted in many editions. The tenth edition was published in numbers in 1733–1734, and it is interesting to observe that the 'conger's' inventory shows that in 1746 the ten proprietors owned one sixth of the copy (Ward having one twentieth and the Knaptons three twentieths of that sixth, the eight others each having a tenth of that sixth), and had also purchased from Ranew Robinson an additional one-third interest in the work, though each of the partners held only one twelfth of that third, the other two twelfths of Robinson's third having been bought by Birt and Davidson. It is clear from contemporary notations

---

[1] When Thomas Osborne's stock was sold at auction on February 9, 1744, Wicksteed paid £ 59 for one-eighteenth (that is, for 4 in 72) of 'Moll's Geography, Fol. now coming out Weekly', according to a notation in the Longmans, Green copy of the catalogue.

[2] At the sale of Stephen Austen's stock in December 1750 Millar paid three pounds for Austen's one-fifth of 33 shares in 72, according to a manuscript notation in the Longmans, Green copy of the sales catalogue.

on trade-sales catalogues that before the eleventh edition of 1739 was published the title to this work was divided into sixtieths, the notation usually being '50 Books in 3000' when single sixtieths were purchased. After Richard Ford[1] died in 1738 his stock was sold at auction on November 14 of that year, and an annotated catalogue of the sale[2] shows that his ten sixtieths were purchased at prices ranging from £ 26. 15s. to £ 28. 10s. each, all the purchasers except three (J. Oswald, S. Birt, and E. Comyns) being members of the 'conger' formed two months later: Hodges (two sixtieths), Hitch (two sixtieths), Ware, Longman, Ward (one sixtieth each). Further trading in sixtieth shares, though at lower prices, is seen in notations concerning E. Wicksteed's purchase of six sixtieths on February 9, 1744, at the sale of Thomas Osborne's stock. At that sale S. Birt also bought a fraction ('33 in 3000', or two thirds of a sixtieth). When these holdings are tabulated they show very clearly that both the members of the 'conger' and other proprietors regarded investment in Burkitt's work as a safe and profitable venture, in spite of the fact that (as will be noticed presently) Burkitt's estate had to be paid ninepence for every copy sold. The 'conger' continued to purchase promising 'copies', among them Robert Jameson's *Critical and Practical Exposition of the Pentateuch*, which was to have been a complete commentary on the Bible but continued for only 66 numbers in 1747–1748. The proprietors included the Knaptons, Longman and Shewell, Hitch, Hodges, J. and J. Rivington, two newcomers (C. Davis and A. Millar) having replaced the others in the 1739 group.

Multiple ownership of copies would appeal to such proprietors as those just mentioned only if profits were likely to be substantial enough to give each member some return for his investment, and it is also to be assumed that a publishing venture divided into sixtieths which changed hands for twenty-five or thirty pounds each must have yielded a good return. So valuable a property must have been eyed with envy

---

[1] Ford was one of the proprietors of the ninth edition of Burkitt's *Expository Notes* (1729), along with Ranew Robinson, Aaron Ward, M. Wyatt, J. and B. Sprint, and L. Jackson.
[2] Seen at Longmans, Green's London office.

by other booksellers, and without some sort of legal protection the fortunate owners would certainly have suffered from piracy. Some did indeed suffer, though there was a statute providing severe penalties for offenders.

The first formal statute providing copyright in England, An Act for the Encouragement of Learning, by Vesting the Copies of Printed Books in the Authors or Purchasers of such Copies (8 Anne, c. 19), offered protection to all who published books, whether in numbers or in complete volumes. Between the expiry of the earlier Licensing Act in 1694 and the 'Queen Anne Act', as it was called, the author or publisher of a book had no statutory protection of his literary property, though a publisher might claim, and usually did claim, exclusive rights of publication if he were a member of the Stationers' Company.[1] Otherwise an author or publisher could only assume—or hope—that his proprietary right in the copy of a book would be recognized under common law. This insecurity led the booksellers and publishers to petition Parliament in 1703, in 1706, and again in 1709 to provide further protection. The ultimate result was the introduction of a Bill in the House of Commons early in 1709, and it was this Bill that presently emerged as the first Copyright Law of England.

The Act of 8 Anne, c. 19 should have meant that no books could be reprinted without a formal and satisfactory agreement between the man who proposed to reprint and the previous proprietor; but smart publishers with an eye to business and a hearty readiness to defy the law did not hesitate even within the periods of statutory protection to reprint *in toto* or in abridged form all sorts of books, no matter when or by whom they had been previously published. Claims to exclusive

---

[1] For the early history of copyright in England see T. E. Scrutton, *The Law of Copyright* (4th ed., London: Clowes, 1903), A. S. Collins, *Authorship in the Days of Johnson* (London: Routledge, 1928), L. Hanson, *Government and the Press 1695–1763* (London: Humphrey Milford, Oxford University Press, 1936), and F. S. Siebert, *Freedom of the Press in England 1467–1776* (Urbana: University of Illinois Press, 1952). Of special interest are also J. W. Draper, 'Queen Anne's Act', *Modern Language Notes*, XXXVI (1921), 146–54, A.W. Pollard, 'Some Notes on the History of Copyright in England, 1662–1774', *Library*, 4th ser., III (1922–23), 97–114, and R. C. Bald, 'Early Copyright Litigation and its Bibliographical Interest', *Papers of the Bibliographical Society of America*, XXXVI (1942), 81–96.

right under common law or under the statute were occasionally supported by injunctions granted in a court of equity; but often they were either challenged defiantly or completely ignored. Neither the threat of injunctions nor the specific penalties enumerated in the text of the statute eliminated piracy in the publishing business.

In order to understand why the Queen Anne statute led not to clarification but to half a century of confusion and the most involved litigation one must study the actual text of the Act itself.[1] The preamble makes a clear statement that printers, booksellers, and other persons had been printing, reprinting, and publishing books and other writings without the consent of the authors and proprietors thereof. The object of the statute was to prevent such practices for the future, and its two central provisions were (1) that the authors or proprietors of books already in print when the statute became effective (April 10, 1710) were to enjoy exclusive rights of publication for the next twenty-one years 'and no longer' —that is, until April 10, 1731 —and (2) that the author or proprietor of any new book published after April 10, 1710, was to have exclusive right of publication for fourteen years from the date of publication 'and no longer'; but a curious postscript in Clause XI provided that after the expiration of the said term of fourteen years the sole right of printing or disposing of copies was to return to the authors, if still living, for a second term of fourteen years. It was not made clear whether this modification of the very explicit term of fourteen years 'and no longer' was to apply even if the author had assigned his right to someone else within the first term. If that were to be the interpretation, then obviously an author could not legally assign his copy for any term extending beyond fourteen years from the date of first publication, and no matter what price he had received for surrendering the copyright the title would automatically revert to him. This limitation might conceivably have conferred financial benefits on the author of a really successful book, but the main intent in all the clauses of this Act for the Encouragement of Learning seems to have been to encourage booksellers rather than authors. Clause XI is but one of many left inexplicit.

[1] See Appendix A.

In the matter of penalties for infringement the Queen Anne statute was — or seemed to be — explicit enough. Anyone printing, reprinting, importing, or causing to be printed, reprinted, or imported, a book which another claimed as his literary property, without the owner's consent in writing, would be required to forfeit the printed copies or parts thereof and to pay a penny for every sheet of the pirated work found in the offender's possession.

So much for the proposed treatment of offenders found guilty of infringing the statute. Those whom the Act was intended to benefit can hardly have appreciated the protection offered, however, for the simple reason that no book was protected unless (1) the title (or the previous proprietor's consent) had been entered in the Stationers' Register before publication, (2) nine copies of the book, 'upon the best Paper', had been delivered to the warehouse-keeper at Stationers' Hall (for distribution to nine important libraries named in Clause V), and (3) all actions against supposed offenders were initiated within three months of the alleged offence. The Act specifically excluded from protection all books in foreign languages printed 'beyond the Seas'.[1] Most curious of all is Clause IX, which seems quite clearly to leave all printing monopolies and common law claims to literary property entirely unaffected, for it provided that

... nothing in this Act contained shall extend, or be construed to extend, either to prejudice or confirm any Right that the said Universities, or any of them, or any Person or Persons have, or claim to have, to the printing or reprinting any Book or Copy already printed, or hereafter to be printed.

[1] In 1734 Samuel Buckley, a London stationer, petitioned the House of Commons to grant him special protection for his sumptuous edition, in seven folio volumes and on imported paper, of *Historia sui Temporis* in Latin, by Jacques Auguste de Thou (alias Thuanus). The Act of 7 George II, c. 24 granted the desired protection for fourteen years. Within a month (beginning in March 1734) an English translation of de Thou's work was being issued in fortnightly numbers, 'beautifully printed on a fine Genoa Paper'. The proprietor, Alexander Lyon of Russell Street, identified the translator as 'M. Cart, Editor of the Original lately publish'd by Mr. Buckley'. As was noticed in Chapter III, a portion of de Thou's work, translated by Rev. Bernard Wilson, had been published in twenty-four numbers in 1728-30.

To those who drew up the final text of the Queen Anne statute these provisions doubtless seemed adequate both for books already in print and for books not yet published. Subsequent litigation proved the insufficiency of the Act. The courts were called upon to hand down decisions in cases of alleged infringement and to decide whether copyright in a published work had existed at common law before the Statute of Anne, and if so whether the statute did or did not affect that right. The whole complicated story is to be traced only in the petitions subsequently (1735, 1737, 1739) presented to the House of Commons demanding improved legislation, in the texts of the bills proposed but rejected, in the affidavits and bills in Chancery praying interim or perpetual injunctions against piratical publishers, and in the reports of various cases argued and adjudged in one or another of the courts of law.

A noticeable feature of the litigation arising out of alleged infringements of the Queen Anne statute is the fact that many decisions were subsequently reversed. As Sir Roger de Coverley said in another case, much might be said on both sides —and often a great deal *was* said. It was seldom difficult to prove that a book allegedly the property of one party had been reprinted by another; the uncertainty came over the question of whether any guilt attached to the act of reprinting the said book. When Andrew Millar and sixteen associated London booksellers charged twenty booksellers of Edinburgh and four booksellers of Glasgow with having invaded their copyright in certain works (including Ephraim Chambers' *Cyclopædia*) the Lords of Council and Session at Edinburgh in April 1743 found that there lay no action of damages in the case, and then when the case was heard again, decided that an action of damages did lie.

The most ample evidence of the legal uncertainties resulting from the Queen Anne statute is to be found in Sir James Burrow's full report of the case of Andrew Millar *versus* Robert Taylor (Court of King's Bench) over the property right in James Thomson's *Seasons* in 1769,[1] in Lord Coalston's and James Boswell's printed reports of the case of *Hinton* v. *Donaldson* over a Scottish edition of Stackhouse's *History of*

[1] 4 Burr. 2303.

the Bible (Court of Session, July 1773),[1] and in Josiah Brown's detailed account of the deliberations in the House of Lords on the appeal in the case of *Donaldson* v. *Beckett* in 1774.[2] These particular cases fall out-side the period covered by the present study, but the reports throw much light on the conditions under which number books were pub-lished before 1750.

Especially illuminating also are the statements made to a Parlia-mentary Committee in 1774[3] by William Johnston, a retired book-seller, who declared that he 'never imagined the Act of Queen Anne interfered with the common law right', that he 'always understood that when a man sells all his right and title for ever, it means a common law right, independent of any statute', and that he 'never saw or heard of any assignment where the second term of 14 years, mentioned in the Act of Queen Anne, was reserved to the author'.[4] Johnston's testi-mony is particularly interesting as a commentary on Clause II of the Queen Anne statute:

---

[1] The facts and legal principles of the *Hinton* v. *Donaldson* cause were set forth by Ilay Campbell, one of the counsel for the defendants, in *Information for Alexander Donaldson and John Wood, Booksellers in Edinburgh, and James Meurose, Bookseller in Kilmar-noch, Defenders; against John Hinton, Bookseller in London, and Alexander M'Conochie, Writer in Edinburgh, his Attorney, Pursuers.* This 82-page pamphlet, marked 'Lord Coalston Reporter', was published January 2, 1773, over six months before the case was heard. Boswell, who was also one of the counsel for the defendants, must have taken great satisfaction in the Court's eleven-to-one decision on July 28, 1773 to dismiss the action. It was he who (according to the title page) in 1774 'published' the text of the formal summons, together with a report of the speeches by nine of the judges and the Lord President. Boswell's 37-page pamphlet is entitled *The Decision of the Court of Session upon the Question of Literary Property; in the Cause John Hinton* ... *against Alexander Donaldson and John Wood* ... *and James Meurose* ..., and was printed by James Donaldson for Alexander Donaldson, who had a shop at No. 48, St. Paul's Churchyard, London, as well as one in Edinburgh. The case of *Hinton* v. *Donaldson* is also reported in the *Scots Magazine*, XXXV (1773), 497 f., and XXXVI (1774), 9–17, 65–7.
[2] 2 Bro. Cases in Par. 129. A full and often diverting account of this appeal in the House of Lords is to be found in *The Parliamentary History of England, from the earliest Period to the Year 1803*, (London, 1813), XVIII, cols. 953–1003. Condensed reports of the arguments of counsel and the opinions of judges on this appeal are printed in the *Scots Magazine*, XXXVI (1774), 121–6, 185–94, 233–7, and 530–4.
[3] *The Parliamentary History of England* (London, 1813), XVII, cols. 1078–1110.
[4] On this last point see also the report of *Carnan* v. *Bowles* (2 Bro. Cha. Rep. 80).

Being asked, why it was not the custom of those who are possessed of copy-right, to enter them in the books of the Stationers' Company? He said, he could only answer for himself, that he never thought the penalties prescribed by the Act of the eighth of queen Anne were worth contending for, as a much shorter and more complete relief might be had, by filing a bill in Chancery; that the trade of a bookseller is circumscribed by no law, nor any bye-law of the Stationers' Company; and every man that pleases may set up in the business, without an hour's servitude to the trade.

It is easy to see why the publishers found it more convenient to file a bill in Chancery, with an affidavit stating the grounds of their application, than to prosecute under the Act of Queen Anne. *Ex parte* injunctions were much simpler and much less costly than prosecutions, and although they were interlocutory, not final, they normally were effective in restraining publication by a rival, even if profits were not recovered and penalties exacted.

It has been pointed out[1] that in 1739 such an injunction did not hinder Robert Walker from completing the publication of Milton's *Paradise Lost* in twelve numbers, in spite of the fact that Tonson's *prima facie* evidence of property rights in the work had been recognized by the High Court of Chancery. Walker's subsequent publication of *Paradise Lost* in sixteen threepenny numbers (weekly, from October 30, 1751, to February 12, 1752) was once again carried to completion in defiance of Tonson,[2] whose bill, filed in Chancery November 26, 1751, brought an answer from Walker on December 12, 1751, but no effective action from the court until the injunction was granted on April 30, 1752, eleven weeks after Walker had triumphantly advertised (in the *Ladies Magazine* for February 8-22, 1752) the final number of the series. Walker's achievement in twice completing number-book editions of a great work in defiance both of the proprietor and of the law was not duplicated by any of his contemporaries, though he and other publishers may often have been challenged. Both R. Penny and W. Rayner got into trouble with the King's Printer for invading his monopoly of printing the Holy Bible. Rayner defied Baskett,

---

[1] Bald, *art. cit.*, p. 92 f.
[2] *Tonson* v. *Walker and Marchant* (1752). See 3 Swan. 672 and 4 Burr. 2325.

declaring in the Preface to *The Compleat History of the Old and New Testament: Or, a Family Bible,* 'with Critical and Explanatory Annotations . . . by S. Smith, D.D.', (published in 174 numbers in 1735–7) that 'the word of God ought not to be the property of any one person, or set of men', and that 'the interest of heaven is no way concerned, whether God's word be printed by J. Baskett, or W. Rayner'. Penny, less brazen, in advertising the monthly numbers of the New Testament, annotated by Rev. John Lindsay in 1734, relieved the anxiety of his customers by a forthright statement in the *St. James's Evening Post* number 2966 (November 2, 1734) that he had come to terms with Baskett:

> N.B. In Order to prevent any Distrust, which might arise from the Report of a Suit in Equity depending between Mr. Baskett, his Majesty's Printer, and Myself, in relation to my Right of Printing the Text of the New Testament, . . . I do hereby acquaint the Publick that the said Suit is compromised, and that I have paid a valuable Consideration in order to do my Subscribers Justice by finishing the Work in the Manner at first proposed, and in which it is hitherto carried on.

It can hardly be supposed that recognition of special monopolies, obedience to the statute, and fear of prosecution by the powerful 'congers' held all would-be book pirates in check; but there is no evidence that any number book, once begun, was stopped by court action in the period under review.

The matter of the legality of publication was given a curious twist by Lord Chancellor Hardwicke, who insisted in 1740 that the publishing of an abridgment, unless it was merely colourable, was not an infringement of the law of copyright.[1] Preposterous though it now seems, the view was held in 1740 and for many years thereafter that a 'fair' abridgment was not piratical, and that on the other hand it might deserve more praise than the original book because it was more succinct. Again and again in the eighteenth century the proprietors of published books found their bills praying injunctions to restrain piratical publication dismissed by the courts without costs, on the

---

[1] See the reports of *Gyles* v. *Wilcox* (March 6, 1740) by John Tracy Atkyns (2 Atk. 141) and Thomas Barnardiston (Barn. C. 368).

ground that the pirate was invading no property right since he was printing an abridgment. Thus, for instance, Robert Dodsley in 1761 was helpless to prevent Kinnersley, the proprietor of the *Grand Magazine of Magazines*, from reprinting large portions of Samuel Johnson's *The Prince of Abyssinia* minus the moral reflections.[1] The deletion of the philosophy made the book in point of fact a different book, as the author would doubtless be the first to agree, though hardly with approval.

Among the thirty-one sections of the 'Considerations on the Case of Dr. Trapp's Sermons' (*Gentleman's Magazine* for July 1787) —attributed by Boswell to Samuel Johnson —is the assertion that 'to abridge a book is no violation of the right of the proprietor, because to be subject to the hazard of an abridgment was an original condition of the property'. The whole argument was based on the assumption that a long and tedious work *ought* to be abbreviated, for the sake of the reader. 'By this method the original author becomes, perhaps, of less value, but these inconveniencies give way to the advantage received by mankind, from the easier propagation of knowledge.' From the piratical publisher's point of view this principle is admirable, but it seems to be a strange means of encouraging honest efforts to write or print original works.

In 1774 John Newbery must have felt particularly elated when, instead of having to defer to a threatened injunction from the Court of King's Bench for publishing an unauthorized edition (abridged) of Dr. Hawkesworth's *Voyages*, he learned that the Court praised his edition, which (according to Capel Lofft's report of the case)[2] 'might be read in the fourth part of the time, and all the substance preserved, and conveyed in language as good or better than in the original, and in a more agreeable and useful manner'. It is shocking to find in Lofft's report the statement that Lord Chancellor Apsley and Mr. Justice Blackstone spent some hours together discussing the principle of the thing,

---

[1] Amb. 403. Johnson's views on copyright are brought together by Sir Arnold McNair in *Dr. Johnson and the Law* (Cambridge University Press, 1948), pp. 96 ff.
[2] Lofft 775.

and were agreed that an abridgment, where the understanding is employed in retrenching unnecessary and uninteresting circumstances, which rather deaden the narration, is not an act of plagiarism upon the original work, nor against any property of the author in it, but an allowable and meritorious work.

Here the implication seems to be that there is nothing piratical about the reprinting of someone else's copy if it has been vigorously blue-pencilled.

That, however, was not the official view during the period under discussion. Thirty-five years before the Apsley-Blackstone pronouncement Lord Chancellor Hardwicke, according to a report by Barnardiston,[1] insisted that mere deletion did not alter the identity of a copy.

And where the second Book has no otherwise differ'd from the former than by reducing or shortening the Stile, or by leaving out some of the Words of the first Book, the second Book has been construed the same with the former.

His Lordship referred to a case *(Read* v. *Hodges)* 'determined on a Motion the 9th of May last' [that is, 1739] concerning two versions of a biography of Peter the Great.

The second Book that was published no otherwise varied from the first, than by leaving out certain Parts of the former, and only by that Means shortening it, and the Court was of Opinion, that an Injunction ought to be granted to restrain the Printing of that second Book.

It was unfortunate that the men who prepared the text of the Queen Anne statute on copyright gave no thought to abridgments.

As a result of that omission there were some proprietors who despaired of being able to enjoy without interference the total protection nominally provided by the statute and had recourse to special licences or patents issued in the name of the King himself. These patents, presumably obtained only on payment of considerable fees, conferred on petitioners exactly the same benefits as those provided by the Copyright Act, with the important addition of protection against abridgment. The proprietors of at least a dozen large works published in numbers in the 1740's petitioned the King for special licences and

[1] Barn. C. 368.

GEORGE R.

GEORGE the Second, by the Grace of God, King of *Great-Britain*, *France*, and *Ireland*, Defender of the Faith, &c. *To all to whom these Presents shall come, Greeting.* Whereas DENNIS COETLOGON, Gentleman, has by his Petition humbly represented unto Us, that he hath with great Labour and Expence compiled from the best Authors, both antient and modern,

An UNIVERSAL HISTORY *of* ARTS *and* SCIENCES;

Containing all Sciences, either divine or human, and all the Arts, either liberal or mechanical, in a more concise and clear Method than heretofore used in any other Work of the Kind; the whole adapted to the meanest Capacity, alphabetically digested, and illustrated with Astronomical and other curious Tables and Prints, which the Petitioner, with the utmost Submission, apprehends may be of the greatest Service to the Publick, as it will be reducing each Art and Science to a regular System, at an easy Rate to the Purchaser, and thereby much encourage every Branch of Learning or Mechanicks; and as the said Work is near finished, and when compleated will cost him upwards of one Thousand Pounds : He therefore being desirous to reap the Fruit of his Labour, and enjoy the full Profits and Benefits that may arise from printing, publishing, and vending the same, without any other Person interfering in his just Property, which he cannot prevent without applying to Us, for Our Royal Licence and Protection : The Petitioner has therefore humbly pray'd Us to grant him Our Royal Licence and Protection, for the sole Printing, Publishing, and Vending the said Work in as ample Manner and Form as hath been done in Cases of the like Nature. We being willing to give all due Encouragement to such a useful Work, are graciously pleased to condescend to his Request ; and do therefore by these Presents, so far as may be agreeable to the Statute in that Behalf made and provided, grant unto the said *Dennis Coetlogon*, his Executors, Administrators, and Assigns, Our Royal Privilege and Licence for the sole Printing, Publishing, and Vending the said Work, for and during the Term of fourteen Years, to be computed from the Date hereof, strictly forbidding and prohibiting all Our Subjects within our Kingdoms and Dominions, to reprint or abridge the same, either in the like, or in any other Volume or Volumes whatsoever, or to import, buy, vend, utter, or distribute any Copies thereof, reprinted beyond the Seas, during the aforesaid Term of fourteen Years, without the Consent and Approbation of the said *Dennis Coetlogon*, his Heirs, Executors, Administrators and Assigns, under their Hands and Seals first had and obtained, as they and very of them offending therein, will answer the contrary at their Peril : Whereof the Commissioners and other Officers of our Customs, the Master, Wardens, and Company of Stationers of Our City of *London*, and all other our Officers and Ministers, whom it may concern, are to take Notice, that due Obedience be given to Our Pleasure herein signified. Given at Our Court at St. *James's* the Thirteenth Day of *March*, 1740-1, in the Fourteenth Year of Our Reign.

By His Majesty's Command,

HARRINGTON.

7. The Royal licence for *Universal History of Arts and Sciences*

drew particular attention to the fact that without such licenses they could not keep other booksellers from interfering in their property rights. Several books so protected have been mentioned earlier in this chapter. The petitioners did not usually have long to wait for an official response. Thus the 'humble Petition of Dennis Coetlogon Gent' for the sole privilege of publishing his *Universal History of Arts and Sciences* was dated March 5, 1740/41,[1] and the license was dated March 13, 1740/41.[2] It is curious that during the next six years the successive weekly numbers of this *Universal History of Arts and Sciences* were entered in the Stationers' Register by John Hart on behalf of Coetlogon. This double precaution—and double expense—must have been sought because the compiler, after suffering the horrors of imprisonment in Newgate for many weeks in 1737,[3] had spent 'upwards of One Thousand Pounds' in the preparation of the work—or so he declared in his petition to the King.

There was also undoubtedly some aura of dignity as well as of security about a work which could be advertised as published 'with His Majesty's Royal License'. The full texts of such licences, duly recorded in the Warrant Books in the Public Record Office, were usually displayed in long advertisements in the newspapers, and were often reproduced on the covers of individual numbers or on the verso of the title pages of completed volumes. In 1739 the four proprietors of *The Universal History, from the Earliest Account of Time to the Present*—Edward Symon, Thomas Osborne, John Wood, and James Crokatt[4]—felt that this extensive work, which at first had encountered many delays, was now so valuable that they wished to protect themselves against more forms of piracy than those specified in the statute. They must have been very well pleased when their petition was granted on March 24,

---

[1] Public Record Office, State Papers Domestic (George II), 36, bundle 55, item 63.
[2] Public Record Office, Warrant Books, S. P. 44, vol. 367, pp. 205–7.
[3] Coetlogon's pathetic letters requesting relief are in the Public Record Office, S. P. 36, bundle 42, item 97, and bundle 43, item 34.
[4] This work had been initiated early in 1730 by J. Batley, E. Symon, N. Prevost, T. Osborne, J. Crokatt, and T. Payne. Apparently Prevost and Payne soon dropped out. By July 1737 Wood and Batley held shares jointly (along with Symon, Osborne, and Crokatt); by 1739 Wood had taken over Batley's share.

1739. The full text of the royal licence, as it appeared in the *Daily Advertiser* number 2565 (April 13, 1739),[1] is worth studying, not only because it exhibits the usual formula for such documents but also because it gives in capital letters particular warning against abridgment:

GEORGE R.

GEORGE the Second, by the Grace of God, King of Great Britain, France and Ireland, Defender of the Faith, &c. to all whom these Presents shall come, Greeting: Whereas *Edward Symon, Thomas Osborne, John Wood*, and *James Crokatt*, of Our City of London, Booksellers, have by their Petition humbly represented unto Us, that they have spent many Years, and expended several thousand Pounds in procuring, buying of Books, and employing a Number of learned Gentlemen in the compiling, writing, and publishing, AN UNIVERSAL HIS-TORY, FROM THE EARLIEST ACCOUNT OF TIME TO THE PRESENT; collected from the best Authors both Antient and Modern; in drawing of Maps, making Chronological and other Tables, for the better illustrating the same, to be comprised in Eight Volumes in Folio; a Work hitherto attempted in vain by other Nations; which the Petitioners, with the utmost Submission apprehend may be of great Service to the Publick, as it will be reducing a very extensive but very useful Science to a regular System or Digest, at an easy Rate to the Purchaser, and thereby much encourage and promote a necessary Branch of Learning: And as this Undertaking is near finish'd, they are desirous of reaping the Fruits of their Labour, and of enjoying the full Profit and Benefit that may arise from Printing, Publishing and Vending the same, without any other Person interfering in their just Property; which they cannot prevent without applying to Us for Our Royal License and Protection: Therefore they have humbly prayed Us to grant them Our Royal Licence and Protection for the sole Printing, Publishing and Vending the said Work, in as ample Manner and Form as has been done in Cases of the same Nature. We being willing to give all due Encouragement to such a useful Work, are graciously pleas'd to condescend to their Request; And do therefore by these Presents, so far as may be agreeable to the Statute in that Behalf made and provided, grant unto the said *Edward Symon, Thomas Osborne*,

---

[1] An official manuscript copy of the text of the licence is in the Warrant Book in the Public Record Office, S. P. 44, Vol. 368, pp. 150-2.

John Wood, and *James Crokatt*, their Executors, Administrators and Assigns, Our Royal Privilege and Licence for the sole Printing, Publishing and Vending the said Work for and during the Term of Fourteen Years, to be computed from the Date hereof; strictly forbidding and prohibiting all our Subjects within Our Kingdoms and Dominions to Reprint or ABRIDGE the same, either in the like, or any other Volume or Volumes whatsoever, or to import, buy, vend, utter, or distribute any Copies thereof reprinted beyond the Seas, during the aforesaid Term of Fourteen Years, without the Consent or Approbation of the said *Edward Symon, Thomas Osborne, John Wood*, and *James Crokatt*, their Heirs, Executors, Administrators and Assigns, under their Hands and Seals first had and obtain'd, as they and every of them offending therein will answer the contrary at their Peril. Whereof the Commissioners, and other Officers of Our Customs, the Master, Wardens, and Company of Stationers, of Our City of London, and all other Our Officers and Ministers, whom it may concern, are to take Notice, that due Obedience be given to Our Pleasure herein signified.

Given at Our Court at St. James's, the 24th Day of March, 1738/9, in the Twelfth Year of Our Reign.

By His MAJESTY'S *Command*

HOLLES NEWCASTLE.

Once again it is obvious that efforts to preserve a property right are evidence of the value put upon that property. It was no mere desire to observe a formality that led Stephen Austen in December 1741 to apply to the King's Most Excellent Majesty for a royal licence. He had 'expended a very considerable Sum of Money' in purchasing the copy of *A New History of the Holy Bible* from the author, the Rev. Thomas Stackhouse, whose additional labours in revising the work would (Austen declared) 'be attended with a still further great Expence and Trouble'. Like other petitioners, Austen was 'very desirous of reaping the Fruits of his great Expence and Labour'; but he knew—or at any rate he asserted—that only a royal licence could protect him against interference and enable him to enjoy the 'full Profit and Benefit . . . from Printing and Vending' the work. He had a very real fear of losing some of the expected profits, for, he declared, 'some other Persons are at this Time actually making Preparations in order to reprint the Same

without his Consent'. Austen's licence, issued January 8, 1742, gave
him sole rights of publication for fourteen years.[1]

Royal licences were, of course, sought by publishers of other works
than those issued in numbers, as the Warrant Books in the Public
Record Office make abundantly clear. Yet newspaper advertisements
of another work by Thomas Stackhouse, the third edition of his
Compleat Body of Speculative and Practical Divinity, indicate that the proprietor, T. Cox, apparently believed the fee for a royal licence to be
unavoidable if the edition were to be published in numbers. In the
Norwich Gazette number 1850 (March 20, 1742) Cox announced that
he had that day published proposals for printing Stackhouse's *Compleat
Body* in one folio volume for a guinea in sheets (instead of thirty shillings
bound, as the two former editions had been priced), provided that
subscribers entered their names and paid five shillings down before the
first day of the following June. After that date the price was to be
advanced, 'so that all who come after that Time, will intirely lose the
Benefit of Subscribing'. Then followed an illuminating note:

> The extraordinary Success that hath attended Books published
> Weekly at Six-Pence per Number, had once determined the Proprietor
> to publish this in the same Manner. But when he considered the great
> unnecessary Expence of a Royal Licence, and other additional Charges
> that do particularly attend that Manner of Publication, he thought
> that saving such Expence, and applying it to the Subscribers Advan-
> tage, by reducing the Price of the Book as above, would be the most
> effectual Means of increasing the Numbers of Subscriptions.

Two months later, however, Cox advertised in the same paper, number
1859 (May 22, 1742), that on Saturday, June 12, he would publish
the first number of Stackhouse's book, and that the work would be

---

[1] Stackhouse's *History of the Bible* was still worth quarrelling over in 1773, when the
Scottish Court of Session heard and dismissed the charge laid by John Hinton of
London that Alexander Donaldson and John Wood of Edinburgh and James
Meurose of Kilmarnoch had invaded his property by publishing 10,000 copies of
Stackhouse's book in 1765. Hinton had acquired title to *The History of the Bible* by
marrying Stephen Austen's widow in 1752. Stackhouse had assigned his right to
Austen by deed dated January 8, 1740 (i.e., 1741), and Austen's will, dated March
20, 1745 (i.e., 1746), conveyed the property to his wife.

continued in forty-two weekly numbers, each containing six sheets for six pence. He said nothing about a royal licence, but declared that he would have endangered his sales if he had kept to his former decision to publish the entire work at one time. To publish in numbers, apparently, was the better way—but Cox was prepared to offer the work in *both* forms, and at the same total price:

> Proposals have been published in the News-Papers, both in Town and Country, to print the said Book at One Guinea a Book in Sheets; Five Shillings to be paid down, and the rest at the Delivery: But as several large Books have since that Time been proposed to the Publick in the weekly Method, I am at last prevailed on to comply with the present Mode, rather than be under any Disadvantage in the Sale of the said Books; and therefore will deliver the same according the former Proposals, or weekly Six Sheets for Six Pence.

The 'several large Books . . . proposed to the Publick in the weekly Method' included Dr. James's *Medicinal Dictionary* and Archbishop Tillotson's *Works*.

This sequence of advertisements by T. Cox shows very well that publication in numbers was sometimes felt to be the surer method of reaping profits. Obviously Cox thought it would be disadvantageous not to publish in numbers, even though that manner of publication would involve additional charges. The first of the two passages quoted above seems to include the fee for a royal licence among the special costs of publishing in numbers, but with one or two exceptions[1] the texts of the licences make no reference to publication in numbers and it is hard to see why Cox believed this to be an inescapable charge. Some books not published in numbers—Richardson's *Pamela*, for example— were granted royal licences, and most number books were published without this costly distinction. There is in fact no perceptible correlation between the petitioning for a royal licence and publication in numbers. Some of the licensed works were reprints or revised versions of books published earlier without royal licence, though in one instance

[1] The seventeen proprietors of Chambers's *Cyclopædia* were granted a royal licence dated April 17, 1741, and in the text of the licence there is reference to their intention to publish 'a certain Number of Sheets Weekly'.

it was the earlier edition, not in numbers, which had the licence.[1]

Presumably the 'great unnecessary Expence' of a royal licence was incurred only when a proprietor was particularly anxious to reduce the risk of piracy or abridgment, though such prominence was usually given to the official document in newspaper advertisements or on the blue covers of the numbers themselves that one supposes the additional expense arose in the desire to impress the public with what was regarded as a hall-mark of quality. For one reason or another, royal licences became very common in 1743 and 1744. On October 18, 1743, Thomas Astley was granted a royal licence for his *New General Collection of Voyages and Travels*; the ten partners in the 1739 Conger (already mentioned), together with six others, were named sole proprietors of *A Complete System of Geography* ('preserving all that is useful in ye fourth and last Edition of the compleat Geographer, published under the Name of Herman Moll') when Lord Cartaret signed the King's licence on December 5, 1743; and eight days later five proprietors (T. Longman, T. Osborne, J. Shuckburgh, C. Hitch, and S. Austen) were granted exclusive rights in the third edition of Thomas Salmon's *Modern History, or the Present State of All Nations*. These royal licences cannot have been sought to protect reprinted works, for although the three works just mentioned, like the revision (licensed February 23, 1744) of John Harris' *Navigantium atque Itinerantium Bibliotheca*, were old works republished in numbers, two new works were likewise given royal protection: *Biographia Britannica* (for which a licence was issued to twenty proprietors on September 26, 1744), and John Marchant's *Exposition on the Books of the Old Testament* (licensed October 30, 1744). The 'other additional Charges' mentioned by Cox as particularly attending the publishing of a work in numbers may have embraced no more than the cost of the blue paper covers for each number, the separate stitching of the fascicules, and the very

---

[1] By a royal licence dated May 19, 1732, James Gibbs, architect, was granted fourteen years' exclusive right to publish his *Rules for Drawing the Several Parts of Architecture*, and Gibbs engaged William Bowyer to print the work for him later that year. The same licence presumably protected the second edition, with text reset, when it was published in twenty-one weekly numbers by A. Bettesworth and C. Hitch, W. Innys and R. Manby, and J. and P. Knapton in 1738.

By the LORDS JUSTICES.

HARDWICKE, *C.* | ARGYLL,
GRAFTON, | TWEEDDALE.

To all to whom thefe Prefents fhall come, Greeting,

WHEREAS THOMAS ASTLEY, of the City of *London*, Bookfeller, hath humbly reprefented unto Us, That he hath been at a very great Expence and Charge in purchafing feveral new *Eng-lifh* Manufcripts of Voyages and Travels, and in Tranflating divers other Books of Voyages and Travels, out of feveral Languages, into *Englifh*, and in Engraving Maps and other Plates for the fame, intending to Print a New General Collection of the faid

VOYAGES and TRAVELS,

In feveral Volumes in Quarto, Improved with CHARTS *of the feveral Divifions of the Ocean, and entire new* MAPS *of each Country; alfo felect* CUTS, *reprefenting Cities, Antiquities, Animals, Vegetables, the Habits of the People, and other Things remarkable in their Kind; with new Difcourfes and Obfervations thereupon;* which Work may be of great Advantage, as well to Trade as Navigation; and he having humbly befought Us to grant to him, the faid *Thomas Aftley*,

His MAJESTY's Royal Privilege *and* Licence,

For the fole Printing and Publifhing the fame for the Term of fourteen Years; we being inclined to encourage

An UNDERTAKING *of fuch* Publick Ufe *and* Benefit,

Are pleafed to condefcend to his Requeft, and do by thefe Prefents, in his MAJESTY's Name, (as far as may be agreeable to the Statute in that Cafe made and provided) grant unto the faid *Thomas Aftley*, his Heirs, Executors, Adminiftrators, and Affigns,

HIS MAJESTY's ROYAL PRIVILEGE *and* LICENCE,

For the fole Printing, Publifhing, and Vending the faid Work, during the Term of Fourteen Years, to be computed from the Day of the Date hereof, ftrictly forbidding and prohibiting all his Majefty's Subjects, with-in his Kingdoms and Dominions, to Re-print or Abridge the fame, or any Part of them, either in the like, or any other Volume or Volumes whatfoever; or to Copy or Counterfeit the Sculptures or Maps thereof, ei-ther in Great or in Small, during the faid Term; or to Import, Buy, Vend, Utter, or Diftribute, any Copies of the fame, or any Part thereof, Re-printed beyond the Seas, within the faid Term, without the Confent of the faid *Thomas Aftley*, his Heirs, Executors, Adminiftrators, or Affigns, by Writing under his or their Hands and Seals, firft had and obtained, as they will anfwer the Contrary at their Peril; whereof the Commif-fioners and other Officers of His Majefty's Cuftoms, the Mafter, Wardens, and Company of Stationers are to take Notice, that due Obedience be rendered to this His Majefty's Pleafure herein declared.

Given at *Whitehall*, the 18th Day of *October*, 1743, in the Seventeenth Year of his Majefty's Reign,

By their Excellencies Command,

E. WESTON.

Official licence of Astley's *Voyages*

considerable increase in the man-hours and postal charges required each week to place the numbers in the hands of subscribers. When the successive fascicules of a work published in numbers were entered in the Stationers' Register there was, of course, the sixpenny charge for each entry—a relatively small sum even if there were many parts, but it further reduced the net profits. Most number books were not entered in the Stationers' Register, but the records of those that were entered show that in most cases the required fee was paid and that the required nine copies were deposited. This last was a much more considerable item of expenditure.

It is of interest to find that the nine copies deposited with the clerk of Stationers' Hall were shipped to the favoured libraries on request as the law required. Manuscript records in the Bodleian Library show that it was the regular practice of the Stationers' Hall clerk to ship to the keeper of books at Oxford a bundle of the publications which had been registered and deposited at the Hall during the previous six months, the books being sent unbound at Michaelmas and Lady Day, the shipping charges being paid by the recipient, and the clerk receiving (at least from Oxford) a semi-annual fee of half a guinea. Presumably the clerk or warehouse-keeper of the Stationers' Company sent similar parcels of books to the eight other libraries named in the statute—the Royal Library, the Cambridge University Library, the library of Sion College, the libraries of the four universities in Scotland, and the Advocates' Library in Edinburgh. Indeed, the statute provided for a fine of five pounds for every copy not so delivered, plus the value of the copy itself. But the statute also stipulated that such delivery was to be made within ten days after demand by the keepers of the respective libraries, and it is possible that the clerk shipped books only if and when he was requested to do so. The Bodleian records indicate that the Rev. Mr. Bowles and after him Mr. Robert Fysher, both of Oriel College, were regular in their requests for the semi-annual shipments.

That the clerk at Stationers' Hall also took his duties seriously and was anxious to keep his records straight is apparent from a letter which Joseph Collyer, clerk of the Stationers' Company, wrote to Mr. Bowles

'at the Publick Library at Oxford' on May 16, 1723:[1] 'I sent your
Books Lady day last', said Collyer, 'but have heard nothing of your
haveing received them, nor any answer to two of three Letters I sent
you, which I wonder at'. He asked Mr. Bowles for a line or two. A few
years later Collyer's successor wrote to Mr. Bowles expressing regret
for a short delay in sending the half-yearly consignment of books.
Thomas Simpson's letter[2] on 'Xber 8th 1726' shows that he had no
time to bother with punctuation:

Sir.
I have this day Sent to Mr Godfreys Your Carrier what Books I
have received to Register Since Michalmas Last I had Sent y^u them
last weeke According to my Promise but Hapned to be to Late for the
Carryer underneath you have an Acc^t of the Above Parcell Sent &
Directed to y^o & hope will come Safe.

Apparently that parcel and the one sent six months earlier both
reached Mr. Bowles, for the Bodleian records for 1726 show that the
expenditures during that year included one guinea 'Pd the Clark (Mr
Tho. Simpson) of Stat^{rs} Hall for his Trouble in sending two Parcels of
Books according to Custom as by Rec^t'; and this same account in-
cludes 7s. 6d. 'Pd Mr Godfrey for the Carriage of ye said Books, &c.'[3]
Along with such accounts as these the Bodleian records also fortunately list all the books received by the librarian during the period.
Among these are most of the number books that were entered in the
Stationers' Register, though some of these are no longer on the
Bodleian shelves. The first number of Stephen Switzer's *Practical Husbandman*, which had been entered on June 8, 1733, was received at the
Bodleian in the shipment at Michaelmas that same year; and all twenty-
one numbers of Demetrius Cantemir's *History of . . . the Othman Empire*
were received during 1734 and 1735: No. 1 at Lady Day, 1735, Nos.
2–11 at Michaelmas that same year, and Nos. 12–21 at Michaelmas,
1736. For some reason or other the early numbers of Coetlogon's
Universal History of Arts and Sciences were not listed as having been

[1] Bodleian Library MS. record: 'Stationers Hall Lists 1650–1764', fol. 16.
[2] *Ibid.*, fol. 17.
[3] Bodleian Library MS. record for the eighteenth century, Register C, fol. 105.

received from the Stationers' Company, though John Hart had entered them on behalf of the author at fairly regular intervals from April 22 to September 17, 1741. No. 23 of this work was included in the shipment at Michaelmas, 1741, and from then onwards the numbers came along in half-yearly batches: Nos. 24-44 at Lady Day, 1742, Nos. 45-60 at Michaelmas that year, Nos. 61-100 in 1743, and the 109 numbers of Volume II during the next four years.

From this time forward, at least well into the second half of the eighteenth century, the Bodleian received a copy of every work published in numbers which had been entered in the Stationers' Register. Between 1742 and 1749 these were nine in number:[1] *The Pleasant . . . Adventures of Mr. Robert Drury*, John Marchant's *Exposition on . . . the New Testament*, the same author's *Exposition on . . . the Old Testament*, Thomas Rowland's *General Treatise of Architecture*, Tindal's continuation of Rapin's *History of England*, John Russell's *Letters from a Young Painter Abroad*, Teresia Constantia Phillips's *Apology*, *The Modern Story Teller*, and William Duff's *New and Full . . . History of Scotland*. During 1739 the Bodleian also received, not from the Stationers' Company but by gift from the University, the last eighteen volumes of Thomas Salmon's *Modern History*, which had been published in numbers (at first monthly, then fortnightly, then weekly) from 1724 to 1738. In 1742, by order of Dr. Leigh, Vice-Chancellor of the University, the Bodleian Library paid Mrs. Gagnier £14 for the ten volumes of *A General Dictionary Historical and Critical*, which Bernard, Birch, and Lockman, leaning heavily on Pierre Bayle, had written for publication in monthly numbers from 1733 to 1741. The Library had not received either of these large works from Stationers' Hall for the simple reason that the respective publishers had not entered them in the Register. The trouble and cost of entering the successive numbers, together with the retail value of the nine sets that would have had to

---

[1] The shipment of books from the Stationers' Company to the Bodleian Library at Michaelmas, 1744, also included 'Trial betw. Campbell & Craig n° 1'. This was presumably the first number of *The Trial at Bar between Campbell Craig, Lessee of James Annesley, Esq; Plaintiff, And the Right Honourable Richard Earl of Anglesey, Defendant*, published in numbers by Robert Walker in 1744.

be deposited, must have seemed too high a price to pay for the kind of protection the Queen Anne Statute provided.

Naturally, from the proprietor's point of view, what mattered most in the making and handling of a number book was the net difference between the total of all costs and the gross returns. As one looks back over two centuries it is easy to say that many an eighteenth-century bookseller who started to publish a book in numbers was a foolish optimist, though it must be granted that the estimates of profit were quite as often too low as too high. In any case, the extra charges incurred by publishing a book in fascicules rather than as whole volumes were usually more than counterbalanced by the increased sales which resulted from piecemeal publication.

It must have been extremely difficult to estimate in advance what the critical difference would be between outgo and income. On the debit side would go the following items of cost: purchase price of copy from former proprietor, or else copy-money to author, compiler, translator; fee for entry in the Stationers' Register, together with the value of the nine deposited copies; fee for a royal patent, or for special permission from the holder of a monopoly; charges for paper, including that required for the blue covers; cost of printing, folding, collating, and stitching the fascicules; the possible payment of a pamphlet tax seemingly required by Clause 101 in An Act for Laying Several Duties upon . . . Certain Printed Papers, Pamphlets (10 Anne, c. 19); the cost of newspaper advertisements, printed proposals, and specimen sheets, together with any cuts, maps, excess sheets, or premiums offered gratis to regular subscribers; charges for cartage and for ultimate distribution to individual customers through wholesalers, retail agents in London and the country, hawkers, and all who undertook to deliver the numbers to regular subscribers and collect the monthly or weekly payment; and a reasonable share of what is commonly lumped together as 'overhead'. On the credit side of the account would go the gross total of so many numbers actually sold and paid for, together with the market value of remainders and the investment value of the copy. This list comprises no very complicated financial structure, but it indicates at how many points the miscalculations and the fluctuations of supply and demand could be deceptive and ruinous. When each 'unit' sold for sixpence the margin of profit on each must have been small; the total profit would depend on the net cost of each and the number sold. Fortunately there are enough surviving records to show quite clearly the actual cost of procuring the copy, producing the numbers, promoting the sales, and distributing the fascicules as they were printed.

The first step, and one involving a primary cost, was the procuring of suitable copy from an author, a translator, a compiler, or another proprietor. Petitions for royal licences often refer to the large expenditures required for the preparation of copy, though usually only by the citing of such round numbers as De Coetlogon's 'upwards of One Thousand Pounds' spent (so he declared) in compiling his *Universal History of Arts and Sciences* in 1741, and the 'several thousand Pounds' said to have been required for the preparation of the *Universal History from the Earliest Account of Time to the Present*. The large sums paid to Smollett for writing his *History of England*, and the less generous payments which Thomas Stackhouse tried to collect from Thomas Edlin, have been mentioned in earlier chapters. Nicholas Tindal was said by the Earl of Egmont in 1735 to have been paid by the Knaptons 'scarce ten shillings a day' for his money-making translation of Rapin.[1] Other translators—John Ozell, John Stevens, Stephen Whatley, Thomas Lediard—probably worked for equally slender fees. Lediard, not as translator but as author, apparently surrendered the copyright of his *Naval History of England* in return for a specified number of copies,

[1] *Diary of the First Earl of Egmont*, entry for March 17, 1734-5, Hist. MSS. Comm (London: H. M. Stationery Office, 1923), II, 161. I am indebted for this reference to Alan D. McKillop, who quotes the passage in his *Samuel Richardson, Printer and Novelist* (Chapel Hill: University of North Carolina Press, 1936), p. 309. Tindal undoubtedly got other rewards for his translation of Rapin. The *London Magazine* for July 1733 made the announcement that on Wednesday, July 4, 'The Rev. Mr. Tindal presented his Royal Highness the Prince of Wales with his first Volume of his Translation of M. Rapin's History of England; when his Royal Highness was pleased to present him with a curious Gold Medal, weighing upwards of ten Ounces, valued at between 40 and 50 £.' News items in *All-Alive and Merry* in 1740 reported that on January 18 Tindal was appointed 'Chaplain to one of the Regiments of Marines', and on November 3 that 'On Friday the Rev. Mr. Tindal, Translator of Rapin's History of England, was collated by the Lord Bishop of Winchester, to the Rectory of Alverstock in Hampshire, a Living of 400 £ a year.'

for the proposals issued some weeks in advance of the first number, published February 2, 1734, indicated that a certain number of copies were 'for the Benefit of the Compiler'. Unnamed hackwriters were probably numerous, overworked, and (all things considered) underpaid, among them many an Iscariot Hackney,[1] many a Mr. Quibble,[2] many a catchpenny bookseller's drudge like those who worked for Edmund Curll and like those encountered by Peregrine Pickle in the book-cobbling sweatshops of London—pathetic creatures who, 'without any pretensions to literature, earned a very genteel subsistence by undertaking work for booksellers, in which reputation was not at all concerned'.[3] Smollett was probably not distorting the facts when he referred to one such 'author' who 'professed all manner of translation, at so much per sheet, and actually kept five or six amanuenses continually employed, like so many clerks in a counting house', another who 'projected a variety of plans for new dictionaries, which were executed under his eye by day-labourers', and a third whose province was 'histories and voyages, collected or abridged by understrappers of the same class'. Such nameless ones gave little except bulk in return for their paltry fees; others had names that carried some weight, and may even have been paid enough for their number-book copy to sustain their bodies, if not their souls.

More respectable sums changed hands in the preparation of the extensive revision and translation of Pierre Bayle's famous *Dictionnaire historique et critique* made by John Peter Bernard, Thomas Birch, John Lockman, and a few other contributors, who preferred to remain anonymous. Among the Birch manuscripts in the British Museum are several statements and receipts[4] showing the sums paid for contributions to the *General Dictionary*. One of these is Birch's own estimate of expected payments for his share in the revising of the first two volumes. The basic rate was seven shillings and sixpence per sheet, but it had been agreed that he would get a guinea for each sheet of the biogra-

---

[1] A 'prostitute Scribbler' in Richard Savage's pamphlet, *An Author to be Lett* (1729).
[2] One of Mr. Bookweight's hacks in Fielding's play, *The Author's Farce* (revised 1734).
[3] Tobias Smollett, *Peregrine Pickle* (1751), Chapter XCIII.
[4] Add. MS. 4256, fols. 36, 39, 40, 41, 42, 43, 56, 57, 58, 61.

phy of Bayle—thirty-two sheets, 'corrected and enlarged'—and thirteen guineas for extra work. The account shows that for doing nine
numbers and two sheets of Volume I he expected £ 27. 15s., and for
doing twenty-seven numbers and four sheets of Volume II he expected
£ 82. 10s. These sums, together with the returns for special chores,
amounted to £ 158. 6s. Another account lists the sums (ranging from
six to fifteen guineas) paid monthly by Mr. Manby from May 17,
1735, to February 17, 1736, for revising the third volume, the total
amount for 243 sheets being £ 122. 12s. 6d. (180 sheets at 7s. 6d.,
and 63 sheets at 17s. 6d. supplied to Mr. Reily, who was 'distressed
for Copy'). These payments by Manby are puzzling, for he was one of
the proprietors of a rival translation of Bayle. Several receipts preserved among the Birch papers show sums of money paid by Birch to
John Martyn and to George Sale for their contributions to various
numbers of the *General Dictionary*. Most interesting of all is a copy of
the agreement signed on April 29, 1734, by which the proprietors
agreed to pay Bernard, Birch, and Lockman at the rate of one pound
five shillings per sheet, 'to be paid to them from time to time at the
publication of each and every Monthly Number', for compiling and
translating 'such Books and Writings as shall be proper to compose
and compleatly finish and perfect the said Book'. The terms of the
agreement specify a penalty of fifty pounds, chargeable against all three
of the authors if the printing of any monthly number should be
hindered by lack of copy.

Fees paid for the initial writing, compiling, or translating of a work
about to be published or in course of publication in numbers were
based, presumably, on the expectation, not the certainty, of profits.
There was no guarantee that a new work would 'take', and the cost
for new copy was probably never very great during the period here
being considered. Among the manuscripts in the British Museum is a
document[1] drawn up on August 4, 1739, showing that John Nourse
paid Godfrey Smith and his son eight guineas for one third share of
Benjamin Baddam's *Memoirs of the Royal Society. A New Abridgment of
the Philosophical Transactions*, 'two Volumes & seven numbers of ye third

[1] British Museum, Add. MS. 38,730, fol. 176.

Volume of which is already published & wch is to be continued . . . weekly in numbers'. Francis Cogan was also a sharer in Baddam's *Memoirs* at this time, though on October 1, 1742,[1] Cogan sold to Nourse his sixth share and also the complete books and separate numbers remaining on Cogan's own shelves or in the hands of T. Cooper, one of the regular distributors. The price paid by Nourse for this one-sixth share cannot be determined from this agreement, since the ownership of one other copy and a substantial stock of two other books changed hands at the same time for a total sum of £ 220.

When a work had already demonstrated by extensive sales that it was a money maker, the prices paid for shares of the copy were sometimes surprisingly high. On September 28, 1737, John Nourse gave Alexander Blackwell notes for £ 150 in payment for one third share in the five hundred superb original plates of Mrs. Elizabeth Blackwell's *Curious Herbal*, eighty numbers of which had by that date been published.[2] Reference was made earlier in this chapter to the prices paid by members of a conger for single sixtieths of Burkitt's *Expository Notes* shortly before the eleventh edition was published in 1739. At the auction sale of Richard Ford, deceased, on November 14, 1738, eight men paid £ 273 for ten sixtieths of Burkitt's book, which indicates that the whole copy was then valued at something over £ 1600. But that sum did not represent the total outlay for copy, since a notation in the catalogue[3] of Ford's holdings warned purchasers that a royalty (as we should now call it) of nine pence had to be paid to the Burkitt estate for every copy of every impression. This notice was repeated in a somewhat different form —'There is 9d. a Book to be paid to the Widow' —in the catalogue of the sale of Thomas Osborne's stock on February 9, 1744, when 'a tenth of a sixth' was sold for £ 12. In an edition of 3000 copies the widow's ninepenny royalty would reduce the profits to the proprietors by £ 112. 10s. The cost of printing, promoting, and delivering the 3000 copies would therefore include

---

[1] British Museum, Add. MS. 38,729, fol. 29.
[2] *Ibid.*, fol. 33.
[3] The sums paid at the trade sales mentioned in this paragraph are recorded in contemporary notations in the Longmans, Green copies of the original catalogues.

Memorandum   London october 2, 1740

wee acknowledge to have sold to M.r John Nourse his
Executors, & assignes &c for the consideration of twenty
five pounds, one Sixth Share of our copy right plates &
Books of a Book intitled a curious Herbal &c containing
five hundred of various plants &c one hundred and twenty
five Description plates &c and wee hereby intitle them to the
preceding profits of the said Share to have and to hold in
the Same ample manner he has and does injoy of one
third Share purchased of us in September the 28.th 1737
which with the abovementiond one third makes the half
of the whole work —

wee promise to make a bill of Sale of the abovementiond
Share when he thinks fit to demand it

                  witness our hands

                         Alexander Blackwell

                         Elizabeth Blackwell

Received oc:ber 2.d 1740 of M.r John Nourse Seventy five
pounds for one Sixth Share for the consideration
above mentioned   by me   Elizabeth Blackwell

9. Memorandum of assignment of a one-sixth share in Elizabeth Blackwell's *Curious Herbal*

the investment in the copy (£ 1600 minus the subsequent market value of the copy), the widow's royalties for the whole impression (£ 112. 10s.), together with the usual charges for paper, type setting, running off, folding, collating, stitching, covering with blue paper, and distribution, including allowance to the trade.

Higher prices for even smaller fractions of another work—the fourth edition (1741) of Chambers' *Cyclopædia*—are noted in the Longmans, Green copies of trade-sales catalogues for 1741 and 1742; and when Andrew Millar and sixteen others charged a group of Edinburgh and Glasgow booksellers in April 1743 with having invaded their rights to certain books, Millar testified that the copy of the *Cyclopædia* had been purchased by himself and his associates 'at a very great Price', and that he himself had paid 'no less than 100 £ Sterling for a 64th Share thereof'.[1] Six thousand four hundred pounds is a considerable sum for the copy of a book which had first been published in 1728 and had been twice reprinted. One might suspect the plaintiffs in a case of alleged piracy of citing impressively large round numbers to prove the extent of their injury, but there is acceptable evidence that Millar was not exaggerating. The value of shares in Chambers' *Cyclopædia* rose steadily. On November 20, 1740, before the fourth edition was announced, Richard Hett paid £ 63 for a sixty-fourth share formerly owned by Ranew Robinson; at the sale of E. Symon's stock on September 1, 1741, Hett bought four more sixty-fourths for £ 292; on October 27, 1741, Andrew Millar paid £ 378 for five sixty-fourths; and less than a year later (at the sale of Francis Gosling's stock on October 5, 1742) Daniel Browne, who already owned two sixty-fourths, paid £ 105 each for two more. With so high a valuation on this work it is not surprising that the proprietors were anxious to protect their rights; they entered the two volumes in the Stationers' Register on March 24, 1741, and secured a royal patent shortly afterwards (on April 17, 1741). They had invested heavily, and could afford to run no risk of losing part of their market. Andrew Millar also put money into the *Universal History*, for on September 30,

---

[1] A printed report of the case is at the British Museum (816. m. 12).

1740, he paid £ 106 for two twelfths of that work, then in course of publication in numbers.

One further instance of substantial investment in copy is that when Thomas Osborne's eighteenth-share in Moll's *Geography* was offered at auction on February 9, 1744, E. Wicksteed took it for £ 59. It was pointed out above that the 1739 conger held shares listed as '33 in 72' in this work. On the basis of the price paid by Wicksteed in 1744 the value of the whole would be £ 1062, and the conger's holdings in this copy would be worth about £ 489.

These figures show that, for at least a few of the number books, the cost of procuring copy was considerable. Reference has already been made to the additional costs sometimes thought to be necessary for retaining unchallengeable ownership: the fee for entering titles in the Stationers' Register, the cost of supplying the nine copies required by the Statute, the fee for royal licences, and special items of cost, such as the ninepence per copy paid to Burkitt's widow and the 'valuable Consideration' paid by Robert Penny to Mr. Baskett, who held the monopoly of printing the text of the Bible. Then there were to be reckoned the costs of production, promotion, and distribution, all inescapable if profits were to accrue. Fortunately, contemporary documents are extant to show what sums had to go for printing and paper, that is, for setting up the type, for running the sheets through the press, for folding, stitching, and covering with blue paper the collated sheets in each fascicule, and for delivering the bundles of finished numbers to the proprietors. The two most revealing extant records are the ledgers of William Strahan and of William Bowyer, both busy and successful printers. Strahan's Ledger A, covering the years from 1739 to 1768,[1] has numerous entries showing exactly how many copies of certain numbers were printed and at what cost. For instance, Strahan's account shows that on January 7, 1745, he charged Thomas Osborne £ 100. 18s. for printing 14 numbers (the letters R and S, which filled 70

---

[1] Through the kind permission of Mr. R. A. Austen-Leigh, who has this precious record in his possession, and with the consent of Dr. Laurence Hanson of the Bodleian Library (which has a microfilm copy), I am able to refer to specific pages and figures.

sheets) of Dr. James's *Medicinal Dictionary*, the rate for printing one thousand copies of each being £ 1. 8*s*. per sheet and the charge for extraordinary corrections in these 70 sheets being £ 2. 18*s*. Osborne settled the account (which also included charges of £ 17. 3*s*. for re-composing sheet J and printing the letters W, X, Y, and Z, with the Explanation of the Tables) by sending Strahan twenty-six sets of the complete work. Osborne's gross income from one thousand copies of each number, if all were sold at the advertised price of one shilling, would have been £ 50, which would mean nearly £ 600 gross profit on the fourteen numbers referred to in Strahan's account; but he doubt-less allowed a discount to J. Roberts, named in the imprint as dealer, and there would in all probability be some remainders.

On the matter of Osborne's profits from Dr. James's *Medicinal Dictionary* it is interesting to note the observation—perhaps written by Samuel Johnson, who told Boswell that he had helped Dr. James in writing the Proposals—that some subscribers might complain of the price—one shilling for five sheets—when other publications had six sheets in each shilling number. The reason for the difference, it was pointed out in the printed Proposals, was that the proprietors of other works issued in numbers had already recovered the cost of the copy and all other expenses by the sale of earlier editions, which had likewise brought in considerable profit even before the edition in numbers was undertaken. This statement about profits could be challenged, but there was justice in the claim that the *Medicinal Dictionary* was a new work and that every sheet was well filled with 'a great Quantity of Matter'. One would like to know what copy-money Dr. James re-ceived, and what compensation Johnson received for his small share in the writing of the work.[1]

No figures are available showing what copy-money was paid to George Turnbull, William Guthrie, and John Lockman for translating Blainville's *Travels* in 1742; but the Strahan accounts show very clearly

---

[1] Dr. L. F. Powell quotes Rev. John Hussey as having stated that Johnson received five guineas from Dr. James for writing the Dedication to Dr. Mead. See *Boswell's Life of Johnson*, ed. G. B. Hill, rev. and enl. L. F. Powell (6 vols, Oxford: Clarendon Press, 1934, 1950), I, p. 159, n. 3.

the costs of paper and printing. For the printing of the first thirteen of the fortnightly numbers of Blainville the proprietor, D. Soyer, paid Strahan—always very promptly—the sum of £ 172. 4s. 6d., though this amount included one guinea for printing 2000 proposals and £ 1. 4s. for the four reams of paper required for them. The printing of 1250 copies of each quarto number at £ 1. 4s. 6d. per sheet came to £ 7. 19s. 3d., since 6½ sheets were printed, the extra half-sheet presumably comprising the cover, though in most other cases the cover was printed separately on blue paper rather than on the regular stock. For each number 16¼ reams of paper were required, and at twelve shillings per ream that came to £ 9. 15s. Since Soyer continued to have Strahan run off 1250 copies of each number it is to be presumed that the sales remained fairly constant at well over a thousand, and as the bill for paper and printing could be paid out of the gross returns on the sale of one third of the quantity produced, the profits on the whole must have been considerable. Soyer would, of course, have to allow the usual 15 per cent trade discount to his selling agents. The imprint indicates that the numbers of Blainville's *Travels* were sold by 'J. Noon, at White-Hart, near Mercers-Chapel, Cheapside; R. Dodsley, at Tully's Head, in Pall-Mall; and at the Bar of Old Slaughter's Coffee-House, in St. Martin's Lane'.

During the same years in which Blainville's *Travels* were selling for a shilling every fortnight Joseph Davidson, at the Angel in the Poultry, Cheapside, was finding ready sale for the Latin originals and prose translations of Horace and Virgil which he issued somewhat less regularly in shilling octavo numbers. Davidson paid Strahan at the rate of £ 1. 6s. per sheet for printing 1000 copies of numbers 4, 6, 8, 9, and 10,[1] though Strahan's records do not show a charge for paper, which Davidson must therefore have supplied. Only 750 copies of some numbers of the *Works* of Horace were printed in the first run, but as Davidson had Strahan reprint numbers 3, 4, and 5, it is clear that his sales were well over 1000, though the second edition of number 4 (350 copies) was not required until December 13, 1742, many months after number 4 was first printed (May 6, 1739). In the meantime the

[1] Numbers 4, 8, and 9 had six sheets each; numbers 6 and 10 had 7¼ sheets each.

smaller quantity (750 copies) of number 5 (first printed on October 22, 1739) had been exhausted, and a second run, 500 copies, was delivered by Strahan on June 1, 1742.

The sales of Davidson's *Virgil* were steadier, though they settled back somewhat after the first two monthly numbers came out in November and December 1741 in editions of 1500 each, for which Strahan was paid at the rate of £ 2. 10s. per sheet. Only 1250 copies of the third number, published at the end of January 1742, were printed, and thereafter the sales were apparently such as to justify the printing of 1000 copies of the next seven numbers. With number 7 (July 1742) Strahan's rate for printing a thousand was reduced from £ 2. 7s. to £ 2. 5s. per sheet. These charges, though higher than those for printing *Horace*, presumably do not include the cost of paper; and no reference is made to the customary blue paper covers. It appears that Davidson both antagonized a competitor and feared for his own rights in these translations of Horace and Virgil. Early in 1741 J. Oswald (at the Rose and Crown, near the Mansion House) inserted advertisements in the *Weekly Miscellany* accusing Davidson of publishing inferior imitations of the translations of Horace made by David Watson, M.A., of St. Leonard's College, St. Andrews. Oswald insisted that Watson's translations, which represented the study and labour of more than six years, would be found to differ very much in substance, method, and price from the edition 'now publishing in Numbers by another Person, who form'd his Plan only from a View of this Copy'. But Davidson continued his numbers of Horace, soon began to publish Virgil in the same manner, and eventually (1747) brought out Ovid likewise, 'with the Latin annex'd', in shilling numbers. On February 24, 1742, Davidson secured a royal licence; and on the following May 10 Strahan entered in Davidson's account a charge of four guineas for printing five thousand copies of new proposals and specimens of Horace and Virgil.

The issuing of printed proposals and specimen pages of a projected work to be published in numbers added to the cost, but rather as an item of promotion than of production. There is one other kind of charge which might have affected the basic cost of producing number books, for a fascicule is in its dimensions the equivalent of a pamphlet, and the Stamp Act (10 Anne, c. 19)[1] contained a clause which required that during a thirty-two year period beginning on August 1, 1712, the publisher of every 'Pamphlet or Paper, being larger than One Whole Sheet, and not exceeding Six Sheets in Octavo, or in a lesser Page, or not exceeding Twelve Sheets in Quarto, or Twenty Sheets in Folio' should pay a tax at the rate of two shillings for each sheet in a single copy of the publication, regardless of the number of copies in the impression. Clause CXI stipulated that within six days[2] of the printing of such a pamphlet one copy should be brought to the office of the Commissioners in order that the title and the number of sheets in the publication should be registered in 'a Book to be kept there for that purpose', and the duty paid. There is evidence[3] that the penny-a-sheet tax on newspapers was evaded by proprietors who entered them as pamphlets and paid the lower tax; but as Dr. Laurence Hanson observes,[4] the pamphlet tax seems not to have been enforced, even for publications quite properly classified as pamphlets within the meaning of the Act. So far as fascicules issued weekly or monthly were concerned, only one piece of evidence has come to light showing that a work announced in newspapers as published in numbers was registered as a pamphlet and the tax paid. This work, *Christianity Set in a True Light, in XII Discourses, Political and Historical*, 'By a Pagan Philosopher newly converted', has been attributed to Alberto Radicati, Count di Passerano. Apparently only the first number was published. The portion issued by J. Peele in 1730 for a shilling—nine octavo half-sheets, with signatures [A]-I—contained 'a Preliminary Discourse' (pp. i-xxxix), a list of the contents of all twelve discourses (pp. xl-[xliii]), and the complete text of Discourse I (pp. 1-20); but page 20 has the

[1] An Act for laying several Duties upon all Sope and Paper made in Great Britain, or imported into the same . . . ; And upon several Kinds of stampt Vellum, Parchment, and Paper; And upon certain printed Papers, Pamphlets, and Advertisements . . .

[2] For pamphlets published outside London and Westminster the time allowed was fourteen days.

[3] See the discussion of this point in Chapter II above.

[4] Laurence Hanson, *Government and the Press 1695-1763* (London: Humphrey Milford, Oxford University Press, 1936), p. 11.

catchword 'Discourse II', and the publication is clearly to be regarded
as the first fascicule of a larger work rather than as a complete and independent pamphlet. The British Museum copy bears what seems to
be the official record of registration. On the verso of the half title is a
manuscript note:

Stamp Office, Lincoln's Inn
Register'd & Enter'd according to the Statute, containing four Sheets
& an half of paper, the Duty Nine Shillings
$$\text{J\small OHN P\small AIN Reg}^{\text{tr}}.$$
£ o : 9 : o
N⁰

The blank that follows the heading 'N⁰' suggests that Mr. Pain was
not keeping very careful records; but one would like to see his register,
none the less. It is probable that the Commissioners and Registrars
usually recognized the booksellers' claim that a fascicule was not a
pamphlet but part of a book. Peele must have had a good reason for
preferring to pay the nine shillings tax rather than the sixpenny fee
which he would have had to pay for entering the title in the Stationers'
Register.

Profits from the publication of a book depend very largely on the
effectiveness of the promotion, and it has already been indicated that
the publishers of books in numbers usually issued printed proposals
and specimen pages gratis, gave advance notice in newspaper advertisements, and in some cases continued to advertise the successive
numbers as they appeared. The critical period for promoting a number
book would doubtless have been the few weeks just before and after
the first number was published. Newspaper advertisements were usually inserted for a standard and uniform charge of two shillings each,
but it cannot be assumed that that part of the cost was negligible, for
there would have to be more frequent announcements for the successive numbers than for a book published as a complete unit. After John
Nourse had acquired one half the rights of Mrs. Blackwell's *Curious
Herbal*[1] his accounts show expenditures of £ 5. 8*s*. for 'Advertise-

[1] The transfer of one sixth share for £75 is recorded in a memorandum dated October 2, 1740 (British Museum, Add. MS. 38,729, fol. 38). According to the assignment

ments in ye Country Papers', and £ 5. 6s. 6d. for 'd^o in London Papers', though it is not clear over what period of time these expenditures were spread.[1] There would be some slight expense for the circulating of proposals and specimen sheets; the actual cost of printing these, even in large quantities, cannot have been heavy in comparison with the basic costs for copy, paper, and press work. Soyer paid Strahan only £ 2. 5s. for printing 2000 copies of his proposals of the translation of Blainville's *Travels*, and Joseph Davidson spent only four guineas for five thousand copies of proposals and specimen pages of the works of Horace and Virgil in Latin and English. It is not known what Edward Cave had to pay for the 6000 proposals he circulated in hopes of procuring a thousand subscribers for the translation of Jean-Baptiste du Halde's history of China, which he intended to issue in numbers, eight sheets fortnightly for a shilling or twenty sheets monthly for half a crown.

Other means of promoting sales included news printed free of charge on the blue paper covers[2] and (rarely) special offers of premiums such as Cave referred to in the *Gentleman's Magazine* for August 1736 in hopes of attracting subscribers to the du Halde work. Although the proposals had been put into circulation in November 1735, there had not yet been 'Encouragement sufficient to begin Work on the Scheme', in spite of the plan to donate fifty pounds of the profits 'for the Encouragement of Artists' and to 'make a Dividend of ye further Profit among the first Thousand Subscribers, as Encouragers of the Work'. The few who had subscribed were becoming impatient, and Cave now requested them to procure additional subscriptions among their friends, sending in the names as soon as possible so that plans could be made for printing the proper number of books. Then in September Cave advertised as ready for the press the two folio volumes of *A*

dated September 28, 1737 (British Museum, Add. MS. 38,729, fol. 31 f.) Nourse had purchased one third of the total work for £150.

[1] In British Museum Add. MS. 38, 729, fol. 47, the charges for advertisements stand between entries for November 14, [1743] and two items belonging to 1744; but the next entry, undated, is nine shillings for 'Advertisements in The York Courant omitted 1741'.

[2] See the last two paragraphs of Chapter II above.

Description of China and Chinese Tartary, with Korea and Tibet,[1] 'containing the Geography and History, as well Natural as Civil, of those
Countries', and 'illustrated with all the Cuts and Maps in the Original
on 64 Copper Plates'. Cave's advertisement repeated the 'condition'
announced ten months before to the effect that while the work was
printing it would be delivered in sheets, twenty each month for half
a crown or eight sheets fortnightly for a shilling. There must have been
further delays, for a change in the scheme of profit sharing was announced in October, and two months later advance notice was given
in the *Gentleman's Magazine* that eight sheets of the *Description of China*
would be published with the magazine on Tuesday, February 1, 1737.
By July of the following year the work had obviously not been long in
the hands of the subscribers, for a correspondent in the *Gentleman's
Magazine* for that month thanked 'Sylvanus Urban' (Cave used this
nom de plume) for 'having undertaken, at so great an Expence, to convey
to English Readers the most copious and accurate Account yet published of that remote and celebrated People'. From the beginning of
the venture, then, the proprietor clearly thought it advantageous to
issue the *Description of China* in parts, and put much effort into promoting the sale; but he probably lost money.[2]

Apart from a reasonable allowance for 'overhead' the only other
consideration which would affect the net returns would be costs of
distributing the numbers as they came from the press. The elaborate
network of agents and vendors sometimes employed in the distribution
of number books will be discussed in the next chapter. Here it is enough
to recognize that the proprietors' net profits must have been affected

---

[1] Not to be confused with R. Brooke's translation of the same work published by
J. Watts in December 1736 at £1. 4s. in four volumes octavo under the title *The General History of China, Chinese Tartary, Corea, and Thibet*. For the inevitable controversy
over the two translations see the *Grub-Street Journal* numbers 354, 363 ff., and James
T. Hillhouse, *The Grub-Street Journal* (Durham: Duke University Press, 1928), pp.
163–5.

[2] Samuel Johnson, in his biography of Cave in the *Gentleman's Magazine* for February
1754, declared that the considerable fortune acquired by Cave through the publication of the *Gentleman's Magazine* would have been yet larger 'had he not rashly and
wantonly impaired it by innumerable projects, of which I know not that ever one
succeeded'.

by the allowances made to the trade—that is, to wholesalers or jobbers (if any), and to retailers, whether shopkeepers or hawkers. Both the wholesaler and the retailer expected a profit, though the only risk involved was of having unsold stock left on the shelves—a condition less embarrassing with number books than with the much more expensive complete volumes. What proportion of the price paid by the customer found its way into the pockets of the proprietors? Or, to put the question the other way, what portion of the retail price went to the middlemen and the retailer? Detailed figures showing the several trade discounts allowed to distributors of number books have apparently not survived, but there is enough evidence to show that allowances made to jobbers and local agents in town and country must have reduced considerably the gross returns to the proprietors.

Small enterprises were sometimes handled entirely by the single proprietor, who in one or two instances was the author or compiler himself. He would have to pay only small commissions to hawkers or to the delivery boy who took the numbers to the houses of regular subscribers. When many booksellers shared in a more ambitious enterprise it is quite likely that they named a warehouse-keeper—probably one of their own group—to act as custodian and to distribute the numbers to the several proprietors according to the shares held, a procedure which would certainly be necessary when a large group such as the 1739 conger controlled only part of a copy.

In a letter dated March 12, 1776, and already referred to at the beginning of this chapter, Dr. Samuel Johnson mentioned 'the regular profit of ten per cent. which is expected in the wholesale trade'. Johnson pointed out that between thirty and thirty-five per cent of the retail price of ordinary books must be reckoned as profit for the distributors. There are more definite figures than these. Advertisements of J. Rio's *Compleat History of the Civil Wars in England*, issued in sixpenny numbers in 1733, indicated that no money was to be paid by the customers until the delivery of the numbers, and that those gentlemen who subscribed for six would receive a seventh gratis. That seems to have been a common allowance to wholesalers and retailers alike.

When John Nourse on November 25, 1736,[1] indicated his willingness to act as agent of the Society for the Encouragement of Learning, he said he would handle the books if he might have one book for every six he disposed of. Nourse, Andrew Millar, and John Gray were officially appointed Booksellers to the Society, and specific articles of contract were agreed to.[2] The percentage allowed for wholesaling the Society's books did not remain fixed, however, as letters by Charles Rivington, John Osborne, William Davies, Paul Vaillant, George Strahan, John Brindley, Samuel Baker, and Thomas Osborne[3] show. On December 26, 1739, Thomas Osborne said he would be willing to handle the Society's books for fifteen per cent, clear of all expense, though he said it would be more expedient to allow him twenty-five per cent so that he could leave a margin of profit for country booksellers. Two days later Millar, Gray, and Nourse accepted the conditions then proposed for their handling the Society's publications, but added, 'As for the allowance to be given us for our Trouble, We Submit intirely to ye Committee.' As was to be expected, the partners in this sort of joint undertaking, like those engaged directly in publication, traded among themselves at especially favourable terms. At the retail level there were doubtless similar concessions, but these would not affect the net profits of the owners of copy.

Figures for cartage, postage, hawkers' commissions, and other costs of distribution are not available, though all of these must have affected the financial side of the number-book trade.

Profits are determined, however, not by total costs alone. Two things must be regarded: the net cost per unit and the number of units sold with some margin of profit. How extensive were the sales of number books? What are the evidences that the trade was profitable? Figures have been cited in Chapter I and earlier in this present chapter to show that many hundreds and sometimes thousands of copies of the weekly or monthly numbers were printed, and presumably most of

[1] Nourse's letter, together with others on the same subject, is to be seen in British Museum Add. MS. 6190.
[2] These articles are set forth in the Society's Register, British Museum Add. MS. 6186.
[3] British Museum Add. MS. 6190.

them were sold. Nicholas Tindal's translation of Rapin's *Histoire d'Angleterre*, published in monthly and then in weekly numbers by James and John Knapton, was a phenomenal success.[1] When Thomas Osborne and Jacob Robinson advertised in the *St. James's Evening Post* number 5606 (December 24, 1745) that the final number in Volume VII of *The Harleian Miscellany* was published that day, they added that of the one thousand sets in the impression not fifty were left. An enormous document[2] in the Public Record Office dated April 17, 1739, sets forth the complaint of Jacob and Richard Tonson and their associates (John Oswald, Samuel Birt, Edward Wicksteed, Richard Chandler, James Hutton, Richard and Bethell Wellington, John Brindley, and John New) against Robert Walker for allegedly infringing their copyright in the text of Milton's *Paradise Lost*, Dr. Bentley's notes, and Elijah Fenton's biography of Milton. The Tonsons *et al.* asserted that Robert Walker of London and James Abree of Canterbury, knowing that the right of publication was vested in Tonson and associates, had announced their intention to publish *Paradise Lost* in twelve twopenny weekly numbers beginning on April 4. In the two weeks between that date and the date of the bill Walker, Abree, and their unknown confederates had 'printed or caused or procured to be printed in Great Britain or in parts beyond the Seas several thousands or other greater Quantities or copies of the said poem....' It is emphatically asserted that Walker and his confederates 'Have published the same, or some part thereof in Numbers Books or Parcells and have taken in Subscriptions for and have sold and delivered or caused to be sold and delivered to Subscribers and others severall thousand Surreptitious Copies....' It is further declared that Walker and his 'copartners in the said illicit Trade' have 'got and acquired great Sums of Money thereby'. As Professor Bald has pointed

---

[1] The author of the account of George Vertue in the Supplement to *Biographia Britannica*, Volume VI, Part II (1766), pp. 245–9, cites that distinguished engraver's own memoirs to the effect that Tindal's translation of Rapin 'had a prodigious run', and that 'Thousands were sold every week.'

[2] Public Record Office, Chancery Proceedings, C. 12, bundle 1214, item 66. This manuscript shows how complicated the ownership of a valuable copy might become as a result of the subdivision and sale of the shares.

out,[1] the injunction desired by Tonson was awarded on May 5, 1739, but the twelve numbers of *Paradise Lost* were published nevertheless. What is of chief interest at the moment is the obvious distress of Tonson and the others at the size of Walker's piratical edition in numbers, and at the great financial loss which the lawful proprietors had consequently to face. Publication in numbers was in this case not a matter of handing the fascicules one by one to single customers who called at the door —as Constantia Phillips's effort seems to have been. It was big business.

Lacking more exact figures showing the sales of a particular number book before 1750,[2] one may see evidence of success at least by implication in (a) the reprinting of single numbers, (b) the ready sale of odd lots and remainders when a bookseller's stock was auctioned off, (c) the bringing out of 'continuations' (as both Knapton and Mechell did with their rival translations of Rapin), and (d) the publishing of a second edition in numbers —though in the last case it is obvious that a so-called second edition was sometimes only the issuing of unsold sheets with a new title page. In the *Daily Advertiser* number 2480 (January 4, 1739) the publishers of Baddam's *Memoirs of the Royal Society* announced that as there had been a greater demand for the work than had been expected they were reprinting the first numbers. References have been made earlier in this chapter to the reprinting of Davidson's *Horace* and *Virgil*, and to Blomefield's successive reprintings of early numbers of his *History of . . . Norfolk*. It is a fact, however, that even when a number book sold well enough to require a reprinting of the earlier parts the net gains were sometimes negligible. In 1740 a crusading enthusiast, J. Lewis by name —who was losing money on his penny paper, the *Christian's Amusement* —found himself working on a very narrow margin in the weekly piecemeal publication of 'that excellent Book, *Luther upon Galatians*'. Obviously his stock of paper was small and he had to depend on weekly payments by subscribers in order to continue the

[1] R. C. Bald, 'Early Copyright Litigation and its Bibliographical Interest', *Papers of the Bibliographical Society of America*, XXXVI (1942), 81–96.
[2] The fact that 13,000 copies of Smollett's *History of England* in fascicules were sold weekly in 1758–1760 was noted in Chapter I.

publication. When there was apparently a demand for back numbers he was willing in his evangelistic zeal to reprint them, but he insisted on a small payment in advance. The first number of the *Christian's Amusement*, issued early in September 1740, had this announcement concerning *Luther upon Galatians:*

> This Book (that it may come easy to the Publick) I am now Printing by Subscription, at Two-Pence Half-Penny a Week .... Next Saturday a new Edition of the first Number will be ready for fresh Subscribers; for all that I have printed have been bought up so eagerly that I have none left. Therefore as I am oblig'd to print it all over again, those Persons who are willing to embrace the Opportunity of having it, are desired to come in before they are all gone a second time; for I cannot afford to lay any by to wait Peoples Leisure.
>
> If you think it too much trouble to come to my House to subscribe, you may give Orders to the Person that serves you with this Paper, pa[y]ing Two-pence Half-penny earnest at the Time of Subscribing, and you shall have the last Number without Money.

The following week Lewis, with a surprising frankness, made this statement:

> Those who are willing to have *Luther upon the Galatians* at Two-pence half-penny a Week, are desired to bring in their Subscriptions as soon as they can, for I know not how to begin the first Number again, till I get more Subscribers, for want of Money to buy Paper.

Not all men of business make such a clean confession of their parlous financial state.

It has been shown that the purchase of copies often required a considerable initial cash outlay by a publisher or group intending to issue a work in numbers. By the same token these copies represented valuable assets, and their eventual resale brought further clear profit to the proprietor who had been so fortunate as to have 'made his account' by the sale of numbers as they were published. Less certain as valuable assets were the little batches of unsold separate numbers left on the shelves; but annotations in the Longmans, Green copies of the trade-sales catalogues indicate that they were anything but a dead loss. At the sale of Richard Williamson's stock of books, quires, and copies on November 29, 1737, several of the lots comprised small quantities of numbers, and they were bought at respectable prices. Astley paid £ 2. 11s. for Lot 8, which consisted of thirty-seven numbers of Bayle's *Critical Dictionary* (5 of number 1, 4 of numbers 2 and 4, 6 of number 3, and 3 of numbers 5, 6, 7, 8, 9, and 10). Astley could handle these, of course, because (unlike Williamson) he was one of the proprietors of the work. Williamson had also left on his shelves single copies of the rival translation of Bayle, listed as the *General Dictionary*. These (numbers 25, 26, 27 of Volume III and a copy of Volume IV complete) were bought for thirty shillings. Lot 36 in the same sale was an interesting assortment of odd numbers of the *General Dictionary* (2), the *Universal History* (4), Burkitt's *Expository Notes on the New Testament* (70), Wilson's translation of de Thou's *Historia sui temporis* (5), L'Estrange's *Josephus* (3), and Barclay's *Universal Traveller* (18). These 102 numbers were bought by 'W. & L.' for £1. 15s. When Francis Gosling's stock was auctioned on October 5, 1742, Longman paid £ 3. 2s. for two hundred odd numbers of Chambers' *Dictionary* (that is, *Cyclopædia*), and Osborn (probably John) bought twelve bundles of odd numbers of Tournefort's *Herbal* for two guineas. Most clearly indicating the value of remainders as still vendible assets is the lengthy tabulation of odd numbers of Bayle's *Dictionary* in the catalogue of Joseph Hazard's sale of stock on October 9, 1739. Benjamin Barker bought a few complete sets of the five-volume edition in large and small paper, 99 copies of single volumes, and small quantities (from 1 to 27 copies each) of most of the 148 numbers in the five-volume translation of Bayle. Barker paid £ 8. 5s. for these 818 odd numbers. These would have retailed for a shilling each, five times the price at which they were taken off Hazard's hands, but that difference is not all due to depreciation, since there was ordinarily a liberal allowance to the trade, and in any case the lot would not be considered a bargain at auction if the price were close to the normal wholesale rate. The really significant thing is that so extensive a stock should have changed hands at a substantial figure more than six years after the first numbers in the long series had been published.

That a book published in numbers was regarded as a 'going concern' is shown also by the fact[1] that at the sale of Edward Symon's stock on September 1, 1741, Thomas Osborne bought Lots 63, 64, 65, and 66 for £ 60 each, one lot consisting of a twelfth share in the copy of the *Universal History*, together with the following quire stock:

> 11 copies of Volume I complete
> 14 copies of Volume I lacking No. 1
> 9 copies of Volume I lacking Nos. 1 and 2
> 13 copies of Volume I lacking Nos. 1, 2, and 3
> 4 copies of Volume III complete
> 11 copies of Volume IV complete
> 22 copies of Volume V complete
> 50 copies of No. 1 in Volume VI
> 52 copies of No. 3 in Volume VI
> 58 copies of Nos. 2, 4, 5, 6, 7, 8 in Volume VI.

Several works —J. Baker's *History of the Inquisition*, Baddam's *Memoirs of the Royal Society*, Bickham's *Universal Penman* and *British Monarchy*, Stackhouse's *History of the Bible*, one of the two translations of *The Roman History*, both translations of Rapin, L'Estrange's *Josephus*, Thomas Salmon's *Modern History*, Foxe's *Book of Martyrs*, and the *Universal History*—had 'second' editions in numbers a few years after the first. It is easy to see that some of these are genuine editions, for the type has been reset; others just as obviously are simply the unsold remainders with a new title page. Except for the volume title page there is no visible difference between one issue of J. Baker's *History of the Inquisition* 'Printed for and sold by O. Payne ... 1736' and that bearing the imprint 'Printed and Sold by Joseph Marshall ... M.DCC.XXXIV'.

It is important, however, to distinguish between a genuine second edition in numbers and the issuing of a whole volume made up of left-over fascicules. In one case the original impression was not large enough to glut the market; in the other case the impression was too large. Occasionally one comes upon a copy of the eleventh edition (1739) of Burkitt's *Expository Notes* in which one or more sheets from the tenth

[1] According to the comtemporary figures given in the Longmans, Green copy of the catalogue.

edition, published in numbers in 1733-1734, are gathered in with newly printed sheets not bearing the usual number-book signatures. The New York Public Library copy of Burkitt (1739) has only one sheet (Fff) bearing the tell-tale signature, 'Numb. XI'. But this work was so popular and so frequently reprinted[1] that there cannot have been any considerable quantity of unusable fascicules.

Sometimes, to be sure, the second printing was piratical, and the profits went neither to the original author nor to the lawful proprietor. The fact that a book published in numbers in London was shortly afterwards reprinted in numbers in Dublin—as was Patrick Barclay's *Universal Traveller* in 1733-1735—shows only that profits were coming to two sets of proprietors at the same time. The Irish publisher of the *Universal Traveller* may have enjoyed a larger net profit, since he presumably got his copy without having to pay the author or the London publisher for it; he had simply to purchase a single copy of each number at the regular rate and then set up the text from the fonts of type in his own printing shop. The law did not touch him.

Likewise the publishing of a French-language edition in numbers —Tindal's notes to Rapin's *History of England*, for example, or Thomas Salmon's *Modern History*—cannot prove what profits were made; it merely implies that profits were expected to be high enough to justify the added cost of translation.

Leaving out of account second editions, piracies, continuations, and translations, one can see that the publishing of a book in numbers was in many cases expensive but ultimately profitable. Though each fascicule was only a fragment of a book —whether it comprised two sheets or twenty sheets—its selling price of three halfpence or twopence per sheet held promise of profit if enough units were sold. When Claude Du Bosc advertised that the weekly numbers of *The Ceremonies and Religious Customs of the Various Nations of the Known World* were to begin early in March 1733 he promised that this enormous work, illustrated

---

[1] The Yale University Library has an incomplete and undated copy of a folio edition obviously published in numbers of two sheets each, with pages numbered to 1006. This is not the twelfth edition, which has unnumbered pages and (except that it lacks number-book signatures) is similar in format to the tenth and eleventh editions.

with more than 172 copper plates, would comprise four large volumes in folio; although the total price would amount to £ 5. 10s. by the time the last of the weekly numbers appeared, this was no more than half the price of the original, and in any case, said Du Bosc, subscribers would pay only three halfpence per sheet. Who could complain of high prices at that very reasonable rate? Perhaps it is the same as saying that a two-dollar ticket to the symphony concert will enable one to enjoy the playing of a hundred men at the low price of two cents per musician. The transaction in either case is profitable for the proprietor only if enough people are willing to pay the price for the whole set.

CHAPTER VI

PRODUCTION, PROMOTION, DISTRIBUTION

In the preceding chapter some attention was paid to the costs of procuring copy, of having that copy set up in type, and of getting the fascicules into the readers' hands with maximum profit to the proprietors. It is expedient in this chapter to consider certain mechanical aspects of production and sale which are peculiar to the publishing of books in numbers.

A number book, sometimes called 'subscription book', is simply an ordinary book, printed sheet by sheet as ordinary books are, but having its sheets released to the purchasers as soon as printed instead of being kept in stacks in the printer's or publisher's warehouse until all can be collated and gathered into a volume. It was by no means unusual in the eighteenth century for a customer to buy a book in the form of a bundle of separate sheets and then take them to a binder, who would fold,[1] collate, stitch, and bind them for a small fee. It was a common practice in advertising a book to quote three different prices, one for the work 'in sheets', another slightly higher for the sheets folded, gathered, and stitched, and a third for the book ready bound in calf or sheepskin. Sometimes the price was given as so much per sheet, with the total price not given at all. When a new edition of Dr. William Cave's *Scriptorum Ecclesiasticorum Historia Literaria* was advertised in 1736 as in the press, the cost to the customer was announced thus: 'Subscribers to pay One Guinea down, Price Three Half-pence per Sheet'. When J. Osborn advertised a new translation of *Gil Blas* in four pocket volumes in 1748, the prices listed were '6s. in Sheets, 7s. stitch'd, 8s. bound'. Neither of these books was issued in numbers, but it is obvious that there would have been no mechanical difficulty in issuing them in that manner if the publisher had desired to do so, since in those years there was no lack of customers ready to buy small

---

[1] It may have been the regular practice for the printer's assistants to fold the sheets of all books; certainly books sold in 'numbers' must have been folded, collated, and 'stitch'd in blue Paper' before leaving the printing office.

batches of sheets with the ink hardly dry as they came from the flat-bed manual presses.

Many books were issued both in numbers and in complete volumes, so that customers unwilling or unable to buy a whole work at one time might manage to purchase it piecemeal. When the Knaptons and five other booksellers (Thomas Cox, Richard Ford, Richard Hett, Aaron Ward, and Thomas Longman) advertised their 'very beautiful and correct' edition of Matthew Henry's *Exposition on the Old and New Testament* in August 1736, they announced that eight sheets would be published every Saturday, beginning on September 4, at the price of one shilling, in order to accommodate 'such Persons who do not chuse to purchase this excellent Work together, or whose Abilities will not permit them to do so'. The total price, incidentally, was not to exceed five guineas and a half, which the publishers said was 'near one Third less' than the six volumes of the previous edition could be bought for. For many weeks, beginning on May 2, 1741, the proprietors of Ephraim Chambers' *Cyclopædia* issued three sheets of that work every Saturday for sixpence, but they indicated that the complete folio volumes could also be purchased.

The issuing of completed volumes of books currently sold in numbers is admirably illustrated by advertisements of *The Weekly Novelist* in 1735.[1] This 'select Collection of the best Novels, Moral, Political, &c., with other Pieces of Love and Gallantry, written by the most approved Authors' was published on Fridays at fourpence per number beginning September 12, 1735. As each number contained three sheets in twelves, 'printed on a neat small Letter and a good Dutch Paper', the persons who subscribed for the first fifteen numbers had by

[1] Not to be confused with the *New Weekly Novelist*, published in numbers towards the end of the century by Alexander Hogg of Paternoster Row, a proprietor who made vast sums of money by publishing number books. Hogg's weekly batch of fiction in the *New Weekly Novelist* consisted of translations made from French by Lewis Porney, a teacher of the French language at Richmond and formerly (according to the title page of his *Essai Philosophique & Pratique sur L'education des Jeunes Seigneurs & Gentils-hommes*, 1772) 'Professeur de Langue Françoise á Eton'. Following the example of his predecessors in the number-book trade, Hogg also issued left-over sheets of the *New Weekly Novelist* as a volume, to which he gave the title *A New and complete collection of interesting Romances and Novels*.

the middle of December accumulated over a thousand pages of fiction. According to an advertisement in the *Whitehall Evening Post* number 2935 (December 11, 1735) these fifteen numbers comprised a new edition of Mrs. Manley's *New Atalantis*, and three different prices were quoted for the complete work: '4*d.* per Number, or 5*s.* 6*d.* sew'd up in blue Paper; bound 7*s.* 6*d.*'

It strikes one immediately that this issuing of books in weekly numbers made it imperative to identify each number as it came out. The easiest way was to assign a serial number to each fascicule. This was most commonly done by marking the blue paper covers, but as these were almost invariably removed it is now often quite impossible to tell from an examination of the bound volumes where one number ended and the next began, or even (without other evidence) to know that the work was issued in fascicules. Only the details in advertisements or other external evidences can enable one, for example, to recognize the successive fascicules in *The Weekly Novelist*, just mentioned. That is true of Dr. James's *Medicinal Dictionary* (1743–1745), *The Harleian Miscellany* (1744–1746), Defoe's *Religious Courtship* (1740–1741), Baker's *Chronicle of the Kings of England* (1732–1733), Tillemont's *Ecclesiastical Memoirs* (1731–1735), John Wilford's *Memorials and Characters* (1739–1741), du Halde's *Description of China* (1736–1741), John Philips's *Authentic Journal of . . . Anson* (1744), the octavo edition of Rapin's *History of England* (Tindal's translation, 1725–1731), the third edition of John Strype's *Annals of the Reformation of the Church of England* (1735–1737), Wilson's translation of de Thou (1728–1730), Fleury's *Ecclesiastical History* (1726–1731), William Maitland's *History . . . of . . . London* (1737–1739), James Dodson's *Anti-logarithmic Canon* (1740–1743), and a dozen other books, all known to have been published in numbers in the editions seen, though bearing no visible sign of weekly or monthly publication. The blue paper covers of the separate fascicules doubtless bore serial numbers, but these covers would naturally be removed when the volumes were bound.

The use of clearly distinguishable serial numbers on the blue paper covers would be particularly important to prevent confusion in the minds of customers who purchased the translation of Jean Frédéric Bernard's *Cérémonies et coutumes religieuses de tous les peuples du monde* which Claude Du Bosc published in weekly fascicules in 1733 and later years, for he published the numbers of Volumes I and IV on alternate Saturdays, and later did the same with the numbers of Volumes II and III.[1]

In a few works issued piecemeal the serial number was printed at the top of each page, as in Moxon's *Mechanick Exercises* (1678 and following years), or at the top of the even-numbered pages, as in the four octavo volumes of Rapin's *Acta Regia* translated by Stephen Whatley (1725–1727). This edition of *Acta Regia* also had the serial number on a separate title page printed for each monthly number, and the same is true of *Atlas Geographus* (1708 and later years), and its sequel, *Magna Britannia* (1714–1731).

But most books that reached their readers in weekly or monthly fascicules bore —and of course still bear —unmistakable marks of their mode of publication, namely, special signatures affixed to the first page of each sheet. Most number books in folio have serial numbers as part of the signature, but many quarto and octavo works lack them. Thus the folio edition of *Acta Regia* (1732–1733) in weekly numbers has signatures from 'Numb. I' to 'Numb. XLII' along with the normal letter signatures [A] to 10H at the foot of the first page of the sheet. That is the usual position of number-book signatures, and that is the usual form, though the abbreviation is sometimes 'No.' instead of 'Numb.' and in some works all the numerals of the signatures are arabic instead of roman. In several of the most carefully printed number books —the eleventh edition of Ralegh's *History of the World* (1735–1736), for example —the signature of the first sheet in each fascicule is in roman numerals and the signatures of the remaining sheets in the fascicule are in arabic numerals.

---

[1] The reason for this awkward alternation may be that Du Bosc had two separate printers at work on the project, for William Jackson, whose name as printer stands on the title pages of all seven volumes, may have engaged an unnamed printer to assist him. But if such alternation was necessary, why was it not the fascicules of Volumes I and II that alternated?

A few works published in numbers have quite unusual signatures, doubtless because an effort was being made to simplify the collating when the fascicules were later assembled into volumes. For instance, each sheet of Patrick Barclay's *Universal Traveller* (folio, 1733-1735) bears three kinds of signature, one showing to which fascicule it belonged, another showing where it belonged in the sequence of sheets within the fascicule, and the third the usual letter signature showing what place the individual sheet had in the whole series of the volume; thus the eight sheets of the twenty-fifth fascicule have signatures as follows:

No. XXV.	1.	9I
No. XXV.	2.	9K

and son on, to

No. XXV.	8.	9Q

As the pagination is continuous throughout the volume and every page has its catchword, it is hard to suppose that any owner or binder could misplace any sheet of this work. Dr. Daniel Scott's *Appendix to the Greek Thesaurus* (folio, 1744-1746) has separate series of fascicule signatures and sheet numbers in each of the two volumes, the five sheets of the fourth fascicule in Volume II being marked thus:

Vol. II.	No. IV.	1.	R
Vol. II.	No. IV.	2.	S
Vol. II.	No. IV.	3.	T
Vol. II.	No. IV.	4.	U
Vol. II.	No. IV.	5.	X

A less complicated set of signatures is to be observed in the twelve handsome octavo volumes of Archbishop Tillotson's works, published in sixpenny weekly numbers in 1742-1744, and also available volume by volume every two months as the fascicules accumulated. The pagination and the regular letter signatures are continuous throughout the twelve volumes, but each of the eight fascicules in a volume is distinguished from the others by a small arabic numeral placed under the volume number at the foot of the first page of each sheet. The seven (or eight, or nine) half-sheets comprising a fascicule are not serially numbered, but each is marked to show which fascicule it belongs to. Thus the signatures of the nine half-sheets making up fascicule 8 in the fifth volume run from

Vol. V   10 K
8

to

Vol. V   10 S
8

The maximum complexity in number-book signatures is to be seen in the double series —one in roman numerals for the first of the eight sheets in each monthly fascicule, one in arabic numerals for both sheets of each weekly number —in R. Penny's text of the New Testament, with annotations by John Court and John Lindsay, in 1733–1735. The sheets of the third monthly fascicule of this work have the following signatures:

No. III.   No. 9.   S
No. 9.   T
No. 10.   U
No. 10.   X
No. 11.   Y
No. 11.   Z
No. 12.   Aa
No. 12.   Bb

and the next sheet is signed

No. IV.   No. 13.   Cc

With the publication of the eighth monthly fascicule the issuing of two sheets weekly apparently came to an end, for thereafter only the roman numeral signatures (No. IX, No. X, and so on) were used.

When every sheet or half-sheet bears a serial number it can usually be inferred that each of these sheet or half-sheet units was published by itself. Occasionally, however, that is clearly not the proper inference. Nor is it right to assume that the consecutive numbering of *every* sheet in a volume does nothing more than provide an unnecessary parallel to the regular letter signatures. These numerals doubtless proved useful when, for example, the publisher of a work issued in fascicules made up of three sheets wished to issue a plate instead of one of the sheets, at no extra charge. In such a case the serial numbers on the printed sheets are not strictly speaking fascicule signatures at all; the fascicule signature of each group of three sheets (or two sheets and a plate) would undoubtedly be printed on the blue paper cover. The only numeral signatures now visible in the 157 sheets of Jacob Hooper's *Impartial History of the Rebellion* (1738) run from 1 to 182, but at irregular intervals one of the numbers is omitted, obviously to make room for one of the 25 plates; the letter signatures, on the other hand, are not interrupted. Thus the printer, guided by the normal letter signatures, could keep the sheets of letterpress in order, the binder would insert a plate wherever there was a gap in the numeral signatures, and the customer would be assured by the numbers on the blue paper covers that his fascicules were consecutive.

It was noted at the end of Chapter V that occasionally odd remainders were incorporated into bound volumes in which most of the sheets were newly printed from reset type. It should be pointed out that there are no number-book signatures in the New York Public Library copy of Lediard's *Naval History of England* (1733-1735), though the copy in the National Library of Scotland has the special signatures. In other respects the two copies appear to be identical, but obviously the sheets in these two copies were from different impressions.

There is one other feature peculiar to the publication of a book in fascicules, and that is the fairly consistent practice of issuing the title page and preliminary matter in the final number or numbers of a volume rather than in the first number. As a result, the imprint of the completed volume may list proprietors who had no share in the work when it first began to appear in numbers. It is also frequently true that the date in the imprint may be as much as two or three years later than the date on which the earliest fascicules reached subscribers. Thus the two folio volumes comprising the eleventh edition of Ralegh's *History of the World* are both dated 1736; but there is ample evidence in newspaper advertisements and contemporary lists of publications that the proprietors had begun to issue the fascicules of this edition early in 1735. To add to the confusion, the same proprietors had issued the same work in the same form (sixpenny weekly numbers) two whole years earlier in what they mistakenly called the 'Seventh 'edition. Misled by this real error on the publishers' part, the nineteenth-century Ralegh bibliographer, T. N. Brushfield, declared that the few title pages which he had seen with the date 1733 were 'fraudulent'.[1] Brushfield did not know that an edition actually had been published in weekly fascicules of four sheets each, beginning on February 3, 1733. Again, the date of the royal licence for the publishing of *A Complete System of Geography* is December 5, 1743, and it is known that the numbers began to appear early in 1744. But both volumes have the date 1747 in the imprint. There may have been a special title page for Volume I dated 1745, for the Preface to Volume I (included in number 84, the penultimate fascicule of that volume) is dated November 30, 1745; but doubtless the general title pages, both dated 1747, were issued when the last of the 144 numbers was printed early in 1747. There are other examples of this time-gap between the date on the title page and the date on which the first fascicule reached the readers.

The main problem of the proprietors was to get not only the first fascicule but all the fascicules into the hands of the largest possible number of regular purchasers. Figures concerning the cost of doing this were cited in the preceding chapter; other aspects of the process will be considered here. Publishers of number books were no different from the publishers of other books in the twofold objective of persuading customers to desire their books and making it easy for them to purchase those books. The number-book business was a new field, however, and special efforts had to be made to induce customers to *begin* taking the numbers regularly. Early in the development of the trade it was necessary to overcome a natural reluctance which some people had against buying slender packets of sheets instead of whole books. One of the very early number books, John Stevens's *New Collection of Voyages and Travels* (1708 and later), had in the first number a reassuring observation that although each of the monthly parts might look slight, as being 'a Stitch'd Pamphlet', the successive fascicules

[1] T. N. Brushfield, *A Bibliography of Sir Walter Ralegh Kt.* (2nd ed., Exeter: Commin, 1908), p. 95.

would soon take shape as a complete work, just as if it had been printed all at once. By the second quarter of the century there was less necessity to convince readers that a book issued in fascicules was none the less a book. People then did not need to be persuaded to accept the new mode of publication; the advertising was used rather to promote particular books. It was recognized that once a subscriber had paid for a few weekly or monthly numbers there was a strong likelihood that he would keep on buying them as they came out, partly because he already had a financial interest in a commodity not valuable unless complete, partly because human beings yield very readily to a periodic custom once its rhythm is established.

The proprietors of number books used every means they could think of to establish that rhythm—to induce the customer to begin taking the fascicules and then to keep on buying them until he was so far caught by the habit that he would not stop. Proposals and advertisements sometimes emphasized the essential quality of the works themselves, for publishers naturally tried to convince potential subscribers that they would receive good value for their money; but eighteenth-century puffs and blurbs seem very mild in comparison with those of our own time. Often, indeed, there was no attempt to argue readers into accepting a work, beyond the claim that the writing, compiling, or translating had been done by 'an eminent hand', or that it had never appeared before in England. In 1732 Thomas Edlin assured pious buyers of John Campbell's *New and Complete History of the Holy Bible* that it would 'afford a proper and religious Exercise for every Sunday'. A little later (in December 1733) the Knaptons appealed to the potential customer's interests by claiming that Burkitt's *Expository Notes* were 'designed to encourage the Reading of the Scriptures in Private Families, and to render the daily Perusal of them profitable and delightful'. In issuing Ralegh's *History of the World* in weekly numbers both in 1733 and again in 1735 the Knaptons and their associates asserted that their edition was 'correctly printed from the only genuine and uncorrupted Edition publish'd by the Author himself',[1] and promised

[1] See Brushfield, *op. cit.*, and also Louise Creighton, 'Sir Walter Ralegh', *Cambridge History of English Literature*, IV, p. 63.

their subscribers not only Ralegh's text but an account of his life, the story of his trial, an index to the work, a picture of the author, and a set of maps.

The lures to buy were never very subtle, and importunate urging was less common than one would expect. Often the proprietor meekly suggested that persons 'willing to encourage so entertaining a Work by becoming Subscribers' should send their names and addresses to him or speak to the vendors of newspapers. Or he might insist that his number book was quite different from a work already in print, as when E. Symon assured the public that John Strype's *Annals of the Reformation of the Church of England*, about to be issued in fascicules, would not interfere with Bishop Burnet's account, 'that being only the History of the Origin and Rise of it'. Strype's work, he declared, was 'supported by Records, Papers of State, Original Letters, &c.', and as evidence of the author's abilities to write such a book Symon printed the recommendation formally prepared and signed by twenty-four of the 'then Bishops'. Some months later (in November 1737) J. Huggonson went a little farther in praising the thirty weekly numbers of *The Art of Painting* by Gérard de Lairesse (translated by J. F. Fritsch), asserting that the book, originally published at Amsterdam, had been received 'with the greatest Applause' on the continent. Earlier in 1737, when E. Holloway (near the Blue Last in Salisbury Court, Fleet Street) advertised in the *London Spy Revived* number 81 (January 31) that the fortnightly numbers of *The Doctrine of the Old and New Testament . . . by Way of Question and Answer* would make three neat octavo volumes, he (or she) added bluntly that the work might justly be looked upon as 'the cheapest and usefullest Book that was ever printed'. During the same year Thomas Harper, copper-plate printer in Dogwell-Court, White-Fryars, tried something new in the way of lure when he advertised *The Musical Entertainer* at sixpence per monthly number. This work, he said, would consist of select Italian, English, and Scotch songs, favourite cantatas, 'the Words Composed by the Best Poets, and set to Musick by the most eminent Masters, adapted to the Voice, Violin, German and Common Flute, Harpsichord, or Spinet, with the thorough Bass to each Song'. Then came Harper's special offer: 'ingenious Persons' were urged to send in their own compositions, post paid. How could a publisher of music better please potential customers than by offering to print their compositions?

Once in a while a proprietor raised his voice like a circus barker and tried to describe his forthcoming number book in terms calculated to attract the unwary. In March 1738 W. Rayner and W. Lloyd announced that the first number of their *Compleat History and Antiquities of the Antient Egyptians, Babylonians, Romans, Carthaginians, Assyrians, Medes, Persians, and Grecians* would be published on 'Wednesday the 22d of March Instant, positively'. Not satisfied with simply stating the usual details, Rayner and Lloyd insisted that the book was a tremendous bargain because it contained so much. According to them the history of any *one* of the nations mentioned in the title would afford 'such a surprising Variety of Events as must engage the Attention of, and afford the most agreeable Entertainment imaginable to every curious Reader'. They then became really importunate:

But when he has travelled thro' the History of one Nation, and stands, as it were, amazed at the great Exploits that have been atchieved by the Heroes, whose Lives he has been traversing with the utmost Delight and Astonishment; to be then led to another Scene full as glorious and entertaining as the last; and the Truth of every Fact attested by the most eminent Historians, whose Veracity was never called in Question: When all this shall appear unexceptionably true, nothing surely can give the Mind a more rational Amusement, than a Work, which comprehends in its Compass all these Particulars.

That, said Rayner and Lloyd, was the sort of work they were offering to the public. 'We dare appeal to the Judgment of every impartial Reader, after he has perused a few of the first Numbers.'

The problem, of course, was how to induce readers to begin the perusal. The usual procedure was to issue printed proposals, which were widely distributed, and sometimes these proposals were themselves announced in newspapers as available gratis at numerous places named in the notice. The principle was that potential customers were more likely to purchase a new work if they heard about it well in advance and knew exactly when the first number was to be published. It is a principle which still has value. If readers have been told that a book

is about to appear they will greet its publication with a certain degree
of recognition, if not of eagerness. These proposals set forth the 'conditions' of publication, giving the full title of the work, naming the
author, translator, or compiler, specifying the size of the page (folio,
quarto, octavo, duodecimo), indicating the number of sheets or pages
in each fascicule, stating the price, stipulating the date of publication
of the first number and the interval between numbers, enumerating
special features such as plates, maps, notes, and tables, describing the
paper and type, listing the proprietors, and mentioning the places
where subscriptions would be received. Sometimes these proposals
and 'conditions' were reprinted in full in close-packed newspaper advertisements announcing the actual publication of the first number.
Usage differed in the announcing of subsequent numbers. Some publishers felt it desirable to repeat or expand the original advertisement
in the newspapers, adjusting the date and the serial number as the
series progressed. The proprietors of Tindal's translation of Calmet
made a point of indicating in each number of *Antiquities Sacred and
Profane* (1724) the date of the next number, saying (in number 10) that
no other notice would be given in future; but this was an unusual
arrangement. Ordinarily there were notices in the newspapers saying,
'This Day is Publish'd . . . Numb. XXII. . . .'

For the later numbers probably the best advertisements of all were
the elaborate title pages of the separate numbers, or the descriptive
details printed in eye-catching type on the blue covers. A few proprietors printed the full text of the original proposals on the blue
covers of the earliest numbers, and some made similar use of the royal
licences if these had been granted. Many books seem to have required
only the initial boost, being carried to completion with a minimum of
advertising, on the principle (one would like to suppose) that good
wine needs no bush. Perhaps the most convincing evidence of success
in number-book publishing is to be seen in the almost perfunctory
notices of this or that series of fascicules well advanced beyond the
first few weeks or months of the run, such notices serving mainly to
indicate to regular customers that it was again time to come in and
pick up the current number.

But the first notices had to be detailed, explicit, and if possible enticing. When the substance of a book was itself enticing it was easy enough to attract attention by simply enumerating the lurid contents, perhaps throwing in a few adjectives for good measure. Mention was made in Chapter II of the efforts of Read and Rayner to persuade customers to buy their sordid accounts of criminals. Another purveyor of the same sorry stuff was John Wilford, whose advertisements of *Select Trials at the Sessions-House in the Old Baily* (published in sixpenny fortnightly numbers in 1734) listed hair-raising varieties of crime. Wilford's announcement of the third number, in the *Daily Advertiser* number 1024 (May 11, 1734), enumerates both the rogues and their crimes, together with some of their victims:

> This Number . . . contains the remarkable Trials of George Duffus for Sodomy; Mary Harvey and Ann Parker for privately stealing Money from Dr. Cassel; Butler Fox for robbing Sir Edward Lawrence on the Highway . . .; Christopher Kraft for ravishing Sarah Pearse; George Nicholas for forging a Bank Note; James Shaw and Richard Norton for Robbery and Murder, &c.

Wilford made a practice of listing the contents of back numbers, and when advertising the numbers of Volume II he included a comprehensive note concerning Volume I. This, he said (in the *Daily Advertiser* number 1218, December 21, 1734), contained upwards of three hundred trials, among them 77 of highwaymen, 53 of murderers, 31 'of Whores for privately stealing, which are very entertaining', 10 of shoplifters, 62 of housebreakers, 11 for rapes and attempts to ravish, 'several of which are very humorous', and small groups of trials for less common misdemeanours, among them 'returning from Transportation' and 'endeavouring to set up a new Mint'. These trials, said Wilford, were not only 'very necessary' for all lawyers, Justices of the Peace, and other persons concerned in prosecutions, but were 'very useful and entertaining to the generality of Readers'.

Wilford was equally enthusiastic about a somewhat less successful venture two years later. In the *London Spy Revived* number 5 (August 6, 1736) he advertised as just published at a shilling the first number of what he called 'A choice, useful, and most entertaining Collection of memorable and genuine Histories, mostly Tragical; the greatest Part of them extracted from the most credible Writers of the last Century'. He offered to deliver these choice pieces either monthly or 'in a less Quantity' weekly, and listed the stories included in the first set, presumably hoping that he would catch customers by dangling lascivious bait. Like the modern warning that a cinema film is 'adult entertainment' the titles were designed to emphasize the viciousness of the stories. The series began with 'The Incestuous Brother and Sister' and 'The Curried Adulterers'. Then followed such morsels as 'The Wife's Diabolical Contrivance to rid herself of two Husbands at once', 'The Double Fratricide', and 'A Modern English Story of a misguided young Beauty's Ruin'. It is to the everlasting credit of English readers that they rejected this sort of slop. Wilford announced four weeks later that he had not yet obtained enough subscribers to enable him to continue, accounting for the lack of response by saying that the publication had been started at the 'very worst Time in the Year' and that he had 'not advertised much'. He promised that when he had a few more subscribers the work would be 'prosecuted with Vigor, and the utmost Regularity'. But it was not until the middle of November that he announced fresh proposals and found additional adjectives to describe these choice, pleasant, useful, entertaining, memorable and genuine histories by foreign authors of undoubted credit and veracity. It is fairly certain that this kind of advertising did not pay.

If the main purpose of advertising was to set forth the essential facts —what the product was, how much it would cost, where and when it might be obtained—then Robert Penny should have reaped his reward, for his Proposals (reprinted in full in his *British Observator* early in August 1733) stated these facts about a forthcoming edition of the New Testament, and included a modest paragraph recommending the critical and explanatory notes. Penny's Proposals will serve to illustrate the general tone of such invitations to buy:

PROPOSALS for Printing by Subscription, the NEW TES-TAMENT, with Critical and Explanatory Notes, extracted from the Writings of the Celebrated Grotius, Hammond, Calmet, Locke, Poole, Whitby, and other curious modern Annotators. In one Volume in Folio.

The Use of these Notes will Explain itself without the Compiler's entring into Particulars, or giving a distinct Character of the several Great Men above. And what the Advantage is that flows from a Perusal of good Books, is too well known to those, who make serious and grave Authors the Study of their leisure Moments, to need any manner of Illustration. Reading, but especially an Endeavour to understand sublime Subjects on Religion, is not only a fine, but a profitable Employment, as it helps to divest the Soul of abundance of its Prejudices, and to instruct it in Things it never knew before. Is any Man, then, desirous of being acquainted with true Knowledge, or of obtaining these two important Ends, let him have Recourse to our Critical Remarks, where, at one View, will be seen what the best modern Commentators have remark'd on the Text and Doctrines of the New Testament.

In order to render this Work, as Universal as it is Useful, it will be publish'd according to the following Conditions.

I. That this Work will contain about 200 Sheets, printed on a fine Dutch Demy Paper, and good Character.

II. That two Sheets shall be publish'd every Week, at the Price of Three-Pence, and deliver'd to the Subscribers own Houses.

III. Those Persons who cannot conveniently come to any of the Places under-mentioned to subscribe, may, by speaking to those Persons who supply them with the News-Papers, have this Work sent Weekly, either in Town or Country.

IV. That the first two Sheets will be publish'd on Thursday the 16th of August next, and to be continu'd every Thursday till the Whole is finish'd.

V. Gentlemen that would not be troubled with Weekly Subscriptions, may have them deliver'd Monthly, stitch'd up in Blue Paper, on paying One Shilling.

VI. The Names of the Subscribers shall be printed and deliver'd to every one of them, Gratis, at the end of the Work.

Printed by R. PENNY, in *Wine-Office-Court, Fleet-street*, where Subscriptions are taken in; as also by Mrs. Dodd, at the Peacock without Temple-Bar; Mrs. Nutt and Mrs. Cooke, at the Royal-Exchange; Mrs. Charlton the Corner of Swithin's-Alley near the Royal-Exchange; J. Chrichley at the London Gazette, Charing-Cross; J. Milan, the Corner of Buckingham-Court, near the Admiralty Office; W. Shropshire in New Bond-Street; J. Booth in Barking-Alley, near Great Tower-Hill; T. Payne in Bishopsgate-Street; S. Lye, Printseller, in Leaden-Hall Street.

The very restraint of these Proposals may have attracted people who made 'serious and grave Authors the Study of their leisure Moments', though they may secretly have looked with some eagerness on the prospect of seeing their names on the printed list of genteel subscribers.

Eagerness among the subscribers is less easily detected now than is the burst of enthusiasm that occasionally emerges in newspaper advertisements of number books, though none of these announcements parallel in extravagance the contemporary notices of anodyne necklaces, wonder-working nostrums, and many varieties of preparations designed to sweeten, beautify, or invigorate. In 1741 Charles Corbett, eager to convince potential customers that a work of established popularity—Thomas Harper had published it in monthly numbers in 1737—urged intending subscribers to *The Musical Entertainer* to be 'speedy' in sending in their names. His advertisement in Dodsley's *Publick Register; or, the Weekly Magazine* number 3 (January 17, 1741) exhibits most of the talking points of a high-pressure salesman: production about to begin; a list of 'eminent' contributors; expert designing and engraving; 'beautiful' pictures; masterly editing by a man with three names; finished product to be two handsome folio volumes; imported paper, both superfine and thick; convenient terms; punctual delivery of numbers; extras gratis, including one's name in print as subscriber; specimens available for inspection; nothing like it heretofore or hereafter; distinguished clientele; edition practically limited; ground-floor opportunity—and hurry! hurry! hurry! Corbett's announcement is importunate but not fulsome:

The Copper Plates being entirely finished, of that Beautiful Work, entitled, The Musical Entertainer. Consisting of Select Italian, English, and Scotch Songs, and set to Musick, by

Purcel,	Stanley,
Handell,	Boyce,
Corelli,	Munro,
Green,	Leveridge,
Carey,	Festing,
Vincent	

And other eminent Masters; adapted to the Voice, Violin, German and Common Flutes, Harpsichord and Spinnet; all neatly engraved on

Copper Plates. At the Head of which is a beautiful Picture, adapted to the Song: Designed by *Gravelot* and others, and Engraved by George Bickham, Jun. And now carefully corrected; a Thorough Bass added to each Song, and made entirely compleat, By Mr. John Frederick Lampe. The Whole making two handsome Folio Volumes, containing Two Hundred Plates, besides Frontispieces and Tables, is proposed to be deliver'd by Subscription, on the following

CONDITIONS

I. That it shall be carefully printed on a Superfine Thick *Genoa* Paper.

II. That a Number containing Four Plates shall be punctually deliver'd every Saturday, sew'd up in Blue Covers, for Six-Pence.

III. That at the End of each Volume shall be given *Gratis* a beautiful Frontispiece, and a Table to the Songs.

IV. That a List of the Subscribers shall be printed and given *Gratis* at the End of the Work.

SUBSCRIPTIONS are taken in by CHARLES CORBETT, Book-seller and Publisher, at *Addison's Head*, over-against St. *Dunstan's* church, in *Fleetstreet*; where a Specimen of this present beautiful Edition may be seen.

N.B. Those Gentlemen and Ladies therefore who are willing to become Subscribers to this Work so universally admired, and now faithfully corrected, the like of which never was before (nor in all Probability ever will be again) published, are desired to be speedy in sending in their Names to the above *Charles Corbett*, he intending to print no more (or at least a very few) than what are really subscribed for.

Somewhat heartier puffs were used to boost the sale of several number books advertised in *All-Alive and Merry*, in which it was announced on Saturday, April 23, 1740, that

On Monday last was publish'd, containing Twelve Pages, at the Price of One Half-Penny, No. 25 of The UNIVERSAL SONGSTER. A Work which is designed for the Amusement of Every Body, and intended as a Specifick against the Spleen, Vapours, and Melancholy, proceeding from either Love, Wine, Grief, or Bad Weather. This Collection will consist of all the best English and Scots Songs, and will be compris'd in 26 Numbers, in which will be near 400 Songs, at the small Expence of One Shilling; and great Care shall be taken that they shall be correctly printed.

Two months earlier the same daily paper carried lively advertisements of the twenty-three numbers of a work described as 'fit to be read at this Juncture by all True Hearts and Sound Bottoms'. Each number contained sixteen large octavo pages, and the price was only a penny, delivered every Wednesday to subscribers, and also 'sold of the Persons who serve the News'. The full title has a hearty ring about it:

England's Triumph; or Spanish Cowardice expos'd. Being a complete History of the many signal Victories gained for over 400 Years past by the Royal Navy and Merchant Ships of Great Britain over the insulting and haughty Spaniards. Wherein will be given a genuine Account of all the Expeditions, Voyages, Adventures, &c. of the English Admirals from the Year 1350 down to 1739, whose Successes have already filled all Europe with Amazement.
By Capt. Charles Jenkins, who has too sensibly felt the Effects of Spanish Tyranny.

Here is the famous Jenkins wreaking a terrible vengeance for his mutilated ear! Surely no true hearts, no sound bottoms, could resist the opportunity to purchase such a document of reprisal at a penny every Vednesday.

A few months later Thomas Cooper, lacking a name so much in the news as that of Jenkins, made the most of blank anonymity by frankly announcing that his *Supplement to Dr. Harris's Lexicon Technicum*, published in thirty fortnightly numbers at a shilling each in 1741-1742, was by 'a Society of Gentlemen', but he assured his public that this supplement, together with the two original volumes, would make 'the most useful Set of Books and compleat Body of Arts and Sciences yet extant', and be a 'very considerable Improvement of Mr. Chambers' Cyclopædia'.

There is more than a little suspicion attached to the claim that a work is the product of a board of learned editors whose names one cannot discover; but several number books —like many other books published in the eighteenth century —were announced as 'by eminent Hands', or 'by a Society of Gentlemen'. Perhaps the *Annotations on the Holy Bible* issued in sixpenny weekly numbers (beginning in September 1735) by J. and T. Read were really, as the advertisements declared, the work of 'a Select Body of Divines'; but one cannot help suspecting that sometimes these alleged 'gentlemen' and 'divines' were not quite either, since it is so easy to conceal a set of 'poor founder'd Hackneys' under honourable terms. Even when no 'eminent Hands' were given credit for a work there might be a row of imposing names in the background to guarantee the quality. When J. Wilford published in fortnightly parts, beginning in December 1734, *The History of the Life and Death of our Blessed Lord and Saviour Jesus Christ*, he said that the compiler, 'a Divine of the Church of England', had found his material in 'the Writings of Taylor, Hammond, Whitby, Grotius, Dupin, Calmet, Prideaux, Basnage, Cave, &c.' If the pillaging of ten or a dozen authors indicates scholarship, then even more deserving of popular acclaim was the same Wilford's *Memorials and Characters of many excellent and Worthy Persons, of all Ranks, and of both Sexes*, issued in monthly parts at a shilling each in 1739–1741; for the unnamed compiler advertised that his basic material had been obtained from 'above 150 different Authors, several scarce Pieces, and some original Manuscripts'.

Anonymity cannot always be taken as a sign of inferiority, and a publisher can sometimes make something of the fact that a person prefers to conceal his identity, or (better still!) is forced to do so. In the public mind there is all the difference in the world between an author who is merely nameless and one who is compelled by circumstances to write *incognito*. The very holding back of an author's name may even lead to romantic conjectures that boost sales. J. Brindley found it to be otherwise, however, when he urged liberal-minded Englishmen to read a translated *History of the Popes* in 1732, for neither the promise of surprising disclosures nor the concealment of the author's name produced a response sufficient to justify the continuance of the work. But Brindley tried hard enough to evoke interest, as appears in the announcement of No. 2 in the *Daily Advertiser* number 552 (November 7, 1732):

This History is compiled from the very best Authorities . . ., and is a Work which ought to do Honour to any Man; but the Author being a Frenchman, and actually residing in France, is oblig'd to conceal his Name. This is observ'd, in order to obviate the Prejudices some may contract against an Anonymous Work; and they may be assur'd, it is inferior to no History, whether Civil, or Ecclesiastical, in the French Tongue.

Should the hired scribbler's name be too obscure for use in publicity, there was always an alternative to anonymity: he could be screened behind a fictitious name high-sounding enough to be impressive in advertising. There were some number books for which the personal attention of a distinguished authority was claimed, but it is mildly amusing to find that the proprietor of certain theological works published in fascicules was unable to devise a more impressive name for his distinguished expert than Smith. Later in the century[1] successful number-book publishers like John Cooke and John Payne used such weighty names as 'George Augustus Hervey' and 'William Frederick Melmoth' to give their manufactured tomes an air of erudition. The *Gentleman's Magazine* for April 1779 attacked this particular fraud in a special article exposing the weakness and inaccuracy of one of Cooke's sixpenny number books, brazenly labelled *The Modern Universal British Traveller; or, a new, complete, and accurate Tour through England, Wales, Scotland, and the neighbouring Islands, comprising all that is worthy of Observation in Great-Britain. With Maps, Landscapes, Views, &c.* Cooke announced that the articles respecting England were by 'Charles Burlington Esq.', those relating to Wales by 'David Llewellyn Rees, Gent.', and those descriptive of Scotland by 'Alexander Murray, M.A.'[2] A letter in the *Gentleman's Magazine* for June 1779 commended the proprietor of that periodical for exposing the specious disguise of 'great' names, and mentioned additional examples of books advertised under fictitious names. The following month another correspondent referred to a thoroughgoing exposure of these frauds by the *St. James's Evening*

[1] See C.H. Timperley, *Encyclopedia* (1839), p. 838, n.

[2] John Nichols, *Literary Anecdotes of the Eighteenth Century* (London, 1812), II, p. 729 f., quotes William Lemoine's account (1783) of Robert Sanders, 'a self-styled LL.D.', who compiled *The Modern Universal British Traveller* and many other number books, using various *noms de plume*. Among the works by Sanders the best known was *The Universal Family Bible*, 'by the Rev. Henry Southwell, D.D. Lemoine says that this was not a fictitious name, but the real name of a clergyman who was paid a hundred guineas for the use of his dignified name (including the 'D.D.'), Sanders being paid only twenty-five or twenty-six shillings per sheet.

Post in 1778. But earlier in the century W. Rayner could invent no more persuasive name for his allegedly erudite compiler than 'S. Smith, D.D.', whose scriptural annotations and biblical biographies brought great gains to Rayner. It may be that the pen was actually wielded by a man named Smith, but the 'D.D.' was probably gratuitous. Perhaps Rayner hoped the very simplicity of the name would give the impression of genuineness.[1]

So humble a name did not disarm the vigorous critic who, writing in the *Grub-Street Journal* number 334 (May 20, 1736), accused the 'Sett of Pirates who have no other End but filthy Lucre' of publishing altered and adulterated extracts from the Bible, and condemned the publisher's pretence that the scholarly annotations were by a distinguished theologian:

> Amongst all the licentious practices, by which this Nation is distinguished at this Time, from all the Nations in the World; I am persuaded, nothing can equal that audacious Liberty which some have lately assumed in printing the sacred Oracles of the living God, without any Authority or Privilege . . . .

What particularly infuriated the writer of this letter was the weekly publication of 'those Writings that were given by the Inspiration of the Holy Ghost', and the fact that even the usual legal restraints seemed ineffectual in curbing the traffic:

> For we plainly see, of what little Efficacy an Injunction out of Chancery (the only Remedy in such Cases) is, to restrain any one from printing The Holy Bible. Is it credible, that a Christian Nation, that boasts of having the purest Religion in the World, should have no Laws to punish so atrocious an Attempt, as publishing the Sacred Books, the Fountains of Truth, with Corruptions and Imperfections; but should

---

[1] The use of 'great' names was not unknown earlier in the century, as those familiar with Edmund Curll's title pages are aware. On the other hand there were doubtless many real persons named S. Smith. Among them was one Samuel Smith, who on February 23, 1731, preached a famous sermon on the necessity of establishing a colony across the Atlantic in Georgia. It is curious to observe that when young Samuel Johnson wrote to Edward Cave on November 25, 1734, offering to contribute articles to the *Gentleman's Magazine* he left his letter unsigned, merely concluding, 'Your letter, by being directed to S. Smith, to be left at the Castle in Birmingham, Warwickshire, will reach Your humble Servant.'

suffer them to be mangled, retailed, and parcelled out amongst the People, like any ordinary History or Romance?

And in order to carry on the Fraud with more Success, and to impose upon the Ignorant, the Editor of one of these Works has the Assurance to make use of a fictitious Author for his *Annotations*, which he tells are written by S. Smith, D.D., tho' it is well known, that they are only collected from the Works of many learned Divines; and this Doctor of Divinity was never heard of before. But the Editor thought the Name of a Doctor of Divinity, real or imaginary, of no small Weight towards insnaring the Populace. But, what is really diverting, this imaginary Divine is not only indebted for his *Annotations* to his Neighbours, but even for his Peruke, which is taken from a Print of Rapin's, by the Dexterity of the Engraver. So that the Word of God is ushered into the World with Forgery and Imposture.

William Rayner was not deterred by anything in the *Grub-Street Journal* from keeping the prolific 'S. Smith, D.D.' busy, for early in 1737 he advertised two more works by the same compiler, to be published as weekly number books. The earlier of these, *The History of the Lives, Actions, Travels, Sufferings, and Deaths of our Blessed Saviour and his Twelve Apostles,* 'extracted from the best Authors', was 'to be comprised in about thirty Numbers, and rendered the compleatest Work of the Kind yet extant'. There were to be maps and cuts, and the numbers, 'in large Octavo . . . stitched in blue Paper', were for sale at twopence each. The other book by 'Dr. Smith' was labelled *The Christian's Guide; or, the Holy Bible by Way of Question and Answer.* It was to fill about 250 sheets in folio, and each number was to contain three sheets and a large folio cut.

However specious some of the claims to learned authorship may have been, very few publishers of number books deliberately misled prospective customers in the matter of price. Certainly there was no very egregious deception in T. Read's notice about *The Several Love Letters that passed between a Nobleman and his Sister, under the borrowed Names of Silvia and Philander* (published every Monday during the first four months of 1735 at fourpence for four sheets in folio) for he merely observed, 'These Letters are so well known, and so much admired, that there is no need of saying any thing to recommend them at this time, but that this Edition will be much cheaper than any one yet published.' When the first number of *The Military History of his Serene Highness Prince Eugene of Savoy* was announced as published on Thursday, November 27, 1735, the sponsoring booksellers in London, Norwich, Peterborough, Dublin, and Exeter said that the total cost for the whole series of weekly one-shilling numbers would be 'about 2 £. 16s.' Earlier that same month T. Read advertised the first number of Thomas Burnet's *State of the Dead and of Departed Souls at the Resurrection*, stating clearly that it was to be continued in weekly numbers, forty-eight octavo pages for sixpence, 'till the whole is finish'd, which will be in 10 Weeks'. It would be surprising if there were no rogues among the publishers of number books in a century notorious for roguery; but the majority seem not to have tried offering a pig in a poke. The customer could blame no one but himself if he found that he was getting less than he bargained for.

Subscribers to books in fascicules might even get more than they bargained for. In some of the proposals and advertisements the publishers offered to supply gratis any issues that should prove necessary to complete a work if it went beyond the expected number of parts. In the *London and Country Journal* number 13 (March 27, 1739) was advertised *The Life and Reign of that excellent Princess Queen Elizabeth*; each of the thirty-nine twopenny numbers was to contain twelve quarto pages, and any additional numbers were to be supplied without charge. When H. Goreham advertised in *Rayner's London Morning Advertiser* number 1186¹ (September 15, 1742) that on the ensuing Saturday he would publish at twopence the first number of a work alluringly entitled *The Female Robbers. Or a General History of the Lives and Adventures of the most famous Highway-women, Pyratesses, Street-Robbers, Shop-lifters, &c.*, he said that the work would make one neat volume in twelves, adorned with cuts engraved by the best masters, and promised that 'if it exceeds above Fifteen Numbers the rest shall be given gratis'.

There were other special ways of attracting attention to a number book. Edward Cave's offer to rebate a share of the profits to the first thousand subscribers of the translation of du Halde's *Description* . . .

¹ Incorrectly numbered 117.

de la Chine (1735) was mentioned in the preceding chapter. No doubt it was supposed by the proprietors of *The Universal History* that dedicating it to the Duke of Marlborough would attract readers,[1] in much the same way as it was supposed a royal licence might. There were also enticements which could be effective only with particular books. In advertising the second volume[2] of *The Practising Scrivener* early in 1733 G. Bird pointed out that the fortnightly numbers would be so printed as to make each of the legal forms end with the sheet, in order that purchasers could have their books interleaved. The proprietors of *A New Method of Putting in Perspective all Natural Objects* (1734) declared that although the work was allowed by all who had seen it to be 'sufficient to instruct the meanest Capacities', some purchasers might find it difficult to master; for them—the ones who were meaner than the meanest—the author provided individual instruction free of charge. They had only to apply. A few authors or proprietors attempted to gain favour by attacking rival publications, as when Thomas Stackhouse labelled John Campbell's *History of the Bible* a 'Hodge-Podge', and Thomas Astley referred to other collections of voyages as 'Sorry Trash'.

Most of the efforts to promote sales by advertising and criticism were positive. The Preface to Astley's *New General Collection of Voyages and Travels*, Volume I, enumerated defects in other collections, but more energy and thought went into the positive claims of merit set forth in the printed proposals and on the title pages of the four large

---

[1] Several other works published in numbers were dedicated to high and mighty patrons. Dr. Richard Bundy dedicated his translation of *Histoire romaine*, by Catrou and Rouillé, to Frederick Prince of Wales. The successive volumes of *The Harleian Miscellany* were dedicated to George II, the Prince of Wales, the Duke of Marlborough, the Duke of Rutland, the Earl of Bath, the Earl of Dysart, the Earl of Chesterfield, and Lord Gower. The anonymous compiler of Astley's *New General Collection of Voyages and Travels* dedicated its four volumes to 'the Honourable Edward Vernon, Esq., vice-admiral of the Red, and Member of Parliament for Ipswich', 'the Honourable George Anson, Esq., Rear-Admiral of the White, One of the Lords of the Admiralty and Member of Parliament for Hedon in Yorkshire', 'His Grace John Duke of Bedford, First Lord-Commissioner of the Admiralty', and 'the Right Honourable Philip Dormer, Earl of Chesterfield'.

[2] An advertisement in the *Daily Advertiser* number 628 (February 3, 1733) stated that the 'other' volume would 'soon after follow'.

quarto volumes. These Proposals, as printed on the original blue
paper covers of the third number, dated December 3, 1743, have a
decidedly aggressive tone; at every point the high-pressure salesman
seems to be choosing the terms:

PROPOSALS

For Printing Weekly by Subscription; With His Majesty's Royal
Privilege and Licence (Gentlemen sending in their Names only) A New
General Collection of Voyages and Travels, more Copious, Methodical
and Accurate, than any hitherto published: Consisting of above Five
Hundred of the most esteemed Relations, (Many of them now first
Translated from Foreign Languages.) Being designed, Both to supply
the Imperfections of Dr. Harris's Collection, And continue it down to
this Time. The Whole interspersed with the most remarkable Expeditions, Sea Fights, Shipwrecks, Captivities, Escapes, and other
Entertaining Adventures, as well by Land as Sea; and Improved not
only with select Cuts, taken from the several Authors; and Charts and
Maps entirely new, accomodated to the Work; but also With so much
of Modern History and Geography, as may serve to illustrate the
present State of All Nations.

The 'conditions' which followed gave the usual details of weekly publication, and the prospective subscribers were left in no doubt where
the numbers could be obtained every Saturday morning:

Proposals are deliver'd, and Subscriptions taken in by Thomas
Astley, at the Rose in St. Paul's Church-Yard, London: Also by the
Booksellers at the two Universities of Oxford and Cambridge; and by
the Booksellers and Printers in all the Cities and noted Towns in
Great-Britain and Ireland.

To strengthen the impression that the work was important, Astley
printed on the verso of the title page of individual fascicules the full
text of the royal licence as issued in the King's name on October 18,
1743, by 'the Lords Justices Hardwicke, Grafton, Argyll, Tweed-
dale' and signed on their behalf by E. Weston. The 197-word description on the title pages of the four volumes is equally persuasive.

One of the most carefully studied efforts to 'soften' prospective
subscribers is seen in letters purporting to have come from readers of
Robert Walker's *Cambridge Journal, and Weekly Flying Post*. In spite of

its too-coaxing tone the letter from 'J.K.' in number 60 (November 9, 1745) urging Walker to publish John Foxe's *Book of Martyrs* in weekly numbers might almost be taken as genuine if it did not also appear in numbers 61 and 62. The shallowness of Walker's artifice is established by the fact that the letter —including its sanctimonious 'May God give a Blessing to the Undertaking' —had been used practically word for word as the Preface to Walker's edition of Foxe some four years earlier. An equally disingenuous epistle was printed in the *Cambridge Journal* number 63 (November 30, 1745). This time 'A.B.C.D. &c.' explained that he spoke for the members of a friendly group of country neighbours who made a practice of assembling once a week to discuss the articles in the Saturday paper. They had been particularly interested in the letter of 'J. K.' and were unanimous in the opinion that Foxe's book ought to be republished 'out of Hand; and the sooner the better'. Then came the writer's *coup de maître:* 'It is therefore our joint Request, that you will begin and publish this bloody History as soon as possible . . . .' One is not surprised to read in the very next number of the *Cambridge Journal* the detailed proposals for printing the 'bloody History' in weekly fascicules by subscription, with 'Cuts design'd to . . . represent the different Tortures they put several of the Martyrs to'.

In much better taste were the claims of merit advanced in the Preface to the first of the eight quarto volumes comprising *The Harleian Miscellany*, published in weekly numbers in 1744-1746. Most of the details were matters of fact intended to inform rather than persuade. It was promised that care would be taken to 'mingle Use and Pleasure through the whole Collection'. It was admitted that not every subject would be relished by every reader, but the buyer was assured that each number would 'repay his generous Subscription'. There is a quiet dignity in the justification offered for publishing the tracts from the Earl of Oxford's library:

Since the Advantages of preserving these small Tracts are so numerous; our Attempt to unite them in Volumes cannot be thought either useless or unseasonable; for there is no other Method of securing them from Accidents; and they have already been so long neglected, that this Design cannot be delayed, without hazarding the Loss of many Pieces, which deserve to be transmitted to another Age.

One further inducement to buy the weekly numbers of *The Harleian Miscellany* was the price. It was pointed out on the verso of the title page in the second volume, and presumably also on the covers of individual numbers, that many choice pieces which had never been sold separately under five, or ten, or twenty shillings would 'besides others in every Number, be sold as usual for One Shilling'.

The specific advantages of buying a book in numbers rather than in complete volumes were obvious enough without coercion or cajolery by the dealers: one paid for the fascicules only as they were delivered; the total price was in some cases less than would have been paid for other editions; unless the work was a reprint the fascicules reached purchasers sooner than the complete volumes did; often the opportunity was given of beginning at any time to take the numbers at regular intervals — it was not necessary for late starters to take a dozen back numbers all at once; some proprietors gave subscribers the option of taking a work in either weekly or monthly numbers as they preferred; invariably subscribers had the opportunity of getting odd numbers to complete their sets, and sometimes to replace faulty sheets with corrected ones free of charge; and the numbers, protected by blue paper covers, were easily obtained from many vendors, or were delivered promptly to those who entered their names as regular subscribers.

This last point was of the greatest importance, for any interruption in the delivery of the numbers at regular intervals would have been most inconvenient, if not disastrous. When delays were unavoidable, as when an intervening holiday made it impossible to keep to the regular day of publication, the proprietors — at least after 1732 — usually were careful to insert a notice in the newspapers.

In the matter of distributing fascicules it is easy to recognize that in the second quarter of the eighteenth century many proprietors counted on inducing a large number of regular subscribers to file their names and addresses either with one of the named proprietors or with an appointed agent. Others apparently looked to the 'Booksellers of

Town and Country' or to the street hawkers for their periodical turn-over. In the preceding chapter it was shown that occasionally the author himself, or the man who did the printing, undertook to distribute the numbers month by month or week by week; but the maximum success normally came to the congers or groups of interested proprietors who collectively provided wide coverage of London and Westminster, where most of the fascicules were sold. Something approaching the same widespread distribution could be achieved by a single proprietor who made particular arrangements with a selected group of retailers to handle the numbers. Wholesale distribution apparently remained in the hands of the proprietor, and if there were several sharers in a large enterprise local retailers presumably sent their orders to any one of the booksellers named in the proposals, in the advertisements, in the imprints of the individual numbers (if there were separate title pages), or on the blue paper covers. Each proprietor in a company would undoubtedly enjoy the profits from the sale of his share of the total number published, whether he disposed of them one by one or in quantities, and if he ran short he could buy odd copies from fellow-proprietors at a special rate.

Advertising was in the first instance a responsibility of the proprietors, though it is to be supposed that booksellers in the provincial towns paid at least part of the cost of advertisements in local newspapers. Many little shops in out of the way places doubtless kept a small stock of a few particular number books. For example, Mrs. Holloway in Salisbury Court, Fleet Street, advertised in the *London Spy Revived* number 246 (February 17, 1738) that she sold by wholesale or retail all sorts of ballads, histories, riddle-books, and added that her customers could get from her the works of Mr. Edward Ward, or any single number to complete their sets, and also *The History of the Bible by Way of Question and Answer*, in three octavo volumes, or any single number of the same. Local delivery to individual subscribers was nearly always undertaken by the retailers, to whom both in London and in rural districts the subscribers presumably sent their names. Yet the proposals of Thomas Lediard's *Naval History of England* (1734) announced that it was the publishers who would attend to the distribution:

For the Convenience of those who are desirous to read this History as it comes from the Press, five Sheets will be publish'd every Week, and punctually deliver'd by the Publishers, at the Places desir'd, for Six-pence.

Since the imprint on the completed volume (1735) is 'London: Printed for John Wilcox, at Virgil's Head, opposite the New Church, and Olive Payne, at Horace's Head, in Round Court, both in the Strand', it is to be assumed that only those two could be regarded as the publishers; but the dealers from whom proposals could be obtained and by whom subscriptions were taken in included also J. Wilford (behind the Chapterhouse in St. Paul's Churchyard), Mr. Mount (on Tower-hill), Mr. Macey (at the Hermitage-bridge), Mr. Eades (at King Edward's Stairs, Wapping), Mr. Brotherton and Mr. Whitridge (in Cornhill), Mr. Motte (at Temple-bar), Mr. Lewis (in Russel-street, Covent-garden), Mr. Stagg (in Westminster-hall), Mr. Jackson and Mr. Jolliffe (near St. James's), Mr. Brindley (in New Bond-street), and Lediard himself (at his House in Smith's square, Westminster). It is likely that the successive numbers could be purchased at any of these places.

Thomas Osborne made more elaborate arrangements for distributing the numbers of *The Harleian Miscellany* in 1744 and following years, as is clear from the list of forty-one booksellers in London—including Mr. Robinson, who handled 250 sets—and the much longer list of country booksellers. In this case the subscribers probably received their numbers through the nearest agent, but Osborne requested them to send their own names to him as 'Proprietor' or to Jacob Robinson, 'the Publisher', if they wished to be listed.

Many details concerning the distributing of weekly, fortnightly, and monthly numbers are explicitly recorded in newspaper advertisements and other contemporary documents. The notice in the *Daily Advertiser* number 531 (October 13, 1732) announcing the first of the sixteen fortnightly numbers of Edward Oakley's *Magazine of Architecture* invited each subscriber to 'enter his Name, Profession, and Place of Abode' so that the numbers might be delivered properly, and added that subscriptions would be taken in by Oakley himself, at the Three Doves in Brewers Street, Golden Square, by B. Creake, at the Red Bible in Ave Mary Lane, near St. Paul's, by W. Waring, at the Bible in Jermyn Street, St. James's, and by the booksellers of London and Westminster. John Marchant's appointment of Benjamin Cole and John Pelham to 'deliver out' the numbers of his *Exposition on the Books of the New Testament* was noticed in an earlier chapter. These two named agents presumably did all the wholesaling of this particular work, at least until Marchant assigned his copyright to R. Walker.[1]

Single proprietors naturally wished to enjoy maximum profits, but they usually saw the wisdom of appointing—and mentioning in the press—a larger number of retail agents than Marchant did. In J. Janeway's numerous advertisements of *The Lives . . . of the . . . Highwaymen and of the . . . Pirates* in 1733 and 1734 the prospective purchasers were told that they could begin to take the numbers at any time and could have them delivered by any of the news carriers or by any one of a dozen persons in the various branches of the bookselling business who were assisting him in the sale and distribution. The list shows that Janeway, whose own establishment was at the Golden Ball, near Water Lane, Fleet Street, was providing plenty of outlets for the Londoners who might be interested in getting weekly doses of criminal biography. Besides 'the Pamphlet-Sellers in Town and Country' there was a copper-plate printer (Mr. Wyatt, next the Vine Tavern in Long Acre); there was a bookbinder (Mr. Pool, at the Lamb in Houndsditch); there were three other booksellers (Mr. Shropshire, in New Bond Street, Mr. Payne, near the South Sea House, and Mr. Orpe, near Ram Tavern, Tooley Street); there were two printsellers (Mr. Dickenson, in the Strand, and Mr. Lye, near the India House, Leadenhall Street); and there were the following dealers whose precise business was not indicated: Mr. Clare, over against St. Andrew's Church, Holborn; Mr. Bell, in Long's Court, Leicester Fields; Mr. Phillmore, at the Three Compasses in Creed Lane, near St. Paul's; Mr. Hester, under Whitefriars Gate; Mr. Dean, in Spicer Street, Spittlefields; Mr. Kent, in George Street, Princess Street; and Mr. Amey, near George Tavern, Charing Cross. At these places proposals were given

[1] See above, p. 140.

gratis and subscriptions received. Janeway also made a particular point of inviting subscriptions by post, for his advertisements included the note that any person, 'by sending a Letter to the above Places', might have the numbers sent weekly according to directions, in either town or country. And to assure his customers near and far that their two-penny patronage was really a matter of personal concern to the proprietor, Janeway urged them to report any negligence on the part of the distributors:

If any of our Subscribers are neglected, and will please to send to J. Janeway by the Penny-Post, the Postage shall be allowed, and particular Care shall be taken for the Future.

As a result of this solicitude Janeway was able to report very early that the work was meeting 'more than common Encouragement'.

One of the most prolific proprietors of books in numbers, Robert Walker, had so many of these going at the same time that the local vendors must have had difficulty in keeping their circulation untangled. In his own *London and Country Journal*, which was accompanied by *The History of the Old and New Testament*, Walker found it necessary in number 28 (July 10, 1739) of this newspaper to reassure disgruntled customers, and incidentally to warn his delinquent agents, that he would personally see to it that in future his paper and its supplement would be delivered promptly to all subscribers:

Complaint having been made to me, that several of the Customers to this Work have not been regularly serv'd, I desire that if for the future the Person who serves these Parts should be negligent, and not punctually attend his Business, that my Subscribers will send me Word, and I will take Care they shall be serv'd by another.

Walker occasionally had to apologize for other irregularities in the delivery of numbers. On June 12, 1740, he placed at the head of the first column in his *London and Country Journal* a special note concerning an interruption in the established service:

We hope our Customers will excuse their being not regularly serv'd with their Books last Week; which was entirely owing to a Quarrel between the Coachmen who travel that Road: But we have taken such effectual Care, that no such Neglect shall happen for the future.

Walker's various notices in the *London and Country Journal* show that he had designated agents who attended to the distribution of his number books in the West country. Chief of these local vendors was Joseph Collett, 'the Person who serves the Cities of Bristol, Bath, Gloucester, &c. with the History of the Bible, the History of England, the Life and Reign of Queen Anne, &c.' A notice in the *London and Country Journal* number 70 (September 18, 1740) and the next two issues drew attention to Collett's change of location from next door to the Golden Heart on St. Phillips's Plain, Bristol, to the Sign of the Bible in Castle Street, where customers could be supplied with Bostock's Cordial, Daffey's Elixir, Ward's Pectoral Tincture, the Hippo Drops, Ointment for Piles, and 'any Books printed by R. Walker in London'. There is no doubt that Collett, and Thomas Moreman of Bath (who is mentioned in an earlier notice in Walker's paper), took full responsibility for the local delivery of numbers. A formal advertisement in the *London and Country Journal* number 43 (March 13, 1740) enumerated a dozen works 'published by Subscription Weekly', and urged all who desired to take in any of them to apply to 'their Friend, Jos. Collett', who said they could be assured of having any of the books delivered weekly at their own houses or wherever they should direct him to leave them.

Other publishers of number books made clear announcements of their agents' names and addresses to make it easy for the customers to enter the subscriptions or to pick up the fascicules regularly. Thus Claude Du Bosc, engraver, offering in weekly numbers at a shilling each a translation of Bernard's *Cérémonies et coutumes religeuses* to rival that published by Nicholas Prevost (1733) named nine other printsellers as his agents, giving full details of their addresses; and he announced that people living at a distance from London who found difficulty in procuring the weekly numbers punctually could 'treat with Mr. Du Bosc and have them deliver'd Monthly or Quarterly' as might suit their convenience.

When a work was published by a large number of proprietors —for example, *Acta Regia*, and *Biographia Britannica*[1] —there was seldom any necessity to designate additional vendors, though (as was pointed out earlier) it is by no means certain that all names in the imprint are those of financially interested proprietors. It is likely, none the less, that many retailers stocked number books in which they had no proprietary interest, and that Londoners could procure without difficulty at least the most reputable of the works published in fascicules.

It is of much interest to find that the record of books delivered to the customers of one retail bookseller in London has survived. The 'Gentleman's Ledger B' kept by Robert Gosling for the years 1730–1740[2] shows that many number books were charged to customers who had accounts at Gosling's shop, the Mitre and Crown, against St. Dunstan's Church, Fleet Street. Folio 32 of this unique document shows that on April 1, 1731, Henry Lussan, Esq., was charged four shillings for numbers 88, 89, 90, 91 of *Magna Britannia*, and two days later was sent number 92. On November 1, 1735, John Phillips bought both folio volumes of Rapin's *History of England* in quires, together with the forty-two Heads of Kings and the 'sett of Monuments' which the Knaptons had engaged George Vertue to design and engrave to go with Tindal's translation of Rapin. Phillips was charged two guineas for the text, one guinea for the Heads of Kings, 12s. 6d. for the Monuments, and an extra ten shillings for having the two volumes bound and lettered. During the next two years another customer, Thomas Dowse, Junior, was charged £1. 11s. for 31 numbers of 'Military History', £1. 9s. for 29 numbers of the second volume of this same work, 2s. 6d. each for sewing these two volumes in boards, with leather back, and an extra shilling for a missing number in the

---

[1] On Friday, March 8, 1745, the Earl of Egmont recorded in his diary a variety of experiences:

Went to the Bank of England and bought 250£. stock in 3 per cent annuities, 1726. Called at Knapton's shop in Paul's Churchyard and bespoke *Bibliotheca Britannica*. Went at night to Hendel's oratorio called 'Sampson'.

See R. A. Roberts (ed.), *Manuscripts of the Earl of Egmont. Diary of the First Earl of Egmont (Viscount Percival)*, III (London: H. M. Stationery Office, 1923), p. 309. His Grace was undoubtedly referring to *Biographia Britannica*. Samuel Johnson made the same kind of mistake in referring to the work as *Bibliographia Britannica*.

[2] Bodleian MS. Eng. Misc. c. 296.

first volume. On September 6, 1736, the Rev. Mr. Church was charged 10s. 6d. for '3 nos. of Universal History Viz^t 1. 2. 3. 3^d voll.'; and in 1739 (July 6 and November 30) Edward Fleming, Esq., purchased five numbers of the fifth volume of the same work.

One of Gosling's heaviest buyers of books, both in numbers and in complete volumes, was Thomas Dowse, Senior, who bought odd numbers of Rapin's *History of England* and *Acta Regia* in 1738, but did not pay for these and for 148 numbers of Bayle's *Dictionary* until October 14, 1741, by which time Dowse's bill amounted to £ 87. 4s. 9d. Presumably scores of booksellers kept similar accounts, though ordinarily the numbers were sold strictly for cash. It was expected that every number would be paid for on delivery, and J. Wilford was only following the regular practice when he stated in the proposals of *The History of . . . Jesus Christ*, dated October 29, 1734, that, 'As no money is desired before the Delivery of the Numbers, so none will be deliver'd on Trust.' Prominent Londoners who were regular subscribers doubtless made special arrangements for getting the numbers 'on Trust', and it is unlikely that such men as the Earl of Chesterfield or the Earl of Egmont would be required to pay sixpence a week for the books they both bought in numbers.

It must have been difficult to keep track of all the copies distributed in the provincial towns, even when country subscribers were served by local dealers. In spite of the fact that prompt delivery and collection of the weekly subscription must have taxed the wits of all who were involved, there is no doubt that a substantial part of the trade in numbers was with customers living outside London. One or two publishers apparently had two separate publication days, one for city subscribers, the other for country folk, though it is not clear why that was necessary, nor which of the two was the earlier. An advertisement of Batty Langley's *Principles of Antient Masonry* in the *Daily Advertiser* number 609 (January 12, 1733) indicated that the first number of this enormous work, printed on Royal paper, would be published and delivered to subscribers 'On Monday the 15th, and Saturday the 20th Instant', and that the subsequent numbers would continue to appear on those two days each week. No provincial dealers are named in the advertisement or in the imprint on the title page of the complete work (1736).

In the attempt to estimate the extent of the distribution of number books one may study with profit the lists of subscribers bound in with some copies on present-day library shelves. It is conceivable that some of these lists may have been padded for effect, but there is strong reason to believe that the lists were more often incomplete. The long list of subscribers to the first volume of Herman Moll's *Atlas Geographus* (published monthly for several years beginning in May 1708) includes names and addresses of many persons living in provincial towns —among them Samuel Johnson's father, who was a bookseller in Lichfield. But in listing the 761 subscribers (including, by the way, Hans Sloane and Alexander Pope) the proprietors insisted that they were enumerating only the subscribers whose names had been sent in.

Note: Those that are omitted (for we are informed several were sent that never came to our Hand) shall be inserted when Asia comes out, if they please to send them.

It is perfectly clear that local dealers had the responsibility of supplying customers in their own regions with the successive numbers of *Atlas Geographus*, for the London proprietors repeatedly urged the provincial booksellers to send in the names of people who regularly took the numbers. Later in the century Thomas Astley listed 1048 subscribers to the first volume of his *New General Collection of Voyages and Travels* (with general title page dated 1745), and added 69 names when Volume II was completed; but he said the list was not complete:

N.B. Notwithstanding our repeated Request to the Booksellers in the Country and others, to send in their Lists of Subscribers, we have as yet been able to procure scarce half of them, which we hope will be our Excuse to those worthy Subscribers who do not find their Names in our List.

Lists in Volumes III and IV, however, added only 92 names, but these included two local dealers, Mr. Micklewright of Reading, who took 10 sets, and Mr. Jonathan Moore of Newport in the Isle of Wight, who took 12 sets.

It is difficult to reach even a reasonably close conjecture concerning

the total circulation of Astley's *Voyages*, for among the 1048 names in
the first list are the following:

Mr. Peter Brown, Bookseller in Bristol	25 Sets
Mr. Martyn Bryson, Bookseller in Newcastle	50 Sets
Mr. Charles Hitch, Bookseller in London	50 Sets
Mrs. Martha Lewis, Bookseller in Bristol	106 Sets
Mr. William Miller, Bookseller in Edinburgh	25 Sets
Mrs. Sarah Newton, Bookseller in Manchester	25 Sets
Mr. John Rivington, Bookseller in London	75 Sets.

There were a few other subscribers who took two or three sets each,
among them His Excellency General Oglethorpe (two sets), but one
cannot simply add all these extra copies (350–375 sets) to the total
represented by the other names, for in all probability many of the
individuals named in the list were among those served by local dealers
who handled twenty-five or more sets. Mr. Brown and Mrs. Lewis of
Bristol between them distributed 131 sets of the numbers in Volume I;
but Astley listed 77 individual subscribers as living in Bristol, all of
them doubtless served by one or other of the two dealers in that city.

Alphabetical lists of subscribers are bound with copies of several
other works published in numbers, among them George Bickham's
*The British Monarchy: Or, a New Chorographical Description of all the Do-
minions Subject to the King of Great Britain* (1743 and following years),
Francis Blomefield's *History of . . . Norfolk* (1736 and following years),
Richard Bundy's translation of *The Roman History* (1728–1737), De
Coetlogon's *Universal History of Arts and Sciences* (1741 and following
years), Demetrius Cantemir's *History of the Othman Empire* (1734–
1735), *The Harleian Miscellany* (1744–1746), William Maitland's
History of London (1737–1739), John Mottley's *Survey of . . . London
and Westminster* (1733–1734), the third edition of John Strype's
Annals of the Reformation of the Church of England (1735), Tillemont's
Ecclesiastical Memoirs (1733–1735), and J. Wilford's *Memorials and
Characters* (1739–1741). All of these lists, and particularly the last
two, show that subscribers to number books included people of every
level of society from the lowliest to the loftiest—bishops, earls, university professors, curates, members of the Royal Society, country

squires, lawyers, librarians, schoolmasters, organists, grocers, joiners, silversmiths, surgeons, druggists, cheese-factors, lightermen—and the total number of individual English men and women in one list of subscribers or another reaches into the tens of thousands. They represent a substantial cross section of the nation. If Mrs. Jennings of the Old Bailey, London, appears among the subscribers to Wilford's *Memorials and Characters*, so also do the Archbishop of Canterbury, the Warden of Manchester College, and a distinguished Professor of Botany at Cambridge University. Books published in numbers were sent to some of the finest dwellings in England as well as to the poorest. They reached the hands of Alexander Pope and Dr. Pepusch, of Richard Savage and Samuel Johnson; they were delivered to Viscount Torrington, to the Rev. Dr. Knight, Prebendary of Ely, to Abraham Fowler, Esq., Gentleman Gaoler of the Tower of London, to Mrs. Jones, at a Boarding School for young Ladies, at Stepney, and to Her Grace the Duchess Dowager of St. Albans; they even crossed the sea in ships and were put ashore in Jamaica and New England. Fascicules found favour everywhere.

CHAPTER VII

FOR EVERY TASTE AND POCKET

Thus far the financial gains and the mechanism of producing and vending books in fascicules have been discussed. It is now time to consider
in what senses the customers may be said to have profited by being
able to buy books piecemeal. Did the customers really get their
money's worth? Are any of the books published in parts in Fielding's
time worth reading now, or were they all 'folio lumps'? Did the
number-book trade really extend or improve the reading habits of
Englishmen two hundred years ago? 'One of the peculiarities which
distinguish the present age is the multiplication of books', Johnson
wrote in his eighty-fifth 'Idler' essay (December 1, 1759). 'Every day
brings new advertisements of literary undertakings', he went on,
'and we are flattered with repeated promises of growing wise on
easier terms than our progenitors.' Had this superfetation any lasting
cultural significance?

Many of the works Johnson had in mind were compilations, and although he did not feel that all of them were useless he said that their
effect was seldom of any long duration. That could be said of most
books published in any generation, and it is no reflection on the contemporary usefulness of number books to say that most of them
deserved the oblivion into which they sank before their first purchasers
had passed away. They were useful in their time. Johnson himself wrote
in 1741 (in the Proposals for printing Dr. James's *Medicinal Dictionary*),
'It is doubtless of Importance to the Happiness of Mankind, that whatever is generally useful should be generally known; and he therefore
that diffuses Science, may with Justice claim, among the Benefactors to
the Public, the next Rank to him that improves it.' If all the works
published in fascicules by the middle of the eighteenth century were
gathered into one place the heap would be vast indeed; if all were
removed which have ceased to be valuable except as curiosities, the
sizable heap would be reduced to a five-foot shelf. *Habent sua fata libelli*,
one might say; yet *'libelli'* is hardly the appropriate word, for when the

fascicules were put together into complete volumes they bulked too large to be labelled with a diminutive term. A twelve-pound book is no '*libellus*'.

For some of the number books impressive bulk is perhaps the only merit which could ever have been claimed, and the kindest dismissal one can give them is to suggest that their usefulness as articles of furniture would not have been materially affected if the pages had all been left blank. It would be easy to let oneself be cynically facetious and say that weekly and monthly numbers were doubtless more convenient for wrapping fish and for other humble uses than ordinary books must have been; but such purposes could be better served by newspapers and supplements, the paper of which was only ordinary newsprint. The number books were generally well printed on superior paper. It is not necessary to take the word of the advertisers, who in the 1730's and 1740's frequently drew attention to the 'fine Dutch Paper and good Letter', or declared that the work proposed would be 'beautifully and correctly printed'. Surviving copies of number books show that in many of them — both reprints and first editions — the paper and presswork were of high quality. In this respect there are surprisingly few number books as bad as Blomefield's *History of Norfolk* (printed in his rectory at Fersfield), Purbeck's *History of the Turkish Empire*, Charles Jenkins' *England's Triumph*, Tindal's *History of Essex*, and the wretchedly printed *Life, Adventures, and Many and Great Vicissitudes of Fortune of Simon, Lord Lovat, the Head of the Family of Frasers, from His Birth at Beaufort, near Inverness, in the Highlands of Scotland, 1668, to the Time of his being taken by Capt. Millar after three Days Search, in a hollow Tree, on the Coasts of Knoidart and Arisaig* (1746). This last book, printed for John Threkeld, near St. Paul's, is a word-for-word reprinting, on bad paper and battered type, of the Rev. Archibald Arbuthnot's strongly anti-Jacobite work which Robert Walker had just published in twelve numbers. Probably the worst of the number books have not survived, but surely there cannot have been many less prepossessing than the seventy-nine dingy little half-sheet fascicules of a book printed for R. Offtey, next St. Sepulchre's Church, in 1744. It bore the title *An Impartial History of the Life and Reign of her Late Majesty Queen Anne of*

Immortal Memory: Wherein all the Transactions of that Memorable Period are faithfully compiled from the Best Authorities. It was one of the three or four biographies of Queen Anne which were issued in numbers, none of the others being quite so pathetically bad as this one. It has incredible flaws of workmanship. If it dazzled the eyes of chambermaids it was only because the print showed through from the other side of the paper. Either Offtey was short of the roman capital E or he had a personal preference for the ones that lean, for he frequently (not invariably) used the italic capital *E* with letters of the other font. The work was 'adorn'd' with several 'curious Cuts' —and 'curious' (in our modern colloquial sense) is the right word to describe them. 'Never was a history . . . [so] full of surprising events', said the writer of the Preface, 'nor cuts better adapted to the history . . . .' It is true; the cuts are a perfect match for the surprisingly bad history. The plate delivered with number 18 shows 'The Taking and Plundering Port St. Mary's, where the Soldiers got drunk, ravish'd the Nuns, &c.' What shocking brutality must lurk behind that '&c.'! The little that shows in the picture is feeble enough. The cut of 'The Taking of Gibraltar' in number 48 is like that used to illustrate a broadside ballad. Most 'curious' of all is the using of identical portraits for more than one person. The cut marked 'Philip of Spain' in number 11 appears in number 34 with the label 'Charles VI. Emperor of Germany'; and in other numbers it was easy to alter the superscription 'The Illustrious John, Duke of Marlborough' when the same portrait was used for 'The Illustrious James, Duke of Ormond'. One cannot help feeling that the cut was standard equipment in Offtey's shop, ready to be used for any illustrious duke whose portrait was called for in the copy. There were other tawdry efforts at elegance among the number books, but none so feebly pretentious as this.

The list of works excellently printed on fine paper is much longer. Demetrius Cantemir's *History of the Othman Empire*, Whiston's *Josephus*, Tillotson's *Works*, and Ralegh's *History of the World* are just four out of a hundred works that could take their place —and indeed have taken their place —alongside the best standard pieces of presswork from the eighteenth century.

Neither bulk nor good presswork is evidence of enduring quality in the intellectual substance of number books. If few of the early number books can still be read with profit it is mainly because most of them fall into Thomas De Quincey's category of literature of knowledge rather than that of power, and they have simply become outmoded by the progress of knowledge itself. In their time many of them served a useful purpose, and that is as true of reprints, compilations, abridgments, and translations as it is of first editions, since the fact that a particular book has been printed before is as likely to indicate its usefulness as is the fact that another one is printed for the first time. Instead of condemning the scriptural commentaries, histories of England, and books of travel as superficial and unscholarly, one should recognize that in the eyes of readers who had had no books at all these things, in cheap weekly parts, had a value in the eighteenth century which would be less in the twentieth century only because cheap books are now on every counter. The number books were not usually compounded of the precious life-blood of master spirits. For that matter, few books of any age are.

To us in the twentieth century there is nothing strange in the fact that quite ordinary persons are able and willing to buy excellent books reasonably well printed at prices considerably lower than those charged for a haircut, an adequate meal, or an evening of films at the cinema. It is curious to find that two centuries ago some consternation was expressed both at the novelty of books in fascicules and at the unprecedented interest in reading shown by those not reckoned as belonging to the 'polite' part of town. Just when both of these phenomena were becoming noticeable there appeared in the *Grub-Street Journal* number 247 (September 19, 1734) a vigorous protest against publishing books in small, inexpensive portions. In a communication signed 'B.T.' the complaint was made that poor people were actually so eager for learning that they went without food and clothing to buy number books. In the fiery terms that usually distinguish this outspoken journal the correspondent denounced what he called the current 'national *Insania* in Learning', which he said was 'never more diffusive and petulant than at this Juncture':

Amongst several Monstrosities, I take notice of that strange Mad-
ness of publishing Books by piece-meal, at six or twelve Pennyworth a
Week. Translations of Greek, Latin, and French Authors, are retailed
after this Manner. You have Bayle's *Dictionary* and Rapin's *History* from
two Places, with the daily Squabbles of Book-sellers and Translators
about them. The Bible can't escape. I bought, the other Day, three
Pennyworth of the Gospel, made easy and familiar to Porters, Carmen,
and Chimney-Sweepers: But how? Why, by Scraps taken out of
Grotius, Hammond, &c. One that runs may read and understand the
Scriptures with such extraordinary Helps. They are publishing
Burkit[t]'s *expository Notes* in the same Way.

Then, in answer to the hypothetical question raised by 'some sensible
and Religious Author or Bookseller' why the common people should
be kept in ignorance of things necessary to their eternal salvation or
tending to the improvement of their minds, merely because they
happen not to have money enough to buy a book in folio at once,
'B.T.' became ironic:

Let them know the History of their own Country from Rapin; and
that of all other Ages and Nations from Raleigh. It nearly concerns
them to inform themselves of the *Antiquities of the Jews* from Josephus;
and of the Opinions of Men in Politics and Philosophy from Mr. Bayle.
Well, what an Age of Wit and Learning have I the happiness to live
in! In which so many Persons in the lowest Stations of Life, are more
intent upon cultivating their Minds, than upon feeding and cloathing
their Bodies. You shall see a Fellow spend Six-pence upon a Number
of Rapin, or Three-pence upon a Bit of St. Matthew's Gospel, when
perhaps his Wife and Children want a Bit of Bread, and himself a Pair
of Breeches. I used to think that nineteen in twenty of the Species were
designed by Nature for Trade and Manufactures; and that to take
them off to read Books, was the Way to do them Harm, to make them,
not wiser or better, but impertinent, troublesome, and factious.

'B.T.' was certainly no very gracious patron of literature for the masses.
We now can see that he was far behind the times. What would he have
said had he foreseen that a little more than a century later the English
people would regularly buy 50,000 copies of the monthly parts of
Vanity Fair, and that two centuries later ordinary readers would buy
'pocket' books literally by the million?

With his curious disdain of popular culture in mind, one is startled to find the explosive correspondent of the *Grub-Street Journal* going on to complain that these number-book translations were inaccurate. To be sure, for porters, carmen, and chimney-sweepers 'it's no Matter how Books are translated'; but none the less the work displeased the critic. Those who compared the translations with the originals found incredible instances of negligence and stupidity, said 'B.T.'

. . . and no Wonder, when Booksellers and Compositors turn Authors and Editors. The Publishers of Rapin, if they were not the Beginners of all this, have at least brought it into vogue. Their gains are so great, that others are still encouraged to undertake something; and I am credibly informed that the Knaptons will get 8 or 10,000 £ by that History. And yet upon Trial I find the Translation a very ordinary one; and that the Translator seems not to understand either French or English well enough for such an undertaking.

'B.T.' goes on to condemn such indefatigable translators as Nicholas Tindal and Thomas Stackhouse—though not naming them—as 'poor founder'd Hackneys . . . hurried on by the Booksellers, thro' thick and thin, and forc'd to perform their Stage within the Time prefixed'. This solicitude for accuracy in translation is hardly consistent with the correspondent's disparaging remarks on lowly readers and on the books which they indiscreetly bought in vast number—remarks which would perhaps carry more weight if it had not been the practice of the *Grub-Street Journal* to print display advertisements of the despised number books, including the very translation of Rapin so severely censured by 'B.T.'

There is no need to labour the point that works published in fascicules before 1750 had their value for many readers in their own century. Some of them still have value. It is unlikely that any twentieth-century poet will be moved to write oriental eclogues, as William Collins was, by reading Salmon's account of Persia in his *Modern History*; but the recent interest in the history of science confers a certain present-day usefulness on Baddam's abridgment of the Royal Society's *Transactions* from 1665 to 1735, and many a historian of our time would be glad to own both *Acta Regia* and *The Harleian Miscellany*.

Some of those old works still bring high prices in the book market: Elizabeth Blackwell's *Curious Herbal*, the six volumes of *Biographia Britannica*, and Herrera's *History of . . . America* stand in the dealers' catalogues at figures much higher than many other books published at the same time. Edward Ward's *London Spy*, James Gibbs's *Rules for Drawing the Several Parts of Architecture*, and portions of George Bickham's *Universal Penman* have been reprinted in the twentieth century. The criminal biographies compiled by Alexander Smith and Charles Johnson still make fascinating reading. Stackhouse's *History of the Bible* is among the titles in Everyman's Library. John Mottley's *New Survey of . . . London and Westminster* is not the only eighteenth-century number book still on the open shelves in the great circular reading room of the British Museum.

A few years ago it was suggested in a study of the economic history of the book trade in England that publishing in numbers did not become so common in the eighteenth century as publishing 'by subscription', and that the reason was the paucity of suitable material.[1] In the period here under examination publishing 'by subscription' was still, as formerly, a means of guaranteeing sales by the simple expedient of requiring part of the total price in advance, the rest to be paid on the delivery of the complete work. The truth is that the phrase 'published by subscription' was also regularly used to designate the issuing of works in weekly or monthly fascicules, though normally no money was paid in advance when the subscribers entered their names to receive the successive numbers. In fact, the books published in fascicules were often called 'subscription books'. As for the alleged lack of acceptable material, it is obvious from the list in Appendix B at the end of this book that there was plenty of choice for all levels of society. There were biographies, histories, books of travel, encyclopedias, commentaries on Holy Writ, translated Latin classics, collections of songs, treatises on mathematics, topography, astronomy, architecture, officinal herbs, painting, calligraphy—what not? If *Joe Miller's Jests, Refin'd and Improv'd* (1746) was among them, so also was James Pater-

[1] Marjorie Plant, *The English-Book Trade. An Economic History of the Making and Sale of Books* (London: George Allen & Unwin, 1939), p. 233.

son's *Complete Commentary . . . on Milton's Paradise Lost* (1744). People who did not care for Archibald Arbuthnot's *Memoirs of the Remarkable Life and Surprizing Adventures of Miss Jenny Cameron* (1746) could get the works of Dr. Isaac Barrow, Master of Trintity College, Cambridge, and teacher of Isaac Newton; those who spurned *The Wood-Lark, a Collection of Songs, Cantatas, Airs* (1744), could perhaps find pleasure in reading *An Authentic Journal of the late Expedition under the Command of Commodore Anson*, by John Philips, midshipman of the *Centurion* (1744). There was something for every taste, whether the readers lived in Ratcliff Highway or in Lambeth Palace.

One of the most convincing pieces of contemporary evidence that books published in fascicules were numerous and diversified is to be seen in a list printed in the supplement to the *Gentleman's Magazine* for 1744. The list, headed 'Books publish'd periodically, January 1745', with sub-heading 'State of Periodical Publications, at London, Weekly', shows that a large number of London's most reputable publishers were using in the aggregate vast quantities of paper every week in order to satisfy a popular demand strong enough to provide a market simultaneously for five different travel books, four separate histories of England, three treatises in geography, and eight other varied works including a medical dictionary, *The Harleian Miscellany*, the works of Dr. Isaac Barrow, a curious treatise by the versatile Dr. James Parsons, and an appendix to the Greek Thesaurus—all of these issued in fascicules. Here is the list, with italics and capitals as in the original:

> *State of Periodical Publications, at* London,
> *Weekly.*
>
> I. *James's* Medicinal Dictionary, No. CLI.
> 1*s. T. Osborne, Roberts.*
>
> II. *Rapin's* history of *England,* translated
> by *Tindall,* No. LVIII 4 sheets, in folio pr. 6*d.*
> *Knapton.*
>
> III. A new general collection of voyages
> and travels, No. LIX. three sheets in 4to. or
> two sheets with a map, pr. 6*d. Astley.*

IV. *Salmon's* modern history, or present
state of all nations, No. LIII. 4 sheets in folio
6*d*. *Longman, Hitch*, and five more.

V. A complete system of geography, being a description of all the countries of the
known world; illustrated with 70 maps, new
drawn and engraved, 4 sheets 6*d*. No. XLV.
Innys, Knapton, and 16 more.

VI. The works of Dr *Isaac Barrow*, published by Dr *John Tillotson*. No. XLVIII.
in Folio, 6 sheets, one week, 5 sheets another,
6*d*. *Millar, Tonson, Roberts*.

VII. A new general history of *England*,
from the invasion of *J. Cæsar*, to the death
of k. *George* I. down to the revolution, by
W. Guthrie, Esq; and from the revolution,
by another hand. No. XLV. 3 sheets Folio
for 6*d*. *Waller*.

VIII. A collection of voyages and travels,
formerly printed by *Churchill*, Illustrated
with above 300 maps and cuts, curiously engraven on copper, No. LXXVI, LXXVII,
being the 35th and 36th numbers in Vol. 2,
Lintot, J. Osborne.

IX. Dr *Harris's* complete collection of
voyages and travels, illustrated with charts,
maps and cuts, No. XXXVI. 4 sheets 6*d*.
or with a map, 3 sheets, the whole to make
2 volumes in Folio. *Woodward, Browne*,
and 14 more.

X. *Harleian* miscellany a collection of
scarce tracts and pamphlets, found in the
late earl of *Oxford's* library, No. IV. Vol.
4. *T. Osborne*. 1*s*.

XI. The history of *England*, during the
reigns of K. *Wm*, Q *Anne* and K. *George* the
first, being a supplement to *Rapin, Guthrie,
Eachard*, &c. illustrated and adorn'd with
heads, maps, &c. to be delivered to subscri-

bers gratis, No. XXXVI. 3 sheets in Folio, 6*d. Waller.*

XII. The continuation of Mr *Rapin de Thoyras's* history of England, containing the reigns of K. *Wm,* Q_*Mary,* Q_. *Anne* and K. *George* I, illustrated with heads of kings, queens, and eminent persons, engraved by Mr *Houbraken;* also whole sheet maps, plans of battles, medals and other copper plates beautifully engraved. No. XXXVI. 4 sheets 6*d. Knapton.*

XIII. The theatre of the present war in the *Netherlands,* and upon the *Rhine.* No. XVII. Price 3*d. Brindley, Corbet.*

XIV. Travels into the inland parts of *Africa:* containing a description of the several nations for six hundred miles up the river *Gambia;* with an accurate map of that river, and ten other copper plates. The whole about fourteen numbers, at 4*d.* each. *Collyer.*

XV. Geography methodized: Or, a new system of General Geography, augmented with several necessary branches omitted by *Gordon* and former authors, whose errors and defects are pointed out and rectify'd. In nine numbers, at 4*d.* each *Collyer.*

XVI. Memoirs of a man of quality. Giving an account of many surprizing adventures, in his travels thro' *England, France, Germany, Turkey, Spain, Portugal* and *Italy.* The whole about fifteen numbers, at 4*d.* each. *Collyer.*

XVII. Polite tales for young gentlemen and ladies, from the most celebrated authors, prose and verse. By a lady. 4 sheets 6*d.* No. X. *Bickerton.*

XVIII. An appendix to the *Greek Thesaurus* of *H. Stephens,* and the *Greek Lexicons* of *Constantine* and *Scapula;* by *Daniel Scot,* L.L.D. No. XXX. *Noon,* 1*s.* 6*d.*

XIX. Political cabinet, No. VI. for *December*, which concludes Vol. I. *Roberts* 1s.

XX. The microscopical theatre of seeds, by *James Parsons*, M.D. F.R.S. No. VI.

Even a list so comprehensive as this does not exhaust the categories of number books. No mention is made, for instance, of the threepenny numbers of *Universal Harmony; or, the Gentleman and Lady's Social Companion*, published by Jacob Robinson late in 1744. This and a dozen other collections of songs issued in weekly or monthly numbers before 1750 were designed to provide agreeable entertainment in the form of vocal music during a period which is often referred to as the dark age of music in England.

'Agreeable entertainment', however, is a very loose term. Presumably all number books were printed with the hope of satisfying some interest or other. One man's meat is another man's poison. From the point of view of a man like Samuel Johnson there was indubitably some poison in the pabulum provided by number books published in Johnson's first years in London, though many of them were respectable enough. The man who admitted that he was insensible to the power of music would not be interested in the collections of songs just mentioned, and he would probably look with disdain (if anything) upon *The Ladies Miscellany; or travelling Adventures* (sold at Furnivall's Inn Coffee-House at a shilling per number in 1737). As a newcomer to London he would be eager to look into *The History, Antiquities, and present State of the Cities of London, Westminster, &c.*, by William Maitland, F.R.S. (published in shilling numbers in 1737). He may never have bothered to look at the Rev. Francis Blomefield's *Essay towards a topographical History of the County of Norfolk*, though his own pseudo-antiquarian *Marmor Norfolciense* of 1739 shows that he counted on the current interest in the researches of local historians to make his *jeu d'esprit* against Walpole seem authentic.[1] His feeling for history may

[1] Johnson's antiquarian interest was genuine enough, as Boswell frequently points out. When Johnson, on Thursday, October 19, 1769, urged Boswell to proceed with the collections he was making on the antiquities of Scotland, he said, 'Make a large book; a folio.' Boswell asked of what use it would be. Johnson replied, 'Never mind the use; do it.'

have led him to glance at *The History and Antiquities of Northamptonshire*, by John Bridges (in shilling numbers published by S. Gibbons in 1739). As the author of a tragedy based on a Turkish story he would certainly have noticed Demetrius Cantemir's *History of the Othman Empire* (published monthly in twenty-one folio numbers in 1735–36). His biographical interests would lead him to explore the Rev. Arthur Jones's *Lives of the most Ancient Philosophers* (published in sixpenny numbers in 1737),[1] *The Historical and Biographical Memoirs* 'from the French of Brantom' (published by J. Critchley in threepenny numbers in 1741), and *Biographia Britannica; or, the Lives of the most eminent Persons who have flourished in Great Britain and Ireland from the earliest Ages down to the present Times* (published in weekly numbers, three sheets each, by Innys, Longman, and others, beginning in 1745). The last named, indeed, Johnson had an opportunity of editing when a second edition was proposed.

How many of these and other number books Johnson actually set eyes upon is of course not known; he cannot have missed seeing them in the booksellers' shops and in the hands of the persons who hawked newspapers and pamphlets. To some of them he may well have felt attracted. His name stands in the list of subscribers to Lediard's continuation of Rapin's *History of England* (Volume III, 1737), and he owned Chambers' *Cyclopædia* in the number-book edition of 1741.[2] According to Boswell, Dr. Adam Smith once observed that Johnson 'knew more books than any man alive'. He was fond of reading sermons, and as he came to have a high regard for those of Dr. Samuel Clarke it would not have displeased Johnson to see in the *Champion; or Evening Advertiser* number 378 (April 20, 1742) an announcement that the first number of Clarke's *Sermons* had just been published.

[1] According to Boswell, Johnson himself had some thoughts of preparing a work dealing with the 'Lives of the Philosophers, written with a polite air, in such a manner as may divert as well as instruct', and another comprising 'Lives of Illustrious Persons, as well of the active as the learned, in imitation of Plutarch'. These were among the projects mentioned in the list Johnson gave to Bennet Langton. See L. F. Powell's revised edition of *Boswell's Life of Johnson* (Oxford: Clarendon Press, 1934, 1950), IV, p. 381, n. 1.
[2] Boswell quotes Stockdale's report that Johnson would like to have edited a second edition of this voluminous work in 1774. See L. F. Powell, *op. cit.*, II, p. 203, n. 3.

Boswell transcribed the resolves Johnson recorded in his journal on July 13, 1755, 'to read the Scriptures methodically with such helps as are at hand', and 'to read books of Divinity, either speculative or practical' —which perhaps indicates that Johnson had *not* dipped into Stackhouse's *Compleat Body of Speculative and Practical Divinity* (reprinted in weekly numbers in 1742) and the numerous commentaries, all issued in numbers, by Matthew Henry, John Gill, Robert Jameson, John Marchant, Samuel Humphreys, and 'S. Smith, D.D.' Johnson's interests were multifarious, and it is not improbable that he glanced with considerable interest at such things as Albinus's *Anatomical Tables* (1747), *Acta Germanica* (1744), and Thomas Salmon's *Present State of the Universities and the five adjacent Counties* (1743). In these and some others Johnson would doubtless have found 'agreeable entertainment'; a good many of the less erudite ones he would certainly have thought too thin and dull to bother with. It is not hard to draw a line between the number books which Johnson could have enjoyed and those he would not have endured.

It adds interest to the history of number books that Johnson himself had a hand in the preparation of two of them, and that the second edition of his own great *Dictionary* was sold in numbers in 1755.[1] He helped to write the Proposals (dated June 24, 1741) of Dr. Robert James's *Medicinal Dictionary*, which began to appear in February 1742, also writing the Dedication to Dr. Richard Mead and at least one of the articles in the work itself—the account of Dr. Herman Boerhaave earlier printed in the *Gentleman's Magazine*. Johnson also wrote the Proposals (dated November 1, 1742) for the catalogue of the Earl of Oxford's great library, which Thomas Osborne had purchased for £13,000, and Boswell states that it was Johnson who wrote for this catalogue 'the Latin accounts of the books'. The first two volumes of *Bibliotheca Harleiana; or, a Catalogue of the Library of the Late Earl of Oxford* were to be sold to subscribers for a total price of ten shillings, half to be paid at the time of subscribing and the rest on delivery of the two

[1] See Philip Babcock Gove, 'Notes on Serialization and Competitive Publishing: Johnson's and Bailey's Dictionaries, 1755', *Oxford Bibliographical Society Proceedings and Papers*, V (1936-39), [305]-322.

volumes 'some Time in February next'. But Osborne decided also to issue the catalogue in weekly parts, as is explained in the final paragraph of 'An Account of the Harleian Library' attached to the Proposals of the catalogue:

> As it is imagined that the approaching Sale of so great and eminent a Collection will excite, in an uncommon Degree, the Curiosity of the Public, it is intended not only to receive Subscriptions, as already mentioned, but to publish this Catalogue in Twelve Numbers, by five Sheets a Week, at One Shilling each Number, of which the first will be delivered on Saturday the Fourth of December.[1]

This octavo catalogue was continued in three subsequent volumes, but it was explained in the Preface to the first of the three additional volumes that it had proved to be impracticable to prepare annotations as originally planned without 'more hands than could be procured, or more time than the necessity of a speedy sale would allow'.

Presently Osborne decided to reprint some of the pamphlets and manuscripts themselves. Proposals were prepared for distribution and also published in the *Gentleman's Magazine* for December 1743, announcing that six sheets would be published for a shilling every Saturday morning beginning March 24, 1744, no money being required until each number was delivered. This work was continued with great success for two years, the last number of the eighth volume being published by March 25, 1746. The whole work, including the thirty-nine numbers (168 pages) of a supplementary catalogue issued with some of the weekly numbers in Volumes III to VII, extended to over 5,000 quarto pages, and according to newspaper advertisements the sales were about a thousand copies. The eight-page Introduction which Johnson wrote for the *Miscellany* undoubtedly caught the eye of many whose names were eventually listed as subscribers. No more important book was first published in fascicules before 1750 than *The Harleian Miscellany: or, a Collection of Scarce, Curious, and Entertaining Pamphlets and Tracts, As well in Manuscript as in Print, Found in the Late Earl of*

---

[1] An advertisement in the *London Evening Post* number 2346 (November 23, 1742) altered the date to 'the 11th of December next'. These Proposals were reprinted by the Oxford University Press in 1926, with an introduction by R.W. Chapman.

Oxford's Library. The story that Johnson knocked down Osborne, the proprietor of the collection, for interfering with Johnson's time-consuming enjoyment of these 'scarce, curious, and entertaining' pieces testifies to the interest they had for the century's greatest critic.

In one way or another it is still true that the books published in fascicules before 1750 are all 'scarce, curious, and entertaining'. A most unusual exhibition could be assembled if one were to bring together a copy of every book so issued by the middle of the eighteenth century. Certainly they would make a strangely assorted room-full. It would add interest to such a collection if one arranged them in general classes by subject. The largest section would be occupied by the *Universal History*, the fat folio and quarto histories by Rapin, Ralegh, Baker, Guthrie, de Thou, Ralph, Robinson, Cantemir, Duff, N. Salmon, T. Salmon, Josephus, Keating, Maitland, Marchant, Lord Herbert of Cherbury, and lesser works by Boyse, Nalson, Piossens, Bridges, Purbeck, Rio, with George Vertue's *Monuments of the Kings*, and *Heads of the Most Illustrious Persons of Great Britain* at the side. Here would be found Bickham's *British Monarchy*, the two editions of *Acta Regia*, the several collections of state trials, and Lediard's *Naval History of England*.

Nearby would be the books of geography, topography, and travel, a large group including the Astley and Harris collections, Moll's *Atlas Geographus* and *A New Description of England and Wales*, Stevens's *View of the Universe*, *Magna Britannia*, Blomefield's *Norfolk*, du Halde's *Description of China*, Mottley's *Survey of London and Westminster*, Ward's *London Spy*, and reports of away-from-home experiences of Charles Thompson, de Blainville, Francis Moore, John Cockburn, and J. Philips.

Another large group would bring together the many volumes of Biblical commentary, church history, and treatises on morality. Here one would put Matthew Henry, William Burkitt, Thomas Stackhouse and his rival, John Campbell, Samuel Parker, John Strype, de Tillemont, Ellies-Dupin, Claude Fleury, Jacques Lenfant, Augustin Calmet, Gilbert Burnet, Isaac Barrow, Samuel Clarke, Archbishop Tillotson, Samuel Humphreys, Laurence Clarke, and some anonymous 'divines'.

A good deal of space would be taken up by biography and pseudo-biography, chief places going to the six folio volumes of *Biographia Britannica*. *The History of the Popes* would stand next to Salmon's *Lives of the English Bishops*, and near Wilford's *Memorials and Characters* would go accounts of Peter the Great, the Rev. George Whitefield, Philip Quarll, James Wyatt, Constantia Phillips, Charles XII of Sweden, and a succession of English highwaymen.

There would also be a small group of encyclopedias, notably those of Chambers and de Coetlogon, together with the rival adaptations of Bayle. Here also would go the supplement to John Harris's *Lexicon Technicum*, and close by could be placed *Bibliotheca Anatomica, Medica, Chirurgica*, Dr. James's *Medicinal Dictionary*, Benjamin Martin's *Philosophia Britannica*, Baddam's *Memoirs of the Royal Society, The Philosophical History . . . of the Royal Academy of Sciences at Paris*, as well as special scientific works such as the herbals of de Tournefort and Mrs. Blackwell, the *Anatomical Tables* of Albinus, Neale's *Uranographia Britannica*, and the *Physical Disquisitions* of Dr. John Tennent.

It is hard to think that anyone except a half-wit could visit such an exhibition without finding something to catch his eye for a moment or two. Mathematicians inspecting the collection would be interested in J. Dougharty's *Mathematical Digests*, in James Dodson's *Anti-logarithmic Canon*, perhaps even in Joseph Champion's *Practical Arithmetick* and C. Price's book on *The Construction of . . . Mathematical Instruments*. The more practically minded visitors would see a little group of works on various arts and crafts, most interesting of all being the earliest of the number books, Joseph Moxon's *Mechanick Exercises*. Here would be seen Bickham's *Universal Penman*, Samuel Palmer's *General History of Printing*, C. Bird's *Practising Scrivener*, and Stephen Switzer's *Practical Husbandman and Planter*. The same viewers might be interested in another small group of books dealing with the fine arts of painting and architecture: works by Gérard de Lairesse, Palladio, James Gibbs, Edward Oakley, Batty Langley, and Thomas Rowland. Students of classics would find volumes of Ovid, Horace, and Virgil, together with Daniel Scott's *Appendix to the Greek Thesaurus*. Students of music would see a dozen different collections of songs, most of them published anonymously, among them the rivals: *The British Miscellany, or the Harmonious Grove*, and *The British Musical Miscellany, or, the Delightful Grove*. Readers of verse would be interested to see *Paradise Lost* on the same table as *Hudibras Redivivus*; and most literary historians would make a point of examining Thomson's *Seasons* if a copy of the quarto edition in numbers (1733) could be found for the display.

Over in one corner visitors would look hopefully at the number books belonging in the category of prose fiction, a surprisingly small set.[1] Besides *The Weekly Novelist* (1735–1736), translations of *Don Quixote*, Marivaux' *Vie de Marianne*,[2] and Prévost's *Mémoires et avantures d'un homme de qualité*, there were fictitious autobiographies, best represented by what appears from the title to be a kind of handbook on seduction: *The Fortunate Country Maid, Being the Entertaining Memoirs of the Present celebrated Marchiness of L - - - V - - - . Who from a Cottage became a Lady of the First Quality in the Court of France, by her Steady Adherence to the Principles of Virtue and Honour. Wherein are Displayed, the Various and Vile Artifices imployed by Men of Intrigue, for Seducing of Young Women; with Suitable Reflections* (1740–1741). These are a disappointing lot, even though one's eye would notice that Defoe is represented by *Madagascar*, and that one Mrs. Slade, 'late a Nun', had contributed the fourteen numbers of her *Nunnery Tales; or the Amours of the Priests and Nuns*. The only book in this group likely to attract more than a passing glance would be the sixpenny numbers of M. Mechell's *The Modern Story-Teller; or, General Entertainer* (1748).[3]

---

[1] As was shown in Chapter II, many works of fiction were printed in newspapers as continued serials. It should be noted also that Mrs. Eliza Haywood's *Female Spectator* (1744–1746), like the earlier *Monthly Amusement* (1709) and the *Records of Love; or, Weekly Amusements for the Fair* (1710), was almost wholly given over to prose fiction. See Graham Pollard, 'Serial Fiction', in John Carter, ed., *New Paths in Book Collecting: Essays by Various Hands* (London: Constable, [1934]), pp. 247–77.

[2] See Alan D. McKillop, *Samuel Richardson, Printer and Novelist* (Chapel Hill: University of North Carolina Press, 1936), p. 90.

[3] On December 23, 1748, M. Mechell, the sole proprietor, entered in the Stationers' Register the first number of her 'Modern Story-Teller, or General Entertainer in two Volumes'. The second number of Volume I was likewise entered on January 4, 1749, and numbers 3 and 4 on February 3. No later numbers were entered in the Stationers' Register.

To anyone knowing nothing of these number books a large collection of them would have little more interest than any other equally varied collection of old books. Once their peculiar mode of publication is known, they take on a unique interest. An informed guide could easily point out the earliest, the largest, the most expensive, the most successful. He would not be content to point to the outside of each book; he would wish to open them up and show the characteristic number-book signatures. He would draw attention to the excellence of the paper and type in William Whiston's *Josephus* and in the twelve volumes of Tillotson's *Works*; he would point out the numerous and carefully engraved maps by Herman Moll and Emanuel Bowen, the magnificent portrait of Thomas Lediard in *The Naval History of England*, the excellent plates in Gibbs's *Rules for Drawing*, in Chambers' *Cyclopædia*, in Elizabeth Blackwell's *Curious Herbal*; he would show what kinds of documents are in *Acta Regia* and *The Harleian Miscellany*; and he would open *The Medicinal Dictionary* so that one could read the Dedication which Samuel Johnson wrote to Dr. Mead on behalf of Robert James, M.D., who compiled the work.

Interested visitors might care to be shown the numerous pairs of rival editions in numbers—one *History of the Bible* by Stackhouse, another by Campbell; one translation of Rapin by Tindal, another by Kelly and Morgan; the several editions of Josephus, the competing adaptations of Bayle's *Dictionnaire*, the several biographies of Queen Anne. If the visitors had read this present book they might ask to have pointed out to them the handwritten signatures of Teresia Constantia Phillips on every copy of the numbers of her *Apology*, and (if they could be found) the signatures of John Frederick Lampe on the covers of the numbers of his *Lyra Britannica, a Collection of Ballads and Ariettas*. They might also like to see the numerous works published in fascicules by Robert Walker, especially the piratical *Paradise Lost* of 1739, which got Walker into serious trouble.

Visitors from the United States might ask to see Samuel Parker's *Bibliotheca Biblica*, since a few numbers of this work had made their way to the Mather library in New England; and they would like to look at the case histories of colonial planters in the *Physical Disquisitions* of John

Tennent, M.D., who on the basis of his professional experience on both sides of the Atlantic recommended as a sure cure of various diseases 'a Plant growing plentifully in North America, named Senecka Rattle-Snake-Root'. Americans would also like to see Captain John Stevens's *New Collection of Voyages and Travels*, which included in numbers 5, 6, 7, and 8 John Lawson's detailed account of North Carolina, where he was Surveyor General. Lawson's dictionary of native Indian words and his observations on swearing and the use of rum in colonial territories make unusually interesting reading even two and a half centuries later; they must have proved really exciting to the first readers in 1709.

Only a person who had made a particular study of fascicules stitched in blue paper, however, would know enough about them to ask for a view of the following ten particularly curious specimens, each selected for a different reason. One of these would be *The Art of Painting* (1737), John Frederick Fritsch's translation of a work by Gérard de Lairesse which strongly influenced the young Robert Browning—though in an edition not published until half a century later. Another would be Samuel Boyse's *Historical View of the Transactions of Europe from the Commencement of the War with Spain in 1739 to the Insurrection in Scotland in 1745* (1746), one's interest being less in the work than in the prolific and impecunious writer, who is reported to have had some tastes in food and dress, but who occasionally lacked a shirt, being forced to write for his bread while sitting up in bed with his writing arm thrust through a hole in a blanket.[1] Next among the curiosities might be number 1, the only part published, of Dr. Herman Boerhaave's *Elementa Chemiæ* (1732), this being a translation ('by a Gentleman of the University of Oxford') of the distinguished physician's own text of the lectures delivered by him annually at Leyden. Both the authentic text and that issued eight years earlier by Boerhaave's students — without his consent—proved very popular in the original Latin and in numerous translations.[2] The proposed edition of *The Ele-*

[1] Several stories about Boyse's hardships are conveniently brought together in L. F. Powell's edition of *Boswell's Life of Johnson* (Oxford: Clarendon Press, 1934, 1950), IV, p. 407, n. 4, and *ibid.*, p. 446.
[2] See Tenney L. Davis, 'The Vicissitudes of Boerhaave's Textbook of Chemistry', *Isis*, X (1928), 33–46.

ments of Chemistry in fascicules did not get beyond the first number. Certainly deserving a place among the show pieces would be the gigantic plates, 22 inches by 29 inches, of Bernard Siegfried Albinus's *Tables of the Skeleton and Muscles of the Human Body* (1747). What makes several of these particularly interesting is the studied nonchalance of the posing skeletons, for in these well executed plates each skeleton was provided with a decorative background to make it look natural, and it appears that when the time came to be drawn each skeleton walked well into the foreground so as to look its best. Most entertaining of all is the fourth plate in the series, into which the designer thoughtfully introduced a female rhinoceros in the flesh, busily occupied in cropping the grass behind the unperturbed skeleton. A note (translated from the Latin in the original just published at Leyden) explains that the picture of the animal was drawn to scale from an actual rhinoceros seen in 1742, 'being two and a half years old, as the keepers reported'. It was thought that a picture of so rare a beast would make a more agreeable background for a skeleton than any design that could be created from the imagination. Whether the use of such ornamentation would be distracting for students of anatomy is perhaps open to question. Certainly the youthful rhino and the elderly skeleton are mutually indifferent.

Somewhere in the set of surprising number books should be included *A General and True History of the Lives and Actions of the Most Famous Highwaymen, Murderers, Street-Robbers &c. To which is added A Genuine Account of the Voyages and Plunders of the most Noted Pirates. Interspersed with several Remarkable Tryals of the most Notorious Malefactors, at the Sessions-House in the Old Bailey, London. Adorn'd with the Effigies, and other material Transactions of the most Remarkable Offenders.* Though this work combines Alexander Smith's earlier book on highwaymen with Charles Johnson's equally popular book on pirates, this whole set of 108 numbers (printed at R. Walker's shop at the sign of the Printing-press, over against the Swan Tavern in the High Street, Birmingham, in 1742) is attributed on the general title page to Capt. Charles Johnson.[1] One

---

[1] Smith was likewise left unmentioned in advertisements of another number-book edition of the combined works in 1733–1734.

choice morsel which might catch the eye (and turn the stomach) of a casual reader has anatomical interest rather different from that provided by Albinus's *Tables*. In the ninth number of the series is a story 'as well attested as any Historical fact can be', yet one admitted to be 'almost incredible, for the monstrous and unparallel'd Barbarities that it relates'. This is the account of Sawney Beane, a bloodthirsty villain if ever there was one. Sawney, who was born eight or nine mles east of Edinburgh during the reign of Queen Elizabeth, in course of time took up with a woman 'as viciously inclined as himself'. They and their numerous offspring lived in a great cave by the seaside on the shore of Galloway county. The place was solitary and lonesome; and when the tide came up, the water went for 'near two hundred Yards into their subterraneous Habitation, which reached almost a Mile under Ground'. For upwards of twenty-five years the family lived in isolation, 'without going into any City, Town, or Village', supporting themselves wholly by robbing unwary passers-by. What distinguished Sawney and his household from most other notorious rogues was their practice of invariably killing and eating all the persons they robbed.

As soon as they had robb'd and murder'd any Man, Woman, or Child, they used to carry off the Carcass to the Den, where cutting it into Quarters, they would pickle the mangled Limbs, and afterwards eat it; this being their only Sustenance.

It appears that food was abundant. Sawney's victims were so numerous that the spacious larder was often too full to hold more. The result of this congestion was that on dark nights Sawney and family 'frequently threw Legs and Arms of the unhappy Wretches they had murder'd into the Sea, at a great distance from their bloody Habitation'. Naturally the victims were missed at home, and many a harmless stranger, many an innocent innkeeper was hanged for Sawney's crime. Finally one frantic victim escaped, and told the amazed authorities what ghastly things he had seen and what ghastlier things he suspected. Thereupon the King himself—James of Scotland—organized a posse to bring the abominable Sawney to justice. Persistent bloodhounds eventually led the members of the search party to the inner recesses of the cave, where they saw a horrifying sight:

...Legs, Arms, Thighs, Hands and Feet of Men, Women, and Children, were hung up in Rows, like dried Beef. A great many Limbs lay in Pickle; and Watches, Rings, Swords, Pistols, ... Cloaths ... were found, thrown together in Heaps, or hung up against the Sides of the Den.

Sawney and company were seized and taken to Leith, where 'without any Process' they were executed in most barbarous fashion, unrepentant, 'cursing and venting the most dreadful Imprecations to the very last Gasp of Life'.

Dr. James Parsons was also an expert at dissection, as one gathers from the titles of his lectures to the Royal Society and his printed papers,[1] but it was only his treatise on the internal structure of seeds that was issued in fascicules (1745). 'The Design of this Work', Dr. Parsons said, was 'not only to reduce the System of Botany to a more easy Method for the English Reader' but also to demonstrate 'the surprising Appearances of the minute Parts contained in the Seeds of Vegetables.' He was a very ardent and enthusiastic scientist.

The Discoveries, which in the Progress of the Work arise before me, are not to be equal'd in any part of Nature, for their Beauty and curious Structure; the Examination of which will not only entertain the Reader, but raise in his Mind the highest Notions of the Power and 'Wisdom of the Divine Creator. And as this minute Inspection of dry Seeds, and their Dissection, have never been attempted before, I make no Doubt, but I shall have contributed towards laying a Foundation for some more new and useful Knowledge of the Vegetable World, than has hitherto been exhibited.

Though only the first of four volumes in this notable pioneer work was published, it is interesting to see and handle *The Microscopical Theatre of Seeds: Being A Short View of the particular Marks, Characters, Contents,*

---

[1] Among these are *A Mechanical and Critical Enquiry into the Nature of Hermaphrodites* (1741), *A Description of the Human Urinary Bladder and Parts Belonging to It; with Anatomical Figures Showing its Make, Situation, etc.* (1742), and *Philosophical Observations on the Analogy between the Propagation of Animals and That of Vegetables* (1752). That Parsons's interests were not exclusively anatomical and physiological appears from the title of a late work, *Remains of Japhet: Being Historical Enquiries into the Affinity and Origin of the European Languages* (1767).

and Natural Dimensions of All the Seeds of the Shops, Flower and Kitchen-Gardens, &c. With Many other Curious Observations and Discoveries, which could not be known without the Assistance of the Microscope. To which are added, The Etymology, Synonyma, Description of Plant and Flower, an Account of their Virtues, and an Explanation of Botanical Terms, with proper Indexes: Which render it compleatly Useful to all Botanists, Gardeners, Seedsmen &c. and Entertaining to all Curious Observers of Nature. Illustrated with Figures of the Seeds considerably Magnified for their better Observation, and engraven on Copper Plates by the best Hands.

One could turn with ease from a scientific treatise in botany to a survey of the two universities. Thomas Salmon, busy with his *Modern History* and his *Collection of Proceedings and Trials against State Prisoners*, yet found time to begin (he did not finish) a work which he called *The Present State of the Universities and of the Five Adjacent Counties, of Cambridge, Huntington, Bedford, Buckingham, and Oxford*. That this was not a perfunctory and dull enumeration of facts is suggested by subtitles in the numbers dealing with Oxford: 'The necessary Expences at the University', 'The Influence a vicious Age has on the University', 'The several Classes of Under-graduates', and 'Of the Conceit some Academics discover of their own Parts and Learning'.

Pride in one's mastery of complicated matters is pardonable, however, if there are tangible and beneficial results. One would like to see number 1 of *Thacker's Cookery*, which was announced in the *Newcastle Courant* for March 29, 1746, as 'ready to be delivered to the Subscribers', for according to the advertisement this sixpenny fascicule contained useful instructions for housekeepers, 'with particular Directions for salting and preserving all manner of Butchers Meat'. (Just the thing for Sawney Beane!) There were also recipes for various dishes, including several sorts of puddings, and 'many other Things interspers'd too tedious to mention'. It would seem that the public found the whole thing too tedious, for there is no trace of the first number. Thacker named agents in Durham, Newcastle, Stockton, York, Bishopauckland, and Sunderland, assuring subscribers that 'whatsoever' might be left of the impression when completed would all be taken into the author's hand, and would not be sold 'under Nine Shillings the

Set to any one whatsoever'. But John Thacker's *Art of Cookery* was not published in Newcastle until 1758, by which time Thacker had been appointed 'Cook to the Honourable and Reverend the Dean and Chapter in Durham'. It would be pleasant to see whether the number advertised in 1746 contained recipes for preparing such dishes as 'Tongue and Udder', 'Mutton cuebob'd', and 'Pulpotoon of Pigeons'; and it would be especially pleasing to see whether that single number gave (as the 1758 edition did) 'a few useful Instructions how to manage Things that have been left after Company have been at Dinner, and they unexpectedly stay Supper'.

The rarity of some number books may be their chief attraction, and perhaps their only merit, though there may be associations that attach a supervenient interest. One need not feel greatly disappointed if there is no surviving copy of George Bickham's piratical and short-lived imitation of Mrs. Blackwell's *Curious Herbal*, or if there is no trace of the spurious numbers against which the anonymous proprietors of *Authentick Memoirs of the Life and Conduct of her Grace Sarah, late Dutchess of Marlborough* warned readers in 1744;[1] but because of the link with Samuel Richardson's first novel it would interest literary historians, if no others, to see the few numbers of *Pamela, or Virtue Rewarded, A Heroick Poem* which were published in London in 1741. A passage of over a hundred lines was quoted in the *Scots Magazine* for October 1741, with the comment that it was the work of 'no mean genius'.

If 'genius' implies transcendent mental ability or extraordinary imaginative endowment, one cannot apply it indiscriminately to the minds which produced the books published in numbers between 1678 and 1750. Some of the books came from the pens, if not the minds, of hired hacks, among whom must be counted 'S. Smith, D.D.' and others who stood behind an invented name or a merciful veil of anonimity. There were also earnest and hopeful authors who were ready

---

[1] Attached to an advertisement in a clipping from the *Sherborne Mercury* in the Hasle-wood Collection at the British Museum is the warning, 'N. B. The Publick may be assured, that whatever Accounts of her Grace may be published in Numbers, by any other Persons, are spurious, and a great Imposition.'

enough to put their names on title pages but simply could not rise above mediocrity in the far too numerous pages that followed those title pages. With a few notable exceptions the eighteenth-century people who wrote books to be published in fascicules before 1750 were an undistinguished lot, but there was a large company of others, venerable men 'of no mean genius', who had never heard of number books but who provided solid and sometimes brilliant matter to fill the fascicules. To say that number books were trashy is to call in question the reputation of Moses, St. Paul, Virgil, Horace, Josephus, John Foxe, Martin Luther, Shakespeare, Sir Walter Ralegh, Cervantes, John Milton, Archbishop Tillotson, several bishops, and a dozen Frenchmen with impressive names. None of these had anything directly to do with eighteenth-century number books, and they gained nothing—except posthumous readers—from the fact that their writings were reprinted in those weekly and monthly packets of sheets.

There were two groups of people who did gain, however—the publishers, and the people. Among those who made or tried to make money by publishing number books there were a few opportunists who paid little attention to property rights or to the literary standards of what they printed so long as the numbers sold. None of these aggressive enjoyers of the number-book trade made quite so many attempts to profit by it as Robert Walker, to whom must go the credit—if that is the right word—of printing and publishing more books in fascicules than any other proprietor before 1750—and he did not stop then.

It would be tiresome to enumerate all the works which bore Walker's imprint, or which he published without acknowledging his responsibility for doing so. (It would be much more tiresome to read the books!) Certainly Walker provided a varied diet of reading matter for those who bought his newspapers containing instalments and supplements.[1] In those papers, especially in his *London and Country Journal*, he advertised the works he issued in fascicules, usually giving advance notice of each new work, later announcing the publication of the first two or three numbers, and then leaving the publicity to his numerous local agents. It is clear that he was both printer and publisher, that he at

[1] See the end of Chapter II above.

one time or another occupied several premises in London, and that he had shops of his own in Cambridge and Birmingham. The advertisements of his proposed series of cheap playbooks show that in January 1735 he had a printing establishment at Shakespeare's Head in Turn-again-lane, Snowhill, and also a shop in Exchange Alley, Cornhill. The imprint of *The Military History of . . . Prince Eugene of Savoy*, printed by Walker later that year, shows that he had a shop next to the White-Horse Inn, Fleet Street. In 1743 his address was 'the British Oil Ware-house in Fleet-lane', and a few years later he was 'at the Corner of Elliott's Court, in the Little Old Bailey'. Many of the books advertised in his own newspapers prove upon examination to have as imprint only the anonymous 'London: Printed for the Booksellers in Town and Country', and it is necessary to seek elsewhere for evidence that they were from his presses. He apparently had some sort of working agreement with James Stanton, who turned from distilling to printing in 1736, and both were mentioned in Tonson's bill against the piratical printers of *Paradise Lost* in 1739, though the imprint of the completed volume states simply that it was 'Printed for a Company of Stationers'.

The years 1740 and 1741 seem to have been a particularly active period in the Walker establishments, if (as seems likely) it can be assumed from the tone and position of the notices in Walker's *London and Country Journal* that most of the number books listed there were sponsored by or printed by him. A list of books 'publish'd by subscription Weekly' and available from Jos. Collett of Bristol was printed in the final column of that paper on March 17, 1740, and repeated, with additions, in later numbers. Nine works published in fascicules are in this list, along with the *Country Magazine, or Weekly Pacquet* and the *Journal* itself ('with the History of the Holy Bible'):

The Tryal of the Seven Bishops in the Reign of King James the Second
The Tryal of King Charles the First, by J. Nalson
The Account of Sir George Byng's Destroying the Spanish Fleet off the Coast of Sicily
Mr. Whitefield's Sermons
. . . the History of his Life by an Impartial Hand
Bishop Beveridge's Private Thoughts upon Religion, digested into

Twelve Articles, &c.

The Adventures of Telemachus the Son of Ulysses, written by the Archbishop and Duke of Cambray

The Account of the Rebellion in the Reign of King Charles I

The History of England, by James Robinson, Esq.

A similar list in number 47 (April 10, 1740) adds:

History of the Reign of Queen Anne.

To these may be added a piratical edition of Oldys's *Life of Sir Walter Ralegh, The History of . . . Peter the First, The Beauties of the English Stage,* Lord Herbert of Cherbury's *Life and Reign of King Henry VIII,* an adaptation of John Foxe's *Book of Martyrs, An Impartial Account of . . . the Inquisition, A Select . . . Account of the Lives . . . of the most Remarkable Convicts from the Year* 1700 *to the Year* 1741. All of these were issued in numbers and began during 1740 or 1741. There were others in later years, all of them published by Walker, among them *A General and True History of . . . Highwaymen . . . and Pirates* (1742), Samuel Simpson's *Agreeable Historian* (1744), Arbuthnot's *Memoirs of . . . Jenny Cameron* (1746), and the same author's *Life . . . of Simon, Lord Lovat* (1746). Doubtless several more will eventually be identified as Walker's. If money was made by printing in numbers, Robert Walker must have made it; and he had no monopoly.

Most of those who had financial interests in number books during the first few decades of the business were among the recognized elite of the book trade. There were, in fact, very few well-known publishers of the period who did not at one time or another have a share in a number book, and most of them presumably made a profit therefrom. For instance, there are the publishers whom Samuel Johnson met in one way or another in the first dozen years of his work in London: Edward Cave, proprietor of the *Gentleman's Magazine;* Thomas Osborne, whom Johnson once banged on the head with a big book; John Wilcox, who looked at Johnson's robust frame and told him that instead of taking up writing as a career he should rather buy a porter's knot, but was none the less regarded by Johnson as one of his best friends; Robert Dodsley, whom Johnson affectionately called 'Doddy' —the man who paid him ten guineas for *London* and fifteen for *The*

Vanity of Human Wishes; Thomas Longman, who with Andrew Millar, Charles Hitch, and the two Knaptons (John and Paul; James had died in 1736) joined Dodsley in inducing Johnson to undertake the writing of the *Dictionary*; James Roberts, who published Johnson's *Life of Savage* and who, incidentally, was proprietor of at least twenty different newspapers. All of these men published number books.

Equally reputable publishers in their day were James Brindley and John Nourse, two of the booksellers named by the Society for the Encouragement of Learning to handle the publications of that organization; John Peele, called by Nichols 'a very considerable bookseller'; James Crokatt, whom Nichols declared to have been 'the greatest literary projector of the age'; Samuel Birt, who according to H. R. Plomer had an interest in all the important publications of his day;[1] Thomas Cooper, publisher of many newspapers and pamphlets; Mary Cooper (widow of Thomas), who, like John Watts, published many of Henry Fielding's works; Richard Hett, Treasurer of the Stationers' Company; W. and J. Innys, Bernard and Henry Lintot, John Newbery, Charles Rivington—these and scores of others, whose names and addresses are given in Appendix C, printed or published books in fascicules, and most of them made money at it.

No one supposes that the enduring worth of a book is indicated by the extent of its sales or by the number of persons who pocket substantial profits from the business of publishing it; but there may be truth in the assertion that the temper and the cultural vigour of a past generation are reflected in the uses to which middle-class money was put, aside from that needed to satisfy the basic necessities of shelter, food, and clothing. We have seen that a writer in the *Grub-Street Journal* in 1734 deplored the fact that so many persons in the 'lowest Stations of Life' were 'more intent upon cultivating their Minds than upon feeding and cloathing their Bodies'. The man who wrote those words was lagging behind the times, for the thing he deplored is now seen to have been one of the most exciting developments of the cen-

[1] H. R. Plomer, G. H. Bushnell, and E. R. McC. Dix, *A Dictionary of the Printers and Booksellers Who Were at Work in England Scotland and Ireland from 1726 to 1775* (Oxford: University Press, for the Bibliographical Society, 1932 [for 1930]), pp. 26, 67.

tury. A more percipient observer writing in the *Grub-Street Journal* two years earlier (October 26, 1732) saw great merit in the new mode of publishing, for it added to the number of readers: 'This Method of Weekly Publication allures Multitudes to peruse Books into which they would otherwise never have looked.' That simple contemporary statement sums up the whole of the development set forth in the seven chapters of this book. If it is true—and it is—that some of the weekly books were trash, and that some of those ostensibly more respectable turn out to be badly printed abridgments of unread and unreadable 'folio lumps', an inspection of surviving copies shows that many were valuable in substance and commendable in physical make-up. Even if there were no long lists of 'polite' subscribers to prove the point, one can see that many works issued in fascicules deserved the patronage of the most cultured readers in Britain. People in the upper levels of society would probably have bought these books no matter how they were published; what makes the issuing of fascicules really significant is that this mode of publication made it possible and easy for middle- and lower-class Englishmen to buy and to read books. That is an admirable habit. It is a habit which not even television and other astounding twentieth-century diversions have been able to break.

APPENDIX A

TEXT OF THE FIRST COPYRIGHT ACT

(8 ANNE, C. 19)

The text is here reproduced from *The Statutes at Large, Beginning with the Seventh Year of the Reign of Queen Anne, and continued to he End of the Eighth and last Session of the Fifth Parliament of Great Britain*, March 7, 1722 (London: John Baskett, E. and R. Nutt, Robert Gosling, 1724), LV, 147–50. Varieties of type (black-letter and italics) are ignored.

AN ACT FOR THE ENCOURAGEMENT OF LEARNING, BY VESTING THE COPIES OF PRINTED BOOKS IN THE AUTHORS OR PURCHASERS OF SUCH COPIES, DURING THE TIMES THEREIN MENTIONED

Whereas Printers, Booksellers, and other Persons have of late frequently taken the Liberty of printing, reprinting, and publishing, or causing to be printed, reprinted, and published Books, and other Writings, without the Consent of the Authors or Proprietors of such Books and Writings, to their very great Detriment, and too often to the Ruin of them and their Families: For preventing therefore such Practices for the future, and for the Encouragement of learned Men to compose and write useful Books; May it please your Majesty, that it may be Enacted, and be it Enacted by the Queens most Excellent Majesty, by and with the Advice and Consent of the Lords Spiritual and Temporal, and Commons in this present Parliament assembled, and by the Authority of the same, That from and after the Tenth Day of April, One thousand seven hundred and ten, the Author of any Book or Books already printed, who hath not transferred to any other the Copy or Copies of such Book or Books, Share or Shares thereof,

or the Bookseller or Booksellers, Printer, or Printers, or any other
Person or Persons, who hath or have purchased or acquired the Copy
or Copies of any Book or Books, in order to print or reprint the same,
shall have the sole Right and Liberty of printing such Book and Books
for the Term of One and twenty Years, to commence from the said
Tenth Day of April, and no longer; and that the Author of any Book
or Books already composed, and not printed and published, or that
shall hereafter be composed, and his Assignee or Assigns, shall have
the sole Liberty of printing and reprinting such Book and Books for
the Term of Fourteen Years, to commence from the Day of the first
publishing the same, and no longer; And that if any other Bookseller,
Printer, or other Person whatsoever, from and after the Tenth Day
of April, One thousand seven hundred and ten, within the times
granted and limited by this Act, as aforesaid, shall print, reprint, or
import, or cause to be printed, reprinted, or imported, any such Book
or Books, without the Consent of the Proprietor or Proprietors thereof
first had and obtained in Writing, signed in the Presence of Two or
more Credible Witnesses, or knowing the same to be so printed or
reprinted, without the Consent of the Proprietors, shall sell, publish,
expose to Sale, or cause to be sold, published, or exposed to Sale,
any such Book or Books, without such Consent had and obtained,
as aforesaid, Then such Offender or Offenders shall forfeit such
Book or Books, and all and every Sheet or Sheets, being part of such
Book or Books, to the Proprietor or Proprietors of the Copy thereof,
who shall forthwith Damask, and make Waste Paper of them: And
further, That every such Offender or Offenders shall forfeit One
Pen[n]y for every Sheet which shall be found in his, her, or their
Custody, either printed or printing, published, or exposed to Sale,
contrary to the true Intent and Meaning of this Act, the One Moiety
thereof to the Queens most Excellent Majesty, Her Heirs and Successors, and the other Moiety thereof to any Person or Persons that
shall sue for the same, to be recovered in any of her Majesties
Courts of Record at Westminster, by Action of Debt, Bill, Plaint, or
Information, in which no Wager of Law, Essoign, Privilege, or
Protection, or more than one Imparlance shall be allowed.

II And whereas many Persons may through Ignorance offend against this Act, unless some Provision be made, whereby the Property in every such Book, as is intended by this Act to be secured to the Proprietor or Proprietors thereof, may be ascertained, as likewise the Consent of such Proprietor or Proprietors for the printing or reprinting of such Book or Books may from time to time be known; Be it therefore further enacted by the Authority aforesaid, That nothing in this Act contained shall be construed to extend to subject any Bookseller, Printer, or other Person whatsoever, to the Forfeitures or Penalties therein mentioned, for or by reason of the printing or reprinting of any Book or Books without such Consent, as aforesaid, unless the Title to the Copy of [misprinted or] such Book or Books hereafter published shall, before such Publication, be entred [thus] in the Register-Book of the Company of Stationers, in such manner as hath been usual; which Register-Book shall at all times be kept at the Hall of the said Company, and unless such Consent of the Proprietor or Proprietors be in like manner entred, as aforesaid, for every of which several Entries, Six Pence shall be paid, and no more; which said Register-Book may, at all seasonable and convenient times, be resorted to, and inspected by any Bookseller, Printer, or other Person, for the Purpose before mentioned, without any Fee or Reward; and the Clerk of the said Company of Stationers, shall, when and as often as thereunto required, give a Certificate under his Hand of such Entry or Entries, and for every such Certificate may take a Fee not exceeding Six Pence.

III Provided nevertheless, That if the Clerk of the said Company of Stationers for the time being, shall refuse or neglect to register, or make such Entry or Entries, or to give such Certificate, being thereunto required by the Author or Proprietor of such Copy or Copies, in the presence of Two or more Credible Witnesses, That then such Person and Persons so refusing, Notice being first and duly given of such Refusal, by an Advertisement in the *Gazette*, shall have the like Benefit, as if such Entry or Entries, Certificate or Certificates had been duly made and given; and that the Clerks so refusing, shall, for any such Offence, forfeit to the Proprietor of such Copy or Copies the Sum of Twenty Pounds, to be recovered in any of Her Majesties Courts of Record at Westminster, by Action of Debt, Bill, Plaint, or Information, in which no Wager of Law, Essoign, Privilege, or Protection, or more than one Imparlance shall be allowed.

IV [This section names the authorities to whom complaint may be made of 'high and unreasonable' prices of books, and who have power to limit and settle the prices.]

V Provided always, and it is hereby Enacted, That Nine Copies of each Book or Books, upon the best Paper, that from and after the said Tenth Day of April, One thousand seven hundred and ten, shall be printed and published, as aforesaid, or reprinted and published with Additions, shall, by the Printer and Printers thereof, be delivered to the Warehouse-keeper of the said Company of Stationers for the time being, at the Hall of the said Company, before such Publication made, for the Use of the Royal Library, the Libraries of the Universities of Oxford and Cambridge, the Libraries of the Four Universities in Scotland, the Library of Sion College in London, and the Library commonly called the Library belonging to the Faculty of Advocates at Edinburgh respectively; which said Warehouse-keeper, is hereby required, within Ten Days after Demand by the Keepers of the respective Libraries, or any Person or Persons by them or any of them authorized to demand the said Copy, to deliver the same, for the Use of the aforesaid Libraries; and if any Proprietor, Bookseller, or Printer, or the said Warehouse-keeper of the said Company of Stationers, shall not observe the Direction of this Act therein, That then he and they, so making Default in not delivering the said printed Copies, as aforesaid, shall forfeit, besides the Value of the said printed Copies, the Sum of Five Pounds for every Copy not so delivered, as also the Value of the said printed Copy not so delivered, the same to be recovered by the Queens Majesty, Her Heirs and Successors, and by the Chancellor, Masters, and Scholars of any of the said Universities, and by the President and Fellows of Sion College, and the said

Faculty of Advocates at Edinburgh, with their full Costs respectively.

VI Provided always, and be it further Enacted, That if any Person or Persons incur the Penalties contained in this Act, in that part of Great Britain called Scotland, they shall be recoverable by any Action before the Court of Session there.

VII Provided, That nothing in this Act contained, do extend, or shall be construed to extend to prohibit the Importation, Vending, or Selling of any Books in Greek, Latin, or any other Foreign Language printed beyond the Seas; Any thing in this Act contained to the contrary notwithstanding.

VIII And be it further Enacted by the Authority aforesaid, That if any Action or Suit shall be commenced or brought against any Person or Persons whatsoever, for doing or causing to be done any thing in pursuance of this Act, the Defendants in such Action may plead the General Issue, and give the Special Matter in Evidence; and if upon such Action a Verdict be given for the Defendant, or the Plaintiff become nonsuited, or discontinue his Action, then the Defendant shall have and recover his full Costs, for which he shall have the same Remedy as a Defendant in any case of Law hath.

IX Provided, That nothing in this Act contained shall extend, or be construed to extend, either to prejudice or confirm any Right that the said Universities, or any of them, or any Person or Persons have, or claim to have, to the printing or reprinting any Book or Copy already printed, or hereafter to be printed.

X Provided, nevertheless, That all Actions, Suits, Bills, Indictments, or Informations for any Offence that shall be committed against this Act, shall be brought, sued, and commenced within Three Months next after such Offence committed, or else the same shall be void and of none effect.

XI Provided always, That after the Expiration of the said Term of
Fourteen Years, the sole Right of printing or disposing of Copies shall
return to the Authors thereof, if they are then living, for another Term
of Fourteen Years.

SHORT-TITLE CATALOGUE OF BOOKS PUBLISHED IN FASCICULES BEFORE 1750

Omitted from this list are all newspapers and periodicals published as such, and works intended to be published in fewer than four numbers or at intervals of more than one month. Also omitted are three works mentioned at the beginning of Chapter II as early examples of works issued in cumulative weekly or monthly portions. Books printed serially as instalments of varying length in the columns of newspapers or periodicals are excluded when it is apparent that subscribers were not expected to preserve and bind the portions, but detachable supplements are included, since these differ in no important respects from fascicules published independently. Works comprising consecutively numbered units—such as *The Phenix: Or a revival of Scarce and Valuable Pieces* (2 vols., London: J. Morphew, 1707, 1708)—are excluded if it is clear that they were not published in fascicules. Series of plays issued singly are also omitted, but the plays published as supplements (one sheet at a time) to *Cotes's Weekly Journal* (1734) and the work published in fascicules under the title *Beauties of the English Stage* (1738) are included because each number was part of a volume, not a complete play issued by itself.

Titles are here listed as they are found on title pages of fascicules or (more often) of completed volumes published in fascicules, but subtitles are reproduced only if they are needed to indicate the nature and scope of the work. Titles of books not actually seen—here marked with an asterisk—are listed as they appear in contemporary notices or advertisements. No attempt is made to give full and exact bibliographical descriptions, since these would have added considerably to the bulk but not to the general interest or usefulness of this book.

In this Catalogue books are grouped by years according to the date on which the first fascicule was published; when this date cannot be ascertained the date in the imprint of the first completed volume is used. In either case the discrepancy due to the practice of changing the year date on March 25 has been attended to by a silent adjustment. As was pointed out in the Note on Dates which stands immediately before the first chapter above, the year specified in the imprint of a volume depends on whether the title page was issued with the first fascicule or with the final one. The folio volume of James Robinson's *Compleat and Impartial History of England* has the date MDCCXXXIX in the imprint because the title page was included in the first fascicule, issued by Robert Walker in February 1739/40. Again, the first of the twenty-one numbers of Demetrius Cantemir's *History of the . . . Othman Empire* was entered in the Stationers' Register by the three Knaptons on 'March 14, 1734', and the general title page has the date MDCCXXXIV. By modern reckoning the year was really 1735; no subscriber saw any number of this book during the year we now call 1734. In this instance the Knaptons deviated from their customary practice, for like most other publishers—Walker's practice being exceptional—they normally issued the title page with the final number, not with the first. Had they issued the title page with the last number, the date in the imprint of this particular book would have been MDCCXXXVI, for No. 21 was entered in the Stationers' Register on May 7, 1736. The work would still have been listed here as belonging to the year 1735, since it is evident that the first fascicule was issued in that year.

Because the exact dates on which the initial fascicules of some books were published cannot be ascertained, the arrangement within each annual group in this Catalogue is not chronological but alphabetical, according to the surname of the author or compiler, if that name is given on the title page or can be otherwise established beyond question. When the name of the author or compiler is not known the title takes its place in the alphabetical sequence according to its first word, the definite and indefinite articles being disregarded.

Immediately after the title the number of volumes (if more than one) is indicated, followed by information concerning earlier editions, if that published in numbers was not the first. Translators, if any, are named at this point.

In a separate paragraph the imprints of the volumes (occasionally the imprints of fascicules) are then given, with the names but not the addresses of printers, proprietors, or distributors; the addresses are listed in Appendix C. Then come as many of the following details as have been ascertained: the size of the page (folio, quarto, octavo, duodecimo); the number of sheets in each fascicule; the frequency of issue (daily, thrice weekly, weekly, fortnightly, monthly, irregularly); the price per number; the total number of fascicules or pages in each volume; a note about plates and maps, if any; an indication of whether the copies seen have special fascicule signatures; the dates of the first and last (or other) numbers; additional information (entry in the Stationers' Register, the granting of a Royal licence, litigation, lists of subscribers, etc.); cross-references to other editions in fascicules within the period covered.

For economy of space the following abbreviations, and others, are used in this Catalogue:

ad.	advertisement, or advertised in
comp.	compiler
con.	continuation, continued, continuous
da.	daily
ent.	entered
fasc. sig.	special number-book signature(s)
fol.	folio
fort.	fortnightly
imp.	imprint
inc.	incomplete
irreg.	published irregularly
mo.	monthly
no. 1, 2, 3, etc.	the successive fascicules of a number book
pag.	pagination
pl.	plate(s)
port.	portrait
prop.	proprietor
pub.	published
rem.	remainders

rep.	reprint, or reprinted
Roy. lic.	Royal licence
s.	shilling(s)
sh.	sheet(s)
sig.	regular letter signatures.
Sta. Reg.	Stationers' Register
supp.	supplement
trans.	translation, translator, translated by
w.	weekly
4to	quarto
8vo	octavo
12mo	duodecimo

Serial numbers of fascicules are here uniformly given in arabic numerals, though many of the originals have roman numerals.

1678

CARE, HENRY. *The Weekly Pacquet of Advice from Rome*. 6 vols.
 Imp., VOL. III—London, Printed for, and to be sold by Langley
 Curtis . . . 1682.
 4to; single sh. ea.; 1s. ea.; VOL. I, nos 1 (Dec. 3, 1678) to 31 (July 4,
 1679), VOL. II, nos 1 (July 11, 1679) to 47 (May 28, 1680), VOL. III,
 nos 1 (June 4, 1680) to 80 (Dec. 16, 1681), VOL. IV, nos 1 (Dec. 23,
 1681) to 35 (Aug. 18, 1682), VOL. V, nos 1 (Aug. 25, 1682) to 47 (July
 13, 1683), VOL. VI, nos 1 (Jan. 5, 1689) to 3 (Feb. 8, 1689); Bodleian
 Library has also a spurious ed. of VOL. V by W. Salmon, nos 1 (Aug.
 25, 1682) to 36 (Apr. 27, 1683); pag. and sigs. con., new series in ea.
 vol.; rep. in nos, 1735.

MOXON, JOSEPH. *Mechanick Exercises, or, The Doctrine of Handy-
works*. 2 vols.
 Imp., no. 1—London, Printed for Joseph Moxon . . . 167, [i.e.,
 1678].
 Imp., VOL. II—London. Printed for Joseph Moxon . . . 1683.
 4to; 2, 2½, or 3 sh. ea.; mo. and irreg.; VOL. I, 14 nos (242 pp.), VOL.
 II, 24 nos (394 pp.); port. and pl.; serial no. on t.p. and at top of pp.;
 ea. no. complete in itself, but pag. and sigs. con., new series in ea. vol.;
 t.p. of no. 1 has 'Began Jan. 1. 1677. And intended to be Monthly
 continued.' VOL. I rep. in nos, 1693-1701.

1679

The Weekly Pacquet of Advice from Germany; or, The History of the Reformation of Religion There.

Imp. at end of no. 17—To be sold at the Phoenix in St. Paul's Church-yard. 1680.

4to; single sh. ea.; w.; fasc. nos at top of p.; ea. no. complete in itself, but pag. and sigs. con.; no. 18 dated Jan. 21, 1679/80.

1693

MOXON, JOSEPH. *Mechanick Exercises: or, The Doctrine of Handy-Works.*

Rep. from first ed., pub. in nos, 1678-1683.

Copy seen at Library of Congress has 12 title pages, with imp.—London, Printed and Sold by J. Moxon, 1693 [or] London, Printed and Sold by J. Moxon, 1694 [or] London, Printed and Sold by J. Moxon ..., 1694.

4to; 2 sh. ea.; mo. and irreg.; 6d.; 14 nos (234 pp.); port. and pl.; serial no. at top of every page ('Numb. I' to 'Numb. XIV', with omissions) not regularly altered for successive fascicules.

1698

WARD, EDWARD. *The London Spy.* 2 vols.

Imp., Parts 1 to 5—London, Printed for J. Nutt ... 1698.

Imp., Parts 6 to 12, and VOL. II, Parts 1 to 6—London, Printed and Sold by J. How ... 1699 (1700).

fol.; 4 sh. ea.; 6d. ea.; mo.; 18 nos; serial no. on ea. t.p.; no. 1 pub. Nov. 1698; rep. in nos as supp., 1736 and 1737.

1705

WARD, EDWARD. *Hudibras Redivivus: or, a Burlesque Poem on the Times.* 24 parts (2 vols.)

Imp. of first part—London, Printed: And Sold by B. Bragge ..., 1705. Price 6d. [others 1706, 1707].

4to; 3½ sh. ea.; mo.; 6d.; 12 parts in ea. vol., ea. part with sep. sigs., pag., and t.p. with 'Part the First', etc.; No. 8 listed *History of the Works of the Learned* April 1706 among 'Books Publish'd this Month ... Sold by B. Bragg'.

1708

MOLL, HERMAN. *Atlas Geographus; or, a Compleat System of Geography, Ancient and Modern.* 5 vols.

Imp., VOL. 1—In the Savoy: Printed by John Nutt; and Sold by

Benjamin Barker and Charles King . . .; Benjamin Tooke . . .; William Taylor . . .; Henry Clemens . . .; Richard Parker and Ralph Smith . . .; and John Morphew . . . MDCCVIII.

4to; mo.; 1s. ea.; maps and pl.; serial no. on sep. t.p. of ea. fasc.; no. 1 pub. May 1708; no. 28 pub. Sept. 1710; ad. the *Tatler*; rep. in nos, 1711-1717; con. in *Magna Britannia Antiqua & Nova* (1714-1731); has list of subscribers.

STEVENS, JOHN, comp., trans., and ed. *A View of the Universe; or a New Collection of Voyages and Travels* [also referred to as *A New Collection of Voyages and Travels*]. 2 vols.
Comprises seven separate works, ea. with sep. t.p. and sep. pag.:
    VOL. I: Bartolomeo de Argensola, *The Discovery and Conquest of the Molucco and Philippine Islands* (260 pp., plus index); John Lawson, *A New Voyage to Carolina* (258 pp.); Pedro Cieza de Leon, *The Seventeen Years Travels of Peter de Cieza through the Mighty Kingdom of Peru* (244 pp., plus contents and index);
    VOL. II: Sieur Mouette, *The Travels of Sieur Mouette in Fez and Morrocco* (115 pp., plus index); Pedro Teixeira, *The Travels of Peter Teixeira from India to Italy by Land* (81 pp., plus contents and index); François Cauche, *A Voyage to Madagascar, the Adjacent Islands, and Coast of Africk* (77 pp., plus index); F. Balthazar Tellez, comp., *The Travels of the Jesuits in Ethiopia* (264 pp., plus contents and index).
    Imp. of no. [1] for Dec. 1708—London Printed, and Sold by J. Knapton . . .; J. Round . . .; N. Cliffe . . .; E. Sanger . . .; and A. Collins . . . 1708.
    Imp. of no. [14] for Jan. 1710—London Printed for J. Knapton . . .; A. Bell . . .; D. Midwinter . . .; W. Taylor . . .; and Sold by J. Round . . .; N. Cliffe . . .; E. Sanger . . .; A. Collins . . .; and J. Baker . . .; 1710.
4to; mo.; 1s. ea.; maps and pl.; sep. t.p. for ea. fasc. as well as for ea. work; reissued in 2 vols., 1711, with new t.p.

1709
Bibliotheca Anatomica, Medica, Chirurgica, &c. 3 vols.
Based on 2nd ed. (2 vols, Geneva, 1699) of *Bibliotheca anatomica sive recens in anatomia inventorum thesaurus locupletissimus*, by Daniel Le Clerc and Jean Jacques Manget.
    Imp. of no. 1 (from ad. in the *Tatler* number 93, Nov. 12, 1709)—In the Savoy: Printed by John Nutt; and sold by W. Lewis . . .; Dan. Brown . . .; J. Pemberton . . .; R. Knaplock . . .; R. Wilkin . . .;

M. Atkins . . .; W. Taylor . . .; T. Horne . . .; A. Bell . . .; and
J. Morphew.

4to; mo.; 1s. ea.; VOL. I, 746 pp.; VOL. II, 687 pp., VOL. III, 654 pp.;
no. 1 pub. Nov. 1709; no. 13 pub. Nov. 1710. [Some of these details
are from K. F. Russell, 'A Bibliography of Anatomical Books Published in English before 1800', *Bulletin of the History of Medicine*, XXII
(1949), 291.]

1710

CERVANTES-SAAVEDRA, MIGUEL DE. *The Life and Notable
Adventures of That Renowned Knight, Don Quixote de la Mancha.* 'Merrily
Translated into Hudibrastick Verse. By Edward Ward.' 2 vols. [VOL.
II not pub. in nos.]
    Imp., VOL. I —London: Printed for T. Norris . . .; A. Bettes-
worth . . .; J. Harding . . .; and Sold by J. Woodward . . . MDCCXI.
Imp. of VOL. II adds E. Curl[l] . . .; and R. Gosling . . ., and is dated
MDCCXII.

8vo; mo.; VOL. I, 475 pp.; no. 1 pub. Oct. 1710; no. 3 ent. Sta. Reg.
Jan. 16, 1711, by W. Taylor, T. Norris, A. Bettesworth, T. Woodward, and B. Lintot.

1711

MOLL, HERMAN. *Atlas Geographus: or, a Compleat System of Geography.
Ancient and Modern.* 5 vols.
Rep. from 1st ed., 1708, in 4to nos.
    Imp., VOLS I and II —In the Savoy: Printed by John Nutt; and Sold
by Benjamin Barker and Charles King . . .; Benjamin Tooke . . .;
William Taylor . . .; Henry Clemens . . .; Richard Parker and Ralph
Smith . . .; and John Morphew . . . MDCCXI [VOL. III, MDCCXII;
VOL. IV, MDCCXIV].
    Imp., VOL. V —In the Savoy: Printed by Eliz. Nutt, for John Nichol-
son . . .; and sold by John Morphew . . . MDCCXVII.

4to; mo.; 1s. ea.; VOL. I, nos 1 to 15, 16 plus 978 pp.; VOL. II, pp.
979-1772, VOL. III, 16 plus 851 pp., VOL. IV, 808 pp., VOL. V, nos 1
to 17, 807 pp.; maps and pl.; list of subscribers; con. in *Magna Britannia
Antiqua & Nova* (1714-1731).

1714

COX, THOMAS and HALL, ANTHONY. *Magna Britannia et Hibernia,
Antiqua & Nova; or, A New Survey of Great Britain.* Collected and Composed by An Impartial Hand. 6 vols.

Pub. as sep. portion of *Atlas Geographus* (1711-1717). Section on Ireland not pub.

> Imp., VOLS I and II—In the Savoy: Printed by Eliz. Nutt; and sold by M. Nutt . . ., and J. Morphew . . . MDCCXX.
>
> Imp., VOLS III, IV, V, and VI—In the Savoy: Printed by E. and R. Nutt; and Sold by T. Cox . . . MDCCXXIV [MDCCXXVII, MDCCXXX, MDCCXXXI].

4to; mo. and irreg.; 1*s*. ea.; VOL. I, 8 plus 752 pp., VOL. II, pp. 753-1516, VOL. III, 762 pp., VOL. IV, 912 pp., VOL. V, 920 pp., VOL. VI, 710 pp.; maps and pl.; no. 3 listed in Lintot's *Monthly Catalogue* number 5 (Sept. 1714), other nos thereafter.

1718

TOURNEFORT, JOSEPH PITTON DE. *The Compleat Herbal: or, the Botanical Institutions of Mr. Tournefort.* Carefully translated from the Original Latin. With large Additions. 2 vols.

> Imp., VOLS I and II—London: Printed for R. Bonwicke, Tim. Goodwin, John Walthoe, S. Wotton, Sam. Manship, Rich. Wilkin, Benj. Tooke, Ralph Smith, and Tho. Ward; and are to be Sold by J. Morphew . . . 1719 [VOL. II, MDCCXXX].
>
> Imp., no. 16 same as imp. of VOL. I, but has Matt. Wotton instead of S. Wotton, and date 1718.
>
> Imp., no. 22 —London. Printed for J. Walthoe, R. Wilkin, J. and J. Bonwicke, S. Birt, T. Ward, and T. Osborn. MDCCXXVIII.

4to; mo.; 1*s*. ea.; VOL. I, 626 pp., VOL. II, 650 pp. plus index, 10 pp.; pl.; serial no. on sep. t.p. of ea. fasc.

1719

The History of King-Killers: or, the 30th of January Commemorated. 2 vols. 8vo; mo.? 12 nos.

1720

PARKER, SAMUEL. *Bibliotheca Biblica. Being a Commentary upon All the Books of the Old and New Testament.* 5 vols.

> Imp., VOL. I—Oxford: Printed at the Theater; for William and John Innys . . .; London. 1720.
>
> Imp., VOLS II, III, IV, and V—Oxford, Printed at the Theater, for Charles Rivington . . . London. 1722. [VOL. III, 1725, VOL. IV, 1728, VOL. V, 1735].

4to; mo. and irreg.; but ea. no. assigned to a particular month; 1*s*. 6*d*. ea.; VOL. I, 4 plus 981 plus 35 pp., VOL. II, 448 plus 49 pp., VOL. III,

387 plus 93 pp., VOL. IV, 489 plus 25 pp., VOL. V, 10 plus 693 plus 69 pp.; numerous ads. refer to nos as pub.

1724

CALMET, D. AUGUSTIN. *Antiquities Sacred and Profane, Or, a Collection of Curious and Critical Dissertations on the Old and New Testament.* 'Done into English from the French, with Notes, by a Clergyman of the Church of England' [Rev. Nicholas Tindal].

Imp.—London; Printed for J. Roberts . . .; S. Wilmot, in Oxford; and C. Crownfield, in Cambridge. MDCCXXIV.

Imp. of no. 3—London; Printed for J. Roberts . . .; and Sold by J. Knapton . . .; J. Pemberton, and T. Woodward . . .; T. Cox . . .; S. Wilmot . . .; C. Crownfield . . . MDCCXXIV.

4to; mo. and irreg.; 1s. ea.; ea. no. complete in itself, with pag. in several series having no relation to fasc.; VOL. 1 ad. to have 15 nos and about 90 sh.; serial no. on sep. t.p. of ea. no.; no. 2 ad. the *Weekly Journal, or Saturday's Post* number 288 (May 2, 1724) as pub. 'This Day'. no. 11 ad. to be pub. June 30, 1725; no. 13 dated 1726.

HERRERA Y TORDESILLAS, ANTONIO DE. *The General History of the Vast Continent and Islands of America, Commonly Call'd, the West-Indies.* 6 vols.

Trans. from the Spanish original (2 vols., Madrid, 1601) by John Stevens.

Imp., VOLS I and II—London: Printed for Jer. Batley . . . MDCCXXV [VOLS III, IV, V, and VI, MDCCXXVI].

8vo; mo.; 1s. ea.; VOL. I, 6 plus 380 pp., VOL. II, 436 pp., VOL. III, 418 pp., VOL. IV, 422 pp., VOL. V, 430 pp., VOL. VI, 408 pp., plus index; maps and pl.; no. 5 ad. the *Evening Post* number 2441 (Mar. 18, 1725) as pub. 'This Day'; no. 13 pub. Nov. 1725.

SALMON, THOMAS. *Modern History; or, the Present State of All Nations.* 31 vols.

Imp. varies; usually—London: Printed for the Author: And sold by J. Roberts . . .; and the Booksellers in Town and Country.

8vo; mo., then fort., then w.; 1s. ea.; 450 to 600 pp. in ea. vol.; no. 1, 'for the Month of June' ad. the *British Journal* number 95 (July 11, 1724); no. 146, first of VOL. XXV, ad. *St. James's Evening Post* number 2965 (Oct. 31, 1734); VOL. XXXI dated 1738; rep. in fol. nos, w., 1744-1746.

1725

CATROU, François and ROUILLE, Pierre Julien. *The Roman History: with Notes.* 6 vols.

Trans. Richard Bundy, from *Histoire romaine, depuis la fondation de Rome*, 20 vols (Paris, 1725-1737).

Imp., VOL. I—London: Printed by J. Bettenham, for T. Woodward and J. Peele. MDCCXXVIII; VOLS II and III, MDCCXXIX; VOL. IV, MDCCXXX; VOL. V—London: Printed by J. Bettenham, for the Editor; And Sold by A. Bettesworth and C. Hitch . . .; and W. Sargeant . . . MDCCXXXVI; VOL. VI, MDCCXXXVII.

fol.; mo.: 1s. 6d. ea.; VOL. I, 616 pp.; VOL. II, 627 pp. plus tables (43 pp.); VOL. III, 574 pp. plus tables (16 pp.); VOL. IV, 648 pp. plus tables (28 pp.); VOL. V, 585 pp. plus tables (14 pp.); VOL. VI, 231 pp. plus tables (7 pp.) plus index (pp. 233-593). No. 1 ad. in the *Evening Post* number 2508 (Aug. 21, 1725) as to be pub. 'speedily'. VOL. I has list of subscribers.

CATROU, François and ROUILLE, Pierre Julien. *The Roman History.*

Trans John Ozell, from *Histoire romaine, depuis la fondation de Rome*, 20 vols. (Paris, 1725-1737).

Imp., no. XI—London, Printed for W. and J. Innys . . .; J. Osborn and T. Longman . . .; G. Strahan . . .; W. Mears . . .; J. Pemberton . . .; T. Edlin . . . 1725.

8vo; mo. (irreg.); 1s. 6d. ea.; nos 1 (Aug. 1725)—16 (April 1729); nos 17, 18, 19 pub. May 1732; 3 nos ea. mo. thereafter.

CERVANTES SAAVEDRA, Miguel de. *The Life and Actions of that Ingenious Gentleman Don Quixote de la Mancha.*

Imp. of no. 1—London: Printed for Thomas Woodward . . .; and John Peele . . . MDCCXXV. (Price 1s. 6d.) [Imp. also in Spanish].

8vo; mo.; copy seen at Houghton Library has 24 plus 172 pp.; inc. (Book III, chap. XV, begins on p. 172); No. 1 ad. *Evening Post* number 2512 (Aug. 31, 1725) as pub. 'This Day . . . In Spanish and English. The English being an entire new Translation, with . . . Notes'.

RAPIN DE THOYRAS, Paul de. *The History of England, as Well Ecclesiastical as Civil.* Done into English from the French [*Histoire d'Angleterre*, The Hague, 1724], with large and useful Notes [and a summary of the whole] . . ., by N. Tindal. 15 vols.

Imp., all vols.—London: Printed for James and John Knapton . . . MDCCXXVII [in copies seen, VOL. IX has date MDCCXXIX, VOLS II,

IV, V, VI have 1731, VOLS III, VII, X, XI XII, XIII, XIV, XV have MDCCXXXI, VOL. VIII has 1732].

8vo; mo.; 1s. ea.; VOL. I, 10 plus 434 plus note on tables (3 pp.) and index (15 pp.), VOL. II, 3 plus 452 pp. plus index (12 pp.), VOL. III, 531 pp. plus index (21 pp.), VOL. IV, 484 pp. plus index (24 pp.), VOL. V, 478 pp. plus index (28 pp.), VOL. VI, 502 pp. plus index (26 pp.), VOL. VII, 706 pp. plus index (21 pp.), VOL. VIII, 511 pp. plus index (46 pp.), VOL. IX, 612 pp. plus index (33 pp.), VOL. X, 5 plus 575 pp. plus index (16 pp.), VOL. XI, 569 pp. plus index (19 pp.), VOL. XII, 2 plus 587 pp. plus index (36 pp.), VOL. XIII, 24 plus 473 pp. plus index (47 pp.), VOL. XIV, 468 pp. plus index (38 pp.), VOL. XV, 287 plus 444 pp. plus index (25 pp.); no. 1 pub. June or July 1725; Tindal's Dedication of VOL. II: 'From on Board the Torbay in the Bay of Revel in the Gulf of Finland, July 12, 1726'; Dedication of VOL. IV: 'From on Board the Torbay in Gibraltar-Bay, Sept. 4, 1727'; Dedication of VOL. VI is dated 'Great Waltham in Essex, September 10th, 1728'; maps and tables; rep. in w. nos, 1732, and again, 1743.

RAPIN DE THOYRAS, PAUL DE. *Acta Regia: Or, An Account of the Treaties, Letters, and Instruments between the Monarchs of England and Foreign Powers, publish'd in Mr. Rymer's Foedera* ... Translated [by Stephen Whatley] from the French of M. Rapin, as publish'd by M. Le Clerc. 4 vols.

It is explained in the Introduction that Rapin's abridgment of Rymer's *Foedera* (19 folio vols) was first pub. in Le Clerc's *Bibliothèques*, that the portions there pub. were gathered in a fol. vol. by 'the illustrious Pensionary Fagel', that only 30 copies of this fol. vol. were printed, and that Whatley had the good fortune to find a copy in the library of an English gentleman, Martin Folkes, who 'generously lent him his Book, of which the following Sheets are an exact Translation'.

Imp., VOLS I, II—London: Printed for J. Darby, A. Bettesworth, F. Fayram, J. Pemberton, C. Rivington, J. Hooke, F. Clay, J. Batley, and E. Symon. MDCCXXVI [VOLS III, IV, same, with 1727].

8vo; mo.; 1s. ea.; VOL. I, nos I-VI (400 pp. plus index, 36 pp.), VOL. II, nos VII-XII (427 pp. plus index, 28 pp.), VOL. III, nos XIII-XVIII (420 pp. plus index, 40 pp.); VOL. IV, nos XIX-XXV (542 pp. plus index, 36 pp., and Life of Rapin, 28 pp.) Serial no. on sep. t.p. of ea. no. and at top of ea. even-numbered p. No. 1 for Sept. 1725.

SALMON, THOMAS. *Modern History; or, The Present State of all Nations.* Translated into French [from original ed., in nos, 1724].

mo.; 1s. ea.; no. 1 ad. in the *Evening Post* number 2457 (April 24, 1725) as pub. 'This Day . . . . Sold by James Crokatt, J. Graves, J. Jackson, C. King, C. Rivington, J. Brotherton, J. Clark, P. Vaillant, and Mr. Woodman'.

1726

FLEURY, CLAUDE. *The Ecclesiastical History of M. L'Abbé Fleury, with the Chronology of M. Tillemont.* 5 vols.
Trans. from Fleury's *Histoire ecclésiastique* (Paris, 1722) by Henry Herbert (VOLS I and II), and G. Adams (VOLS III, IV, and V).
  Imp., VOLS I, II—London: Printed by T. Wood, for James Crokatt . . . 1727; VOLS III, IV, V—London: Printed for W. Innys. 1728 [1730; 1732].
  4to; 15 sh. ea.; mo. (irreg.); 3s. ea.; VOL. I, (615 pp. plus index); VOL. II, (916 pp.); VOL. III, nos 12-17 (706 pp.); VOL. IV, nos 18-23 (695 pp.); VOL. V, nos 24-? (728 pp.) no. 1 ad. in the *Daily Post* number 2063 (May 5, 1726) as 'now published'. No. 28 listed in the *Monthly Chronicle* October 1731; has list of subscribers.

Sepulchrorum Inscriptiones.
According to Plomer (*A Dictionary of the Printers . . . from 1726 to 1775,* p. 66), a work on epitaphs bearing this title was published in monthly parts by B. Creake in 1726.

1728

LENFANT, JACQUES. *History of the Council of Constance,* Done into English, from the last Edition, printed at Amsterdam, 1727. 2 vols.
Trans. Stephen Whatley.
  Imp., VOL. I—London: Printed for Thomas Cox . . ., Thomas Astley . . ., Stephen Austen . . ., Lawton Gilliver . . ., MDCCXXVIII.
  Imp. VOL. II—London: Printed for A. Bettesworth, C. Rivington, J. Batley, T. Cox, J. Clarke, R. Hett, T. Astley, S. Austen, J. Gray and L. Gilliver, MDCCXXX.
  4to; 15 sh. ea.; mo. (irreg.); 3s. ea.; about 10 nos; VOL. I, 62 plus 636 pp.; VOL. II, 603 pp.; plates. Proposals announced no. 1 to be pub. April 6, [1728]; dedication dated March 1, 1729/30. Two vols complete ad. March 1730.

SALMON, NATHANIEL. *A New Survey of England.* 2 vols.
8vo; irreg.; 1s. ea.; 11 nos; maps; no. 1 listed in the *Monthly Chronicle* April 1728, 'To be continued Monthly, or as often as conveniently it may . . . Sold by J. Roberts'. No. XI, 'last', listed *ibid.*, Aug. 1730.

THOU, Jacques Auguste de, *alias* THUANUS. *History of his own Time.* 2 vols.

Trans. Rev. Bernard Wilson, from Latin original, *Historia sui temporis* (Geneva, 1720).

Imp. vol. 1—London: Printed by E. Say, and sold by W. Meadows..., B. Motte and T. Worral..., J. Stagg..., T. Jackson..., and B. Farnsworth at Newark. MDCCXXIX. Imp. vol. ii adds F. Fayram, T. Green, and J. Roberts, and is dated MDCCXXX.

fol.; 16 sh. ea.; mo.; 6d. to 2s. ea.; 24 nos; vol. 1, 699 pp. and index; vol. ii, pp. [i]-cxli plus 568. No. 1 listed in the *Monthly Chronicle* March 1728 as pub. Feb.

1729

FLOURNOIS, Gédéon. **Religious Novels.* Translated from the French, *Entretiens des voyageurs sur la mer.* With Additions.

French original pub. Cologne, 1704.

No. 1 listed in the *Monthly Chronicle* July 1729 as 'Printed for J. Roberts. Price 1s.'.

PALMER, Samuel. *The General History of Printing.*

Imp. no. 1 (March)—London: Printed by the Author, and sold at his Printing-House...; also by J. Roberts..., and by most Booksellers in Town and Country. MDCCXIX. (Price 2s. 6d.) Imp. of vol.—London: Printed by the Author, and sold by his Widow at his late Printing-House...; also by J. Roberts..., and by most Booksellers in Town and Country. MDCCXXXII.

4to; mo. (irreg.); 2s. 6d. ea.; vii plus 400 pp.; inc.; serial nos on sep. t.p. of fasc.; no. 1 listed in the *Monthly Chronicle* April 1729. Reissued with new t.p. 1733.

PIOSSENS, ..., Chevalier de. *Memoirs of the Regency of His Royal Highness the late Duke of Orleans.*

A trans. of *Mémoires de la régence de ... Mgr. le Duc d'Orléans durant la minorité de Louis XV* (Paris 1729).

Imp.—London: Printed for J. Crokatt ... 1729.

8vo; 10 hf. sh. ea.; mo.; 1s. ea.; no. 1 has 80 pp., text running on; no. 1, listed in the *Monthly Chronicle* May 1729; no. 3 listed *ibid.* July 1729; note in no. 1: 'The Second Number of this Work will be publish'd in a few Days; and the Heads mention'd in the Title for the First Volume, will be added to the Sixth Pamphlet, which will compleat it.' Whole work pub. 1732.

RAPIN DE THOYRAS, PAUL DE. *Histoire d'Angleterre par Mr. d'Rapin Thoyras, avec les Notes ajoutées par Mr. Tyndal Marquées d'un Asterisque, traduits en François.
mo.; 1s. ea.; at least 52 nos; 'Nombre I' listed in the Monthly Chronicle Feb. 1729 as 'Printed for J. Roberts . . .'; no. 24 (April 1730) and later nos ad. as 'Printed for T. Astley'; no. 52, 'which compleats VOL. IX', pub. Dec. 1731.

1730
*Memorials of Affairs of State, during the . . . Reign of King William III. No. 1 ad. in the Monthly Chronicle Jan. 1730 as 'Printed for P. Meighan. Price 1s'.

RADICATI, ALBERTO, COUNT DI PASSERANO. Christianity Set in a True Light. By a Pagan Philosopher newly converted.
Imp.—London: Printed for J. Peele . . .; and Sold by the Booksellers of London and Westminster. 1730. [Price One Shilling].
8vo; 9 hf. shs.; mo.; 1s. ea.; prelim. plus 44 pp. plus 20 pp. in the only no. pub.; no. 1 listed in the Echo; or, Edinburgh Weekly Journal number 69 (April 29, 1730), 'To be continued Monthly'; licensed as pamphlet.

SALE, GEORGE, John Campbell, and others. An Universal History, from the Earliest Account of Time to the Present. Compiled from Original Authors. 7 vols.
Imp. VOL. 1—London: Printed for J. Batley . . .; E. Symon . . ; T. Osborne . . .; and J. Crokatt. MDCCXXXVI [VOL. II, MDCCXXXVII]. fol.; 20 sh. ea.; mo. (irreg.); 3s. 6d. ea.; VOL. I, nos 1-XIII; other vols. 10, 11, or 12 nos ea.; maps, pl., tables; no. 1 listed in the Monthly Chronicle May 1730; no. 6 ad. in Daily Advertiser number 434 (June 22, 1732); no. 10 ad. ibid. number 1218 (Dec. 24, 1734); no. 13, 'which concludes VOL. I', listed at 10s. 6d. in London Magazine Feb. 1736; no. 1 of VOL. III ad. St. James's Evening Post number 4291 (July 5, 1737) as pub. 'This Day'; VOL. IV completed by April 13, 1739; no. 2 of VOL. V ad. Weekly Miscellany (Aug. 4, 1739); Roy. lic. Mar. 24, 1738/39; second ed., 8vo, 1747-1766.

1731
GROSVENOR, BENJAMIN. The Mourner: or, the Afflicted Relieved. Imp.—London: Printed for Richard Hett . . . MDCCXXXI.
12mo; 12 nos; Preface dated Mar. 30, 1731; listed in Monthly Chronicle April 1731, 'In Twelve Numbers. 1s. 6d.'.

MORGAN, J. *Phoenix Britannicus; Being a Miscellaneous Collection of Scarce and Curious Tracts . . . Prose and Verse.*

Imp., VOL. I—London: Printed for the Compiler, and T. Edlin . . .; and J. Wilford . . . M.DCC.XXXII. Price (Unbound) Fifteen Shillings.

4to; mo. (irreg.); 2s. 6d.; VOL. I, Nos I to 6 (6 plus 4 plus 6 plus 2 plus 584 pp.); no more pub.? fasc. sigs.; No. I is marked 'for January 1731', but is listed *Monthly Chronicle* April 1731; Nos 2, 3, 4, 5 listed *ibid.* Aug., Oct., and Dec. 1731 as 'Printed for J. Wilford'.

SALMON, NATHANIEL. *The Lives of the English Bishops, from the Restauration to the Revolution.*

Imp. Part I—London: Printed for C. Rivington . . . MDCCXXXI;
Imp. Part II—London: Printed for J. Roberts . . . MDCCXXXI.

8vo; irreg.; 1s. ea.; publication in nos discontinued after Part II; remainder (pp. 163-402) all pub. together by J. Roberts in 1733; serial nos on sep. t.p. of Parts I and II; Part I listed *Monthly Chronicle* July 1731. Part II listed *ibid.*, Sept. 1731.

1732

BAKER, SIR RICHARD. *A Chronicle of the Kings of England . . . to the Death of King James the First . . . With a Continuation to the Year 1660.* By E. Phillips. [and] A Second Continuation [to the death of King George I].

Rep. from ed. pub. by Ballard, Motte, Williamson, and others (London, 1730).

Imp.—London, Printed for Samuel Ballard . . .; Benjamin Motte . . .; Richard Williamson . . .; Samuel Birt . . .; John Stagg . . .; Thomas Osborne . . .; and Charles Davis . . . MDCCXXXIII.

fol.; 5 sh. ea.; w.; 6d. ea.; vol. has 20 plus 918 plus 12 pp (48 nos); no. 1 ad. *Daily Advertiser* number 577 (Dec. 6, 1732) as to be pub. Dec. 13.

BARCLAY, PATRICK. *The Universal Traveller: Or, A Complete Account of the most Remarkable Voyages and Travels.*

Imp.—London: Printed for J. Purser, and T. Read . . .; and S. Hester . . . MDCCXXXV.

fol.; 2 sh. w. for 3d., or 8 sh. mo. for 1s.; 25 mo. nos; maps; fasc. sigs.; vol. has 12 plus 795 plus 12 pp.; no. 1 ad. *Daily Advertiser* number 580 (Dec. 9, 1732) as pub. 'This Day' . . . Sold by Abr. Holbeche . . .; Sam. Hester . . .; the Widow Davis . . .; and A. Weddell . . .;' rep. in nos, Dublin, 1733.

BOERHAAVE, HERMAN. *Elements of Chemistry*. Being the Annual Lectures of Herman Boerhaave, M.D. In two Volumes . . . English'd by a Gentleman of the University of Oxford.
No. 1 listed in *Gentleman's Magazine* January 1732. Advance notice in *Monthly Chronicle* October 1731: 'to be continued in Numbers at 1*s*. 6*d*. each. Printed for J. Clark. N.B. This work is to be translated from the Author's own Book [*Elementa Chemiae*], just printed in Holland, each Exemplar being sign'd with his own Hand, and will contain about 150 Sheets in 4to, Eight of which, at least, shall be published in each Number, till the Whole is finished'. Listed in *Gentleman's Magazine* May 1732: 'Dr. Boerhaave's Elements of Chymistry, faithfully abridg'd from the genuine Edition, publish'd and sign'd by himself at Leyden. Printed for J. Wilford, pr. 7*s*. with Cuts.' Apparently only the first fascicule was pub.

BRUYS, FRANÇOIS. **The History of the Popes, from St. Peter down to Benedict XIII, inclusively*. Translated from the French Original just publish'd at the Hague.
Trans. of *Histoire des Papes, depuis St. Pierre jusqu'à Benoit XIII* 5 vols. (La Haye, 1732-1734).
mo.; 1*s*. ea.; no. 1 listed in *London Magazine* Sept. 1732 as 'Printed for J. Batley'; no. 2 ad. in *Daily Advertiser* number 552 (Nov. 7, 1732) as 'Just publish'd . . . . The Author being a Frenchman, and actually residing in France, is oblig'd to conceal his Name.'

CAMPBELL, JOHN. *A New Complete History of the Holy Bible, As contained in the Writings of the Old and New Testament*. 2 vols.
Begun by Thomas Stackhouse in Sept. 1732. When Stackhouse refused in Nov. 1732 to continue, Edlin engaged Campbell to carry on the work.
Imp.—London: Printed and Sold by T. Edlin . . . MDCCXXXIII [VOL. II, MDCCXXXIV].
fol.; 3 sh. ea.; w.; 6*d*.; VOL. I, 44 plus 512 plus 164 pp.; VOL. II, 612 pp.; pl., 3*d*. ea. to subscribers, 6*d*. ea. to others; no. 48 ad. *Cotes's Weekly Journal* number 1 (May 11, 1734) as pub. 'This Day'.

COLBATCH, JOHN. *The Generous Physician, or Medicine made easy*.
Imp.—London: Printed for J. Roberts . . .: and sold by the Booksellers of London and Westminster. (Price One Shilling and Sixpence). n.d.
8vo; fort.; 6*d*.; vol. has 4 plus 90 pp.; inc.; no. 1 ad. *Daily Advertiser*

number 585 (Dec. 15, 1732) as pub. 'This Day' under the title *Dr. Colbatch's Legacy, or, the Family Physician.*

*Compleat Collection of English and Scotch Songs and Ballads, A. w.; *6d.* ea.; 8 hf. sh. in ea.; nos 1, 2, 3 listed *London Magazine* Nov. 1732 as 'Printed for W. Bickerton, T. Astley, S. Austen, and R. Willock.' Nos 4, 5, 6, 7 listed *ibid.* Dec. 1732; no. 9 listed *ibid.* May 1733.

*Construction and Principal Uses of all Mathematical Instruments, The. fort.; *6d.* ea.; 4 sh. ea.; no. 3 ad. *Whitehall Evening-Post* number 2293 (Jan. 9, 1733) as pub. 'This Day . . . by C. Price . . ., neat Pocket Volumes . . . by Several Hands'.

EISENMENGER, JOHANN ANDREAS. **The Traditions of the Jews; with the Expositions and Doctrines of the Rabbins.* Translated [by Rev. John Peter Stehelin] from the High Dutch [first pub. Frankfurt, 1700; 2nd ed. Königsberg, 1711]. 2 vols.
  Imp., No. 1 —London: Printed for G. Smith . . ., and Sold by J. Brotherton . . .; and Steph. Austen . . . M.DCC.XXXII. (Price 1*s*).
  Imp., VOL. 1—London: Printed for J. Brotherton, and sold by J. Wilford, 1732 [VOL. II, 1734].
8vo; copy of no. 1 seen at Library of Congress has 6 plus 80 pp.; no. 3, 'which compleats VOL. 1', ad. *Daily Advertiser* number 436 (June 23, 1732) as pub. 'This Day . . . Price 4*s*. Sew'd. Those who have bought Numb. I and II, may have Numb. III to compleat the First Volume at 2*s*. and 6*d*.'

JOSEPHUS, FLAVIUS. *The Works of Flavius Josephus which are Extant* . . . Translated from the Original Greek, according to Dr. Hudson's Edition. By John Court . . . with . . . Notes, Tables, Maps.
  Imp. of one early no.—London: Printed by R. Penny, at Mr. Jane-way's . . . M.DCC.XXXII.
  Imp. of vol.—London: Printed by R. Penny . . ., and J. Janeway . . . M.DCC.XXXIII.
fol.; 134 nos; vol. has 978 pp. plus index; maps; fasc. sigs.

JOSEPHUS, FLAVIUS. *The Works of Flavius Josephus.* Translated into English by Sir Roger L'Estrange, Knight . . . Fifth Edition. Previous ed. 1725.
  Imp.—London: Printed for James, John, and Paul Knapton . . .;

D. Midwinter and A. Ward . . .; A. Bettesworth and C. Hitch, John Osborn and T. Longman, and J. Batley . . .; J. Pemberton . . .; C. Rivington . . .; F. Clay . . .; R. Williamson . . .; R. Hett . . .; T. Hatchett . . . And Sold by T. Warner . . . MDCCXXXIII. fol.; 3 sh. ea.; w.; 6d. ea.; 50 nos; vol. has 18 plus 917 plus 28 pp.; fasc. sigs.; no. 9 ad. *Whitehall Evening-Post* number 2292 (Jan. 6, 1733); total to be 250 sh., issued 5 sh. w.; reissued 1739.

KEATING, GEOFFREY. *History of Ireland.*
Trans. from Irish original by Darby O'Connor (1721).
6 sh. ea.; w.; 6d.; 30 nos; no. 1 ad. *Daily Advertiser* number 604 (Oct. 7, 1732) as pub. 'This Day . . . Printed for B. Creake . . ., and W. Waring . . .; and sold by the Booksellers of London and Westminster'.

NOTE: References to the *Daily Advertiser* here and elsewhere in this list are to the serial numbers as they appear in the originals. The numbers are inconsistent, for number 606 (Oct. 10, 1732) is followed by number 529 (October 11, 1732).

Milton Restor'd, and Bentley Depos'd.
8vo.; 6d.; no. 2 listed *Gentleman's Magazine* Mar. 1732.

OAKLEY, EDWARD. *The Magazine of Architecture, Perspective, and Sculpture.* Second Edition.
Rep. from first ed. (Westminster:Printed by A. Campbell, for the Author . . . & B. Creake . . . MDCCXXX).
10 hf. sh. ea.; fort.; 1s. ea., or 1s. 6d. ea. on Royal paper; 16 nos; total 80 sh. (31½ sh. presswork and 97 plates); Proposals in *Daily Advertiser* number 531 (Oct. 13, 1732) announce no. 1 to be pub. Oct. 16: 'Subscriptions are taken in by the Author, at the Three Doves in Brewers Street, Golden-square; B. Creake . . .; W. Waring . . .; and by the Booksellers of London and Westminster'.

PALLADIO, ANDREA. *The First Book of Palladio's Architecture.* Correctly copied from the first Edition, printed at Venice, Anno Dom. MDLXX. Based on Andrea Palladio's *I quattro libri del'architettura* (Venice, 1570).
fol.; 3½ sh. ea.; w.; 6d. ea.; vol. to have 20 sh. fol. and 30 fol. pl.; Proposals in *Daily Advertiser* number 559 (Nov. 15, 1732) announce this to be 'engrav'd and printed by Ben. Cole', and 'Subscriptions are taken in by the Undertaker . . . .; and J. Clark . . . .' No. 1 ad. *ibid.* number 564

(Nov. 21, 1732) as pub. Nov. 18. Cole expected to pub. the three other books 'in the same Manner, and on the same Terms'. Rem. may have made up *Andrea Palladio's Architecture in Four Books* (London: Printed for Benjⁿ Cole Engraver . . . & John Wilcox . . . MDCCXXXVI).

RAPIN DE THOYRAS, PAUL DE. *Acta Regia: Being the Account which Mr. Rapin de Thoyras Published of the History of England . . . grounded upon those Records which . . . are collected in . . . Mr. Rymer's Foedera.* Rep. from ed. in 8vo nos pub. 1725.

Imp.—London: Printed for James, John and Paul Knapton . . .; D. Midwinter . . .; A. Bettesworth and C. Hitch . . .; C. Rivington . . .; J. Pemberton . . .; J. Osborn and T. Longman . . .; F. Clay . . .; J. Batley . . .; A. Ward . . .; R. Hett . . .; T. Hatchett . . . n.d.

fol.; 5 sh. ea.; w.; 6d. ea.; 43 nos; vol. has 828 plus 32 pp.; fasc. sigs; no. 1 listed *Gentleman's Magazine* Nov. 1732; Dedication by Stephen Whatley dated Dec. 20, 1733.

RAPIN DE THOYRAS, PAUL DE. *The History of England.* Second Edition. 2 vols.
Trans. by Nicholas Tindal, from French original pub. at the Hague in 1724. Rep. from ed. in 8vo nos pub. by Knaptons 1725-1731.

Imp.—London: Printed for James, John and Paul Knapton . . . MDCCXXXII [VOL. II, MDCCXXXIII].

fol.; 5 sh. ea.; w.; 6d. ea.; VOL. I, nos I-XLIII; VOL. II, nos XLIV-LXXXIV; fasc. sigs.; no. 1 ad. *Daily Advertiser* number 472 (Aug. 5, 1732) as pub. 'This Day'; continuation pub. in 103 fol. nos, 1736; Third ed. pub. by Knaptons in nos, 1743.

RAPIN DE THOYRAS, PAUL DE. *The History of England.* Written originally in French by M. Rapin Thoyras. Translated into English by John Kelly of the Inner Temple, Esq. [VOL. II has 'Translated by Joseph Morgan, Gent.']. 2 vols.

Imp.—London: Printed for James Mechell . . . MDCCXXXII [VOL. II, MDCCXXXIII].

fol.; 4 sh. ea.; w.; 6d. ea.; VOL. I, nos 1-53 (14 plus 822 pp.), VOL. II, nos 1-58 (936 pp.); fasc. sigs.; no. 1 pub. June 3, 1732; continuation pub. in nos by Mechell, 1735. Mechell indicated in the first volume of the continuation of this work that Kelly had disagreed with him while the nos of VOL. I were being pub., and that Kelly had 'printed some Numbers on his own account'.

RAPIN DE THOYRAS, PAUL DE. *The History of England.*
Kelly's trans. of Rapin's *Histoire d'Angleterre* (see preceding item).
8vo; 1 hf. sh. (8 pp.) ea.; w.; pub. as supp. to the *Historical Journal* (printed and sold by R. Barlow, London); pp. 89-96 attached to the *Historical Journal* number 12 (Aug. 26, 1732).

STACKHOUSE, THOMAS. *A New History of the Holy Bible.*
fol.; 3 sh. ea.; w.; 6d. ea.; no. 1 ad. *Daily Advertiser* number 596 (Sept. 27, 1732) as pub. 'This Day . . . . Subscriptions . . . taken in by Tho. Edlin'; was to have contained 200 sh.; inc. (discontinued after a few nos; started anew with no. 1, Feb. 3, 1733).

TILLEMONT, LOUIS SEBASTIEN LE NAIN DE. *Ecclesiastical Memoirs of the Six First Centuries.* 2 vols.
Trans. Thomas Deacon.
Imp., VOL. 1—London: Printed for the Benefit of the Translator; and Sold by J. Wilford . . ., and W. Clayton, Bookseller in Manchester. MDCCXXXIII.
Imp., VOL. II—London: Printed for the Translator; and Sold by W. Clayton, Bookseller in Manchester. MDCCXXXV.
fol.; mo.; 2s. 6d. ea.; VOL. I, nos 1-12 (668 pp.); VOL. II, nos 1-5 (36 plus 594 pp.); inc.; no. 1 listed in *Monthly Chronicle* Dec. 1731; has list of subscribers.

TINDAL, NICHOLAS. *The History of Essex.*
Imp., no. 1 —London: Printed by H. Woodfall; and Sold by J. and J. Knapton . . .; Mr. Green, at Chelmsford; Mrs. Oliver, at Norwich; Mr. Bailey, at St. Edmunds-bury; Mr. Holman, at Sudbury; Mr. Humphry jun. at Halsted; Mr. Creighton, at Ipswich; and by others at Saffron-Walden, Braintree, Colchester, and the rest of the Towns of Essex. [1732].
4to; 7 sh. ea.; 1s. 6d. ea.; to make 3 vols., but only nos 1 and 2 pub.; fasc. sigs.

1733
BARCLAY, PATRICK. *The Universal Traveller: Or, a Complete Account of the most Remarkable Voyages and Travels of the Eminent Men of our own and other Nations to the present Time.*
Rep. from the ed. in nos, London, 1732.
Imp.—Dublin. Printed by R. Reilly . . . for Stearne Brock . . . MDCCXXXV.
fol.; 10 sh. ea.; mo.? 22 nos; 858 plus 20 pp.; maps; fasc. sigs.

BAYLE, PIERRE. *The Dictionary Historical and Critical.* Second Edition. To which is prefixed, The Life of the Author, Revised, Corrected, and Enlarged, by Mr. Des Maizeaux. 5 vols.
Trans. from *Dictionnaire historique et critique*, 4th ed., 4 vols (Amsterdam, 1730). First ed. in English pub. 1710, based on 2nd ed. of the original, 3 vols. (Rotterdam, 1702).
    Imp. of VOL. 1–London: Printed for J., J. and P. Knapton; D. Midwinter; J. Brotherton; A. Bettesworth and C. Hitch; J. Hazard; J. Tonson; W. Innys and R. Manby; J. Osborne and T. Longman; T. Ward and E. Wicksteed; W. Meadows; T. Woodward; B. Motte; W. Hinchliffe; J. Walthoe, jun.; E. Symon; T. Cox; A. Ward; D. Browne; S. Birt; W. Bickerton; T. Astley; S. Austen; L. Gilliver; H. Lintot; H. Whitridge; R. Willock. MDCCXXXIV. [VOL. V, MDCCXXXVIII].
fol.; 8 sh. ea.; fort.; 1s. ea.; 148 nos; fasc. sigs.; no. 1 pub. Jan. 1733.

BAYLE, PIERRE. *A General Dictionary, Historical and Critical.* 10 vols.
Trans. and ed. (with considerable additions) by John Peter Bernard, Thomas Birch, John Lockman, and others. from *Dictionnaire historique et critique*, 4th ed., 4 vols. (Amsterdam, 1730). 10 vols.
    Imp.–VOL. 1–London. Printed by James Bettenham, for G. Strahan, J. Clarke, T. Hatchet . . .; J. Gray, J. Batley . . .; T. Worrall, J. Shuckburgh . . .; J. Wilcox, A. Millar, C. Corbet . . .; T. Osborne . . .; J. Brindley . . .; and C. Ward and R. Chandler, and sold at their Shop in Scarborough. MDCCXXXIV. [VOLS. II and III have MDCCXXXV; VOL. IV has MDCCXXXVI; VOL. V has MDCCXXXVII; VOLS. VI and VII have MDCCXXXVIII; VOLS. VIII and IX have MDCCXXXIX; VOL. X has MDCCXLI; imp. of VOL. IV omits T. Worrall and adds J. Wood; imp. of VOL. V adds G. Hawkins; imp. of VOL. VI omits J. Batley; imp. of VOL. X adds C. Woodward]. Some copies of VOL. I have the imp.–London: Printed; And Sold by J. Roberts . . . and Paul Vaillant . . . MDCCXXXIV. This work is ad. in *Daily Advertiser* number 674 (March 29, 1733) as 'to be continu'd Monthly (As advertis'd by Mr. Payne) . . . . Printed for and sold by Nicholas Prevost . . .; Mr. Gyles . . .; Mr. Harding . . .; Mr. Crokatt . . .; Mr. Brindley . . .; Mess. Clements and Wilmot, at Oxford; Mess. Crownfield and Thurlborne, at Cambridge; Mess. Leake and Cobb, at Bath; and Mr. Hillyard, at York'.
fol.; 20 sh. ea.; mo.; 3s.; Preface points out that ea. vol. 'will contain but nine monthly Numbers, whereas it was designed before to contain twelve'; VOL. I, 2 plus 4 plus 30 plus 712 pp.; VOL. II, 718 pp.; VOL. III, 724 pp.; VOL. IV, 715 pp.; VOL. V., 716 pp.; VOL. VI, 716 pp.;

VOL. VII, 828 pp.; VOL. VIII, 832 pp.; VOL. IX, 716 pp.; VOL. X, 588 pp. plus index, sigs. 71-9Y; no. 1 pub. March 1733.

BERNARD, JEAN FRÉDÉRIC. *The Ceremonies and Religious Customs of the various Nations of the known World* . . . Faithfully translated into English by a Gentleman, some time since of St. John's College in Oxford. 7 vols.
Trans. from *Cérémonies et coutumes religieuses de tous les peuples du monde*, 8 vols. (Amsterdam, 1723-1743).
    Imp., VOLS I and III—London: Printed by William Jackson, for Claude Du Bosc, Engraver . . . MDCCXXXIII. [VOLS II and IV, MDCCXXXIV; VOL. V, MDCCXXXVI; VOL. VI, MDCCXXXVII; VOL. VII, MDCCXXXIX].
fol.; 4 sh. plus 2 prints, or 6 sh. plus 1 print, or 8 sh.; w.; 1s. ea.; pl. by Picart; no. 1 ad. *Daily Advertiser* number 662 (Mar. 15, 1733) as pub. Mar. 10. Total pr. to be £5. 10s. 'Proposals may be seen at the Places where Subscriptions are taken in, viz. Claude Dubosc . . .; Thomas Bowles . . .; Philip Overton . . .; Thomas Glass . . .; John Bowles . . .; James Regnier . . .; John Hulton . . .; Peter Foudrinier . . .; John King . . .; Mrs. Marbeck . . . .'

BICKHAM, GEORGE. *The Universal Penman.*
    Imp.—London: Printed for the author, and Sent to the Subscribers, if Living within the Bills of Mortality. n.d.
fol.; 4 hf. sh. ea.; irreg.; 6d.; 52 nos; 208 fols.; Address to Subscribers dated Aug. 1733; pl. variously dated 1733, 1734, 1735, 1736, 1737, 1738 . . .; rep. in nos, 1742.

BIRD, G. *The Practising Scrivener and Modern Conveyancer.* 2 vols.?
Presumably rep. from ed. pub. in 4 vols., VOL. 1 of which comprises 102 sh. and has the imp.—In the Savoy: Printed by E. and R. Nutt and R. Gosling, (Assigns of E. Sayer, Esq;) for J. Stagg . . ., and D. Browne . . . MDCCXXIX.
8 sh. ea.; fort.; 1s.; no. 1 of VOL. II ad. *Daily Advertiser* number 628 (Feb. 3, 1733) as pub. Jan. 25; 'The other Volume . . . will soon after follow . . . . Each Volume . . . . will contain about 200 Sheets'; agents named: Roberts, Stagg, Brown, Worrall, Batley, Meadows.

British Miscellany, or the Harmonious Grove, The.
8vo; 12 songs in ea. no.; mo.; 1s. ea.; no. 1 ad. *Daily Advertiser* number 861 (Nov. 2, 1733) as pub. 'This Day . . . Printed for Daniel Wright . . .; Dan. Wright jun. . . .; and T. Wright . . .; the whole will be comprised

in two large Volumes in 8vo., containing 288 Songs, 12 of which will be publish'd Monthly at 1*s.*'

British Musical Miscellany: Or, The Delightful Grove, The. Being a Collection of Celebrated English and Scotch Songs. By the Best Masters. 6 vols.
Imp.—London. Printed for & Sold by I. Walsh . . . n.d.
4to; mo.; 1*s.* ea.; 4 plus 145 pp. in ea. vol.; no. 1, 'Publish'd for Nov. 1733' ad. *Daily Advertiser* number 897 (Dec. 14, 1733) as pub. 'This Day'; no. 8 ad. June 1735.

BURKITT, WILLIAM. *Expository Notes, with practical Observations, on the New Testament.* Tenth Edition.
Imp.—London: Printed for James, John, and P. Knapton . . .; D. Midwinter, R. Robinson, C. Rivington . . .; A. Bettesworth and C. Hitch, J. Osborn and T. Longman, Jer. Batley . . .; J. Downing . . .; R. Ford, R. Hett . . .; F. Clay . . .; A. Ward . . .; T. Ward and E. Wicksteed . . .; J. Clarke . . .; T. Hatchett . . . MDCCXXXIV.
fol.; 5 sh. ea.; w.; 6*d.* ea.; 44 nos; fasc. sigs.; no. 1 ad. *Daily Advertiser* number 892 (Dec. 8, 1733) as pub. 'This Day', with J. Pemberton included among the proprietors.

BURNET, GILBERT. *The History of the Reformation of the Church of England.*
Taken from the Writings of the Right Reverend Father in God, Gilbert, Lord Bishop of Sarum, and others.
Imp.—London: Printed by J. Read . . . MDCCXXXVII.
fol.; single sh. ea. no. (as detachable supp. to *Read's Weekly Journal; or, British Gazetteer*), or 2 sh. fort. for 2*d.*, or 4 sh. mo. for 4*d.*; 139 nos; 560 pp.; fasc. sigs.; first single sh. supp. issued Sept. 29, 1733; seventh mo. no. ad. *Read's Weekly Journal* number 472 (April 6, 1734).

CAMDEN, WILLIAM. *Britannia.*
Rep. from Gibson's English trans. (1695, 1722) of *Britannia, sive florentissimorum regnorum, Angliae, Scotiae, Hiberniae Chorographica descriptio* (1586).
4to.; single hf. sh. pub. as supp. to the *British Observator* (printed and sold by R. Penny); pp. 65-68 (sig. no. IX I) attached to number 9 (May 5, 1733).

CHAMPION, JOSEPH. **Practical Arithmetick.* Second Edition.
8vo; 2 hf. sh. (16 pp.) ea.; fort.; 3*d.* ea; no. 1 ad. *Daily Advertiser* number

666 (Mar. 20, 1733) as pub. 'This Day . . . . Subscriptions will be taken in till May next, and no longer, at Sidebotham's St. Martin's Le Grand Coffee-House; Halfmoon Coffee-House, Cheapside; Mr. King, at the Globe in the Poultry; Mr. Evendon, in Leadenhall-street, and by the Author . . . at the Golden Pea in the Old Change, Cheapside'.

Collection of the most remarkable Trials of Persons for High Treason, Murder, Rapes, Heresy, Bigamy, Patricide, Sodomy, Burglary, Bills of Attainder, Impeachments &c. 5 vols.
fol.; single sh. as supp. to *Penny London Post* Mon., Wed., and Fri., or 12 sh. mo. for 1s.; fourth mo. no. ad. *Daily Advertiser* number 901 (Dec. 19, 1733) as pub. 'This Day . . . . The General Title, with a compleat Index to this Work, shall be deliver'd gratis when the Collection is finish'd. Printed and Sold by T. Read . . .; and at the Pamphlet-shops at the Royal Exchange, Temple Bar, and Charing Cross.' No. 32 (11th of VOL. III) ad. *St. James's Evening Post* number 4062 (Jan. 17, 1736) as pub. Jan. 12 at 1s.

COURT, JOHN and LINDSAY, JOHN. *The New Testament . . . with Critical and Explanatory Notes* [by Court 'as far as the 10th Chapter of S. Luke'].
   Imp.—London: Printed by R. Penny . . . MDCCXXXVI.
fol.; 2 sh. w. for 3d., or 8 sh. mo. for 1s.; 27 mo. nos; 895 pp.; fasc. sigs., sep. series for w. and mo. nos; proposals pub. Aug. 4, 1733; no. 1 ad. *British Observator* number 23 (Aug. 18, 1733) as pub. Aug. 16; reissued 1737 with new t.p.: *A Critical and Practical Commentary on the New Testament*, Printed for D. Farmer . . . and J. Robinson.

FOXE, JOHN. *Book of Martyrs.*
w.; 2 sh. ea.; 3d. ea.; listed *Gentleman's Magazine* January 1733; ad. of similar work by Lyndar (*Daily Advertiser* number 778, July 28, 1733) refers to 'a Weekly Work already begun . . . a mere Abstract of the English Book of Martyrs'.

History of Scotland, The.
fol.; 2 sh.; w.; supp. to the *British Mercury, or Weekly Pacquet* (printed by William Rayner); or 8 sh. mo. for 1s.; no. 1 ad. *Daily Advertiser* number 818 (Sept. 13, 1733) to be pub. Sept. 15.

History of the Conquest of Mexico, or New Spain.
single sh. as supp. to the *Original London Post: Or, Heathcote's Intelligence*, Mon., Wed., and Fri. 'The Title Page, Preface, and Contents

to be given Gratis, when the Volume is compleated ... To be had only of B. Buckeridge ... and of the Persons that carry the News Papers, at the small Expence of One Penny.' Ad. *Daily Advertiser* number 864 (October 16, 1733).

*KING, GILES. *Heads of all the Kings and Queens from K. William the Conqueror to K. William III, together with Plates of ... Battles.*
2 prints ea.; mo.; 3*d.* ea. pl.; 40 pl. in all; nos 1 and 2 ad. *Daily Advertiser* number 602 (Jan. 5, 1733) as to be pub. the next day; 'Design'd as Ornaments for the History of England, publishing Weekly. ... may be had of Messrs. Millan and Chrichley ...; W. Shropshire ...; D. Gardiner ...; T. Corbett ...; J. Janeway ...; E. Nutt ...; at the Picture-shop near the East-India House in Leadenhall-street, and by most of the Book and Pamphlet-sellers in London and West-minster'.

LANGLEY, BATTY. *Ancient Masonry, both in Theory and Practice.*
Imp. —London: Printed for, and sold by the Author, at Parliament-stairs, near Old Palace-Yard, Westminster, J. Milan ..., and J. Huggonson ... MDCCXXXVI.
fol. (Royal paper); 2, 3, or 4 sh. ea.; w.; 6*d.* ea.; 434 pp. and 465 pl.; fasc. sigs. in nos 1-19; no. 1 ad. *Daily Advertiser* number 609 (Jan. 12, 1733) to be pub. 'on Monday the 15th and Saturday the 20th In-stant .... Printed by J. Chrichley'. Intro. dated Jan. 15, 1732 [i.e., 1733]. Advertisement to Reader dated Sept. 10, 1736.

LANGLEY, BATTY. **The Young Builder's Rudiments; teaching by Question and Answer the most useful Parts of Geometry, Architecture, Mechanicks, Mensuration several Ways, and Perspective.*
4to; 5 sh. ea.; fort.; pl. by Vandergucht and Cole; no. 1 ad. *Daily Advertiser* number 605 (Jan. 8, 1733) as pub. 'This Day .... Subscrip-tions are taken in by J. Millan ...; and by the Booksellers in London and Westminster.'

LYNDAR, HARRY (of the Inner Temple, Esq.). **A Book of Martyrs the best Preservative against Popery; or, a compleat History of the Sufferings Protestants have been subjected to.*
4 sh. ea.; w.; 6*d.* ea.; no. 2 ad. *Daily Advertiser* number 778 (July 28, 1733): 'Subscriptions ... taken in ... by J. Roberts ...; Stephen Fitzer ...; E. Nutt ...; A. Dodd ...; J. Crichley ...; J. Millan ...; J. Jolliffe ...; W. Shropshire ...; Webb ... in Greenwich; G. Allen ... at Eaton; and W. Ayres ... in Reading.'

MOLL, HERMAN. *A New Description of England and Wales, with the adjacent Islands.*
First ed. pub. 1724.
  Imp.—London: Printed for J. Wilford . . .; T. Bowles . . ., C. Rivington . . .; and J. Bowles . . . MDCCXXXIII.
6 sh. ea.; w.; 1s. ea.; 19 nos; 50 maps by Moll; no. 1 listed in the *Bee* number 8 (March 31, 1733) among 'Books and Pamphlets publish'd from Thursday March the 22d to Thursday March the 29th'.

RALEGH, SIR WALTER. *The History of the World.* The Seventh Edition, printed from the Edition publish'd in the Author's Lifetime, and revis'd by Himself. To which is Added, The Life of the Author, newly compil'd . . .; Also his Trial.
First ed. 1614.
  Imp.—London: Printed for J. J. and P. Knapton, G. Conyers, R. Knaplock, D. Midwinter and A. Ward, A. Bettesworth and C. Hitch, J. Tonson, B. Sprint, J. Osborn and T. Longman, R. Robinson, B. Motte, J. Walthoe junior, J. Wilford, J. Clarke, T. Wotton, and H. Lintott. MDCCXXXIII.
fol.; 4 sh. ea.; w.; 6d. ea.; fasc. sigs.; proposals in the *Whitehall Evening Post* number 2294 (Jan. 11, 1733) announce no. 1 to be pub. Feb. 3; no. 51, 'which finishes the Body of the Work', ad. *ibid.* number 2455 (Jan. 24, 1734) as pub. Jan. 19; no. 52 (8 sh. for 1s.) ad. *St. James's Evening Post* number 3014 (Feb. 15, 1735) and no. 53 (8 sh. for 1s.) ad. *ibid.* to be pub. the following week 'for greater Expedition'; reissued or rep. 1735-1736 in fol. nos as the 'Eleventh Edition'.

RIO, J. (late Rector of Rodney-Stoke, and Prebendary of Wells in Somersetshire). * *Compleat History of the Civil Wars in England.*
6d. ea.; pl.; no. 1 ad. *Daily Advertiser* number 730 (June 2, 1733) to be pub. June 30: 'Subscriptions are taken in by W. Jackson . . ., J. Smith . . .; J. Milan . . .; J. Critchley . . .; Mr. Lewis . . .; R. Phillimore . . .; Mr. Lye . . . .' Six nos pub., then discontinued for some months; new proposals pub. Aug. 10, 1734: 'Subscriptions taken in by J. Wilford . . .; G. Strahan . . .; B. Motte . . .; J. Fox . . .; and W. Jackson . . .; as likewise by most Booksellers in Town and Country.'

SEYMOUR, ROBERT, alias John Mottley. *A Survey of the Cities of London and Westminster, Borough of Southwark, and Parts Adjacent.* 2 vols.
  Imp., VOL. 1—London. Printed for T. Read . . . MDCCXXXIII [Some copies have J. Read . . . MDCCXXXIV]; VOL. II, London . . . T. Read [or J. Read] . . . MDCCXXXV.

fol.; 4 sh. ea.; w.; *6d.* ea.; VOL. I, 54 nos (822 pp.); VOL. II, 57 nos (918 pp.); map; fasc. sigs.; no. 1 probably pub. April 28, 1733; no. 15 ad. *Daily Advertiser* number 783 (Aug. 3, 1733) as to be pub. the next day; no. 22 of VOL. II ad. *St. James's Evening Post* number 2962 (Oct. 24, 1734); has list of subscribers.

SMITH, ALEXANDER and JOHNSON, CHARLES. *A General History of the Lives and Adventures of the Most Famous Highwaymen, Murderers, Street Robbers, &c. To which is added, A Genuine Account of the Voyages and Plunders of the most Notorious Pyrates.* Interspersed with several diverting Tales, and pleasant Songs.
   Imp.—London: Printed for and Sold by J. Janeway . . .; and by the Booksellers of London and Westminster. MDCCXXXIV.
   fol.; 2 sh. ea.; w.; *2d.* (or 8 sh. mo. for *8d.*); 73 nos (484 pp. plus index, 2 pp.); fasc. sigs.; No. 1 ad. *Daily Advertiser* number 754 (June 30, 1733) as pub. June 23; also pub. in nos, 1742.

*State Tryals for High Treason, Murder, Rapes, Sodomy . . . from . . . 1407 down to the present Time. 2 vols.
   fol.; single sh. pub. as supp. to the *Compleat Historian, or the Oxford Penny-Post*, Mon., Wed., and Fri., or 3 sh. w. for *2d.*, or 9 sh. for *6d.* every 3 weeks; 1st 6d. no. ad. *Daily Advertiser* number 825 (Sept. 21, 1733) as to be pub. Sept. 22, 'Printed by William Rayner, Prisoner in the King's Bench, and sold at his Printing-Office . . .; and by the Booksellers, Pamphlet-sellers, and News-carriers in Town and Country'.

STACKHOUSE, THOMAS. *A New History of the Holy Bible.* 2 vols.
   Imp., VOL. I and II—London: Printed for the Author, and sold at his House in Theobald's Court, and by the Booksellers in Town and Country. MDCCXXXVII. Lambeth Palace copy (VOL. II only) has t.p. (perhaps from a fasc.) with imp.—London: Printed for the Author, and sold by T. Payne . . ., and the Booksellers in Town and Country. MDCCXXXIII.
   fol.; 4 sh. ea.; fort.; *6d.* ea. (Royal paper, *1s.*); 111 nos (68 plus 1616 plus 32 pp.); cuts; fasc. sigs.; proposals pub. Dec. 22, 1732: 'Subscriptions . . . taken in by Mr. Ballard, at Paul's Coffee-House in . . ., by T. Payne . . . and by [Stackhouse] at Mr. Gauden's, in King Street, Bloomsbury'; no. 1 pub. Feb. 3, 1733; rep. in fol. nos, 1742.

SWITZER, STEPHEN. **The Practical Husbandman & Planter.*
   mo.; *2s. 6d.* ea.; no. 1, for the month of April, entered in Sta. Reg. June 8, 1733.

THOMSON, JAMES. *Four Seasons, &c.
4to; fort.; 2s. or 3s. ea.; 6 pl. 'design'd by Mr. Kent'; proposals ad. *Daily Advertiser* number 605 (Jan. 8, 1733) as available from J. Millan, and the booksellers in London and Westminster; nos to 'begin to be deliver'd on Monday the 22d Instant'.

VERTUE, GEORGE and others (Du Bosc, Schley, Yver). *The Heads of the Kings of England*, proper for Mr. Rapin's History, Translated by N. Tindal, M.A. . . . Also, Twenty Plates of the Monuments of the Kings of England.
    Imp. of vol. –London: Printed for James, John and Paul Knapton . . . MDCCXXXVI.
fol. (14 × 18½ inches); 6d. ea.; pl. variously dated 1733, 1734, 1735, 1736.

1734
BAKER, REV. J. *The History of the Inquisition . . . in . . . Spain, Portugal, &c. and in both the Indies*. Compiled and Translated by the Reverend J. Baker, M.A.
    Imp.–London: Printed and Sold by Joseph Marshall . . .; and George Davies and Robert Spencer . . . M.DCC.XXXIV.
4to; 4 sh. ea.; 17 nos; 8 plus 532 plus 4 pp.; pl.; fasc. sigs.; reissued with new t.p. *(A Complete History of the Inquisition)*, 1736.

Complete Collection of State-Trials and Proceedings upon High Treason . . . from the Reign of King Richard III. to the present Time, A.
fol.; 24 sh. ea.; mo.; 1s. 6d.; or 2 sh. Mon., Wed., Fri., for 1½d.; total to be 1500 sh.; first mo. no. ad. *Daily Advertiser* number 1066 (June 29, 1734) as pub. 'This Day . . . Printed for and sold by W. Harris . . ., and by most Booksellers in Town and Country'.

FIELDING, HENRY. *The Miser*.
Rep. from ed. pub. 1733 by J. Watts.
fol.; single sh. ea.; w.; supp. to *Cotes's Weekly Journal: Or, the English Stage-Player* (London: Printed by J. Taylor, at T. Edlin's . . .); 2d. for 1 sh. of news and 1 sh. of text; presumably began with number 5 (June 8, 1734).

History of the Inquisitions of the Kingdom of Spain, Portugal, &c., The.
4to; 4 sh. ea.; fort.; 6d. ea.; no. 1 pub. Feb. 16, 1734; pl.; pub. by J. Janeway.

History of the Life and Death of . . . Jesus Christ . . . . To which will be added The Lives and Travels of the Apostles. By a Divine of the Church of England.
fol.; 4 sh. ea.; fort.; 6d. ea.; 'near 150 Sheets'; pl.; proposals dated October 29, 1734; no. 1 pub. Dec. 7, 1734; 'Subscriptions . . . taken in by J. Wilford . . .; and by the Booksellers of London and Westminster.' No. 39 ad. *Daily Journal*, May 22, 1736.

Honey-suckle, The. Consisting of Poems, Epigrams, Songs, Tales, Odes, Translations, &c. never before made Publick. By a Society of Gentlemen.
Imp.—London, Printed for Charles Corbett, 1734.
8vo; mo.; 1s. ea.; 6 nos; 372 pp.; no. 1 ad. *Daily Advertiser* number 947 (Feb. 11, 1734) as pub. 'This Day'; no. 6, 'which compleats a Volume', listed in *London Magazine* July 1734.

LEDIARD, THOMAS. *The Naval History of England . . . from the Norman Conquest, 1066, to the Conclusion of 1734.* 2 vols., usually bound as one.
Imp.—London: Printed for John Wilcox . . ., and Olive Payne . . . MDCCXXXV.
fol.; 5 sh. ea.; 6d. (later nos, 20 sh. for 2s.); 20 nos (4 plus 20 plus 12 plus 933 pp.); port.; fasc. sigs. (lacking in some copies); proposals in *Daily Advertiser* number 918 (Jan. 8, 1734) give title as *A Compleat and Impartial History of all the memorable Naval Expeditions . . . of the English Nation*; no. 1 pub. Feb. 2, 1734; no. 19 ad. *Daily Advertiser* number 1210 (Dec. 14, 1734) as pub. 'This Day . . . . The Remainder will be publish'd, without any further Delay, immediately after the Holidays, and carry the History down to the present Time.' Dedication dated Feb, 13, 1734/5.

New Method of Putting in Perspective all Natural Objects, A.
4 copper plates and 4 pp. of letterpress fort.; 1s. ea. no.; total 16s.; no. 2 ad. *Daily Advertiser* number 991 (April 3, 1734) as pub. April 2; 'Proposals are given gratis, and Subscriptions taken in, at Mr. Vaughan's Fan shop in Russel-court, Drury-lane; Mr. Glass's . . .; the Globe in the Poultry; and Mr. Fourdrenier . . . .'

Questions and Answers.
fol.; single sh. w. as supp. to the *Weekly Oracle: or, Universal Library* (London; Printed for T. Read); also in mo. nos, 4 sh. ea.; 6d. ea., 'stitch'd up in Blue Paper'; 70 nos; no. 1, Sat. Dec. 7, 1734.

Select Trials for Murders, . . . *at the Sessions-House in the Old Bailey.* To which are Added, Genuine Accounts of the Lives . . . of the most Eminent Convicts . . . 1720, to 1724 [VOL. II, 1724, to 1732]. 2 vols.

   Imp.—London: Printed for J. Wilford . . . M.DCC.XXXIV [VOL. II, M.DCC.XXXV].

8vo; 5 hf. sh. ea.; fort.; *6d.*; VOL. I, nos 1-12 (2 plus 8 plus 480 pp.); VOL. II, nos 13-26 (6 plus 500 pp.); fasc sigs.; no. 3 ad. *Daily Advertiser* number 1024 (May 11, 1734) as pub. 'This Day'; no. 19, 'Being the 7th Number of the 2d Volume', ad. *Daily Advertiser* number 1218 (Dec. 21, 1734).

SHAKESPEARE, WILLIAM. *Julius Caesar.*
fol.; single sh. ea.; w.; supp. to *Cotes's Weekly Journal: or, the English Stage-Player* (London: Printed by J. Taylor, at T. Edlin's); *2d.* for 1 sh. of news and 1 sh. of text; 5 nos; no. 1 pub. May 11, 1734.

SHAKESPEARE, WILLIAM. *The Merry Wives of Windsor.*
   Imp.—London: Printed by R. Walker . . . MDCCXXXIV.
12mo; single sh. ea.; w.; 1*d.*; 'Advertisement' dated Sept. 6, 1734, in Jacob Tonson's ed. of *The Merry Wives of Windsor* (1734) states that Walker had pub. proposals for printing plays by Shakespeare and others in single penny sh. w., and that Walker had already pub. the first 2 sh. of *The Merry Wives of Windsor.*

THOU, JACQUES AUGUSTE DE, *alias* THUANUS.* *History of His Time.*
A trans. by 'M. Cart' of *Historia sui temporis,* 6 vols (Geneva, 1720); 7 vols. (London, 1734).
8 sh. ea.; fort.; 1*s.*; no. 2 ad. *Fog's Weekly Journal* number 283 (April 6, 1734) as pub. 'This Day' by Alexander Lyon.

1735
*Annotations on the Holy Bible. By a Select Body of Divines of the Church of England.
5 sh. ea.; w.; *6d.* ea.; no. 1 ad. *Weekly Oracle: or, Universal Library* number 33 (July 19, 1735) to be pub. July 28, 'Printed and sold by J. Read . . ., E. Nutt, R. Charlton, and M. Cook . . .; A. Dodd . . .; and by the Booksellers in Town and Country; and by the Persons who carry the News'; publication of no. 3 deferred 'for some Weeks'; no. 8 ad. *Weekly Oracle* number 47 (October 25, 1735).

BEHN, Aphra. *Love-letters between a nobleman* [Forde Grey, Earl of Tankerville] *and his sister* [sister-in-law, Lady Henrietta Berkeley]; *with the history of their adventures.*
First ed. pub. 1684; 5th ed. pub. 1718; 6th ed. pub. 1735 by J. Tonson, G. Strahan, W. Mears, S. Ballard, D. Brown, F. Clay, and B. Motte.
Imp.—London: Printed by T. Read... M DCC XXXV.
fol.; 4 sh. ea.; w.; 4*d.*; 18 nos. (283 pp.); no. 13 ad. *Weekly Oracle* number 19 (April 12, 1735) as to be pub. April 14; total to take four months.

BURNET, Thomas. *A treatise concerning the State of the Dead, and of Departed Souls, at the Resurrection.* Translated from the Original Latin [*De Statu mortuorum et resurgentium liber*] of Dr. Burnet.
Imp.—London: Printed, and Sold by the Booksellers of London and Westminster. MDCCXXXVII.
8vo; 3 sh. ea.; w.; 6*d.* ea.; 10 nos; 408 pp.; no. 1 ad. *Weekly Oracle* number 48 (November 1, 1735) to be pub. Nov. 10, 'Printed and Sold by T. Read'.

CANTEMIR, Demetrius (Prince of Moldavia). *The History of the Growth and Decay of the Othman Empire.* Translated into English, from the Author's own Manuscript [in Latin], by N. Tindal, M.A.
Imp.—London: Printed and sold by James, John and Paul Knapton... MDCCXXXIV [i.e., 1735].
fol.; 6 sh. plus a head; fort.; 1*s.* ea.; 21 nos; 41 plus 460 pp.; fasc. sigs.; no. 1 ent. Sta. Reg. Mar. 14, 1735; nos 2-21 ent. Sta. Reg. May 21, 1735 to May 7, 1736; has list of subscribers.

CARE, Henry. *The History of Popery.* 2 vols.
Rep., 'with such Alterations of Phrase as may be more suitable to the Taste of the Age, and such Additions as may better accommodate it to the present State of Popery in Great Britain', from the *Weekly Pacquet of Advice from Rome* (1678-1683).
Imp.—London: Printed for J. Oswald... MDCCXXXV [VOL. II, MDCCXXXVI].
4to; nos 1-9, 1½sh. ea., pr. 2*d.*; nos 10-39, 4½ sh. ea., pr. 6*d.*; w.; VOL. I, 481 plus 13 pp.; VOL. II, 676 pp.; pl.; no. 1 ad. *Daily Advertiser* number 1292 (March 20, 1735) to be pub. March 25; '... a few will be printed on fine large Paper, at the Price of Three-pence.... Printed for J. Roberts....'

CHARLES I (KING). *The Works of King Charles I. Both Civil and Sacred.
fol.; 6 sh. ea.; w.; 6d. ea.; no. 1 ad. Weekly Oracle: or, Universal Library number 26 (May 31, 1735) as to be pub. June 9; 'Subscriptions are taken in by T. Read . . ., and by most Booksellers in Town and Country, as also by the Persons who carry News-Papers'; final no. ad. ibid. number 45 (October 11, 1735) as pub. Oct. 6.

DUMONT, JEAN (Baron of Carelscroon) and ROUSSET DE MISSY, JEAN. The Military History of his Serene Highness Prince Eugene of Savoy: As also, of his Grace the Duke of Marlborough . . .; and his Serene Highness the Prince of Nassau Friesland. Written originally in French by Messrs. Dumont and Rousset, and now first translated into English.
Imp.—London: Printed by R. Walker . . . MDCCXXXV.
4to; w.; 1s. ea.; no. 1 ad. Fog's Weekly Journal number 368 (Nov. 22, 1735) as to be pub. Nov. 27; ' . . . and the Whole will Amount to about £ 2. 16s'.

*English Champion; or, the Reform'd Knight, The. By Palmerin of England.
w.; 3d. ea.; 52 nos, to make 4 vols; no. 1 ad. St. James's Evening Post number 3017 (Feb. 22, 1735) as to be pub. March 1: 'Subscriptions . . . taken in, and the Numbers sold by J. Stephens . . ., and by the Booksellers and Pamphlet-Shops of London and Westminster.'

FENELON, FRANÇOIS DE SALIGNAC DE LA MOTHE-. *A New and Accurate Edition of the Works of the late Celebrated M. de Fenelon. In French and English. To which will be prefix'd, Some Memoirs of his Lordship's Life; written originally in French by Mr. Ramsay, Author of the Travels of Cyrus. By [i.e., presumably trans. by] N. Gifford, of the Inner Temple, Gent.
fol.; 5 sh. (or 3 sh. and a print) ea.; 6d.; pl.; proposals dated Dec. 10, 1734 announce no. 1 to be pub. Mar. 8; 'Subscriptions . . . taken in by J. Wilford . . . .'

*History of England.
Pub. as supp. to the Parrot: Or Pretty Poll's Morning Post (ad. Queen Anne's Weekly Journal number 4, Dec. 6, 1735). See above, p. 69.

HUMPHREYS, SAMUEL. The Sacred Books of the Old and New Testament, Recited at Large: and illustrated with Critical and Explanatory Annotations. 3 vols.

Imp.—London: Printed by R. Penny . . ., MDCCXXXV [VOL. II,
MDCCXXXVII; VOL. III, MDCCXXXIX].
fol.; 5 sh. ea.; 8d. ea. with map or cut; fort.? VOL. I, nos 1-60 (pp.
[1]-1206); VOL. II, nos 61-117 (pp. 1207-2409); VOL. III, nos 118-?
(pp. 2410-?); proposals and ads. pub. July 24, 1735 announce no. 1 to
be pub. Aug. 9; completed by Mar. 23, 1739.

JOSEPHUS, FLAVIUS. *The Genuine Works of Flavius Josephus.* Translated from the Original Greek, according to Havercamp's accurate
Edition. [also] eight Dissertations . . . By William Whiston, M. A. Sometime Professor of the Mathematicks in the University of Cambridge.
Imp.—London, Printed by W. Bowyer for the Author; and are to
be sold by John Whiston . . . MDCCXXXVII.
fol.; 12 sh. ea.; 152 plus 1024 plus 76 pp.; maps; fasc. sigs.; Whiston's
note, p. [1023]: 'N.B. I began this version . . . on December the 9th,
A.D. 1734 . . . and finished it on Jan. 6. 1736/7 . . . .'

LEDIARD, THOMAS. *The History of England, By M. Rapin de Thoyras,
Continued, from the Abdication of King James II, to the Accession of . . .
K. George I.* By Thomas Lediard.
Perhaps based on con. in French by David Durand. Pub. as VOL. III
of Rapin's *History of England* (trans. Kelly and Morgan), 1732-1733.
Imp.—London printed by and for, the sole Proprietor, J. Mechell . . . MDCCXXXVI.
fol.; 4 sh. ea.; w.; 6d. ea.; 25 nos (to end of reign of Queen Anne), 412
pp. plus index to the con. (12 pp.) plus summary of con. (12 pp.); fasc.
sigs.; no. 6 of con. ad. *St. James's Evening Post* number 4062 (Jan. 17,
1736).

LEDIARD, THOMAS. *The History of England, Written Originally in
French, as far as the Revolution, By M. Rapin de Thoyras; Translated into
English . . . . The Reigns of King William III and Queen Mary: And also that
of Queen Anne, Are Impartially continued,* By Thomas Lediard. A more
extended work than the preceding, but similarly pub. as VOL. III of
Rapin's *History of England* (trans Kelly and Morgan), 1732-1733.
Imp.—London: Printed by James Mechell . . . MDCCXXXVII.
fol.; 4 sh. ea.; w.; 6d. ea.; nos 1-46; 784 pp. plus index to 3 vols (49 pp.)
plus summary of 3 vols. (93 pp.); fasc. sigs.; list of subscribers.

MANLEY, MARY DE LA RIVIÈRE. *Secret Memoirs and Manners of
Several Persons of Quality of Both Sexes. From the New Atalantis.* The
Seventh Edition. 4 vols.

Imp.—London: Printed by J. Watson . . .; Sold by A. Dodd . . .;
and by most of the Booksellers in London and Westminster.
MDCCXXXVI.
12 mo; 3 sh. or 6 hf. sh. ea.; w.; 4*d*. ea.; 15 nos; VOL. I, 226 pp.; VOL. II,
272 pp.; VOL. III, 279 pp.; VOL. IV, 280 pp.; running head title on ea.
p., The New Atalantis; proposals dated Sept. 19, 1735 indicate that
this seventh ed. was pub. under the title *The Weekly Novelist, a Select
Collection of the Best Novels, Moral, Political, &c.* See below, *s.v.* Gautier
de Costes de la Calprenède, 1736.

'MOLIERE'. *Plays in English translation.
Pub. as supp. to the *Parrot: Or Pretty Poll's Morning Post* (ad.
Queen Anne's Weekly Journal number 4 (Dec. 6, 1735). See above,
p. 69.

Old and New Testament, or the Family Bible, with Annotations. By Permission of his Majesty's Printer.
fol.; 6 sh. ea.; 1*s*. ea.; fort.; proposals in *St. James's Evening Post* number
3012 (Feb. 11, 1735); no. 1 ad. in R. Penny's *British Observator* number
108 (March 8, 1735) as pub. Mar. 1; apparently discontinued because
of objections from the King's Printer; ad. in *St. James's Evening Post*
number 3082 (July 24, 1735) of Penny's proposals for printing Samuel
Humphreys's *Sacred Books of the Old and New Testament (q.v.)* has note
probably referring to the work beginning March 1:
'N.B. It having been render'd necessary for me, in Consequence of the
Construction of the Articles executed between Mr. Basket, (his
Majesty's Printer) and myself, to begin this Undertaking in another
Manner, I do hereby promise to exchange the Numbers already
deliver'd out, gratis . . . .'

RALEGH, SIR WALTER. *The History of the World* . . . . The Eleventh
Edition, printed from a Copy revis'd by Himself. To which is Prefix'd,
The Life of the Author, newly compil'd . . . By Mr. Oldys. Also his
Trial, with some Additions. 2 vols.
Imp., VOLS. I and II—London: Printed for G. Conyers, J. J. and
P. Knapton, D. Midwinter, A. Bettesworth and C. Hitch, B. Sprint,
R. Robinson, B. Motte, J. Walthoe, A. Ward, J. Clarke, S. Birt,
T. Wotton, T. Longman, H. Whitridge, H. Lintot, and J. and
R. Tonson. MDCCXXXVI.
fol.; 4 sh. ea.; 53 nos; VOL. I, 250 plus 8 plus 32 plus 24 plus 370 pp.;
VOL. II pp. 371 – [818] plus 24 plus 20 pp.; port., maps; fasc. sigs.;
appears to be reissue or rep. of the 'Seventh Edition' pub. in w. nos

1733-1734 (or 1735), with the addition of the Life by William Oldys (which lacks fasc. sigs.).

SALMON, Thomas. *A new Abridgement and Critical Review of the State Trials* . . . from the Reign of King Richard II, down to . . . the Tenth Year of the Reign of . . . King George II.

  Imp.—London: Printed for J. and J. Hazard . . .; W. Mears . . .; J. Mechell . . .; J. Applebee . . .; C. Ward and R. Chandler . . ., and at their Shops in York and Scarborough. MDCCXXXVIII. [Price Bound One Pound Ten Shillings.]

fol.; 8 sh. ea.; mo.; 1s. ea.; 29 nos; 12 plus 922 plus 8 pp.; fasc. sigs.; no. 11 ad. *London Daily Post, and General Advertiser* number 576 (Sept. 4, 1736) as pub. 'This Day . . . Printed for Messrs. Knapton, Bettesworth, Hitch, Rivington, Hazard, Brotherton, Symon, Hatchett, Clarke, Mears, Pemberton, Isted, Corbett, Stone, Jackson, and most other Booksellers in Town and Country.'

SMITH, Samuel. *The Compleat History of the Old and New Testament: Or, a Family Bible*. With . . . Annotations . . . By S. Smith, D.D. 2 vols.

  Imp.—London: Printed by W. Rayner. MDCCXXXV.

VOL. II has title *The History of the Family Bible: Being the New Testament*, Containing, The Lives . . . Of our Blessed Saviour Jesus Christ, and his Twelve Apostles. With . . . Notes.

  Imp., VOL. II—London: Printed by W. Rayner and Sold by the Booksellers of London and Westminster. MDCCXXXVII.

fol.; 4 sh. ea.; fort.; 6d. ea.; VOL. I, nos 1-64; VOL. II, nos 65-110; maps and cuts; fasc. sigs.; no. 3 ad. *Daily Advertiser* number 1294 (March 22, 1735) as to be pub. Mar. 27. 'Subscriptions are taken in by A. Dodd . . .; M. Charleton . . .; at the Seven Stars in Russel-court, Drury-lane; by W. Rayner . . .; by most Booksellers in Town and Country; and by the Hawkers of News, of whom may be had the First and Second Number.' VOL. II rep. in 8vo nos, 1737, by Rayner, under the title *The History of the Lives, Actions, . . . of our Blessed Saviour, and his Twelve Apostles* . . . By S. Smith, D.D.; rep. or reissued in 1739; rep. in 1741.

SMITH, Samuel. *The Family Companion: Or, Annotations upon the Holy Bible*. Being a New and Compleat History of the Old and New Testament. Together with the Lives, Actions, . . . of Our Blessed Saviour and his Twelve Apostles.

  Imp.—London: Printed by W. Rayner, for J. Wilford . . . MDCCXXXV.

fol.; 4 sh. ea.; 78 nos; fasc. sigs.; not the same as *The Compleat History of the Old and New Testament: Or, a Family Bible.*

STRYPE, JOHN. *Annals of the Reformation of the Church of England.* 4 vols.
Imp., VOLS I and II—London. Printed for Edward Symon . . . MDCCXXXV. [VOLS III and IV, MDCCXXXVII].
fol.; 5 sh. ea.; w.; 6d. ea.; no. 1 ad. *Daily Advertiser* number 1274 (Feb. 27, 1735) as pub. 'Subscriptions are taken in by E. Symon . . .; as likewise by most Booksellers in Town or Country.' No. 39 ad. *Weekly Miscellany* number 154 (Nov. 22, 1735) as pub. Nov. 20; has list of subscribers.

1736
BLOMEFIELD, FRANCIS. *An Essay towards a Topographical History of the County of Norfolk.* 3 vols.
Imp., VOL. I—Printed at Fersfield in the Year of our Lord, MDCCXXXIX.
Imp., VOL. II—Printed at Norwich in the Year of our Lord MDCCXLV.
Imp., VOL. III—Lynn: Printed, and Sold by W. Whittingham; and R. Baldwin . . ., London. 1769.
fol.; mo.; 1s. ea.; VOL. I, 4 plus 808 pp.; VOL. II, 913 pp.; VOL. III, 870 pp.; no. 1 pub. March 1736; Intro. dated March 25, 1736; p. 771 of VOL. I has 'Finis. Fersfield, Dec. 25, 1739'; no. 1 of VOL. II listed *Scots Magazine* May 1741; MS. note in British Museum copy of VOL. II, p. 902: 'Mr Blomefield died at Norwich on Friday Jany 17th 1752. The 3d Vol of this Work not being finished. Altho he lived to see 670 pages of it published which came out in 21 Numbers.' Cambridge copy has list of subscribers.

BOWES, SIR ROBERT. **The Letters of Sir Robert Bowes, of Streatham-Castle . . . During the Time of his Embassy from Queen Elizabeth to King James VI.*
Proposals dated at Durham Aug. 12, 1736 pub. in *Gentleman's Magazine* Aug. 1736. No. 1 to be pub. Nov. 1736; work to be pub. 6 fol. sh. mo. or oftener for 1s.

BROWNE, SIR THOMAS. *The Works of Sir Thomas Browne: Hydriotaphia: or Urn Burial.* Fourth Edition. [Also] *The Garden of Cyrus.*
Imp. of *Hydriotaphia*—London: Printed for E. Curll . . . 1736.
Imp. of *The Garden of Cyrus*—London: Printed in the Year 1736.

8vo; 1s. 6d. ea.; sigs. continuous but sep. pag.; no. 1, 6 plus 60 pp.; no. 2, 6 plus 40 pp.; no. 2 of 'The Works of Sir Thomas Browne' listed *London Magazine* Sept. 1736.

Choice, useful, and most entertaining Collection of ... Histories, mostly Tragical ... of the last Century, A.
fol.; 12 sh. mo. for 1s., or 'a less Quantity' w.; no. 1 ad. *London Spy Reviv'd* number 5 (Aug. 6, 1736) as just pub., 'Printed for J. Wilford ...; where Proposals may be had; as likewise of most Booksellers and Pamphlet Shops in Town and Country.' Publication interrupted till Nov. 17, 1736.

DEFOE, DANIEL. *The Wonderful Life and most surprising Adventures of Robinson Crusoe, of York, Mariner.*
Pub. as single sh. supp. to *Walker's Half-Penny London Spy*; no. 15. ad. in *Queen Anne's Weekly Magazine* number 42 (Aug. 28, 1736. See above, p. 69.

FARQUHAR, GEORGE. *The Recruiting Officer.*
Pub. as single sh. supp. to the *Weekly Spectator, and English Theatre*; no. 1 ad. *Queen Anne's Weekly Magazine* number 37 (July 24, 1736). See above, p. 69.

HENRY, MATTHEW. *An Exposition on the Old and New Testament.*
Fourth Edition. 5 vols.
Imp.—London: Printed for John and Paul Knapton ...; Thomas Cox ...; Richard Ford and Richard Hett ...; Aaron Ward ...; and Thomas Longman ... 1737 [VOL. V, 1738].
fol.; 8 sh. ea.; w.; 1s. ea.; VOL. I, nos 1-28; VOL. II, nos 29-53; VOL. III, nos 54-78; VOL. IV, nos 79-98; VOL. V, nos 99-118; fasc. sigs.; no. 1 ad. *Whitehall Evening Post* number 3047 (Aug. 28, 1736) as to be pub. Sept. 4.

History and Antiquities of Berkshire ... [and] the several Histories and Antiquities of the neighbouring Counties, The.
Pub. as single sh. supp. to the *Reading Mercury: Or, The London Spy;* ad. *London Evening Post* number 1370 (Aug. 28, 1736).

JOSEPHUS, FLAVIUS. *A Compleat Collection of the Genuine Works of Flavius Josephus,* Faithfully Translated from the Original Greek ... with Notes, and ... Observations upon the Writings of Josephus. By H. Jackson, Gent.

Imp.—London: Printed and sold by J. Brindley . . ., J. Worral . . .,
O. Payne . . .; J. Jolliffe . . .; W. Shropshire . . .; C. Corbett . . ., and Mr.
Norton . . .; as likewise by Mssieurs Rogers and Cooper . . . 1736.
fol.; 8 sh. ea.; 25 nos; maps, cuts; fasc. sigs.; 774 plus 15 pp.

LA CALPRENEDE, GAUTIER DE COSTES DE. *Hymen's Præludia:
Or, Love's Master-Piece*: Being that So-much-admir'd Romance, intitled, Cleopatra . . . Elegantly render'd into English, By Robert
Loveday. 8 vols.
Loveday's trans. of VOLS I-III pub. London, 1652-1655; trans. of re-
mainder by John Coles, James Webb, and John Davies pub. London,
1655-1665.
  Imp.—London: Printed and Sold by J. Watson . . . MDCCXXXVI.
12 mo; 3 sh. ea.; w.; 4d. ea.; no. 11, 'which concludes VOL. II of Cleo-
patra . . . Being no. XXVI of the Weekly Novelist', ad. *London Daily
Post, and General Advertiser* number 489 (May 26, 1736) as to be pub.
May 28. See *s.v.* Mary de la Rivière Manley, 1735.

*Naval Transactions and Sea Fights of the English Nation, from the Year
1693, to this Time.* Collected from Lediard's and Burchet's Naval
Histories, and other authentick Authorities.
Pub. as single sh. supp., w., to the *Distillers Universal Magazine* (proprietor James Stanton); no. 1 ad. *London Spy Revived* number 24 (Sept.
20, 1736) as to be pub. Sept. 25, 1736; no. 10 ad. Nov. 27, 1736.

NELSON, ROBERT. *A Companion for the Festivals and Fasts of the
Church of England.*
First ed. London, 1704; 16th ed. London, 1736, printed for J. Walthoe, R. Wilkin, J. and J. Bonwicke, S. Birt, and T. Ward and
E. Wicksteed.
8vo; single sh. ea.; w.; 2d. ea.; 27 nos; pl.; no. 1 ad. *London Spy Revived*
number 63 (Dec. 20, 1736) as pub. 'This Day . . . . Subscriptions are
taken in by J. Stanton, Distiller . . ., and by the several Hawkers of
News-papers; to whom such Persons who intend to become Subscribers, are desired to speak immediately.'

'SEYMOUR, ROBERT', *alias* John Mottley. *Survey of the Cities of
London and Westminster.*
Rep. from ed. in nos pub. 1733-1735 by T. Read.
Pub. as single sh. supp., w.. to the *Distillers Universal Magazine* (pro-
prietor James Stanton); no. 1 ad. *London Spy Revived* number 24 (Sept.
20, 1736) as to be pub. Sept. 25, 1736. No. 7 ad. Nov. 6, 1736.

TINDAL, NICHOLAS. *A Continuation of Mr. Rapin de Thoyras's History of England, from the Revolution to the Accession of King George I.* 2 vols. Pub. as VOLS III and IV of Rapin (trans. Tindal), 1732. Advance notice in *Daily Advertiser* number 1204 (Dec. 7, 1734): '. . . the Continuation of M. de Rapin de Thoyras's History of England, written in French, which will shortly be publish'd in Holland, is now translating into English, with large Improvements and additional Notes, By N. Tindal . . .; And will speedily be publish'd Weekly, by J. J. and P. Knapton'. This suggests that Tindal trans. and amplified the con. by David Durand pub. at The Hague in 1735. Tindal added an abridgment both of his own trans. of Rapin and of the new con.
fol.; w.; 4 sh. ea.; *6d.* ea.; proposals pub. Feb. 5, 1735; no. 1 listed *London Magazine* April 1736 as pub.; whole work, including con. and abridgment, rep. in nos as 'Third Edition' in 1743-1747.

WARD, Edward. *The London Spy.*
Apparently this work, first pub. in mo. nos, 1698, was pub. as supp. regularly filling p. 1 of the *Reading Mercury; or, the London Spy.*

1737
BICKHAM, GEORGE. *The Musical Entertainer.* Engrav'd by George Bickham junr. 2 vols.
Imp.—London Printed for & Sold by Geo: Bickham . . . n.d.
fol.; 4 hf. sh. ea.; mo.; *6d.* ea.; VOL. I, nos 1-25; VOL. II, nos 1-25; nos 4 (March 1737) and 10 (July 1737) ad. as 'Printed and Sold by Thomas Harper'; no. 14 of VOL. II (March 1739) ad. as pub. by T. Cooper; rep. or reissued in nos by Charles Corbett in 1740.

BLACKWELL, ELIZABETH. *A Curious Herbal containing five Hundred Cuts of the most useful Plants which are now used in the Practice of Physick.* Engraved on Folio Copper Plates after Drawings taken from the Life. By Elizabeth Blackwell. To which is added a short Description of ye Plants and their Common Uses in Physick. 2 vols.
Nos sold by Samuel Harding. John Nourse gradually obtained title by mortgage and assignment. Ad. in the *Country Journal: or, the Craftsman* number 617 (May 6, 1738) includes this note: 'The first Volume [i.e., 252 prints], and what is finish'd of the second [i.e., 132 prints], is sold by Samuel Harding, Booksellers, in St. Martin's-Lane; and no where else: At which Place the Numbers will be deliver'd weekly to the Subscribers, till the Work is finish'd.' Copies are found bearing the imprint of Samuel Harding, 1737, and others with the imprint: London, Printed for J. Nourse . . . 1739.

fol.; 4 prints in ea. no.; w.; 1s. ea., plain; 2s. ea., coloured; 1s. 6d. ea., large paper, plain; 3s. ea., large paper, coloured; 125 nos; VOL. I, nos 1-63; VOL. II, nos 64-125; prints numbered consecutively; Dedication of VOL. I to Richard Mead, M.D., dated at Chelsea 'ye 14th of July, 1737'; Dedication of VOL. II to Robert Nicholls dated 8th Aug. 1737'; nos 123, 124, 125 ad. *Daily Advertiser* number 2480 (Jan. 4, 1739); a spurious ed. of this work was started in April-May 1738; rep. or re-issued in nos, 1741.

CLARKE, LAURENCE. *A Compleat History of . . . Jesus Christ: with the Lives . . . of the Apostles and Evangelists . . . to which is prefixed The Life of the Blessed Virgin Mary.*
   Imp.—London: Printed for the Author, and sold by the Booksellers in Town and Country. MDCCXXXVII.
Pub. under the title, the *Universal Weekly Register: with the Life of Christ and his Apostles*, with news on the covers.
4to; single sh. (8 pp.) ea.; w.; 2d. ea.; 728 pp.; pl.; fasc. sigs.; no. 1 ad. *London Spy Revived* number 127 (May 16, 1737) as to be pub. May 21; intending subscribers asked to give notice to Mr. James Stanton, Distiller; rep. or reissued in nos, 1741.

CLARKE, LAURENCE. *A Compleat History of the Holy Bible.* 2 vols.
   Imp.—London: Printed for the Author, and sold by the Booksellers in Town and Country. MDCCXXXVII [VOL. II, same].
4to; 2 sh. and one cut ea.; w.; 4d. ea.; 78 nos; VOL. I, pp. 1-616 plus index (pp. 1-46); VOL. II, pp. 619-722, plus 390 pp. plus index (pp. 47-84); fasc. sigs.; proposals in *Grub-street Journal* number 371 (Feb. 3, 1737) announce no. 1 as to be pub. Feb. 14; intending subscribers asked to give notice to 'Mr. James Stanton, Distiller, . . . whom I [i.e., Laurence Clarke] have (being the sole Proprietor) empowered to publish the Work for me Weekly'; nos to be 'stitch'd up in white Paper instead of Blue, and have the whole Week's News . . . printed thereon, . . . with the Prices of Goods . . . , &c.'

CLARKE, LAURENCE. *The History of the Holy Bible.*
w.; free supp. to R. Walker's *Warwick and Staffordshire Journal: with the History of the Holy Bible* number 11 (Oct. 29, 1737) to number 149 (June 19, 1740).

Doctrine of the Old and New Testament; being a Key to the Holy Scriptures . . . by Way of Question and Answer, The. 3 vols.
This is probably the same as *The History of the Bible by Way of Question*

and Answer ad. by Mrs. Holloway in *London Spy Revived* number 246 (Feb. 17, 1738) as 'neatly Printed in three Volumes Octavo with Cuts, or any single Number to complete . . . Volumes'.
8vo; 2 sh. ea.; fort.; 2*d*. ea.; about 35 nos; no. 1 ad. *London Spy Revived* number 81 (Jan. 31, 1737) as to be pub. Feb. 5, 'Printed and Sold by E. Holloway . . . and may be had of all Persons that carry the News.' No. 17 of VOL. III ad. *ibid.* number 228 (Jan. 6, 1738) as to be pub. Jan. 7.

DU HALDE, JEAN BAPTISTE. *A Description of the Empire of China and Chinese Tartary.* From the French of P. J. B. Du Halde, Jesuit: with Notes Geographical, Historical, and Critical; and Other Improvements, particularly in the Maps, By the Translator. 2 vols.
Based on Du Halde's *Description géographique, historique . . . de l'empire de la Chine et de la Tartarie chinoise,* 4 vols. (Paris, 1735) and 4 vols. (La Haye, 1736). Translator identified as John Green by G. R. Crone and R. A. Skelton, 'English Collections of Voyages and Travels, 1625-1846', in Edward Lynam, ed., *Richard Hakluyt & His Successors* (London: Hakluyt Society, 1946), p. 100. See also G. R. Crone, 'A Note on Bradock Mead, alias John Green', *Library,* ser. 5, VI (1951), 42 f.
Imp., VOL. I—London: Printed by T. Gardner . . ., for Edward Cave . . . MDCCXXXVIII.
Imp., VOL. II—London: Printed by Edward Cave . . . MDCCXLI fol.; 20 sh. mo. for 2*s*. 6*d*., or 8 sh. fort. for 1*s*.; VOL. I, nos 1-30 (678 pp.); VOL. II nos 31-52 (388 pp. plus index); ad. *Gentleman's Magazine* Aug., Sept., Oct., Dec., 1736 to begin Feb. 1737; no. 31 pub. Nov. 6, 1738; no. 52 (last) listed *Gentleman's Magazine* Mar. 1742 as pub.

DU HALDE, JEAN BAPTISTE. *The General History of China, Chinese, Tartars, Corea and Thibet,* being an Historical, Geographical, Chronological, Political, and Physical Description.
Presumably based on Du Halde's *Description géographique, historique, chronologique, politique, et physique de l'Empire de la Chine et de la Tartarie chinoise,* 4 vols. (Paris, 1735; La Haye, 1736), an English trans. of which. was being pub. in nos by Edward Cave.
fol.; 6 sh. ea.; 4*d*.; to be about 30 nos, making one vol.; proposals ad. *London Spy Revived* number 75 (Jan. 17, 1737): 'Subscriptions are taken in by W. Rayner . . ., and by the Carriers of News.'

ELLIES-DUPIN, LOUIS. *The History of the Jewish and Christian Church in every Age, From the Beginning of the World, to the Seventeenth*

Century. By Way of Question and Answer. Written originally in French by Lewis Elli Dupin, Doctor of Sorbonne, and Regius Professor of Divinity at Paris.
Presumably based on the English trans. (4 vols., 1724) of Dupin's *Histoire de l'Eglise en abrégé: depuis le commencement du monde jusqu'au présent,* 3rd ed., 4 vols. (Paris, 1719).
8vo; 3 hf. sh. (24 pp.) ea.; w.; 2*d.*; to be about 150 sh.; no. 1 ad. *Rayner's Morning Advertiser* number 174 (Jan. 31, 1737) as to be pub. Feb. 5, 'Printed by A. Ilive, and sold by the Booksellers in Town and Country, and by the Carriers of News'.

*Exposition on the Common-Prayer.
w.; free supp. to R. Walker's *Warwick and Staffordshire Journal: with the Exposition on the Common-Prayer* number 3 (Sept. 3, 1737) to number 10 (October 22, 1737).

*General View of the World.
The Longmans, Green copy of a trade-sale catalogue has notation showing that at the auction sale of Richard Williamson's stock on Tuesday, November 29, 1737, S. Birt paid 17*s.* for *Magna Britannia,* numbers 62 to 92 inclusive, together with 'General View of the World, 3 vols. and some odd Numbers'.

History of the Incarnation, Life, Doctrine, and Miracles; the Death, Resurrection, and Ascension, of . . . Jesus Christ . . . To which are added, The Lives . . . of the Twelve Apostles, The. By a Divine of the Church of England.
Imp.—London: Printed for Arthur Bettesworth and Charles Hitch . . . MDCCXXXVIII.
fol.; 4 sh. ea.; 56 nos; 16 plus 875 plus 16 pp.; fasc. sigs.

JONES, REV. ARTHUR. **Lives of the most Ancient Philosophers.*
May have had some connection with *The Lives and most remarkable Maxims of the Antient Philosophers . . . extracted from Diogenes Laertius* (London, 1702), or with the translation (London, 1726) of Fénelon's *Abrégé des vies des anciens philosophes* (Paris, 1726).
No. 1 listed *Gentleman's Magazine* Mar. 1737, 'price 6*d.*'.

*Ladies Miscellany; or travelling Adventures, The.
No. 1 listed in *Gentleman's Magazine* Aug. 1737 as 'Sold at Furnivall's Inn Coffee-House pr 1*s.*'.

LAIRESSE, GÉRARD DE. *The Art of Painting, in all its Branches.*

Trans. John Frederick Fritsch from *Het groot schilderboek* (Amsterdam: W. de Coup, 1707).

 Imp.—London: Printed for the Author, and sold by J. Brotherton . . ., W. Hinchliffe . . ., J. Oswald . . ., A. Bettesworth and C. Hitch, and J. Wood . . ., C. Rivington, C. Foster, J. Clark . . ., L. Gilliver and J. Clarke . . ., S. Sympson . . ., S. Harding, J. Regnier . . ., J. Millan . . ., J. Crichley, J. Fox, J. Jackson, J. Brindley, J. Clark . . ., and J. Huggonson . . . 1738.

4to; 3 sh. ea.; 28 nos; 654 pp.; pl.; fasc. sigs.; no. 9 ad. *Literary Courier of Grub Street* number 1 (Jan. 5, 1738).

Life and Reign of her Late excellent Majesty Queen Anne, The.

 Imp.—London: Printed for the Compiler, and sold by the Dealers in Books in Town and Country. MDCCXXXVIII.

8vo; 3 hf. sh. (24 pp.) ea.; w.; 2*d*. ea.; 40 nos; 783 plus 11 pp.; cuts; fasc. sigs.; no. 1 ad. *London Spy Revived* number 202 (Nov. 7, 1737) as to be pub. Nov. 16 by James Stanton, Distiller and Printer, 'and may be had of the Hawkers of this and other News-Papers'; rep. in 148 nos, 1740, with slight changes.

MAITLAND, WILLIAM. *The History of London, from its Foundation by the Romans to the Present Time.*

 Imp.—London: S. Richardson, 1739.

fol.; 6 sh. ea.; fort.? 1*s*. ea.; 8 plus 8 plus 800 plus 14 pp.; map, pl.; no. 1 ad. *London Daily Post, and General Advertiser* number 776 (Apr. 26, 1737) as pub. 'This Day . . . sold by the Author, at the Dial opposite the Old Jewry in the Poultry'; no. 23 ad. *Daily Post* number 5830 (May 18, 1738) as pub. May 12; has list of subscribers.

*Most Remarkable Sea Fights and Expeditions of the English Nation, from . . . 1665, to this Present Time, The.

Ad. *London Spy Revived* number 71 (Jan. 7, 1737) as to be pub. as supp., single sh. w., to new *Oxford Magazine, or Universal Library* (proprietor Robert Walker), number 2 of which was ad. *London Spy Revived* number 74 (Jan. 15, 1737) as to be pub. Jan. 16.

SMITH, SAMUEL. *The Christian's Guide; or, the Holy Bible By Way of Question and Answer.* Being an Exposition of the Old and New Testament.

 Imp.—London: Printed by W. Rayner, and sold by the Booksellers of London and Westminster. MDCCXXXVIII.

fol.; 3 sh. ea.; w.; 3*d*. ea.; 127 nos; 1492 pp.; cuts; fasc. sigs.; proposals ad. *Rayner's Morning Advertiser* number 176 (Feb. 4, 1737) as to be pub. 'speedily'.

SMITH, SAMUEL. **History of the Lives, Actions, Travels, Sufferings and Deaths of our Blessed Saviour, and his Twelve Apostles, The.*
Apparently a rep. of part of VOL. II of Smith's *The Complete History of the Old and New Testament; or, a Family Bible*, pub. in fol. nos 1735.
8vo; 3 hf. sh. ea.; w.; 2d. ea.; 30 nos; maps, cuts; no. 1 ad. *London Spy Revived* number 71 (Jan. 7, 1737) as to be pub. Jan. 8, 'Printed by W. Rayner . . ., and sold by the Hawkers of News.'

*Trial at Large of Dr. Henry Sacheverel, The.
Ad. *London Spy Revived* number 71 (Jan. 7, 1737) as to be pub. as supp., single sh. w., to new *Oxford Magazine, or Universal Library* (proprietor Robert Walker), number 2 of which was ad. *London Spy Revived* number 74 (Jan. 14, 1737).

*Universal Musician, The.
No. 1 listed *London Magazine* Sept. 1737 as 'Printed for W. Lloyd, 6d.'; no. 2 listed *Gentleman's Magazine* Sept. 1737.

VERTUE, GEORGE. **The Heads of the Most Illustrious Persons of Great Britain.*
fol.; 4 pl. ea.; mo. (irreg.); 4s. ea. (no. 5 and later nos 5s. ea.); proposals listed *London Magazine* Feb. 1737: no. 1 (containing 4 Heads at 1s. ea.) to be pub. Mar. 1; no. 2 ad. *Common Sense: Or, the Englishman's Journal* number 10 (Apr. 10, 1737) as 'Printed for J. and P. Knapton'. No. 12 ad. *Daily Advertiser* number 2762 (Nov. 29, 1739) as pub. 'This Day'.

WARD, EDWARD. **Works.*
Apparently pub. as single sh. supp., Mon., Wed., Fri., to *London Spy Revived*, number 225 (Dec. 30, 1737) of which has note: 'N.B. Mr. Ward's Works being compleated in the *London Spy*, we shall, notwithstanding, continue tht Title to our Paper, and for the Entertainment of our Readers, insert the *Persian Tales* in one Sheet, and the most material Occurrences, Foreign and Domestick, in our other.' Number 246 (Feb. 17, 1738) of *London Spy Revived* had ad. by Mrs. Holloway, 'Of whom may be had the Works of Mr. Edward Ward, or any single Number to complete Sets . . .'.

*Whole Duty of a Woman, The: Or, An infallible Guide to the Fair Sex.
4to; 3 sh. ea.; w.; 3d. ea.; about 20 nos; no. 1 ad. *London Spy Revived*

number 128 (May 18, 1737) as to be pub. May 21. 'Printed and Sold by T. Read . . ., where Subscriptions are taking in, who will likewise send the Sheets as published, to any Part of the Town, on receiving Notice by Letter, or from any of the Persons who carry the News'; perhaps related to *The Whole Duty of a Woman: or, a Guide to the Female Sex. From the Age of Sixteen to Sixty, Written by a Lady*, of which the eighth edition was pub. by Bettesworth and Hitch, R. Ware, and J. Hodges in 1739.

1738

BADDAM, BENJAMIN. *Memoirs of the Royal Society*; Being a New Abridgment of the Philosophical Transactions . . . The whole carefully abridg'd from the Originals . . . By Mr. Baddam. 10 vols.
Imp.—London: Printed by G. Smith . . . for the Editor . . .; J. James . . .; W. Shropshire . . .; J. Millan . . .; T. Wright . . .; N. Adams . . . MDCCXXXVIII. [VOLS II-IV, MDCCXXXIX; VOLS V-VIII, MDCCXL; VOLS IX, X, MDCCXLI].
8vo; 5 sh. ea.; w.; 6*d*. ea.; 13 nos in ea. vol.; fasc. sigs. in VOLS IV-X; no. 3 ad. *Daily Advertiser* number 2480 (Jan. 4, 1739) as pub.; completed before end of 1741; some early nos rep. and pub. in vol. with t.p. marked 'The Second Edition'; one-third of the copy sold by Godfrey Smith, Jr. and Sr., to John Nourse on Aug. 14, 1739 [British Museum, Add. MS. 38,730, fol. 176]; one-sixth of the copy sold by Francis Cogan to John Nourse on October 1, 1742 [British Museum, Add. MS. 38,729, fol. 29].

Beauties of the English Stage; or, Select Plays from the Best Dramatick Authors, The. [Title from ads.; vols. seen lack general t.p.] 9 vols.
Comprises complete texts of 36 plays by Elizabethan, Restoration, and eighteenth-century dramatists, 4 plays in ea. vol.
Imp. of ea. play in VOL. I—London: Printed for the Booksellers, in Town and Country. MDCCXXXIX.
Imp. of ea. play in VOLS. VI and VIII and of the first two plays in VOL. IX—London: Printed for the Booksellers in Town and Country. MDCCXL.
Imp. of last 2 plays in VOL. IX—London: Printed for the Booksellers in Town and Country. MDCCXLI.
12mo; 3 hf. sh. (36 pp.) ea.; w.; 2*d*.; 9 or 10 nos in ea. vol.; cuts; fasc. sigs. (new series 1 to 9 or 1 to 10 in ea. vol.); no. 1 ad. *Warwick and Staffordshire Journal* number 68 (Nov. 30, 1738) as to be pub. Dec. 7, 1738; note, *ibid.*, 'N.B. The Title of the above Work has been alter'd since the Publication of the Proposals and instead of the Universal

Theatre will be entituled, The Beauties of the English Stage'; next 6 nos announced w. in *Warwick and Staffordshire Journal;* rep. or re-issued by R. Walker in 1740.

BLACKWELL, ELIZABETH. **A Curious Herbal.*
Ad. in *Country Journal; or, the Craftsman* number 617 (May 6, 1738) warned customers against 'a spurious and base Copy' of the authorized ed. sold by Samuel Harding; one number of the pirated ed. was pub. and sold by printsellers and engravers named in the ad.: George Bickham, jun., Philip Overton, John King, Thomas Bakewell, John Tinny, Samuel Simpson, Stephen Lye, Thomas Harper. Chancery bills, affidavits, and answers in this case are in the Public Record Office (CII, bundle 1543 (11); C11, bundle 1546 (6); and C31, bundle 101 (560)).

BROWN, THOMAS. *Amusements Serious and Comical, calculated for the Meridian of London.*
Probably rep. from 7th ed. of *Works* (1730).
pub. as supp. (filling p. 1, Mon., Wed., Fri.) in the *London Spy Revived*, numbers 226 (Jan. 2, 1738) to 257 (Mar. 15, 1738) and later numbers, with fasc. sigs. no. 1 (regular sig. A) to no. xxxii (regular sig. Ii).

BUTLER, JAMES (Second Duke of Ormonde). *Memoirs of the Life of His Grace, James, late Duke of Ormond . . .* Extracted from his own private Memoirs, lately printed at the Hague, in French; and now first translated into English.
    Imp.—London: Printed by and for J. Stanton . . . MDCCXXXVIII. 8vo; 3 hf. sh. ea.; w.; 2d.; 16 nos; 384 pp.; cut; fasc. sigs.; no. 1 ad. *London Spy Revived* number 227 (Jan. 4, 1738) as to be pub. Jan. 9; no. 1 also ad. R. Walker's *Warwick and Staffordshire Journal* number 25 (Feb. 2, 1738) as to be pub. Feb. 10, whole to have about 18 nos; different trans. of same work pub. in nos by Applebee in 1741.

CHAMBERLEN, PAUL. *An Impartial History of the Life and Reign of Our late Most Gracious Sovereign Queen Anne.*
    Imp.—London: Printed for W. Lloyd . . ., and sold by the Book-
    sellers of London and Westminster. MDCCXXXVIII.
fol.; 3 sh. ea.; w.; 48 nos; 514 pp.; cuts; fasc. sigs.

*Collection of Select Sermons, by the most eminent English Divines, ancient and modern, A.
fol.; 6 sh. ea.; fort.; 6d. ea.; no. 1 ad. *Weekly Miscellany* number 287 (June 23, 1738) as to be pub. June 24 by J. Janeway.

*Compleat History and Antiquities of the Antient Egyptians, Babylonians, Romans, Carthaginians, Assyrians, Medes, Persians, and Grecians, The.
fol.; 4 sh. ea.; w.; 6d.; 50 nos (one vol.); maps, cuts; proposals in Read's Weekly Journal; or, British Gazetteer number 705 (Mar. 11, 1738); no. 1 ad. to be pub. Mar. 22: 'Subscriptions... taken by W. Rayner...; W. Lloyd...; and the Booksellers in Town and Country.'

*Curious Relations; or, the Entertaining Correspondent.
Listed in Gentleman's Magazine Jan. 1738 as 'Printed for G. Smith. Price 4d. each Week'.

GIBBS, JAMES. Rules for Drawing the several Parts of Architecture. The Second Edition.
First edition, 1732.
 Imp.—London: Printed for A. Bettesworth and C. Hitch . . .; W. Innys and R. Manby . . .; and J. and P. Knapton . . . MDCCXXXVIII.
fol.; w.; 1s.; 21 nos (8 plus 40 pp. and 64 pl.); no. 1 ad. Salisbury Journal number 20 (June 5, 1738) as pub. 'This Day'; no. 21 ad. ibid. number 39 (Oct. 23, 1738) as pub.; Roy. lic. dated May 19, 1738.

*History of the Holy Bible, The.
Presumably the work by Laurence Clarke pub. as supp. to Walker's Warwick and Staffordshire Journal in 1737.
Supp. to Robert Walker's Derbyshire Journal with the History of the Holy Bible, number 2 of which is dated May 31, 1738. See G. A. Cranfield, A Hand-list of English Provincial Newspapers and Periodicals 1700-1760 (Cambridge: Bowes & Bowes, 1952), p. 7.

HOOPER, JACOB. An Impartial History of the Rebellion and Civil Wars in England, During the Reign of King Charles the First.
 Imp.—London: Printed, and Sold by all the Booksellers in Town and Country. M.DCC.XXXVIII.
fol.; 3 sh. ea. (or 2 sh. and pl.); w.; 3d.; 61 (?) nos (628 pp. and 25 pl.; the 157 sh. are numbered with arabic numerals 1 to 182, one of these serial numbers being omitted, with no interruption in pag. or regular sigs., whenever a pl. was issued); no. 1 ad. by R. Walker in Warwick and Staffordshire Journal number 52 (Aug. 10, 1738) as to be pub. Aug. 17, whole to be finished in 14 months: 'Country Farmers, or others living at a Distance, may have 'em left for them, so that they may take them home with them on a Market Day.' Rep. as supp. to Cambridge Journal, 1747.

Humorous Companion; or, Wit in all Shapes, The.
No. 3 ad. *London Farthing-Post* Dec. 18, 1738, as to be pub. 'next Tuesday ... and may be had of the Persons who carry this Paper'. *The London Farthing-Post* was 'Printed and Sold by J. Harwood ....'

Impartial Account of many Barbarous Cruelties Exercised by the Inquisition in Spain, Portugal, and Italy, An.
　　Imp.—London: Printed, and Sold by the Booksellers in Town and Country. MDCCXXXVIII.
8vo; 2 hf. sh. ea. (no. 6, single sh. with 4 cuts); w.; 2*d.*; 14 nos (27 sh., 432 pp.); 5 pl.; sh. numbered 1 to 27; no. 1. ad. by R. Walker, 'Printer of the above Work', in *Warwick and Staffordshire Journal* number 68 (Nov. 30, 1738) as to be pub. Dec. 7; rep. or reissued by Walker in 14 nos in 1741, and in 10 nos in 1745.

Lady's Curiosity: Or, Weekly Apollo. By 'Nestor Druid, Gent'.
No. 8 ad. *Country Journal: or, the Craftsman* number 650 (Dec. 23, 1738), as 'Printed and sold by W. Rayner ... It will be covered with a Wrapper, giving the Week's News'.

Persian Tales.
Apparently pub. as single sh. supp. (Mon., Wed., Fri.) to the *London Spy Revived.* Number 225 (Dec. 30, 1737) of that paper has note: 'N.B. Mr. Ward's Works being compleated in the *London Spy*, we shall, notwithstanding, continue the Title to our Paper and for the Entertainment of our Readers, insert the *Persian Tales* in one Sheet, and the most material Occurrences ... in our other.'

Reign of the Victorious Queen Elizabeth, The.
Ad. R. Walker's *Queen Anne's Weekly Magazine* number 142 (July 29, 1738) as to be pub. as w. supp. to J. Stanton's *New Half-Penny Post* beginning in number 1, due to appear Aug. 2, 1738. To run 50 weeks, 'at the End of which the Work will make a compleat Volume'. Number 12 of the *New Half-Penny Post* ad. in *Queen Anne's Weekly Magazine* number 146 (Aug. 26, 1738), with a warning against 'a spurious life of Queen Elizabeth being published on whited-brown Paper, old batter'd Letter, and incorrectly Printed'. See above, p. 69.

RICHARDS, WILLIAM. *The Compleat Penman; or Young Clerk's Companion.*
4to; 8 pl. ea.; fort.; 6*d.*; 12 nos; no. 2 ad. *Warwick and Staffordshire Journal* number 32 (Mar. 23, 1738) as to be pub. Mar. 25; proposals delivered

and subscriptions taken by Mr. Richards, the Compiler; Mr. Benj. Cole . . .; Mr. King . . .; Mr. Hitch . . .; Mr. Hodges . . .; Mr. Wilcox . . .; Mr. Clark . . .; and Mr. Dicey in Northampton.

Universal Fabulist, The. Consisting of . . . Tales and Fables, with additional Poems . . . Extracted from the Writings of the most approved Authors, both Ancient and Modern.
8vo; 4 pl. ea.; w.; 2d.; total 100 pl.; no. 1 ad. R. Walker's *Warwick and Staffordshire Journal* number 54 (Aug. 24, 1738) as pub. 'This Day'; no publisher named.

WHITEFIELD, GEORGE. *The Christian's Companion: or, Sermons on Several Subjects.*
Imp. —London: Printed and Sold by the Booksellers in Town and Country. MDCCXXXVIII.
8vo; 3 hf. sh. (24 pp.) ea.; w.; 2d. ; 13 nos; cut.; fasc. sigs.; sep. pag. for ea. section of the work; no. 1 ad. *London Spy Revived* number 251 (Mar. 1, 1738) as to be pub. Mar. 6; prospective subscribers invited to 'give Notice by Letter or otherwise, to the Printer and Publisher, James Stanton . . ., or to any of the Hawkers, or other Persons, who serve out Books or News Papers'.

1739
ADDISON, JOSEPH. *Spectator* essays on *Paradise Lost.*
12mo; w.; 2d.; 4 nos; ad. in R. Walker's *Warwick and Staffordshire Journal* number 97 (June 20, 1739): 'Several of the Customers to Milton's Paradise Lost, having express'd their Desire of having the Great Mr. Addison's Notes on that celebrated Poem, collected from the Spectator, printed at the End of this Work, as what will be very proper to embellish and explain many Passages in that valuable Book; this is published, to certify the Subscribers, that these Notes will be printed on the same Paper and Letter with the Work, so that they may be bound up with it, and will make out Four Numbers, at Two Pence each Number; and by speaking to the Person who has served them with that Work lately published at Two Pence per Week, they may be carefully served with the same.'

[BOYER, JEAN BAPTISTE DE (Marquis d'Argens)?] *Jewish Letters.*
This is probably a trans. of *Lettres juives, ou correspondance philosophique, historique, & critique, entre un Juif . . . & ses correspondans en divers endroits,* 6 vols. (The Hague, 1738). A trans. of the first 40 letters was pub. in London by D. Browne in 1739.

Gentleman's Magazine June 1739 has letter from 'Philo-Christus' addressed 'To the Translator of the Jewish Letters, publishing in numbers at Newcastle upon Tyne'.

BRIDGES, JOHN. *The History and Antiquities of Northamptonshire.* Title page missing in copy seen. Prepared for publication by Dr. Samuel Jebb and (later) Rev. Peter Whalley.
fol.; 1s. ea.; 164 pp.; inc.; MS. note, dated March 16, 1748/49, in British Museum copy: 'These are all ye Numbers publish'd by Mr. Bridges.' No. 1 ad. *Daily Advertiser* number 2527 (Feb. 28, 1739) as pub. Feb. 26: 'Numbers will be deliver'd regularly . . . by John Fowler and William Dicey in Northampton . . . and S. Gibbons . . ., J. & R. Tonson . . .; E. Symon and J. Crokatt, L. Gilliver and J. Clarke.' See John Nichols, *Literary Anecdotes* (London, 1812), II, pp. 61, 105f and n., 700f.

*British Melody; or, The Musical Magazine, The. Consisting of . . . the most approv'd English and Scotch Songs.
Completed work ad. *Warwick and Staffordshire Journal* number 115 (Oct. 25, 1739) as 'Just Published. Printed for, and sold by the Proprietor, Benjamin Cole, Engraver . . . . N.B. Those Persons that have the former Numbers may have their Books compleated.'

CORBETT, THOMAS. **A True Account of the Expedition of the British Fleet in Sicily in the Years* 1718, 1719, *and* 1720.
This is probably a piracy of *An Account of the Expedition of the British Fleet to Sicily*, pub. by J. and R. Tonson in 1739.
8vo; 3 hf. sh. ea. (or 12mo, single sh. or 2 hf. sh. ea.); 24 pp. ea.; w.; 2d. ea.; to have 5 nos; no. 1 ad. R. Walker's *London and Country Journal* number 29 (Dec. 6, 1739) as to be pub. Dec. 19 and 20.

FINCH, HENEAGE. *The Indictment . . . of Twenty-Nine Regicides, the Murthurers of King Charles I.*
Imp.—London: Printed for the Booksellers in Town and Country. MDCCXXXIX.
4to; single hf. sh. ea.; 70 nos; 280 pp.; fasc. sigs.; rep. in nos, 1740.

FRANSHAM, JOHN, of Norwich. **The World in Miniature: or, The Entertaining Traveller. Giving an Account of every Thing necessary and curious . . . belonging to each Country.*
Ad. as to have 8 nos, 3 sh. (72 pp., 12mo) in ea.; fort.; 6d.; no. 2 ad. *Daily Advertiser* number 2762 (Nov. 29, 1739) as pub., 'Printed for John Torbuck'; 'Second Edition' in 2 vols. has imp. (VOL. I)—Lon-

don: Printed, and Sold by John Torbuck . . .; Mess. Astley and Austen . . .; T. Osborne . . .; A. Millar . . .; J. Hodges and T. Harris . . .
1741; VOL. I of this 'Second Edition' has 336 pp. (28 hf. sh., 12mo);
pl.; tables.

Genius of the Antients; or, The Wisdom of Greece and Rome, The. Being
a Collection of the Sayings . . . of great Persons mention'd by the
Greek and Roman Writers.
pub. as single sh. supp., mo., to *Pasquin: or, The Emblematist*, which was
printed for C. Corbett at 6*d.*; no. I pub. Sept. 1739.

*History of the Life and Reign of that Excellent Princess Queen Elizabeth,
The . . .: as also, The Trial, Sufferings, and Death of Mary Queen of Scots.
With The . . . Divorce of King Henry VIII.*
   Imp.—London: Printed, and sold by the Booksellers in Town and
   Country. MDCCXXXIX.
4to; single hf. sh. ea.; 113 nos; 436 pp.; cuts; fasc. sigs.; *The Life and
Reign of that Excellent Princess Queen Elizabeth* was ad. R. Walker's
London and Country Journal number 13 (March 27, 1739) as to begin
'about the Tenth or Twelfth of April': whole to have 39 4to nos
('excess of 39 gratis'), 12 pp. (i.e., 3 hf. sh.) ea., w., at 2*d.*, with cuts;
no publisher named, but subscribers invited to speak to 'the Persons
who serve the *History of the Bible*'; no. I ad. *ibid.* number 15 (April 10,
1739) as pub. that day; the 113 single hf. sh. are doubtless the same ed.
as that proposed in nos of 3 hf. sh. ea.

History of the Old and New Testament, The. 2 vols.
Pub. as supp. to R. Walker's *London and Country Journal: with the
History of the Old and New Testament.* This paper was issued in two
series, one pub. on Tuesdays, beginning Jan, 2, 1739, the other pub.
in Thursdays beginning twenty-two weeks later. The supp. came to
an end in number 149 (Nov. 3, 1741) of the Tuesday series and presumably in the same number (March 4, 1742) of the other series.

*History of the Rise and Fall of that famous Favourite of Q. Elizabeth, the
Earl of Essex, The.*
single. sh. or hf. sh.; w.? ½*d.* ea.; no. I ad. at end of *The Life of Charlotta
Du Pont*, pub. in nos, 1739, *q.v.*

History of the World.
This is possibly a rep. of Ralegh's *History of the World.*
Pub. as supp., gratis, to the *Hereford Journal.*

HORATIUS FLACCUS, Quintus. *Odes.
mo. (irreg.); 1s. ea.; no. 4 of 'Horace's Odes, &c. Translated into
English prose' listed Gentleman's Magazine May 1740 as pub. by
J. Davidson.

JENKINS, Charles. England's Triumph: or, Spanish Cowardice expos'd.
Being a Compleat History of the Many Victories Gain'd by the
Royal Navy and Merchant Ships of Great Britain, For the Term
of Four Hundred Years past, over the insulting and haughty
Spaniards.
    Imp.—London: Printed in the Year MDCCXXXIX.
8vo; 2 hf. sh. ea.; w.; 1d. ea.; 358 pp.; 23 nos; pl.; fasc. sigs.

*Lady's Delight; or Universal Songster, The.
12mo; single hf. sh. (12 pp.) ea.; w. or fort.; total to make 3 vols, containing 'above 1000 Songs'; total cost to be not more than 3s. 3d.;
no. 23 ad. All-Alive and Merry, Feb. 4, [1740] as pub. 'this Morning';
no. 26 (last of VOL. I) ad. ibid., Feb. 26, [1740] as pub. Feb. 22, and
no. 1 of VOL. II as pub. 'this Day', no publisher named: 'VOL. I may
be had of the News Carriers, neatly bound, for 18 Pence.'

Life of Charlotta Du Pont, An English Lady, The. Taken from her own
Memoirs.
    Imp.—London: Printed in the Year 1739.
8vo; single hf. sh. (8 pp.) ea.; 25 nos; 200 pp.; fasc. sigs.

Memorials and Characters of Divers Eminent and Worthy Persons. Now
first selected from the most celebrated Writers of the Church of
England, as well as private Information.
    Imp.—London: Printed for J. Wilford. 1741.
fol.; 8 sh. ea.; mo. (irreg.); 1s. ea.; 26 nos; 8 plus 788 plus 42 plus 2 pp.;
no. 1 ad. Daily Advertiser number 2482 (Jan. 6, 1739); no. 26 listed
Gentleman's Magazine May 1741; has list of subscribers.

MILTON, John. Paradise Lost. A Poem in Twelve Books. To which is
prefix'd, An Account of his Life [by Elijah Fenton].
    Imp.—London: Printed for a Company of Stationers. MDCCXXXIX.
12mo; 3 hf. sh. (36 pp.) ea.; w.; 2d. ea.; 12 nos; cuts; fasc. sigs.;
no. 1 ad. R. Walker's London and Country Journal number 15
(April 10, 1739) as pub. that day; Walker and others formally
challenged by Tonson and associates for this piratical printing. See
above, pp. 188-9.

MILTON, JOHN. *Paradise Regain'd: A Poem. In Four Books. To which is added, Samson Agonistes, and Poems on several Occasions. Written by John Milton.
12mo; 3 hf. sh. (36 pp.) ea. (or single sh. with 4 cuts); w.; 2d.; 9 nos; 8 cuts; no. 1 ad. *Warwick and Staffordshire Journal* number 105 (Aug. 16, 1739) as pub. 'This Day'; intending subscribers invited to 'speak to the Person who serves this Place with the History of the Bible and other Books printed by R. Walker'.

*Moral Philosopher: or, Instructive and Entertaining Essays on various Subjects, Divine, Moral, and Political, The.
8vo; 2d. ea.; to make 20 nos; no. 2 ad. *Daily Advertiser* number 2613 (June 8, 1739) as pub. 'This Day . . . Printed for M. Watson'.

*New Vocal Miscellany, or Merry Companion, A.
w.; 2d. ea.; no. 14 ad. W. Rayner's *Universal Weekly Journal* May 5, 1739: 'Subscriptions taken in by W. Rayner'.

Proceedings and Tryal . . . of the . . . Lord Archbishop of Canterbury, and the [seven Bishops], The.
Imp. —London: Printed for the Booksellers in Town and Country. MDCCXXXIX.
8vo; single sh. ea.; w.; 2d. ea.; 27 nos; 432 pp.; cut; fasc. sigs.; no. 1 ad. R. Walker's *London and Country Journal* number 25 (Nov. 8, 1739) as to be pub. Nov. 14 and 15; but this ad. states that there are to be 14 nos.

SALMON, NATHANIEL. *The History and Antiquities of Essex.*
Imp. —London: Printed by W. Bowyer, And Sold by J. Cooke, Bookbinder . . . MDCCXL.
fol.; 6 sh. ea.; 1s. ea.; 19 nos; inc.; 460 pp.; fasc. sigs.; no more pub.; no. 1 listed *Scots Magazine* Nov. 1739, 'The whole to consist of 21 numbers. 1s. each'.

SALMON, THOMAS. *A Collection of Proceedings and Trials against State-Prisoners . . . from the Norman Conquest to this present Time.* Compiled by the Editor of the Four First Volumes of State-Trials in Folio [1st ed., 1719; 2nd ed., 6 vols fol., 1730, plus 2 vols, 1735].
Imp. —London: Printed for J. Wilcox 1741; colophon at end: Printed by C. Jephson.
fol.; 8 sh. ea.; 1s. ea.; 20 nos; 610 plus 6 pp.; fasc. sigs.; no. 1 ad. *Daily Advertiser* number 2758 (Nov. 24, 1739) as pub. 'This Day . . . . Subscriptions . . . taken in by Mr. Hodges . . .; Mr. Brotherton . . .; Mr.

Davidson . . .; Mr. Rivington . . .; Mr. Corbett . . .; Mr. Waller . . .; Mr. Wilcox . . .; Mr. Stagg . . .; Mr. Dodsley . . .; Mr. Jolliffe . . .; Mr. Brindley . . .; Mr. Thurlbourn, at Cambridge; and Mr. Fletcher, at Oxford.'

SMITH, SAMUEL. *The Compleat History of the Old and New Testament: or a Family Bible:* with large Annotations. 2 vols.

Imp.—London: Printed for the Author, and Sold by the Booksellers. MDCCXXXIX.

Title of VOL. II—*The History of the Family Bible: Being the New Testament,* with Large Annotations.

Imp., VOL. II—London: Printed for the Author, and Sold by the Booksellers. MDCCXXXIX.

This is a rep. or reissue of Smith's *Compleat History of the Old and New Testament,* pub. in nos by W. Rayner in 1735.

fol.; double series of fasc. sigs., one marking w.(?) nos of 2 sh. ea., the other marking fort.(?) nos of 4 sh. ea.; VOL. I, nos [1]-64; VOL. II, nos [65]-110.

TUCKER, JOSIAH, Dean of Gloucester. *The Life and Particular Proceedings of the Rev. Mr. George Whitefield.* By an Impartial Hand. 8vo; 3 hf. sh. ea.; w.; 2d. ea.; 4 nos; 96 pp.; cuts. ad. R. Walker's *London and Country Journal* number 39 (Dec. 6, 1739) to begin on Dec. 19 and 20.

WHITEFIELD, GEORGE. *The Christian's Companion: or, Sermons on Several Subjects.*

Imp.—London: Printed and Sold by the Booksellers in Town and Country. MDCCXXXIX.

8vo; 3 hf. sh. ea.; 14 nos; 336 pp.; cut; fasc. sigs.; ad. Robert Walker's *London and Country Journal* number 28 (July 10, 1739) as to begin the following week.

1740

Account of the Rebellion in the Reign of King Charles I, The.

May be later nos, or reissue, or rep., of Jacob Hooper's *Impartial History of the Rebellion and Civil Wars in England, During the Reign of King Charles the First,* pub. in nos, probably by R. Walker, in 1738.

w.? 3d.; listed in R. Walker's *London and Country Journal* number 43 (Mar. 13, 1740) as being pub. in nos.

Beauties of the English Stage; or, Select Plays from the best Dramatick Authors, The. 9 vols.

Rep. or reissue of work pub. in nos beginning Dec. 7, 1738.
12mo? w.; 36 pp. ea.; 2d.; 9 or 10 nos in ea. vol.; 4 plays in ea. vol.;
no. 1 ad. R. Walker's *London and Country Journal* number 60 (July
10, 1740): 'Apply to the Person that serves this Place with the
History of the Bible, printed by Walker.'

BEVERIDGE, WILLIAM. *Private Thoughts upon a Christian Life.*
12th ed. pub. 1730.
    Imp.—London: Printed, and Sold by the Booksellers in Town and
Country. MDCCXL.
3 hf. sh. (24 pp.) ea.; 12 nos; fasc. sigs.

BEVERIDGE, WILLIAM. *Private Thoughts upon Religion.*
    Imp.—London: Printed, and Sold by the Booksellers in Town and
Country. MDCCXL.
3 hf. sh. (24 pp.) ea.; w.; 2d. ea.; 10 nos; fasc. sigs.; listed R. Walker's
London and Country Journal number 35 (Jan. 17, 1740) as to begin
Jan. 29.

BICKHAM, GEORGE, Jr. *The Musical Entertainer.* Engrav'd by
George Bickham junr. Now carefully Corrected by Mr. John Frederick
Lampe. 2 vols.
VOL. II has title *Bickham's Musical Entertainer.*
Rep. or reissued from ed. in nos 1737.
    Imp.—London Printed for & Sold by Charles Corbett . . . n.d.
fol.; 4 pl. (words and music) ea.; w.; 6d. ea.; total 200 pl.; VOL. I, nos
1-25; VOL. II, nos 1-25; fasc. sigs.; No. 1 ad. *Salisbury Journal* number
135 (Aug. 26, 1740) as to be pub. Aug. 30.

CLARKE, LAURENCE. **A compleat and full History of . . . Jesus
Christ: with the Lives . . . of the Twelve Apostles, and Four Evangelists. To
which will be prefixed the Life of the Virgin Mary.*
Probably rep. from ed. pub. in nos by James Stanton in 1737.
4to; single sh. ea.; w.; 2d.; news on covers; no. 1 ad. by R. Walker in
his *Warwick and Staffordshire Journal* number 149 (June 18, 1740) [the
final number of the series to which Clarke's *History of the Bible* was
attached as supp.] as to be pub. 'Next Week'; rep. or reissued in nos.
by Walker in 1741.

COCKBURN, JOHN. *The Unfortunate Englishmen: Or, A Faithful
Narrative of the Distresses and Adventures of John Cockburn and five other
English Mariners.* The Second Edition.

For earlier ed. see above, p. 47.

Imp. —London: Printed and Sold by the Booksellers of London and Westminster. MDCCXL.

8vo; 4 hf. sh. (32 pp.) ea.; w.; 2*d*. ea.; 6 nos; 190 pp.; cut; fasc. sigs.; no. 1 ad. *All-Alive and Merry* Oct. 1, [1740] as pub. 'This Day'; no. 6 ad. *ibid.* Oct. 18, [1740] as to be pub. Oct. 25.

DEFOE, DANIEL. *Religious Courtship.*
8vo; 3 hf. sh. ea.; w.; 2*d*.; 15 or 16 nos; ad. R. Walker's *London and Country Journal* number 79 (Nov. 20, 1740) as to begin Dec. 3 and 4. 5th ed. pub. 1737; 6th ed. pub. in 1741 by J. Hodges.

DODSON, JAMES. *The Anti-logarithmic Canon.* Being a table of numbers, consisting of eleven places of figures, corresponding to all logarithms under 100000.

Imp. —London: Printed for James Dodson and John Wilcox . . ., 1742.

fol.; 1*s*. ea.; 306 pp.; nos 1 and 2 listed *Scots Magazine* June 1740; completed work listed at £1. 2*s*. 6*d*. in *London Magazine* Sept. 1742.

Father's Advice to His Son, or the Whole Duty of a Youth, The.
8vo; 16 pp. ea.; w.; announced *All-Alive and Merry* Sept. 7, [1740] as to have 6 or 7 nos.

FENELON, FRANÇOIS DE SALIGNAC DE LA MOTHE-.* *The Adventures of Telemachus . . . and* [by another hand] *The Adventures of Aristonous.*
8vo; 3 hf. sh. ea.; w.; 2*d*. ea.; 24 nos.; cuts; no. 1 ad. R. Walker's *London and Country Journal* number 55 (Jan. 15, 1740 as to be pub. Jan. 29 and 30. Probably issued as rival to the 15th ed. of the trans. by Littlebury and Boyer, pub. in 2 vols 12mo (1740) by Brotherton and fifteen others.

FINCH, HENEAGE. *The Indictment, Tryal . . . of Twenty nine Regicides.* Probably a piracy of the ed. in 70 nos, 1739.
4to; 3 hf. sh. ea.; w.; 2*d*. ea.; 23 nos; listed R. Walker's *London and Country Journal* number 42 (Mar. 6, 1740): 'And as the Trial of King Charles I . . . is just finish'd, and met with a kind Reception, 'tis hop'd that the Trial of his Murderers will be favourably received.'

HERBERT OF CHERBURY, EDWARD (Baron). *The Life and Reign of King Henry VIII.* First pub. 1649.

Imp.—London: Printed and sold by the Booksellers in Town and Country. MDCCXLI.

4to; single sh. ea.; w.; 2d. ea.; 60 nos; 480 pp.; fasc. sigs.; no. 1 ad. R. Walker's *London and Country Journal* number 79 (Nov. 20, 1740) as to be pub. Dec. 3 and 4; to be issued in 46 nos.: first 12 nos, 2 sh. ea.; next 12 nos, single sh. ea.; next 12 nos, 2 sh. ea.; next 10 nos, single sh. ea., overplus gratis; but ea. sh. is numbered.

History of the Life and Reign Of her Late Majesty Queen Anne, The.
Rep., with slight changes, of *The Life and Reign of . . . Queen Anne,* pub. in 8vo nos, 1737.
     Imp.—London, Printed and Sold by the Booksellers in Town and Country. MDCCXL.
fol.; single sh. ea.; 148 nos; 520 pp.; cuts; fasc. sigs.; ad. R. Walker's *London and Country Journal* as to begin Wed. and Thurs., April 2 and 3, 1740, with title *An Impartial History of the Reign of her late most excellent Majesty Queen Anne,* to make one small fol. vol., to have about 56 nos, 3 sh. ea., w., 3d. ea.; notice to be given to 'the Person who serves this Place with . . . Books printed by R. Walker'.

*History of the Life of Peter the First, late Emperor of Russia.
Probably based on John Mottley's *History of the Life of Peter I,* 3 vols. (London: J. Read, 1739), or on John Banks's *History of the Life and Reign of the Czar Peter the Great* (London: J. Hodges, 1740).
fol.; 3 sh. (or cut and 2 sh.) ea.; w.; to have about 36 nos, excess gratis; cuts; ad. R. Walker's *London and Country Journal* number 58 (June 26, 1740): 'Apply to the Person that serves this Place with the History of the Bible, Printed by R. Walker in London.'

*Honey-Suckle, The.
Perhaps a rep. of *The Honey-Suckle,* pub. by Corbett in nos, 1734. ½d. ea.; no. 1 ad. *All-Alive and Merry,* various nos, Nov. 1740.

JOSEPHUS, FLAVIUS. **Compleat Collection of the Genuine Works of Flavius Josephus.* By [i.e., ed. by] James Wilson.
4to; single sh. ea.; w.; 2d.; 104 sh.; news on covers; maps, cuts; no. 1 ad. by R. Walker in his *Warwick and Staffordshire Journal* number 149 (June 18, 1740) as to be pub. 'Next Week'; same rep. or reissued in nos by Walker in 1741.

LAMPE, JOHN FREDERICK. **Lyra Britannica, a Collection of Ballads and Ariettas,* the Words and Musick entirely new.

6d. ea.; no. 2 ad. *Daily Advertiser* number 2985 (Aug. 15, 1740) as to be pub. Aug. 16: 'To be had of C. Corbett . . ., and at all the Musick Shops, Musick Sellers, and Pamphlet-Shops, in Town and Country . . . . N.B. To prevent Imposition by incorrect or pirated Editions, each Number will be sign'd at the Bottom of the Cover by Mr. Lampe.'

LANGLEY, GILBERT. *The Life, extraordinary Adventures, and sur-prising Exploits, of that well-known and famous Beau and Town-Rake, Gilbert Langley. Written by himself.
8vo; 3 hf. sh. ea.; w.? 2d. ea.; 10 nos; no. 3 ad. in unidentified and un-dated newspaper with imp.—London: Printed for J. Nicholson, near the Sessions-House, in the Great Old-Baily., as to be pub. 'To-morrow . . . Printed by J. Webb . . ., and may be had of all News-Sellers.'

Life and Military Actions of his Royal Highness Prince Eugene of Savoy, The. Probably based on the trans. of Dumont pub. in nos by Walker in 1735.
8vo; 2 sh. ea.; w.; to make 12 nos, total 2s.; excess gratis; no. 1 ad. R. Walker's *London and Country Journal* number 60 (July 10, 1740): 'Apply to the Person that serves this Place with the History of the Bible, printed by R. Walker.'

LUTHER, MARTIN. *A Commentary on St. Paul's Epistle to the Gala-tians.* British Museum cat. records no ed. of an English trans. between 1644 and 1760.
w.; 2½d. ea.; announced in the *Christian's Amusement* numbers 1 and 2 (undated, but a letter in number 2 is dated Sept. 12, 1740): 'This Book I [i.e., J. Lewis, printer of the *Christian's Amusement*] am now Printing by Subscription, at Two-Pence Half-Penny a Week'; num-ber 20 of the same paper has note: 'This is to give Notice, That all the first Numbers of *Luther upon the Galatians* are printed over again . . . .'

MOUHY, CHARLES DE FIEUX (Chevalier de). *The Fortunate Country Maid. Being the Entertaining Memoirs of the Present Celebrated Marchioness of L—V—. Who from a Cottage became a lady of the first quality in the court of France . . .* [title from ad. of 2nd ed. in *Norwich Gazette* number 1843 (Jan. 30, 1742)].
Nos 1 and 2 listed *Scots Magazine* April 1740 at 1s. ea.; no. 5 (last) listed *London Magazine* Feb. 1741 as 'Printed for F. Needham'.

NALSON, J. *The Tryal of King Charles the First,* with additions by J. Nalson.

Imp.—London: Printed and Sold by the Booksellers in Town and Country. MDCCXL.

8vo; 3 hf. sh. ea.; w.? 2*d.* ea.; 11 nos; 262 pp.; fasc. sigs.; no. 1 ad. R. Walker's *London and Country Journal* number 32 (Dec. 27, 1739) as to be pub. Jan. 2 and 3, 1740; rep., much abridged, as free supp. to *Oxford Flying Weekly Journal* [conjectured date 1746].

OLDYS, WILLIAM. *The Life of Sir Walter Ralegh.*
The New York Public Library card has this note: 'Apparently an unauthorized reprint, with slight changes, of Oldys's life of Ralegh, which first appeared prefixed to the 1736 edition of Ralegh's History of the World'.
Imp.—London: Printed for the Booksellers in Town and Country. MDCCXL.

8vo; 3 hf. sh. ea.; w.; 24 nos; 576 pp.; cut; no. 1 ad. R. Walker's *London and Country Journal* number 58 (June 26, 1740).

ROBINSON, JAMES. *A Compleat and Impartial History of England, from the Conquest of Britain by Julius Caesar to the End of the Reign of King George the First.* Faithfully collected from Rapin, Echard, Kennet, and other Historians.
Imp.—London: Printed for the Booksellers in Town and Country. MDCCXXXIX.

fol.; 3 sh. ea.; w.; 6*d.* ea.; 90 nos; 860 plus 4 pp.; pl.; fasc. sigs.; no. 1 ad. R. Walker's *London and Country Journal* number 54 (Jan. 8, 1740) as to be pub. Feb. 5 and 6, 1740; work mentioned *ibid.* number 123 (May 5, 1741) as completed; but no. 1 also ad. *Kentish Post, or Canterbury News Letter* number 2397 (Oct. 29, 1740) as to be pub. Nov. 4 and 5, 1740, the whole to have 215 sh. and 55 pl., 65 nos; nos 1-55 to have 3 sh. of letterpress and one cut; nos 56-65 to have 5 sh. ea.; overplus gratis. This notice is signed by R. Walker, presumably the proprietor.

Young Lady's Companion; or, Beauty's Looking-Glass, The. Written by a Person of Quality.
Imp.—London: Printed and Sold by the Booksellers of London and Westminster. 1740
8vo; single sh. ea.; w.; 1*d.* ea.; 4 nos; cut; 68 pp.; fasc. sigs.; announced in *All-Alive and Merry* Sept. 7, [1740], as 'now finished'.

1741
Acta Germanica; or the Literary Memoirs of Germany. Done from the Latin and High-Dutch, by a Society of Gentlemen.

Imp. —London: Printed for and by G. Smith . . . MDCCXLII.
4to; 3 sh. ea.; w.; 6d. ea.; 8 plus 460 plus 14 pp.; cuts; no. 1 listed
Gentleman's Magazine Dec. 1741 as pub.

BENNET, GEORGE. *Pamela; or Virtue Rewarded, a heroick poem.*
A versification of Richardson's *Pamela; or, Virtue Rewarded* (1740).
Ad. *Daily Advertiser* July 24 and Aug. 12, 1741; note with passage
(110 lines) quoted in *Scots Magazine* Oct. 1741 says,' . . . began to be
published lately at London, in numbers; but the work now seems
dropt'. See Alan D. McKillop, *Samuel Richardson, Printer and Novelist*
(Chapel Hill: University of North Carolina Press, 1936), p. 70 and
n. 129.

BLACKWELL, ELIZABETH. *A Curious Herbal.*
Rep. or reissue of work originally pub. in nos, 1737-1739.
fol.; 4 prints in ea. no.; w.; 1s. plain, 2s. coloured; no. 1 ad. *Champion*
number 301 (Oct. 15, 1741) as to be pub. Nov. 2, 'Printed for J.
Nourse'.

BRANTÔME, PIERRE DE BOURDEILLE (Seigneur de). *The
Historical and Biographical Memoirs.*
Trans. from *Mémoires de Messire Pierre de Bourdeille, seigneur de Brantôme*,
of which there were several ed. in the seventeenth century. No. 1
listed *Gentleman's Magazine* Feb. 1741, 'From the French of Brantom . . . Printed for J. Crichley. pr. 3d.'

BUTLER, JAMES (Second Duke of Ormonde). *Memoirs of the Life of
the Late Duke of Ormond.* Written by Himself . . . Translated from the
French.
Not the same trans. as that pub. in 16 nos by J. Stanton in 1738.
Imp. —London: Printed by E. Applebee . . . 1741.
8vo; 3 hf. sh. ea.; 13 nos; 312 pp.; fasc sigs.

CLARKE, LAURENCE. *A Compleat . . . History of . . . Christ,
. . . the Twelve Apostles, . . . the Four Evangelists, . . . and the Virgin
Mary.*
Rep. or reissued from the ed. pub. in nos by J. Stanton in 1737-1738.
4to; single sh.; w.; 2d. ea.; 99 nos; 30 cuts; no. 1 ad. R. Walker's
London and Country Journal number 149 (Nov. 3, 1741) as to be pub. the
next week; news on the covers; same also pub. as supp. to the *London
and Country Journal*, new series beginning with number 1 (Tues., Nov.
10, 1741).

CHAMBERS, Ephraim. *Cyclopædia: or, an Universal Dictionary of Arts and Sciences.* The Fourth Edition. 2 vols.

Imp., vols I and II—London: Printed for D. Midwinter, J. Senex, R. Gosling, W. Innys, C. Rivington, A. Ward, J. and P. Knapton, E. Symon, S. Birt, D. Brown, T. Longman, R. Hett, C. Hitch, J. Shuckburgh, J. Pemberton, A. Millar, and the Executors of J. Darby. MDCCXLI.

fol.; 3 sh. ea.; w.; 6*d*. ea.; pp. not numbered; VOL. I, sigs. to 5Oo; VOL. II, sigs. 5Pp to 13 Kk; no. 1 pub. May 2, 1741; whole work ent. Sta. Reg. March 24, 1741; Roy. lic. dated April 17, 1741.

*Christian Library; containing a Variety of Discourses on all the necessary Points of Doctrine, The.
No. 1 listed*London Magazine* Feb. 1741 as 'Printed for F. Cogan, price 6*d*. . . . to be continued'.

COETLOGON, Chevalier Dennis de. *An Universal History of Arts and Sciences.* 2 vols.

Imp.—London: Printed and Sold by John Hart . . . MDCCXLV.

fol.; 3 sh. w. for 6*d*., or 12 sh. mo. for 2*s*.; VOL. I, nos 1-100 (1204 plus 24 pp.); VOL. II ,nos 1-[109] (1244 plus 26 pp.); pl.; fasc. sigs.; no. 1 ad. R. Walker's *London and Country Journal* number 97 (Mar. 26, 1741) as to be pub. April 22; no. 1 ent. Sta. Reg. April 22, 1741; all subsequent nos of both vols ent. Sta. Reg. April 29, 1741 to June 2, 1747; Roy. lic. dated March 13, 1740-1; has list of subscribers.

Complete history of the present war with Spain, A.
Imp.—London, Printed in the Year 1742.
8vo; 6*d*.; 44 pp.; no more pub.? Listed *Scots Magazine* Dec. 1741 as 'published in numbers'.

DEFOE, Daniel? *The Pleasant, and Surprizing Adventures of Mr. Robert Drury, During his Fifteen Years Captivity on the Island of Madagascar.* First pub. 1729, by W. Meadows.

Imp.—London, Printed, and Sold by W. Meadows . . .; T. Astley . . .; and B. Milles . . . 1743.

8vo; 10 plus 470 pp.; fasc. sig. in no. 1 only; no. 1 ent. Sta. Reg. Dec. 9, 1741 by Bryan Milles as proprietor of the whole; no. 2 ent. *ibid*. Jan. 15, 1742; no. 3 ent. *ibid*. Feb. 1, 1742.

FONTENELLE, Bernard le Bovier de. *The Philosophical History and Memoirs of the Royal Academy of Sciences at Paris; or, An*

Abridgment of all the Papers relating to Natural Philosophy . . .
publish'd by the Members of that Illustrious Society, from . . . 1699
to 1720. Translated and Abridged By John Martyn, F.R.S. Professor
of Botany in the University of Cambridge; and Ephraim Chambers,
F.R.S. Author of the Universal Dictionary of Arts and Sciences. 5 vols.
    Imp. of all vols. —London: Printed for John and Paul Knapton . . . ;
    and John Nourse . . . MDCCXLII.
8vo; 5 hf. sh. ea.; w.; *6d.*; VOL. I, nos 1-12 (456 plus 14 pp.); VOL. II,
nos 13-23 (407 pp. plus index plus 10 pp.); VOL. III, nos 24-34 (422 pp.
plus index); VOL. IV, nos 35-45 (410 pp. plus index plus 26 pp.); VOL.
V, nos 46-56 (416 pp. plus index); pl.; fasc. sigs.; no. 1 listed *Scots
Magazine* Nov. 1741.

FOXE, JOHN. *The Book of Martyrs: Containing an Account of the Sufferings and Death of the Protestants In the Reign of Queen Mary the First.*
Revised and Corrected by an Impartial Hand.
Latin original first pub. 1559; first ed. in English pub. 1563; frequently
rep.
    Imp. —London: Printed & Sold for the Proprietor. M.D.C.C.X.L.I.
fol.; 3 sh. ea. (or 2 sh. and cut); w.; *4d.*; 70 nos; 713 pp.; 29 cuts; fasc.
sigs.; ad. R. Walker's *London and Country Journal* number 103 (Thurs.,
May 7, 1741): 'Such Persons as are desirous of taking in this valuable
Work, are desired to apply to the Person who serves this Place with
Books and News Papers printed in London by R. Walker.' Rep. or
reissued in nos by Walker in 1745.

HARRIS, JOHN. *A Supplement to Dr. Harris's Dictionary of Arts and
Sciences.* By a Society of Gentlemen.
Harris's *Lexicon Technicum Magnum; or an Universal English Dictionary
of Arts and Sciences* was first pub. 1702; the fifth ed. was pub. in 2 fol.
vols in 1736.
    Imp. —London: Printed for the Authors; and Sold by M. Cooper...;
    J. Clarke and T. Comyns . . .; C. Bathurst . . .; T. Gardner . . .;
    and most other Booksellers in Town and Country. MDCCXLIV.
fol.; fort.; 1*s.* ea.; pages not numbered; sigs. A-11S; pl.; nos 1 and 2
listed *London Magazine* Aug. 1741, 'to be continued in about 30 Numbers, price 1*s.* each. Printed for T. Cooper'.

**Impartial Account of many Barbarous Cruelties Exercised by the Inquisition
in Spain, Portugal, and Italy, An.*
Rep. or reissue of work with same title pub. in 27 sh. and 5 cuts in
1738.

8vo; w.?; 2*d*.; 14 nos; 27 sh. and 5 cuts; no. 1 ad. *London and Country Journal* number 136 (Thurs., Dec. 24, 1741) as 'Printed and Sold by R. Walker . . .; and may be had of the Person who serves this News Paper.' Rep. or reissued in nos by Walker in 1745.

JOSEPHUS, FLAVIUS. **Compleat Collection of the Genuine Works of Flavius Josephus.* By [i.e., ed. by] James Wilson.
4to; single sh. ea.; w.; 104 sh. in all; 2*d*. ea.; maps, cuts; no. 1 ad. R. Walker's *London and Country Journal* number 149 (Nov. 3, 1741) as to be pub. the following week; 'stitch'd up in a large Cover, . . . on which Cover will be printed the whole Week's News, Foreign and Domestick'.

LUTHER, MARTIN. **A Commentary on St. Paul's Epistle to the Galatians.*
Nine ed. of an anonymous trans. of this Commentary were pub. between 1575 and 1644. This may be a rep. of the ed. in nos pub. in 1740.
w.? 4*d*. ea.; 25 nos; no. 1 of 'Luther on the Galatians' listed *Scots Magazine* Jan. 1741: 'To make 25, at 4*d*. each'.

Musical Companion: or, Lady's Magazine, The. Being a Complete Collection Of . . . English and Scotch Songs, Airs, Catches, &c. [words only].
Imp. —London: Printed for T. Read . . . MDCCXLI.
8vo; 2 sh. ea.; 12 nos (388 pp.); fasc. sigs.

Pamela in High Life: Or, Virtue Rewarded.
This is one of the anonymous sequels to Part I of Richardson's *Pamela; or, Virtue Rewarded* (1740).
Imp. (cancelled t.p.) —London: Printed in the Year, MDCCXLI.
Imp. (substituted t.p.) —London: Printed for Mary Kingman . . . 1741.
Ad. *Daily Advertiser*, Sept. 29 and Oct. 15, 1741. See Alan D. McKillop. *Samuel Richardson, Printer and Novelist* (Chapel Hill: University of North Carolina Press, 1936), p. 56 f.

PURBECK, REV. MR. *The Present State of the Turkish Empire.* Collected from the best Authors by the Rev. Mr. Purbeck.
Imp. —London: Printed by T. Totteridge . . . n.d.
8vo; 3 hf. sh. ea.; w.; 2*d*.; 23 nos; 502 pp.; cuts; fasc. sigs.; no. 1 ad. *Robinson Crusoe's London Daily Evening Post* Sept. 21, 1741, under the

title *A Compleat History of the Turkish Empire from its Origin to the Present Time* as to be pub. in 17 nos., 8vo, 3 hf. sh. w. for 2*d*.

SMITH, SAMUEL. *The Old and New Testament, or, a Family Bible. With large Annotations.* 2 vols.
Rep. from ed. in nos, 1735.
fol.; 4 sh. ea.; w.; 6*d*. ea.; to make about 300 sh.; no. 1 ad. *London Morning Advertiser* number 949 (Oct. 12, 1741) as pub. 'This Day . . . Subscriptions are taken in by H. Goreham . . . . This will be cover'd with Admiral Vernon's Weekly Journal, which will not only contain the common News, but the Life, History, and Memoirs of that Magnanimous and renown'd Admiral.' William Rayner was the proprietor.

VERGILIUS MARO, PUBLIUS. *The Works of Virgil*, translated into English Prose . . . with the Latin Text . . . and . . . Notes.
mo.; 1*s*. ea.; no. 1 ad. *Champion* number 308 (Oct. 31, 1741) as to be pub. Nov. 5, 'Printed for J. Davidson . . . .'

1742
ADAMS, GEORGE. *A System of Divinity.*
No. 1 listed *Scots Magazine* Nov. 1742.

Bibliotheca Harleiana: Or, A Catalogue of the Library of the late Earl of Oxford. Purchased by Thomas Osborne, Bookseller, in Gray's Inn. 2 vols. [continued in VOLS III, IV, and V].
8vo; 5 sh. ea.; w.; 1*s*. ea.; 12 nos; proposals dated Nov. 1, 1742 announced no. 1 as to be pub. Dec. 4; no. 1 pub. Dec. 11, 1742.

BICKHAM, GEORGE. *The Universal Penman.*
Rep. or reissued in nos from 1st ed. in nos, 1733-1741.

BLAINVILLE, J. DE. *Travels through Holland, Germany, Switzerland, and other parts of Europe, but especially Italy.* 3 vols.
Trans. by W. Guthrie, George Turnbull, D. Soyer, and J. Lockman. Imp.—London: Printed by W. Strahan for the Proprietor; and sold by J. Noon . . .; by R. Dodsley . . .; and at the Bar of Old Slaughter's Coffee-House, in St. Martin's Lane. MDCCXLIII [VOL. II, MDCCXLIII; VOL. III, MDCCXLV].
4to; 6 sh. ea.; fort.; 1*s*. ea.; VOL. I, nos 1-13 (12 plus 12 plus 564 pp. plus index); VOL. II, nos 14, 15 (no other fasc. sigs.), (586 pp. plus contents and index); VOL. III, 593 pp. plus contents and index; nos 1 and 2 listed *Scots Magazine* July 1742: 'Translated from the Author's

Original MS. by G. Turnbull, L.L.D.'; Preface to VOL. III by J. Lockman, dated July 23, 1744, promised a fourth vol.

CLARKE, SAMUEL, D.D. *Sermons.*
No. 1 ad. *Champion, or Evening Advertiser* number 379 (April 20, 1742) as pub. 'This Day'.

Female Robbers, The. Or a General History of the Lives and Adventures of the most famous Highway-women, Pyratesses, Street-Robbers, Shoplifters, &c.
12mo; 2d. ea.; to have 15 nos, excess gratis; cuts; no. 1 ad. *Rayner's London Morning Advertiser* number 1186 [incorrectly numbered 117] (Sept. 15, 1742) as to be pub. Sept. 18: 'Those Persons who are willing to encourage so Entertaining a Work by becoming Subscribers, may be regularly serv'd, by sending their Names and Places of Abode to H. Goreham . . ., or by speaking to the Persons that carry the News'. No. 6 ad. *ibid.* number 1205 (Nov. 3, 1742) as to be pub. Nov. 6.

HORATIUS FLACCUS, QUINTUS. *The Satires, Epistles, and Art of Poetry of Horace Translated into English Prose* . . . With the Latin Text in the Opposite Page; and . . . Notes . . . And a Preface to each Satire and Epistle.
Imp.—London: Printed for Joseph Davidson . . . MDCCXLIII.
8vo; 18 plus 632 plus 16 pp.; Roy. lic. dated Feb. 24, 1741/42; rep. 1748, 'Third Edition'.

JAMES, ROBERT, M.D. *A Medicinal Dictionary*; including Physic, Surgery, Anatomy, Chymistry and Botany, In all their Branches relating to Medicine. Together with a History of Drugs . . . and an Introductory Preface. 3 vols.
Imp.—London: Printed for T. Osborne . . .; and Sold by J. Roberts . . . MDCCXLIII [VOL. II, MDCCXLV; VOL. III, MDCCXLV].
fol.; 5 sh. ea.; fort.; 1s. ea.; Preface of VOL. I, 99 pp.; pp. of text not numbered. VOL. I, sigs. B-11N; VOL. II, A-13S; VOL. III, A*-†K; proposals dated June 24, 1741; no. 1 ad. *Norwich Gazette* number 1849 (Mar. 13, 1742) as pub. Feb. 4; no. 151 listed supp. (Jan. 1745) to *Gentleman's Magazine* for 1744; completed by Aug. 17, 1745.

Life of Oliver Cromwell, The.
This may be a reprinting of *The Life of Oliver Cromwell*, 4th. ed., printed for J. Brotherton and T. Cox in Sept. 1741.
8vo; single hf. sh. ea.; thrice w., Mon., Wed., Fri.; ¼d. ea.; port; no. 2

ad. *Rayner's London Morning Advertiser* number 1188 (Sept. 20, 1742)
as to be pub. Sept. 22: 'To be had of all Persons who serve News and
Subscription Books'. No. 43 ad. *ibid.* number 1230 (Dec. 30, 1742) as
pub. 'This Day'.

MARCHANT, JOHN. *An Exposition on the Books of the New Testament.*
    Imp.—London: Printed for the Author, and Sold by the Book-
    sellers in Town and Country. MDCCXLIII.
fol.; 2 sh. ea.; w.; 3*d.* ea.; 110 nos; 880 pp.; pl.; fasc. sigs.; no. 1 ad.
Champion Nov. 11, 1742 as to be pub. Nov. 17: 'And I have appointed
Mr. Benjamin Cole, Engraver . . . and Mr. John Pelham, of New
Shoreham in Sussex, to deliver out the Books for me.' All nos ent.
Sta. Reg. by John Marchant, sole proprietor: no. 1 on Nov. 24, 1742,
to no. 110 on Feb. 2, 1745; followed by similar work on the Old
Testament (in nos, 1745).

New Anatomical Tables.
irreg.; 1*s.* 6*d.* ea.; pl.; no. 1, 'representing the general structure of the
bones, and the compleat skeleton of a man', listed *Scots Magazine* Jan.
1742; no. 2, 'representing the skeleton of a woman', listed *ibid.* March
1742; nos 3 and 4 'representing all the parts of the human body, with
explanations', listed *ibid.* Dec. 1742; no. 5, 'representing the common
teguments of the body . . .', listed *ibid.* March 1743 as pub. at Edinburgh; no. 6 listed *ibid.* March 1744.

SCOTT, DANIEL, LL. D. *Appendix ad thesaurum grecæ linguæ ab Hen.
Stephano constructum.* 2 vols.
    Imp.—Londini, typis Jac. Bettenham, veneunt apud Joh. Noon . . .
    1745 [VOL. II, 1746].
fol.; 1*s.* 6*d.* ea.; 64 nos; VOL. I, nos 1-31 (1264 cols); VOL. II, nos 1-33
(1312 cols); fasc. sigs.; no. 1 listed *Scots Magazine* June 1742; no. 30
listed supp. (Jan. 1745) to *Gentleman's Magazine* for 1744; no. 33 (last
of VOL. II) listed *London Magazine* June 1746.

*Select and Impartial Account of the Lives, Behaviour, and Dying Words, of
the most remarkable Convicts, from the Year 1700 to the Year 1741, A.*
10 nos 4*d.* ea.; 72 pp. ea. [i.e. 3 sh. 12mo?]; no. 1 ad. R. Walker's
London and Country Journal number 136 (Dec. 24, 1741) as to begin the
following week: 'Printed and Sold by R. Walker . . .; and may be had
of the Person who serves this News Paper.'

[SMITH, ALEXANDER] and JOHNSON, CHARLES. *A General*

and True History of the Lives and Actions of the most Famous Highwaymen, Murderers, Street-Robbers, &c. To which is added, A Genuine Account of the Voyages and Plunders of the most noted Pirates. Interspersed with several Remarkable Tryals of the most Notorious Malefactors, at the Sessions-House in the Old Baily London.

Rep., with omissions and changes in sequence, of the ed. in nos by Janeway in 1733.

Imp.—Birmingham: Printed by R. Walker, at the Sign of the Printing-Press, over-against the Swan-Tavern in the High-Street. MDCCXLII.

fol.; single sh. ea.; 108 nos; 428 pp.; pl.; fasc. sigs.; rep. in 8vo nos, 1747, with authorship attributed to James Macklecan.

STACKHOUSE, THOMAS. *A Compleat Body of Speculative and Practical Divinity.* The Third Edition.

First pub. 1729.

Imp.—London: Printed for T. Cox . . . MDCCXLIII.

fol.; 5 sh. ea.; w.; 6*d.* ea.; 50 nos; 6 plus 980 plus 16 pp.; fasc. sigs.; first four nos listed *London Magazine* Sept. 1742; whole vol. listed *ibid.* Sept. 1743 at £1. 10*s.*

STACKHOUSE, THOMAS. *A New History of the Holy Bible.* The Second Edition. 2 vols.

Rep. from first ed., pub. in nos, 1732-1735.

Imp.—London: Printed for Stephen Austen . . . 1742 [VOL. II, 1744]. fol.; 4 sh. ea.; 6*d.* ea.; 111 nos; 60 plus 8 plus 1650 plus 50 pp.; maps, pl.; fasc. sigs.; Roy. lic. dated Jan. 8, 1742 issued to Stephen Austen; proposals dated Jan. 12, 1742; no. 1 ad. *Kentish Post, or Canterbury News Letter* number 2527 (Jan. 27, 1742) as to be pub. Feb. 6; Dedication dated April 7, 1744.

TILLOTSON, JOHN. *Sermons on several Subjects and Occasions,* By the most Reverend Dr. John Tillotson, Late Lord Archbishop of Canterbury. 12 vols.

Imp.—London: Printed for R. Ware, A. Ward, J. and P. Knapton, T. Longman, R. Hett, C. Hitch, S. Austen, J. and R. Tonson, J. Wood, J. and H. Pemberton, and J. Rivington. MDCCXLII [VOL. II omits J. Wood, adds J. Hodges; VOLS. III and IV, same as II; VOL. V same as II, but has date MDCCXLIII; VOL. VI same as II, with date MDCCXLII; VOLS. VII, VIII, IX, X same as III and IV, with date MDCCXLIII; VOL. XI same, but with date MDCCXLIV; VOL. XII same, but with date MDCCXLIII].

8vo; 7 hf. sh. ea.; w.; 6d. ea.; 8 nos in ea. vol.; port.; fasc. sigs.; no. 1 ad. *Norwich Gazette* number 1854 (April 17, 1742) as to be pub. May 1.

1743

ADLERFELD, Gustavus. *The Genuine History of Charles XII King of Sweden.* Translated by James Ford.
Perhaps based on anon. English trans. pub. 1740 in 3 vols. 8vo by the Knaptons, Hodges, Millar, and Nourse; original Swedish MS. trans. to French by Adlerfeld's son in 1740.
8vo; 2 sh. ea.; w.; 3d. ea.; to have about 30 nos, excess over 35 gratis; cuts; no. 1 ad. *Kentish Post, or Canterbury News Letter* number 2735 (Dec. 21, 1743) as to be pub. Dec. 17, 1743, at London, 'Printed . . . and sold by R. Walker . . . .'

American Traveller, The . . . a new . . . collection . . . containing a compleat account of . . . the West Indies.
   Imp.—London: Printed and sold by J. Fuller . . ., and by most of the Booksellers in Town and Country.
8vo; 3 hf. sh. ea.; 18 nos; 398 pp.; fasc. sigs.

BICKHAM, George. *The British Monarchy*: Or, a New Chorographical Description of all the Dominions Subject to the King of Great Britain. 2 vols.
   Imp., vol. 1—Publish'd according to Act of Parliament, October 1st, 1743, and Sold by G. Bickham . . ., & by the Booksellers & Printsellers in Town and Country. n.d.
   Imp., vol. 11—Printed for & Sold by him [George Bickham] in Numbers 6d. each 25 in the Whole of this Volume Of whom may be had the first Volume Neatly Bound 15s.
fol.; 6d. ea.; engraved maps and plates; a few plates variously dated 1744, 1747, 1749; has list of subscribers.

[GREEN, John]. *A New General Collection of Voyages and Travels:* consisting of the most esteemed Relations, which have been hitherto published in any Language. 4 vols.
For a discussion of evidence that the editor was John Green, see G. R. Crone and R. A. Skelton, 'English Collections of Voyages and Travels, 1625-1846', in Edward Lynam, ed., *Richard Hakluyt & His Successors* (London: Hakluyt Society, 1946), p. 100; see also G. R. Crone, 'A Note on Bradock Mead, alias John Green', *Library*, ser. 5, VI (1951), 42f.

Imp., VOL. I—London: Printed for Thomas Astley . . . MDCCXLV [VOL. II, same; VOL. III, MDCCXLVI; VOL. IV, MDCCXLVII]. 4to; 3 sh. ea.; or 2 sh. and map; w.; 6d. ea.; 164 nos; VOL. I, nos 1-33 (680 pp.); VOL. II, nos 34-79 (732 pp.); VOL. III, nos 80-117 (605 pp.); VOL. IV, nos 118-164 (751 plus 34 pp.); maps and pl.; fasc. sigs.; no. 1 listed *Scots Magazine* Dec. 1743; no. 59 listed supp. (Jan. 1745) to *Gentleman's Magazine* for 1744; Roy. lic. dated Oct. 18, 1743; list of subscribers.

LONGUEVILLE, PETER. *The History and Surprizing Adventures of Mr. Philip Quarll, the English Hermit.* This is doubtless based on *The Hermit; or, the unparalleled Sufferings of Mr. Philip Quarll, an Englishman* (1727). See Arundell Esdaile, 'Author and Publisher in 1727. "The English Hermit"', *Library*, ser. 4, II (1921-1922), 185-192. 16 pp. ea.; twice weekly; no. 17 ad. *London Morning Advertiser* number 1269 (April 26, 1743) as pub.

RAPIN DE THOYRAS, PAUL DE. *The History of England.* Written in French by Mr. Rapin de Thoyras. Translated into English, with Additional Notes, by N. Tindal. The Third Edition. 2 vols. Rep. from 2nd ed., pub. in nos, 1732-1735. Imp., VOLS I and II—London: Printed for John and Paul Knapton . . . MDCCXLIII. fol.; 5 sh. ea.; w.; 84 nos; VOL. I, nos 1-43 (10 plus 849 pp.); VOL. II, nos 44-84 (10 plus 807 plus 16 pp.); maps, cuts, port.; fasc. sigs.; followed by fol. nos of Tindal's con. (probably based on con. in French by David Durand) and Tindal's abridgment of the whole work. See 1744, *s.v.* Tindal.

ROWLAND, THOMAS. *A General Treatise of Architecture in Seven Books.* No. 1 listed *London Magazine* Sept. 1743 as 'Sold by J. Robinson. 2s.'; nos 1-4 ent. Sta. Reg. by Thomas Rowland Aug. 17, Oct. 6, Nov. 3, 1743, and Jan. 24, 1744.

SALMON, THOMAS. *The Present State of the Universities and of the Five Adjacent Counties.* Imp. of 'Numb. 1 for the Month of July' —London: Printed for the sole Benefit of the Author, and sold by J. Roberts . . . (Price One Shilling). 8vo; 10 hf. sh. ea.; mo.; 1s. ea.; was to have made 2 vols. of 6 nos ea.; VOL. I, apparently inc., has 476 pp.; no. 1 listed *Scots Magazine* Aug.

1743; no. 6 listed *Gentleman's Magazine* June 1744 as pub. or sold by Gardner.

SIMPSON, SAMUEL. *The Agreeable Historian, Or the Compleat English Traveller*: Giving a Geographical Description of every County in . . . England. 3 vols.
>Imp., VOLS I, II, III—London: Printed by R. Walker . . ., and Sold by the Booksellers in Town and Country, 1746.

8vo; single sh. (16 pp.) ea.; w.; 3*d.* ea.; 109 nos; VOL. I, nos 1-35 (554 pp.); VOL. II, nos 36-74 (638 pp.); VOL. III, nos 75-109 (pp. 639-1194); maps; fasc. sigs.; no. 23 ad. *St. James's Evening Post* number 5351 (May 5, 1744) as 'Sold by T. Read'.

SLADE, MRS, 'late a Nun'. *The Nunnery Tales; or the Amours of the Priests and Nuns.*
No. 14, 'which compleats the Volume', ad. *London Morning Advertiser* number 1296 (April 26, 1743) as pub. 'This Day... Printed by T. Davis...'

THOMPSON, CHARLES. *The Travels of the Late Charles Thompson, Esq.* 3 vols.
>Imp.—Reading, Printed by J. Newbury and C. Micklewright, at the Bible and Crown in the Market-Place. MDCCXLIV.

8vo; 2 sh. (32 pp.) ea.; w.; 3*d.* ea.; 50 nos.; VOL. I, nos 1-17; VOL. II, nos 18-32; VOL. III, nos 33-50; proposals issued May 30, 1743, indicate that the ed. was pub. 'from the Author's original Manuscripts . . .' and that no. 1 was to be pub. June 27.

Trial at Bar, between Campbell Craig, Lessee of James Annesley, Esq.; Plaintiff, And the Right Honourable Richard Earl of Anglesey, Defendant, The. This is a summary account of the famous trial conducted in Dublin in Nov. 1743. See Andrew Lang, *The Annesley Case* (Edinburgh and London: Hodge, 1912).
>Imp.—London: Printed for M. Cooper . . ., and sold by the Booksellers and Printers in all the Cities and noted Towns in Great Britain and Ireland. MDCCXLIII.

fol.; 1*s.* ea.; 150 pp.; no. 4 ad. *General Evening Post* number 1625 (Feb. 18, 1744) as pub. at 1*s.*, 'printed for M. Cooper'.

1744
Agreeable Companion; or, an Universal Medley of Wit and Good Humour, The.
>Imp.—London. Printed for W. Bickerton . . .; and sold by the Booksellers in Town and Country. MDCCXLV.

12mo; 2 sh. ea.; w.; 8 nos; total 384 pp.; listed *Scots Magazine* Dec.
1744 as 'Published in numbers'; second vol. planned, but not to be
pub. in nos.

**Authentick Memoirs of the Life and Conduct of her Grace Sarah, late
Dutchess of Marlborough.*
24. pp. ea.; w.; 2*d*. ea.; to have 8 or 9 nos; no. 1 ad. in clipping from
[*Sherborne*] *Mercury* as to be pub. Dec. 3, 1744; 'Printed by Order of
the Proprietors: And by their Appointment, and published by
B. Collins, Bookseller in Salisbury; and Sold by R. Baldwin, at Newport in the Isle of Wight; T. Burrough, in Devizes, C. Wooddeson,
at Yeovil in Somerset, and by the Men who carry this *Mercury*.'

BARROW, Isaac, D. D., Master of Trinity College, Cambridge.
*The Works of Dr. Isaac Barrow, published [i.e., edited] by Dr. John
Tillotson.
Probably rep. of 5th ed., pub. by Millar and Tonson in 1741.
fol.; 6 sh. ea. (5 sh. on alternate weeks); w.; 6*d*. ea.; no. 48 listed in the
supp. (Jan. 1745) of the *Gentleman's Magazine* for 1744 as pub. by Millar,
Tonson, Roberts.

BOLTON, S. *A Complete System of Geography.* Being a Description
of All the Countries, Islands, Cities, Chief Towns, Harbours, Lakes,
and Rivers, Mountains, Mines, &c. of the Known World. 2 vols.
    Imp., VOLS I and II—London: Printed for William Innys, Richard
    Ware, Aaron Ward, J. and P. Knapton, John Clarke, Thomas Long-
    man and Thomas Shewell, Thomas Osborne, Henry Whitridge,
    Richard Hett, Charles Hitch, Stephen Austen, Edward Comyns,
    James Hodges, Andrew Millar, Thomas Corbett, and John Riving-
    ton. 1747.
fol.; 4 sh. ea.; w.; 6*d*. ea.; VOL. I, nos 1-85 (28 plus 1013 pp.); VOL. II,
nos 86-144 (804 plus 24 pp.); 70 maps by E. Bowen; fasc. sigs.; no. 3
ad. *General Evening Post* number 1625 (Feb. 18, 1744); no. 45 listed in
supp. (Jan. 1745) to the *Gentleman's Magazine* for 1744 as pub. by
'Innys, Knapton, and 16 more'; completed work ad. *General Evening
Post* number 2246 (March 1, 1748); Roy. lic. dated Dec. 5, 1743;
Preface, signed by S. Bolton, dated Nov. 30, 1745.

Collection of Voyages and Travels, A. . . To which is prefixed, An Introductory Discourse (supposed to be written by the Celebrated
Mr. Locke) intitled, The Whole History of Navigation from its Original to this Time. The Third Edition. 6 vols.

Rep. of *A Collection of Voyages and Travels*, pub. in 4 vols. fol. by Awnsham and John Churchill in 1704 and reissued or rep. in 1732 with two additional vols.

    Imp., VOL. I—London: Printed by Assignment from Mssrs. Churchill, For Henry Lintot; and John Osborn . . . MDCCXLIV [VOLS II, III, IV have MDCCXLV; VOLS V, VI have M.DCC.XLVI]. fol.; 5 sh. ea.; w.; 6*d.*; VOL. I, nos [1]-39 (8 plus 29 plus 64 plus 4 plus 668 pp.); VOL. II, nos 40-87 (2 plus 744 pp.); VOL. III, nos 88-137 (794 pp.); VOL. IV, nos 138-179 (780 pp.); VOL. V, nos 180-223 (708 pp.); VOL. VI, nos 224-271 (824 pp., plus index, sigs. 9Z-11B); maps, pl.; no. 9 ad. *St. James's Evening Post* number 5351 (May 5, 1744); nos 76 and 77, 'being the 35th and 36th numbers in vol. 2', listed in supp. (Jan. 1745) to *Gentleman's Magazine* for 1744 as pub. by Lintot and J. Osborne; fasc. sigs.

FANCOURT, SAMUEL. *The Gentleman and Ladies Growing and Circulating Library . . . in Crane-Court, Fleet Street.*
Catalogue, issued in parts, 1744-1746.

Flanders Delineated or, a View of the Austrian and French Netherlands . . . By an Officer of the Allied Army now in Flanders.
    Imp.—Reading, Printed and Sold by J. Newbery and C. Micklewright . . .; and by Most Booksellers and News-Carriers in Great Britain. MDCCXLV.
8vo; 2 sh. ea.; w.; 2*d.*; 12 nos (4 plus 310 pp.); maps; fasc. sigs.; listed *Gentleman's Magazine* Sept. 1744 as 'Publishing in weekly Numbers, at 2*d.* each, by Robinson', and *ibid.* Dec. 1744 as pub. 'pr. 3*s.* 6*d.* Newbery'.

Fortune's Favourite: containing, Memoirs Of the many Hardships and Sufferings, together with The surprizing Deliverance . . . of Jacobo Anglicano, a Young Nobleman [i.e., James Annesley].
    Imp.—London: Printed for the Author; And Sold by the Booksellers in Town and Country, 1744.
8vo; 4 hf. sh. ea.; 12 nos (384 pp.); announced in no. 13 of *The Trial at Bar . . .*, pub. by R. Walker, as about to begin; fasc. sigs.

Geography Methodized; Or, a New System of General Geography.
Possible related to *Geography Reformed: or, a New System of General Geography*, pub. E. Cave, 1739.
9 nos; w.; 4*d.* ea.; listed in supp. (Jan. 1745) to *Gentleman's Magazine* for 1744 as pub. by Collyer.

GUTHRIE, WILLIAM. *A General History of England, from the Invasion of the Romans under Julius Cæsar, to the Late Rebellion in* MDCLXXXVIII. Title, VOL. II, *A General History of England, Beginning with the Reign of Edward the Second, and Ending with that of Henry the Eighth.* Title, VOL. III, *A General History of England, from Edward the Sixth, to the Restoration of King Charles the Second.* 4 vols.

    Imp., VOL. I—London: Printed by Daniel Browne, for T. Waller . . . MDCCXLIV.

    Imp., VOL. II—London: Printed for T. Waller . . . MDCCXLVII.

    Imp., VOLS III and IV—London: Printed for T. Waller, MDCCLI. fol.; 3 sh. ea.; w.; 6*d.* ea.; VOL. I, nos 1-83 (4 plus 962 pp. plus index); VOL. II, nos 84-179 (1130 pp. plus index); VOLS III and IV, nos 1-115 (1396 pp. plus index); no. 1 ad. *General Evening Post* number 1625 (Feb. 18, 1744); VOL. I completed Oct. 26, 1745; VOL. II completed Nov. 21, 1747; An ad. in *Whitehall Evening-Post* number 277 (Nov. 21, 1747) by T. Waller refers to Guthrie's *History of England* and adds: 'N.B. The Continuation of this Work, which brings it down to the present Times, is now publishing. The First Volume is finished, and as far as no. 36 of the Second, which is likewise a supplement to Rapin, Kennet, and Eachard.' No. 45 of this con., 'by another hand', is listed in supp. (Jan. 1745) to the *Gentleman's Magazine* for 1744; like Guthrie's work, this con. was pub. in fol., 3 sh. ea., w.; 6*d.* ea.

Harleian Miscellany, The; or, a Collection of Scarce, Curious, and Entertaining Pamphlets and Tracts, As well in Manuscript as in Print, Found in the Late Earl of Oxford's Library. 8 vols.

    Imp., all vols—London: Printed for T. Osborne . . . MDCCXLIV [VOL. II, same; VOLS III, IV, V, 1745; VOLS VI, VII, VIII, 1746]. 4to; 6 sh. ea.; w.; 1*s.* ea.; VOL. I, 16 plus 8 plus 608 pp.; VOL. II, 12 plus 612 pp.; VOL. III, 12 plus 556 pp. plus nos 1-11 of Oldys's *Copious and Exact Catalogue,* (pp. 1-56); VOL. IV, 12 plus 572 pp. plus nos 12-21 of *Catalogue* (pp. 57-96); VOL. V, 12 plus 576 pp. plus nos 22-31 of *Catalogue* (pp. 97-136); VOL. VI, 12 plus 584 pp. plus nos 32-38 of *Catalogue* (pp. 137-164); VOL. VII, 12 plus 608 plus no. 39 of *Catalogue* (pp. 165-168) VOL. VIII, 12 plus 612 pp.; proposals pub. *Gentleman's Magazine* end of run for 1743), announcing no. 1 as to be pub. March 24, 1744; no. 13 (last of VOL. VII) ad. *St. James's Evening Post* number 5606 (Dec. 24, 1745) as pub. 'This Day'; completed March 25, 1746; has list of subscribers.

HARRIS, JOHN. *Navigantium atque Itinerantium Bibliotheca. Or, a Complete Collection of Voyages and Travels.* Consisting of above Six hundred of the most Authentic Writers . . . Originally published in Two Volumes in Folio, By John Harris, D. D. and F.R.S. Now Carefully Revised, With Large Additions, and Continued down to the Present Time. 2 vols.

Editing attributed to John Campbell.

> Imp., VOL. I—London: Printed for T. Woodward, A. Ward, S. Birt, D. Browne, T. Longman, R. Hett, C. Hitch, H. Whitridge, S. Austen, J. Hodges, J. Robinson, B. Dod, T. Harris, J. Hinton, and J. Rivington. M.DCC.XLIV.

> Imp., VOL. II—London: Printed for T. Woodward, A. Ward, S. Birt, D. Browne, T. Longman, R. Hett, C. Hitch, H. Whitridge, S. Austen, J. Hodges, J. Fuller, J. Robinson, B. Dod, J. Hinton, J. and J. Rivington, J. Ward. M.DCC.XLVIII [i.e., 1749].

fol.; 4 sh. ea., or 3 sh. and map. w.; 6d. ea.; VOL. I, 69 nos (28 plus 984 pp.); VOL. II, nos 70-143 (8 plus 1056 pp. plus index); port., maps, cuts; fasc. sigs.; no. 1 pub. in April 1744; Dedication of VOL. I dated Dec. 3, 1745, issued with no. 69; no. 140 [sic] 'and last; with a copious index' listed *Gentleman's Magazine* Feb. 1749; Roy. lic. dated Feb. 23, 1743/44.

HARRISON (CONYERS). *An Impartial History of the Life and Reign Of her Late Majesty Queen Anne Of Immortal Memory.*

> Imp.—London: Printed and Sold by R, Walker . . .; and the Booksellers in Town and Country. MDCCXLV.

4to; 75 sh. (596 pp.), numbered [1] to 96, with omissions; pl.; may be the ed. pub. as free w. supp. to the *Cambridge Journal and Weekly Flying Post*. See R. Bowes, 'On the first and other early Cambridge Newspapers', *Proceedings of the Cambridge Antiquarian Society*, VIII (1895, for 1891-1894), 348.

Impartial History of the Life and Reign of her Late Majesty Queen Anne, An.

> Imp.—Printed for R. Offtey . . . 1744.

4to; single sh. ea.; 79 nos; 620 pp.; pl.; fasc. sigs.

MOORE, FRANCIS. **Travels into the Inland Parts of Africa*: containing a description of the Several Nations for . . . Six Hundred Miles up the River Gambia.

Rep. from the ed. pub. in London, 1738, by Edward Cave, or from the 2nd ed., 1740. Same work also included in VOL. II of the *New General Collection of Voyages and Travels* pub. in nos by Astley in 1743. Listed in supp. (Jan. 1745) to *Gentleman's Magazine* for 1744: 'The whole about fourteen numbers, at 4d. each. Collyer.'

OLDYS, WILLIAM. *A copious and exact Catalogue of Pamphlets in the Harleian Library.*
4to; w.; 39 nos (168 pp.); fasc. sigs.; issued with the nos of *The Harleian Miscellany* (1744).

OVIDIUS NASO, PUBLIUS. **The Epistles of Ovid*, translated into English Prose, with the Latin.
irreg.; 1s. ea.; no. 1 listed *Gentleman's Magazine* Sept. 1744; no. 3, 'which compleats the whole. Printed for J. Davidson', listed *London Magazine* Feb. 1746.

PARSONS, JAMES. *The Microscopical Theatre of Seeds.* Being a Short View of the Particular Marks, Characters, Contents, and Natural Dimensions of All the Seeds of the Shops, Flower and Kitchen Gardens, &c.
    Imp.—London: Printed for F. Needham . . .; and sold by M. Cooper . . . 1745.
8vo; 1s. ea.; to make 4 vols; VOL. 1 complete has 348 pp.; no more pub.; pl. by R. Parr; listed *Gentleman's Magazine* Nov. 1744: 'pr. 1s. each no. Cooper'; no. 6 listed in supp. (Jan. 1745) to *Gentleman's Magazine* for 1744 as pub. at 1s. by 'Wilcox, Dodsley, &c.'; trans. to German by G. L. Huth, pub. Nürnberg, 1747.

PATERSON, JAMES. *A Complete Commentary, with . . . Notes on Milton's Paradise Lost*, by James Paterson, M.A., and Philologist.
    Imp.—London: Printed by the Proprietor, R. Walker . . . 1744. [Library of Congress copy has 1743].
12mo; 512 pp.; no. 1 listed *Gentleman's Magazine* April 1744 as 'to be continued. pr. 3d. Bickerton'.

PHILIPS, JOHN. *An Authentic Journal of the late Expedition under the Command of Commodore Anson* . . . By John Philips, Midshipman of the Centurion.
    Imp.—London: Printed for J. Robinson . . . 1744.
8vo; w.; 6d. ea.; 516 pp.; listed *Gentleman's Magazine* Sept. 1744 as 'Publishing weekly, at 6d. each no. Robinson.'

*Polite Tales for Young Gentlemen and Ladies, from the Most Celebrated Authors, Prose and Verse. By a Lady.
4 sh. ea.; w.; 6d. ea.; listed in *Gentleman's Magazine* Nov. 1744 as 'publishing in numbers at 6d. each'; no. 10 listed in supp. (Jan. 1745) to *Gentleman's Magazine* for 1744 as pub. by Brotherton.

PREVOST d'Exiles, Antoine-François. *Memoirs of a man of quality.* Giving an account of many surprizing adventures, in his travels thro' England, France, Germany, Turkey, Spain, Portugal, and Italy. VOL. I of the first English trans. of Prevost's *Mémoires et avantures d'un homme de qualité* (1728) was 'Printed and sold by J. Wilford' in 1738; VOL. I, 'Second Edition', and VOL. II were 'Printed for E. Cave' in 1742.
Listed in supp. (Jan. 1745) to *Gentleman's Magazine* for 1744: 'The whole about fifteen numbers, at 4*d.* each. Collyer.'

RALPH, James. *The History of England: during the Reigns of K. William, Q. Anne, and K. George I.* With an Introductory Review of the Reigns of the Royal Brothers, Charles and James . . . By a Lover of Truth and Liberty. 2 vols.
    Imp., VOL. I—London: Printed by Daniel Browne, for F. Cogan . . .; and T. Waller . . . MDCCXLIV.
    Imp., VOL. II—London: Printed by Daniel Browne, for T. Waller . . . MDCCXLVI.
fol.; 3 sh. ea.; w.; 6*d.* ea.; VOL. I, nos 1-90 (1078 plus 5 pp.); VOL. II, nos 1-86 (1024 plus 8 pp.); maps, pl.; fasc. sigs.; no. 36 listed in supp. (Jan. 1745) to *Gentleman's Magazine* for 1744 as pub. by Waller, and there described as 'a supplement to Rapin, Guthrie, Eachard, &c.'

SALMON, Thomas. *Modern History: or, the Present State of all Nations.* Third Edition. 3 vols.
1st ed. pub. in 8vo nos, 1724-1738; 2nd ed. pub. in 3 vols 4to, 1739.
    Imp., VOL. I—London: Printed for T. Longman, T. Osborne, J. Shuckburgh, C. Hitch, S. Austen, J. Rivington. 1744; VOL. II adds J. Hinton; VOL. III adds T. Shewell, and has date 1746.
fol.; 4 sh. ea.; w.; 6*d.* ea.; 143 nos; VOL. I, nos 1-50 (777 pp. plus index); VOL. II, nos 51-103 (832 pp. plus index); VOL. III, nos 104-143 (628 pp. plus index); maps, pl.; fasc. sigs.; no. 6 ad. *General Evening Post* number 1625 (Feb. 18, 1744) as pub.; no. 53 listed in supp. (Jan. 1745) to *Gentleman's Magazine* for 1744 as pub. by 'Longman, Hitch, and five more'; Roy. lic. dated Dec. 30, 1743 granted sole rights for 14 years to T. Longman, T. Osborne, J. Shuckburgh, C. Hitch, and S. Austen.

Theatre of the present War in the Netherlands, and upon the Rhine, The. 8vo; w.; 3*d.* ea.; maps, pl.; no. 17 listed in supp. (Jan. 1745) to *Gentleman's Magazine* for 1744 as pub. by Brindley and Corbett; complete vol. listed *Gentleman's Magazine* Sept. 1744 as pub. for '7*s.* 6*d.* together, or in weekly Numbers at 3*d.* each. Brindley'.

TINDAL, NICHOLAS. *The History of England, by Mr. Rapin de Thoyras. Continued from the Revolution to the Accession of King George II.* By N. Tindal. 2 vols. (bound as 3).

Rep. from ed. in nos, 1736, with addition of material for reign of George I; pub. as VOLS III and IV of Rapin (trans. Tindal), 3rd ed., *q.v.*

Imp., VOL. III [i.e., VOL. I of the continuation]—London: Printed for John and Paul Knapton ... MDCCXLIV [VOL. IV, Part I—MDCCXLV; VOL. IV, Part II—MDCCXLVII].

fol.; 4 sh. ea.; w.; *6d.* ea.; VOL. III, nos 1-34; VOL. IV, Part I, nos 35-82; VOL. IV, Part II, nos 83-119 and six others lacking fasc. sigs. (but fasc. sigs. indicate that VOL. III was to comprise nos 1-51 and VOL IV. nos 52-119 etc.); maps, pl.; fasc. sigs.; no. 1 ad. *St. James's Evening Post* number 5351 (May 5, 1744); no. 36 listed in supp. (Jan. 1745) of *Gentleman's Magazine* for 1744; no. 125, 'compleating the whole', listed *Gentleman's Magazine* March 1747; Dedication by Tindal to his Royal Highness William Duke of Cumberland dated March 25, 1747.

Trial at Bar between Campbell Craig, Lessee of James Annesley, Esq; Plaintiff, And the Right Honourable Richard Earl of Anglesey, Defendant, The.
This is one of the many reports of the famous trial conducted in Dublin in Nov. 1743. Not the same as *The Trial at Bar* pub. in nos by Cooper in 1743; not the same as *The Trial at Large* pub. in nos by Watson in 1744. Added at end, in nos 13 (part) and 14, is *The Trial of James Annesley and Joseph Ridding ... July 15, 1742, for the Murder of Thomas Egglestone.*

Imp.—London: Printed by and for the Proprietor, R. Walker ... MDCCXLIV.

mixed 8vo hf. sh. and small 4to sh., all of 8 pp.; 4 of these sh. or hf. sh. ea. (no. 5 has 3 4to sh.; no. 6 has 2 8vo hf. sh and 3 4to sh.; no. 8 has 3 8vo hf. sh.); 14 nos (398 pp. plus pp. 399-488: *Trial of ... Annesley and ... Ridding*); fasc. sigs.; no. 13 has this announcement (p. 398):

The Hardships and Sufferings that this young Gentleman, Mr. Annesley, underwent, during the time of his Transportation Abroad, are so many and various, and were of so long Continuance, that they would swell this Volume to too great a Thickness to be bound up with this; therefore it will be printed by itself, and will make a neat Pocket Volume in twelve Numbers, and will be done in the Manner of a Novel.

Trial at Large, between James Annesley, Esq; Plaintiff, And the Right Honourable Richard Earl of Anglesey, Defendant, The.

Imp.—London: Re-printed from the Original Copy printed at Dublin, for J. Watson . . . M.DCC.XLIV.
8vo; 3 hf. sh. ea.; 14 nos; 336 pp.; fasc. sigs.

Trial at Large between the Honourable James Annesley, Esq. and the Rt. Honourable the Earl of Anglesea, The.
This may be the same as *The Trial at Bar* pub. in shilling fol. nos by Cooper in 1743.
fol.; irreg.; 1s. ea.; no. 1 ad. *Bristol Oracle* number 28 (Jan. 21, 1744) as pub. 'This Day . . . London: Printed, and sold by Benj. Hickey, Bookseller in Nicholas-street, Bristol . . . Price One Shilling . . . N.B. No. II will be publish'd with all the convenient Speed that Care in so remarkable a Trial as this will admit.'

Universal Harmony; or, the gentleman and Lady's Social Companion. Consisting of a great variety of . . . English and Scots Songs, Cantatas . . . Set to Music for the Voice, Violin, Hautboy, German and Common Flute; with a thorough Bass for the Organ, Harpsichord, Spinnet, &c. By the Best Masters.
Imp.—London: Printed for the Proprietors, n.d.
4to; 103 engraved pl.; listed *Gentleman's Magazine* Dec. 1744 as 'Publish'd in numbers at 3d. each. Robinson'; same also issued with new t.p.: imp.—London: Printed for J. Newberry . . . 1745.

Useful and Entertaining Collection of Letters upon Various Subjects, An.
Imp.—London: Printed for W. Bickerton . . . M.DCC.XLV.
4to; w.; 3d.; 2 plus 436 plus 8 pp.; listed *Gentleman's Magazine* Sept. 1744 as pub. by Bickerton 'In weekly Numbers, at 3d. each'.

Wood-Lark, The. A Collection of Songs, Cantatas, Airs.
w.; 2d ea.; to have 12 nos; 50 songs in ea. no.; No. 1 ad. *Penny London Morning Advertiser* number 165 (May 18, 1744).

1745
Acta Germanica.
Probably a rep. or continuation of *Acta Germanica; or the Literary Memoirs of Germany*, pub. in nos, 1741.
w.; 6d ea.; no. 6 of VOL. II listed in *Gentleman's Magazine* April 1745 as pub. (or sold) by Robinson.

Atlantis Reviv'd, The: Or, A select Collection of Novels . . . By a Gentleman.

8vo; 3 sh. ea.; w.; *6d.*; to make 2 vols.; no. 1 pub. July 27, 1745; proposals in *Cambridge Journal* number 48 (Aug. 17, 1745): 'Subscriptions are taken in by Charles Corbett . . .; Thomas Harris . . .; Thomas Merrill, Bookseller, in Cambridge; and William Hayhow, Bookseller, in Ely; Also by all the Booksellers and New[s]-Carriers in Town and Country.'

FOXE, JOHN. *The Book of Martyrs: Being an Account of the Sufferings and Death of the Protestants in the Reign of Queen Mary I*. Revised and Corrected by an Impartial Hand.
Rep. or reissue of ed. in nos pub. 1741.
fol.; 5 sh. ea. (or 4 sh. with cut); w.; *6d.*; 30 pl.; no. 1 ad. *Cambridge Journal* number 66 (Dec. 21, 1745); whole to have about 40 nos; subscribers invited to apply to R. Walker, Mr. Stemson in Stamford, Mr. Hayhow in Ely, or 'any of the Men who deliver this Journal'.

GILL, JOHN. *An Exposition of the New Testament*.
fol.; 1s. ea.; 76 nos; 'Gill's exposition of the New Testament. At 1s. each number' listed *Scots Magazine* June 1745; completed 3 vols. 'containing 76 numbers' listed *Gentleman's Magazine* Aug. 1748: 'The Revelations may be had alone in 6 numbers. Ward.'

Impartial Account of many barbarous Cruelties exercised in the Inquisition in Spain, Portugal, and Italy, An.
Rep. of work pub. in 14 nos in 1738 and 1741.
8vo; 3 sh. (48 pp.) ea.; w.; *3d.*; 10 nos; no. 1 ad. *Cambridge Journal* number 60 (Nov. 7, 1745) as pub. 'This Day . . .; may be had of R. Walker, at the New Printing Office in Cambridge; Mr. Hayhow in Ely; Mr. Stemson in Stamford; and the Men who carry this Journal'.

MARCHANT, JOHN. *An Exposition on the Books of the Old Testament*. Follows same author's *Exposition on the . . . New Testament*, pub. in nos, 1742.
   Imp.—London: Printed and Sold by R. Walker . . .: Sold also at his Shop next the Theatre-Coffee-House in Cambridge; and by most Booksellers in Town and Country. M.DCC.XLV.
fol.; 2 sh. ea.; w.; *3d.*; 145 nos (1160 pp.); pl.; fasc. sigs.; no. 19 ad. *Cambridge Journal* number 36 (May 25, 1745) as pub. 'This Day'; Marchant stated *ibid.* that he had 'sold and assign'd the Copy-right of both these my Works' to R. Walker, but all nos ent. Sta. Reg. by Marchant as sole prop.: nos 1 and 2 on Feb. 9, 1745, nos 143, 144, and 145 on Oct. 22, 1747; Roy. lic.

OLDYS, William and others. *Biographia Britannica: or, the Lives of the Most eminent Persons... in Great Britain and Ireland.* 6 vols in 7.

Imp., VOL. I—London: Printed for W. Innys, W. Meadows, J. Walthoe, T. Cox, A. Ward, J. and P. Knapton, T. Osborne, S. Birt, D. Browne, T. Longman and T. Shewell, H. Whitridge, R. Hett, C. Hitch, T. Astley, S. Austen, C. Davis, R. Manby and H. S. Cox, C. Bathurst, J. and R. Tonson and S. Draper, J. Robinson, J. Hinton, J. and J. Rivington, and M. Cooper. MDCCXLVII.

Imp., VOL. II—same, but omits A. Ward, T. Shewell, adds J. Ward, and has date MDCCXLVIII.

Imp., VOL. III—same as in VOL. II, but omits S. Austen, and has date MDCCL.

Imp., VOL. IV—London: Printed for W. Meadows, J. Walthoe, T. Osborne and J. Shipton, D. Browne, H. Whitridge, C. Hitch and L. Hawes, R. Manby, J. and R. Tonson, John Rivington, H. S. Cox, C. Bathurst, J. Robinson, J. Rivington and J. Fletcher, L. Davis and C. Reymers, J. Ward, W. Johnston, J. Richardson, T. Longman, P. Davey and B. Law, and M. Cooper. MDCCLVII.

Imp., VOL. V—same as in VOL. IV, but omits J. Shipton, H. S. Cox, J. Robinson, adds R. Baldwin, T. Kearsley, and has date MDCCLX.

Imp., VOL. VI, Part I—London: Printed for J. Walthoe, T. Osborne, H. Whitridge, C. Hitch and L. Hawes, R. Manby, J. and R. Tonson, H. Woodfall, J. Rivington, C. Bathurst, L. Davis and C. Reymers, R. Baldwin, W. Johnston, G. Keith, J. Richardson, T. Longman, B. Law and Co., G. Kearsley, and J. Hinxman. MDCCLXIII.

Imp., VOL. VI, Part II—London: Printed for J. Walthoe, T. Osborne, H. Whitridge, J. and R. Tonson, H. Woodfall, C. Bathurst, J. Rivington, L. Davis and C. Reymers, R. Baldwin, L. Hawes and W. Clarke and R. Collins, W. Johnston, G. Keith, T. Longman, B. Law, and M. Richardson. MDCCLXVI.

fol.; 3 sh. ea.; w.; 6*d.* ea.; 366 nos; 4388 pp. plus Supplement (260 pp.) plus index (44 pp.); fasc. sigs.; Listed *Scots Magazine* Mar. 1745: 'In numbers, 6*d.* each'; Roy. lic. dated Dec. 26, 1744.

*Parent's Weekly Present to his Children, The.
Listed *London Magazine* Sept. 1745 as 'Publishing in Numbers at 2*d.* each. Printed for T. Gardner.'

PICKERING, ? **Pickering's New Dictionary of the Bible.*
Listed *Gentleman's Magazine* June 1745 as 'in numbers at 1*s.* each'; No. 7 listed among the 'Periodical Publications at the End of the

Year' following the annual Index to the Register of Books in *Gentleman's Magazine* for 1745 as pub. by 'Wilcox &c.'.

*Protestant Miscellany, The. Containing several choice Pieces both in Verse and Prose, relating to the . . . church at Rome.
8vo; 3 hf. sh. (24 pp.) ea.; w.; 2*d* ea.; about 10 nos; cuts; no. 1 ad. *St. James's Evening Post* number 5592 (Nov. 19, 1745) as to be pub. Nov. 23 . . . 'Printed for T. Read . . . and to be had of those Persons who carry the News'.

*Soldier's Pocket Companion, The; Or, The Manual Exercise of our British Foot.
8vo; 16 pl. ea.; w.; 6*d*.; 7 nos, to contain 'near 100 Plates, besides Letter-press Work'; no. 1 ad. *Cambridge Journal* number 62 (Nov. 23, 1745) as pub. 'This Day'; prop., B. Cole.

TENNENT, JOHN. *Physical Disquisitions: Demonstrating the Real Causes of the Blood's Morbid Rarefaction and Stagnation.*
Imp.—London: Printed for W. Payne . . .; and sold by the Booksellers in Town and Country. 1745.
8vo; 6*d*.; copy seen (inc.) has 8 plus 120 pp.; cut; listed *London Magazine* July 1745 as 'Publishing in Numbers at 6*d*. each. Printed for J. Collyer.'

*Universal Harmony; Or, the Gentleman and Lady's Social Companion.
Rep. or reissue of work pub. in nos, 1744.
4to; ea. no. to have 5 songs, with music; no. 8 ad. *Cambridge Journal* number 36 (May 25, 1745) as pub. 'This Day'; but same ad. states that 22 nos have already been pub.; persons willing to contribute songs ('No indecent songs shall be inserted.') are invited to send them to J. Robinson . . ., J. Newbery . . ., or R. Walker, next the Theatre Coffee House, Cambridge; completed work ad. *Cambridge Journal* number 55 (Oct. 5, 1745) at 7*s*. 6*d*.

1746

ARBUTHNOT, ARCHIBALD. *Memoirs of the remarkable Life and surprizing Adventures of Miss Jenny Cameron.*
Imp.—London: Printed and Sold by R. Walker . . .; and by the Booksellers in Town and Country, MDCCXLVI.
4to; 3 sh. ea.; 2*d*. ea.; 12 nos; 280 pp.; cut; fasc. sigs.; no. 1 ad. in newspaper clipping, dated in manuscript Nov. 1746 (probably the *Salisbury Journal*), in the Haslewood Collection (British Museum) as pub. 'This

Day: ... give timely Notice to my Printer and Publisher, R. Walker ...; or to B. Collins, in Salisbury; R. Woolridge in Shaston; R. Baldwin at Newport in the Isle of Wight, or to any of the Persons who serve the Salisbury Journal.'

ARBUTHNOT, ARCHIBALD. *The Life, Adventures, And Many and Great Vicissitudes of Fortune of Simon, Lord Lovat.*
> Imp. —London: Printed and Sold for the Author by R. Walker ...; and at his Printing-Office, next the Theatre Coffee-House in Cambridge. MDCCXLVI.
> 4to; 3 sh. ea.; 12 nos; 280 pp.; fasc. sigs.

ARBUTHNOT, ARCHIBALD. *The Life, Adventures, and Many and Great Vicissitudes of Fortune of Simon, Lord Lovat.*
Rep., with minor changes, from work of same title pub. in nos. by R. Walker in 1746; see preceding item in this catalogue.
> Imp. —London: Printed for John Threkeld ... 1746.
> 4to; single sh. (8 pp.) ea.; 48 nos; 306 pp.; fasc. sigs.

BOYSE, SAMUEL. *An Historical View of the Transactions of Europe from the Commencement of the War with Spain in 1739, to the Insurrection in Scotland in 1745 ... To which is added, An Impartial History of the Late Rebellion ... By S. Boyse, M.A. 3 vols.*
> Imp., VOLS I and II—Reading, Printed by and for D. Henry in Friarstreet; and sold by J. Robinson ..., London, and by all the Booksellers in Great Britain and Ireland. MDCCXLVII [VOL. III, MDCXLVIII, for MDCCXLVIII].
> 8vo; VOL. I, 14 plus 424 pp.; VOL. II, 22 plus 178 pp.; VOL. III, 183 plus 5 pp.; no. 1 ad. *Henry's Winchester Journal* number 142 (June 30, 1746).

*Essay towards a New Version of the Old Testament, An. By the Author of the Hebrew Language Asserted [i.e., *The Majesty and Singular Copiousness of the Hebrew Language Asserted* (London, 1744); author not identified].
Nos 1 and 2 listed in *Gentleman's Magazine* May 1746 as pub. by Roberts at 6d. ea.

Foundling Hospital for Wit.
1s. ea.; no. 3 listed in *Gentleman's Magazine* June 1746.

*General History of the Trials of the Three Lords at Westminster, A.
8vo; 3 hf. sh. (24 pp.) ea.; w.; 2d. ea.; about 18 nos, no. 1 ad. in news-

paper clipping, dated in manuscript No. 1746 (probably the *Salisbury Journal*), in the Haslewood Collection, British Museum, as pub. 'This Day'; author and publisher not indicated; latter probably R. Walker, printer and publisher of the other work (Arbuthnot's *Memoirs of . . . Jenny Cameron*) ad. in the same column.

*History of the rebellion 1745 and 1746, The. With an account of . . . the clans . . . .
This may be the work referred to in the ad. of Andrew Henderson's *History of the Rebellion, 1745 and 1746, General Evening Post* number 2282 (May 10, 1748): a 'pyracy of this only authentick History . . . now carrying on, by a common, notorious, impudent Plunderer'. Listed *Scots Magazine* August 1746 as pub. in numbers '(three of which are published). 4*d*. each. Edinburgh.'

MARCHANT, JOHN. *The History of the Present Rebellion.*
Imp. —London: Printed for the Author, and Sold by R. Walker . . . , and at his Printing Office in Cambridge. 1746.
4to; 4 sh. ea.; w.; 3*d*. ea.; 13 nos; 416 pp.; fasc. sigs.; no. 1 ad. *Henry's Winchester Journal* number 128 (March 31, 1746) as to be pub. April 5.

MIDON, FRANCIS. *The History of the Surprizing Rise and Sudden Fall of Masaniello, The Fisherman of Naples.*
Rep., with minor changes, from ed. 'Printed for C. Davis . . . and T. Green . . . 1729.'
Imp. —Oxford: Printed by R. Walker and W. Jackson. To be delivered gratis to the Customers to the Oxford Flying Weekly Journal. n.d. [Catalogue of Yale University Library suggests date as *ca.* 1746.]
8vo; single hf. sh.; 5 nos; 104 pp.; fasc. sigs.

MOTTLEY, JOHN. **Joe Miller's Jests, Refined and Improv'd.*
First printed London, 1739; 8th ed. London, 1745; numerous later eds.
8vo; single hf. sh. ea.; da.; ¼*d*. ea.; announced on last p. of *The Life . . . of Simon, Lord Lovat,* pub. in nos by Threkeld (London, 1746), as to be comprised in 50 nos, 'one of which will be publish'd every Day, and may be had of the News Carriers'; no. 1 to be pub. 'On Monday next, November 17, 1746 . . . eight Pages . . . (Price One Farthing)'.

NALSON, J. *The Trial of King Charles the First*. With Additions, by J. Nalson.
Abridged from work pub. in 11 nos (262 pp.) in 1740.
  Imp.—Oxford: Printed by R. Walker and W. Jackson. To be delivered gratis to the Customers to the Oxford Flying Weekly Journal. [Date unknown. Catalogue of Yale University Library dates '*ca.* 1746' another supp. (Midon's *History of . . . Masaniello*) bound with this.]
8vo single hf. sh. (8 pp.) ea.; w.; free supp.; 12 nos; 92 pp.; fasc. sigs.

STACKHOUSE, THOMAS. *A New and Accurate Exposition of the Apostles Creed.*
fol.; 4 sh. ea.; fort.; 6*d.* ea.; inc.? No. 5 ad. *Whitehall Evening Post* number 34 (May 3, 1746) as to be pub. May 8: 'The Book . . . will be published for the Benefit of the Author and his Family, at his House in Eagle Court in the Strand.' See next item.

STACKHOUSE, THOMAS. *A New and Practical Exposition of the Apostles Creed.*
  Imp.—London: Printed for Thomas Longman and Thomas Shewell, and Charles Hitch . . .; Richard Manby and Henry Shute Cox . . .; and John and James Rivington . . . MDCCXLVII.
fol.; 4 sh. ea.; w.; 6*d.* ea.; 28 nos; 28 plus 2 plus 436 pp.; proposals dated Oct. 1, 1746 pub. *Ipswich Journal* number 402 (Oct. 25, 1746) and no. 1 ad. *ibid.* as pub. Oct. 18; but apparently Stackhouse had begun to pub. this work in 6*d.* nos, fort., earlier in 1746. See preceding item.

Thacker's Cookery.
Perhaps inc. and unrecorded ed. of John Thacker's *The Art of Cookery* (Newcastle upon Tyne: Printed by I. Thompson and Company, 1758).
mo.; 6*d.* ea.; to be 12 nos; no. 1 ad. *Newcastle Journal* number 364 (March 29, 1746) as pub. that day: 'Subscriptions are taken in by Mr. Alderman Aisley, and Mr. Richardson, Booksellers in Durham; Mr. Bryson, Mr. Akenhead, Mr. Fleming, and Mr. Harrison, Booksellers in Newcastle; Mr. Bell, Bookseller in Stockton; Messrs Barstow and Stabler, Booksellers in York; Mr. Green, Upholsterer in Bishopsauckland; and Mr. Thomas Hall, Hardwareman in Sunderland.'

Winter Evening Tales. Consisting of several Curious and Entertaining Novels.
24 pp. ea.; w.; 1½*d.* ea.; 8 nos; no. 1 ad. on final p. of *The Life . . . of Simon, Lord Lovat*, pub. in nos (London: Threkeld, 1746), followed by

ad. of *Joe Miller's Jests*, both apparently to be pub. 'On Monday next, November 17, 1746 . . . '.

*Wit a-la-mode.
Nos 1 and 2 listed *Gentleman's Magazine* June 1746 as pub. at 6*d*. ea.

1747

ALBINUS, BERNARD SIEGFRIED. *Tables of the Skeleton and Muscles of the Human Body* . . . [with explanations] Translated from the Latin [Bernardi Siegfried Albini *Tabulæ sceleti et musculorum corporis humani* (Lugduni: Verbeck, 1747), with 25 pl., variously dated 1739-1747].
    Imp.—London: Printed for John and Paul Knapton. M.DCC.XLIX. large fol.; fort. and irreg.; 2*s*. 6*d*.; 25 pl., ea. followed by 2 or more pp. of explanation; pl. variously dated 1747, 1748, 1749; nos 1 and 2 listed *Scots Magazine* Nov. 1747: 'To be continued, a no. once a fortnight'.

FIELDING, HENRY. *The Mock Doctor: or, The Dumb Lady Cur'd* . . . Done from Moliere. Fifth Edition.
    Imp.—Oxford: Printed by R. Walker and W. Jackson. MDCCXLVII. And given Gratis to the *Oxford Flying Weekly Journal* and *Cirencester Gazette.*
8vo; single hf. sh. ea.; 4 (perhaps 5) nos; fasc. sigs.

HOOPER, JACOB. **Impartial History of the Rebellion and Civil Wars in England, during the Reign of King Charles I.*
Rep. from work originally pub. 1738. John Nichols (*Literary Anecdotes,* II, p. 726) mistakenly supposed this to have been Clarendon's *History of the Rebellion.* Identified by R. Bowes in paper 'On the first and other early Cambridge Newspapers', *Proceedings of the Cambridge Antiquarian Society,* VIII (1895, for 1891-1894), 348.
8vo; single hf. sh. ea.; w.; free supp. to *Cambridge Journal and Flying Post* from *ca.* 1747 to 1750.

JAMESON, ROBERT. *A Critical and Practical Exposition of the Pentateuch, with Notes.*
    Imp.—London: Printed for J. and P. Knapton . . ., T. Longman and T. Shewel . . ., C. Hitch . . ., C. Davis . . ., J. Hodges . . ., A. Millar . . ., and J. and J. Rivington . . . MDCCXLVIII.
fol.; 3 sh. ea.; w.; 6*d*. ea.; 66 nos. (12 plus 779 pp.); work was intended to fill 5 vols; no. 1 pub. Jan. 3, 1747; listed *London Magazine* Jan. 1747

under title *A Critical and Practical Exposition of the Bible*, 'Publish'd weekly in Numbers at 6*d*. each.'

LILLO, GEORGE. *The London Merchant: or, The History of George Barnwell*. The tenth edition. With great Additions and Improvements, by the Author.

    Imp.—Oxford: Printed by R. Walker and W. Jackson. And given Gratis to the constant Customers to the *Oxford Flying Weekly Journal* and *Cirencester Gazette*. n.d.

8vo; single hf. sh. ea.; nos 1 to 7 (64 pp.; no fasc. sig. for pp. [i] — [viii]; first fasc. sig. is Numb. I, on p. [9], sig. B); fasc. sigs.

LINDSAY, JOHN. *A Brief History of England, Both in Church and State*. By Way of Question and Answer. Faithfully extracted from the most authentic Histories and Records.

    Imp.—London: Printed for the Author. MDCCXLVIII.

8vo; 8 plus 376 plus 32 pp.; Preface dated 17 Oct. 1747; apparently pub. in fasc.; p. 376 has note: 'This Work having already extended to the Length and Size of a convenient Volume, it is thought proper to make a stop here, at this Grand AEra [i.e., 1689]: From whence, God willing, (if Health, Leisure and Opportunity permit) the same may be continued in another Volume.'

[LOCKMAN, JOHN]. *A New History of England. By Question and Answer*. Extracted from the most celebrated English Historians, particularly M. Rapin de Thoyras. Sixth Edition.

w.; 6*d*.; this work together with the same author's *New Roman History* to have 16 nos; 32 pl.; no. 1 pub. Feb. 14, 1747; proposals for reprinting this work 'by a Weekly Subscription' pub. *Ipswich Journal* number 421 (Mar. 7, 1747); prop., Thomas Astley, agent, R. Baldwin.

[LOCKMAN, JOHN]. *A New Roman History, by Question and Answer*. Extracted from the best Authors, both Ancient and Modern. Second Edition.

w.; 6*d*.; this work along with the same author's *New History of England* to have 16 nos; 16 pl.; no. 1 pub. Feb. 14, 1747; proposals for reprinting this work 'by a Weekly Subscription' pub. *Ipswich Journal* number 421 (Mar. 7, 1747); prop., Thomas Astley, agent, R. Baldwin.

MACKLECAN, JAMES. *A General and True History of the Lives and Actions of the most famous Highwaymen, Murderers, Street Robbers, &c., To which is added, a genuine Account of the Voyages and Plunders of the most*

noted Pirates, Interspersed with several remarkable Trials of the most notorious Malefactors, at the Sessions-House in the Old Baily, &c. By Capt. James Macklecan. 2 vols.
Probably rep. of work (by Alexander Smith and Charles Johnson) with similar title pub. in fol. nos by R. Walker in Birmingham in 1742. 8vo; 16 pp. ea.; w.; 1*d*.; no. 26 ad. *Oxford Flying Weekly Journal, and Cirencester Gazette* number 79 (Mar. 7, 1748) as pub. 'This Day' and available from 'the Printers of this Paper', i.e., R. Walker and W. Jackson, at the New Printing Office near Carfax Conduit, Oxford.; rep. in 20 nos, 8vo, by R. Walker in 1748.

MARTIN, Benjamin. *Philosophia Britannica.
Probably rep. of Benjamin Martin's *Philosophia Britannica; or A New ... System of the Newtonian Philosophy, Astronomy and Geography*, pub. in 2 vols. 8vo, both with imp. — Reading. Printed by C. Micklewright and Co. for the Author; and for M. Cooper . . ., London; R. Raikes at Gloucester; B. Collins at Salisbury; and J. Leake, and W. Frederick at Bath. MDCCXLVII.
    Nos. 1 and 2 listed *Gentleman's Magazine* Dec. 1747 as pub. by M. Cooper at 6*d*. ea.: 'To be comprised in 30 Numbers.'

OVIDIUS NASO, Publius. *Metamorphosis. A new translation . . . in Prose, with the Latin annex'd.
No. 1 listed *London Magazine* Jan. 1747; no. 3 listed *Gentleman's Magazine* Sept. 1747, 'pr. 1*s*. Davidson'.

RUSSELL, John. *Letters from a Young Painter Abroad to his Friends in England.
mo.; 6*d*.; no. 1 listed *Gentleman's Magazine* Mar. 1747 as pub. by 'Russel'; nos 1 to 7 (the last) ent. Sta. Reg. by William Russell, the sole prop., Mar. 20, Apr. 8, Apr. 28, May 16, June 10, July 9, Sept. 15, 1747; on May 14, 1750, 'Richd Russel' ent. *ibid.* the whole work in 2 vols. (2nd ed. of VOL. I).

*Wonders of Nature and Art, The.
3*d*. ea.; 56 nos; nos 55 and 56 ('being the last') ad. *Ipswich Journal* number 551 (Sept. 2, 1749): 'Printed and Sold by C. Corbett . . ., and W. Creighton in Ipswich; also by most Booksellers and Country Printers; and by the Men who Carry this News'; whole work in 4 pocket vols ad. *ibid.* number 572 (Jan. 27, 1750).

WYATT, James. *The Life and Surprizing Adventures of James

Wyatt . . . Written by Himself.
8vo; 3*d*. ea.; cuts; no. 1 listed *London Magazine* Nov. 1741, 'pr. 3*d*. Cook'.

1748

*Amusements of Aix la Chapelle, The,
Possibly related to *Amusements des eaux d' Aix-la-Chapelle* by Charles Louis, Baron de Pöllnitz, 3 vols. (Amsterdam, 1736).
mo.; 6*d*. ea.; cuts; no. 1 listed *London Magazine* May 1748 as pub.; no. 5, 'which compleats Volume I', listed *Gentleman's Magazine* Sept. 1748 as printed for M. Payne.

DOUGHARTY, J. **Mathematical Digests.*
No. 1 listed *Gentleman's Magazine* Dec. 1748 as pub. by Reeve at 2*s*. 6*d*.

DUTFIELD, JAMES. **A . . . Natural History of English Moths and Butterflies.*
fol.; 6 nos; inc.; listed in Albert R. Corns and Archibald Sparke, *A Bibliography of Unfinished Books in the English Language* (London: Quaritch, 1915), p. 76, as pub. in London, 1748-1749.

KITCHIN, THOMAS. **The Small English Atlas; being a new and accurate set of maps.*
This is doubtless Thomas Kitchin's *The Small English Atlas . . . Maps of all the Counties in England and Wales*, 12mo (London, 1748), listed by E. G. Cox, *A Reference Guide to the Literature of Travel*, VOL. III (Seattle: University of Washington Press, 1949), p. 547, or the same work (by Thomas Kitchin and Thomas Jefferys), 4to (London, 1749) listed *op. cit.*, p. 592.
Listed in *Gentleman's Magazine* Nov. 1748 as 'published in numbers at 6*d*. each. Payne'.

*Love and Avarice. Or, The Fatal Consequences of Preferring Love to Beauty. Done in the Manner of a Novel . . . By a Lady of Shropshire.
8vo; w.; 245 pp.; complete work ad. *Penny London Post, or, the Morning Advertiser* number 798 (June 24, 1748) at 1*s*. 6*d*. in blue covers, or 1*s*. 4*d*. 'in the Numbers, as they were publish'd by Subscription Weekly . . . . Printed for . . . T. Ward'.

*Love's Magazine; or, the Lady's Cabinet Unlock'd. By Penelope Graveairs, Widow.
w.; no. 3 ad. *Penny London Post, or, the Morning Advertiser* number 1024 (Nov. 11, 1748) as 'Printed for T. Ward.'

MACKLECAN, James. *A General and true History of the Lives and Actions of the most famous Highwaymen, Murderers, Street-Robbers, &c. To which is added, A genuine Account of the Voyages and Plunders of the most noted Pirates. Interspersed with several remarkable Trials of the most notorious Malefactors, at the Sessions-House in the Old Baily, &c. By Capt. James Macklecan.

Rep. or reissue of ed. pub. in nos by R. Walker in 1747.

8vo; 2 sh. ea.; 2d.; 20 nos; no. 1 ad. by R. Walker in the *Cambridge Journal* number 181 (March 5, 1748) as to be pub. Mar. 19.

Modern Story-Teller, or General Entertainer, The. 2 vols. (Only VOL. 1 pub. in fascicules.)

Imp., VOLS. 1 and 11—London Printed for the Author, and Sold by M. Mechell . . .; and by all the Booksellers in Town and Country. [n.d.]

12mo; 6d.; VOL. 1, 6 plus 32 plus 264 pp.; (VOL. 11, 2 plus 284 pp.); no. 1 listed *Gentleman's Magazine* Dec. 1748 as pub.; no. 1 ent. Sta. Reg., Dec. 23, 1748, by M. Mechell, sole proprietor of the whole work; no. 2 likewise on Jan. 4, 1749, nos 3 and 4 on Feb. 2, 1749.

NEALE, J. *Uranographia Britannica; or, a new Survey of the Heavens.* 50 large copper plates; nos 1, 2, 3, 4 listed *Gentleman's Magazine* April 1748: '. . . a two guinea subscription is also kept open, which has met with all the encouragement, from the best judges, that so elegant and useful a work justly deserves. Neale, in Leadenhall-Street, &c.'

PHILLIPS [MUILMAN], Teresia Constantia. *An Apology for the Conduct of Mrs. Teresia Constantia Phillips.* 3 vols.

Imp., VOL. 1—N.B. Such extraordinary Care has been taken to intimidate the Booksellers, in order to stifle this Work, that Mrs. Phillips is obliged to publish it herself, and only at her House in Craig's Court, Charing Cross; and to prevent Imposition, each Book will be signed with her own Hand.

Imp., VOLS 11 and 111—London: Printed for the Author, and Sold at her House in Craig's Court, Charing-Cross. MDCCXLVIII [VOL. III, MDCCXLIX].

8vo; 6, 7, or 8 hf. sh. ea.; 1s. ea.; VOL. 1, nos 1-6; VOL. 11, nos 1-5; VOL. III, nos 1-6; fasc. sigs.; nos 1 and 2 listed *Gentleman's Magazine* April 1748 as pub., 'pr. 1s. each. Griffith.'; no. 1 ent. Sta. Reg. April 11, 1748 by Teresia Constantia Phillips (sole proprietor); likewise other nos to no. 3 of VOL. 11, ent. Oct. 29, 1748; a 'Second Edition' was ad. in 1748.

1749

Counter-Apology: or, Genuine Confession, A. Being a Caution to the Fair Sex in General. Containing the Secret History . . . of M — — P — —. Written by herself.

Apparently an attempt to profit by the notoriety attached to Teresia Constantia Phillips's *Apology*, pub. in nos 1748.

  Imp.—London: Printed for R. Young . . . MDCCXLIX. (Price One
  Shilling.)

8vo; no 1 has 62 pp.; no more pub.?

DUFF, WILLIAM. *A New and Full Critical, Biographical, and Geographical History of Scotland . . . from Robert Bruce, to the present Time.* By an Impartial Hand.

  Imp.—London: Printed for the Author, and sold by the Booksellers
  of London and Westminster. MDCCXLIX.

fol.; 3 sh. ea.; w.; 30 nos; inc.; 8 plus 364 pp. (misnumbered 360); port.; fasc. sigs.; no. 1 ent. Sta. Reg. Aug. 5, 1749; nos 2-30 ent. *ibid.* Aug. 12, 1749 to Oct. 1, 1750.

*Gentleman's Travels through Portugal, Spain, and Galicia, A.
Listed in *Bristol Journal* number 1662 (Aug. 12, 1749) as 'just publish'd . . . to be continued'.

HOOKE, (ANDREW). *Bristollia: or, Memoirs of the City of Bristol, Both Civil and Ecclesiastical.*

  Imp.—London: Printed for J. Hodges . . .; and Sold by B. Hickey
  and J. Palmer . . .

8vo; 8 or 9 hf. sh. ea.; 1s. ea.; no. 1, 10 plus 62 pp.; no. 11, 8 plus 56 pp.; no more pub.; no. 1 listed *Scots Magazine* Feb. 1749.

*Unfortunate Duchess; or, The Lucky Gamester, The.
Rep. from 'a Novel founded on a True Story' pub. 1739.
8vo; free supp. to the *Cambridge Journal and Flying Post*, in number 239 of which (April 15, 1749) it is announced as to begin immediately, according to R. Bowes, 'On the first and other early Cambridge Newspapers', *Proceedings of the Cambridge Antiquarian Society*, VIII (1895, for 1891-1894), 348.

A LIST OF BOOKSELLERS, PRINTERS, AND OTHERS WHO HAD SOME SHARE IN THE PRODUCTION OR THE DISTRIBUTION OF NUMBER BOOKS IN LONDON AND WESTMINSTER BEFORE 1750

A few authors who printed or published their own works (Rev. Francis Blomefield and Mrs. Constantia Phillips, for example) are not included in this list. Addresses, where given, are taken from printed proposals, advertisements, or imprints of books published in numbers.

ADAMS, N.: optician to their Royal Highnesses the Prince and Princesses of Wales, at the Golden Spectacles, Charing Cross

APPLEBEE, E.: in Wine Office Court, Fleet Street

APPLEBEE, John: Bolt Court, near the Leg Tavern, Fleet Street

ASTLEY, Thomas: at the Rose, in St. Paul's Churchyard; in Paternoster Row

ATKINS, M.: at the Golden Ball, in St. Paul's Churchyard

AUSTEN, Stephen: at the Angel and Bible in St. Paul's Churchyard

BAKER, J.: in Paternoster Row

BALDWIN, Robert: in Paternoster Row

BALLARD, Samuel: in Little Britain

BARKER, Benjamin: in Westminster Hall

BARLOW, R.: at the Corner of Red Cross Alley, Jewin Street

BATHURST, Charles: in Fleet Street

BATLEY, Jeremiah: at the Dove in Paternoster Row

BELL, Andrew: at the Cross Keys, in Cornhill

BETTENHAM, James: printer

BETTESWORTH, Arthur: at the Red Lyon, on London Bridge; later (with Charles Hitch) at the Red Lyon, in Paternoster Row

BICKERTON, Weaver: in the Temple Exchange, Fleet Street

BICKHAM, George: in James Street, Bunhill Fields

BICKHAM, George, Jr.: engraver, at the corner of Bedford-Bury, New Street, Covent Garden

BIRT, Samuel: in Ave Mary Lane

BONWICKE, R.

BOOTH, J.: in Barking Alley, near Great Tower Hill

BOWLES, John: printseller, at the Black Horse in Cornhill

BOWLES, Thomas: printseller, next the Chapter House, in St. Paul's Churchyard

BOWYER, William: printer

BRAGG, Benjamin: Ave Mary Lane; at the Raven in Paternoster Row, against Ivy Lane

BRINDLEY, James: New Bond Street

BROTHERTON, John: at the Bible, in Cornhill, near the Royal Exchange

BROWNE, Daniel: printer, without Temple Bar

BUCKERIDGE, B.: in Baldon's Gardens, Leather Lane

CAVE, Edward: at St. John's Gate

CHANDLER, Richard: (with Caesar Ward) at the Ship between the Temple Gates in Fleet Street

CHARLTON, Richard: at the Royal Exchange

CHARLTON, Mrs.: the Corner of Swithin's Alley near the Royal Exchange

CHRICHLEY, J.: at the corner of Craig's Court, Charing Cross

CLARK[E], J.: near Warwick Court in Gray's Inn

CLARKE, J.: (with T. Comyns) under the Royal Exchange

CLARK[E], J.: in the Poultry; in Duck Lane

CLAY, F.: without Temple Bar

CLEMENS, Henry: at the Half Moon, in St. Paul's Churchyard

CLIFFE, N.: at the Golden Candlestick, in Cheapside

COGAN, Francis: at the Middle Temple Gate

COLE, Benjamin: at the corner of King's Head Court, near Fetter Lane, Holborn

COLLINS, A.: at the Black Boy, in Fleet Street

COLLYER, J.

COMYNS, T.: (with J. Clarke) under the Royal Exchange

CONYERS, George

COOK, M.: at the Royal Exchange

COOKE, J.: bookbinder, next to the Red Hart, Fetter Lane

COOKE, Mrs. M.: at the Royal Exchange

COOPER, M.: at the Globe in Paternoster Row

COOPER, Thomas: at the Globe in Paternoster Row

COOPER, —: (with — Rogers) near Bishopsgate

CORBETT, Charles: bookseller and publisher, in the Strand; at Addison's Head, over against St. Dunstan's Church in Fleet Street

COX, Henry Shute: on Ludgate Hill

COX, Thomas: at the corner of Swithin's Alley, Cornhill; at the Lamb, under the Royal Exchange, Cornhill; at the Lamb, under the Piazza, at the Royal Exchange, Cornhill

CREAKE, Benzaleel: at the Red Bible in Ave Mary Lane, near St. Paul's

CROKATT, James: at the Golden Key near the Inner Temple Gate in Fleet Street

CURLL, Edmund: at the Dial, in Fleet Street; at Pope's Head, in Rose Street, Covent Garden

CURTIS, Langley: at the Sign of Sir Edmundbury Godfrey, near Fleet Bridge

DARBY, John

DAVENPORT, S.: philosophical instrument maker, the upper end of High Holborn

DAVIDSON, Joseph: at the Angel in the Poultry, Cheapside

DAVIES, George: (with Robert Spencer) at the Golden Ball in White Fryers

DAVIS, Charles: opposite Gray's Inn, Holborn; in Paternoster Row

DAVIS, widow: in Frying Pan Alley in Wood Street

DAVIS, T.: printer, opposite the Plough in Black Horse Alley, Fleet Street

DICKINSON, —: printseller, in the Strand

DOD[D], Anne: without Temple Bar; at the Peacock, without Temple Bar

DOD[D], Benjamin

DODSLEY, Robert: at Tully's Head, in Pall Mall

DODSON, James: at the Hand and Pen in Warwick Lane

DOWNING, Joseph: printer, in Bartholomew Close

DRAPER, Somerset

DU BOSC, Claude: engraver, at the Golden Head in Charles Street, Covent Garden

EADES, Mr.: at King Edward's Stairs, Wapping

EDLIN, Thomas: at the Prince's Arms, over against Exeter Exchange in the Strand

FARMER, D.: at the King's Arms in St. Paul's Churchyard, near Cheapside

FAYRAM, Francis: under the Royal Exchange

FEALES, William: Rowe's Head, the corner of Essex Street, in the Strand

FITZER, Stephen: at the Three Bibles in the Minories

FORD, Richard: in the Poultry

FOSTER, G.

FOUDRINIER, Peter: stationer and printseller, at the corner of Craig's Court, Charing Cross; opposite to the Ship Tavern, Charing Cross

FOX, J.: in Westminster Hall

FULLER, John: at the Dove in Creed Lane

GARDINER, D.: in Little Turnstile, High Holborn

GARDNER, Thomas: printer, opposite St. Clement's Church in the Strand; in Bartholomew Close

GIBBONS, Samuel: by the Great Door of the Temple Church

GILLIVER, Lawton: over against St. Dunstan's Church in Fleet Street

GLASS, Thomas: printseller, next the Royal Exchange Stairs in Cornhill

GOODWIN, Timothy

GOREHAM, H.: in Wine Office Court, Fleet Street

GOSLING, Francis

GOSLING, Robert: at the Mitre in Fleet Street; at the Mitre and Crown against Fetter Lane in Fleet Street; at the Mitre and Crown, against St. Dunstan's Church, Fleet Street

GRAVES, J.: St. James's Street

GRAY, John: in the Poultry

GREEN, T.: over against the Meuse Gate, Charing Cross

GRIFFITHS, Ralph: bookseller and publisher, at the Dunciad in Ludgate Street

GYLES, Fletcher

HARDING, J.: at the upper end of St. Martin's Lane

HARDING, Samuel

HARPER, Thomas: copper plate printer, in Dogwell Court, White Fryars

HARRIS, Thomas: at the Looking Glass and Bible on London Bridge

HARRIS, W.: in Meeting House Court, Black Friars

HART, John: printer, in Popping's Court, Fleet Street

HARWOOD, J.: in Goulding Lane, near Playhouse Yard

HATCHETT, T.: under the Royal Exchange

HAWKINS, G.: in Fleet Street

HAZARD, Joseph: (with J. Hazard) against Stationers' Hall

HAZARD, J.: (with Joseph Hazard) against Stationers' Hall

HENRY, D.: printer, in Friar Street

HESTER, Sam.: at the Corner of White Friars, in Fleet Street

HETT, Richard: in the Poultry

HINCHLIFFE, William

HINTON, John

HITCH, Charles: (with A. Bettesworth) at the Red Lyon, in Paternoster Row

HODGES, James: at the Looking Glass, over against St. Magnus Church, London Bridge

HOLBECHE, Abr.: at the Bible and Crown in Barbican

HOLLOWAY, Mrs. E.: near the Blue Last in Salisbury Court, Fleet Street

HOOKE, J.

HORNE, T.: under the Royal Exchange

HOW, J.: in the Ram Head Inn Yard in Fenchurch Street

HUGGONSON, J.: printer, near Sergeants Inn, in Chancery Lane

HULTON, John: printseller, at the corner of Pall Mall, facing the Haymarket

ILIVE, Abraham: printer

INNYS, John: (with William Innys) at the Prince's Arms, at the West end of St. Paul's

INNYS, William: (with John Innys) at the Prince's Arms, at the West end of St. Paul's; (with R. Manby) at the West end of St. Paul's

ISTED, J.: at the Golden Ball near St. Dunstan's Church in Fleet Street.

JACKSON, J.: in Pall Mall, near St. James's; near St. James's House; near St. James's Gate

JACKSON, T.: in Pall Mall

JACKSON, William: printer, at the Printing Office, the corner of Red Cross Alley in Jewin Street

JAMES, J.: bookseller, at Horace's Head, under the Royal Exchange

JANEWAY, J.: printer, at the Golden Ball near Water Lane End, Fleet Street; in White Fryars, near Fleet Street

JEPHSON, C.: printer, in Wine Office Court, Fleet Street

JOLLIFFE, J.: at the Bible in St. James's Street

KING, Charles: in Westminster Hall

KING, John: printseller, in the Poultry, near Stocks Market

KINGMAN, Mary: at the Corner of Swithin's Alley, near the Royal Exchange

KNAPLOCK, R.: at the Bishop's Head, in St. Paul's Churchyard

KNAPTON, James: (with John and Paul Knapton) St. Paul's Churchyard; at the Crown in Ludgate Street, near the West end of St. Paul's

KNAPTON, John: (with James and Paul Knapton) St. Paul's Churchyard; at the Crown in Ludgate Street, near the West end of St. Paul's

KNAPTON, Paul: (with James and John Knapton) St. Paul's Churchyard; at the Crown in Ludgate Street, near the West end of St. Paul's

LANGLEY, Batty: at Parliament Stairs, near Old Palace Yard, Westminster

LEWIS, Mr.: in Flower de Luce Court, Fleet Street

LEWIS, John: in Bartholomew Close

LEWIS, W.: Russell Street, Covent Garden

LINTOT, Henry

LLOYD, William: next the King's Arms Tavern in Chancery Lane, near Fleet Street

LONGMAN, Thomas: (with Thomas Shewell) in Paternoster Row

LYE, S.: printseller, near the India House, Leadenhall Street

LYON, Alexander: in Russell Street, Covent Garden

MACEY, B.: at the Hermitage Bridge

MANBY, Richard: (with Henry Shute Cox) on Ludgate Hill; (with W. Innys), at the West end of St. Paul's

MANSHIP, Sam.

MARBECK, Mrs.: printseller, in Westminster Hall

MARSHALL, Joseph: printer, at the Bible in Newgate Street

MEADOWS, W.: in Cornhill; at the Angel, near the Royal Exchange

MEARS, W.: without Temple Bar; on Ludgate Hill

MECHELL, James: printer and publisher, at the King's Arms, near Red Lion Street, High Holborn; at the King's Arms, next the Three Cups Inn, High Holborn; at the King's Arms, next the Leg Tavern, in Fleet Street

MECHELL, Mrs. M.: at the King's Arms in Fleet Street

MEERE, T.: (with E. Holloway) at the Blue Last in Salisbury Court, Fleet Street

MEIGHAN, P.

MIDWINTER, Daniel: in St. Paul's Churchyard

MILLAN, John: bookseller, the corner of Buckingham Court, near the Admiralty Office; opposite the Admiralty Office, Charing Cross

MILLAR, Andrew: opposite Katharine Street in the Strand

MILLES, Bryan: in Houndsditch, near Bishopsgate

MORGAN, J.

MORPHEW, John: near Stationers' Hall

MOTTE, Benjamin: at the Middle Temple Gate, in Fleet Street

MOUNT, Mr.: on Tower Hill

MOXON, Joseph: at the sign of the Atlas on Ludgate Hill; on the West side of Fleet Ditch, at the sign of the Atlas; at the Atlas in Warwick Lane, and at his Shop in Westminster Hall right against the Parliament Stairs

NEALE, J.: in Leadenhall Street

NEEDHAM, F.: bookseller, opposite Gray's Inn, in Holborn

NEWBERY, John: at the Bible and Crown, without Temple Bar

NICHOLSON, John: at the King's Arms in Little Britain; near the Sessions House in the Great Old Bailey.

NOON, J.: at the White Hart, near Mercers Chapel, Cheapside

NORRIS, T.: at the Looking Glass

NORTON, Mr.: in Finch Lane, near the Royal Exchange

NOURSE, John: at the Lamb without Temple Bar

NUTT, Edward: at the Royal Exchange

NUTT, Elizabeth: printer, in the Savoy

NUTT, J.: near Stationers' Hall

NUTT, John: printer, in the Savoy

NUTT, M.: in Exeter Exchange in the Strand

OFFTEY, R.: near St. Sepulchre's Church

ORPE, Mr.: bookseller, near the Ram Tavern, Tooley Street

OSBORN, J.: (with T. Longman) in Paternoster Row

OSBORNE, Thomas: in Gray's Inn

OSWALD, J.: at the Rose and Crown in the Poultry, near Stocks Market

OVERTON, Philip: printseller, near St. Dunstan's Church, Fleet Street

PALMER, Samuel: printer, printing house in Bartholomew Close

PARKER, Richard: (with Ralph Smith) under the Piazza of the Royal Exchange

PAYNE, Olive: at Horace's Head in Round Court in the Strand, over against York Buildings

PAYNE, Thomas: bookseller, near the South Sea House, Bishopsgate Street

PEELE, John: at Locke's Head, in Paternoster Row

PEMBERTON, John: at the Buck and Sun against St. Dunstan's Church in Fleet Street

PEMBERTON, H.

PENNY, Robert: Wine Office Court, Fleet Street

PHILLIMORE, R.: bookseller, near Ludgate

PREVOST, Nicholas: at the Ship opposite Southampton Street in the Strand

PRICE, C.: in the Fleet

PURSER, J.: in White Fryars

RAYNER, William: Printing Office in Marygold Court, near Exeter Exchange in the Strand; at the Rising Sun in Angel Court, near the King's Bench, Southwark; near St. George's Church, Southwark; the Bible, in Wine Office Court, Fleet Street

READ, James: printer, in White Fryars

READ, Thomas: Dogwell Court, White-Fryars, Fleet Street

REEVE, —

REGNIER, James: printseller, at the Golden Ball in Newport Street, near Longacre

REILY, R.: printer

RICHARDSON, Samuel: printer

RIVINGTON, Charles: bookseller, at the Bible and Crown in St. Paul's Churchyard

RIVINGTON, James: (with John Rivington) in St. Paul's Churchyard

RIVINGTON, John: (with James Rivington) in St. Paul's Churchyard

ROBERTS, James: near the Oxford Arms in Warwick Lane

ROBINSON, Jacob: next the One Tun Tavern near Hungerford Market, in the Strand; at the Golden Lion in Ludgate Street

ROBINSON, Mr.: at St. Saviour's Dock, Southwark

ROBINSON, Ranew: in St. Paul's Churchyard

ROGERS, —: (with — Cooper) stationers, near Bishopsgate Street

ROUND, I.: in Exchange Alley, in Cornhill

RUSSELL, William: at Horace's Head, without Temple Bar

SANGER, Edward: at the Post House, in Fleet Street

SARGEANT, W.: stationer, in Great Newport Street, near Newport Market

SAY, Edward: printer

SENEX, J.

SHEWELL, Thomas: (with Thomas Longman) in Paternoster Row

SHROPSHIRE, William: over against the Duke of Grafton's in New Bond Street; in Old Bond Street

SHUCKBURGH, John: in Fleet Street

SMITH, Godfrey, Sr.: printer, in Stanhope Street, near Clare Market

SMITH, Godfrey, Jr.: printer, in Stanhope Street, near Clare Market

SMITH, G.: in Prince's Street, Spittle Fields

SMITH, J.: bookseller, over against the King's Arms in New Bond Street

SMITH, Ralph: (with Richard Parker) under the Piazza of the Royal Exchange

SPENCER, Robert: (with George Davies) at the Golden Ball in White Fryars

SPRINT, B.

STAGG. John: in Westminster Hall

STANTON, James: distiller and printer, at the Empty Gallon Pot, in Black and White Court in the Old Baily; at the Empty Gallon Pot, the corner of Seacoal Lane, next Fleet Street

STEPHENS, J.: at the Bible in Butchers Row, without Temple Bar

STONE, J.

STRAHAN, G.: at the Royal Exchange; at the Golden Ball in Cornhill

STRAHAN, W.: printer

SYMON, Edward: over against the Royal Exchange in Cornhill

SYMPSON, S.

TAYLOR, William: at the Ship in Paternoster Row

THREKELD, John: near St. Paul's

TONSON, Jacob: near Catherine Street, in the Strand

TONSON, R.: near Catherine Street, in the Strand

TOOKE, Benjamin: at the Middle Temple Gate

TORBUCK, John: Clare Court, near Drury Lane

TOTTERIDGE, T.: printer, opposite to the Elephant and Castle in Fleet Lane

VAILLANT, Paul: in the Strand; over against Southampton Street, in the Strand

VAN DER ESCH, Henry

VAUGHAN, Mr.: Fan Shop in Russell Court, Drury Lane

WALKER, Robert: printer and publisher, at Shakespeare's Head in Turn-again Lane, Snowhill; in Exchange Alley, Cornhill; next the White Horse Inn, Fleet Street; at the British Oil Warehouse in Fleet Lane; the corner of Elliott's Court, in the Little Old Bailey; also had shops in Oxford, Cambridge, and Birmingham.

WALLER, T.: in the Temple; at the Crown and Mitre, opposite to Fetter Lane, in Fleet Street

WALSH, John: music printer and instrument maker to His Majesty, at the Harp and Hautboy in Catherine Street in the Strand

WALTHOE, John

WALTHOE, John, Jr.

WARD, Aaron: in Little Britain

WARD, Caesar: (with Richard Chandler) at the Ship between the Temple Gates in Fleet Street

WARD, Thomas: (with E. Wicksteed) in the Inner Temple Lane

WARE, Richard

WARING, W.: at the Bible in Jermyn Street, St. James's

WARNER, T.: at the Black Boy, in Paternoster Row

WATSON, James: in Wardrobe Court, Great Carter Lane

WATSON, M.: next the King's Arms Tavern in Chancery Lane

WATTS, John

WEBB, J.: printer, in the Old Bailey

WEDDELL, A.: against Catherine Street in the Strand

WHISTON, John: bookseller, at Mr. Boyle's Head, Fleet Street

WHITRIDGE, Henry: the corner of Castle Alley, in Cornhill

WICKSTEED, E.: (with T. Ward) in the Inner Temple Lane

WILCOX, John: at Virgil's Head, opposite the New Church in the Strand

WILFORD, John: at the Three Flower-de-luces, behind St. Paul's Chapter House

WILKIN, Richard: at the King's Head in St. Paul's Churchyard

WILLIAMSON, Richard: near Gray's Inn Gate, Holborn
WILLOCK, R.
WOOD,: J. in Paternoster Row
WOOD, T.: printer
WOODFALL, Henry, Jr.: printer, at the Rose and Crown in Little Britain
WOODMAN, James: in Covent Garden
WOODWARD, J.: in Scalding Alley, over against Stocks Market
WOODWARD, T.: at the Half Moon, over against St. Dunstan's Church in Fleet Street
WORRALL, Thomas: Fleet Street; at the Dove in Bell Yard, near Lincoln's Inn
WOTTON, Matthew
WOTTON, S.
WOTTON, Thomas
WRIGHT, Daniel: next the Sun Tavern in Holborn
WRIGHT, Daniel, Jr.: at the Golden Bass, near the Pump in St. Paul's Churchyard
WRIGHT, T.: at the Golden Harp on London Bridge; at the Violin and Harp on London Bridge
WRIGHT, T.: mathematical instrument maker to His Majesty, Fleet Street
WYATT, —: copper plate printer, next the Vine Tavern in Longacre
YOUNG, R.: in Duke's Court, near St. Martin's Lane

BIBLIOGRAPHY

This is a selected list of books and articles which have been found useful in the writing of the present book. The list does not include the 'primary sources' of information, which consist mainly of the works published in fascicules before 1750 (see Appendix B), contemporary newspapers, printed proposals, the Stationers' Register, the statutes dealing with copyright and the tax on paper, the English [Law] Reports, certain State papers, annotated trade-sales catalogues, letters and diaries, pamphlets, dedications, and a few manuscript records kept by printers and booksellers.

BOOKS

BOSWELL, James. *Boswell's Life of Johnson*, ed. G. B. Hill, rev. and enl. L. F. Powell. 6 vols. Oxford: Clarendon Press, 1934, 1950.

CHUBB, Thomas. *The Printed Maps in the Atlases of Great Britain and Ireland. A Bibliography*, 1579-1870. London: Homeland Association.

COLLINS, A. S. *Authorship in the Days of Johnson. Being a Study of the Relation between Author, Patron, Publisher, and Public*, 1726-1780. London: Routledge, 1928.

CARLSON, C. Lennart. *The First Magazine. A History of the Gentleman's Magazine*. Providence: Brown University, 1938.

COLLET, C. D. *History of the Taxes on Knowledge; Their Origin and Repeal*. London: Watts, [1933].

CORDASCO, Francesco. *A Register of 18th Century Bibliographies and References*. Chicago: V. Giorgio, 1950.

COX, Edward Godfrey. *A Reference Guide to the Literature of Travel, Including Voyages, Geographical Descriptions, Adventures, Shipwrecks and Expeditions*. [subtitle of VOL. III: *Including Tours, Descriptions, Towns, Histories and Antiquities, Surveys, Ancient and Present State, Etc.*] 3 vols. VOL. I, Seattle: University of Washington, 1935; VOL. II, Seattle: University of Washington, 1938; VOL. III, Seattle: University of Washington Press, 1949.

CRANE, R. S. and F. B. Kaye. *A Census of British Newspapers and Periodicals* 1620-1800. Chapel Hill: University of North Carolina Press, 1927.

CRANFIELD, G. A. *A Handlist of English Provincial Newspapers and Periodicals* 1700-1760. Cambridge: Bowes & Bowes, for the Cambridge Bibliographical Society, 1952.

GROSE, Clyde Leclare. *A Select Bibliography of British History* 1660-1760. Chicago: University of Chicago Press, [1939].

HANSON, Laurence. *Government and the Press* 1695-1763. London: Oxford University Press, 1936.

HILLHOUSE, James T. *The Grub-Street Journal.* Durham: Duke University Press, 1928.

KNIGHT, Charles. *The Old Printer and the Modern Press.* London: John Murray, 1854.

LOWNDES, William Thomas. *The Bibliographer's Manual of English Literature*, rev. Henry G. Bohn. 4 vols. London: Bell, 1857-1864.

MORISON, Stanley. *The English Newspaper. Some Account of the Physical Development of Journals Printed in London between 1622 and the Present Day.* Cambridge: University Press, 1932.

MUMBY, Frank Arthur. *Publishing and Bookselling. A History from the Earliest Times to the Present Day.* London: Cape, [1930].

NICHOLS, John. *Literary Anecdotes of the Eighteenth Century: Comprising Biographical Memoirs of William Bowyer, Printer . . ., and . . . Friends.* 6 vols. London, 1812. Followed by VOL. VII, Part i (1813), VOL. VIII (1814), VOL. IX (1815), and VOL. VII, Part ii (1816).

PARGELLIS, Stanley and D. J. Medley. *Bibliography of British History: the Eighteenth Century* 1714-1789. Oxford: Clarendon Press, 1951.

Parliamentary History of England, from the Earliest Period to the Year 1803. VOL. XVII. London, 1813.

PARTRIDGE, R. C. Barrington. *The History of the Legal Deposit of Books throughout the British Empire.* London: Library Association, 1938.

PLANT, Marjorie. *The English Book Trade. An Economic History of the Making and Sale of Books.* London: Allen & Unwin, [1939].

PLOMER, H. R., G. H. Bushnell, and E. R. McC. Dix. *A Dictionary of the Printers and Booksellers Who Were at Work in England, Scotland and Ireland from* 1726 *to* 1775. London: Oxford University Press, for the Bibliographical Society, 1932 (for 1930).

ROBERTS, William. *The Earlier History of English Bookselling.* London: Sampson Low, Marston, 1892.

SALE, William M., Jr. *Samuel Richardson: Master Printer.* Ithaca, New York: Cornell University Press, 1950.

SCRUTTON, Thomas Edward. *The Law of Copyright.* 4th ed. London: Clowes, 1903.

SHAW, William A., ed. *Calendar of Treasury Books and Papers . . . Preserved in Her Majesty's Public Record Office.* 5 vols. [VOL. I, 1729-1730; VOL. II, 1731-1734; VOL. III, 1735-1738; VOL. IV, 1739-1741; VOL. V, 1742-1745]. London: H. M. Stationery Office, 1897-1903.

STAUFFER, Donald A. *The Art of Biography in Eighteenth Century England.* 2 vols. Princeton: Princeton University Press, 1941.
TIMPERLEY, C. H. *A Dictionary of Printers and Printing.* London: Johnson, 1839.
TURNER, Sydney R. *The Newspaper Tax Stamps of Great Britain. The First Issue* 1712-1757. n.p.: Sydney R. Turner, [1936].
WEED, Katherine K. and R. P. Bond. *Studies of British Newspapers and Periodicals from their Beginnings to* 1800. *A Bibliography.* No. 2 of *Studies in Philology*: Extra Series. Chapel Hill: University of North Carolina Press, 1946.

ARTICLES

ALDIS, H. G. 'Book Production and Distribution, 1625-1800', *Cambridge History of English Literature*, XI, 311-342.
ASPINALL, A. 'Statistical Accounts of the London Newspapers in the Eighteenth Century', *English Historical Review*, LXIII(1948), 210-232.
BALD, R. C. 'Early Copyright Litigation and its Bibliographical Interest', *Papers of the Bibliographical Society of America*, XXXVI(1942), 81-96.
BLAGDEN, Cyprian. 'Booksellers' Trade Sales 1718-1768', *Library*, 5th ser., V(1951), 243-257.
CHAPMAN, R. W. 'Eighteenth-century Booksellers'. *Book-collector's Quarterly*, IX (1933), 25-36.
CHAPMAN, R. W. 'Eighteenth-century Imprints', *Library*, 4th ser., XI(1931), 503f.
CHAPMAN, R. W. 'The Numbering of Editions in the Eighteenth Century', *Review of English Studies*, III (1927), 77-79.
CRONE, G. R. and R. A. Skelton. 'English Collections of Voyages and Travels, 1625-1846', in Edward Lynam, ed., *Richard Hakluyt & His Successors*. London: Hakluyt Society, 1946, pp. 63-140.
DAVIS, Herbert. 'Bowyer's Paper Stock Ledger', *Library*, 5th ser., VI(1951), 73-87.
DRAPER, John W. 'Queen Anne's Act. A Note on English Copyright', *Modern Language Notes*, XXXVI (1921), 146-154.
GOVE, Philip Babcock. 'Notes on Serialization and Competitive Publishing: Johnson's and Bailey's Dictionaries, 1755', *Oxford Bibliographical Society Proceedings & Papers*, V (1936-1939), [305]-322.
GREG, W. W. 'Old Style—New Style', in *Joseph Quincy Adams Memorial Studies*, ed. James G. McManaway, Giles E. Dawson, Edwin E. Willoughby. Washington: Folger Shakespeare Library, 1948, pp. 563-569.

HAZEN, A. T. 'One Meaning of the Imprint', *Library*, 5th ser., VI (1951), 120-123.

HEAL, Ambrose. 'London Booksellers 1700-1750', *Notes & Queries*, CLXII (1932), 46-47, 116-120.

MUIR, P. H. 'The Bickhams and their *Universal Penman*', *Library*, 4th ser., XXV (1945), 162-184 and plates; also anonymous letter, *ibid.*, XXVI (1946), 196.

OSBORN, J. M. 'Thomas Birch and the *General Dictionary*', *Modern Philology*, XXXVI (1938), 25-46.

POLLARD, Alfred W. 'Some Notes on the History of Copyright in England, 1662-1774', *Library*, 4th ser., III (1922-1923), 97-114.

POLLARD, Graham. 'Notes on the Size of the Sheet', *Library*, 4th ser., XXII (1941), 105-137.

POLLARD, Graham. 'Serial Fiction', in John Carter, ed., *New Paths in Book Collecting*. London: Constable, [1934].

SUTHERLAND, James R. 'The Circulation of Newspapers and Literary Periodicals, 1700-30', *Transactions of the Bibliographical Society*, 2nd ser., XV (1935), 110-124.

SUTHERLAND, James R. 'Lost Journals', *Periodical Post Boy*, VI (March 1950), [1]-4.

WOOD, Frederick T. 'Notes on London Booksellers and Publishers, 1700-1750', *Notes & Queries*, CLXI (1931), 39-42, and *passim*.

WOOD, Frederick T. 'Pirate Printing in the XVIII Century', *Notes & Queries*, CLIX (1930), 381-384, 400-403.

INDEX

Initial articles, both definite and indefinite, are omitted from all titles in English. Names in imprints are omitted. For these, see Appendix B, *passim.*

Abree, James, 188

abridgments, 28, 30, 39, 47, 48 ,66, 72, 160–2, 164–5, 305

Account of the Expedition of the British Fleet, 316

Account of the Plague at Marseilles, as instalments, 30

Account of the Rebellion, 320

Account of Voyages (Hawkesworth), 161

Acts of Parliament, xiii, 23, 31, 32, 53, 54, 70, 154–7, 155 n., 172, 182, and Appendix A

Acta Germanica, 244, 325, 344

Acta Regia (Rapin-Whatley), monthly, 97, 277; weekly, 123, 198, 285; shares in, 151–2; odd numbers retailed, 228; usefulness of, 237

Adams, George, 278, 330.

Addison, Joseph, 26, 315; see *Cato;* see *Spectator* essays

Adlerfeld, Gustavus, 334

Admiral Vernon's Weekly Journal, 74, 330

advantages of buying fascicules, 14, 88, 134 n., 221, 232

Adventures of Aristonous, 322

Adventures of Telemachus (Fénelon), 322

advertising of fascicules, 142–5, 203–12; costs of, 5, 183–4, 222

Agreeable Companion, 336

Agreeable Historian (Simpson), 336

Albinus, Bernard Siegfried, 244, 251, 351

All-Alive and Merry, 44–50, 52.

All the Expeditions, Sea-Fights, 69

allowance to dealers, 18, 177, 179, 180, 186–7

America, description of, 124; history of, 89

American Traveller, 334

Amhurst, Nicholas, 108

Amusements des eaux d'Aix-la-Chapelle (de Pöllnitz), 354

Amusements of Aix la Chapelle, 354

Amusements Serious and Comical (Brown), 63, 312

Anatomical Tables, 244

Ancient Masonry (Langley), 128, 228, 291

Andrea Palladio's Architecture, 285

Aniello, Tomaso, 72

Annesley, James, case of, as serial, 43; in numbers, 171 n., 336, 343, 344; fiction about, 338, 343: *Memoirs* of, as serial, 46, 50

Annotations on the Holy Bible, 212–3

Annals of the Reformation of the Church of England (Strype), 197, 204, 302

anonymity, 121, 140, 146–7, 212–16, 251 n., 255

Anson, Commodore, 43; see *Authentic Journal*

Anti-logarithmic Canon (Dodson), 197, 322

Anti-Pamela (Haywood), instalments of, 46, 48, 49

Antiquities Sacred and Prophane (Calmet-Tindal), 94–5, 206, 275

Apology for the Conduct of Mrs . . . Phillips, 143–6, 171, 355

Appendix ad thesaurum grecæ linguæ (Scott), 148, 199, 332

Applebee, John, 22, 39–40, 60

Apsley, Lord Chancellor, 161–2

Arabian Nights' Entertainments, instalments of, 35, 36, 38, 38 n.

Arbuthnot, Rev. Archibald, 233, 347, 348

Archbishop of Canterbury, 142, 231, 319; see Tillotson

Argensola, Bartolomeo de, 88, 272

Art of Cookery (Thacker), 254, 255, 350

Art of Painting (de Lairesse-Fritsch), 214, 250, 308

Asia, description of, 124

Atlantis Reviv'd, 344

Atlas Geographus (Moll), 83–6, 198, 229, 271, 273

Aubin, Penelope, see *Life and Adventures of Lady Lucy*

Austen-Leigh, R. A., 178 n.

Authentic Journal of the late Expedition under . . .Anson (Philips), instalments of, 43, 43 n.; in fascicules, 43 n., 197, 341

Authentick Memoires of . . . Sarah. late Dutchess of Marlborough, 255, 337

author as distributor, 137, 139, 141, 145, 146, 223

author as proprietor, 136, 137, 139, 141, 143–6, 186

Author to be Lett (Savage), 23

Author's Farce (Fielding), 174 n.

author's signature on fascicules, 145, 249, 324

authorship, difficulties of, 135, 141, 142, 143, 145; expenses of, 141, 163, 165, 173

Aventures merveilleuses (Gueullette), translation of, as serial, 36

B. *Berington's Evening Post*, 108

Barnardiston, Thomas, 162

Baddam, Benjamin, 175, 311

Baker, J., 192, 294

Baker, Sir Richard, 125, 150, 281

Bald, R. C., 154 n., 188–9

Banks, John, 323

Barclay, Dr. Patrick, 124, 281, 286

Barrow, Dr. Isaac, 239, 337

Bartholomew, A. T., 119 n.

Baskett, J., 159, 178, 300

Bayle, Pierre, see *Dictionary Historical;* see *Dictionnaire historique et critique;* see *General Dictionary*

Beane, Sawney, story of, 252–3

Beauties of the English Stage, 19 n., 267, 311, 321–2

Bee, 55–6, 57

Behn, Aphra, 297; see *Lord Grey's . . . Love-Letters;* see *Oroonoko;* see *Several Love Letters*

Bellamira (Sedley), 114

Bennet, George, 326

Bentley, Dr. Richard, 119, 188

Bernard, Jean Frédéric, 129, 288; see *Ceremonies and Religious Customs*

Bernard, John Peter, 174–5, 287; see *General Dictionary*

Beveridge, William, 321

Bibliotheca Anatomica, 89–90, 272

Bibliotheca Biblica (Parker), 101, 249, 274

Bibliotheca Harleiana, 244–5, 330; see *Harleian Miscellany*

Bickham, George, 255; see *British Monarchy*, 139, 192, 334; see *Musical Entertainer*, 305, 321; see *Universal Penman*, 130–1, 139, 192, 238, 288, 330

Biographia Britannica (Oldys and others), 151, 168, 238, 243, 346

Birch, Rev. Thomas, 115, 174–5, 287

Bird, G., 129, 218, 288

Birt, Samuel, 86 n., 259

Blackstone, Sir William, 161–2

Blackwell, Alexander, 176

Blackwell, Elizabeth, 176, 305, 312, 326; see *Curious Herbal*

Blagden, Cyprian, 151 n.

Blainville, J. de, 148, 330

Blomefield, Rev. Francis, 140–2, 302; see *Essay Towards a . . . History of Norfolk*

blue paper covers, 6, 7, 47, 65–6, 197, 222, and *passim*

Bodleian Library, records of, 169, 170–1

Boerhaave, Dr. Herman, 244, 282; see *Elementa Chemiæ*

Bolton, S., 337, see *Complete System of Geography*

Book of Martyrs (Foxe), 129, 192, 220, 290, 328, 345

Book of Martyrs the best Preservative against Popery (Lyndar), 291

Book-binder . . . Confuted (Stackhouse), 109, 112–13

books, imitation, 12

books as ornaments, 11–12

books ordered by the yard, 12

booksellers' problem, 15, 25

Boswell, James, 157, 158 n., 179, 242 n.

Bowes, R., 351, 356

Bowes, Sir Robert, 302
Bowles, Rev. Mr., 169–70
Bowyer, William, 178
Boyer, Jean Baptiste de, 315
Boyse, Samuel, 250, 348
Brantôme, Pierre de Bourdeille, Seigneur de, 326
Brice, Andrew, of Exeter, 29, 20, 33, 34, 60
Brice's Weekly Journal, 29
Bridges, John, 316
Brief Historical . . . Account of all the Empires, instalments of, 37
Brief History of England (Lindsay), 352
Brindley, James, 213
Bristollia (Hooke), 356
Britannia (Camden), 56, 57, 61–2, 85, 289
Britannia & Hibernia, 84–5
British Intelligence, or Universal Advertiser, 50 n., 54
British Melody, 316
British Mercury, 37, 290
British Mercury, or Weekly Pacquet, 68
British Miscellany; or the Harmonious Grove, 288
British Monarchy (Bickham), 139, 192, 334
British Musical Miscellany, 289
British Observator, 56–7, 61–2, 289
British Traveller, instalments of, 46, 48, 49
Brown, Josiah, 158
Brown, Tom, 82 n.; see *Amusements Serious and Comical*; see *Infallible Astrologer*
Browne, Sir Thomas, works of, 302
Browning, Robert, 250
Brushfield, T. N., 202
Bruys, François, 121, 282
Budgell, Eustace, 55–6, 57
Bundy, Dr. Richard, 98, 100, 110, 218 n., 276
Burkitt, William, 127, 152, 289
Burn, Thomas, bookseller in Oxford, 18
Burnet, Bishop Gilbert, 38, 114, 289
Burnet, Thomas, 297
Burrow, Sir James, 157
Butler, James (Duke of Ormonde), 312, 326

Caius College Library, 142
Calmet, Augustin, 94, 275
Cambridge Journal and Flying Post, 73, 351, 356
Camden, William, see *Britannia*
Campbell, Dr. John, 111, 280, 282, 340; see *History of the Bible*; see *New and Compleat History of the Holy Bible*
Cantabrigians, reading matter for, 73
Cantemir, Demetrius, 170, 297; see *History of the Othman Empire*
Captain Singleton (Defoe), instalments of, 30
Care, Henry, 75, 78, 79, 270, 297
Carnan, William, of Reading, 63
Cart, M., 296
Case of Authors . . . Stated (Ralph), 134–5
cases, court: *Carnan v. Bowles*, 158 n.; *Donaldson v. Beckett*, 158; *Gyles v. Wilcox*, 160 n.; *Hinton v. Donaldson*, 157, 158 n.; *Millar v. Taylor*, 157; *Read v. Hodges*, 162; *Tonson v. Walker and Marchant*, 159 n.
Catalogue of Books Printed . . . at London, 1
catchwords, 27, 35, 60
Cato (Addison), 17
Catrou, François, 98, 276
Cauche, François, 272
Cave, Edward, 58, 184–5, 258
Cave, William, 195
Celenia; or, the History of Hyempsal, instalments of, 40
Ceremonies and Religious Customs (Bernard), 193, 288
Cérémonies et coutumes religieuses (Bernard), 129, 298, 226, 288
Cervantes-Saavedra, Miguel de, 35, 40, 82, 97–8, 273, 276; see *Don Quixote*; see *Exemplary Novels*; see *Story of the Liberal Lover*
Chamberlen, Paul, 312
Chambers, Ephraim, 10, 327, 328; see *Cyclopædia*
Champion, Joseph, 129, 289
Chapman, R. W., 133 n.
Charles I, works of, 298
Chesterfield, Earl of, 228

Chinese Tales (Gueullette), instalments of, 34, 36

Choice . . .Collection of . . .Histories, 207–8, 303

Christian's Amusement, 189–90

Christian Library, 327

Christianity Set in a True Light (Radicati), 93, 182–3, 280

Christian's Companion (Whitefield), 305, 320

Christian's Guide (Smith), 216, 309

Chronicle of the Kings of England (Baker), 58, 125, 150, 197, 271

Churchman's Last Shift; or, Loyalist's Weekly Journal, 38 n.

Cieza de Leon, Pedro, 272

Clarke, Laurence, 74, 306, 313, 321, 326; see *Compleat . . . History of . . . Jesus Christ*; see *Compleat History of the Holy Bible*; see *History of the Holy Bible*; see *Life of the Blessed Virgin Mary*; see *Lives . . . of the Apostles*

Clarke, Dr. Samuel, 243, 331

classical literature, 37, 64, 148, 180–1, 247; see Horace, Ovid, Virgil

Coalston, Lord, 157, 158 n.

Cockburn, John, 47, 321; see *Distresses and Adventures*; see *Journey over Land*: see *Unfortunate Englishman*

Coetlogon, Dennis de, 163, 170, 173, 327; see *Universal History of Arts and Sciences*

Colbatch, John, 282; see *Dr. Colbatch's Legacy*; see *Generous Physician*

Coleridge, Samuel Taylor, 100 n.

Collection of Plays by Eminent Hands, 16

Collection of Select Sermons, 312

Collection of . . . Trials, 290

Collection of . . . Trials against State Prisoners, 319

Collection of Voyages and Travels, 337

Collett, Joseph, of Bristol, 226

Collins, William, 237

Collyer, Joseph, Clerk of the Stationers' Company, 169–70

Colman, George, 41 n.

Comedian; or, Philosophical Enquirer, 107, 108

Commentary on St. Paul's Epistle to the Galatians (Luther), 324, 329

Common Sense, 45

Compleat and Impartial History of England (Robinson), 146–7, 268, 325

Compleat Body of Divinity (Stackhouse), 109, 110, 166, 244, 333

Compleat Collection of . . . Songs, 123, 283

Compleat Collection of the Works of. . . Josephus (ed. Jackson), 303

Compleat Collection of the . . . Works of . . . Josephus (ed. Wilson), 74 323, 329

Compleat English Gentleman (Defoe), 11

Compleat Herbal (Tournefort), 90–1, 191, 274

Compleat Historian, or the Oxford Penny-Post, 67, 293

Compleat History of Executions, 22

Compleat . . . History of . . . Jesus Christ (Clarke), 74, 306, 321, 326

Compleat . . . History of . . . Naval Expeditions (Lediard), 295

Compleat History . . . of the Antient Egyptians, 205, 313

Compleat History of the Civil Wars in England (Rio), 129, 286, 292

Compleat History of the Holy Bible (Clarke), 306

Compleat History of the Old and New Testament (Smith), 160, 301, 320

Compleat History of the Turkish Empire, 329–30

Compleat Linguist (Henley), 24

Compleat Penman (Williams), 314

Complete Collection of State Trials, 294

Complete Commentary . . . on Milton's Paradise Lost (Paterson), 341

Complete History of the Inquisition (Baker), 192, 294

Complete History of the Present War with Spain, 327

Complete System of Geography (Moll-Bolton), 168, 202, 337

Conant, Martha P., 36 n.

conditions, text of, 20, 209, 211

congers, 5, 149, 151–3, 168, 178, 222

Congreve, William, plays of, 19 n.

Conscious Lovers (Steele), 17

Constantine the Great (Lee), 17, 19

Construction . . . of Mathematical Instruments, 122, 283

continuations, 40, 96, 108, 109, 125, 147, 150, 171, 189, 243, 281, 285, 299, 305, 339, 343

Conyers, George, 91

Cooke, John, 6, 214

Cooper, Mary, 259

Cooper, Thomas, 212, 259

copies, assignment of shares in, 137, 140, 151 n., 152–3, 175–6, 183 n.; joint ownership of, see proprietors, groups of; value of shares in, 114, 118–19, 123, 150–3, 163, 165, 176, 177, 178, 190, 192; see also trade sales of copies

Copious and Exact Catalogue (Oldys), 339, 341; see *Harleian Miscellany*

copyright, 28–9, 30, 31, 48, 57, 97, 106, 114, 137, 145, 154–62, 177, 188, 193; assignment of, 137, 140, 146, 173; early history of, 154 n.; litigation over, 9, 157–9, 161, 166n., 177, 188–9; penalties for infringement of, 156, 262; provided by special Act, 156 n.; retained by author, 136, 137, 138, 139; violation of, 29, 30, 117; see copies; see royal licences

Copyright Act, text of, 261–6

Corbett, Charles, 64, 210–11

Corbett, Thomas, 316

Corns, Albert R., 354

costs of advertising, 5, 183–4, 222; of printing, 6, 178–9; of production, 17, 84, 172

Cotes, Cornelius, 64–5

Cotes's Weekly Journal; or, the English Stage-Player, 64–5, 267, 294, 296

Counter-Apology, 356

Country Wife (Wycherley), 17

Course of Academical Lectures (Henley), 24

Court, John, 117, 132, 283, 290; see *New Testament . . . with Notes*

Cowley, J., 59

Cox, Thomas, 86, 273

Crabbe, George, quoted, 9

Craftsman, 108

Cranfield, Dr. G. A., 73, 313

Crébillon, Claude Prosper Jolyot de, 41

Creighton, Louise, 213 n.

Critical . . . Commentary on the New Testament (Court and Lindsay), 290

Critical Dictionary (Bayle), 191

Critical . . . Exposition of the Bible (Jameson), 352

Critical . . . Exposition of the Pentateuch (Jameson), 153, 351

Crokatt, James, 259

Crone, G. R., 89 n., 307, 334

Crownfield, C., of Cambridge, 94

Curious Herbal (Blackwell), 238, 305, 326; pirated, 312; share in bought by Nourse, 176, 183

Curious Relations, 313

Curll, Edmund, 33, 82, 87 n., 119, 174, 215 n.

Cyclopædia (Chambers), 8, 157, 167 n., 177, 191, 196, 243, 327

Cynthia, instalments of, 36–7

Czar of Muscovy's Travels, instalments of, 39

dates in imprints, xiii, xiv, 17, 78 n., 86, 201, 267–8, and Appendix B

dating before 1753, xiii-xiv

D'Aulnoy, Countess, 36

Davies, Godfrey, 37 n.

Davis, Tenney L., 250 n.

Dawson, Dr. Giles E., 19 n.

Deacon, Thomas, 138, 286; see *Ecclesiastical Memoirs* (Tillemont)

dedications to men of influence, 218

De Statu mortuorum (Burnet), 297

Defoe, Daniel, 2, 11, 28, 30, 36, 36 n., 41 n., 76, 77, 303, 322, 327; see *Captain Singleton*; see *Compleat English Gentleman*; see *Four Years' Voyages of . . . Roberts*; see *Religious Courtship*; see *Robinson Crusoe*

De Quincey, Thomas, 235

Derbyshire Journal, 313

Description . . . de l'empire de la Chine (du Halde), 307

Description of China (du Halde), 184–5, 197, 217–18, 307

Devil turn'd Hermit, instalments of, 52

De Vinne, Theo. L., 80 n.

Diana (Montemayor), instalments of, 40

Dickens, Charles, 3

Dictionary, Johnson's, 7, 244

Dictionary Historical and Critical (Bayle), 115, 228, 287

Dictionnaire historique et critique (Bayle), 174; 287; see *Dictionary Historical and Critical*; see *General Dictionary*

difficulties in delivery of fascicules, 225–6

difficulties in writing for publication in fascicules, 124–5, 128, 141; see also Stackhouse, 109–13

Digby, John, 40 n.

Discovery . . . of the . . . Philippine Islands (Argensola), 88, 272

Distillers Universal Magazine, 69, 70–1, 304

distribution of fascicules and supplements, 66, 67, 68, 95, 124, 139–40, 147, 185–6, 209, 221–31

Distresses and Adventures of John Cockburne, instalments of, 46; see *Journey over Land*

Doctrine of the Old and New Testament, 204, 306

Dodsley, Robert, 58–60, 258, 259

Dodson, James, 197, 322

Don Quixote (Cervantes-Philips), 97–8; instalments of, 34

Don Quixote, Life of (Ward), 82

Dottin, Paul, 36 n., 41 n.

Dougharty, J., 354

Dr. Colbatch's Legacy, 121–2, 283

Dryden, John, plays of, 16

Duff, William, 140, 171, 356

Du Halde, Jean Baptiste, 307; see *Description of China*; see *General History of China*

Dumont, Jean, 298, 324

Dunton, John, 77, 80

Dupin, Louis Ellies, see Ellies-Dupin

duplicate editions of newspapers, 48–50, 68, 228, 317

Durand, David, 299, 305, 335

Dutfield, James, 354

Ecclesiastical History (Fleury), 100, 197, 278

Ecclesiastical Memoirs (Tillemont-Deacon), 138, 197, 286

Echo (Edinburgh), 11

Edlin, Thomas, 98, 99, 106, 109–13, 173, 203

Egmont, Earl of, 173 n., 227 n., 228

Eisenmenger, Johann Andreas, 283

Electra (Sophocles), instalments of translation, 37

Elementa Chemiæ (Boerhaave), 250, 282

Elements of Chemistry (Boerhaave), 282

Ellies-Dupin, Louis, 307

England's Triumph (Jenkins), 146, 212, 233, 318

English Champion, 298

English Guzman; or Captain Hilton's Memoirs, 76

Englishman, 108

engraved cuts, 17, 64, 71, 74, 83, 87, 90, 95, 97, 103, 107, 127, 128, 129, 130, 131, 139, 176, 185, 194, 201, 204, 210–11, 216, 217, 219, 220, 227, 234, 249, 251, and Appendix B *passim*

Entertaining Traveller, instalments of, 51

enticements to buy, special, 71, 184–5, 217–18; see also advertising of fascicules, engraved cuts, premiums to subscribers, promotion of sales

Entick, John, 23; see *Speculum Latinum*; see *Speculum Linguarum*

Entretiens des voyageurs (Flournois), 279

Epistles of Ovid, 341

Esdaile, Arundell, 36 n., 37 n., 40 n., 335

Essay towards a . . . History . . . of Norfolk (Blomefield), 140–2, 233, 242, 302

Essay towards a New Version of the Old Testament, 348

Etherege, Sir George, see *Man of Mode*

Exemplary Novels (Cervantes), instalments of, 35, 35 n.

Exposition of the Common Prayer, 308

Exposition of the New Testament (Gill), 345

Exposition on . . . the New Testament (Marchant), 139–40, 171, 224, 332

Exposition on the Old and New Testament (Henry), 150, 196, 303

Exposition on . . . the Old Testament (Marchant), 140, 168, 171, 345
Expository Notes . . . on the New Testament (Burkitt), 127, 152, 176, 191, 192–3, 203, 289; royalties on, 176

Fables of Aesop (L'Estrange), 114
Fair Penitent (Rowe), 17
Faithful Account of the Distresses of John Cockburne, 37
Faithful Account . . . of the Mahometans (Pitts), instalments of, 44
Faithful Collections, 23
Faithful Narrative of the . . . Work at Kilsyth (Robe), 23
Familiar Letters from a Beautiful Young Damsel, instalments of, 49; see *Anti-Pamela*
Family Companion (Smith), 301
Fanatical Persecution, instalments of, 27
Fancourt, Samuel, 338
Farley, Samuel, 29, 30, 33
Farley's Exeter Journal, 30
Farquhar, George, see *Recruiting Officer*
fascicule signatures, 8, 101, 125–6, 198–201; omitted, 8, 125, 197, 198; see Appendix B *passim*
Fatal Secret; or Constancy in Distress (Haywood), instalments of, 27–8
Father's Advice to His Son, 322
Fate of Majesty, instalments of, 27
Feales, William, 16, 17–19, 21
Female Deserters (Hearne), instalments of, 28
Female Robbers, 217, 331
Female Spectator, 248 n.
Fénelon François de Salignac de la Mothe, 298, 308, 322
Fenton, Elijah, 188, 318
fictitious names, 44, 50, 128, 214–6
Fielding, Henry, 2, 3, 7, 125, 174 n., 294, 351; see *Author's Farce*; see *Joseph Andrews*; see *Mock Doctor*; see *Miser*; see *Tom Jones*
Finch, Heneage, 316, 322
First Book of Palladio's Architecture, 284
Flanders, description of, see *Flanders Delineated*; see *Travels through Flanders*

Flanders Delineated, 338
Fletcher, Mr., bookseller in Oxford, 18
Fleury, Abbé Claude, see *Ecclesiastical History*
Flournois, Gédéon, 279
Foedera (Rymer), 97, 285
Folger Shakespeare Library, 19 n.
Fontenelle, Bernard le Bovier de, 327
Ford, James, 334
Fortunate Country Maid (de Mouhy), 248, 324
Fortune's Favourite, 338
Foundling Hospital for Wit, 348
Four Books of Architecture (Palladio), 117
Four Years' Voyages of Captain George Roberts (Defoe?), instalments of, 36
Foxe, John, 129, 290, 328, 345; see *Book of Martyrs*
Fransham, John, 316
Freeman, A., 50–1, 53
Freinshemius, 40
frequency, change of, 92, 105, 200
Fritsch, John Frederick, 138, 309; see *Art of Painting*
Full and Just Account of . . . the Ottoman Empire (Hill), 48 n.
Fysher, Robert, 169

Garden of Cyrus (Browne), 302
General and True History of . . . Highwaymen (Macklecan), 352
General Dictionary, Historical and Critical (Bayle-Bernard-Birch-Lockman), 115–16, 171, 174–5, 191, 287
General History of . . . America (Herrera y Tordesillas), 89, 275
General History of China (du Halde), 307
General History of England (Guthrie), 148, 339
General History of . . . Highwaymen (Smith), 131–2, 224, 251–3, 293, 332–3
General History of Ireland, see *History of Ireland*
General History of Printing (Palmer), 102–3, 279
General History of the Pyrates (Johnson), 29–30, 33, 224, 293

General History of the Trials. . . at West-
    minster, 348
General London Evening Mercury, 42 n.,
    43 n.
General Treatise of Architecture (Rowland),
    171, 335
General View of the World, 86 n., 308
Generous London Morning Advertiser, 43, 74
Generous Physician (Colbatch), 122, 282
Genius of the Antients, 64, 317
Gentleman and Ladies . . . Circulating Library
    (Fancourt), 338
Gentleman's Magazine, 126, 214, 239–42,
    and passim
Gentleman's Travels through Portugal, 356
Genuine Account of Richard Turpin, instal-
    ments of, 41
Genuine Account of the . . . Pirates (Mackle-
    can), 352–3, 355
Genuine Account of the . . . Pyrates (John-
    son), 132, 293, 333
Genuine History of Charles XII (Adlerfeld-
    Ford), 334
Genuine Works of Flavius Josephus (Whis-
    ton), 299
Geography (Moll), 152, 168, 178, 202;
    see Atlas Geographus
Geography Methodized, 338
Geography Reformed, 338
Gibbs, James, 168 n., 313
Gifford, N., 298
Gil Blas, 195
Gill, John, 345
Gomez, Madeleine Angélique Poisson
    de, 42, 42 n.
Gosling, Francis, sale of stock, 91
Gosling, Robert, 82, 227–8
Gove, Philip Babcock, 244 n.
Gray, John, 187
Great Britain's Rules of Health, 83
Green, John, 307, 334; see New General
    Collection of Voyages
Gregory, Dr., 84
Grenville, Rt. Hon. Thomas, 27; library
    of, 27 n.
Grosvenor, Benjamin, 280
Grub-Street Journal, 2, 5, 105–6

Gueullette, Thomas, 36, 40; see Aven-
    tures merveilleuses; see Chinese Tales; see
    Mogul Tales; see Sultanas of Guzarat
Gulliver's Travels (Swift), instalments of,
    34, 36; spurious continuation of, 40
Guthrie, William, 148, 330, 339

hackwriters, 174, 213, 237, 255
Hakluytus Posthumus, 89
Half-Penny London Journal, 34
Half-Penny London Journal; or, The British
    Oracle, 34
Hall, Rev. Anthony, 86, 273
Hamlet (Shakespeare), 17
Hanson, Dr. Laurence, 178 n., 182 n.
Hardwicke, Lord Chancellor, 160, 162
Harleian Miscellany, 188, 197, 218 n., 220–
    1, 223, 237, 245–6, 339; see Bibliotheca
    Harleiana; see Copious and Exact Catalogue
Harper, Thomas, 204
Harris, John, 150, 328, 339, 340; see
    Lexicon Technicum; see Navigantium
    atque itinerantium bibliotheca
Harrison, Conyers, 340
Harrison, James, 6
Hastings, Warren, 10
Haywood, Eliza, 28, 43, 43 n., 48 n.;
    see Anti-Pamela; see Familiar Letters
    from a Beautiful Young Damsel; see Fatal
    Secret; see Love in Excess
Heads of all the Kings and Queens (King), 291
Heads of the Kings of England (Vertue and
    others), 294
Heads of the Most Illustrious Persons
    (Vertue), 310
Hearne, Mary, 28; see Female Deserters;
    see Lover's Week
Heathcote, William, 27–9, 30, 39, 56,
    60, 61
Henley, John, 24–5; see Compleat Linguist;
    see Course of Academical Lectures; see
    Oratory Transactions
Henry, Matthew, 150, 303; see Ex-
    position on the Old and New Testament
Herbert, Edward (Baron Herbert of
    Cherbury), 322
Herbert, Henry, 278

Hereford Journal, 317

Hermit (Longueville), 335

Herrera y Tordesillas, Antonio de, 89, 275

Hett, Richard, 259

Hill, Aaron, 48, 48 n.

Hillhouse, James T., 24 n.

Histoire d'Angleterre (Rapin de Thoyras), 58, 96, 108, 188; with Tindal's notes in French, 96, 280; see also *History of England*

Histoire de l'Eglise (Ellies-Dupin), 308

Histoire ecclésiastique (Fleury), 278

Histoire romaine (Catrou-Rouillé), 218 n.; see *Roman History*

Historia sui temporis (Thuanus), see *History of His Own Time* (de Thou)

Historical and Biographical Memoirs (Brantôme), 243, 326

Historical . . . Description of all the Counties in England (Cowley), instalments of, 59

Historical Journal, 61

Historical View of the Transactions of Europe (Boyse), 250, 348

History and Antiquities of Berkshire, 63, 303

History and Antiquities of Essex (Salmon), 93, 121 n., 319

History and Antiquities of Northamptonshire (Bridges), 243, 316

History and Cruelties of the Inquisitions, instalments of, 46, 50

History of . . . America (Herrera y Tordesillas), 238

History of . . . Czar Peter the Great (Banks), 323

History of England, 61, 69, 298

History of England (Ralph), 135, 148, 342

History of England (Rapin-Kelly-Morgan), 5, 46, 106–8, 109, 285, 286; Lediard's continuation of, 147, 243, 299

History of England (Rapin-Tindal), 5, 96–7, 106–8, 120, 123, 135, 193, 197, 227, 228, 276, 305; second edition, 107–8, 285; third edition, 335; Tindal's continuation of, 171, 305, 343

History of England (Smollett), 5–6, 173

History of England, by Way of Question and

Answer (Lockman), instalments of, 41, 46

History of Essex (Tindal), 119–20, 233, 286

History of Executions, 22

History of His Own Time (Burnet), instalments of, 39

History of His Own Time (de Thou), 100, 156 n., 191, 197, 279, 296

History of Ireland (Keating-O'Connor), 122, 284

History of . . . Jesus Christ, 213, 295, 308

History of King-Killers, 274

History . . . of . . . London, Westminster (Maitland), 139, 197, 242, 309

History of . . . Masaniello (Midan), 72, 349

History . . . of Mr. Philip Quarll (Longueville), 335

History of Norfolk (Blomefield), see *Essay Towards a . . . History . . . of Norfolk*

History of Osman the 19th (de Gomez-Williams), instalments of, 42

History of . . . our Blessed Saviour (Smith), 216, 301, 310

History of Popery (Care), 297; see *Weekly Pacquet of Advice from Rome*

History of . . . Queen Anne, 323

History of . . . Queen Elizabeth, 317

History of Scotland, 68, 129, 290; see *New . . . History of Scotland*

History of Tarquinius, Lucretia, and Brutus, instalments of, 46, 50

History of the Bible (Campbell), 111, 218; see *New and Compleat History of the Holy Bible*

History of the Bible (Stackhouse), 109–13, 137, 157–8, 192, 238

History of the Bible by Way of Question and Answer, 222, 306

History of the Conquest of Mexico, 62–3

History of the Council of Constance (Lenfant-Whatley), 103, 278

History of . . . the Earl of Essex, 317

History of the Family Bible (Smith), 301, 320

History of the Holy Bible, 313

History of the Holy Bible (Clarke), 306

History of the Inquisition (Baker), 192, 294

History of the Jewish and Christian Church (Ellies-Dupin), 307

History of the Life of Peter I (Mottley), 323

History of the Life of Peter the First, 323

History of the Old and New Testament, 68, 317

History of the Othman Empire (Cantemir), 170, 234, 243, 268, 297

History of the Popes (Bruys), 121, 312, 282

History of the Present Rebellion (Marchant), 349

History of the Pyrates (Johnson), instalments of, 29, 30, 33, 34

History of the Rebellion 1745 and 1746, 349

History of the Reformation of the Church of England (Burnet), 62, 129, 289

History of the Revolution in Portugal (Vertot), instalments of, 42

History of the Town of Tournay, instalments of, 43

History of the Turkish Empire (Purbeck), 233; see *Present State of the Turkish Empire*

History of the Works of the Learned, 1

History of the World, 317

History of the World (Ralegh), 131, 150, 198, 201, 203, 234, 292, 300, 317

Hitch, Charles, 259

Hogg, Alexander, 6, 196 n.

Holloway, Mrs., 222

Homer, 7

Honey-suckle, 295, 323

Hooke, Andrew, 356

Hooper, Jacob, 313, 320, 351; see *Impartial History of the Rebellion*

Horace, 318, 331; quoted, 110

Horatius Flaccus, Quintus, 318, 331

Hudibras Redivivus (Ward), 82, 271

Humorous Companion, 314

Humphreys, Samuel, 298, 300

Hussey, Rev. John, 179 n.

Hussey, Nicholas, 141

Hutchins, H. C., 48 n., 82 n.

Hydriotaphia (Browne), 302

Hymen's Præludia (La Calprenède-Loveday), 304

I quattro libri del'architettura (Palladio), 284

Ilive, T., and sons, 44

Impartial Account of Many Barbarous Cruelties, 314, 328, 345

Impartial History of . . . Queen Anne, 233, 323

Impartial History of . . . Queen Anne (Chamberlen), 312

Impartial History of . . . Queen Anne (Harrison), 73, 340

Impartial History of the Late Rebellion (Boyse), 348

Impartial History of the Rebellion (Hooper), 73, 201, 313, 320, 351

imprints, anonymous, 146–8; see proprietors, groups of, and Appendix B *passim*

Indictment . . . of Twenty-Nine Regicides (Finch), 316, 322

Infallible Astrologer (Ward and Brown), 82 n.

instalment printing in newspapers, 4, 8, 10, 25, 26–52, 59, 60, 63

inventory of copies, 151–3; of stock, 17, 191–2

Jackson, H., 119, 303

Jackson, William A., 34 n., 98 n.

Jamaica, fascicules sent to, 231

James, Dr. Robert, 179, 331; see *Medicinal Dictionary*

James, Thomas, 73

Jameson, Robert, 153, 351, see *Critical Exposition of the Bible*; see *Critical Exposition of the Pentateuch*

Jane Shore (Rowe), 17

Jebb, Dr. Samuel, 316

Jenkins, Charles, see *England's Triumph*

Jewish Letters, 315

Joe Miller's Jests (Mottley), 349

Johnson, Charles, 29 n., 30, 132, 293, 332; see *General History of the Pyrates*; see *Genuine Account of the Pirates*; see *History of the Pyrates*; see Macklecan

Johnson, Michael, 84

Johnson, Dr. Samuel, 3, 7, 10, 13, 58, 97 n., 133, 161, 179, 185 n., 186, 215 n., 227 n., 229, 231, 232, 242–6, 249, 258

Johnston, William, 5, 158–9

Jones, Rev. Arthur, 243, 308

Joseph Andrews, 7; instalments of, 46, 50

Josephus, Flavius, 58, 118, 283, 299, 303, 323, 329; works of, 118–19; translated by Court, 138, 283; by Jackson, 303; by L'Estrange, 138, 151, 191, 192, 283; by Whiston, 138, 234, 249; by Wilson, 74, 323, 329

Journey over Land (Cockburn), instalments of, 46, 47; see *Distresses and Adventures*; see *Unfortunate Englishman*

Julius Caesar (Shakespeare), 64, 296

Keating, Geoffrey, 122, 284

Kelly, John, 106, 108, 285, 286; see *History of England*

Kenny, Robert W., 135 n.

Kent, description of, instalments of, 26–7, 60

Kimber, Isaac, 37 n.

King, Giles, 291

King's Printer, 159

Kitchin, Thomas, 354

Knapton, James, John, Paul, 5, 42 n., 61, 87, 106–8, 203, 259, 268, and *passim*

Knight, Charles, 6

Knight, Rev. Dr. Knight, Prebendary of Ely, 231

La Belle Assemblée (de Gomez), 42 n.

La Calprenède, Gautier de Costes de, 304

Ladies Miscellany, 242, 308

Lady's Curiosity, 314

Lady's Delight, 318

Lairesse, Gérard de, 138, 308; see *Art of Painting*

Lampe, John Frederick, 323–4; see *Lyra Britannica*; see *Musical Entertainer*

Langley, Batty, 127, 128, 291; see *Ancient Masonry*; see *Principles of Antient Masonry*; see *Young Builder's Rudiments*

Langley, Gilbert, 324

Laureate Volunteer (Savage), 23

Lawson, John, 89, 250, 272

Lay-Monk, 12

Le Clerc, Daniel, 89, 272

L'Ecumoire, histoire japonaise (Crébillon), instalments of, 41

Le Diable hermite (de Saumery), 52

Lediard, Thomas, 109, 147, 173–4, 295, 299, 304; see *Compleat . . . History of . . . Naval Expeditions*; see *Naval History of England*

Lee, Nathaniel, plays of, 15, 16, 18; see *Constantine the Great*; see *Rival Queens*

Lenfant, Jacques, 103, 278

L'Estrange, Sir Roger, 75, 114, 118, 119, 151, 283; see *Fables of Aesop*; see Josephus, works of

Letter to the Society of Booksellers, 135–6

Letters from a Young Painter Abroad (Russell), 171, 353

Letters of Abelard and Heloise, instalments of, 41

Letters of Sir Robert Bowes, 302

Lettres juives (Boyer), 315

Lewis, J., 189–90

Lexicon Technicum (Harris), 328; supplement to, 212

libraries, rural, 11–13, 14

Licensing Act, expiry of, 154

Life and Adventures of Lady Lucy (Aubin), instalments of, 34

Life and Adventures of Robinson Crusoe, see *Robinson Crusoe*

Life and Most Surprising Adventures of Robinson Crusoe, see *Robinson Crusoe*

Life and Reign of King Henry VIII (Herbert of Cherbury), 322

Life and Reign of . . . Queen Anne, 309

Life and Reign of . . . Queen Elizabeth, 217, 317

Life and Surprizing Adventures of Signor Rozelli (Olivier), instalments of, 52

Life of Alexander the Great (Quintus Curtius), instalments of, 39–40

Life of Charles XII of Sweden (Voltaire), instalments of, 39, 42

Life of Charlotta Du Pont, 318

Life of Cromwell, instalments of, 37

Life . . . of . . . Don Quixote (Cervantes), 276

Life . . . of . . . Don Quixote (Ward), 82, 273

Life . . . of . . . Gilbert Langley, 324

Life . . . of James Wyatt, 354

Life of John Sheppard, instalments of, 34

Life of Olivier Cromwell, 331; instalments of, 43

Life of Osman the Great (de Gomez-Williams), instalments of, 42

Life . . . of . . . Prince Eugene of Savoy, 324

Life . . . of Simon Lord Lovat (Arbuthnot), 233, 348

Life of Sir Walter Ralegh (Oldys), 325

Life of the Blessed Virgin Mary (Clarke), 306

Life . . . of the Rev. Mr. George Whitefield (Tucker), 320

Lillo, George, 352

Lincoln's Inn, 54, 183

Lindsay, John, 132, 290, 352; see *Brief History of England;* see *New Testament . . . with Notes*

Linnell, Rev. C. L. S., 141 n.

Literary Magazine, 102, 103

Lives . . . of the Apostles, 295

Lives . . . of the Apostles (Clarke), 306

Lives of the Twelve Apostles, 308

Lives of the English Bishops (Salmon), 93, 281

Lives of the English Sovereigns, instalments of, 39

Lives of the . . . Philosophers (Jones), 243, 308

Lives of the Sovereigns, instalments of, 38 n.

Lockman, John, 46, 115, 129, 174–5, 287, 330, 331, 352; see *History of England;* see *New History of England;* see *Roman History*

Lofft, Capel, 161

London and Country Journal, 49, 68, 317, 326

London Evening Advertiser, 50–1, 53

London Journal, 108

London Magazine, 55–6, 57, 126–7

London Merchant (Lillo), 352

London Mercury; or, Great Britain's Weekly Journal, 38

London Morning Advertiser, 43

London Spy (Ward), 63, 69, 80–1, 238, 271, 305

London Spy Revived, 63, 310, 314

London Tatler, 41

Longman, Thomas, 259

Longmans, Green, and Company, 86 n., 91 n., 119 n., 152 n., 153 n., 176 n., 177, 190, 192 n., 308

Longueville, Peter, 335

Lord Grey's . . . Love-Letters (Behn), 69, 297

Lorrain, Paul, 21

Love and Avarice, 354

Love in Excess (Haywood), instalments of, 43

Loveday, Robert, 303

Lover's Week (Hearne), instalments of, 28

Love's Magazine, 354

Luther, Martin, 324, 329; see *Commentary on . . . Epistle to the Galatians*

Luther upon Galatians, 189–90

Lynam, Edward, 89 n., 307, 334

Lyndar, Harry, 129, 291; see *Book of Martyrs the Best Preservative*

Lyra Britannica (Lampe), 249, 323

McKillop, Alan D., 173 n., 326, 329

Macklecan, James, 352, 355

Macky, Mr. 36 n.

McNair, Sir Arnold, 161 n.

Madagascar; or, Robert Drury's Journal, 41 n.; see *Pleasant . . . Adventures of Mr. Robert Drury*

Magazine of Architecture (Oakley), 123, 223, 284

Magna Britannia, 85–6, 198, 227, 273, 308

Maitland, William, 139, 309

Man of Mode (Etherege), 17

Manget, Jean Jacques, 89, 272

Manley, Mary de la Rivière, 197, 299

maps, 5, 83, 85, 86, 87, 185, 204, 216, 219, 249, and Appendix B *passim*

Marchant, John, 139–40, 332, 345, 349; see *Exposition on . . . the New Testament;* see *Exposition on . . . the Old Testament;* see *History of the Present Rebellion*

Marmor Norfolciënse (Johnson), 242

Marriage Dialogues (Ward), instalments of, 38 n.

Martin, Benjamin, 353

Martyn, John, 90, 175, 328

Maslen, Keith I. D., 118 n.

Mathematical Digests (Dougharty), 354

Mather, Cotton, 102

Mather library, 249

Matrimonial Dialogues (Ward), instalments of, 38

Mead, Dr. Richard, 244

Mechanick Exercises (Moxon), 79–80, 136, 198, 270, 271

Mechell, J., 106, 108–9, 147

Medicinal Dictionary (James), 167, 179, 197, 232, 244, 331

Mémoires de Messire de Bourdeille, Seigneur de Brantôme, 326

Mémoires de la régence (de Piossens), 279

Memoirs of a certain Society, instalments of, 59

Memoirs of a Man of Quality (Prévost d'Exiles), 342

Memoirs of an Unfortunate Young Nobleman, instalments of, 46, 50; see Annesley, James

Memoirs of . . . His Grace, James, late Duke of Ormond, 312

Memoirs of Miss Jenny Cameron (Arbuthnot), 347, 349

Memoirs of . . . Signor Rozelli (Olivier), 52

Memoirs of the Life of the Late Duke of Ormond, 326

Memoirs of the Regency of . . . the late Duke of Orleans (de Piossens), 279

Memoirs of the Royal Society (Baddam), 175–6, 189, 192, 311

Memorials and Characters (Wilford), 197, 213, 231, 318

Memorials of Affairs of State, 94, 280

Merry Wives of Windsor (Shakespeare), 17, 19 n., 296

Merryman, A., 44, 45, 47–9

Metamorphoses (Ovid), 353

Microscopical Theatre of Seeds (Parsons), 253–4, 341

Midon, Francis, 72, 349

Military History of . . . Prince Eugene (Dumont and Rousset de Missy), 217, 298

Millar, Andrew, 177, 187, 259

Milton, John, 318, 319; life of, 188, 318; see *Paradise Lost;* see *Paradise Regain'd*

Milton Restor'd and Bentley Depos'd, 119, 284

Miser (Fielding), 64, 294

Miseries . . . of the Inferior Clergy (Stackhouse), 109

Mist, Nathaniel, 29

Mock Doctor (Fielding), 351

Modern History, instalments of, 34

Modern History (Salmon), 14, 34, 92, 136, 168, 171, 192, 193, 237, 275, 342; French translation, 92, 277

Modern Story Teller, 171, 355

Modern Universal British Traveller, 214

Mogul Tales (Gueullette), 40, 60; see *Sultanas of Guzarat*

Molière, plays by, 16, 69; translations of, 300

Moll, Herman, 83, 84, 131, 152, 271, 273, 292; see *Atlas Geographus;* see *Complete System of Geography;* see *New Description of England and Wales*

Montemayor, Jorge de, 40

Monthly Amusement, 35 n.

Monthly Chronicle, 92, 100, 101

Moore, Francis, 340

Moral Philosopher, 319

Morant, Philip, 93, 120

Morden, Robert, 86

Moreman, Thomas, of Bath, 226

Morgan, J., 104, 281

Morgan, Joseph, 285

Morison, Stanley, 31 n.

Most Remarkable Sea Fights, 71, 309

Mottley, John, 128, 292, 304, 323, 349; see *History of the Life of Peter I;* see *Joe Miller's Jests;* see *New Survey of . . . London;* see *Survey of . . . London*

Mouette, Sieur, 272

Mouhy, Charles de Fieux, Chevalier de, 324

Mourner (Grosvenor), 280

Moxon, Joseph, 79–80, 136, 270, 271; see *Mechanick Exercises*

Mr. H. Treby's Narrative of his . . . Shipwreck, instalments of, 30–1

Mr. Stackhouse's Last Stack (Edlin), 112–13

Muilman, Henry, 143–4

Muir, P. H., 131 n.

Murray, Robert H., 89 n.

music, see songs, collections of

Musical Companion, 329

Musical Entertainer (Bickham), 305, 321

Musical Entertainer (Lampe), 204, 210

Nalson, J., 72, 324, 350

Narrative of the Shipwreck, instalments of, 40

Natural History of English Moths (Dutfield), 354

Naval History of England (Lediard), 173, 201, 222–3, 295

Naval Transactions and Sea Fights, 69, 71, 304

Navigantium atque itinerantium bibliotheca (Harris), 150, 168, 339–40

Neale, J., 355

New Abridgement . . . of the State Trials (Salmon), 301

New Anatomical Tables, 332

New and Compleat History of the Holy Bible (Campbell), 112, 203, 282

New Atalantis (Manley), 197, 300

New . . . Collection of . . . Novels, 196 n.

New Collection of Voyages and Travels (Stevens), 87–9, 202, 272

New Description of England and Wales (Moll), 131, 292

New Dictionary of the Bible (Pickering), 346

New England, fascicules sent to, 231, 249

New . . . Exposition of the Apostles Creed (Stackhouse), 113, 137, 350

New General Collection of Voyages (Green), 168, 218, 229–30, 334

New Half-Penny Post, 69, 314

New History of England (Lockman), 352

New . . . History of Scotland (Duff), 140, 171, 356

New History of the Holy Bible (Stackhouse), 165, 166 n., 286, 293, 333; see *History of the Bible* (Stackhouse)

New Method of . . . Perspective, 218, 295

New Roman History (Lockman), 352

New Survey of England (Salmon), 278

New Survey of . . . London (Mottley), 238

New Testament . . . with Notes (Court and Lindsay), 132, 160, 200, 208, 290

New Version of . . . the New Testament, 94

New Vocal Miscellany, 319

New Voyage to Carolina (Lawson), 89, 272

New Weekly Novelist, 196 n.

news printed on covers, 73–4, 306, 314, 326, 329, 330

Nichols, John, 73, 93 n., 101, 109, 121 n., 214 n., 259

Nicholson, John, 43, 50 n., 54, 85

Night Walker, 77, 81

No. I of the Herculean Labour, 99

North Carolina, description of, 250

Norwich, 140, 141 n.

Nourse, John, 175, 176, 183, 187, 259, 305, 311

numbers, each a complete unit, 3, 22, 23, 24, 95

Nunnery Tales (Slade), 336

Nuptial Dialogues (Ward), instalments of, 38 n.

Oakley, Edward, 123, 284

Occasional Paper (Willis)

Occasional Preacher (Wright), 23

O'Connor, Darby, 284

Odes of Horace, 318

Offtey, R., 233–4

Oglethorpe, General, 230

Old and New Testament . . . with Annotations, 300

Old and New Testament . . . with Annotations (Smith), 330

Oldys, William, 300, 325, 339, 341, 346; see *Biographia Britannica*; see

Copious and Exact Catalogue; see *Life of Sir Walter Ralegh*

Oliver, S. P., 41 n.

Olivier, Abbé, 52

opposition to publishing in fascicules, 215–16

opposition to serial publication, 7, 235–7

Oratory Transactions (Henley), 24

Ordinary of Newgate, 21, 22

Oriel College Library, 169

Original London Post; or, Heathcote's Intelligence, 26–9, 62–3, 290

Original Weekly Journal, 40, 60

Ormonde, Duke of, 312, 326

Oroonoko (Behn), 69

Orphan (Otway), 17

Osborn, J. M., 115 n.

Osborne, Thomas, 187, 244, 258

Otway, Thomas, plays of, 16, 19 n., see *Orphan*

Ovidius Naso, Publius, 341, 353; see *Epistles*; see *Metamorphoses*

Oxford, Earl of, 142; library of, 244, 330, 339

Oxford Flying Weekly Journal, 72–3, 325, 349, 350

Oxford Journal; Or The Tradesman's Intelligence, 69

Oxford Magazine, or Universal Library, 71, 309, 310

Oxford Magazine; Or Family Companion, 69

Oxonians, reading matter for, 73

Ozell, John, 35 n., 98–9, 129, 173, 276

Pain, John, Registrar of Pamphlets, 183

Palæographia Britannica (Stukeley), 23

Palæographia Sacra (Stukeley), 23

Palladio, Andrea, 117, 284; see *First Book of Palladio's Architecture*; see *Four Books of Architecture*

Palmer, Samuel, 102–3, 279

Pamela . . . a Heroick Poem (Bennet), 255, 326

Pamela in High Life, 329

Pamela; or, Virtue Rewarded (Richardson), 167, 329; instalments of, 52

pamphlets, tax on, 55–7, 58, 182–3

Paradise Lost (Milton), 119, 159, 188–9, 318, 341; *Spectator* essays on, 315; see *Complete Commentary . . . on . . . Paradise Lost*

Paradise Regain'd (Milton), 319

Parent's Weekly Present to His Children, 346

Parker, G., 29, 30, 35, 36, 39, 56

Parker, Samuel, 101–2, 274

Parker's London News, 29, 35

Parker's Penny Post, 35–7

Parkyn, Rev. Charles, 142

Parrot; Or Pretty Poll's Morning Post, 69, 298, 300

Parsons, Dr. James, 253, 341

Pasquin; or, The Emblematist, 64, 317

Paterson, James, 341

payment, to authors, 5, 104, 106, 110–11, 134–6, 173, 174–5, 179, 214 n.; to compilers, 104; to engravers, 17; to printers, 17, 178–81; to King's Printer, 160, 178; to translators, 97, 104, 173, 174–5

Payne, John, 214

Peele, John, 259

Peisley, A., bookseller in Oxford, 17–18

Penny, Robert, 56, 57, 61, 62, 208

Penny London Morning Advertiser, 43, 50 n.

Penny London Post, 34, 66

Penny London Post; or, The Morning Advertiser, 43, 50 n., 293

Penny Weekly Journal, 38

Pepusch, Dr., 231

Persian Tales, 63, 310, 314

Phenix, 267

Phoenix Britannicus (Morgan), 104, 281

Philosophia Britannica (Martin), 353

Philips, John, 43 n., 239, 341

Phillips, E., 281

Phillips, Mrs. T. C., 143–6, 171, 189, 355

Philosophical History . . . of the Royal Academy of Sciences at Paris (de Fontenelle), 327

Physical Disquisitions (Tennent), 249, 347

Pickering, 346

Pickwick Papers (Dickens), 3, 81

Piggott, Stuart, 23 n.
Pilgrim (de Vega), instalments of, 40
Piossens, Chevalier de, 279
piratical printing, 28, 49, 124, 154, 155, 157, 160, 168, 177, 188, 193, 255, 312, 316, 318, 322, 348; penalties for, 156, and Appendix A
Pitts, Joseph, 44
Plant, Marjorie, 238 n.
playbooks published periodically, 16–21, 267; dwindling sales of, 18
plays as supplements, 64–5
playwrights listed for publication, 20
Pleasant . . . Adventures of Mr. Robert Drury, 148–9, 171, 327; instalments of, 41
Plomer, H. R., 259
Pöllnitz, Charles Louis, Baron de, 354
Polite Tales for Young Gentlemen and Ladies, 341
Pollard, Graham, 3 n., 33 n.
Polly Honeycomb, 41 n.
Poor Robin's Intelligence, 76
Poor Robin's Memoirs, 75
Pope, Alexander, 9, 25 n., 84, 229, 231
Porney, Lewis, 196 n.
Postmaster (Exeter), 30
Pote, Joseph, bookseller in Eton, 18
Powell, Dr. L. F., 179 n.
Practical Arithmetick (Champion), 129, 289
Practical Husbandman (Switzer), 129, 170, 293
Practising Scrivener (Bird), 129, 218, 288
premiums to subscribers, 71, 184–5
Prévost d'Exiles, Antoine François, 342
Principles of Antient Masonry (Langley), 128, 228, 291
Present State of the Turkish Empire (Purbeck), 147–8, 329
Present State of the Universities (Salmon), 244, 254, 335
prices of books, retail, 2, 7, 8, 10, 14, 18, 20, 22, 24, 25, 62, 106, 109, 126, 194, 195, 196, 197, 216–17, 227, 235, 238; wholesale, 17, 18
prices of fascicules, see Appendix B *passim*

Prince of Abyssinia, 161
printers as publishers, 105–6
printers named in imprint, see Appendix B *passim*
printers not named in imprint, 146–7
Proceedings and Tryal . . . of the . . . Archbishop of Canterbury, 319
profits from publishing in fascicules, 5, 6, 18, 97, 133, 237, and chapter V *passim*
promotion of sales, 202–12, 216–21
proposals, cost of printing, 5, 180, 184; printed in newspapers, 205; text of, 208–9, 210–11, 219
proprietor named in imprint, see Appendix B *passim*
proprietor not named in imprint, 146–7
proprietors, change of, 91, 103, 104, 123, 124, 136, 137, 138, 139, 140, 150, 153, 163 n., 176, 177, 178, 183, 192, 201
proprietors, groups of, 5, 82, 84, 87, 90, 91, 95, 98, 103, 104, 114, 115, 116, 118, 119 n., 123, 130, 137, 149, 150, 151–3, 163, 164–5, 168, 186, 188, and see congers; see imprints in Appendix B
Protestant Miscellany, 347
provinces, distribution of fascicules in, 13, 95, 286, 313
provinces, sale of books in, 16, 17–18, 219, 223, 225, 226, 228, 229, 230
Psalmanazar, George, 103
Public Record Office, 163, 164 n., 188
publication in fascicules discontinued, 93, 94, 98, 119, 120–2, 153, 182, 251, 281, 300, 316, 326
publication of fascicules delayed, 99, 119, 130–1, 142, 145, 163, 185, 221
Publick Register; or, the Weekly Magazine, 58–60
publishing by subscription, 19, 238
publishing in fascicules, a stimulus to literacy, x, 2, 6, 14; additional costs of, 166, 168–9, 172; advantages of, 8, 91, 133, 141, 167; disadvantages of, 166; principle of, 3

Purbeck, Rev. Mr., 148, 329
Purchas, Samuel, 89
Purefoy, Henry, 14

quality of literature published in fascicules, 7, 13, 14, 235, and chapter VII *passim*
quality of paper and presswork in fascicules, 14, 233–34, 249
quarrels, 110–13, 114–16, 117
Queen Anne's Weekly Journal, 69
Quintus Curtius, 40

Radicati, Alberto, 93 n., 182, 280
Ralegh, Sir Walter, 131, 150, 292, 300; biography of, 300, 325; see *History of the World*
Ralph, James, 134–35, 148, 342; see *Case of Authors*; see *History of England*
Rapin de Thoyras, Paul de, see *Acta Regia*; see *Histoire d'Angleterre*; see *History of England*
Rawlinson, Richard, 142
Rayner, William, 42, 43, 67–68, 74, 205, 215, 216
Rayner's London Morning Advertiser, 42
Read, James, 39, 62
Read, T., 65–67, 70
reading and drinking, relative merits of, 12–13
Reading Mercury; Or, The London Spy, 63, 303, 305
reading public, extent of, 1–2, 4, 6; expansion of, 25
Read's Weekly Journal; or, British Gazetteer, 62
Records of Love, 248 n.
Recruiting Officer (Farquhar), 69, 303
Reign of the Victorious Queen Elizabeth, 69, 314
Relation of a Voyage to Spain (D'Aulnoy), instalments of, 36
Religious Courtship (Defoe), 197, 322
Religious Novels (Flournois), 279
remainders, 179, 192–93, 196 n., 285; purchase of, 91, 191; sale of, 47, 103, 123, 125, 189, 190–1

reprinting of individual fascicules, 5, 71, 95, 142, 180–1, 189, 190, 311, 324
retail trade in fascicules, records of, 227–8
Rhapsody, 37
Richards, William, 314
Richardson, Colin, 24 n.
Richardson, Samuel, 93, 139
Rio, J., 129, 292
rival publications, 5, 10, 16, 19–21, 29–30, 34, 49–50, 61, 66–7, 79 n., 98–100, 106–9, 111–13, 114–18, 129, 132, 159, 165–6, 175, 181, 218, 226, 248, 249, 285, 312, 314
Rival Queens (Lee), 21
rivalry, 16, 19–20, 29, 43 n., 49, 50 n., and see rival publications
Rix, S. Wilton, 141 n., 142 n.
Robe, Rev. James, 23
Robinson, James, 147, 325
Robinson, Dr. Tancred, 84
Robinson Crusoe (Defoe), abridgment of, 28, 47–4; as supplement, 69; instalments of, 27, 28, 38, 46, 60
Robinson Crusoe's London Daily Evening Post, 51–2, 53
Robert Drury's History of Madagascar, instalments of, 41; see *Pleasant . . . Adventures of Mr. Robert Drury*
Roberts, James, 259
Roman History, 192
Roman History (Catrou-Rouillé-Bundy), 98, 106, 276
Roman History (Catrou-Rouillé-Ozell), 98, 110, 129, 276
Rouillé, Pierre Jeanne, 98, 276
Rousset de Missy, Jean, 298
Rover, instalments of, 37
Rowe, Nicholas, see *Fair Penitent*; see *Jane Shore*
Rowland, Thomas, 171, 335
royal licence, 136, 137, 139, 150, 151, 162–8, 172, 173, 178, 181, 202, 218, 219, and Appendix B *passim*; text of, 164–5
royalties, payment of, 176–7, 178
Rules for Drawing (Gibbs), 168, 238, 313

Russell, John, 171, 353
Rymer, Thomas, 97, 285

Sacred Books of the Old and New Testament
    (Humphreys), 298, 300
Sailor's Advocate, 23
Sale, George, 175, 280
Sale, W. M., 93
Salmon, Nathaniel, 92, 93, 121 n., 278,
    281, 319; see History and Antiquities of
    Essex; see Lives of the English Bishops;
    see New Survey of England
Salmon, Thomas, 92, 136, 275, 276, 301,
    319, 335, 342; see Modern History; see
    New Abridgement of the State Trials; see
    Present State of the Universities
Salmon, William, 79 n.
Samber, Robert, 36
Sanders, Robert, 214
Satires, Epistles, and Art of Poetry (Horace),
    331
Saumery, Pierre Lambert de, 52
Savage, Richard, 23, 174 n., 231; see
    Author to be Lett; see Laureate Volunteer
Scarborough, Earl of, 144
Scott, Daniel, 148, 332
Scriptorum ecclesiasticorum historia (Cave),
    195
Seasons (Thomson), 127, 157, 294
second editions in fascicules, 96, 97,
    107, 123, 131 n., 136, 159, 189, 192,
    193, 201-2, 271, 273, 285, 286, 293,
    297, 304, 320, 321, 322, 323, 326, 328,
    329, 330, 333, 335, 342, 343, 344, 345,
    349, 350, 353
Secret Memoirs (Manley), 299
Sedley, Sir Charles, see Bellamira
Select and Impartial Account of . . . Convicts,
    332
Select Collection of Molière's Comedies, 16
Select Trials at the Sessions-House, 207, 296
Sepulchrorum inscriptiones, 278
series, books published in, 15-25
Sermons (Clarke), 243, 331
Sermons on several Subjects (Tillotson), 333
Seventeen Years Travels of Peter de Cieza,
    272

Several Love Letters (Behn), 216
'Seymour, Robert', see Mottley
Shadwell, Thomas, plays of, 16
Shakespeare, William, plays of, 19,
    19 n., 20-1, 64; see Hamlet; see Julius
    Caesar; see Merry Wives of Windsor
Shaw, W. A., 55 n.
sheets, books sold in, 8, 195; folding of,
    3, 195; size of, 3, 33
Short Narrative of the . . . Work at
    Cambuslang (Robe), 23
Simpson, Samuel, 336
Simpson, Thomas, 170
size of editions, 5, 6, 16-17, 180-1, 187,
    188, 189 n., 245
Skelton, R. A., 89 n., 307, 334
Skimmer (Crébillon), instalments of, 41
Slade, Mrs., 336
Sloane, Dr. Hans, 84, 229
Small English Atlas (Kitchin), 354
Smith, Alexander, 131, 293, 332; see
    General History of . . . Highwaymen; see
    Macklecan
Smith, Adam, 243
Smith, Godfrey, 175, 311
Smith, Samuel, 160, 215-16, 215 n., 301,
    309, 310, 320, 330; see Christian's
    Guide; see Compleat History of the Old
    and New Testament; see Family Com-
    panion; see History of . . . our Blessed
    Saviour; see History of the Family Bible;
    see Old and New Testament
Smollett, Tobias, 5, 6, 173, 174
social classes served by supplements
    and fascicules, 10, 65, 110, 116, 117,
    127, 230-1, 235, 239
Society for the Encouragement of
    Learning, 187, 259
Soldier's Pocket Companion, 347
songs, collections of, 123, 132, 204,
    210-11, 242, 247-8, 283, 288, 289,
    295, 305, 310, 316, 318, 319, 329, 344,
    347
Sophocles, 37
Sophonisba (Lee), 17, 21
Southwell, Rev. Henry, 214 n.
Soyer, D., 330

Spanish Historian, instalments of, 51

Sparke, Archibald, 354

Spectator, 2, 12, 26, 125 n., 315

Speculum Latinum; or, Latin made easy to Scholars (Entick), 24

Speculum Linguarum (Entick), 24

Stackhouse, Rev. Thomas, 39, 109–13, 137, 165, 166, 173, 218, 282, 286, 293, 333, 350; quarrel with Edlin, 110–13; see *Book-binder . . . Confuted*; see *Compleat Body of Divinity*; see *History of the Bible*; see *Miseries . . . of the Inferior Clergy*; see *New . . . Exposition of the Apostles Creed*; see *New History of the Holy Bible*; see *Vana Doctrinæ Emolumenta*

Stackhouse, Thomas, 36 n.

Stamp Act, effects of, 32, 34, 35, 59, 60; provisions of, 31, 56

Stamp Office, 105, 183; Commissioners of, 54–6, 58, 62, 182, 183; enlargement of, 54

Stamp Tax, 30 n., 31–5, 59–60; 62; evasions of, 32–4, 53–8

Stanton, James, 69–71, 257

State of the Dead (Burnet), 217

State Trials (titles vary), 38, 39, 66, 67, 293

Stationers' Company, 159, 169, 171, 259

Stationers' Hall, 156; shipments of books from, 169–71

Stationers' Register, xiii, xiv, 129, 140, 145, 149, 156, 163, 169, 170, 171, 172, 177, 178, 183, 248 n., 268

Stauffer, Donald A., 21 n.

Steele, Sir Richard, 26; see *Conscious Lovers*; see *Tatler*

Stehelin, Rev. John Peter, 283

Stevens, John, 87, 89, 173, 272; see *New Collection of Voyages and Travels*; see *View of the Universe*

Story of the Liberal Lover (Cervantes), instalments of, 35

Strahan, William, 178–80; ledgers of, 148

Strype, John, 197, 302

Stukeley, Rev. William, 23

subjects, variety of, in number books, ix, 9, 238–9, and chapter VII *passim*

subscribers, printed lists of, 10, 84, 100, 120, 138, 139, 142, 209, 229, 230–1, 260, and Appendix B *passim*

'subscription books', use of the term, 52 n., 238

Sultanas of Guzarat (Gueullette), instalments of, 40, 40 n.

Supplement to Dr. Harris's Dictionary, 212, 328

supplements in newspapers, 10, 55, 61–73, 267, 289, 290, 293, 294, 298, 300, 303, 304, 305, 306, 308, 309, 310, 313, 314, 317, 325, 326, 350, 351; not taxed, 55, 57

Sun Fire Office, 37

Surprising . . . Effects of . . . Love, instalments of, 27–8

Surtees, Robert Smith, 3

Survey of . . . London and Westminster ('Seymour', i.e. Mottley), 69, 70, 128–9, 292, 304

Sutherland, Professor James, 68–9

Swift, Jonathan, 2, 119; see *Gulliver's Travels*

Switzer, Stephen, 129, 170, 293

Symon, E., 204

System of Divinity (Adams), 330

Tables of the Skeleton and Muscles (Albinus), 251, 351

Tabulæ sceleti et musculorum corporis humani (Albinus), 351

Tales of Love and Honour, see *Lover's Week*

Tatler, xiv, 2, 26, 83, 90

Taylor, William, 82 n.

Teixeira, Pedro, 272

Tellez, F. Balthazar, 272

Tennent, Dr. John, 250, 347

Thacker, John, 254–5, 350

Thackeray, William Makepeace, 3

Thacker's Cookery, 254–5, 350

Theatre of the present War in the Netherlands, 342

Thompson, Charles, 336

Thomson, James, 127, 157, 294

Thuanus, see de Thou

Thou, Jacques Auguste de, 100, 156 n., 191, 197, 279, 296

Tillemont, Louis Sebastien le Nain de, 138, 286

Tillotson, John, Archbishop of Canterbury, 152, 167, 199–200, 234, 333

Timperley, C. H., 6

Tindal, Rev. Nicholas, 94, 96, 97, 106, 108, 120–1, 173, 275, 276, 280, 285, 286, 297, 305, 335, 343; rewards and honours for, 173 n.; see *Antiquities Sacred and Prophane*; see *History of England*; see *History of Essex*

title page supplied at end of run, 60, 62, 63, 66, 67, 78, 102 n., 201–2, 290, 291

Tom Jones (Fielding), 7, 125

Tonson, Jacob, 16, 17, 19, 20, 188–9

Torrington, Viscount, 231

Tournefort, Joseph Pitton de, 90, 274

trade discount, see allowance to dealers

trade-sales catalogues, see Longmans, Green, and Company

trade sales of copies, 86 n., 91 n., 114 n., 119 n., 152, 153, 176, 177, 190, 192 n., 308

Traditions of the Jews (Eisenmenger), 119, 283

translations unprotected by copyright, 108

Travels into the Inland Parts of Africa (Moore), 340

Travels of Peter Teixeira, 272

Travels of Sieur Mouette, 272

Travels of the Jesuits in Ethiopia (Tellez), 272

Travels of the Late Charles Thompson, 336

Travels through Flanders, instalments of, 43

Travels through Holland (de Blainville), 148, 179, 180, 184, 330

Treasury, Lords of the, 33, 33 n., 54

Treatise concerning the State of the Dead, 297

Trent, W. P., 36 n., 41 n.

Trial at Bar (Annesley), 171 n., 336, 343

Trial at Large (Annesley), 343, 344

Trial at large of Dr. Henry Sacheverel, 71, 310

Trial of Charles Drew, instalments of, 46

Trial of Counsellour Layer, instalments of, 30, 38 n., 60

Trial of King Charles the First (Nalson), 72, 322, 324, 350

Trial . . . of Mary Queen of Scots, 317

Trial of the Hon. James Annesley, instalments of, 43

Tribune (Dublin), 12–13

Trollope, Anthony, 3, 146 n.

True Account of . . . the British Fleet in Sicily (Corbett), 316

Tryals of State Criminals, instalments of 38, 38 n., 39

Tucker, Josiah, 320

Turkish Spy; or, Hill's General History of the Ottoman Empire, instalments of, 46, 48, 49

Turnbull, George, 330, 331

Turner, Sydney, R., 31 n.

Tuttle, Julius Herbert, 102 n.

Tyers, Thomas, 10, 97 n.

Unfortunate Duchess, 73, 356

Unfortunate Englishmen (Cockburn), 47, 321; see *Journey over Land*

Universal Fabulist, 315

Universal Harmony, 242, 344, 347

Universal History (Sale, Campbell, and others), 163, 173, 177, 191, 192, 218, 228, 280

Universal History of Arts and Sciences (de Coetlogon), 163, 164–5, 170–1, 173, 327

Universal London Morning Advertiser, 43

Universal Musician, 310

Universal Penman (Bickham), 130–1, 139, 192, 238, 288, 330

Universal Songster 211

Universal Spectator, 12

Universal Spy; or, London Weekly Magazine, 41

Universal Theatre, 311–12

Universal Traveller (Barclay), 124, 191, 193, 199, 281, 286

Universal Weekly Register, 306

Uranographia Britannica (Neale), 355

Useful and Entertaining Collection of Letters, 344

Van der Gucht, G., 17, 97
Vana Doctrinæ Emolumenta (Stackhouse), 113
Vanity Fair (Thackeray), 236
Vega, Lope de, 40
Vergilius Maro, Publius, works of, 330
Vernon, Edward, Admiral, biography of, 74, 330
Vertot, Abbé de, 42
Vertue, George, 227, 294, 310
View of the Universe (Stevens), 87, 272
Voltaire, 39, 42
Voyage to Madagascar (Cauche), 272
Voyages . . . of Captain Richard Falconer, instalments of, 34

Wager, Sir Charles, 96
Walker, Robert, 16, 17, 19–21, 49, 68–70, 71–3, 119, 140, 147, 159, 188–9, 220, 225–6, 256–8; list of books published serially by, 257–8
Walker's Half-Penny London Spy, 69, 303
Walpole, Sir Robert, 33 n.
Ward, Edward, 38, 63, 80–1, 271, 273, 305; works of, in instalments, 41; in numbers, 222; as supplements, 310; see *Hudibras Redivivus*; see *Infallible Astrologer*; see *Life . . . of Don Quixote*; see *London Spy*; see *Marriage Dialogues*; see *Matrimonial Dialogues*; see *Nuptial Dialogues*; see *Weekly Comedy*
Warwick and Staffordshire Journal, 306, 308
Watson, David, 181
Watts, John, 16, 259
Weekly Amusement; or, Universal Magazine, 41
Weekly Comedy (Ward), 81 n.
Weekly Journal; or, British Gazetteer, 38 n., 39–40
Weekly Novelist, 196, 300
Weekly Oracle; or, Universal Library, 65–6, 295

Weekly Pacquet of Advice from Germany, 78, 271, 297
Weekly Pacquet of Advice from Rome (Care), 77–8, 270
Weekly Spectator, and English Theatre, 69, 303
Wellington, R., 16
West Indies, history of, 89; description of, 334
Whalley, Rev. Peter, 316
Whatley, Stephen, 97, 103, 151, 173, 277, 278; see *Acta Regia*; see *History of the Council of Constance*
Whiston, John, 138
Whiston, William, 118, 138, 299
Whitefield, Rev. George, 315, 320
Whole Duty of a Woman, 310, 311
Wilcox, John, 258
Wilford, John, 55, 109–10, 207, 208, 213, 228
Williams, Richard, 314
Williamson, Richard, 86 n.
Willis, Dr. Richard, 23
Wilmot, S., of Oxford, 94
Wilson, Rev. Bernard, 100 n., 279
Wilson, James, 74, 323
Winter Evening Tales, 350
Wit a-la-mode, 351
Wonderful Life . . . of Robinson Crusoe (Defoe), 303
Wonders of Nature and Art, 353
Woodfall, Henry, 17
Wood-Lark, 344
World in Miniature (Fransham), 316
Wright, Dr. Samuel, 23
Wyatt, James, 354
Wycherley, William, see *Country Wife*

Young Builder's Rudiments (Langley), 127, 291
Young Lady's Companion, 325

For EU product safety concerns, contact us at Calle de José Abascal, 56–1°,
28003 Madrid, Spain or eugpsr@cambridge.org.

www.ingramcontent.com/pod-product-compliance
Ingram Content Group UK Ltd.
Pitfield, Milton Keynes, MK11 3LW, UK
UKHW042210180425
457623UK00011B/125